★ **Trajan's Markets** ⑩
See pages 88–9

★ **San Clemente** ⑫
See pages 186–7

Piazza di Spagna

Via Veneto

Piazza della Rotonda

Quirinal

★ **Santa Maria del Popolo** ⑥
See pages 138–9

★ **Santa Maria Maggiore** ⑬
See pages 172–3

Esquiline

Capitol

Forum

Palatine

Lateran

Caracalla

★ **San Giovanni in Laterano** ⑭
See pages 182–3

Aventine

★ **Santa Maria in Trastevere** ⑤
See pages 212–13

★ **Colosseum** ⑪
See pages 92–5

ROME

EYEWITNESS *TRAVEL GUIDES*

ROME

DK PUBLISHING, INC.

A DK Publishing Book

PROJECT EDITOR Fiona Wild
ART EDITOR Annette Jacobs
EDITORS Ferdie McDonald, Mark Ronan, Anna Streiffert
US EDITORS Mary Ann Lynch, Mary Sutherland
DESIGNER Lisa Kosky
DESIGN ASSISTANT Marisa Renzullo

MANAGING EDITOR Douglas Amrine
MANAGING ART EDITOR Geoff Manders
SENIOR EDITOR Georgina Matthews
SERIES DESIGN CONSULTANT Peter Luff
EDITORIAL DIRECTOR David Lamb
ART DIRECTOR Anne-Marie Bulat

PRODUCTION CONTROLLER Hilary Stephens
PICTURE RESEARCH Catherine O'Rourke
RESEARCH IN ROME Sam Cole
DTP EDITOR Siri Lowe

MAIN CONTRIBUTORS
Olivia Ercoli, Ros Belford, Roberta Mitchell

MAPS
Andrew Heritage, James Mills-Hicks, John Plumer,
Chez Picthall (Dorling Kindersley Cartography)

PHOTOGRAPHERS
John Heseltine, Mike Dunning, Kim Sayer

ILLUSTRATORS
Studio Illibill, Kevin Jones Associates,
Martin Woodward, Robbie Polley
•
This book was produced with the assistance of
Websters International Publishers.

Film outputting bureau Cooling Brown (London)
Reproduced by Colourscan (Singapore)
Printed and bound by Graphicom (Italy)

First American Edition, 1993
4 6 8 10 9 7 5
Published in the United States by
DK Publishing, Inc.,
95 Madison Avenue, New York, New York 10016
Reprinted with revisions 1996, 1997

Library of Congress Cataloging-in-Publication Data
Belford, Ros.
Rome / Ros Belford, Rodney Palmer.
p.   cm. – – (Eyewitness travel guides)
Includes index.
ISBN 1-56458-186-1
1. Rome (Italy) – – Aerial photographs.   2. Rome (Italy) – – Guidebooks.
I. Palmer, Rodney.   II. Title.   III. Series.
DG806.8.B45   1993
914.5'63204929– –dc20   92-53473
CIP
•
Every effort has been made to ensure that the information in this book is as
up-to-date as possible at the time of going to press. However, details such
as telephone numbers, opening hours, prices, gallery hanging arrangements
and travel information are liable to change. The publishers cannot accept
responsibility for any consequences arising from the use of this book.

We would be delighted to receive any corrections and suggestions for
incorporation in the next edition. Please write to the Managing Editor,
Eyewitness Travel Guides, Dorling Kindersley
9 Henrietta Street, London WC2E 8PS, UK.

THROUGHOUT THIS BOOK, FLOORS ARE REFERRED TO IN ACCORDANCE WITH
EUROPEAN USAGE, I.E. THE "FIRST FLOOR" IS ONE FLIGHT UP.

CONTENTS

Colosseum

INTRODUCING ROME

Moses by Michelangelo in
San Pietro in Vincoli

Fresco in Villa Farnesina

ROME
AREA BY AREA

The Tempietto

Arch of Titus

TRAVELERS'
NEEDS

Mosaic in Santa Prassede

SURVIVAL GUIDE

Roman antipasto

The basilica of St. Peter's
in the Vatican City

HOW TO USE THIS GUIDE

THIS EYEWITNESS TRAVEL GUIDE helps you get the most from your stay in Rome with the minimum of practical difficulty. The opening section, *Introducing Rome*, locates the city geographically, sets modern Rome in its historical context and explains how Roman life changes through the year. *Rome at a Glance* is an overview of the city's attractions. The main sightseeing section is section two, *Rome Area by Area*, starting on page 62. It describes all the important sights with maps, photographs and detailed illustrations. In addition, six planned walks take you step by step through special areas of Rome.

Carefully researched tips for hotels, shops and markets, restaurants and cafés, sports and entertainment are found in section three, *Travelers' Needs*, and section four, *Survival Guide* has advice on everything from mailing a letter to catching the Metro.

ROME AREA BY AREA

The city has been divided into the 16 central sight-seeing areas, each separately color-coded. Each chapter opens with a portrait of the area and a list of the sights to be covered. These are located by numbers on an *Area Map*. This is followed by a large-scale *Street-by-Street Map* focusing on the most interesting part of the area. The main body of the chapter consists of detailed descriptions of all the listed sights. Finding your way around the chapter is made simple by the numbering system used throughout. This refers to the order in which the sights are described in the chapter.

Sights at a Glance lists the sights in the area by category: Churches and Temples, Museums and Galleries, Historic Streets and Piazzas, Historic Buildings, Arches and Gates, Columns, Obelisks and Statues, Fountains, Ancient Sites and Parks and Gardens.

The area covered in greater detail on the *Street-by-Street Map* is shaded red.

Numbered circles pinpoint all the listed sights on the *Area Map*. Palazzo Doria Pamphilj, for example, is **❻**.

1 Area Map

For easy reference, the sights in each area are numbered and located on a map of the area. To help the visitor, the map also shows Metro stations and parking areas.

Photographs of distinctive details of buildings help you identify the sights.

Color-coding on each page makes the area easy to find in the book.

2 Street-by-Street Map

This gives a bird's-eye view of the heart of each sightseeing area. To help you locate and identify important sights as you walk around, these are highlighted in stronger color.

A locator map shows you exactly where you are in relation to surrounding areas. The area shown in the *Street-by-Street Map* is marked in red.

Palazzo Doria Pamphilj ❻ is shown on this map as well.

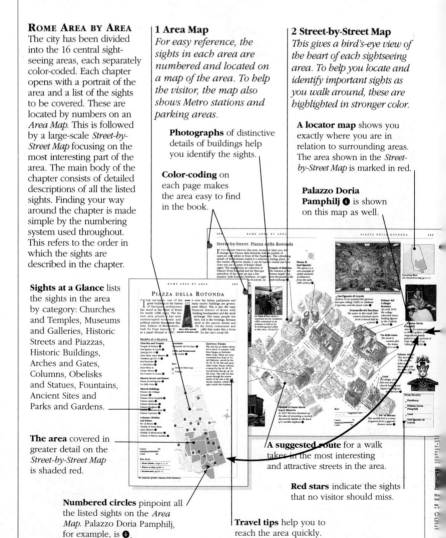

A suggested route for a walk takes in the most interesting and attractive streets in the area.

Red stars indicate the sights that no visitor should miss.

Travel tips help you to reach the area quickly.

ROME AT A GLANCE

Each map in this section covers a specific theme: *Churches and Temples, Museums and Galleries, Fountains and Obelisks, Celebrated Visitors and Residents.* The top sights are shown on the map; other sights are described on the two pages following.

Each sightseeing area is color-coded.

The theme is explored in greater detail on the two pages following the map.

3 Detailed information on each sight

All the important sights in each area are described individually. They are listed in order, following the numbering on the Area Map. Practical information is also provided.

PRACTICAL INFORMATION

Each entry provides all the information needed to visit the sight. A key to the symbols used is inside the back cover.

Map reference to *Street Finder* at back of book

Sight number

Address

Telephone number

Palazzo Doria Pamphilj ❻

Palazzo del Collegio Romano 1A.
Map 5 A4 & 12 E3. ☎ 679 43 65.
🚌 56, 60, 62, 85, 90, 95, 160, 492.
Open 10am–1pm Tue, Fri, Sat & Sun.
Closed public hols. **Adm charge.** ♿
📷 compulsory for private apartments; notify attendant if you want tour. 📷

Opening hours

Useful bus routes

Services and facilities available

4 Rome's major sights

These are given two or more full pages in the sightseeing area in which they are found. Historic buildings are dissected to reveal their interiors; and museums and galleries have color-coded floor plans to help you find important exhibits.

The Visitors' Checklist provides the practical information you will need to plan your visit.

The facade of each major sight is shown to help you spot it quickly.

Red stars indicate the most interesting architectural details of the building, and the most important works of art or exhibits on display inside.

A timeline charts the key events in the history of the building.

INTRODUCING
ROME

Putting Rome on the Map

Since its foundation 2,700 years ago on seven hills near the banks of the River Tiber, Rome has grown into a city of three million people covering 580 sq miles (1,500 sq km) of southern Italy. Within this area is the independent Vatican City State. Rome was made capital of the newly united Italy in 1870. It is about 17 miles (28 km) from the sea and has good rail and road links to many other historic Italian towns and cities.

KEY

☐ Rome and Environs

— Main railway

✈ Airport

═ Motorway

═ A road

0 kilometers   50

0 miles   25

Pisa

Arno

Livorno

Firenze (Florence)

Arezzo

Siena   326

223

Isola
d'Elba

Lago
di Bolsena

Viterbo

Tarquinia

Civitavecchia

(Vatican City) Città

Aerial view looking north over Isola Tiberina

N

M A R

T I R R E N

(TYRRHENIAN SEA

Europe

Rome is in southern Europe, on the same line of latitude as New York. It has two airports and is about 3 hours' flying time from London. Rome is also linked to the rest of Europe by road and rail. It is about 15 hours from Paris by train. It is also at the center of Italy's main road network, parts of which follow the routes of ancient Roman roads.

EUROPE

NORWAY   SWEDEN   FINLAND

ESTONIA

RUSSIAN FED.

DENMARK

LATVIA

LITHUANIA

RUSSIAN FED.

REPUBLIC OF IRELAND   UNITED KINGDOM

NETHERLANDS   POLAND   BELORUSSIA

BELGIUM   GERMANY

LUXEMBOURG   CZECH REPUBLIC   SLOVAKIA   UKRAINE

FRANCE

SWITZERLAND   AUSTRIA   HUNGARY

SLOVENIA   CROATIA   ROMANIA

ITALY   BOSNIA AND HERZEGOVINA   YUGOSLAVIA

BULGARIA

Rome   ALBANIA

SPAIN   GREECE

PORTUGAL

ALGERIA   TUNISIA

ROME AND ENVIRONS

0 kilometers   10

0 miles   5

Pesaro

Via Cassia

Via Flaminia

Via Salaria

Via Nomentana

A1

Via Tiburtina

A24

5

1 Via Aurelia

Grande Raccordo Anulare (GRA)

Città del Vaticano
(Vatican City)

See next page

Via Casilina

6

A12

A2

EUR

Leonardo
da Vinci
(Fiumicino)

Tevere
(Tiber)

Via Cristoforo Colombo

148

(GRA)

Ciampino

Via Appia

7

Rome and Environs
*A major ringroad, the Grande Raccordo
Anulare (GRA), circles the city and links
up with all the main roads into Rome.*

MARE
ADRIATICO
(ADRIATIC SEA)

71

Tevere
(Tiber)

36

3

75

Perugia

Assisi

Lago di
Trasimeno

75

36

3

A24

Terni

2,912 m
(9,554 ft)

Pescara

A1

L'Aquila

Lago
di Bracciano

A25

Bracciano

Tivoli

Subiaco

Parco
Nazionale
d'Abruzzo

del Vaticano

ROMA

Palestrina

Ostia
Antica

Tevere
(Tiber)

Frascati

Anagni

17

O

Velletri

148

Latina

Anzio

213

A2

(Naples) Napoli

Vesuvio
1,277 m
(4,190 ft)

Ercolano

Isola
d'Ischia

Pompei

Isola di Capri

Aerial view of the Forum

Central Rome

MOST OF THE SIGHTS described in this book lie within the old city wall in 16 areas shown on the map below. Each of the areas has its own chapter. If you are on a short visit, you may have to restrict yourself to just a few of the central areas: the Forum to see ancient Rome; the Capitol, Piazza della Rotonda and Piazza Navona for the historic center of the city; Campo de' Fiori for its grand Renaissance palazzi; Piazza di Spagna for its reminders of the 18th-century Grand Tour and its smart modern shops; and the Vatican to see St. Peter's and the center of Roman Catholicism.

PAGES 128–41
Street Finder maps
4, 5

0 meters   500
0 yards   500

Piazza di Spagna

Vatican

Piazza Navona

Piazza della Rotonda

Campo de' Fiori

Janiculum

Trastevere

PAGES 222–49
Street Finder maps
3, 4

PAGES 116–27
Street Finder maps
4, 11, 12

PAGES 142–53
Street Finder maps
4, 8, 11, 12

PAGES 214–21
Street Finder maps
3, 4, 7, 11

PAGES 206–13
Street Finder maps
4, 7, 8, 11

PAGES 102–15
Street Finder maps
4, 5, 12

PAGES 198–205
Street Finder maps
7, 8, 12

Pages 154–65
Street Finder maps
5, 6, 12

Pages 250–55
Street Finder maps
5, 6

Pages 64–75
Street Finder maps
5, 12

Pages 166–75
Street Finder maps
5, 6

Pages 76–95
Street Finder maps
5, 8, 9, 12

Pages 96–101
Street Finder map 8

Pages 188–97
Street Finder maps
8, 9

Pages 176–87
Street Finder maps
6, 9, 10

Via Veneto

Quirinal

Esquiline

Capitol

Forum

Palatine

Lateran

Aventine

Caracalla

THE HISTORY OF ROME

ONE OF THE most ancient cities in Europe, Rome was founded over 2,700 years ago. Since then, it has been continuously inhabited, and, as the headquarters first of the Roman Empire and then of the Catholic Church, it has had an immense impact on the world. Many European languages are based on Latin; many political and legal systems follow the ancient Roman model; and buildings all around the world utilize styles and techniques perfected in ancient Rome. The city itself retains layers of buildings spanning over two millennia. Not surprisingly, all this history can seem a little overwhelming.

Rome began as an Iron Age hut village, founded in the mid-8th century BC. In 616, the Romans' sophisticated Etruscan neighbors seized power but were ousted in 509, when Rome became a Republic. It conquered most of the rest of Italy, then turned its attentions overseas, and by the 1st century BC, it ruled Spain, North Africa and Greece. The expansion of the Empire provided opportunities for power-hungry individuals, and the clashing of egos led to the collapse of democracy. Julius Caesar ruled for a time as dictator, and his nephew, Octavian, became Rome's first emperor, assuming the title Augustus. During the reign of Augustus, Christ was born, and though Christians were persecuted until the 4th century, the new religion took hold, and Rome became its main center.

Even though it was the seat of the papacy, during the Middle Ages Rome went into decline. The city recovered spectacularly in the mid-15th century and for over 200 years was embellished by the greatest artists of the Renaissance and the Baroque. Finally, in 1870, Rome became the capital of the newly unified Italy.

Roman eagle (2nd century AD)

15th-century map of Rome from the north

Detail from 2nd-century AD Roman mosaic from the Temple of Fortune in Palestrina

Rome's Early Development

ACCORDING TO THE HISTORIAN Livy, Romulus founded
Rome in 753 BC. Sometime later, realizing his tribe
was short of females, he invited the neighboring
Sabines to a festival and orchestrated the mass
abduction of their women. Although Livy's account is
pure legend, there is evidence that Rome was founded
around the middle of the 8th century BC, and that the
Romans and Sabines united shortly afterward. Historical
evidence also gives some support to Livy's claim that
after Romulus's death Rome was ruled by a series of
kings, and that in the 7th century BC it was conquered
by the Etruscans and ruled by the Tarquin family. Last
of the dynasty was Tarquinius Superbus (Tarquin
the Proud). His despotic rule led to the Etruscans
being expelled and the founding of a Republic
run by two annually elected consuls. The uprising
was led by Lucius Junius Brutus, the model of the
stern, patriotic Roman Republican.

EXTENT OF THE CITY

☐ *750 BC*   ☐ *Today*

Ceremonial trumpets

Capitoline Quirinal Viminal

Palatine

Aventine Celian Esquiline

The Seven Hills of Rome
*By the 8th century BC, shepherds and
farmers lived on four of Rome's seven hills.
As the population grew, huts were built in the
marshy valley later occupied by the Forum.*

Iron Age Hut
*Early settlers lived
in crude thatch
huts. Traces of
their original
foundations
have been
found on the
Palatine.*

**Augur, digging
foundation**

TEMPLE OF JUPITER
*This Renaissance painting by Perin del
Vaga shows Tarquinius Superbus
founding the Temple of Jupiter on the
Capitol, the sacred citadel of Rome.*

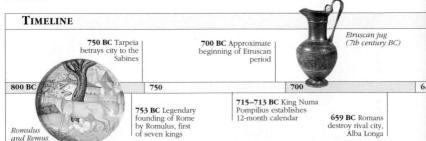

TIMELINE

750 BC Tarpeia
betrays city to the
Sabines

700 BC Approximate
beginning of Etruscan
period

*Etruscan jug
(7th century BC)*

800 BC   **750**   **700**   6

*Romulus
and Remus*

753 BC Legendary
founding of Rome
by Romulus, first
of seven kings

715–713 BC King Numa
Pompilius establishes
12-month calendar

659 BC Romans
destroy rival city,
Alba Longa

☐ **Rome's Early Development**

THE HISTORY OF ROME

The Legend of the She-Wolf
The evil King of Alba threw his baby nephews, Romulus and Remus, into the Tiber but they were washed ashore and suckled by a she-wolf.

Raven, guardian of the citadel

Apollo of Veio
Etruscan culture and religion were influenced by the Greeks. This 5th- or 6th-century statue of the Greek god Apollo comes from Veio, a powerful, wealthy Etruscan city.

King Tarquin, holding the stone worshiped as a thunderbolt

The Legend of Aeneas
Some Roman legends make the Trojan hero Aeneas the grandfather of Romulus and Remus.

WHERE TO SEE ETRUSCAN ROME

The Cloaca Maxima sewer still functions, but there are few other traces of Etruscan Rome. Most finds come from Etruscan sites outside Rome like Tarquinia, with its tomb paintings of sumptuous banquets *(see p271)*, but there are good collections in the Villa Giulia *(pp262–3)* and Vatican Museums *(p238)*. The most famous object, however, is a bronze statue of the legendary she-wolf in the Capitoline Museums *(p73)*. The Antiquarium Forense *(p87)* displays objects from the necropolis that once occupied the site of the Roman Forum.

Funeral urns shaped like huts were used for cremation starting in the mid-8th century BC.

Etruscan jewelry, like this 7th-century BC gold filigree brooch, was lavish. Treasures of this kind have given the Etruscans a reputation for luxurious living.

578 BC Servius Tullius Etruscan King

600 BC Possible date of construction of Cloaca Maxima sewer

565 BC Traditional date of the Servian Wall around Rome's seven hills

Statue of Jupiter

510 BC Temple of Jupiter consecrated on Capitoline

| 600 | 550 | 500 |

616 BC Tarquinius Priscus, first Etruscan king. Forum and Circus Maximus established

534 BC King Servius murdered

509 BC L.J. Brutus expels Etruscans from Rome and founds the Republic

L.J. Brutus

507 BC War against Etruscans. Horatius defends wooden bridge across Tiber

Kings, Consuls and Emperors

ROME HAD OVER 250 RULERS in the 1,200 years between its foundation by Romulus and AD 476, when the last emperor was deposed by the German warrior Odoacer. Romulus was the first of seven kings, overthrown in 509 BC when Rome became a Republic. Authority was held by two annually elected consuls, but provision was made for the appointment of a dictator in times of crisis. In 494 BC, the office of Tribune was set up to protect the plebeians from injustice at the hands of their patrician rulers. Roman democracy, however, was always cosmetic. It was discarded completely in 27 BC, when absolute power was placed in the hands of the emperor.

70–63 BC Pompey

107–87 BC Marius is consul seven times

205 BC Scipio Africanus

218 BC Quintus Fabius Maximus

Romulus; his twin Remus; and the she-wolf who suckled them

456 BC Lucius Quintus Cincinnatus

c753–715 BC Romulus

800 BC	700	600	500	400	300	200	100
SEVEN KINGS			REPUBLIC				
800 BC	700	600	500	400	300	200	100

c715–673 BC Numa Pompilius

396 BC Marcus Furius Camillus

c673–641 BC Tullus Hostilius

c509 BC Lucius Junius Brutus and Horatius Pulvillus

133 BC Tiberius Gracchus

122–121 BC Gaius Gracchus

c641–616 BC Ancus Marcius

c534–509 BC Tarquinius Superbus

82–80 BC Sulla

c579–534 BC Servius Tullius

63 BC Cicero

616–579 BC Tarquinius Priscus

60–50 BC Triumvirate of Julius Caesar, Pompey and Crassus

45–44 BC Julius Caesar is sole ruler

Tarquinius Priscus consulting an augur

Julius Caesar, whose rise to power marked the end of the Roman Republic

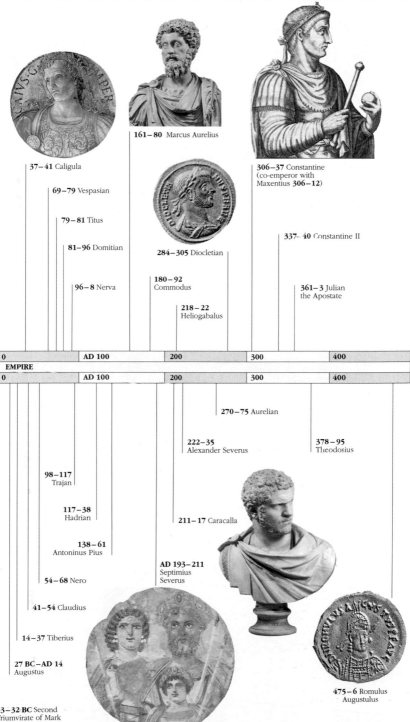

37–41 Caligula

69–79 Vespasian

79–81 Titus

81–96 Domitian

96–8 Nerva

161–80 Marcus Aurelius

284–305 Diocletian

180–92 Commodus

218–22 Heliogabalus

306–37 Constantine (co-emperor with Maxentius 306–12)

337–40 Constantine II

361–3 Julian the Apostate

| 0 | AD 100 | 200 | 300 | 400 |

EMPIRE

| 0 | AD 100 | 200 | 300 | 400 |

270–75 Aurelian

222–35 Alexander Severus

378–95 Theodosius

98–117 Trajan

117–38 Hadrian

138–61 Antoninus Pius

211–17 Caracalla

AD 193–211 Septimius Severus

54–68 Nero

41–54 Claudius

14–37 Tiberius

27 BC–AD 14 Augustus

43–32 BC Second Triumvirate of Mark Antony, Octavian and Lepidus

475–6 Romulus Augustulus

Septimius Severus and family

The Roman Republic

B Y THE MID-2ND CENTURY BC, Rome controlled the west Mediterranean, policing and defending it with massive armies. The troops had more loyalty to the generals than to distant politicians, giving men like Marius, Sulla, Pompey and Caesar the muscle to seize political power. Meanwhile, peasants whose land had been destroyed during the invasion of Hannibal in 219 BC had flooded into Rome. They were followed by slaves and freedmen from conquered lands such as Greece, swelling the population to half a million. There was plenty of work for immigrants: constructing roads, aqueducts, markets and temples, all financed by taxes on Rome's expanding trade.

Bronze coin, showing Temple of Vesta (c 57 BC)

EXTENT OF THE CITY

▨ *400 BC*   ☐ *Today*

Cut stone blocks

Covered water channels

Arch spanning road

The gradient of an aqueduct was about 1 in 1,000.

How an Aqueduct Worked
Water from a spring in the hills was collected in a reservoir to build up pressure and ensure a steady supply to the city.

High ground

Cleaning vent

Reservoir

Underground water channel

Arches carrying water across low ground

Cicero Denounces Catiline
In 62 BC, Catiline planned a coup. Cicero discovered the plot and persuaded the Senate to condemn the conspirators to death.

TIMELINE

499 BC Battle against Latin tribes; Temple of Castor and Pollux built to commemorate the victory

396 BC Definitive victory over rival Etruscan city, Veio

380 BC Servian Wall rebuilt

Via Appia

312 BC Construction of Via Appia and Rome's first aqueduct, the Aqua Appia

500 BC	450 BC	400 BC	350 BC	300 BC

Relief of Capitoline geese

390 BC Rome invaded by Celtic Gauls: quacking geese on Capitoline hill warn of impending attack

264–241 BC First Punic War (against Carthage)

☐ **Roman Republic**

Roman Street
In the 1st century BC, most buildings in Rome were made from brick and concrete. Only a few public buildings were of marble.

AQUEDUCT (2ND CENTURY BC)

Rome owed much of its prosperity to its skilled civil engineers. When the city's wells were no longer sufficient, aqueducts were built to bring water from surrounding hills. Some were over 50 miles (80 km) long.

Arches for maintaining a constant gradient over low-lying land

Temple of Juno
The ruins of this 197 BC temple are embedded in the church of San Nicola in Carcere (see p152). Romans consulted their gods before all important ventures.

Scipio Africanus
In 202 BC, the Roman general Scipio defeated Hannibal. Rome replaced Carthage as master of the Mediterranean.

WHERE TO SEE REPUBLICAN ROME

This fresco depicting a group of slaves building a wall can be seen at the Museo Nazionale Romano *(see p163).*

The Temple of Saturn, first built in 497 BC, now consists of eight majestic columns overlooking the Forum at the end of the Via Sacra *(see p83).*

Rome's loveliest Republican buildings are the two Temples of the Forum Boarium *(see p203).* Four more temples can be seen in the Area Sacra of Largo Argentina *(p150).* Most monuments from this period, however, lie underground. Only a few, like the Tomb of the Scipios *(p195),* have been excavated. One of the bridges leading to Tiber Island *(p152),* the Ponte Fabricio, dates from the 1st century BC and is still used by pedestrians.

Ponte Fabricio, built in 62 BC

250 BC	200 BC	150 BC	100 BC

220 BC Via Flaminia built, linking Rome to the Adriatic coast

168 BC Victory in Macedonian War completes Roman conquest of Greece

133–120 BC Gracchi brothers killed for trying to introduce land reforms

51 BC Caesar conquers Gaul

218–202 BC Second Punic War; Scipio Africanus defeats Carthaginians

Hannibal

149–146 BC Third Punic War; Carthage destroyed

71 BC Spartacus's slave revolt crushed by Crassus and Pompey

60 BC Rome has three joint rulers: Pompey, Crassus and Caesar

Imperial Rome

I̲N 44 BC, Caesar became dictator for life, only to be assassinated a month later. The result was 17 years of civil war, which ended in 27 BC, when Augustus became Rome's first emperor. The Empire expanded in fits and starts, but by the late 3rd century it was so huge that Diocletian decided to place it under the rule of four emperors. Thanks to trade and taxes from its vast domains, Rome was the most magnificent city in the world, studded with the lavish buildings of emperors advertising their civic munificence and military triumphs.

Statue of Bacchus, god of wine

EXTENT OF THE CITY

☐ *AD 250*   ☐ *Today*

Cross-vaulted ceiling with mosaic decoration

Natatio (swimming pool)

Apotheosis of Augustus
The first and perhaps the greatest Roman emperor, Augustus ruled for 27 years and was deified by the Senate after his death.

ROMA CAPVT MVNDI

The baths could hold up to 3,000 people. They met to gossip in the central *frigidarium* (cold room).

Area for exercise and gymnastics

The Roman Empire under Trajan
By the 2nd century AD, the Roman Empire stretched from Britain to Syria, and Rome was known as the Caput Mundi, *the head of the world.*

TIMELINE

49 BC Caesar crosses the Rubicon and takes Rome	**27** Augustus becomes first emperor	*Emperor Nero*	**64** Fire during Nero's rule destroys much of city	**65** First persecution of Christians under Nero
				72 Colosseum begun

50 BC	**0**	**AD 50**	**100**

| **44** Caesar becomes dictator for life and is murdered by Brutus and Cassius | **13** Ara Pacis is erected to celebrate the peace Augustus has secured in the Empire | **AD 42** St. Peter the Apostle comes to Rome | **67** St. Peter is crucified and St. Paul executed in Rome |

Statue of St. Peter in San Paolo fuori le Mura

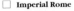
☐ **Imperial Rome**

Roman Revelry
Banquets could last for ten hours, with numerous courses. In order to continue eating, guests would retire to a small room to vomit between courses.

BATHS OF DIOCLETIAN (AD 298)
Rome's public baths were not just places to keep clean. They also had bars, libraries, barbershops, brothels and sports facilities.

WHERE TO SEE IMPERIAL ROME

There are relics of Imperial Rome throughout the city center, some hidden below churches and palazzi, others – like the Forum *(see pp76–87)*, the Palatine *(pp97–101)* and the Imperial Fora *(pp88–91)* – fully excavated. The magnificence of the era, however, is best conveyed by the Pantheon *(pp110–11)* and the Colosseum *(pp92–5)*.

The Arch of Titus *(p87)*, erected in the Forum in AD 81, commemorates Emperor Titus's sack of Jerusalem in AD 70.

Tepidarium **(warm room)**

Virgil (70–19 BC)
Virgil was Rome's greatest epic poet. His most famous work is the Aeneid, *the story of the Trojan hero, Aeneas, and his journey to the future site of Rome.*

A relief of Mithras, a popular Persian god (3rd century AD), can be seen beneath the church of San Clemente *(pp186–7)*.

164–80 Plague rages in Roman Empire

212 Citizenship granted to virtually all inhabitants of the Empire

270 Aurelian Wall begun

Section of Aurelian Wall

| 150 | 200 | 250 |

125 Hadrian redesigns the Pantheon

Mosaic from the Baths of Caracalla

216 Baths of Caracalla completed

247 Rome's Millennium is celebrated

284 Empire divided into West and East

Early Christian Rome

Crucifixion in Santa Maria Antiqua

I**N THE** 1**ST CENTURY AD**, during the reign of Tiberius, a rebellious pacifist was crucified in a distant corner of the Empire. This was nothing unusual, but within a few years, the followers of that man – Jesus Christ – became notorious in Rome, and they and Christ's teachings were perceived as a threat to public order, and many Christians were executed. Even so, the new religion spread through all levels of Roman society. When the Apostles Peter and Paul arrived in Rome, there was a small Christian community, and in spite of persecution by the state, Christianity flourished. In AD 313, the Emperor Constantine issued an edict granting Christians freedom of worship and soon after founded a shrine on the site of St. Peter's tomb. This secured Rome's position as a center of Christianity, but in the 5th century Rome's political importance declined, and the city fell to Goths and other invaders.

EXTENT OF THE CITY

▨ *AD 395*　　□ *Today*

St. Paul

Youthful, beardless representation of Christ

Classical-style border decorated with fruit

4TH-CENTURY MOSAIC, SANTA COSTANZA
Beautiful mosaics, often with palm trees and other Oriental motifs suggesting Jerusalem, helped spread the message of early Christianity.

Santo Stefano Rotondo
This 17th-century engraving shows how a Roman temple (top) might have been transformed (above) into the 5th-century round church of Santo Stefano.

The Good Shepherd
The pagan image of a shepherd sacrificing a lamb became a Christian symbol.

TIMELINE

300	350	400	450
c320 Building of first St. Peter's	**356** Legendary founding of Santa Maria Maggiore		**455** Rome sacked again by Vandals
		Gold solidus of Theodosius	
		410 Rome sacked by Alaric's Goths	
312 Control of Empire won by Constantine after battle at Milvian Bridge	*Battle of the Milvian Bridge*	**395** Division of the Empire between Ravenna and Constantinople	**422** Founding of Santa Sabina
	380 Emperor Theodosius makes Christianity the official religion of the Roman Empire		

□ **Early Christian Rome**

Epigraph of Peter and Paul
This is one of hundreds of early Christian graffiti housed in the Lapidary Gallery of the Vatican (see p237).

(see p237)

WHERE TO SEE EARLY CHRISTIAN ROME
There are traces of early Christianity all over Rome. Many ancient churches were built over early Christian meeting places and sites of martyrdoms: among them are San Clemente *(see pp186–7)*, Santa Pudenziana *(p171)* and Santa Cecilia *(p211)*. Outside the walls of the old city are miles of underground catacombs *(pp265–6)*, many decorated with Christian frescoes, while the Vatican's Pio-Christian Museum *(p240)* has the best collection of early Christian art.

Crucifixion, Santa Sabina
This 5th-century panel on the door of Santa Sabina (see p204) is one of the earliest known representations of the Crucifixion. Interestingly, Christ's cross is not actually shown.

This statuette, carved out of bone, is embedded in the rock of the Catacombs of San Panfilo, just off the Via Salaria (**map** 2 F4).

St. Peter receiving peace from the Savior

Lambs symbolizing the Christian flock

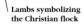

Constantine's Cross
Constantine's vision of the True Cross during the Battle of the Milvian Bridge made him convert to Christianity.

The Cross of Justin, in the Treasury of St. Peter's *(p232)*, was given to Rome by the Emperor Justin in AD 578.

475 Fall of Western Roman Empire; Byzantium becomes seat of Empire

A Byzantine image of St. Paul

609 Pantheon is consecrated as a Christian church

500 | **550** | **600**

496 Anastasius II is first pope to assume title *Pontifex Maximus*

590–604 Pope Gregory the Great strengthens the papacy

630 Sant'Agnese fuori le Mura is built in Roman Byzantine style

The Papacy

THE POPE is considered Christ's representative on earth, claiming his authority from St. Peter, the first Bishop of Rome. Though some popes have been great thinkers and reformers, the role has rarely been purely spiritual. In the Middle Ages, many popes were involved in power struggles with the Holy Roman Emperor. Renaissance popes like Julius II and Leo X, the patrons of Raphael and Michelangelo, lived as luxuriously as any secular prince. The popes listed here include all those who exercised significant political or religious influence, up as far as the end of the Counter Reformation, when the power of the papacy began to wane.

St. Ludovic Kneels before Boniface VIII by Simone Martini

314–35 St. Sylvester I

222–30 St. Urban I

217–22 St. Callixtus I

590–604 St. Gregory the Great

496–8 St. Anastasius II

Gregory the Great leading a procession to end the plague

931–5 John XI

891–6 Formosus

955–64 John XII

1227–41 Gregory IX

1216–27 Honorius III Savelli

0	200	400	600	800	1000	1200

PAPACY BASED IN ROME

0	200	400	600	800	1000	1200

336–7 St. Mark

352–66 Liberius

90–9 St. Clement

42–67 St. Peter

579–90 Pelagius II

608–15 St. Boniface IV

731–41 St. Gregory III

772–95 Adrian I

1047–8 Benedict IX

1073–85 St. Gregory VII

1099–1118 Paschal II

1130–43 Innocent II

1154–9 Adrian IV

847–55 St. Leo IV

817–24 St. Paschal I

1198–1216 Innocent III

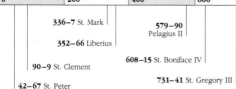

St. Peter, from a mosaic in Santa Prassede (see p171)

795–816 St. Leo III

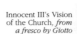

Innocent III's Vision of the Church, from a fresco by Giotto

Portrait of Gregory XIII
by Lavinia Fontana

1559–65 Pius IV Medici

1555–9 Paul IV

1523–34
Clement VII Medici

1513–21 Leo X Medici

1492–1503
Alexander
VI Borgia

1572–85 Gregory XIII Boncompagni

1670–76 Clement X Altieri

1294–1303
Boniface VIII

1484–92
Innocent VIII Cybo

1667–9 Clement IX

1471–84 Sixtus IV della Rovere

1655–67
Alexander VII Chigi

1464–71 Paul II Barbo

1605 Leo XI
Medici

1458–64
Pius II Piccolomini

1700–21 Clement XI

1300	1400	1500	1600	1700
AVIGNON	PAPACY AGAIN BASED IN ROME			
1300	1400	1500	1600	1700

1417–31
Martin V Colonna

1644–55 Innocent X Pamphilj

1447–55
Nicholas V

1585–90
Sixtus V

1623–44 Urban VIII Barberini

1592–1605
Clement VIII
Aldobrandini

Nicholas V Receiving a
Book, illustration from a
contemporary manuscript

1503–13 Julius II della Rovere

1605–21 Paul V
Borghese

Urban VIII Approving a Building
Project in the Vatican's Gallery
of Tapestries (see p241)

Raphael's portrait of Julius II

1534–49 Paul III Farnese

Paul III Gives his Approval to
the Capuchin Order by
Sebastiano Ricci

Medieval Rome

Mosaic, San Clemente

SUPPLANTED BY CONSTANTINOPLE as capital of the Empire in the 4th century, Rome was reduced to a few thousand inhabitants by the early Middle Ages; its power was just a memory, its monuments little more than weed-covered ruins. In the 8th and 9th centuries, the growing importance of the papacy revived the city and made it once more a center of power. But continual conflicts between the Pope and the Holy Roman Emperor soon weakened the papacy. The 10th, 11th and 12th centuries were among the bleakest in Roman history: violent conflict with invaders left Rome poverty-stricken, and the constantly warring local barons tore apart what remained of the city. In 1309, the papacy was forced to move to Avignon, leaving Rome to slide into further squalor and strife.

EXTENT OF THE CITY

▨ 1300   ☐ Today

San Giovanni in Laterano

Aurelian Wall

Charlemagne Crowned in St. Peter's
On Christmas Day in 800, Charlemagne was made emperor of the Holy Roman Empire, a new Christian dominion to replace that of ancient Rome.

Column of Trajan

Column of Marcus Aurelius

Madonna and Child Mosaic
The Chapel of St. Zeno (817–24) in the church of Santa Prassede (see p171) has some of the best examples of Byzantine mosaics in Rome.

MEDIEVAL PLAN OF ROME
Maps like this one, illustrating the principal features of the city, were produced for pilgrims, the tourists of the Middle Ages.

TIMELINE

725 King Ine of Wessex founds the first hostel for pilgrims in the Borgo

852 The Vatican is fortified with walls following a raid by Saracens

Emperor Otto I

961 King Otto the Great becomes first German Holy Roman Emperor

700	800	900	1000

778 Charlemagne, King of the Franks, conquers Italy

800 Charlemagne crowned emperor in St. Peter's

880–932 Rome is ruled by two women, Theodora and then her daughter, Marozia

☐ **Medieval Rome**

Stefaneschi Triptych *(1315)*
Giotto and his pupils painted this triptych for Cardinal Stefaneschi as an altarpiece for St. Peter's. It is now in the Vatican Museums (see p240).

WHERE TO SEE MEDIEVAL ROME

Among the most interesting churches of the period are San Clemente, with a fine apse mosaic and Cosmati floor *(see pp186–7)*, Santa Maria in Trastevere *(pp212–13)* and Santa Maria sopra Minerva, Rome's only Gothic church *(p108)*. Santa Cecilia in Trastevere *(p211)* has a Cavallini fresco, and there is fine Cosmati work in Santa Maria in Cosmedin *(p202)*.

Charlemagne's Dalmatic in the Treasury of St. Peter's *(p232)* was supposedly worn by the Holy Roman Emperor at his coronation. In fact, the richly embroidered vestment probably dates from the 14th century.

Colosseum
Capitol
Pyramid of Caius Cestius
Old St. Peter's
Castel Sant'Angelo
Pantheon

Cosmati Tabernacle
Marblework by the Cosmati family, like this tabernacle in Santa Sabina (see p204), *decorates many of Rome's medieval churches.*

Santa Sabina *(p204)* on the Aventine Hill has a medieval bell-tower.

1084 Rome is attacked by Normans

1108 San Clemente is rebuilt

1200 Rome an independent commune under Arnaldo di Brescia

1309 Pope Clement V moves the papacy to Avignon

1300 First Holy Year proclaimed by Pope Boniface VIII

1348 Black Death strikes Rome

1100

1200

1300

Mosaic facade, Santa Maria in Trastevere (pp212–13)

1232 Cloister of San Giovanni in Laterano completed

1140 Santa Maria in Trastevere is restored

Cola di Rienzo

1347 Cola di Rienzo – an Italian patriot – tries to restore the Roman Republic

Renaissance Rome

POPE NICHOLAS V came to the throne in 1447 determined to make Rome a city fit for the papacy. Among his successors, men like Julius II and Leo X eagerly followed his lead, and the city's appearance was transformed. The Classical ideals of the Renaissance inspired artists, architects and craftsmen, such as Michelangelo, Bramante, Raphael and Cellini, to build and decorate the churches and palaces of a newly confident Rome.

Detail of Botticelli's *Youth of Moses* (1480s)

EXTENT OF THE CITY

☐ 1500   ☐ Today

Hemispherical dome

Balustrade of small columns

Classical colonnade of 16 Doric columns

School of Athens by Raphael
In this fresco (see p243), Raphael complimented many of his peers by representing them as ancient Greek philosophers. The building shown is based on a design by Bramante.

THE TEMPIETTO
The Tempietto (1502) at San Pietro in Montorio (see p219) was one of Bramante's first works in Rome. A simple, perfectly proportioned miniature Classical temple, it is a model of High Renaissance architecture.

Cosmati-style mosaic floor

Palazzo Caprini
Bramante's design had a strong influence on later Renaissance palazzi. Parts of the building survive in Palazzo dei Convertendi (see p227).

TIMELINE

1377 Papacy returns to Rome from Avignon under Pope Gregory XI

1409–15 Papacy moves to Pisa

1452 Demolition of old St. Peter's basilica begins

1444 Birth of Bramante

| 1350 | | 1400 | | 1450 |

1378–1417 The Great Schism, a division in the papacy in Avignon

1417 Pope Martin V ends the Great Schism in the papacy

Pope Martin V, reigned 1417–31

☐ **Renaissance Rome**

Sack of Rome
In 1527, the unruly troops of Charles V of Spain pillaged the city, destroying countless works of art. Pope Clement VII took refuge in Castel Sant'Angelo.

Pope Nicholas V
Nicholas ordered the demolition of the old St. Peter's.

Statue of St. Peter, believed to have been crucified on this site

Underground chapel

WHERE TO SEE RENAISSANCE ROME

The Campo de' Fiori area *(see pp142–53)* is full of grand Renaissance palazzi, especially along Via Giulia *(pp276–7)*. Across the river stands the delightful Villa Farnesina *(pp220–21)*. The most typical church of the period is Santa Maria del Popolo *(pp138–9)*, and the best collection of Renaissance art is in the Vatican Museums *(pp234–47)*. These include the Sistine Chapel *(pp244–7)* and the Raphael Rooms *(pp242–3)*.

The Madonna di Foligno by Raphael *(1511–12)* is one of the fine Renaissance paintings in the Vatican Pinacoteca *(p241)*.

The Pietà, commissioned for St. Peter's in 1501, was one of Michelangelo's first sculptures executed in Rome *(p233)*.

1483 Birth of Raphael

1486 Building of Palazzo della Cancelleria

1519 Frescoes completed in Villa Farnesina

1527 Troops of Emperor Charles V sack Rome

Emperor Charles

1500

1550

1475 Birth of Michelangelo

1506 Pope Julius II orders start of work on new St. Peter's

1508 Michelangelo begins painting the Sistine Chapel ceiling

Cumaean Sibyl, Sistine Chapel

1547 Pope Paul III appoints Michelangelo architect of St. Peter's

Baroque Rome

B Y THE 16TH CENTURY, the Catholic Church
had become immensely rich – one of
the chief criticisms of the Protestant
reformers. The display of grandeur and
extravagance by the papal court contrasted
sharply with the poverty of the people, and
Baroque wealthy Roman society was characterized by
putto sumptuous luxury and a ceaseless round
of entertainment. To make the Catholic faith more
appealing than Protestantism, scores of churches were
built, and monuments and fountains were erected to
glorify the Holy See. The finest architects in the ornate,
dramatic style of the Baroque were
Bernini and Borromini.

EXTENT OF THE CITY

■ *1645*   □ *Today*

**Ceiling portraying
heavenly scenes**

**Monument to Pope
Alexander VII**
*This Bernini tomb in
St. Peter's* (pp230–33)
*includes a skeleton
brandishing an
hourglass.*

**Gian Lorenzo
Bernini** *(1598–1680)*
*The favorite artist of
the papacy, Bernini
transformed Rome with
his churches, palaces,
statues and fountains.*

**Holy Family
fresco**

**Tapestry of Pope
Urban VIII**
*Bernini's most devoted
patron, Pope Urban
VIII Barberini
(1623– 44), is shown
here receiving the
homage of the nations.*

A marble rose marks the
best place to stand to
appreciate the illusion of
space created by the artist.

TIMELINE

1568 The Jesuits build the
Gesù, prototypical church
of the early Baroque

Altar carving from the Gesù

1595 Annibale Carracci begins
to fresco Palazzo Farnese

1624 Bernini's sculpture
of *Apollo and Daphne*

1626 Work on
St. Peter's is
completed

1550	1575	1600	1625

1571 Birth of Caravaggio

1585 Pope Sixtus V
plans new streets

1600 Philosopher Giordano Bruno
is burned at the stake for heresy

Galileo

1633 Galileo
condemned to
death in Rome
for heresy

□ **Baroque Rome**

Illusionistic beams in ceiling

Chapel painted on flat slanting wall

Figures painted to be viewed from an angle

Queen Christina of Sweden
In a coup for Catholicism, Christina renounced Protestantism and abdicated her throne. In 1655, she moved to Rome, where she became the center of a lively literary and scientific circle.

St. Ignatius, founder of the Jesuits

San Carlo alle Quattro Fontane
One of Borromini's most influential designs was this tiny oval church (see p161) on the Quirinal Hill.

Francesco Borromini
(1599–1667)
In the many churches he built in Rome, Borromini made use of revolutionary geometric forms.

POZZO CORRIDOR
The use of perspective to create an illusion of depth and space was a favorite Baroque device. Andrea Pozzo painted this illusionistic corridor in the 1680s in the Rooms of St. Ignatius near the Gesù (see pp114–15).

1651 Bernini redesigns much of Piazza Navona

Bernini's Fontana dei Fiumi in Piazza Navona

1694 Palazzo di Montecitorio is completed

1735 Spanish Steps are designed

1732 Works start on Trevi Fountain

1650	1675	1700	1725

1657 Borromini completes Sant'Agnese in Agone

Bonnie Prince Charlie, pretender to the throne of England

1656 Work starts on Bernini's colonnade for St. Peter's square

1721 Bonnie Prince Charlie is born in Rome

1734 Clement XII makes Palazzo Nuovo world's first public museum

Understanding Rome's Architecture

Arch of Titus

THE ARCHITECTURE of Imperial Rome kept alive the Classical styles of ancient Greece, at the same time developing new, uniquely Roman forms based on the arch, the vault and the dome. The next important period was the 12th century, when many Romanesque churches were built. The Renaissance saw a return to Classical ideals, inspired by the example of Florence, but in the 17th century Rome found a style of its own again in the flamboyance of the Baroque.

The entablature above these columns has both straight and arched sections (Hadrian's Villa).

CLASSICAL ROME

Most Roman buildings were of concrete faced with brick, but from the 1st century BC, the Romans started to imitate earlier Greek models, using marble to decorate temples and other public buildings.

Caryatids were sculpted columns, usually in the form of a female figure. Roman caryatids, like this one in the Forum of Augustus, were often copied in detail from earlier Greek examples.

Plain frieze — Corinthian capital — Triangular pediment — Cornice (projecting section along facade) — Architrave (horizontal section resting on columns) — Fluted column shaft — Podium — Cella (inner sanctuary) — Colonnade enclosing portico

Roman temples were usually built on a raised dais or podium, to make them prominent. Many were fronted by a portico, a roofed porch with columns.

The orders of Classical architecture were building styles, each based on a different column design. The three major orders were borrowed by the Romans from the Greeks.

Doric order   Ionic order   Corinthian order

Aedicules were small shrines, framed by two pillars, usually containing a statue of a god.

Coffers were decorative sunken panels that reduced the weight of domed and vaulted ceilings.

EARLY CHRISTIAN AND MEDIEVAL ROME

The first Christian churches in Rome were based on the basilica: oblong, with three naves, each usually ending in an apse. From the 10th to the 13th centuries, most churches were built in the Romanesque style, which used the rounded arches of ancient Rome.

The triumphal arch divides the nave of a church from the apse. Here, in San Paolo fuori le Mura, it is decorated with mosaics.

A tabernacle is used to house the Sacrament for the mass. This 13th-century Gothic wall tabernacle is in San Clemente.

Basilicas in Rome have, in most cases, kept their original rectangular shape. The nave of San Giovanni in Laterano retains its 4th-century floor plan.

RENAISSANCE AND BAROQUE ROME

Renaissance architecture (15th–16th centuries) drew its inspiration directly from Classical models. It revived the use of strict geometric proportions. The Baroque age (late 16th–17th centuries) broke many established rules, favoring grandiose decoration over pure Classical forms.

A baldacchino is a canopy, supported on columns, rising over the main altar. This Baroque example is in St. Peter's.

Putti were a popular decorative feature in the Baroque. A *putto* is a painting or sculpture of a child like a Cupid or cherub.

A loggia is an open-sided gallery or arcade. It may be a separate structure or part of a building, as here at San Saba.

Rusticated masonry decorates the exterior of many Renaissance palazzi. It consists of massive blocks divided by deep joints.

COSMATESQUE SCULPTURE AND MOSAICS

The Cosmati family, active in Rome during the 12th and 13th centuries, have given their name to a particularly Roman style of decoration. They worked in marble, producing various elements for churches, including cloisters, episcopal thrones, tombs, pulpits, fonts and candlesticks. These were often decorated with

Cosmatesque floor, Santa Maria in Cosmedin

bands of colorful mosaic. They also left many fine floor mosaics, usually of white marble with an inlay of red and green porphyry. Ancient Roman columns were cut up to provide the materials. Several other families of stonemasons used a similar style, and their work is also described as Cosmatesque.

Rome during Unification

Garibaldi in his distinctive red shirt

U NDER NAPOLEON, Italy had a brief taste of unity, but by 1815 it was once more divided into many small states, and papal rule was restored in Rome. Over the next 50 years, patriots – led by Mazzini, Garibaldi and others – struggled to create an independent, unified Italy. In 1848, Rome was briefly declared a Republic, but Garibaldi's forces were driven out by French troops. The French continued to protect the pope, while the rest of Italy was united as a kingdom under Vittorio Emanuele of Savoy. In 1870, troops stormed the city, and Rome became capital of Italy.

EXTENT OF THE CITY

▨ *1870*　　☐ *Today*

Porta Pia

Tricolored flag of the new Italian kingdom

Plumed hat of the Bersaglieri, crack troops from Savoy

Allegory of Italy's Liberty
This patriotic poster from 1890 shows the king; his chief minister, Cavour; Garibaldi; and Mazzini. The woman in red represents Italy.

Vittorio Emanuele II
Vittorio Emanuele, King of Piedmont, became the first King of Italy in 1861.

ROYALISTS STORM PORTA PIA
On September 20, 1870, troops of the kingdom of Italy put an end to the papal domination of Rome. They breached the city walls near Porta Pia; the pope retreated, and Rome was made the Italian capital.

TIMELINE

Napoleon Bonaparte

1751 Piranesi's *Views of Rome* revive interest in Classical ruins

1762 Trevi Fountain is completed

1797 Napoleon captures Rome

1799 Napoleon expelled from Italy by Austrians and Russians

1750　　　　　　　　1775　　　　　　　　1800

Piranesi etching of Trajan's Forum

1792 Canova creates the Tomb of Pope Clement XIII, St. Peter's

1800–1801 Napoleon takes Italy again

1807 Birth of Garibaldi

☐ **Rome during Unification**

Garibaldi and Rome

The charismatic leader Giuseppe Garibaldi had taken much of Italy from foreign rule by 1860. Rome still remained a crucial problem. Here he declares "O Roma o morte" (Rome or Death).

Villa Paolina

Giuseppe Verdi (1813–1901)

Verdi, the opera composer, supported unification and in 1861 became a member of Italy's first national parliament.

Breach in Aurelian Wall

A Freed City

This marble plaque was set up at Porta Pia to commemorate the liberation of Rome.

Victor Emmanuel Monument

A vast monument to Italy's first king (see p74) stands at the end of Via del Corso.

S · P · Q · R ·
VRBE · ITALIAE · VINDICATA
INCOLIS · FELICITER · AVCTIS
GEMINOS · FORNICES · CONDIDIT

1816 Work begins on Piazza del Popolo

Fountain in Piazza del Popolo

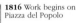

1848 Nationalist uprising in Rome. Pope flees and a Republic is formed

1860 Garibaldi and his 1,000 followers take Sicily and Naples

1870 Royalist troops take Rome, completing the unification of Italy

1825	1850

1820 Revolts throughout Italy

1821 Keats dies in Piazza di Spagna

1849 Pope is restored to power, protected by a French garrison

Pope Pius IX

1861 Kingdom of Italy founded with capital in Turin

Twentieth-Century Rome

World Cup mania

T HE FASCIST DICTATOR Mussolini dreamed of re-creating the immensity, order and power of the old Roman Empire: "Rome," he said, "must appear wonderful to the whole world." He planned to build a massive Palace of Fascism by the Forum. This came to nothing, though he did begin to build a grandiose new complex, EUR, outside the city and razed 15 churches and many medieval houses to create space for wide new roads. Fortunately, most of the old center has survived, leaving the city with one of Europe's most picturesque historic cores.

EXTENT OF THE CITY

☐ *1960s*   ☐ *Today*

Placido Domingo   **José Carreras**   **Luciano Pavarotti**

Mussolini's Plans for Rome
This propaganda poster reflects Mussolini's grandiose projects, such as Via dei Fori Imperiali in the Forum area (see p76) and EUR (p267).

THREE TENORS CONCERT (1990)
Combining Italy's love for music and soccer, this opera recital at the Baths of Caracalla was broadcast live during the World Cup.

Pope John Paul II
John Paul II is the first non-Italian pope since the 1520s. A traditionalist, he exerts a tremendous influence on the lives of the world's Catholics.

TIMELINE

1900	1912	1925	1938
1911 Victor Emmanuel Monument is completed	**1915** Italy enters World War I	**1926** Opposition parties banned	**1946** National referendum establishes Italy as a Republic; King Umberto II exiled
	1922 Fascists march on Rome. Mussolini becomes Prime Minister	**1929** Lateran Treaty creates a separate Vatican state	**1944** Allies liberate Rome from Germans
		Poster for EUR	**1940** Italy enters World War II; work begins on EUR zone

☐ **Twentieth-Century Rome**

Religion in the 20th Century

Rome has attracted pilgrims for centuries, and they continue to come, especially at Easter and for the ever more-frequent beatifications. The city also hosts a large cosmopolitan religious community.

Conductor Zubin Mehta

Poster for *La Dolce Vita*

In the 1950s and '60s Rome was Europe's Hollywood. Ben Hur, Quo Vadis? and Cleopatra were made at the Cinecittà studios, as well as Italian films like Fellini's La Dolce Vita.

Valentino Model

While not as important as Milan for fashion, Rome is still home to some of the industry's leading designers.

City-Center Traffic

Rome's streets are congested, and many buildings have been damaged by pollution. There are plans to close the historic center to traffic.

1960 Olympic Games are held in Rome

1981 Assassination attempt on Pope John Paul II in St Peter's Square

1993 Francesco Rutelli of the Green Party is elected mayor

| 1950 | 1962 | 1975 | 1988 |

1957 Treaty of Rome initiates European Common Market

1962 Second Vatican Council brings about Church reforms

1978 Premier Aldo Moro kidnapped, then killed by Red Brigades; Karol Wojtyla is elected Pope John Paul II

1990 World Cup is held in Rome

ROME AT A GLANCE

ROM ITS EARLY DAYS as a simple settlement of shepherds on the Palatine Hill, Rome grew to rule a vast empire that stretched from northern England to North Africa. Later, after the empire had collapsed, Rome became the center of the Christian world, and artists and architects flocked to work for the popes. The legacy of this history can be seen throughout the city. The following pages are a timesaving summary of the best Rome has to offer. There are sections on churches and temples, museums and galleries, fountains and obelisks, and celebrated visitors and residents. Below are the top attractions no visitor should miss.

ROME'S TOP TOURIST ATTRACTIONS

Capitoline Museums
See pp 70–73.

Colosseum
See pp92–5.

Sistine Chapel
See pp244–7.

Raphael Rooms
See pp242–3.

Trevi Fountain
See p159.

Spanish Steps
See p134.

Castel Sant'Angelo
See pp248–9.

Pantheon
See pp110–11.

St. Peter's
See pp230–33.

Roman Forum
See pp78–87.

Piazza Navona
See p120.

Interior of the Pantheon, by Giovanni Paolo Pannini (1691–1765)

Rome's Best: Churches and Temples

A S THE CENTER of Christianity, Rome has a vast wealth of beautiful and interesting churches. These range from magnificent great basilicas built to assert the importance of the medieval and Renaissance Catholic church, to smaller, humbler buildings where the first Christians gathered, often in secret. Among the most fascinating early churches are those converted from ancient Roman temples. Additions to these over the years have resulted in some intriguing many-layered buildings. A more detailed historical overview of Rome's churches is on pages 44 to 45.

Pantheon
This monumental 2,000-year-old building is one of the largest surviving temples of ancient Rome.

St. Peter's
At 450 ft (136 m) high, Michelangelo's dome is the tallest in the world. Sadly, the artist died before seeing his work completed.

Santa Maria in Trastevere
Built over a very early Christian foundation, this church is famous for its ornate mosaics.

Piazza di Spagna

Vatican

Piazza della Rotonda

Piazza Navona

T I B E R

Janiculum

Campo de' Fiori

Capito

Trastevere

Santa Cecilia in Trastevere
This statue of Cecilia, showing her as she lay when her tomb was uncovered, was sculpted in 1599 by Stefano Maderno.

Santa Maria in Cosmedin
The decorations in this 6th-century church are 12th century and earlier. A restored painting in the apse shows the Virgin, Child and saints.

Santa Maria Maggiore
Rich mosaics and relics contrast with the sober interior form of Santa Maria Maggiore. Among its treasures are vestments bearing the Borghese coat of arms.

Sant'Andrea al Quirinale
Bernini made maximum use of strong, dynamic curves in this oval interior (1658–70), creating a small masterpiece of the Roman Baroque.

Santa Prassede
Magnificent Byzantine mosaics cover the walls and ceilings of this 9th-century church. This Christ with angels is in the Chapel of St. Zeno.

Santa Croce in Gerusalemme
Saints adorn the facade of Santa Croce. Inside are relics of the Cross, brought from Jerusalem by St. Helena.

Via Veneto

Quirinal

Esquiline

Forum

Palatine

Aventine

Caracalla

Lateran

0 meters 500

0 yards 500

San Clemente
Many archaeological layers lie beneath the 12th-century church. This sarcophagus dates from the 4th century.

San Giovanni in Laterano
The original church was built by Constantine, the first Christian emperor. The Chapel of St. Venantius mosaics include the figure of St. Venantius himself.

Exploring Churches and Temples

THERE ARE MORE CHURCHES in Rome than there are days of the year, so you'll have to be selective. Catholic pilgrims have always been drawn to the seven major basilicas: **St. Peter's**, the heart of the Roman Catholic church; **San Giovanni in Laterano**; **San Paolo fuori le Mura**; **Santa Maria Maggiore**; **Santa Croce in Gerusalemme**; **San Lorenzo fuori le Mura** and **San Sebastiano**. These have a wealth of relics, tombs and magnificent works of art from many different periods. Smaller churches can be equally fascinating, especially those that have preserved their original character.

13th-century fresco by Pietro Cavallini in Santa Cecilia

ANCIENT TEMPLES

ONE PAGAN TEMPLE survives virtually unaltered since it was erected in the 2nd century AD. The **Pantheon**, "Temple of all the Gods," has a domed interior quite different in structure from any other church in Rome. It was reconsecrated as a Christian church in the 7th century.

Other Roman temples have been incorporated into Christian churches at various times. Two of these are in the Forum: **Santi Cosma e Damiano** was established in the Temple of Romulus in 526, while San Lorenzo in Miranda was built onto the ruins of the **Temple of Antoninus and Faustina** in the 11th century. The Baroque facade, built in 1602, looms behind the columns of the temple.

Another church that clearly shows its ancient Roman origins is **Santa Costanza**, built as a mausoleum for Constantine's daughter. It is a round church with some splendid 4th-century mosaics.

The impressive domed interior of the Pantheon, which became a church in 609

EARLY CHRISTIAN AND MEDIEVAL CHURCHES

SOME EARLY BASILICAS, the 5th-century **Santa Maria Maggiore** and **Santa Sabina**, for example, retain much of their original structure. Other, even earlier, churches such as the 4th-century **San Paolo fuori le Mura** and **San Giovanni in Laterano** preserve their original basilica shape. San Paolo was rebuilt after an 1823 fire destroyed the original building, and the San Giovanni of today dates from a 1646 reconstruction by Borromini. Both these churches still have their medieval cloisters.

Santa Maria in Trastevere and **Santa Cecilia in Trastevere** were built over houses where the earliest Christian communities met and worshiped in secret, to avoid persecution. One church where the different layers of earlier structures can clearly be seen is **San Clemente**. At its lowest level, it has a Mithraic temple of the 3rd century AD. Other early churches include **Santa Maria in Cosmedin**, with its impressive Romanesque bell tower, and the fortified convent of **Santissimi Quattro Coronati**. Many Roman churches, most notably **Santa Prassede**, contain fine early Christian and medieval mosaics.

Cloister of San Giovanni in Laterano

UNUSUAL FLOOR PLANS

The design of Rome's first churches was based on the ancient basilica, a rectangular building divided into three naves. Since then, there have been many bold departures from this plan – including round churches, square churches based on the shape of the Greek cross, as in Bramante's plan for St. Peter's and, in the Baroque period, even oval and hexagonal ones.

Pantheon (2nd century)

Santa Costanza (4th century)

RENAISSANCE

The greatest undertaking of the Renaissance popes was the rebuilding of **St. Peter's**. Disagreements on the form it should take meant that, although work started in 1506, it was not completed until well into the 17th century. Fortunately, this did not prevent the building of Michelangelo's great dome. In addition to working on St. Peter's, Michelangelo provided the **Sistine Chapel** with its truly magnificent frescoes.

On a completely different scale, another key work of Renaissance architecture is Bramante's tiny **Tempietto** (1499) on the Janiculum. **Santa Maria della Pace** has a Bramante cloister, some frescoes by Raphael and a charming portico by Pietro da Cortona. Also of interest is Michelangelo's imaginative use of the great vaults of the Roman Baths of Diocletian in the church of **Santa Maria degli Angeli**.

There are other churches worth visiting for the sake of

Michelangelo's dramatic dome crowns St. Peter's interior

their outstanding paintings and sculptures. **Santa Maria del Popolo**, for example, has two great paintings by Caravaggio, the Chigi Chapel designed by Raphael and a series of 15th-century frescoes by Pinturicchio. **San Pietro in Vincoli**, besides having the chains with which St. Peter was bound in prison, boasts Michelangelo's awe-inspiring statue of Moses, while **San Luigi dei Francesi** contains three Caravaggios depicting St. Matthew plus frescoes by Domenichino.

BAROQUE

Interior of Rosati's dome in San Carlo ai Catinari (1620)

THE COUNTER REFORMATION inspired the exuberant, lavish style of such churches as the **Gesù** and **Sant' Ignazio di Loyola**. The best-loved examples of Roman Baroque are the later works associated with Bernini, such as the great colonnade and baldacchino he built for **St. Peter's**. Of the smaller churches he designed, perhaps the finest is **Sant' Andrea al Quirinale**, while **Santa Maria della Vittoria** houses his truly astonishing Cornaro Chapel with its dramatic sculpture, *Ecstasy of St. Teresa*. The late Baroque was not all Bernini, however. You should also look for such churches as **San Carlo ai**

Catinari, with a beautiful dome by Rosato Rosati, and the many churches by Bernini's rival, Borromini. **Sant'Agnese in Agone** and **San Carlo alle Quattro Fontane** are famed for the dramatic concave sur-faces of their facades, while **Sant'Ivo alla Sapienza's** complex structure makes it one of the small-scale Baroque masterpieces.

Bramante's St. Peter's (1503)

Sant'Andrea al Quirinale (1658)

Sant'Ivo alla Sapienza (1642)

Rome's Best: Museums and Galleries

THE MUSEUMS OF ROME are among the richest in the world; the Vatican alone contains incomparable collections of Egyptian, Etruscan, Greek, Roman and Early Christian artifacts, as well as frescoes by Michelangelo and Raphael, priceless manuscripts and jewels. Excavations in the 19th century added treasures from ancient Rome that are now displayed in museums throughout the city. The finest Etruscan collections in the world can be enjoyed in the Villa Giulia. More details on Rome's museums and galleries are given on pages 48 and 49.

Vatican Museums
The galleries and long corridors hold priceless artifacts, such as this 9th-century mosaic showing scenes from the life of Christ.

Villa Giulia
Etruscan treasures from Rome's early history are displayed in this beautiful Renaissance villa.

0 meters 500
0 yards 500

Piazza Spagna

Vatican

Piazza della Rotonda

Piazza Navona

T I B E R

Campo de' Fiori

Galleria Spada
This collection's strength lies in its 17th- and 18th-century paintings. Earlier works include a Visitation *by Andrea del Sarto (1486–1530).*

Janiculum

Trastevere

Palazzo Corsini
Included here are works by Caravaggio, Rubens and Van Dyck, as well as a painting of the Baroque sculptor Bernini – a rare portrait by Il Baciccia (1639–1709).

Galleria Doria Pamphilj
Most of the great names of the Renaissance are represented on this gallery's crowded walls. Titian (1485–1576) painted Salomé *early in his career.*

Museo Borghese
The ground-floor galleries house sculpture from ancient Greece and Rome as well as early Bernini masterpieces, such as his David *(1619).*

Museo Nazionale Romano
This fresco, from Livia's Villa (1st century AD) outside Rome, is one of a huge collection of finds from archaeological sites throughout the city.

Palazzo Barberini
The works of art here date mainly from the 13th to the 16th century. This figure of Providence comes from Pietro da Cortona's The Triumph of Divine Providence *(1633–9).*

Palazzo Venezia
The highlights of Rome's most important museum of decorative arts are its Byzantine and medieval collections, including this Byzantine enamel of Christ dating from the 13th century.

Via Veneto

Quirinal

Esquiline

pitol

Forum

Palatine

Caracalla

Lateran

entine

Capitoline Museums: Palazzo dei Conservatori
Pietro da Cortona's Rape of the Sabine Women *(1629) is one of many Baroque paintings in the picture gallery.*

Capitoline Museums: Palazzo Nuovo
Among the sculptures is this head of Giulia Domna (wife of Septimius Severus) from the 2nd century AD.

Exploring Museums and Galleries

Etruscan clay head, Villa Giulia

ROME'S MUSEUMS and galleries boast two major strengths: Greek and Roman archaeological treasures and paintings and sculpture of the Renaissance and the Baroque. The Vatican Museums have superb collections of both, as do, on a smaller scale, the Capitoline Museums. Fine paintings can also be found scattered throughout Rome in museums, galleries and churches *(see pp44–5).*

development of Roman art. Splendid copies of Greek originals can be seen in the **Capitoline Museums**.

In the Forum, occupying two floors of the church of Santa Francesca Romana, is the small but worthwhile **Antiquarium Forense**. For those who enjoy history, the large-scale model at the **Museo della Civiltà Romana** in EUR gives an excellent idea of what ancient Rome looked like in the 4th century AD.

Centurion's breast-plate, Museo della Civiltà Romana

ETRUSCAN ARTIFACTS

5th-century BC Etruscan gold plate with inscription, Villa Giulia

THE ETRUSCANS inhabited an area stretching from Florence to Rome from the 8th century BC and governed Rome from the late 7th century BC *(see pp16–17).* It was the Etruscan custom to bury the dead along with their possessions, and as a result Etruscan artifacts have been excavated from tombs all over central Italy. Three main collections can be seen in Rome. The **Villa Giulia** has been the home of the Museo Nazionale Etrusco since 1889. The villa, designed by Vignola for Pope Julius III's summer outings, is one of Rome's prettiest Renaissance buildings. In addition to the collections, the villa gardens contain

a reconstructed Etruscan temple. Not all of the finds are Etruscan; some of the pottery, statuettes and other artifacts are relics of the Faliscans, Latins and other tribes who inhabited central Italy before the Romans.

The Gregorian Etruscan Museum in the **Vatican Museums** was opened in 1837 to house Etruscan finds from tombs on church-owned land. The Museo Barracco in the **Piccola Farnesina** has statues from the much-older civilizations of ancient Egypt and Assyria.

ANCIENT ROMAN ART

THE ARCHAEOLOGICAL zone in Rome forms a huge open-air museum of evidence of ancient Roman life, while the porticoes and cloisters of the city's churches are filled with ancient sarcophagi and fragments of statuary. The largest important collection can be seen in the **Museo Nazionale Romano** at the Baths of Diocletian in front of the station. The museum's many ancient artifacts include, most notably, a sarcophagus from Livia's Villa at Prima Porta, just north of Rome. Much of this extensive collection is in storage while the rooms are being done. The most important statues are in the **Vatican Museums**, which also have the best of the great Greek works, such as the *Laocoön*, brought to Rome around the 1st century AD. It had tremendous influence on the subsequent

Victory banner, Museo della Civiltà Romana

ART GALLERIES

Muses in Raphael's *Parnassus* (1508–11), Vatican Museums

IN THE PAST, many of Rome's great aristocratic families owned magnificent private collections of painting and sculpture. Some of these are still housed in ancestral palazzi that are open to the public. One is the **Galleria Doria Pamphilj**, which has the greatest concentration of paintings of any palazzo in Rome. It's well worth searching through the dimly lit rooms to find the pearls of the collection, which include works by Raphael, Filippo Lippi, Caravaggio, Titian and Claude Lorrain, as well as a portrait of Pope Innocent X Pamphilj by the Spanish artist Velázquez. The collection of the **Galleria Spada**, begun by Bernardino Spada in 1632, is still in the fine original gallery built for it. The paintings demonstrate 17th-century Roman

Hellenistic faun, Museo Borghese

taste: Rubens, Caravaggio, Guido Reni, Guercino, Domenichino and Jan Brueghel the Elder. The **Galleria Colonna** houses a collection of art from the same period.

Other old family residences are now showcases for state art collections. The Galleria Nazionale d'Arte Antica is divided between **Palazzo Barberini** and **Palazzo Corsini**. Palazzo Barberini, built between 1625 and 1633 by Bernini and others for the Barberini family, houses paintings from the 13th to the 16th century. It also has objets d'art acquired by the state from various private collections. At some future date, the 17th- and 18th-century paintings exhibited in the Palazzo Corsini, on the south side of the Tiber, will be transferred to join the Palazzo Barberini collection.

Another wonderful private collection was that of the Borghese family, also now managed by the state. The **Museo Borghese** is under repair, and only the sculpture on the ground floor can be seen. But it's worth going to see the technically amazing *Apollo and Daphne* by the youthful genius Bernini and the famous statue of Pauline Borghese by Canova.

The **Capitoline Museums** hold collections that were gifts of the popes to the people of Rome. The Pinacoteca (art gallery) in the **Palazzo dei Conservatori** contains works by Titian, Guercino and Van Dyck. There is an art gallery at the **Vatican Museums**, but lovers of Renaissance art will head straight for the Sistine Chapel and the Raphael Rooms. Rome's main modern art collection is in the **Galleria Nazionale d'Arte Moderna**.

SMALLER MUSEUMS

THE MOST IMPORTANT of the smaller collections is the beautifully laid-out medieval museum in **Palazzo Venezia**, which has exhibits ranging from ceramics to sculpture. Rome has a wealth of small specialist museums, including a **Museum of Musical Instruments**; a **Museo del Folklore**, with tableaux showing life in Rome during the last century; and the **Burcardo Theater Museum**.

For those with an interest in the English Romantic poets who lived in Rome in the 19th century, there is the **Keats-Shelley Memorial House**, a museum in the house where John Keats died. If your interest is in the French Empire, the **Museo Napoleonico** has relics and paintings of Napoleon and his family members, many of whom lived in Rome.

Laocoön (**1st century AD**) **in the Vatican's Pio-Clementine Museum**

Finally, for people with a macabre taste, there is a waxworks, the **Museo delle Cere**.

The Deposition (**1604**) **by Caravaggio, the Vatican**

Portrait of Pauline Borghese painted by Kinson (c 1805), now in the Museo Napoleonico

Rome's Best: Fountains and Obelisks

ROME HAS SOME of the loveliest fountains in the world.
Many of them are the work of the greatest sculptors of
the Renaissance and Baroque eras. Some fountains are
flamboyant displays, others quiet trickles of water. Many
are simply drinking fountains, while a few cascade from
the sides of buildings. Obelisks date from far earlier
in the city's history. Although some of them were
commissioned by Roman emperors, many are even
older and were brought to Rome by triumphant
conquering armies. A detailed overview of the city's
fountains and obelisks is on pages 52 and 53.

Piazza San Pietro
*Twin fountains give
life to the splendid
monumental piazza
of St. Peter's. Maderno
designed the one on
the Vatican side in
1614; the other was
later built to match.*

Piazza del Popolo
*19th-century massive
marble lions and
fountains surround an
ancient obelisk in the
center of the piazza.*

Fontana dei Fiumi
*The figures in the
fountain of the four
rivers by Bernini
represent the Ganges,
the Plate, the Danube
and the Nile.*

**Obelisk of Santa Maria
sopra Minerva**
*This Egyptian obelisk,
held up by Bernini's
marble elephant, dates
from the 6th century BC.*

Fontana delle Tartarughe
*One of Rome's more secret fountains,
this jewel of Renaissance sculpture
shows youths helping tortoises into a basin.*

Fontana della Barcaccia
This elegant 1627 fountain is probably the work of Pietro Bernini, father of the more famous Gian Lorenzo.

N

0 meters 500
0 yards 500

Trevi Fountain
The Trevi, inspired by Roman triumphal arches, was designed by Nicola Salvi in 1762. Tradition has it that a coin thrown into the water guarantees a visitor's return to Rome.

iazza
spagna   Via Veneto

Quirinal

Esquiline

apitol

Forum

Palatine

Lateran

Caracalla

ventine

Fontana delle Naiadi
When this fountain was unveiled in 1901, the realistically sensual bronze nymphs caused a storm of protest.

Obelisk of Piazza San Giovanni in Laterano
The oldest obelisk in Rome dates from the 15th century BC. It came to Rome in AD 357, brought here on the orders of Constantine II.

Piazza della Bocca della Verità Fountain
In this 18th-century fountain, built by Carlo Bizzaccheri for Pope Clement XI, water spills over a craggy rock formation where two Tritons hold aloft a large shell.

Exploring Fountains and Obelisks

Fountain of the Amphorae (1920s)

THE POPES who restored the ancient Roman aqueducts used to build fountains to commemorate their deeds of munificence. As a result, fountains of all sizes and shapes punctuate the city, drawing grateful crowds on hot summer evenings. Ancient obelisks provide powerful reminders of the debt Roman civilization owed to the Egyptians. Architects have learned to incorporate them into Roman piazzas in fascinating ways.

The Pantheon Fountain

FOUNTAINS

THE TREVI FOUNTAIN is one of the most famous of all. It is a *mostra*, a monumental fountain built to mark the end of an aqueduct – in this case the Acqua Vergine, built by Marcus Agrippa in 19 BC, although the Trevi itself was not erected until 1762. Other *mostre* are the **Fontana Paola,** built for Pope Paul V in 1612 on the Janiculum, and the less magnificent **Moses Fountain**, commemorating the opening of the Acqua Felice by Pope Sixtus V in 1587.

Almost all Rome's famous piazzas have fountains. In **Piazza San Pietro** there is a matching pair of powerful fountains. Piazza Navona has Bernini's wonderful Baroque **Fontana dei Fiumi** (fountain of the rivers) as its main attraction. The fountain's four figures each represent one of the four principal rivers then known. To the south of this is the smaller **Fontana del Moro** (the Moor), also by Bernini, showing an Ethiopian struggling with a dolphin. At the north end, Neptune wrestles with an octopus on a

19th-century fountain. In Piazza Barberini is the magnificent Bernini creation of 1642–3: the **Fontana del Tritone** with its sea god blowing through a shell.

More recently, large piazzas have been redesigned around fountains. Valadier's great design for **Piazza del Popolo** (1816–20) has marble lions and fountains surrounding the central obelisk plus two more

Fountain of the Four Tiaras located behind St. Peter's

fountains on the east and west sides of the square. The turn of the century saw the opening of the **Fontana delle Naiadi** (nymphs), in Piazza della Repubblica; its earthy figures were a great scandal at the time. The highly original **Fountain of the Amphorae** (map 8 D2) was erected in Piazza dell' Emporio during the 1920s. The same designer, Pietro Lombardi, also created the **Fountain of the Four Tiaras** (map 3 C3) behind the colonnade of St. Peter's.

The city also has a number of smaller, and often very charming fountains. At the foot of the Spanish Steps is the **Fontana della Barcaccia** (the leaking boat) of 1627; the **Fontana delle Tartarughe**

Fontana dei Cavalli Marini

THE TREVI FOUNTAIN

Appropriately for a fountain resembling a stage set, the theatrical Trevi has been the star of many films set in Rome, including romantic films like *Three Coins in a Fountain* and *Roman Holiday*, but also *La Dolce Vita*, Fellini's satirical portrait of Rome in the 1950s. Whatever liberties Anita Ekberg took then, paddling in the fountains of Rome is now forbidden, however tempting it could be in the summer heat.

Anita Ekberg in *La Dolce Vita* (1960)

(the tortoise fountain) has been in the tiny Piazza Mattei since 1581, and by Santa Maria in Domnica is the **Fontana della Navicella** (little boat), created out of an ancient Roman sculpture in the 16th century. In the forecourt of **Santa Sabina** (map 8 D2) water gushes from a huge mask set in an ancient basin. The **Pantheon Fountain** (map 4 F4), from 1575, is by Jacopo della Porta. **Le Quattro Fontane** (four fountains) have stood at the Quirinal hill crossroads since 1593.

Fountains in parks and gardens include the **Galleon Fountain** (1620–21) at the Vatican, and the **Fontana dei Cavalli Marini** (seahorses), of 1791, at Villa Borghese. The somewhat decayed 16th-century terraced gardens of the **Villa d'Este**, with their display of over 500 fountains, are still worth the journey.

Piazza Navona with Fontana dei Fiumi, by Pannini (1691–1765)

The Ovato Fountain at Villa d'Este

OBELISKS

THE MOST ANCIENT and tallest of Rome's obelisks is the **Obelisk of Piazza di San Giovanni in Laterano**. Built of red granite, 100 ft (31 m) high, it came from the Temple of Ammon at Thebes, erected in the 15th century BC. It was brought to Rome in AD 357 by the order of Constantine II and put up in the Circus Maximus. In 1587 it was rediscovered, broken into three pieces, and re-erected in the following year. Next in age is the obelisk in **Piazza del Popolo**, from the 12th or 13th century BC. It was brought to Rome in the

time of Augustus and also erected in the Circus Maximus. The slightly smaller **Obelisk of Piazza Montecitorio** was another of Augustus's trophies.

Other obelisks, such as the one at the top of the Spanish Steps, are Roman imitations of Egyptian originals. The **Obelisk of Piazza dell' Esquilino** and the one in **Piazza del Quirinale** (map 5 B4) first stood at the entrance to the Mausoleum of Augustus. When reerected, most obelisks were mounted on decorative bases, often with statues and fountains at their foot. Others became integral parts of sculptures. Bernini was responsible for the marble elephant balancing the Egyptian **Obelisk of Santa Maria sopra Minerva** on its back, and for the **Fontana**

Obelisk in Piazza del Popolo

dei Fiumi, with an obelisk from the Circus of Maxentius. Another obelisk was added to the remodeled Pantheon Fountain in 1711. The obelisk in **Piazza San Pietro** is Egyptian but does not have the usual hieroglyphics.

The **Obelisk of Axum** was brought by Mussolini's army from Ethiopia in 1937 as a war trophy. It now stands by the United Nations building near the Circus Maximus.

Wall fountain at Villa d'Este

Celebrated Visitors and Residents

Rome exerts a powerful fascination, and foreigners thoughout history have succumbed to its charms, often staying for long periods or even taking up permanent residence. The list of famous visitors is almost endless: painters, sculptors and architects from Rome's very earliest days; writers, poets and musicians; and exiles, pilgrims, religious teachers, philosophers, aesthetes and archaeologists – all have passed through. Their orchestral works, operas, paintings, drawings, drama and literary journals testify to Rome's inspirational effect.

Martin Luther *(1483–1546)*
The religious reformer from Germany came to the convent at Santa Maria del Popolo in 1511. His horror at the corruption he saw led to the Reformation.

J.W. von Goethe *(1749–1832)*
The German poet, philosopher, artist, playwright, botanist and courtier lived at 20 Via del Corso, now a museum.

Sant'Ignazio di Loyola *(1491–1556)*
He came to Rome from Spain in 1537 and founded the Jesuits near what is now the Gesù, the first Jesuit church.

Vatican

Piazza Popol

Piazza della Rot

Piazza Navona

Janiculum

T I B E R

Campo de' Fic

Trastevere

Queen Christina *(1626–89)*
The Swedish queen abdicated in 1654 and came to live in Palazzo Corsini on Via Lungara.

St. Dominic *(1170–1221)*
Founder of the Dominican order, St. Dominic was born in Spain. The order's headquarters were at Santa Sabina on the Aventine.

Jean Auguste Ingres *(1780–1867)*
The 19th-century French painter, leader of the Neoclassical tradition, lived in Rome from 1806 until 1820. He returned in 1834 as director of the French Academy at Villa Medici.

Pauline Borghese
(1780–1825)
Napoleon's sister was the subject of scandal in 1805, when she posed semi-nude for a statue by Canova, which is now in Villa Borghese.

The Exiled Stuarts
James Stuart (1688–1766), unsuccessful claimant to the British throne, came to Rome as an exile. He was presented with Palazzo Balestra by Pope Clement XI and died here.

Via Veneto

Quirinal

Esquiline

pitol

Forum

Palatine

Lateran

Caracalla

Aventine

0 meters 500

0 yards 500

Lord Byron *(1788–1824)*
Though the English poet's stay in the city was brief, the influence on his work was long-lasting. Stanzas in Childe Harold's Pilgrimage *and* Manfred *were inspired by his seeing the Colosseum in moonlight.*

Percy Bysshe Shelley
(1792–1822)
The great English Romantic poet wrote his drama Prometheus Unbound *in the calm of the ruined Baths of Caracalla in 1819.*

Artists and Writers Inspired by Rome

A RTISTS AND WRITERS have been attracted to Rome since Classical times. Many came to work for the emperors; the poets Catullus, Horace, Virgil and Ovid, for example, all enjoyed the patronage of Emperor Augustus. Later on, especially in the Renaissance and Baroque periods, the greatest artists and architects came to Rome to compete for commissions from the popes. However, patronage was not the only magnet. Since the Renaissance, Rome's Classical past and its picturesque ruins have drawn artists, architects and writers from all over Italy and abroad.

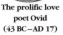

The prolific love poet Ovid (43 BC–AD 17)

Self-portrait by the 18th-century artist Angelica Kauffmann, c 1770

PAINTERS, SCULPTORS AND ARCHITECTS

Diego Velázquez, one of many great 17th-century artists to visit Rome

I N THE EARLY 16th century, artists and architects were summoned from all parts of Italy to realize the grandiose building projects of the popes. From Urbino came Bramante (1444–1514) and Raphael (1483–1520); from Perugia came Perugino (1450–1523); from Florence came Michelangelo (1475–1564) and many others. They worked in the Vatican, on the new St. Peter's and on the decoration of the Sistine Chapel. Artists were often well rewarded, but they also lived in dangerous times. Florentine sculptor and goldsmith Benvenuto Cellini (1500–71) helped defend Castel Sant' Angelo *(see pp248–9)* during the Sack of Rome (1527) but was later imprisoned there and made a dramatic escape. His memoirs tell the story.

Toward the end of the 16th century, church patronage was generous to the Milanese-born Caravaggio (1571–1610), despite his violent character and unruly life. The Carracci family from Bologna also flourished – especially brothers Annibale (1560–1609) and Agostino (1557–1602).

The work of Gian Lorenzo Bernini (1598–1680) can be seen all over Rome. He succeeded Carlo Maderno (1556–1629) as architect of St. Peter's and created its great bronze baldacchino; the splendid colonnade *(see pp230–31);* and numerous fountains, churches and sculptures. His rival for the title of leading architect of the Roman Baroque was Francesco Borromini (1599–1667), whose highly original genius can be appreciated in many Roman churches and palazzi.

In the 17th century, it became common for artists from outside Italy to work in Rome. Diego Velázquez (1599–1660), King Philip IV of Spain's court painter, came in 1628 to study the treasures of the Vatican. Rubens (1577–1640) came from Antwerp to study and carry out commissions. The French artists Nicolas Poussin (1594–1665) and Claude Lorrain (1600–82) lived here for many years.

The Classical revival of the 18th century attracted artists to Rome in unprecedented numbers. From Britain came the Scottish architect Robert Adam (1728–92) and the Swiss artist Angelica Kauffmann (1741–1807), who settled here and was buried with honor in Sant'Andrea delle Fratte. After the Baroque excesses, sculpture turned to the simplicity of Neoclassicism. A leader of this movement was Antonio Canova (1757–1821). Sculptors from all over Europe were influenced by him, including the Dane Bertel Thorvaldsen (1770–1844), who lived in Rome for many years.

Claude Lorrain's view of the Forum, painted in Rome in 1632

WRITERS

Dante (1262–1321) visited Rome during his exile from Florence, and in the *Inferno* he describes the great influx of pilgrims for the first Holy Year (1300). The poet Petrarch (1304–74), born in Arezzo, came to the city in much happier circumstances to be crowned with laurels on the Capitol in 1341. The poet Torquato Tasso (1544–95), from Sorrento, was invited to receive a similar honor, but died soon after his arrival. He is buried in Sant'Onofrio *(see p219)* on the Janiculum.

Torquato Tasso

Two of the first writers from abroad to visit Rome were the French essayist Montaigne (1533–92) and English poet John Milton (1608–74). Then, by the early 18th century, writers seemed to flock to Rome. Edward Gibbon (1737–94) was inspired to write *Decline and Fall of the Roman Empire* when he heard the monks singing the Angelus outside Santa Maria in Aracoeli *(see p69)*. German visitors included J.J. Winckelmann (1717–68),

who wrote influential studies of ancient art, and the poet J.W. von Goethe (1749–1832).

In the Romantic period Rome teemed with English writers: poets Keats, Shelley and Byron, followed by the Brownings and the novelist Charles Dickens. Travel writers in the 19th century included Augustus Hare (1834–1903) and the German historian Ferdinand Gregorovius (1821–91). Much of *The Portrait of a Lady* by American Henry James (1843–1916) is set in Rome.

Modern life in Rome is brilliantly captured by the Roman-born novelist and short-story writer Alberto Moravia (1907–90).

MUSICIANS

Giovanni luigi da Palestrina (1525–94), from the town of that name, became choir-master and organist to the Vatican and composed some of the greatest unaccompanied choral music ever written. In 1770, the 14-year-old Mozart heard Gregorio Allegri's unpublished *Miserere* in the Sistine Chapel and wrote it down from memory. Arcangelo

Portrait of the poet John Keats painted by his friend Joseph Severn in 1819

Corelli (1653–1713), the great violinist and composer of the Baroque age, worked in Rome under the patronage of Cardinal Ottoboni. One of his first commissions was to provide a festival of music for Queen Christina of Sweden.

During the 19th century, the Prix de Rome brought many French musicians to study here at the Villa Medici *(see p135)*. Hector Berlioz (1803–69) owed the inspiration for his popular *Roman Carnival*, the

Giacomo Puccini

overture to his opera *Benvenuto Cellini*, to his two-year stay in Rome. Georges Bizet (1838–75) and Claude Debussy (1862–1918) were also Prix de Rome winners. Franz Liszt (1811–86), after his 50th year, settled in Rome, took minor orders and became known as Abbé Liszt. He wrote *Fountains of the Villa d'Este* while staying at the villa in Tivoli.

More recent, 20th-century musical associations with Rome include the popular works by Ottorino Respighi (1870–1936), *The Fountains of Rome* and *The Pines of Rome*, while Giacomo Puccini (1858–1924) used Roman settings when creating his dramatic tragic opera, *Tosca*.

ROMAN CINEMA

The Cinecittà studios, built in 1937 just outside Rome, are most famous for the films made here in the 1940s, classics of Italian Neorealism such as Roberto Rossellini's *Roma Città Aperta* and Vittorio De Sica's *Sciùscià* and *Ladri di Bicicletta*. In the 1950s, Cinecittà became a center for international productions including the epics *Ben Hur* and *Spartacus*.

The director most strongly associated with Roman cinema is Federico Fellini, whose films *La Dolce Vita* (1960) and *Roma* (1972) present a highly idiosyncratic portrait of the follies of the city. Of all the Roman-born film-makers, perhaps the most famous is the controversial writer Pier Paolo Pasolini (1922–75), who became internationally known with his films *Teorema* (1968) and *Il Decamerone* (1971).

Pier Paolo Pasolini

ROME THROUGH THE YEAR

THE BEST TIMES to visit Rome are spring and autumn, when the weather is usually warm and sometimes even hot enough to sunbathe and swim at the beaches and lakes outside the city. November is best avoided since the weather tends to be gray and extremely rainy, while in high summer, most people (including Romans, who leave the city in droves) find the heat unbearable. Easter and Christmas are obviously very special in Rome, but there are other religious festivals worth seeing at other times in the year, as well as some enjoyable secular events, like the Festa de Noantri in Trastevere and the Flower Festival in Genzano. In villages outside Rome, local celebrations are held to welcome new crops, such as strawberries and beans in the spring, and grapes and truffles in the autumn.

SPRING

EASTER, falling in March or April, marks the official beginning of the tourist season in Rome. Catholics from all over the world flock into the city to make their pilgrimages to the main basilicas and to hear the Pope's Easter Sunday address outside St. Peter's; the less devout come simply to take advantage of the mild weather. Meanwhile, Romans pile into their cars and head for the coast and countryside, so you can expect the roads, the beaches, and the restaurants of the Castelli Romani and Lake Bracciano to be busy.

Temperatures tend to be around 66° F (18° C), but can hit 82° F (28° C), so by mid-May it's usually possible to lunch and dine outside. However, there can still be sudden downpours and temperature swings, so do bring warm

Crowds gathering in St. Peter's square at Easter

clothes and an umbrella. In April, tubs full of colorful azaleas are arranged on the Spanish Steps and along Via Veneto, and once the roses start to flower in the city's Rose Garden overlooking the Circus Maximus, it is opened to the public.

For two weeks from mid-May, Via dei Coronari is lit by candles, lined with plants and hung with banners for the street's antiques fair, while Via Margutta hosts an outdoor art show. In the first week of May, the International Horse Show is held in the Villa Borghese, and toward the end of the month many world-class tennis players flock to Rome to compete in the International Tennis Championships at Foro Italico.

EVENTS

Festa di Santa Francesca Romana (March 9), Santa Francesca Romana. Blessing of the city's cars, buses and trams (see p87).
Festa di San Giuseppe (March 19), Trionfale area. St. Joseph's (and Father's) Day. Street stalls, food and music.
Good Friday (March/April), Colosseum. Procession of the Cross at 9pm led by the pope.
Easter Sunday (March/April), St. Peter's square. Address made by the pope (see p231).
Rome's Birthday (Sunday before April 21), Piazza del Campidoglio.
Festa della Primavera (March/April), Spanish Steps and Trinità dei Monti. Azaleas in the street and concerts.
Art exhibition (April/May), Via Margutta (see p339).
International Horse Show (early May), Villa Borghese (see p350).
Antiques Fair (mid–late May), Via dei Coronari (see p324).
International Tennis Championships (late May), Foro Italico (see p350).

Flowers for sale on the Piazza del Popolo

AVERAGE DAILY HOURS OF SUNSHINE

Hours: 10, 8, 6, 4, 2, 0

Jan Feb Mar Apr May Jun Jul Aug Sep Oct Nov Dec

Sunshine Chart
Rome is famous for its light. June is the sunniest month, but very dry, and without the occasional shower the bright heat can feel intense. In autumn, Rome's southerly position makes the midday sun enjoyably warm.

SUMMER

IN JUNE, a summer season of concerts begins, with performances in some of the city's most beautiful palaces, churches and courtyards. In July and August, opera is usually staged in the Baths of Caracalla and classical drama at Ostia Antica. Throughout the summer there are also contemporary cultural events – film, music of all kinds, dance and theater – staged as part of the Cineporto and Massenzio film festivals *(see p346)* and RomaEuropa. On midsummer evenings, there are stalls and amusements on the Tiber embankments by Castel Sant'Angelo, while in the last two weeks of July

Flower-carpeted streets in Genzano

August, when the temperature often soars to over 104° F (40° C), virtually all Romans flee the city for the sea, and many restaurants, cafés and shops close for the month.

EVENTS

Flower Festival *(June, the Sunday after Corpus Domini),* Genzano, Castelli Romani, south of Rome. Streets are carpeted with flowers.
Festa di San Giovanni *(June 23–24),* Piazza di Porta San Giovanni. Celebrated with meals of snails in tomato sauce, suckling pig, a fair and fireworks display.
RomaEuropa *(late June–late July),* mainly in Villa Medici. Films, dance, theater and concerts *(see p341).*
Festa di San Pietro *(June 29),* many churches. Celebrations mark the feast of St. Peter.

Expo Tevere *(end June–mid-July),* along the Tiber. Arts and crafts, food and wine, music and fireworks *(see p339).*
Festa de Noantri *(last two weeks in July),* the streets of Trastevere. Feasting, processions and entertainment *(see p339 and p341).*
Arts outdoors *(July/August),* Baths of Caracalla, Villa Ada, Ostia Antica, by the Tiber, in parks. Opera, concerts, drama and film *(see p341).*
Festa della Madonna della Neve *(August 5),* Santa Maria Maggiore. Legendary 4th-century fall of snow re-enacted with showers of white flower petals *(see p172).*
Ferragosto *(August 15),* Santa Maria in Trastevere. Midsummer Roman holiday. Almost everything closes down. Celebrations are held for the Feast of the Assumption.

Summer vegetables

Trastevere becomes an open-air party, as the Noantri festival is celebrated with trinket stalls, dining in the street and fireworks. Mid-July is good for shoppers because the sales *(saldi)* begin.

Many Romans leave the city at the end of June, when schools close, but since June and July are busy for tourists, hotels, restaurants and cafés and sights are packed. In

The heat of an August afternoon in front of St. Peter's

AVERAGE MONTHLY RAINFALL

Jan Feb Mar Apr May Jun Jul Aug Sep Oct Nov Dec

Rainfall Chart
Autumn is Rome's rainiest season, with heavy downpours, sometimes lasting for days, especially in November. Rain in summer tends to come in violent – but often extremely refreshing – storms. In winter and early spring, expect a few dull, drizzly days.

AUTUMN

SEPTEMBER AND OCTOBER are the best – and among the most popular – months to visit Rome. The fiery heat of July and August will have cooled a little, but midday can be very hot, and you can still eat and drink outside without feeling chilly until late at night. Visiting Rome in November is not recommended: it is the wettest month of the year, and Roman rainstorms are often very strong and heavy.

At the beginning of October, an artisans' fair is held on Via dell'Orso and adjacent streets, while nearby the antiques galleries of Via dei Coronari hold open house. There are also October antiques fairs in Orvieto and Perugia, two of the loveliest Umbrian hill towns, which are about an hour's drive north of Rome. In November, there's yet another prestigious antiques fair at the papal palace of Viterbo, 40 miles (65 km) north of Rome *(see p271)*.

Autumn is, of course, the season of harvest festivals, and it can be fun to head out to the small towns around Rome to sample local cheeses, sausages, chestnuts

A roast chestnut stall in autumn

and mushrooms. Perhaps the most spectacular of these is the wine festival in Marino (in the Castelli Romani, south of Rome) where wine flows freely from the fountain in the central piazza. In Rome itself, there's a grape festival in early September, the Sagra dell'Uva, held in the Basilica of Constantine in the Forum, where there are grapes for sale, as well as street entertainment. Throughout the autumn and winter, freshly roasted chestnuts can be bought from vendors on street corners, and there is usually a stand on Campo de' Fiori where you can sample the new season's wine, *vino novello*, for free.

On All Souls and All Saints days, which fall on November 1 and 2, the Romans make pilgrimages to the tombs of relatives who are buried in the cemeteries of Prima Porta and Verano. Chrysanthemums are then traditionally placed on their graves, and for this reason they should definitely not be given to friends, hosts and hostesses as thank-you presents for their hospitality. On a much happier note, the classical concert and opera seasons begin again in October and November. Details of performances can be found in *Trovaroma (see p340)* and on posters scattered around the city.

EVENTS

Art fair *(September)*, Via Margutta *(see p339)*.
Sagra dell'Uva *(early September)*, Basilica of Constantine. Harvest festival with grapes selling at bargain prices and lots of folksy street entertainment.
Crafts fair *(last week September/first week October)*, Via dell'Orso, near Piazza Navona *(see p339)*.
Marino Wine Festival *(first Sunday in October)*, Marino. Celebrations include tastings, street entertainment and wine spouting from the fountain in the main piazza.
Antiques Fair *(mid-October)*, Via dei Coronari *(see p339)*.
Festa di Santa Cecilia *(November 22)*, Santa Cecilia in Trastevere and Catacombs of San Callisto.
Vino Novello tasting *(late November)*, Campo de' Fiori.

Autumn in the Villa Doria Pamphilj park

AVERAGE MONTHLY TEMPERATURE

	C°											F°
30												85
24												75
18												65
12												55
6												45
0												32

Jan Feb Mar Apr May Jun Jul Aug Sep Oct Nov Dec

Temperature Chart
The chart shows the average minimum and maximum monthly temperatures. July and August can be unbearably hot, making sightseeing a chore. The cooler days of spring and autumn are ideal to visit Rome, but there are some dull and rainy spells.

WINTER

Rome during one of its rare snowfalls

DURING THE WINTER, Rome is bracingly chilly, but the temperature rarely drops below freezing. Not all buildings are centrally heated, so if you're staying in a small hotel bring warm clothes and request extra blankets as soon as you arrive, because they are often in short supply. Warm up in cafés with hot chocolate or a cappuccino.

The days before Christmas are really great fun in Rome, especially with children. Manger scenes, *presepi*, are set up in many churches, piazzas and public places and

The Befana on Piazza Navona

from mid-December to Twelfth Night, Piazza Navona hosts the Befana, a Christmas market where you can buy manger scenes, decorations and toys.

If you don't have friends in Rome, Christmas can be lonely, since it is such a family event. On New Year's Eve, however, everyone is out on the street to drink sparkling wine and let off fireworks. Watch out for flying dressers, because there's a tradition of throwing out old furniture in the New Year. The Carnival season runs

from late January through to February, celebrated largely by children with costume parties and parades along Via Nazionale, Via Cola di Rienzo and the Pincio. Avoid any teenagers with shaving cream sprays and water balloons.

EVENTS

Festa della Madonna Immacolata *(December 8)*, Piazza di Spagna. Firemen climb up a ladder to place a wreath on the statue of the Virgin Mary.
Befana *(mid-December – mid-January)*, Piazza Navona. Christmas and children's market *(see p120).*
Nativity scenes *(mid-December – mid-January)*, many churches. Life-size scene in St. Peter's square, collection at Santi Cosma e Damiano.
Midnight Mass *(December 24)*, at most churches.
Christmas Day *(December 25)*, St. Peter's square. Blessing by the pope.
New Year's Eve *(December 31)*, all over city. Fireworks displays, furniture thrown out.

PUBLIC HOLIDAYS

New Year's Day (Jan 1)
Epiphany (Jan 6)
Easter Monday
Liberation Day (Apr 25)
Labor Day (May 1)
Ferragosto (Aug 15)
All Saints (Nov 1)
Immaculate Conception (Dec 8)
Christmas Day (Dec 25)
Santo Stefano (Dec 26)

Via Condotti at Christmas

ROME AREA BY AREA

CAPITOL

THE TEMPLE OF JUPITER on the Capitol, the southern summit of the Capitoline Hill, was the center of the ancient Roman world. Reached by a zigzagging path up from the Forum, the temple was the scene of all the most sacred religious and political ceremonies. The hill and its temple came to symbolize Rome's authority as *caput mundi*, head of the world, and the concept of a "capital" city is derived from the Capitol. Throughout the city's history, the Capitol, or Campidoglio as it is called in Italian, has remained the

Hand of colossal statue in Palazzo dei Conservatori

seat of municipal government. Today's city council, the Comune di Roma, meets in the Renaissance splendor of Palazzo Senatorio. Rome's position as a modern capital is seen in the enormous Victor Emmanuel Monument, which blots out the view of the Capitol from Piazza Venezia. The present arrangement of the buildings on the hill dates from the 16th century, when Michelangelo created a beautiful piazza reached by a dramatic flight of steps, the Cordonata. Two of the three buildings around the piazza are now home to the Capitoline Museums.

SIGHTS AT A GLANCE

Churches and Temples
Santa Maria in Aracoeli **7**
Temple of Jupiter **8**
San Marco **12**

Museums and Galleries
*Capitoline Museums:
Palazzo Nuovo pp70–71* **1**
*Capitoline Museums:
Palazzo dei Conservatori
pp72–3* **2**
Palazzo Venezia
and Museum **11**

Historic Buildings
Roman Insula **5**

Historic Streets and Piazzas
Piazza del Campidoglio **3**
Cordonata **4**
Aracoeli Staircase **6**

Ancient Sites
Tarpeian Rock **9**

Monuments
Victor Emmanuel
Monument **10**

GETTING THERE
All the sights in this area are within walking distance of Piazza Venezia. Bus routes converge here from all parts of the city, as do many thousands of motorists. From Termini station you can catch the 64, 65, 70, 75 or 170; from Piazza Barberini the 56, 60 or 492. From St. Peter's and the Vatican the only bus is the 64. Other useful routes include the 44, 46, 57, 90 and 90b.

0 meters   200
0 yards   200

KEY

Street by street map

SEE ALSO
• *Street Finder*, maps 5, 12

Michelangelo's Piazza del Campidoglio

Street by Street: The Capitol and Piazza Venezia

THE CAPITOL, citadel of ancient Rome, is a must stop for every visitor. A broad flight of steps (the Cordonata) leads up to Michelangelo's spectacular Piazza del Campidoglio. This is flanked by the Palazzo Nuovo and the Palazzo dei Conservatori, housing the Capitoline Museums with their fine collections of sculpture and painting. The absence of cars makes the hill a welcome retreat from the squeal of brakes below, but visitors should brave traffic to visit Palazzo Venezia and its museum.

Victor Emmanuel Monument
This huge white marble monument to Italy's first king was completed in 1911 ❿

PIAZZA VENEZIA

PIAZZA VENEZIA

San Marco
The church of the Venetians in Rome has a fine 9th-century apse mosaic ⓬

Palazzo Venezia
The museum's finest exhibits, such as this 13th-century gilded angel decorated with enamel, date from the late Middle Ages ⓫

Roman *Insula*
This is a ruined apartment block dating from imperial Rome ❺

VIA DEL TEATRO DI MARCELLO

Cordonata
Michelangelo's great staircase shifted the orientation of the Capitol to the west ❹

Aracoeli Staircase
When it was built in 1348, the staircase became a center for political debate ❻

KEY

— — — Suggested route

0 meters		75
0 yards		75

★ **Palazzo dei Conservatori**
Displayed in the courtyard in this part of the Capitoline Museums is a fine series of reliefs from the Temple of Hadrian (see p106) ❷

Santa Maria in Aracoeli
The treasures hidden behind the church's brick facade include this 15th-century fresco, The Funeral of St. Bernardino *by Pinturicchio* **7**

LOCATOR MAP
See Central Rome Map pp12–13

★ **Palazzo Nuovo**
This bust of Augustus in the Hall of the Emperors is one of many fine classical sculptures in the Capitoline Museums **1**

Palazzo Senatorio was used by the Roman Senate from about the 12th century. It now houses the offices of the mayor.

★ **Piazza del Campidoglio**
Michelangelo designed both the geometric paving and the facades of the buildings **3**

Temple of Jupiter
This artist's impression shows the gold-and-ivory statue of Jupiter that stood in the temple **8**

Tarpeian Rock
In ancient Rome traitors were thrown to their death from this cliff on the Capitol **9**

STAR SIGHTS

★ **Piazza del Campidoglio**

★ **Palazzo dei Conservatori**

★ **Palazzo Nuovo**

Capitoline Museums: Palazzo Nuovo ❶

See pp70–71.

Capitoline Museums: Palazzo dei Conservatori ❷

See pp72–3.

Piazza del Campidoglio ❸

Map 5 A5 & 12 F5. 🚌 *See **Getting There** p65.*

WHEN EMPEROR Charles V visited Rome in 1536, Pope Paul III Farnese was so embarrassed by the muddy state of the Capitol that he asked Michelangelo to draw up plans for repaving the piazza and for renovating the facades of Palazzo dei Conservatori and Palazzo Senatorio.

Michelangelo came up with the idea of a third building, Palazzo Nuovo, to form a piazza in the shape of a trapezium, embellished with Classical sculptures chosen for their relevance to Rome. Building started in 1546 but progressed so slowly that Michelangelo lived to oversee only the double flight of steps at the entrance of Palazzo Senatorio.

The piazza was completed in the 17th century, the design remaining largely faithful to the original. Two-story pilasters and balustrades interspersed by statues link the buildings thematically. The piazza faces west toward St. Peter's, the Christian equivalent of the Capitol and site of other great commissions executed by Michelangelo for Pope Paul III.

Cordonata ❹

Map 5 A5 & 12 F5. 🚌 *See **Getting There** p65.*

FROM PIAZZA VENEZIA, the Capitol is approached by a gently rising, subtly widening ramp – the Cordonata. At the foot is a pair of granite Egyptian lions, and a 19th-century monument to Cola di Rienzo is on the left, close to where the 14th-century tyrant was executed. The top of the ramp is guarded by restored Classical statues of the Dioscuri, Castor and Pollux.

Roman *Insula* ❺

Piazza d'Aracoeli. **Map** 5 A5 & 12 F4. ☎ *67 10 30 65.* 🚌 *See **Getting There** p65. **Open** by appt only: apply to Ripartizione X (see p367).*

TWO THOUSAND YEARS ago the urban poor of Rome used to make their homes in *insulae* – apartment blocks.

One of the statues of the Dioscuri at the top of the Cordonata

These were often badly maintained by landlords and expensive to rent in a city where land costs were high. This 2nd-century AD tenement block, of barrel-vault construction, is the only survivor from that era. The fourth and fifth stories and part of the sixth remain above current ground level.

In the Middle Ages, a section of these upper stories was converted into a church; its bell tower and 14th-century Madonna in a niche are visible from the street.

During the Fascist years, the area was cleared, and three lower floors emerged. Some 380 people may have lived in the tenement, in the squalid conditions described by the 1st-century AD satirical writers Martial and Juvenal. The latter mentions that he had to climb 200 steps to reach his garret.

This *insula* may once have had more stories. The higher you lived, the more dismal the conditions, as the cramped spaces of the building's upper levels testify.

The Cordonata in an 18th-century painting by Antonio Canaletto

Aracoeli Staircase ⑥

Piazza d'Aracoeli. **Map** 5 A5 & 12 F4.
🚌 *See **Getting There** p65.*

THE ARACOELI Staircase
contains 124 marble steps
(122 if you start from the
right) and was completed in
1348, some say in thanks for
the passing of the Black
Death, but more probably in
preparation for the 1350
Holy Year.

The 14th-century tribune-
turned-tyrant Cola di Rienzo
harangued the masses from
the Aracoeli Staircase; 17th-
century foreigners slept on
the steps, until Prince Caffarelli,
who lived on the hill, scared
them off by rolling stone-filled
barrels down upon them.

Popular belief has it that by
climbing the steps on your
knees you can win the
national lottery. From the top
is a good view of Rome, with
the domes of Sant' Andrea
della Valle and St. Peter's
slightly to the right.

Aracoeli Staircase

Santa Maria in Aracoeli ⑦

Piazza d'Aracoeli (entrances via
Aracoeli Staircase and door behind
Palazzo Nuovo). **Map** 5 A5 & 12 F4.
📞 679 81 55. 🚌 *See **Getting There**
p65.* **Open** 7am–noon, 4–5:30pm
(Jun–Sep: 6:30pm) daily.

DATING FROM AT LEAST the
6th century, the church
of Santa Maria in Aracoeli, or
St. Mary of the Altar in the
Sky, stands on the northern
summit of the Capitoline, on

Ceiling commemorating Battle of Lepanto in nave of Santa Maria in Aracoeli

the site of the ancient temple
to Juno. Its 22 columns were
taken from various ancient
buildings; the inscription on
the third column to the left
explains that it comes *"a
cubiculo Augustorum"* – from
the bedroom of the emperors.

The church of the Roman
senators and people, Santa
Maria in Aracoeli has been
used to celebrate many
triumphs over adversity. Its
ceiling, with naval motifs,
commemorates the Battle of
Lepanto (1571) and was built
under Pope Gregory XIII
Boncompagni, whose family
crest, the dragon, can be seen
towards the altar end.

Many other Roman families
and individuals are honored
by memorials in the church.
To the right of the entrance
door, the tombstone of
archdeacon Giovanni Crivelli,
rather than being set into the
floor of the church, stands
eternally at attention, partly
so that the signature
"Donatelli" (by Donatello)
can be read at eye level.

The frescoes in the first
chapel on the right, painted
by Pinturicchio in the 1480s
in the beautifully clear style
of the early Renaissance,
relate the life and death of
St. Bernardino of Siena. On
the left wall, the perspective
of *The Burial of the Saint*
slants to the right, taking
into account the position of
the viewer from just outside
the chapel.

The church is most famous,
however, for an icon with
apparently miraculous powers,
the *Santo Bambino*, a 15th-
century olive-wood figure of
the Christ child which was
carved out of a tree from the
garden of Gethsemane. Its
powers are said to include
resurrecting the dead, and it
is sometimes summoned to
the bedsides of the gravely ill.
The original figure was stolen
in 1994 but has now been
replaced by a replica.

At Christmas the Christ
Child is moved to a
picturesque crèche (second
chapel to the left), but usually
it is located in the sacristy, as
is the panel of the *Holy
Family* from the workshop of
Giulio Romano.

**The miraculous olive-wood Christ
Child at Santa Maria in Aracoeli**

Capitoline Museums:
Palazzo Nuovo ❶

A COLLECTION of Classical statues has been kept on the Capitoline Hill since the Renaissance. The first group of bronze sculptures was given to the city by Pope Sixtus IV in 1471, and more additions were made by Pope Sixtus V in 1586. The Palazzo Nuovo was designed by Michelangelo as part of the renovation of the Piazza del Campidoglio, and after its completion in 1654, a number of the statues were transferred there. In 1734, Pope Clement XII Corsini decreed that the building be turned into the world's first public museum.

Hall of the Philosophers
The hall contains a rich mix of portraits of Greek politicians, scientists and literary figures. They are Roman copies that decorated the libraries, villas and gardens of the wealthy in ancient times.

MUSEUM GUIDE
The two floors of the Palazzo Nuovo are devoted chiefly to sculpture. Most of the finest works, such as the Capitoline Venus, are Roman copies of Greek masterpieces. There are also two collections of busts assembled in the 18th century for visitors eager to identify all the philosophers and poets of ancient Greece and the rulers of ancient Rome. The price of entry includes admission to the Palazzo dei Conservatori, which is directly opposite.

Portrait of a Flavian Lady
The woman wears the fanciful and elaborate hairstyle popular among the female aristocracy of the 1st century AD.

Capitoline Venus

3

4　　　　5

First floor　　　**Courtyard**

★ **Marcus Aurelius**
This bronze equestrian statue of the emperor dates from the 2nd century AD. It used to stand on a pedestal in the center of the Campidoglio, but has now been restored and is housed in the Palazzo Nuovo.

Ground floor

4　　　5　　　6

The facade of Palazzo Nuovo was designed by Michelangelo, but the work was actually finished in 1654 by the brothers Carlo and Girolamo Rainaldi.

STAR SCULPTURES

★ **Marcus Aurelius**

★ **Discobolus**

★ **Dying Galatian**

KEY TO FLOOR PLAN

▨ Non-exhibition space

☐ Exhibition space

Mosaic of the Doves
This charming naturalistic mosaic once decorated the floor of Hadrian's Villa at Tivoli (see p269). It shows doves drinking water from a vase.

★ **Discobolus**
The twisted torso was part of a Greek statue of a discus thrower. An 18th-century French sculptor, Monnot, made the additions that turned him into a wounded warrior.

VISITORS' CHECKLIST

Musei Capitolini, Piazza del Campidoglio.
Map 5 A5 & 12 F5.
[67 10 30 69.
44, 46, 64, 70, 81, 110 and many other routes to Piazza Venezia.
Open 9am–7pm Tue–Sat, 9am–1:45pm Sun (last adm: 30 mins before closing). **Closed** Jan 1, Jun 29, Aug 15, Dec 25.
Adm charge (free last Sun of month). Entrance ticket is also valid for Palazzo dei Conservatori.

Red Faun
Found at Tivoli, the famous red marble satyr is a 2nd-century AD version of a Greek original – an example of Hadrian's fondness for all things Greek.

Stairs to ground floor

Stairs to first floor

★ **Dying Galatian**
Great compassion is conveyed in this Roman copy of an original Greek work of the 3rd century BC.

Alexander Severus as Hunter
In this marble of the 3rd century AD, the emperor is posed as Perseus, holding up the head of Medusa the Gorgon after he had killed her in her sleep.

Main entrance

Capitoline Museums: Palazzo dei Conservatori ❷

THE PALAZZO DEI CONSERVATORI was the seat of the city's magistrates during the late Middle Ages. Its frescoed halls are still used occasionally for political meetings, and the ground floor houses the municipal registry office. The palazzo was built by Giacomo della Porta, who carried out Michelangelo's designs for the Piazza del Campidoglio in the mid-16th century. While much of the palazzo is given over to sculpture, the art galleries on the second floor hold works by Veronese, Guercino, Tintoretto, Rubens, Caravaggio, Van Dyck and Titian.

Facade of Palazzo dei Conservatori
Work began on this Michelangelo design in 1563, the year before his death.

MUSEUM GUIDE
The rooms on the first floor are remarkable for their original 16th-and 17th-century decoration and for a number of the Classical statues. The second-floor art gallery houses paintings and a collection of porcelain in room 6. Both the Museo Nuovo and Braccio Nuovo sections are now closed.

Burial and Glory of St. Petronilla
This huge Baroque altar-piece was painted from 1622–3 by Guercino to hang in St. Peter's.

Stairs to second floor

★ **St. John the Baptist**
Painted in 1595–6, Caravaggio's sensual portrait of the young saint presents a highly unorthodox image of the forerunner of Christ.

Stairs to first floor

Second-floor art gallery

Courtyard

Main entrance

The Horatii and Curatii
D'Arpino's fresco was painted in 1613 and depicts a duel taken from early Roman legend.

KEY TO FLOOR PLAN

☐ Garden

☐ Non-exhibition space

☐ Temporarily closed

☐ Exhibition space

Endymion
The youth doomed to sleep forever by the goddess Diana was painted by Pier Francesco Mola (1612–66), who studied under Cavalier d'Arpino.

Braccio Nuovo

Esquiline Venus
The 1st-century BC figure was associated with the cult of Isis.

Museo Nuovo

Roman Garden

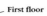
First floor

VISITORS' CHECKLIST

See p71.

STAR EXHIBITS

★ She-Wolf

★ St. John the Baptist by Caravaggio

★ Spinario

Constantine II
The head of a colossal 4th-century AD statue of the emperor has survived, along with a hand and other odd fragments.

★ **Spinario**
This is a charming bronze sculpture from the 1st century BC of a boy trying to remove a thorn from his foot.

★ **She-Wolf**
The Etruscan bronze of the wolf dates from the early 5th century BC. The legendary twins, Romulus and Remus (see pp16–17), were probably added in the 15th century.

Temple of Jupiter ⑧

Via del Tempio di Giove. **Map** 5 A5 & 12 F5. 🚌 See **Getting There** p65.

THE TEMPLE of Jupiter, the most important in ancient Rome, was built in honor of the arch god around 590 BC on the southern summit of the Capitoline Hill. From the few traces that remain, archaeologists have been able to reconstruct the rectangular Greek appearance of the temple as it once stood. In places are remnants of its particularly Roman feature, the podium. Most of this lies beneath the Museo Nuovo wing of the Capitoline Museums (see pp72–3).

By walking around the site, from the podium's southwestern corner in Via del Tempio di Giove to its southeastern corner in Piazzale Caffarelli, visitors can see that the temple was about the same size as the Pantheon.

Ancient coin showing the Temple of Jupiter

Tarpeian Rock ⑨

Via di Monte Caprino and Via del Tempio di Giove. **Map** 5 A5 & 12 F5. 🚌 See **Getting There** p65.

THE SOUTHERN TIP of the Capitoline is called the Tarpeian Rock (Rupe Tarpea), after Tarpeia, the young daughter of Spurius Tarpeius, defender of the Capitol in the 8th-century BC Sabine War.

The Sabines, bent on vengeance for the rape of their women by Romulus and

Sabine soldiers crushing the treacherous Tarpeia with their shields

his men, bribed Tarpeia to let them up to the Capitol. As the Augustan historian Livy records, Tarpeia's reward for her treachery was to be what the sabines wore on their shield arms: heavy gold bracelets and jeweled rings.

The Sabines kept to the letter of the bargain if not to its spirit – they repaid Tarpeia not with their jewelry but by crushing her to death between their shields.

Tarpeia was possibly the only casualty of her act of treachery – as the invading warriors met the Roman defenders, the Sabine women leapt between the two opposing armies, and forced them to become reconciled. All traitors and other condemned criminals were subsequently executed by being thrown over the sheer face of the rock. Today the place is still considered dangerous, and at present it has been fenced off, while surveying work is carried out.

Victor Emmanuel Monument ⑩

Piazza Venezia. **Map** 5 A5 & 12 F4. 🚌 See **Getting There** p65. **Not open** to the public.

KNOWN AS Il Vittoriano, this monument was begun in 1885 and inaugurated in 1911 in honor of Victor Emmanuel II of Savoy, the first king of a unified Italy. The king is depicted here in a gilt bronze equestrian statue, oversized like the monument itself – the statue is 39 ft (12 m) long.

The edifice contains a museum of the Risorgimento, the events that led to unification (see pp36–7). It has, however, been closed since the early 1980s. Built in austere white Brescian marble, the "wedding cake" or "typewriter" (two of the many insulting nicknames given to this unloved white elephant) will never mellow into the ocher tones of surrounding buildings. It is widely held to be the epitome of self-important, insensitive architecture.

Victor Emmanuel Monument in Piazza Venezia

Palazzo Venezia and Museum ⓫

Via del Plebiscito 118. **Map** 5 A4 & 12 E4. **☎** *679 88 65.* **⛟** *See* ***Getting There*** *p65.* **Open** *9am– 2pm Tue–Sat, 9am–1pm Sun (last adm: 30 mins before closing).* **Closed** *public hols.* **Adm charge.** 📷 ♿ ***Temporary exhibitions***.

O NE OF THE first Renaissance civic buildings in Rome, this palazzo has arched windows and doors that are so harmonious the facade was once attributed to the great Humanist architect Leon Battista Alberti (1404–72). It was more probably designed by Giuliano da Maiano, who carved the fine doorway to the piazza.

Pope Paul II

Palazzo Venezia was built in 1455 for the Venetian cardinal Pietro Barbo, who later became Pope Paul II. It was at times a papal residence, at other times the Venetian Embassy before passing into Austrian hands in 1797. Since 1916 it has belonged to the state. In the Fascist era Mussolini used it as his headquarters, addressing crowds from the balcony.

The interior is best seen on a visit to the Museo del Palazzo Venezia, Rome's most underrated museum, which holds first-class collections of early Renaissance painting; painted wood sculptures and Renaissance chests from throughout Italy; tapestries from all over Europe; majolica; silver; Neapolitan ceramic figurines; Renaissance bronzes; arms and armor; Baroque terra-cotta sculptures by Bernini, Algardi and others; and 17th- and 18th-century Italian paintings. There is a marble screen from the Aracoeli convent, which was destroyed to make way for the Victor Emmanuel Monument, and a bust of Paul II, showing him to rank with Martin V and Leo X among the fattest popes. The building also houses the national art library (closed).

Palazzo Venezia with Mussolini's balcony in the center

San Marco ⓬

Piazza San Marco 48. **Map** 5 A4 & 12 F4. **☎** *679 52 05.* **⛟** *See* ***Getting There*** *p65.* **Open** *7:30am–12.30pm & 4–7pm daily.* 🚻 🚫

T HE CHURCH of San Marco was founded in 336 by St. Mark, then pope, in honor of St. Mark the Evangelist. The relics of Pope Mark lie under the altar. The church was restored by Pope Gregory IV in the 9th century – the magnificent apse mosaics date from this period.

Further major rebuilding took place from 1455 –1471, when Pope Paul II Barbo made San Marco the church of the Venetian

Coat of arms of Pope Paul II

community in Rome. The blue-and-gold coffered ceiling is decorated with Pope Paul's heraldic crest, the lion rampant, recalling the lion of St. Mark, the patron saint of Venice. The appearance of the rest of the interior, with its colonnades of Sicilian jasper, was largely the creation of Filippo Barigioni in the 1740s. Complemented by an interesting array of funerary monuments in the aisles, the taste is typical of the late Roman Baroque.

Leon Battista Alberti, whose name is also mentioned tentatively in connection with Palazzo Venezia, may have been the architect of the elegant travertine arcade and loggia of the facade.

San Marco's apse mosaic of Christ, with Gregory IV on the far left

FORUM

THE FORUM was the center of political, commercial and judicial life in ancient Rome. The largest buildings were the basilicas, where legal cases were heard. According to the playwright Plautus, the area teemed with "lawyers and litigants, bankers and brokers, shopkeepers and strumpets, good-for-nothings waiting for a tip from the rich." As

Figure of barbarian on the Arch of Constantine

Rome's population boomed, the Forum became too small. In 46 BC Julius Caesar built a new one, setting a precedent that was followed by emperors from Augustus to Trajan. In addition to the Imperial Forums, emperors erected triumphal arches to themselves, and just to the east Vespasian built the Colosseum, center of entertainment after the business of the day.

SIGHTS AT A GLANCE

Churches and Temples
Temple of Saturn **5**
Temple of Castor and Pollux **8**
Temple of Vesta **9**
Temple of Antoninus and Faustina **11**
Temple of Romulus and Santi Cosma e Damiano **12**
Santa Francesca Romana **14**
Temple of Venus and Rome **17**

Historic Buildings
Basilica Aemilia **1**
Curia **2**
Basilica Julia **7**

House of the Vestal Virgins **10**
Basilica of Constantine and Maxentius **13**
Trajan's Markets pp88–9 **18**
Torre delle Milizie **20**
Casa dei Cavalieri di Rodi **21**
Mamertine Prison **24**
Colosseum pp92–5 **27**

Museums
Antiquarium Forense **15**

KEY
Tour of the Forum maps
M Metro station

Arches and Columns
Arch of Septimius Severus **4**
Column of Phocas **6**
Arch of Titus **16**
Column of Trajan **19**
Arch of Constantine **26**

Ancient Sites
Rostra **3**
Forum of Augustus **22**
Forum of Caesar **23**
Forum of Nerva **25**

GETTING THERE
The simplest way to reach the area is to take the Metro to Colosseo on line B. The Forum's main entrance is on Via dei Fori Imperiali, served by buses 11, 27, 81, 85, 87 and 186. Many more routes go to Piazza Venezia. For Trajan's Markets, take such buses as the 64, 65, 70 and 75 that stop in Via IV Novembre.

SEE ALSO

• *Street Finder*, maps 5, 8, 9, 12

• *Where to Stay* pp294–5

• *Triumphal Arches Walk* pp278–9

0 meters   200
0 yards   200

PIAZZA VENEZIA

LARGO ROMOLO E REMO

M Colosseo

PIAZZA DEL COLOSSEO

PIAZZA DEL COLOSSEO

View of the Forum with the Colosseum rising behind the bell tower of Santa Francesca Romana

A Tour of the Roman Forum: West

To APPRECIATE THE LAYOUT of the Forum before visiting its confusing patchwork of ruined temples and basilicas, it is best to view the whole area from above, from the back of the Capitol. From there you can make out the Via Sacra (the Sacred Way), the route followed through the Forum by religious and triumphal processions toward the Capitol. Up until the 18th century, when archaeological excavations began, the Arch of Septimius Severus and the columns of the Temple of Saturn lay half-buried underground. Excavation of the Forum continues, and the ruins uncovered date from many different periods of Roman history.

The Temple of Vespasian was the point from where Piranesi made this 18th-century engraving of the Forum. Its three columns were then almost completely buried.

Temple of Concord

Portico of the Dii Consentes

Temple of Saturn
The eight surviving columns of this temple stand close to the three columns of the Temple of Vespasian ❺

Rostra
These are the ruins of the platform used for public oratory in the Forum ❸

Basilica Julia
Named after Julius Caesar, who ordered its construction, the basilica housed important law courts ❼

Column of Phocas
One of the very last monuments erected in the Forum, this single column dates from AD 608 ❻

★ Arch of Septimius Severus

A 19th-century engraving shows the arch after the Forum was first excavated ❹

LOCATOR MAP
See Central Rome Map pp12–13

STAR SIGHT

★ **Arch of Septimius Severus**

Santi Luca e Martina
was an early medieval church that was completely rebuilt in 1640 by Pietro da Cortona.

Curia
A modern reconstruction has been built on the site of the chamber of the Roman Senate ❷

KEY

— — — Suggested route

0 meters 75

0 yards 75

Basilica Aemilia
This large meeting hall was razed to the ground in the 5th century AD ❶

Entrance to Forum

The Temple of Julius Caesar was erected in his memory by Augustus on the spot where Caesar's body was cremated after his assassination in 44 BC.

Julius Caesar

To Roman Forum: East
See pp80–81

Temple of Castor and Pollux
A temple to the twin sons of Jupiter stood on this spot from the 5th century BC. This section of cornice and the columns supporting it date from the rebuilding in AD 6 ❽

A Tour of the Roman Forum: East

THE EASTERN END of the Roman Forum is dominated by the massive barrel-vaulted ruins of the Basilica of Constantine. To picture the building as it was in the 4th century AD, you must imagine marble columns, floors and statues, as well as glittering tiles of gilt bronze. The remains of the other important buildings are scanty, though the garden and ponds in the center of the House of the Vestal Virgins make it a very attractive spot. The two churches in this part of the Forum cannot be reached from within the archaeological area but are accessible from the road outside.

The Regia was the office of the Pontifex Maximus, the chief priest of ancient Rome.

To Forum entrance

Temple of Antoninus and Faustina
The portico of this temple, built in AD 141, has been incorporated into the church of San Lorenzo in Miranda **⓫**

VIA SACRA

An early Iron Age necropolis was found here in 1902. Finds from it, such as this burial urn, are displayed in the Antiquarium.

Temple of Vesta
Partly reconstructed, this tiny temple to the goddess of the hearth was one of ancient Rome's most sacred shrines **❾**

Temple of Romulus
This domed building from the 4th century AD has survived as part of the church of Santi Cosma e Damiano **⓬**

★ House of the Vestal Virgins
The priestesses who tended the sacred flame in the Temple of Vesta lived here. The house was a large rectangular building around a central garden **❿**

★ **Basilica of Constantine**
The stark remains of the basilica's huge arches and ceilings give some idea of the original scale and grandeur of the Forum's public buildings ⑬

LOCATOR MAP
See Central Rome Map pp12–13

Santa Francesca Romana
The church takes its name from a saint who cared for the Roman poor in the 15th century ⑭

Antiquarium Forense
A small museum houses archaeological finds made in the Forum. They include this frieze of Aeneas and the Founding of Rome from the Basilica Aemilia ⑮

Colonnade surrounding Temple of Venus and Rome

Temple of Venus and Rome
These extensive ruins are of a magnificent temple built here in AD 135 by the Emperor Hadrian, largely to his own design ⑰

VIA DEI FORI IMPERIALI

VIA SACRA

Ruined Baths

Arch of Titus
This 19th-century reconstruction shows how the arch may have looked when it spanned the flagstoned roadway of the Via Sacra ⑯

STAR SIGHTS

★ **Basilica of Constantine**

★ **House of the Vestal Virgins**

KEY

– – – Suggested route

| 0 meters | 75 |
| 0 yards | 75 |

**Melted coins embedded in the
floor of the Basilica Aemilia**

Basilica Aemilia ❶

See Visitors' Checklist.

ORIGINALLY this building was
a rectangular colonnaded
hall, with a multicolored
marble floor and a bronze-
tiled roof. It was built by the
consuls Marcus Aemilius
Lepidus and Marcus Fulvius
Nobilor in 179 BC. The two
consuls, who were elected
annually, exercised supreme
power over the Republic.

Basilicas in ancient Rome
served no religious purpose;
they were meeting halls for
politicians, moneylenders and
publicani (businessmen con-
tracted by the state to collect
taxes). A consortium of *publicani* agreed to hand over a
specified sum to the state, but
its members were allowed to
collect as much as they

could and keep the difference.
This is why tax collectors in
the Bible were so loathed.

The basilica was
rebuilt many times; it
was finally burned
down when the Goths
sacked Rome in
AD 410. Business seems
to have carried on
until the last moment,
for the pavement is
splashed with tiny
lumps of coins that
melted in the fire.

Curia ❷

See Visitors' Checklist.

A MODERN REPLICA has been
built over the ruins of the
hall where Rome's Senate
(chief council of state) used
to meet. The first Curia stood
on the site now occupied
by the church of Santi
Luca e Martina, but
after the building
was destroyed by
fire in 52 BC, Julius
Caesar built a new
Curia at the edge
of the Forum. This
was restored by
Domitian in AD 94
and, after another
fire, rebuilt by
Diocletian in the 3rd
century. The replica you see
today is based on Diocletian's
Curia. Inside are two relief
panels commissioned by
Trajan to decorate the Rostra.
One shows Trajan destroying
records of unpaid taxes to
free citizens from debt; in the
other he sits on a throne
receiving a mother and child.

Ruins of the Imperial Rostra

Rostra ❸

See Visitors' Checklist.

SPEECHES WERE delivered from
this dais, the most famous –
thanks to Shakespeare –
being Mark Antony's "Friends,
Romans, Countrymen" oration
after the assassination of Julius
Caesar in 44 BC. Caesar
himself had just reorganized
the Forum and this speech
was made from the newly
sited Rostra, which is now
in ruins. In the
following year the
head and hands of
Cicero were put
on display after he
had been put to
death by the
second Triumvirate
(Augustus, Mark
Antony and Marcus
Lepidus). Fulvia,
Mark Antony's
wife, stabbed the
great orator's tongue with a
hairpin. It was also here that
Julia, Augustus's daughter, was
said to have played the
prostitute – one of many
scandalous acts that led to
her banishment.

The dais took its name from
the ships' prows *(rostra)* with
which it was decorated.
Sheathed in iron (for ramming
enemy ships), these prows had
been captured at the Battle of
Antium in the 4th century BC.

Replica of the Curia

Honorary
statue

Relief panel
in balustrade,
showing
Trajan's acts
of charity

Prows of ships
(rostra)

ROSTRA

*This reconstruction
shows the platform for
public speaking in the Forum,
as it looked in Imperial times.*

Arch of Septimius Severus ❹

See Visitors' Checklist.

THIS TRIUMPHAL ARCH, one of the most striking and best-preserved monuments of the Forum, was erected in AD 203 to celebrate the tenth anniversary of the accession of Septimius Severus. The relief panels – largely eroded – celebrate the emperor's victories in Parthia (modern-day Iraq and Iran) and Arabia.

"Barbarian" captives, Arch of Severus

Originally, the inscription along the top of the arch was to Septimius and his two sons, Caracalla and Geta, but after Septimius died, Caracalla murdered Geta and had his brother's name removed. Even so, the holes in which the letters of his name were pegged are still visible.

During the Middle Ages the central arch, half-buried in earth and debris, was used to shelter a barber's shop.

Triumphal arch of the Emperor Septimius Severus

Temple of Saturn ❺

See Visitors' Checklist.

THE MOST PROMINENT of the ruins in the fenced-off area between the Forum and the Capitoline Hill is the Temple of Saturn. It consists of a high platform, eight columns and a section of entablature. There was a temple dedicated to

Ionic capitals on the surviving columns of the Temple of Saturn

Saturn here as early as the 5th century BC, but it had to be rebuilt many times and the current remains date only from the 4th century AD.

Saturn was the mythical god-king of Italy, said to have presided over a prosperous and peaceful Golden Age from which slavery, private property, crime and war were absent. As such, he appealed particularly to the lower classes and slaves. Every year, between December 17 and December 23, Saturn's reign was remembered in a week of sacrifices and feasting known as the Saturnalia.

As long as the revels lasted, the normal social order was turned upside down. Slaves were permitted to drink and dine with (and sometimes even be served by) their masters. Senators and other high-ranking Romans would abandon the aristocratic togas that they usually wore to distinguish them from the lower classes and put on more democratic, loose-fitting gowns. During the holidays all the law courts and schools in the city were closed. No prisoner could be punished, and no war could be declared.

People also celebrated the Saturnalia in their own homes: they exchanged gifts, in particular special wax dolls and wax tapers, and played lighthearted gambling games, the stakes usually being nuts, a symbol of fruitfulness. Much of the spirit and many of the rituals of the festival have been preserved in the Christian celebration of Christmas.

Column of Phocas ❻

See Visitors' Checklist.

THIS COLUMN, 44 ft (13.5 m) high, is one of the few to have remained upright since the day it was put up. Until 1816, when an inquisitive Englishwoman, Lady Elizabeth Foster, widow of the fifth duke of Devonshire, decided to excavate its pedestal, nobody knew what it was. It turned out to be the youngest of the Forum's monuments, erected in AD 608 in honor of the Byzantine emperor Phocas, who had just paid a visit to Rome. The column may have been placed here as a mark of gratitude to Phocas for giving the Pantheon to the pope *(see pp110–11)*.

Slender, fluted Column of Phocas

Remains of the Basilica Julia, a Roman court of civil law

Basilica Julia ❼

See Visitors' Checklist, p82.

THIS IMMENSE basilica, which occupied the area between the Temple of Saturn and the Temple of Castor and Pollux, was begun by Julius Caesar in 54 BC and completed after his death by his great nephew Augustus. It was damaged by fire almost immediately afterward in 9 BC, but was subsequently repaired and dedicated to the emperor's grandsons, Gaius and Lucius.

After numerous sackings and pilferings, only the steps, pavement and column stumps remain. Nevertheless, the ground plan is fairly clear. The basilica had a central hall, measuring 260 ft by 59 ft (82 m by 18 m), surrounded by a double portico. The hall was on three floors, while the outer portico had only two.

The Basilica Julia was the seat of the *centumviri*, a body of 180 magistrates who tried civil law cases. They were split into four chambers of 45 men, and unless a case was particularly complicated, they would all sit separately.

The four courts were, however, divided only by screens or curtains, and the voices of lawyers and cheers and boos of spectators in the upper galleries echoed through the building. Lawyers used to hire crowds of spectators, who would applaud every time the lawyer who was paying them made a point and jeer at his opponents. The clappers and booers must have had a good deal of time on their hands: scratched into the steps are checkerboards where they played dice and other gambling games to while away the time between cases.

TEMPLE OF VESTA

The temple preserved the shape of the original primitive structure made of wooden posts with a thatched roof.

Temple of Castor and Pollux ❽

See Visitors' Checklist, p82.

THE THREE SLENDER fluted columns of this temple form one of the Forum's most beautiful ruins. The first temple here was probably dedicated in 484 BC in honor of the mythical twins and patrons of horsemanship, Castor and Pollux. During the battle of Lake Regillus (496 BC) against the ousted Tarquin kings, the Roman dictator Postumius promised to build a temple to the twins if the Romans were victorious. Some said the twins appeared on the battlefield, helped the Romans to victory and then materialized in the Forum – the temple marks the spot – to announce the news.

The temple, like most buildings in the Forum, was rebuilt many times. The three surviving columns date from the last occasion on which it was rebuilt – by the future Emperor Tiberius after a fire in 12 BC. For a long period the temple housed the city's office of weights and measures, and it was also used at times by a number of bankers.

Corinthian columns of the Temple of Castor and Pollux

Temple of Vesta ❾

See Visitors' Checklist, p82.

THE FORUM'S most elegant temple, a circular building originally surrounded by a ring of 20 fine fluted columns, dates from the 4th century AD, though there had been a temple on the site for far longer. It was partially reconstructed in 1930.

The cult of the Vestals was one of the oldest in Rome, and centered on six Vestal Virgins, who were required to

Cella (sacred inner chamber)

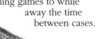

Ring of Corinthian columns

Sacred flame

keep alight the sacred flame of Vesta, the goddess of the hearth. This responsibility was originally entrusted to the daughters of the king, but it then passed to the Vestals, the only group of women priests in Rome. It was no easy task, as the flame was easily blown out by the wind. Any Vestal who allowed the flame to die was whipped by the high priest and dismissed.

The girls, who had to belong to noble families, were selected when they were between six and ten years old. They served for 30 years: the first ten were spent learning their duties, the next ten performing them and the final ten teaching novices. They enjoyed high status and financial security, but were compelled to remain virgins. The penalty for transgressing was to be buried alive, although only ten Vestals are recorded as ever having suffered this fate. The men concerned were whipped to death. When Vestals retired, they were free to live the rest of their lives as ordinary citizens. If they wished they could marry, but few ever did.

Another of the Vestals' duties was to guard the Palladium, a sacred statue of the goddess Pallas Athena. The irreverent Emperor Heliogabalus burgled the temple in the 3rd century AD. He thought he had succeeded in stealing the Palladium, but the Vestals had been warned of his intention and had replaced it with a replica.

Restored section of Temple of Vesta

Central courtyard of the House of the Vestal Virgins

House of the Vestal Virgins ⑩

See Visitors' Checklist, p82.

AS SOON AS a girl became a Vestal she came to live in the House of the Vestal Virgins. Originally this was an enormous complex with about 50 rooms on three stories. The only substantial remains today are some of the rooms around the central courtyard. This space is perhaps the most evocative part of the Forum. Overlooking ponds of water lilies and plump goldfish is a row of eroded, and mostly headless, statues of senior Vestals, dating from the 3rd and 4th centuries AD. The better-preserved examples were transferred to the Museo Nazionale Romano *(see p163)*. On one of the pedestals the inscription has been removed because the Vestal in question suffered some disgrace. It is thought she may have been a certain Claudia, known to have betrayed the cult by converting to Christianity.

Though many of the rooms surrounding the courtyard are well preserved – some even retain flights of steps leading to an upper floor – you are not allowed inside them. If you look into the series of rooms along the south side, however, you might be able to see the remains of a mill,

Honorary statue of a Vestal Virgin

used for grinding the grain with which the Vestals made a special sacrificial cake. The bakery was next door.

Temple of Antoninus and Faustina ⑪

See Visitors' Checklist, p82.

ONE OF THE FORUM'S oddest sights is the Baroque facade of the church of San Lorenzo in Miranda rising above the porch of a Roman temple. First dedicated in AD 141 by the Emperor Antoninus Pius to his late wife Faustina, the temple was rededicated to them both on the death of the emperor. In the 11th century it became a church because it was thought San Lorenzo (St. Lawrence) had been condemned to death there. The current church dates from the 17th century and is closed to the public.

Temple of Antoninus and Faustina

Temple of Romulus and Santi Cosma e Damiano ⑫

See Visitors' Checklist, p82. **Santi Cosma e Damiano** 🛈 699 15 40. **Open** 9am–12:30pm & 3–7pm daily. **Adm charge** for crèche. 🚻 📷 ♿

No one is sure to whom the so-called Temple of Romulus was dedicated, but it wasn't to Romulus, the founder of Rome, or to the son of the Emperor Maxentius.

The temple is a circular brick building, topped by a cupola, with two rectangular side rooms and a concave porch. The heavy, dull bronze doors are original.

Since the 6th century the temple has acted as a vestibule to the church of Santi Cosma e Damiano, which itself occupies an ancient building – a hall in Vespasian's Forum of Peace. The entrance is on Via dei Fori Imperiali. The beautiful carved figures of its 18th-century Neapolitan *presepio* (crèche or Nativity scene) are back on view now, and the church has a vivid Byzantine apse mosaic with Christ pictured against orange clouds.

Roof of the Temple of Romulus

Basilica of Constantine and Maxentius ⑬

See Visitors' Checklist, p82.

The basilica's three vast, coffered barrel vaults are powerful relics of what was the largest building in the Forum. Work began in the early 4th century AD under the Emperor Maxentius. When he was deposed by Constantine after the Battle of the Milvian Bridge in AD 312, work on the massive project continued under the new regime. The building, which like other Roman basilicas was used for the administration of justice and for carrying on business, is often referred to simply as the Basilica of Constantine.

The area covered by the basilica was roughly 330 ft by 215 ft (100 m by 65 m). It was originally designed to have a long nave and aisles running from east to west, but Constantine switched the axis around to create three short broad aisles with the main entrance in the center of the long south wall. The height of the building was 115 ft (35 m). In the apse at the western end, where it could be seen from all over the building, stood a 39 ft (12 m) statue of the emperor, made partly of wood and partly of marble. The giant head, hand and foot are on display in the courtyard of the Palazzo dei Conservatori *(see pp72–3)*. The basilica's roof glittered with gilded tiles until the 7th century, when they were removed and re-used to cover the roof of the old St. Peter's.

The three barrel-vaulted aisles of the basilica were used as law courts.

The octagonal coffers in the vaulted ceiling were originally faced with marble.

The main entrance was added by Constantine in AD 313.

The roof was supported by eight massive Corinthian columns. One now stands in Piazza Santa Maria Maggiore *(see p173)*.

Santa Francesca Romana ⑭

Piazza di Santa Francesca Romana. **Map**
5 B5. 🇮 *679 55 28.* 🚌 *11, 27, 81, 85,
87, 186.* Ⓜ *Colosseo.* **Open** *9:30am–*
12:30pm & 3:30–7pm daily. 🏠 ◎ 🎧

EVERY YEAR on March 9,
devout Roman drivers try
to park as close as possible to
this Baroque church with
a pleasant Romanesque
bell tower. The aim of
their strange pilgrimage
is to have their vehicles
blessed by Santa
Francesca Romana, the
patron saint of
motorists.
Francesca was
a 15th-century
wife and
mother from
Trastevere who
founded a
society of pious

**Bell tower of
Santa Francesca**

women devoted
to helping the
poor and sick.
After she had been canonized
in 1608, the church, which
was originally called Santa
Maria Nova, was rededicated
to Francesca.

The most curious sight
inside the church is a flagstone
with what are reputed to be
the imprints of the knees of
St. Peter and St. Paul. The story
goes that a magician, Simon
Magus, decided to prove that
his powers were superior to
those of the Apostles by
levitating himself above the
Forum. As Simon was in
midair, Peter and Paul fell to
their knees and prayed
fervently for God to show his
divine force. Simon instantly
plummeted to his death.

Antiquarium Forense ⑮

See Visitors' Checklist, p82.

THE FORMER CONVENT of
Santa Francesca Romana
now houses a small museum
and the offices of those in
charge of the excavations of
the Forum. The museum is
currently being reorganized,
and only one or two rooms
are open. They contain Iron
Age burial urns and graves

Dedication to Titus and Vespasian on the Arch of Titus

and their skeletal occupants,
along with some ancient bric-
a-brac exhumed from the
Forum's drains. Fragments of
statues, capitals, friezes and
other architectural decoration
taken from the Forum's
buildings will be on exhibit
when the museum reopens.

Frieze of Aeneas in the Antiquarium Forense

Arch of Titus ⑯

See Visitors' Checklist, p82.

THIS TRIUMPHAL ARCH was
erected in AD 81 by the
Emperor Domitian in honor
of the victories of his brother,
Titus, and his father, Vespasian,
in Judea. In AD 68 the Jews,
weary of being exploited by
unscrupulous Roman officials,
rebelled. A bitter war broke
out, ending two years later in
the fall of Jerusalem and the
start of Jewish Diaspora.

Although the reliefs
inside the arch are
badly eroded, you can
make out a triumphant
procession of Roman
soldiers carrying off
spoils from the Temple
of Jerusalem. The
booty includes the
altar, silver trumpets
and a golden seven-
branched menorah.

Temple of Venus and Rome ⑰

See Visitors' Checklist, p82.

THE EMPEROR Hadrian
designed this temple to
occupy what had been the
vestibule to Nero's
Golden House. Many
of the columns have
been reerected, and
though there is no
access, there is a good
view as you leave the
Forum and also from
the upper tiers of the
Colosseum. The temple,
the largest in Rome,
was dedicated to Roma,
the personification of the city,
and to Venus because she was
the mother of Aeneas, father
of Romulus and Remus. Each
goddess had her own *cella*
(shrine). When the architect
Apollodorus pointed out that
the seated statues in the
niches were too big (had they
tried to "stand," their heads
would have hit the vaults),
Hadrian had him put to death.

**Statue of
goddess**   **Porphyry
column**

Cross-section of Temple of Venus and Rome

Trajan's Markets ⑱

ORIGINALLY CONSIDERED among the wonders of the Classical world, Trajan's Markets now show only a hint of their former splendor. Emperor Trajan and his architect, Apollodorus of Damascus, built this visionary new complex of 150 shops and offices (probably used for administering the corn ration) in the early 2nd century AD. It was the ancient Roman equivalent of the modern shopping center, selling everything from silks and spices imported from the Middle East to fresh fish, fruit and flowers.

The Markets Today
Above the facade stands the 13th-century Torre delle Milizie, built for defensive purposes.

Cross vaulting

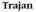

Trajan
The emperor was a benevolent ruler and a successful general.

Main Hall
Twelve shops were built on two floors, and the corn ration was shared out on the upper story. This was a free corn ration given to Roman men to prevent hunger.

Via Biberatica
The main street that runs through the market may have been lined with inns and shops selling pepper and spices.

Small semicircle of shops

Staircase

TIMELINE

AD 100	AD 500	1000	1300	1800	1950
AD 100–112 Building of Trajan's Markets	**472** Invasion by Ricimer the Suevian. Some of his Germanic troops stationed here		**1200s** Torre delle Milizie built on top of the markets	**1572** Convent of Santa Caterina da Siena built over part of markets	**1924** Many medieval houses demolished
AD 117 Death of Trajan	**552** Byzantine takeover of Rome. Markets occupied and fortified by the army		**1300s** Annibaldi and Caetani families vie for control of the area	**1828** First tentative excavations, but importance of site not recognized	**1911–14** Convent demolished
AD 98 Trajan succeeds Nerva as emperor					**1930–33** Markets finally excavated

VISITORS' CHECKLIST

Mercati Traianei, Via IV Novembre.
Map 5 B4. █ 67 10 36 13. ▥
57, 64, 65, 70, 75, 170 to Via IV
Novembre and many routes to
Piazza Venezia. **Open** 9am–7pm
Tue–Sat, 9am–1pm Sun (last adm:
30 mins before closing).
Closed Mon, public hols.
Adm charge, except for last
Sunday of each month. 📷 ♿

The Markets in the 16th Century
*This fanciful fresco depicts a gladiatorial combat
taking place in front of the partly buried remains
of Trajan's Markets.*

A Market Shop
*Shops were built with
arched entrances, their
jambs and lintels
creating rectangular
portals and windows.
A wooden mezzanine
was used for storage.*

Upper Corridor
*Shops on this upper level
were thought to have sold
wine and oil, because
storage jars were
discovered here.*

**Large hall with
semidomed
ceiling**

**Wall dividing
market area from
Forum of Trajan**

Shops on the ground floor of
the large curving semicircle
were smaller than those on
the upper stories. They were
also cooler and probably sold
vegetables, fruit and flowers.

The terrace
over the archway
spanning Via
Biberatica has
a good view of
the Forum of
Trajan below.

MARKET SHOPPING

Shops opened early and closed about
noon. The best ones were decorated
with mosaics of the goods they sold.
Almost all the shopping was done
by men, though women visited the
dressmaker and cobbler. The
tradespeople were almost all
male. In employment records
for the period AD 117 to 193,
the only female shopkeepers
mentioned are three wool-
sellers, two jewelers, a
greengrocer and a
fishwife.

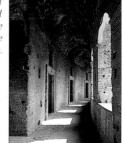

Fish mosaic

Trajan's Markets ⓲

See pp88–9.

Column of Trajan ⓳

Via dei Fori Imperiali. **Map** 5 A4 & 12 F4. *See Visitors' Checklist for Trajan's Markets, p89.*

Detail of Trajan's Column

THIS ELEGANT marble column was inaugurated by Trajan in AD 113, and celebrates his two campaigns in Dacia (Romania) in AD 101–102 and AD 105–106. The column, base and pedestal are 131 ft (40 m) tall – precisely the same height as the spur of the Quirinal Hill, which was excavated to make room for Trajan's Forum. Spiraling up the column are minutely detailed scenes from the campaigns, beginning with the Romans preparing for war and ending with the Dacians being ousted from their homeland. The column is pierced with small windows to illuminate its internal spiral staircase (closed to the public). If you wish to see the reliefs in detail, there is a complete set of casts in the Museo della Civiltà Romana at EUR *(see p267)*.

When Trajan died in AD 117, his ashes, and those of his wife, Plotina, were placed in a golden urn in the column's hollow base. The column's survival was largely thanks to the intervention of Pope Gregory I ("the Great") who reigned from 590 to 604. He was so moved by a relief showing Trajan helping a woman whose son had been killed that he begged God to release the emperor's soul

from hell. God duly appeared to the pope to say that Trajan had been rescued, but asked him not to pray for the souls of any more pagans.

According to legend, when Trajan's ashes were exhumed, his skull and tongue were not only intact, but his tongue told of his release from Hell. The land around the column was then declared sacred and the column spared. The statue of Trajan remained on top of the column until 1587, when it was replaced with one of St. Peter.

Torre delle Milizie ⓴

Mercati Traianei, Via IV Novembre. **Map** 5 B4. *Closed for restoration.*

FOR CENTURIES this massive brick tower was thought to have been the one in which Nero stood watching Rome burn, after he had set it alight in order to clear the city's slums. It is uncertain whether arson was among Nero's crimes, but it is certain that he did not watch the fire from this tower – it was built in the 13th century.

Casa dei Cavalieri di Rodi ㉑

Piazza del Grillo 1. **Map** 5 B5. 67 10 20 70. 11, 27, 81, 85, 87, 186. **Open** by appt only.

Loggia, Casa dei Cavalieri di Rodi

SINCE THE 12TH CENTURY, the crusading order of the Knights of St. John, also known as the Knights of Rhodes (Rodi) or Malta, have had their priorate in this medieval house above the Forum of Augustus. If you are lucky enough to get inside, ask to see the beautiful Cappella di San Giovanni (Chapel of St. John).

Forum of Augustus ㉒

Piazza del Grillo 1. **Map** 5 B5 & 12 F5. 67 10 20 70. 11, 27, 81, 85, 87, 186. **Open** by appt only.

Podium of the Temple of Mars in the Forum of Augustus

THE FORUM of Augustus was built to celebrate Augustus's victory over Julius Caesar's assassins, Brutus and Cassius, at the Battle of Philippi in 41 BC. The temple in its center was dedicated to Mars the Avenger. The forum stretched from a high wall at the foot of the sleazy Suburra quarter to the edge of the Forum of Caesar. At least half of it is now concealed below Mussolini's Via dei Fori Imperiali. The temple is easily identified, with its cracked steps and four Corinthian columns. Originally it had a statue of Mars that looked very like Augustus. In case anyone failed to notice the resemblance, a giant statue of Augustus himself was placed against the Suburra wall.

Forum of Caesar ㉓

Via del Carcere Tulliano. **Map** 5 A5. 67 10 20 70. 11, 27, 81, 85, 87, 186. **Open** by appt only.

THE FIRST of Rome's Imperial forums was built by Julius Caesar. He spent a fortune – most of it booty from his conquest of Gaul – buying up and demolishing houses on the site. The best of these was a temple dedicated in 46 BC to the goddess Venus Genetrix, from whom Caesar claimed descent. The temple contained statues of Caesar and Cleopatra as well as of Venus. All that remains of this temple to vanity is a platform and three Corinthian columns.

The forum was enclosed by a double colonnade that sheltered a row of shops, but this burned down in AD 80 and was rebuilt by Domitian and Trajan. Trajan also added the Basilica Argentaria (an important financial exchange) and a heated public lavatory. The forum is not open to the public, but parts of it are visible from above in Via dei Fori Imperiali.

Mamertine Prison ㉔

Clivo Argentario 1. **Map** 5 A5.
📞 679 29 02. 🚌 81, 85, 87, 186.
Open Apr–Sep: 9am–12:30pm & 2:30–6pm; Oct–Mar: 9am–noon & 2–5pm. **Donation** expected. 📷 🔌

19th-century engraving of guards visiting prisoners in the Mamertine

B ELOW THE 16th-century church of San Giuseppe dei Falegnami (St. Joseph of the Carpenters) is a dank dungeon in which, according to Christian legend, St. Peter was imprisoned. He is said to have caused a spring to bubble up into the cell, and used the water to baptize the two prison guards.

The prison was in an old cistern with access to the city's main sewer (the *cloaca maxima*). The lower cell, the *tullianum*, was used for executions, and bodies were thrown into the sewer. Among the enemies of Rome to be executed here was the Gaulish leader Vercingetorix, defeated by Julius Caesar in 52 BC.

17th-century view of the ruined Forum of Nerva

Forum of Nerva ㉕

Piazza del Grillo 1 (reached through Forum of Augustus). **Map** 5 B5.
📞 67 10 20 70. 🚌 11, 27, 81, 85, 87, 186. **Closed** for excavations.

T HE FORUM of Nerva was begun by Nerva's predecessor, Domitian, and completed in AD 97. Little more than a long corridor with a colonnade along the sides and a Temple of Minerva at one end, it was also known as the Forum Transitorium because it lay between the Forum of Peace built by the Emperor Vespasian in AD 70 and the Forum of Augustus. Vespasian's forum is almost completely covered by Via dei Fori Imperiali, as is much of the Forum of Nerva itself. Excavations have unearthed Renaissance shops

Medallion on the Arch of Constantine

and taverns, and part of the forum, including the base of the temple and two columns that were part of the original colonnade. These support a relief of Minerva above a frieze of young girls learning to sew and weave.

Arch of Constantine ㉖

Between Via di San Gregorio and Piazza del Colosseo. **Map** 8 F1.
🚌 11, 15, 27, 81, 85, 87, 118, 186, 673. 🚇 13, 30b. Ⓜ Colosseo.

T HIS TRIUMPHAL ARCH was dedicated in AD 315 to celebrate Constantine's victory three years before over his co-emperor, Maxentius. Constantine claimed he owed his victory to a vision of Christ, but there is nothing Christian about the arch – in fact, most of the medallions, reliefs and statues were scavenged from earlier monuments. There are statues of Dacian prisoners taken from Trajan's Forum and reliefs of Marcus Aurelius, including one where he distributes bread to the poor. Inside the arch are reliefs of Trajan's victory over the Dacians. These were probably by the artist who worked on the Column of Trajan.

Colosseum ㉗

See pp92–5.

North side of the Arch of Constantine, facing the Colosseum

Colosseum ㉗

R OME'S GREATEST amphitheater was commissioned by the Emperor Vespasian in AD 72 on the marshy site of a lake in the grounds of Nero's palace, the Domus Aurea *(see p175)*. Deadly gladiatorial combats and wild animal fights were staged free of charge by the emperor and wealthy citizens for public viewing.

Outer Wall of the Colosseum
Stone plundered from the facade in the Renaissance was used to build several palaces, bridges and parts of St. Peter's.

The Colosseum was built to a practical design, with its 80 arched entrances allowing easy access to 55,000 spectators, but it is also a building of great beauty. The drawing here shows how it looked in AD 80. It was one of several similar amphitheaters built in the Roman Empire, and some survive at El Djem in North Africa, Nîmes and Arles in France and Verona in northern Italy. Despite being damaged over the years by neglect and theft, it remains a majestic sight to this day.

The Founder of the Colosseum
Vespasian was a professional soldier who became emperor in AD 69, founding the Flavian dynasty.

The outer walls are made of travertine.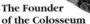

FLORA OF THE COLOSSEUM

By the 19th century, the Colosseum was heavily overgrown. Different micro-climates in various parts of the ruin had created an impressive variety of herbs, grasses and wild flowers. Several botanists were inspired to study and catalog them, and two books were published, one listing 420 different species.

Borage, a herb

The bollards anchored the velarium.

The velarium was a huge awning that shaded spectators from the sun. Supported on poles attached to the upper story of the building, it was then hoisted into position with ropes anchored to bollards outside the stadium.

TIMELINE

80 Vespasian's son, Titus, stages inaugural festival in the amphitheater. It lasts 100 days.

AD 70	100
72 Emperor Vespasian begins work on the Colosseum	**81–96** Amphitheater completed in reign of Domitian

Internal Corridors
These were designed to allow the large and often unruly crowd to move freely and to be seated within ten minutes of arriving at the Colosseum.

VISITORS' CHECKLIST

Piazza del Colosseo. **Map** 9 A1.
[700 42 61. ☰ 11, 27, 81, 85, 87. **M** Colosseo. ☰ 13, 30b to Piazza del Colosseo. **Open** Jan–mid-Mar: 9am–4:30pm Mon, Tue & Thu–Sat (mid-Mar–May: 5:30pm; Jun–Sep: 7pm; Oct: 5pm; Nov–Dec: 4pm), 9am–1pm Wed & Sun **Closed** public hols. **Adm charge**. ☐ & limited.

The vomitorium was the exit used from each numbered section.

Brick formed the inner walls.

The podium was a large terrace where the emperor and the wealthy upper classes had their seats.

Corinthian columns

Ionic columns

Doric columns

Entry routes to take the spectators to their seats were reached by means of staircases to the various levels of the amphitheater.

Arched entrances, 80 in total, were all numbered to let in the vast crowds that attended the fights.

Colossus of Nero
The Colosseum may have acquired its name from this huge gilt-bronze statue that stood near the amphitheater.

A gladiator's shield

230 Colosseum restored by Severus	**404** Gladiatorial combats banned		**1200s** Frangipane family turn Colosseum into a fortress			**1870** All vegetation removed
				15th–16th centuries Ruins used as quarry. Travertine blocks recycled by popes		
200	**400**	**1300**		**1500**	**1700**	**1900**
248 Thousandth anniversary celebration of founding of Rome by Romulus and Remus	**442** Building damaged in an earthquake	**523** Wild animal fights banned	**1312** Emperor Henry VII gives Colosseum to the Senate and people of Rome		**1749** Colosseum dedicated to Passion of Jesus	**1893–6** Structure below arena revealed

How Fights Were Staged in the Arena

THE EMPERORS HELD shows here that often began with animals performing circus tricks. Then on came the gladiators, who fought one another to the death. When one was killed, attendants dressed as Charon, the mythical ferryman of the dead, carried his body off on a stretcher; sand was raked over the blood to make ready for the next bout. A badly wounded gladiator would surrender his fate to the crowd. The "thumbs up" sign from the emperor meant he could live, "thumbs down" that he die, and the victor became an instant hero. Animals were brought here from as far away as North Africa and the Middle East. The games held in AD 248 to mark the 1,000th anniversary of the founding of Rome saw the death of a host of lions, elephants, zebras and elks.

Beneath the Arena
Late 19th-century excavations exposed the network of underground rooms where the animals were kept.

Interior of the Colosseum
The stadium was built in the form of an ellipse, with tiers of seats around a vast central arena.

Emperor's box

Emperor's entrance

Tiers of seats

Consul's box

Consul's entrance

Gladiators' entrance

Layout of underground passages

A complex of rooms, passages and lifts lay beneath the arena.

Roman Gladiators
These were usually slaves, prisoners of war or condemned criminals. Most were men, but there were a few female gladiators.

Dramatic Entrances
Below the sand was a wooden floor through which animals, men and scenery appeared in the arena.

The Colosseum by Antonio Canaletto

This 18th-century view of the Colosseum shows the Meta Sudans fountain (now demolished). Water "sweated" from a metal ball on top of its brick cone.

Metal fencing kept animals penned in, while archers stood by just in case any escaped.

Seating was tiered, and different social classes were segregated.

A winch brought the animal cages up to arena level when they were due to fight.

A ramp and trap door enabled the animal to reach the arena after walking along a corridor.

Cages were actually three-sided lifts that were hoisted to the level where the animals were released.

SEA BATTLES IN THE ARENA

The historian Dion Cassius, writing in the 4th century AD, relates how, 150 years earlier, the Colosseum's arena was flooded to stage a mock sea battle. Scholars now believe that he was mistaken. The spectacle probably took place in the Naumachia of Augustus, a water-filled arena situated across the Tiber in Trastevere.

PALATINE

ACCORDING TO LEGEND, Romulus and Remus were raised here by a wolf in a cave. Traces of Iron Age huts, dating from the 9th century BC, have been found on the Palatine Hill, providing archaeological support for the area's legendary links with the founding of Rome. The Palatine was a very desirable place to live and became home to some of the city's most famous inhabitants. The great orator Cicero had a house here, as did the lyric poet Catullus. Augustus was born on the hill and continued to live here in very modest

Fresco of mask in the House of Augustus

circumstances even when he became emperor. The two buildings identified as the House of Augustus and the House of Livia, his second wife, are among the best preserved. The first emperor's example of frugality was ignored by his successors, Tiberius, Caligula and Domitian, who all built extravagant palaces here. The ruins of Tiberius's palace lie beneath the 16th-century Farnese Gardens. The most extensive ruins are those of the Domus Augustana and Domus Flavia, the two wings of Domitian's palace, and the later extension built by Septimius Severus.

SIGHTS AT A GLANCE

Temples
Temple of Cybele ❻

Historic Buildings
Domus Flavia ❶
Domus Augustana ❸
House of Livia ❺

Ancient Sites
Cryptoporticus ❷
Stadium ❹
Huts of Romulus ❼

Parks and Gardens
Farnese Gardens ❽

SEE ALSO

• *Street Finder*, map 8

GETTING THERE

There are two ways of getting on to the Palatine hill; through either the Roman Forum (from Via dei Fori Imperiali) or through the entrance in Via di San Gregorio. One ticket is valid for both Forum and Palatine. The best buses are the 11, 27, 81, 85, 87 and 186; all stop in Via dei Fori Imperiali near the main entrance. Colosseo Metro station *(see p77)* is also handy.

KEY

■ Tour of the Palatine map

0 meters   200
0 yards   200

Towering ruins of the Palace of Septimius Severus on the Palatine Hill

A Tour of the Palatine

SHADED ON ITS LOWER SLOPES with pines, and scattered in spring with wild flowers, the Palatine is the most pleasant and relaxing of the city's ancient sites. You can reach the hill by walking up from the Roman Forum *(see pp76–7)*. The area is dominated by the ruins of the Domus Flavia and the Domus Augustana, two parts of Domitian's huge palace built at the end of the 1st century AD. What you are able to see depends on where excavations are taking place at the time.

Huts of Romulus
These are traces of a 9th-century BC village on the Palatine ❼

To Farnese Gardens
See p101

House of Augustus

Temple of Cybele
Also known as the Temple of the Magna Mater, this was the center of an important fertility cult ❻

★ **House of Livia**
Many of the wall paintings have survived in the house where Augustus lived with his wife Livia ❺

STAR SIGHTS

★ **Domus Flavia**

★ **House of Livia**

KEY

– – – Suggested route

0 meters　　　　　　　　75

0 yards　　　　　　　　75

★ **Domus Flavia**
This oval fountain was designed to be seen from the dining hall of the palace ❶

Domus Augustana
The Roman emperors lived in this part of the palace, while the Domus Flavia was used for public functions ❸

Cryptoporticus
In this long underground gallery, built by Nero, the stuccoes that decorated the walls and vault have been replaced with copies ②

LOCATOR MAP
See Central Rome Map pp12–13

FORUM

PALATINE

CARACALLA

AVENTINE

Octagonal fountain of the Domus Flavia

The Palatine Museum is housed in a former convent, but has been closed for many years.

Stadium
Part of the Imperial palace, this enclosure may have been used by the emperors as a private garden ④

To Forum entrance

The exedra of the Stadium may have housed a balcony for emperors to view races.

Baths of Septimius Severus

The Palace of Septimius Severus (reigned AD 193–211) was an extension of the Domus Augustana. It projected beyond the hillside, requiring enormous arched supports.

Substructure of palace

Domus Flavia ❶

See Visitors' Checklist.

Marble pavement in the courtyard of the Domus Flavia

I N AD 81, DOMITIAN, the third of the Flavian dynasty of emperors, decided to build a splendid new palace on the Palatine Hill. But the western peak, the Germalus, was covered with houses and temples, while the eastern peak, the Palatium, was very steep. So the emperor's architect, Rabirius, flattened the Palatium and used the soil to fill in the cleft between the two peaks, burying (and thus preserving) a number of Republican-era houses.

The palace had two wings – one official (the Domus Flavia), the other private (the Domus Augustana). It was the main imperial palace for 300 years. At the front of the Domus Flavia, the surviving stubs of columns and fragments of walls trace the shapes of three adjoining rooms. In the first of these, the Basilica, Domitian dispensed his personal brand of justice.

The central Aula Regia was a throne room decorated with 12 black basalt statues. The third room (now covered with corrugated plastic) was the Lararium, a shrine for the household gods known as Lares (usually the owner's ancestors). It may have been used for official ceremonies or by the palace guards.

Fearing assassination, Domitian had the walls of the courtyard covered with shiny marble slabs designed to act as mirrors so that he could see anyone lurking behind him. Ironically, he was assassinated in his bedroom, possibly on the orders of his wife, Domitia. The courtyard is now a pleasant place to pause; the flower beds in the center follow the maze pattern of a sunken fountain pool.

Cryptoporticus ❷

See Visitors' Checklist.

T HE CRYPTOPORTICUS, a series of underground corridors, was built by Nero to connect his Golden House (*see p175*) with the palaces of earlier emperors on the Palatine. A branch leading to the Palace of Domitian was added later. Its vaults are decorated with delicate stucco reliefs – copies of originals, now kept in the Palatine's closed museum.

Domus Augustana ❸

See Visitors' Checklist.

T HIS PART of Domitian's palace was called the Domus Augustana because it was the private residence of the "august" emperors. On the upper level, a high brick wall remains, and visitors can make out the shape of its two courtyards. The far better preserved lower level is closed to the public, though visitors can look down on its sunken courtyard with the geometric foundations of a fountain in its center. Sadly, not visible are the stairs linking the two levels (once lit by sunlight falling on a mirror-paved pool), or the surrounding rooms, paved with colored marble.

Stadium ❹

See Visitors' Checklist.

Stadium viewed from the south

T HE STADIUM on the Palatine was laid out at the same time as the Palace of Domitian. It is not clear whether it was a public stadium, a private track for exercising horses or simply a large garden. The alcove in the eastern wall looks as though it may have held a box from which the emperor could have watched races. It is known, however, that the stadium was used for foot races by the Ostrogothic king Theodoric in the 6th century – he added the small oval-shaped enclosure at the southern end of the site.

Remains of the Domus Augustana and the Palace of Septimius Severus

House of Livia ❺

See Visitors' Checklist. If closed, see the custodian.

Fresco in the House of Livia

T HIS HOUSE dating from the 1st century BC is one of the best preserved on the Palatine. It was probably part of the house in which the Emperor Augustus and his second wife, Livia, lived. Compared with later Imperial palaces, it is a modest home. According to Suetonius, the biographer of Rome's early emperors, Augustus slept in the same small bedroom for 40 years on a low bed that had "a very ordinary coverlet." He wore home-made clothes

Detail of floor mosaic

(woven by Livia; his sister, Octavia; and daughter, Julia), but he was vain enough to wear shoes with extremely thick soles to conceal the fact that he was rather short.

The ground level of the Palatine is now above the house, so visitors walk down steps and along a mosaic-paved corridor into a courtyard. Its imitation marble wall frescoes have been detached in order to preserve them, but they still hang in situ. Though they are very faded, the veining patterns are still visible. Leading off the courtyard are three small reception rooms. The frescoes in the central one include a faded scene of Hermes coming to the rescue of Zeus's beloved Io, who is guarded by the 100-eyed Argos. In the left-hand room are faint frescoes of griffins and other beasts, while the decor in the right-hand room includes colorful landscapes and cityscapes.

Temple of Cybele ❻

See Visitors' Checklist.

O THER THAN a platform with a few column stumps and capitals, there is little to see of the Temple of Cybele, a popular Roman fertility goddess of Asian origin. The priests of the cult castrated themselves in the belief that the sacrifice of their own fertility would guarantee that of the natural world.

The annual festival of Cybele, from March 22 to 24, culminated with frenzied eunuch-priests slashing their bodies to offer blood to the goddess, and the ceremonial castration of novice priests.

Statue of the goddess Cybele

Huts of Romulus ❼

See Visitors' Checklist.

A CCORDING TO LEGEND, after killing his brother, Remus, Romulus founded a village on the Palatine. In the 1940s a series of holes was found filled with earth lighter in color than the surrounding soil. Archaeologists deduced that these holes must originally have held the supporting poles of three Iron Age huts – the first foundations of Rome (*see pp16–17*).

Farnese Gardens ❽

See Visitors' Checklist.

I N THE MID-16TH century Cardinal Alessandro Farnese, grandson of Pope Paul III, bought the ruins of Tiberius's palace on the Palatine. He filled in the ruined building and had Vignola, architect of the interior of the Gesù church, design a garden. The result was one of the first botanical gardens in Europe, its terraces linked by steps stretching from the House of the Vestal Virgins in the Forum to the Palatine's Germalus peak. The gardeners introduced a number of plants to Italy and Europe, among them *Acacia farnesiana*. Farnese was at the center of a flamboyant set that included a number of courtesans, so the parties here were likely to have been somewhat unholy.

The area was dug up during the excavation of the Palatine and relandscaped afterward. Nevertheless, the tree-lined avenues, rose gardens and glorious views still make it an ideal place to unwind.

Farnese pavilions, relics of the age when the Palatine was a private garden

Piazza della Rotonda

THE PANTHEON, one of the great buildings in the history of European architecture, has stood at the heart of Rome for nearly 2,000 years. The historic area around it has seen uninterrupted economic and political activity throughout that time. Palazzo di Montecitorio, built for Pope Innocent X as a papal tribunal in 1697, is now the Italian parliament, and many nearby buildings are government offices. This is also the main financial district of Rome, with banking headquarters and the stock exchange. Not many people live here, but in the evenings, Romans stroll through the narrow streets and fill the restaurants and cafés that make this area a focus of the city's social life.

Bitter apéritif, popular in Roman cafés

Sights at a Glance

Churches and Temples
Temple of Hadrian ❶
Sant'Ignazio di Loyola ❸
Gesù pp114–15 ❾
Santa Maria sopra Minerva ⓫
Pantheon pp110–11 ⓭
Sant'Eustachio ⓮
La Maddalena ⓯
Santa Maria in Campo Marzio ⓲
San Lorenzo in Lucina ⓴

Historic Streets and Piazzas
Piazza di Sant'Ignazio ❷
Via della Gatta ❼

Historic Buildings
Palazzo del Collegio Romano ❹
Palazzo Doria Pamphilj ❻
Palazzo Altieri ❽
Palazzo Baldassini ⓱
Palazzo Borghese ⓳
Palazzo di Montecitorio ㉑
Palazzo Capranica ㉔

Columns, Obelisks and Statues
Pie' di Marmo ❿
Obelisk of Santa Maria sopra Minerva ⓬
Obelisk of Montecitorio ㉒
Column of Marcus Aurelius ㉓

Fountains
Fontanella del Facchino ❺

Cafés and Restaurants
Caffè Giolitti ⓰

Key

▨	Street-by-Street map
P	Parking

Getting There

The area has no Metro station but is about 15 minutes' walk from Spagna or Barberini Metro stops. There are some convenient bus stops in Via del Plebiscito, served by the 56, 64, 70, 90, 492 and many other routes. Piazza Colonna is served by the 56, 60 and 85 and all buses that go up Via del Corso. The only bus that passes through the narrow streets of the area is the 119 electric minibus, which stops right outside the Pantheon.

0 meters   200
0 yards   200

See Also

• *Street Finder*, maps 4, 5, 12
• *Where to Stay* pp294–5
• *Restaurants* pp310–11

The immense granite columns of the Pantheon

Street by Street: Piazza della Rotonda

IF YOU WANDER THROUGH this area, sooner or later you will emerge into Piazza della Rotonda, with its jumble of open-air café tables in front of the Pantheon. The refreshing splash of the fountain makes it a welcome resting place. In this warren of narrow streets, it can be hard to imagine just how close you are to some of Rome's finest sights. The magnificent art collection of Palazzo Doria Pamphilj and the Baroque splendor of the Gesù are just a few minutes' walk from the Pantheon. At night there is always a lively buzz of activity as people dine in style or enjoy the coffee and ice creams for which the area is famous.

Temple of Hadrian
The columns of this Roman temple now form the facade of the stock exchange ❶

Piazza di Sant'Ignazio
The square is a rare example of stylish domestic architecture from the early 18th century ❷

La Tazza d'Oro enjoys a reputation for the wonderful coffee consumed on its premises as well as for its freshly ground coffee to take out. *(See p319.)*

Santa Maria sopra Minerva
The rich decoration of Rome's only Gothic church was added in the 19th century ⓫

★ Pantheon
The awe-inspiring interior of Rome's best-preserved ancient temple is only hinted at from the outside ⓭

PIAZZA DI SANT'IGNAZIO

VIA DI SANT' IGNAZIO

VIA DEL SEMINARIO

PIAZZA DELLA ROTONDA

PIAZZA DELLA MINERVA

Obelisk of Santa Maria sopra Minerva
In 1667, Bernini dreamed up the idea of mounting a recently discovered obelisk on the back of a marble elephant ⓬

★ **Sant'Ignazio di Loyola**
Andrea Pozzo painted this glorious Baroque ceiling (1685) to celebrate St. Ignatius and the Jesuit order ③

Palazzo del Collegio Romano
Up until 1870, the college educated many leading figures in the Catholic Church ④

Fontanella del Facchino
The water in this small 16th-century fountain spurts from a barrel held by a porter ⑤

★ **Palazzo Doria Pamphilj**
Among the masterpieces in the art gallery of this magnificent family palazzo is this portrait of Pope Innocent X by Velázquez (1650) ⑥

LOCATOR MAP
See Central Rome Map pp12–13

Via della Gatta
The street is named after the statue of a cat ⑦

Palazzo Altieri
This enormous 17th-century palazzo is decorated with the arms of Pope Clement X ⑧

★ **Gesù**
The design of the very first Jesuit church had a great impact on religious architecture ⑨

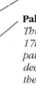

KEY

– – – Suggested route

| 0 meters | 75 |
| 0 yards | 75 |

Pie' di Marmo
This marble foot is a stray fragment from a gigantic Roman statue ⑩

STAR SIGHTS

★ **Pantheon**

★ **Palazzo Doria Pamphilj**

★ **Gesù**

★ **Sant'Ignazio di Loyola**

Temple of Hadrian ❶

La Borsa, Piazza di Pietra. **Map** 4 F3 &
12 E2. 🚌 *56, 60, 71, 81, 85, 90,*
119, 492. **Not open** to the public.

THIS TEMPLE, built to honor
the Emperor Hadrian as a
god, was dedicated by his
successor Antoninus Pius in
AD 145. The remains of
the temple are visible on the
southern side of Piazza di
Pietra, incorporated in a
17th-century building. This
was originally a papal customs
house, completed by Carlo
Fontana and his son in the
1690s. Today the building
houses the Roman Stock
exchange (La Borsa).

Eleven marble Corinthian
columns 49 ft (15 m) high
stand on a base of *peperino*, a
volcanic rock quarried from
the Alban Hills to the south of
Rome. The columns
decorated the northern flank
of the temple, enclosing its
inner shrine, the *cella*. The
peperino wall of the *cella* is
still visible behind the columns,
as is part of the coffered
portico ceiling.

A number of reliefs from
the temple representing
conquered Roman provinces
are now in the courtyard of
the Palazzo dei Conservatori
(see pp72–3). They reflect the
mostly peaceful foreign policy
of Hadrian's reign.

Remains of Hadrian's Temple

Piazza di Sant'Ignazio ❷

Map 4 F4 & 12 E3. 🚌 *56, 60, 71,*
81, 85, 90, 119, 492.

ONE OF THE MAJOR works of
the Roman Rococo, the
piazza (1727–8) is Filippo
Raguzzini's masterpiece. It
offsets the imposing facade of
the church of Sant'Ignazio
with the intimacy of the

Illusionistic ceiling in the crossing of Sant'Ignazio

houses of the bourgeoisie. The
theatrical setting, the curvilinear
design and the playful forms
of its windows, balconies and
balusters mark the piazza as
one of a highly distinctive
group of structures. Along
with Palazzo Doria Pamphilj
(1731), the facade of La
Maddalena (1735) and the
aristocratic Spanish Steps
(1723), it belongs to that happy
moment when Rome's bubbly
Rococo triumphed over
conservative Classicism.

Sant'Ignazio di Loyola ❸

Piazza di Sant'Ignazio. **Map** 4 F4 &
12 E3. ☎ *679 44 06.* 🚌 *56, 60, 71,*
81, 85, 90, 119, 492. **Open** *7:30am–*
12:30pm & 4–7:15pm daily. 🚹 🅾

THE CHURCH was built by
Cardinal Ludovisi in 1626
in honor of St. Ignatius of
Loyola, founder of the Society
of Jesus and the man who
most embodied the zeal of
the Counter-Reformation.

Together with the Gesù *(see
pp114–15)*, Sant'Ignazio forms
the nucleus of the Jesuit area
in Rome. Its vast interior, lined
with precious stones, marble,
stucco and gilt, creates a
thrilling sense of theater. The
church has a Latin-cross plan,
with an apse and many side
chapels. A cupola was planned

but never built, so the space
it would have filled was
covered by a fake perspective
painting. The piers built to
bear the weight of the cupola
help support the observatory
of the Collegio Romano.

Palazzo del Collegio Romano ❹

Piazza del Collegio Romano. **Map** 5 A4
& 12 E3. 🚌 *56, 60, 62, 85, 90, 95,*
160, 492. **Not open** to the public.

SHARING THE SAME BLOCK as
the church of Sant'Ignazio,
the palazzo used to house a
college run by the Jesuits;
many future bishops, cardinals
and popes studied here. The
college was confiscated in
1870 and turned into an
ordinary school. The portals
bear the coat of arms of its
founder, Pope Gregory XIII
Boncompagni, who reigned
from 1572 to 1585. The
facade is also decorated with
a bell, two sundials and a
clock. On the right
is a tower built
in 1787 as an
observatory. Up
until 1925, its time
signal regulated
all the clocks in
the city.

Portal of the
Collegio Romano

Fontanella del Facchino ❺

Via Lata. **Map** 5 A4 & 12 E3. 🚍 *56, 60, 62, 85, 90, 95, 160, 492.*

IL FACCHINO (the Porter), once in the Corso, now set into the wall of the Banco di Roma, was one of Rome's "talking statues" like Pasquino *(see p124)*. Created around 1590, the fountain may have been based on a drawing by Florentine painter Jacopino del Conte. The statue of a man holding a barrel probably represents a member of the Università degli Acquaroli (Fraternity of Water Carriers), though it is also claimed to be of Martin Luther, or of Abbondio Rizzio, a porter who died carrying a barrel.

The Facchino drinking fountain

Palazzo Doria Pamphilj ❻

Piazza del Collegio Romano 1A. **Map** 5 A4 & 12 E3. 📞 679 43 65. 🚍 *56, 60, 62, 85, 90, 95, 160, 492.* **Open** *10am–1pm Mon, Tue, Fri, Sat & Sun.* **Closed** *public hols.* **Adm charge.** ♿ *limited.* 📷 *compulsory for private apartments, otherwise ask.* 📷

PALAZZO DORIA PAMPHILJ is a great island of stone in the heart of Rome, the oldest parts dating from 1435. Through the Corso entrance you can glimpse the 16th-century porticoed courtyard with the coat of arms of the della Rovere family. The next owners were the Aldobrandini family. Between 1601 and 1647 the mansion acquired a second courtyard and flanking wings at the expense of a public bath that stood nearby.

When the Pamphilj family took over, they completed the Piazza del Collegio Romano facade and the Via della Gatta

wing, a splendid chapel and a theater inaugurated by Queen Christina of Sweden in 1684.

In the first half of the 18th century, Gabriele Valvassori created the gallery above the courtyard and a new facade along the Corso, using the highly decorative style of the period known as the *barocchetto*, which now dominates the building. The stairways and salons, the Mirror Gallery and the picture gallery all radiate a joyous sense of light and space.

The family collection in the Doria Pamphilj gallery has over 400 paintings dating from the 15th to the 18th century, including the famous portrait of Pope Innocent X Pamphilj by Velázquez. There are also important works by Titian, Caravaggio, Lorenzo Lotto, Guercino and Claude Lorrain. The rooms in the private apartment have many of their original furnishings on display including splendid Brussels and Gobelins tapestries.

Via della Gatta ❼

Map 5 A4 & 12 E3. 🚍 *56, 60, 62, 85, 90, 95, 160, 492.*

THIS NARROW STREET runs between the great Palazzo Doria Pamphilj and the smaller Palazzo Grazioli. The ancient marble sculpture of a

cat *(gatta)* that gives the street its name can be seen on the first cornice on the corner of Palazzo Grazioli.

Via della Gatta's marble cat

Palazzo Altieri ❽

Via del Gesù 93. **Map** 4 F4 & 12 E3. 🚍 *56, 64, 70, 81, 90 and many other routes. See* **Shops** *p333.*

THE ALTIERI FAMILY is first mentioned in Rome's history in the 9th century. This palazzo was built by the last male heirs, the brothers Cardinal Giambattista di Lorenzo Altieri and Cardinal Emilio Altieri, later Pope Clement X (reigned 1670–76).

Many surrounding houses were demolished to make way for the palazzo, but an old woman called Berta refused to leave, so her hovel was incorporated into the building. Its windows are still visible on the west end of the palazzo. Most of Palazzo Altieri is now occupied by the fabric and clothing business, Bises.

Gesù ❾

See pp114–15.

Caravaggio's *Rest During the Flight into Egypt* in Palazzo Doria Pamphilj

Marble foot from a Roman statue

Pie' di Marmo ⑩

Via di Santo Stefano del Cacco.
Map 4 F4 & 12 E3.   56, 64, 70, 81, 90, 90b, 119.

IT WAS POPULARLY believed in the Middle Ages that half the population of ancient Rome must have been made up of bronze, golden and marble statues. Fragments of these giants, usually gods or emperors, are scattered throughout the city. *Pie' di marmo*, a marble foot, comes from an area dedicated to the Egyptian gods Isis and Serapis and might have been part of a statue in a temple, where tapers burned unattended. These statues, painted and covered with jewels and clothes given by the faithful, were a great fire hazard.

Santa Maria sopra Minerva ⑪

Piazza della Minerva 42. **Map** 4 F4 & 12 E3.   679 39 26.   56, 64, 70, 81, 90, 119. **Open** 7am–noon & 4–7pm daily, but call to check. **Cloister open** 8am–1pm & 3:30–7:30pm daily.   **Concerts**.

FEW OTHER CHURCHES can display such a complete and impressive record of Italian art. Dating from the 13th century, the Minerva is one of the very few examples of Gothic architecture in Rome. It was the traditional stronghold of the Dominicans, whose anti-heretical zeal earned them the punning nickname of *Domini Canes* (the hounds of the Lord).

Built on ancient ruins, supposed to have been the Temple of Minerva, the simple T-shaped vaulted building acquired rich chapels and works of art by which its

many patrons wished to be remembered. Note the Cosmatesque 13th-century tombs and the exquisite works of 15th-century Tuscan and Venetian artists. Native Roman talent of the period can be admired in Antoniazzo Romano's *Annunciation*, featuring Cardinal Juan de Torquemada, uncle of the infamous Spanish Inquisitor.

The more monumental style of the Roman Renaissance is well represented in the tombs of the 16th-century Medici popes, Leo X and his cousin Clement VII, and in the richly decorated Aldobrandini Chapel. Near the steps of the choir is the celebrated sculpture called *Risen Christ*, started by Michelangelo but completed by Raffaele da Montelupo in 1521.

There are also splendid works of art from the Baroque period, including a tomb and a bust by Bernini. The church is visited not only for its art, but also because it contains the tombs of many famous Italians: St. Catherine of Siena, who died here in 1380; the Venetian sculptor Andrea Bregno (died 1506); the Humanist Cardinal Pietro Bembo (died 1547); and Fra Angelico, the Dominican friar and painter, who died in Rome in 1455.

Obelisk of Santa Maria sopra Minerva ⑫

Piazza della Minerva. **Map** 4 F4 & 12 D3.   56, 64, 70, 81, 90, 119.

ORIGINALLY MEANT to decorate Palazzo Barberini as a kind of joke, this exotic elephant and obelisk sculpture is typical of Bernini's inexhaustible imagination. (The elephant was actually sculpted by Ercole Ferrata to Bernini's design.) The old obelisk was found in the garden of the monastery of Santa Maria sopra Minerva, and the friars wanted the monument erected in their piazza. The elephant was provided with its enormous saddlecloth because of a friar's insistence that the gap under the animal's abdomen would undermine its stability. Bernini knew better: you need only look at the Fontana dei Fiumi *(see p120)* in Piazza Navona to appreciate his use of empty space. The elephant, an ancient symbol of intelligence and piety, was chosen as the embodiment of the virtues on which Christians should build true wisdom.

Bernini's Egyptian obelisk and marble elephant

Nave of Santa Maria sopra Minerva

Pantheon ⑬

See pp110–11.

Sant'Eustachio ⑭

Piazza Sant'Eustachio. **Map** 4 F4 & 12 D3. 686 53 34. 70, 81, 87, 90, 90b, 119, 186, 492. **Open** 4–7:30pm Mon–Sat, 9:30am–12:30pm Sun.

T HE ORIGINS of this church go back to early Christian times, when it offered succour to the poor. In medieval times many charitable brotherhoods elected Sant'Eustachio as their patron and had chapels here.

The squat Romanesque bell tower is one of the few surviving parts of the medieval church, which was totally redecorated in the 17th and 18th centuries.

Bell tower of Sant'Eustachio

La Maddalena ⑮

Piazza della Maddalena. **Map** 4 F3 & 12 D2. 679 77 96. 70, 81, 87, 90, 90b, 186, 492. **Open** 7:30am– noon & 5–7:45pm daily.

S ITUATED IN a small piazza near the Pantheon, the Maddalena, with its Rococo facade built in 1735, epitomizes the love of light and movement of the late Baroque. Its curves are reminiscent of Borromini's San Carlo alle Quattro Fontane *(see p161).* The facade has been lovingly restored, despite the protests of diehard Neoclassicists who dismiss its painted stucco as sugar icing.

The small size of the Maddalena did not deter the

The old-fashioned *salone* of the Caffè Giolitti

17th- and 18th-century decorators, who filled the interior with ornament from the floor to the top of the elegant cupola. The organ loft and choir are particularly powerful examples of the Baroque desire to fire the imagination of the faithful.

Many of the paintings and sculptures employ the new Christian imagery of the Counter Reformation. In the niches of the nave, for example, the statues are personifications of virtues such as Humility and Simplicity. There are also scenes from the life of San Camillo, who died in the adjacent convent in 1614. The church belonged to his followers, the Camillians, a preaching order active in Rome's hospitals. Like the Jesuits, they commissioned works of art to convey the force of their religious message.

La Maddalena's stuccoed facade

Caffè Giolitti ⑯

Via degli Uffici del Vicario 40. **Map** 4 F3 & 12 D2. 699 12 43. 56, 60, 90, 119, 492. **Open** 7am–2am Tue–Sun, 7am–3am Sat.

F OUNDED IN 1900, the Caffè Giolitti is the heir to the glittering *Belle Epoque* cafés that lined the nearby Corso in Rome's first days as capital of the new Italian state. Its spacious *salone* accommodates tourists in summer, Roman families on weekends, and on weekdays a varied crowd of office workers, construction workers and officials from the nearby parliament in Palazzo di Montecitorio.

Palazzo Baldassini ⑰

Via delle Coppelle 35. **Map** 4 F3 & 12 D2. 70, 81, 90, 90b, 119. **Not open** to the public.

M ELCHIORRE BALDASSINI built his home in the style of the Florentine Renaissance, skillfully adapted to the more austere surroundings of Rome. With its cornices marking the different floors and wrought-iron window grilles, this is one of the best examples of a Roman palazzo of the early 16th century. It stands in the part of Rome built at the time of Pope Leo X (reigned 1513–21) and still known as the Renaissance Quarter, an area that grew up around the straight streets such as Via di Ripetta and Via della Scrofa.

Pantheon ⑬

IN THE MIDDLE AGES, the Pantheon, the Roman "temple of all the gods," became a church; in time this magnificent building with its awe-inspiring domed interior became a symbol of Rome itself. The rectangular portico screens the vast hemispherical dome: only from inside can its true scale and beauty be appreciated. The rotunda's height and diameter are equal: 140 ft (43.3 m). The opening at the top of the dome, the *oculus*, provides the only light. We owe this marvel of Roman engineering to the Emperor Hadrian (AD 118–125), who designed it to replace an earlier temple built by Marcus Agrippa, son-in-law of Augustus. The shrines that now line the wall of the Pantheon range from the Tomb of Raphael to those of the kings of modern Italy.

★ Interior of the Dome
The dome was cast by pouring concrete mixed with tufa and pumice over a temporary wooden framework.

The portico, enclosed by granite columns

The walls of the drum supporting the dome are 19 ft (6 m) thick.

The immense portico is built on the foundations of Agrippa's temple.

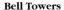

STAR FEATURES

★ **Interior of the Dome**

★ **Tomb of Raphael**

Bell Towers
This 18th-century view by Bernardo Bellotto shows Bernini's much-ridiculed turrets, which were removed in 1883.

Floor Patterning
The marble floor, restored in 1873, preserves the original Roman design.

RAPHAEL AND LA FORNARINA

Raphael, at his own request, was buried here when he died in 1520. He had lived for years with his model, La Fornarina (*see p210*), seen here in a painting by Giulio Romano, but she was excluded from the ceremony of his burial. To the right of his tomb is a memorial to his fiancée, Maria Bibbiena, niece of the artist's patron, Cardinal Dovizi di Bibbiena.

VISITORS' CHECKLIST

Piazza della Rotonda. **Map** 4 F4 & 12 D3. **[** 68 30 02 30.
▥ 64, 70, 75, 119.
Open 9am–5:30pm Mon–Sat (Jul–Sep: 6pm; Oct–Mar: 4:30pm), 9am–1pm Sun & public hols.
Closed Aug 15, Dec 25 & 26.
✝ ◎ & ♫ Concerts. **▯**

Oculus

Coffering
Constructing the dome from hollow decorative coffers reduced its weight.

Relieving Arches
Brick arches embedded in the structure of the wall act as internal buttresses, distributing the weight of the dome.

★ Tomb of Raphael
The artist's body rests below a Madonna by Lorenzetto (1524).

TIMELINE

27–25 BC Marcus Agrippa builds first Pantheon	*M·AGRIPPA·* *Inscription on pediment*	**735** Gregory III roofs the Pantheon in lead	**1305–77** While papal seat is in Avignon, Pantheon is used as fortress and poultry market		**1888** Tomb of King Vittorio Emanuele II completed
30 BC	**AD 100**	**600**		**1100**	**1600**
	AD 118 Hadrian builds new Pantheon	**609** Pope Boniface IV consecrates Pantheon as church of Santa Maria ad Martyres	**663** Byzantine Emperor Constans II strips gilded tiles from the roof	**1632** Urban VIII melts down bronze from portico for Bernini's baldacchino in St. Peter's	

Bernini's curving southern facade of Palazzo di Montecitorio

Santa Maria in Campo Marzio ⑱

Piazza in Campo Marzio 45. **Map** 4 F3 & 12 D2. **(** *678 70 21.* **▦** *56, 60, 90, 90b, 119, 492.* **Closed** *for renovation.*

Around the courtyard through which you enter the church, there are fascinating remnants of medieval houses, once the property of the original monastery. The church itself was rebuilt in 1685 by Antonio de Rossi, using a square Greek-cross plan with a cupola. Above the altar is a 12th-century painting of the Madonna, which gives the church its name.

Palazzo Borghese ⑲

Largo della Fontanella di Borghese. **Map** 4 F3 & 12 D1. **▦** *70, 81, 90, 90b, 119.* **Not open** *to the public.*

The palazzo was acquired in about 1605 by Cardinal Camillo Borghese, just before he became Pope Paul V. Flaminio Ponzio was hired to enlarge the building and give it the grandeur appropriate to the residence of the pope's family. He added a wing overlooking Piazza Borghese and the delightful porticoed courtyard inside. Subsequent enlargements included the building and decoration of a great *nympheum* known as the Bath of Venus. For more than two centuries this palazzo housed the Borghese family's renowned collection of paintings, which was bought

by the Italian state in 1902 and transferred to the Villa Borghese *(see pp260–61).*

Pope Paul V, who commissioned Palazzo Borghese for his family

San Lorenzo in Lucina ⑳

Via in Lucina 16A. **Map** 4 F3 & 12 E1. **(** *687 14 94.* **▦** *70, 81, 90, 90b, 119.* **Open** *8:30am–noon & 4:30–7:30pm daily.* 🚹 📷

The church is one of Rome's oldest Christian places of worship, and was probably built on a well sacred to Juno, protectress of women. It was rebuilt in the 12th century, and today's external appearance is typical of the period: a portico

with reused Roman columns crowned by medieval capitals, a plain triangular pediment and a Romanesque bell tower with colored marble inlay.

In contrast, the interior of the church was totally rebuilt in the 17th century. The old basilica plan was destroyed and the two side naves were replaced by richly decorated Baroque chapels. Don't miss the fine busts in the Fonseca Chapel, designed by Bernini, or the *Crucifixion* by Guido Reni above the main altar. There is also a 19th-century monument honoring French painter Nicolas Poussin, who died in Rome in 1655 and was buried in the church.

Palazzo di Montecitorio ㉑

Piazza di Montecitorio. **Map** 4 F3 & 12 E2. **▦** *56, 60, 85, 90, 90b, 119, 492.* **Not open** *to the public.*

The palazzo's first architect, Bernini, got the job after he presented a silver model of his design to the wife of his patron, Prince Ludovisi. The building was completed in 1697 by Carlo Fontana and became the Papal Tribunal of Justice. In 1871 it was chosen to be Italy's new Chamber of Deputies, and by 1918 it had doubled in size with a second grand facade. The 630 members of parliament are elected by a system of proportional representation that ensures that no single party ever gains an overall majority.

The church of San Lorenzo in Lucina

Emperor Augustus's obelisk

Obelisk of Montecitorio ❷

Piazza di Montecitorio. **Map** 4 F3 & 12 E2. 🚍 *56, 60, 85, 90, 119, 492.*

T HE MEASUREMENT of time in ancient Rome was always a rather hit-and-miss affair: for many years the Romans relied on an imported (and therefore inaccurate) sundial, a trophy from the conquest of Sicily. In 10 BC, the Emperor Augustus laid out a new enormous sundial in the Campus Martius. Its center was roughly in today's Piazza di San Lorenzo in Lucina. The shadow was cast by an enormous granite obelisk Augustus brought back from Heliopolis in Egypt. Unfortunately, this sundial also became inaccurate after only 50 years, possibly as a result of the ground settling.

The obelisk was still in the piazza in the 9th century but then disappeared until it was rediscovered in the reign of Pope Julius II (1503–13). The pope was intrigued by its Egyptian hieroglyphs, thought to hold the key to the wisdom of Adam before the Fall, but it was only under Pope Benedict XIV (reigned 1740–58) that the obelisk was finally unearthed. It was erected in its present location in 1787 by Pope Pius VI.

Column of Marcus Aurelius ❷

Piazza Colonna. **Map** 5 A3 & 12 E2. 🚍 *56, 60, 85, 90, 90b, 119, 492.*

C LEARLY AN IMITATION of the Column of Trajan *(see p90)*, this monument was erected after the death of Marcus Aurelius in AD 180 to commemorate his victories over the barbarian tribes of the Danube. Made 80 years after the original column, this one is very different artistically: the wars of Marcus Aurelius are rendered in simplified pictures in stronger relief, sacrificing Classical proportions for the sake of clarity and immediacy. The spirit of the work is more akin to the 4th-century Arch of Constantine *(see p91)* than to Trajan's monument. Gone are the heroic qualities of the Roman soldiers, by now mostly barbarian mercenaries, and a sense of respect for the vanquished. A new emphasis on the supernatural points to the end of the Hellenistic tradition and the beginning of Christian culture.

Composed of 28 drums of marble, the column was restored in 1588 by Domenico Fontana on the orders of Pope Sixtus V. The emperor's statue on the summit was replaced by a bronze of St. Paul. The 20 spirals of the low relief chronicle the German war of AD 171–3 and (above) the Sarmatic war of AD 174–5. The column is almost 100 ft (30 m) high and 12 ft (3.7 m) in diameter. An internal spiral staircase leads to the top. The easiest way to appreciate the sculptural work, however, is to visit the Museo della Civiltà Romana at EUR *(see p267)* and study the casts of the reliefs.

Palazzo Capranica ❷

Piazza Capranica. **Map** 4 F3 & 12 D2. 🚍 *56, 60, 85, 90, 90b, 119, 492.*

Windows of Palazzo Capranica

O NE OF ROME'S small number of surviving 15th-century buildings, the palazzo was commissioned by Cardinal Domenico Capranica both as his family residence and as a college for higher education. Its fortresslike appearance is a patchwork of subsequent additions, not unusual in the late 15th century when Rome was still hovering between medieval and Renaissance taste. The Gothic-looking windows on the right of the building show the cardinal's coat of arms, and the date 1451 is inscribed on the doorway underneath. The palazzo now houses a popular movie theater.

Relief of the emperor's campaigns on the Column of Marcus Aurelius

Gesù ❾

DATING FROM BETWEEN 1568 and 1584, the Gesù was the first Jesuit church to be built in Rome. Its design epitomizes Counter Reformation Baroque architecture and has been much imitated throughout the Catholic world. The layout proclaims the church's two major functions: a large nave with side pulpits for preaching to great crowds, and a main altar as the centerpiece for the celebration of the mass. The illusionistic decoration in the nave and dome was added a century later. Its message is clear and confident: faithful Catholic worshipers will be joyfully uplifted into the heavens, while Protestants and heretics will be flung into hell's fires.

★ Chapel of Sant'Ignazio
Above its altar is a statue of the saint, framed by gilded lapis lazuli columns. The chapel was built in 1690 to 1700 by Andrea Pozzo, a Jesuit artist.

Triumph of Faith Over Heresy
This vivid Baroque allegory sculpted by Théudon illustrates the great ambition of Jesuit theology.

ST. IGNATIUS AND THE JESUIT ORDER

The Spanish soldier Ignatius Loyola (1491–1556) joined the Church after being wounded in battle in 1521. He came to Rome in 1537 and founded the Jesuits, sending missionaries and teachers all over the world to win souls for Catholicism.

Main entrance

STAR FEATURES

- ★ **Nave Ceiling Decorations**
- ★ **Chapel of Sant'Ignazio**
- ★ **San Roberto Bellarmino**

Allegorical Figures
Antonio Raggi made these stuccoes, which were designed by Il Baciccia to complement the figures on his own nave frescoes.

Madonna della Strada
This 15th-century image, called the Madonna of the Road, was originally displayed on the outer facade of a nearby church of the same name.

VISITORS' CHECKLIST

Piazza del Gesù. **Map** 4 F4 & 12 E4. [678 63 41. 44, 46, 56, 60, 62, 64, 65, 70, 81, 90 and many other routes to Largo di Torre Argentina or Piazza Venezia. **Open** 6am–12:30pm & 4–7:15pm daily.

★ **San Roberto Bellarmino**
Bernini captured the forceful personality of this anti-Protestant theologian, who died in 1621.

The Chapel of St. Francis Xavier is a memorial to the great missionary who died alone on an island off China in 1552.

★ **Nave Ceiling Decorations**
The figures in Il Baciccia's astonishing fresco of the Triumph of the Name of Jesus *spill out onto the coffered vaulting of the nave.*

Cupola Frescoes
The cupola was completed by della Porta to Vignola's design. The frescoes, by Il Baciccia, feature Old Testament figures.

TIMELINE

1540 Founding of the Society of Jesus (the Jesuits)	**1571** Giacomo della Porta's design chosen for the facade	**1696–1700** The Chapel of Sant' Ignazio is designed by Andrea Pozzo, a Jesuit artist	**1773** Pope Clement XIV orders the suppression of the Jesuit order
	1584 Church's consecration		
1500	**1600**		**1700**
1545–63 Council of Trent defines the new Catholic orthodoxy	**1568–71** Vignola builds the church up to the crossing under the patronage of Cardinal Alessandro Farnese		**1670–83** Giovanni Battista Gaulli (Il Baciccia) paints the nave vault, dome and apse
1556 Death of Ignatius		**1622** Ignatius Loyola is canonized	

PIAZZA NAVONA

THE FOUNDATIONS of the buildings surrounding the elongated oval of Piazza Navona were the ruined grandstands of the vast Stadium of Domitian. The piazza today still provides a dramatic spectacle, with the obelisk of the Fontana dei Fiumi in front of the church of Sant' Agnese in Agone as its focal point.

Lion on Fontana dei Fiumi

The predominant style of the area is Baroque, with many of its finest buildings dating from the reign of Innocent X Pamphilj (1644–55), patron of Bernini and Borromini. Of special interest is the complex of the Chiesa Nuova, headquarters of the Filippini, the order founded by San Filippo Neri, the 16th-century "Apostle of Rome."

SIGHTS AT A GLANCE

Churches and Temples
Sant'Agnese in Agone ❹
Santa Maria dell'Anima ❺
Santa Maria della Pace ❻
San Luigi dei Francesi ❼
Sant'Ivo alla Sapienza ❾
Sant'Andrea della Valle ❿
Chiesa Nuova ⓯
Oratorio dei Filippini ⓰
San Salvatore in Lauro ㉑
Sant'Apollinare ㉕

Museums
Palazzo Braschi ⓬
Museo Napoleonico ㉒

Historic Buildings
Palazzo Pamphilj ❸
Palazzo Madama ❽
Palazzo Massimo
alle Colonne ⑪
Torre dell'Orologio ⓱
Palazzo del Banco
di Santo Spirito ⓲
Palazzo Gaddi ⓳
Palazzo Altemps ㉓

Fountains and Statues
Fontana dei Fiumi ❶
Pasquino ⓭

Historic Streets and Piazzas
Piazza Navona ❷
Via del Governo Vecchio ⓮
Via dei Coronari ⑳

Restaurants
Hostaria dell'Orso ㉔

SEE ALSO

- **Street Finder**, maps 4, 11, 12
- **Where to Stay** pp294–5
- **Restaurants** pp310–11

GETTING THERE
This central area is within walking distance of many parts of the city. Much of the area itself is closed to traffic, but it is easily reached by bus. The principal bus routes along Corso Vittorio Emanuele II are the 64 from Termini Station to St. Peter's and the 46. Corso del Rinascimento, which runs parallel to Piazza Navona, is served by several useful bus routes, including the 70, 81, 90 and 492.

KEY

Street-by-Street map

P Parking

Piazza Navona, with the Fontana del Moro and church of Sant'Agnese in Agone

Street by Street: Piazza Navona

NO OTHER PIAZZA in Rome can rival the theatricality of Piazza Navona. Day and night, there is always something going on in the pedestrian area around its three flamboyant fountains. The Baroque is also represented in many of the area's churches. To discover an older Rome, walk along Via del Governo Vecchio and admire the facades of its Renaissance buildings and browse in the fascinating antiques shops.

Oratorio dei Filippini
The musical term oratorio *comes from this place of informal worship*

Torre dell' Orologio
This clock tower by Borromini (1648) is part of the Convent of the Filippini 🅐

Chiesa Nuova
This church was rebuilt in the late 16th century for the order founded by San Filippo Neri 🅑

To Corso Vittorio Emanuele II

Santa Maria della Pace
The medallion shows Pope Alexander VII, who had the church restored by Pietro da Cortona in 1656 🅕

Via del Governo Vecchio
This street preserves a large number of fine Renaissance houses 🅐

Pasquino
Romans hung satirical verses and dialogues on this weatherbeaten statue 🅑

Palazzo Pamphilj
This grand town house was built for Pope Innocent X and his family in the mid-17th century 🅒

STAR SIGHTS

★ **Sant'Andrea della Valle**

★ **San Luigi dei Francesi**

★ **Piazza Navona**

KEY

– – – Suggested route

0 meters	75
0 yards	75

Palazzo Braschi
A late 18th-century building with a splendid balcony, the palazzo houses the Museo di Roma 🅒

MUSEO DI ROMA

Palazzo Massimo alle Colonne
The magnificent curving colonnade (1536) is by Baldassarre Peruzzi 🅑

Sant'Agnese in Agone
Borromini's startling concave facade (1657) dominates one side of Piazza Navona ❹

Santa Maria dell'Anima
For four centuries this has been the German church in Rome ❺

Palazzo Madama
A spread-eagled stone lionskin decorates the central doorway of the palazzo, now the Italian Senate ❽

LOCATOR MAP
See Central Rome Map pp12–13

Fontana dei Fiumi
Bernini designed this fountain supporting an obelisk ❶

★ **San Luigi dei Francesi**
An 18th-century statue of St. Louis stands in a niche in the facade ❼

★ **Piazza Navona**
This unique piazza owes its shape to a Roman racetrack and its stunning decor to the genius of the Roman Baroque ❷

The Fontana del Moro was remodeled in 1653 by Bernini, who designed the central sea god.

Sant'Ivo alla Sapienza
This tiny domed church is one of Borromini's most original creations. He worked on it between 1642 and 1660 ❾

★ **Sant'Andrea della Valle**
The church, with its grandiose facade by Carlo Rainaldi (1665), has gained fame outside Rome as the setting of the first act of Puccini's Tosca ❿

To Campo de' Fiori

Fontana dei Fiumi ❶

Piazza Navona. **Map** 4 E4 & 11 C3.
🚌 70, 81, 87, 90, 90b, 186, 492.

BUILT FOR POPE Innocent X
Pamphilj, this magnificent
fountain in the center of
Piazza Navona was unveiled
in 1651. The pope's coat of
arms, the dove and the olive
branch, decorate the bold
pyramid rock formation
supporting the Egyptian
obelisk, which once stood in
the Circus of Maxentius on
the Appian Way. Bernini
designed the fountain, which
was paid for by means of
highly unpopular taxes on
bread and other staples. The
great rivers then known – the
Ganges, the Danube, the Nile
and the Plate – are
represented by four giants.

The Nile's veiled head
symbolizes the river's
unknown source, but there is
also a legend that the veil
conveys Bernini's dislike for
the nearby Sant'Agnese in
Agone, designed by his rival,
Borromini. Similarly, the

View of Palazzo Pamphilj across Piazza Navona

athletic figure of the Plate,
cringing with arm upraised, is
supposed to express Bernini's
fear that the church will
collapse. Sadly, these widely
believed stories have no basis
in actual fact: Bernini had
completed the fountain before
Borromini even started work
on the church.

Piazza Navona ❷

Map 4 E3 & 11 C2. 🚌 46, 62, 64,
70, 81, 87, 90, 90b, 186, 492.

ROME'S MOST beautiful
Baroque piazza follows
the shape of Domitian's
stadium, which once stood on
this site – some of its arches
are still visible below the
church of Sant'Agnese in
Agone. The *agones* were
athletic contests held in the
1st-century stadium, which
could seat 33,000. The word
Navona is thought to be
a corruption of *in
agone*. The piazza's
unique appearance and
atmosphere were
created in the 17th
century with the
addition of the Fontana
dei Fiumi. The other

fountains, the Fontana di
Nettuno and the Fontana del
Moro, date from the previous
century but have been altered
several times since. The figure
known as Il Moro is a late
work by Bernini.

Up until the 19th century,
Piazza Navona was flooded
during August by stopping
the fountain outlets. The rich
moved around in carriages,
while street urchins paddled
after them.

Today the piazza is a
favorite in all seasons. Each
January 6, it fills with colorful
stalls selling toys and sweets
for the feast of the Befana.

Palazzo Pamphilj ❸

Piazza Navona. **Map** 4 E4 & 11 C3.
🚌 46, 62, 64, 70, 81, 87, 90, 90b,
186, 492. **Not open** to the public.

**Family dove and olive branch on
the facade of Palazzo Pamphilj**

IN 1644 Giovanni Battista
Pamphilj became pope,
assuming the name of
Innocent X. During his ten-
year reign, he heaped riches
on his own family, especially
his domineering sister-in-law,
Olimpia Maidalchini. The
"talking statue" Pasquino *(see
p124)* gave her the nickname
"Olim-pia," Latin for "formerly
virtuous." She lived in the
grand Palazzo Pamphilj,
which has frescoes by Pietro
da Cortona and a gallery by
Borromini. The building is
now the Brazilian embassy.

Symbolic figure of the River Ganges in Bernini's Fontana dei Fiumi

Sant'Agnese in Agone ➍

Piazza Navona. **Map** 4 E4 & 11 C3.
【 679 44 35. ▇ 70, 81, 87, 90,
90b, 492. **Open** 5–6:30pm Mon–Sat,
10am–1pm Sun & public hols.

THIS CHURCH IS believed to
have been founded on the
site of the brothel where, in
AD 304, the young St. Agnes
was exposed naked to force
her to renounce her faith. A
marble relief in the crypt
shows the miraculous growth
of her hair, which fell around
her body to protect her
modesty. She was martyred
on this site and is buried in
the catacombs that bear her
name along the Via
Nomentana *(see p264).*

Today's church was
commissioned by Pope
Innocent X in 1652. The first
architects were a father and
son, Girolamo and Carlo
Rainaldi, but they were
replaced by Borromini,
who worked on the
church from 1653 to
1657. He stuck largely
to the Rainaldi
scheme, except
for the concave
façade designed
to emphasize
the dome. A statue
of St. Agnes on the
façade is said to
be reassuring the
Fontana dei Fiumi's
statue of the River
Plate that the
church is stable.

**Statue of St. Agnes
on Sant'Agnese
façade**

Carlo Saraceni's *Miracle of St. Benno and the Keys of Meissen Cathedral*

tomb by Baldassarre Peruzzi
in Santa Maria dell'Anima. It
stands to the right of
Giulio Romano's
damaged altarpiece and
is redolent of the
pagan Renaissance
spirit the pope had so
condemned during
his brief, rather
gloomy reign, when
patronage of the arts
ground to a halt. Santa
Maria dell'Anima is
the German church in
Rome, and some of its
paintings, such as the
Miracle of St. Benno by
Carlo Saraceni (1618),
illustrate events connected
with the history of Germany.

Santa Maria dell'Anima ➎

Via della Pace 20. **Map** 4 E4 & 11 C2.
【 683 37 29. ▇ 70, 81, 87, 90, 90b,
492. **Open** 7:30am–7pm Mon–Sat,
8am–1pm & 3–7pm Sun.

POPE ADRIAN VI (reigned
1522–3), son of a ship-
builder from Utrecht, was the
last non-Italian pope before
John Paul II. He would have
disapproved of his superb

Santa Maria della Pace ➏

Vicolo dell'Arco della Pace 5. **Map**
4 E3 & 11 C2. **【** 686 11 56. ▇ 70,
81, 87, 90, 90b, 186, 492. **Closed** for
restoration. 🚻 📷 ♿ 2 steps.

A DRUNKEN SOLDIER allegedly
pierced the breast of a
painted Madonna on this site,
causing it to bleed. Pope
Sixtus IV della Rovere

(reigned 1471–84) placated
the Virgin by ordering Baccio
Pontelli to build her a church
if she would bring the war
with Turkey to an end. Peace
was restored, and the church
was named Santa Maria della
Pace (St. Mary of Peace).

The cloister was added by
Bramante in 1504. As in his
famous Tempietto *(see p219),*
he scrupulously followed
Classical rules of proportion
to produce a thoroughly
original result, achieving a
really monumental effect in a
relatively small space.

Pietro da Cortona may have
had Bramante's Tempietto in
mind when he added the
church's charming semi-
circular portico in 1656. The
interior, a short nave ending
under an octagonal cupola,
houses Raphael's famous
frescoes of four *Sybils,* plus
four *Prophets* by his pupil
Timoteo Viti, painted for the
banker Agostino Chigi in 1514.
Baldassarre Peruzzi also did
some work in the church (the
fresco in the first chapel on
the left), as did the architect
Antonio da Sangallo the
Younger, who designed the
second chapel on the right.

San Luigi dei Francesi ❼

Via Santa Giovanna d'Arco.
Map 4 F4 & 12 D2. 🕿 688 27 1. 🚌
70, 81, 87, 90, 90b, 186, 492. **Open**
8am–12:30pm & 3:30–7pm daily.
Closed Thu pm. 🛉 📷 🛉

T HE FRENCH national church
was founded in 1518, but
was not finished until 1589,
with contributions by
Giacomo della Porta and
Domenico Fontana. Visitors
are drawn to the church
because of the many well-
known Frenchmen buried
here and the three
Caravaggios in the fifth
chapel on the left, dedicated
to St. Matthew.

Painted between 1597 and
1602, these were Caravaggio's
first great religious works: the
Calling of St. Matthew, the
Martyrdom of St. Matthew and
St. Matthew and the Angel.
The first version of this last
painting was rejected because
of its vivid realism – never
before had a saint been
shown as a tired
old man with
dirty feet – and
a second
version had
to be painted.
These realistic
works display
a dramatic use
of light.

Caravaggio, whose paintings of St. Matthew hang in San Luigi dei Francesi

**Shield linking symbols of France
and Rome on facade of San Luigi**

Palazzo Madama ❽

Corso del Rinascimento. **Map** 4 F4 &
12 D3. 🚌 70, 81, 87, 90, 90b, 186,
492. **Open** first Sat of month.

T HIS 16TH-CENTURY palazzo
was built for the Medici
family, who had owned a bank
here in the previous century.
It was the residence of the
Medici cardinals, Giovanni
and Giuliano. Both later
became pope, Giovanni as
Leo X and Giuliano as
Clement VII. Caterina de'
Medici, Clement VII's niece,
lived here before she was
married in 1533 to Henry, son
of King Francis I of France.

The palazzo takes its name
from Madama Margherita of

Austria, Emperor Charles V's
illegitimate daughter, who
married Alessandro de' Medici
and, after his death, Ottavio
Farnese. This caused the
fabulous art collection of
the Florentine Medici family
to be broken up; part was
inherited by the Roman
Farnese family.

The spectacular facade, with
its ornate cornice and
whimsical roof details, was
built in the 17th century by
Paolo Maruccelli. Since 1871
the palazzo has been the seat
of the Senate, the upper
house of the Italian parliament.

Cornice of Palazzo Madama

Sant'Ivo alla Sapienza ❾

Corso del Rinascimento 40.
Map 4 F4 & 12 D3. 🚌 70, 81, 87,
90, 90b 186, 492. **Open** for mass
9am–noon Sun. **Closed** Jul &
Aug. 🛉 📷

T HE CHURCH'S lantern
is crowned with a
cross on top of a
dramatic twisted
spiral – a highly
distinctive landmark
from Rome's roof
terraces. Seen up
close, this
Borromini
church is
even more　　**Lantern and spire**
striking. No　　**of Sant'Ivo**
other Baroque
church is quite like it. The
church is based on a design
of astonishing geometrical
complexity, with walls that are
a breathtaking combination of
concave and convex surfaces.
It stands in the small
courtyard of the Palazzo della
Sapienza, seat of the old
University of Rome from the
15th century until 1935.

Sant'Andrea della Valle ❿

Piazza Sant'Andrea della Valle.
Map 4 E4 & 12 D4. 🕿 686 13 39.
🚌 46, 62, 64, 70, 81, 87, 90, 90b,
186, 492. **Open** 7:30am–noon &
4:30–7:30pm. 🕇 📷

Dome of Sant'Andrea della Valle

THIS CHURCH is the scene of the first act of Puccini's opera *Tosca*, though opera fans will not find the Attavanti chapel, which is a poetic invention. The real church has much to recommend it – the recently restored facade shows the flamboyant Baroque style at its best. Inside, a golden light filters through the high windows, showing off the gilded interior. Here lie the two popes of the Sienese Piccolomini family: on the left of the central nave is the tomb of Pius II, the first Humanist pope (reigned 1458–64); Pope Pius III lies opposite – he reigned for less than a month in 1503.

The church is famous for its beautiful dome, the largest in Rome after St. Peter's. It was built by Carlo Maderno from 1622 to 1625 and was painted with splendid frescoes by Domenichino and Giovanni Lanfranco. The latter's extravagant style, seen in the dome fresco *Glory of Paradise*, won him most of the commission, and the jealous Domenichino is said to have tried to kill him. He failed, but Domenichino's jealousy was unnecessary, as shown by his two beautiful

paintings of scenes from the life of St. Andrew around the apse and altar. In the Strozzi Chapel, built in the style of Michelangelo, the altar has copies of the *Leah and Rachel* by Michelangelo in San Pietro in Vincoli *(see p170)*.

Palazzo Massimo alle Colonne ⓫

Corso Vittorio Emanuele II 141.
Map 4 F4 & 11 C3. 🚌 46, 62, 64,
70, 81, 87, 90, 186, 492. **Open**
7am–1pm Mar 16 every year.

Roman column, Palazzo Massimo

DURING THE LAST two years of his life, Baldassarre Peruzzi built this palazzo for the Massimo family, whose home had been destroyed in the sack of Rome in 1527. Peruzzi displayed great ingenuity in dealing with an awkwardly shaped site. The previous building had stood on the ruined Theater of Domitian, which created a curve in the great processional Via Papalis. Peruzzi's convex colonnaded facade follows the line of the street. His originality is also evident in the small square upper windows, the courtyard and the stuccoed vestibule. The entrance in Piazza de' Massimi has a Renaissance-style frescoed facade. A single column from the theater has been set up in the piazza.

The Massimo family, Quintus Fabius Maximus, traced its origins to the

conqueror of Hannibal in the 3rd century BC, and their proud coat of arms is borne by an infant Hercules. Over the years the family produced many great Humanists; in the 19th century a Massimo negotiated peace with Napoleon. On March 16 each year the palazzo opens to the public to celebrate Paolo Massimo's resurrection from the dead by San Filippo Neri in 1538.

Palazzo Braschi ⓬

Piazza San Pantaleo 10. **Map** 4 E4 &
11 C3. 🕿 687 53 45. 🚌 46, 62, 64,
70, 81, 87, 90, 186, 492. **Open** 9am–
1pm Tue–Sun, 5–7:30pm Thu & Sat.
(call to check for the Museo di Roma).

ON ONE SIDE of Piazza San Pantaleo is the last Roman palazzo to be built for the family of a pope. Palazzo Braschi was built in the late 18th century for Pope Pius VI Braschi's nephews by the architect Cosimo Morelli. He gave the building its imposing facade, which looks out on to the piazza.

The palazzo now houses the municipal Museo di Roma. It holds collections of pictures, drawings and everyday objects illustrating life in the city from medieval times until the last century.

Angel with raised wing by Ercole Ferrata, flanking the facade of Sant'Andrea della Valle

Pasquino ⑬

Piazza di Pasquino. **Map** 4 E4 &
11 C3. 🚌 *46, 62, 64, 70, 81, 87,
90, 492.*

**Pasquino, the most famous of
Rome's satirical "talking statues"**

This ROUGH CHUNK of marble
is all that remains of a
Hellenistic group, probably
representing the incident in
Homer's *Iliad* in which
Menelaus shields the body of
the slain Patroclus. For years
it lay as a stepping stone in a
muddy medieval street until it
was erected on this corner in
1501, near the shop of an
outspoken cobbler named
Pasquino. Freedom of speech
was not encouraged in papal
Rome, so the cobbler wrote
out his satirical comments on
current events and attached
them to the statue.

Other Romans were quick
to follow suit, hanging their
maxims and verses on the
statue by night to escape
punishment. Despite the wrath
of the authorities, the sayings
of the "talking statue" (renamed
Pasquino) were part of popular
culture right up until the 19th
century. Other statues started
to "talk" in the same satirical
vein; Pasquino used to conduct
dialogues with another statue
known as Marforio that stood
in Via del Campidoglio and
is now in the courtyard of
Palazzo Nuovo *(see pp 70–
71).* Rome's only English-
language cinema, which is
in Trastevere, is called the
Pasquino *(see p 347).*

Via del Governo
Vecchio ⑭

Map 4 E4 & 11 B3. 🚌 *46, 62, 64.*

The STREET TAKES its name
from Palazzo del Governo
Vecchio, the seat of papal
government in the 17th and
18th centuries. Once part of
the Via Papalis, which led
from the Lateran to St. Peter's,
the street is lined with 15th-
and 16th-century houses and
small workshops. Particularly
interesting are the 15th-
century houses at Nos. 104
and 106. The small palazzo
at No. 123 was once thought
to have been the home of
Bramante. Opposite is
Palazzo del Governo
Vecchio. It is also known
as Palazzo Nardini, after
its founder, whose name
is inscribed on the first-
floor windows along with
the date 1477.

Via del Governo Vecchio

Chiesa Nuova ⑮

Piazza della Chiesa Nuova.
Map 4 E4 & 11 B3. 📞 *687 52 89.*
🚌 *46, 62, 64.* **Open** *8am–noon &
4:30–7pm daily.* 🛉 📷

Facade of the Chiesa Nuova

San FILIPPO NERI (St. Philip
Neri) is the most appealing
of the Counter Reformation
saints. A highly unconventional
reformer, he required his
noble Roman followers to
humble themselves in public.
He made aristocratic young
men parade through the
streets of Rome in rags or even
with a fox's tail tied behind
them and set noblemen to
work as laborers building his
church. With the help of Pope
Gregory XIII, his church was
built in place of an old
medieval one, Santa Maria in
Vallicella, and it has been
known ever since as the
Chiesa Nuova (new church).

Begun in 1575 by Matteo da
Città di Castello and continued
by Martino Longhi the Elder,
it was consecrated in 1599,
although the facade, by Fausto
Rughesi, was finished only
in 1606. Against San Filippo's
wishes, the interior was
decorated after his death;
Pietro da Cortona frescoed the
nave, dome and apse, taking
nearly 20 years. There are
also three paintings by Rubens:
Madonna and Angels above
the altar; *Saints Domitilla,
Nereus and Achilleus* on the
right of the altar; and *Saints
Gregory, Maurus and Papias*
on the left. San Filippo is
buried in his own chapel, to
the left of the altar.

Borromini's facade of the Oratorio

Oratorio dei Filippini ⑯

Piazza della Chiesa Nuova. **Map** 4 E4 & 11 B3. 📞 686 93 74. 🚌 46, 62, 64. **Admission** on request to caretaker. 🚫 **Concerts.**

W ITH THE ADJOINING church and convent, the oratory formed the center of Filippo Neri's religious order, founded in 1575. Its members are commonly known as Filippini. The musical term *oratorio* (a religious text sung by solo voices and chorus) derives from the services held here.

Filippo Neri came to Rome at 18 to work as a tutor. The city was undergoing a period of religious strife and an economic slump after the sack of Rome in 1527. There was also an outbreak of the plague. It was left to newcomers like Neri and Ignazio di Loyola to revive the spiritual life of the city.

Neri formed a brotherhood of laymen who worshiped together and helped pilgrims and the sick *(see Santissima Trinità dei Pellegrini, p146).* He founded the Oratory as a center for religious discourse. Its conspicuous curving brick facade was built by Borromini in 1637 and 1643.

Torre dell' Orologio ⑰

Piazza dell'Orologio. **Map** 4 E4 & 11 B3. 🚌 46, 62, 64.

B ORROMINI BUILT this clock tower to decorate one corner of the Convent of the Oratorians of San Filippo Neri from 1647 to 1648. It is typical of Borromini in that the front and rear are concave and the

sides convex. The mosaic of the Madonna beneath the clock is by Pietro da Cortona, while on the corner of the building is a small tabernacle to the Madonna flanked by angels in the style of Bernini.

Pietro da Cortona (1596–1669)

Palazzo del Banco di Santo Spirito ⑱

Via del Banco di Santo Spirito. **Map** 4 D4 & 11 A2. 🚌 41, 46, 62, 64, 982. **Open** normal banking hours.

F ORMERLY THE MINT of papal Rome, this palazzo is often referred to as the Antica Zecca (old mint). The upper stories of the facade, built by Antonio da Sangallo the Younger in the 1520s, are in the shape of a Roman triumphal arch. Above the arch stand two Baroque statues symbolizing Charity and Thrift, and in the center of the arch above the main entrance an inscription records the founding of the Banco di Santo Spirito by Pope Paul V Borghese in 1605.

Pope Paul was a very shrewd financier who encouraged Romans to deposit their money at the bank by offering the vast estates of the Hospital of Santo Spirito *(see p226)* as security. The system provided for only the rudimentary banking requirements of the population, but business was brisk as people deposited money here, secure in the knowledge that they could get it out simply by presenting a chit. The hospital coffers also gained from the system. The Banco di Santo Spirito still exists but is now part of the Banco di Roma.

Facade of the Banco di Santo Spirito, built to resemble a Roman arch

Palazzo Gaddi ⑲

Via del Banco di Santo Spirito 42.
Map 4 D3 & 11 A2. 🚌 *41, 46, 62, 64, 280.* **Not open** to the public.

Portrait of Michelangelo in his old age by Jacopino del Conte

Traditionally attributed to the Florentine Jacopo Sansovino, Palazzo Gaddi was owned by Florentine families for many generations. Cardinal Gaddi – himself born into a famous Florentine family, the Altoviti – built the palazzo in the 16th century during the reign of Pope Clement VII de' Medici, when the Tuscan colony in Rome flourished. Michelangelo is known to have lived at the palazzo; nearby is the place where the Sienese banker Agostino Chigi set up his first bank in Rome. For years Chigi kept the papal tiara in safe keeping as security against a loan made to Pope Julius II.

Via dei Coronari ⑳

Map 4 D3 & 11 B2. 🚌 *46, 62, 64, 70, 81, 87, 90, 90b, 186, 492.*

Large numbers of medieval pilgrims making their way to St. Peter's walked along this street to cross over the Tiber at Ponte Sant'Angelo. Of the businesses that sprang up to try to part the pilgrims from their money, the most enduring was the selling of rosaries, and the street is still named after the rosary sellers

(coronari). The street followed the course of the ancient Roman Via Recta (straight street), which originally ran from today's Piazza Colonna to the Tiber.

Making one's way through the people in Via dei Coronari could be hazardous. In the Holy Year of 1450, some 200 pilgrims died, crushed by the crowds or drowned in the Tiber. Following the tragedy, Pope Nicholas V demolished the Roman triumphal arch that stood at the entrance to Ponte Sant'Angelo. In the late 15th century, Pope Sixtus IV encouraged the building of private houses and palaces along the street.

Although the rosary sellers have been replaced by antiques dealers, the street still has many original buildings from the 15th and 16th centuries. One of the earliest, at Nos. 156–7, is known as the House of Fiammetta, the mistress of Cesare Borgia.

Antiques shop, Via dei Coronari

San Salvatore in Lauro ㉑

Piazza San Salvatore in Lauro 15.
Map 4 E3 & 11 B2. 📞 *687 51 87.*
🚌 *46, 62, 64, 280.* **Open** *8:30am–noon Mon, Wed, Sat & Sun, 4:30–7pm daily.* ✝

The church is named "in Lauro" after the laurel grove that grew here in ancient times. Today's church was built at the end of the 16th century by

Cloister, San Salvatore in Lauro

Ottaviano Mascherino. The bell tower and sacristy were 18th-century additions by Nicola Salvi, famous for the Trevi Fountain *(see p159).* The church contains the first great altarpiece by the 17th-century artist Pietro da Cortona, *The Birth of Jesus,* in the first chapel to the right.

The adjacent San Giorgio convent, to the left, has a pretty Renaissance cloister, a frescoed refectory and the monument to Pope Eugenius IV (reigned 1431–47), moved here when old St. Peter's was pulled down. An extravagant Venetian, this pope spent thousands of ducats on his gold tiara but requested a "simple, lowly burial place" near his predecessor, Pope Eugenius III. His portrait, by Salviati, is in the refectory.

In 1669 the church became the seat of a pious association, the Confraternity of the Piceni, inhabitants of the Marche region. Fanatically loyal to the pope, the Piceni were traditionally employed as papal soldiers and tax collectors.

Facade of San Salvatore in Lauro

Museo Napoleonico �022

Piazza di Ponte Umberto 1.
Map 4 E3 & 11 C1. 🔔 *68 80 62 86.*
🚌 *70, 81, 87, 90, 90b, 186, 280, 492.*
***Open** 9am–7pm Tue–Sat, 9am–1pm
Sun.* **Adm charge.** 🚷 ♿ 📷 *only.*

Entrance to Museo Napoleonico

THIS MUSEUM contains
memorabilia and portraits
of Napoleon Bonaparte and
his family. Personal relics of
Napoleon himself include an
Indian shawl he wore during
his exile on St. Helena.

After his death in 1821, the
pope allowed many of the
Bonaparte family to settle in
Rome, including his
formidable mother Letizia,
who lived in Palazzo
Misciatelli on Via del Corso
and died there in 1836.
Of her other children,
the most intriguing is
the flighty Pauline, who
married the Roman Prince
Camillo Borghese. The
museum has a cast of her
right breast, made by
Canova in 1805 as a
preparatory study for his
statue of her as a
reclining Venus, now
in the Museo
Borghese *(see
p260–61).*
Portraits and
personal effects of

many other members of the
family are on display,
including court dresses,
uniforms and even a penny-
farthing bicycle that belonged
to Prince Eugène, the son of
Emperor Napoleon III.

The last male of the Roman
branch of the family was
Napoleon Charles, portrayed
in a late 19th-century painting
by Guglielmo de Sanctis. The
collection was assembled in
1927 by the Counts Primoli,
the sons of Charles's sister,
Carlotta Bonaparte.

Palazzo Altemps �023

Via Sant'Apollinare 8. **Map** 4 E3 &
11 C2. 🚌 *70, 81, 87, 90, 90b, 186,
280, 492.* **Not open** to the public.

THE PALAZZO was built for
Girolamo Riario, nephew
of Pope Sixtus IV, and the
Riario coat of arms can still
be seen in the janitor's room.
In the popular uprising that
followed the pope's death in
1484, the building was sacked
and Girolamo fled the city.

In 1568 the palazzo was
bought by Cardinal Marco
Sittico Altemps. His family was
of German origin – the name
is an Italianization of
Hohenems – and extremely
influential in the church. In
1565, when the cardinal's
brother married San Carlo
Borromeo's sister, Ortensia,
Pope Pius IV marked the day
with the last great tournament
to be held in the Vatican's
Belvedere Courtyard *(see
pp234–5).* The
palazzo was
renovated in

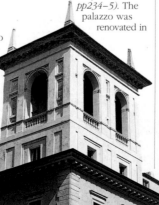

Belvedere of Palazzo Altemps

the 1570s by Martino Longhi
the Elder, who added the
great belvedere, crowned
with obelisks and a marble
unicorn. The Altemps were
ostentatious collectors; the
courtyard and the staircase
leading from it are lined with
ancient sculptures. The
palazzo is now a seminary.

Hostaria dell' Orso �024

Via dei Soldati 25. **Map** 4 E3 & 11 C2.
🔔 *686 42 50.* 🚌 *70, 81, 87, 90, 90b,
186, 280, 492.* **Open** 8pm–midnight
Mon–Sat.

NOW A RESTAURANT, this
ancient inn has a 15th-
century portico and loggia
built with columns taken from
Roman ruins. Legend has it
that Dante once stayed here.
Later visitors to Rome known
to have used the inn include
the 16th-century French writers
Rabelais and Montaigne.

Dante Alighieri (1265–1321)

Sant'Apollinare �025

Piazza Sant'Apollinare 49. **Map** 4 E3 &
11 C2. 🔔 *68 30 80 37.* 🚌 *70, 81, 87,
90, 90b, 186, 492.* **Open** 7:30–10am
Mon–Sat, 7:30–11:30am Sun. ✝ 📷

FOUNDED IN medieval times,
the church was rebuilt by
Ferdinando Fuga in the 18th
century. It is dedicated to the
saint said to have accompanied
St. Peter from Antioch to
Rome; he later became the
first Bishop of Ravenna. At
a special service held every
Sunday, Gregorian chants
are sung by the priests.

PIAZZA DI SPAGNA

By the 16th century, the increase in numbers of visiting pilgrims and ecclesiastics was making life in Rome's already congested medieval center unbearable. A new triangle of roads was built (and is still in place today), to help channel pilgrims as quickly as possible from the city's north gate, the Porta del Popolo, to the Vatican. By the 18th century, hotels had sprung up

Lion fountain in Piazza del Popolo

throughout the district. Today this attractive area offers much more: the superb works of Renaissance and Baroque art in Santa Maria del Popolo and Sant' Andrea delle Fratte; the magnificent reliefs of the restored Ara Pacis; art exhibits in the Villa Medici; views of the city from the Spanish Steps and the Pincio Gardens; plus Rome's most famous shopping streets, centered around Via Condotti.

SIGHTS AT A GLANCE

Churches
Sant'Andrea delle Fratte **1**
Trinità dei Monti **10**
All Saints **12**
Santa Maria dei Miracoli and Santa Maria in Montesanto **14**
Santa Maria del Popolo pp138–9 **17**
San Rocco **21**
Santi Ambrogio e Carlo al Corso **22**

Museums and Galleries
Keats-Shelley Memorial House **7**
Casa di Goethe **13**

Historic Buildings
Collegio di Propaganda Fide **2**
Villa Medici **11**

Arches, Gates and Columns
Colonna dell'Immacolata **3**
Porta del Popolo **18**

Historic Streets and Piazzas
Via Condotti **4**
Piazza di Spagna **6**

Spanish Steps **9**
Piazza del Popolo **16**

Monuments and Tombs
Ara Pacis **19**
Mausoleum of Augustus **20**

Parks and Gardens
Pincio Gardens **15**

Café and Restaurant
Caffè Greco **5**
Babington's Tea Rooms **8**

KEY
▢	Street-by-Street map
M	Metro station
P	Parking
—	City Wall

0 meters 300
0 yards 300

GETTING THERE
For Piazza di Spagna and the shops around Via Condotti, the Spagna Metro station on line A is more convenient than the main bus routes along Via del Corso and Via del Tritone. Stay on until Flaminio Metro if you want to visit Piazza del Popolo. For getting around locally, the 119 minibus, which goes up Via del Babuino, is very handy.

SEE ALSO

The Spanish Steps leading up to the church of Trinità dei Monti

Street by Street: Piazza di Spagna

THE NETWORK of narrow streets between Piazza di Spagna and Via del Corso is one of the liveliest areas in Rome, drawing throngs of tourists and Romans to its discreet and elegant shops. In the 18th century, the area was full of hotels for frivolous English aristocrats doing the Grand Tour, but there were also artists, writers and composers, who took the city's history and culture more seriously.

Caffè Greco
Busts and portraits recall the café's former artistic patrons **5**

★ **Piazza di Spagna**
For almost three centuries, the square with its curious Barcaccia fountain in the center has been the chief meeting place for visitors to Rome **6**

Via delle Carrozze took its name from the carriages of wealthy tourists that used to line up there for repairs.

Via Condotti
This shadowy narrow street has the smartest shops in one of the smartest shopping areas in the world **4**

Bulgari sells very expensive jewelry behind an austere shopfront in Via Condotti.

| 0 meters | 75 |
| 0 yards | 75 |

KEY

– – – Suggested route

Ⓜ Metro station

Trinità dei Monti
This 16th-century church has a spectacular setting and some of the finest views in Rome **⓿**

Babington's Tea Rooms
English tourists are catered to in the style of the 1890s **8**

LOCATOR MAP
See Central Rome Map pp12–13

Colonna dell'Immacolata
A Roman column supports a statue of the Virgin Mary **3**

Collegio di Propaganda Fide
This facade (1665) was one of the last works of the great Francesco Borromini **2**

Sant'Andrea delle Fratte
Pasquale Marini painted The Redemption *to decorate the interior of Borromini's high dome in 1691* **1**

★ Keats-Shelley Memorial House
The library is part of the small museum established in the house where the English poet Keats died in 1821 **7**

★ Spanish Steps
Even obscured by crowds, the steps are one of the glories of late Baroque Rome **9**

STAR SIGHTS

★ **Piazza di Spagna**

★ **Keats-Shelley Memorial House**

★ **Spanish Steps**

Sant'Andrea delle Fratte ❶

Via Sant'Andrea delle Fratte 1.
Map 5 A3. 679 31 91. 119.
Spagna. **Open** 6:30am–12:45pm
& 4–7pm daily.

WHEN SANT'ANDREA delle
Fratte was built in the
12th century, this area was the
northernmost edge of Rome.
Though the church is now
firmly embedded in the city,
its name (*fratte* means
"thickets") recalls its old setting.

The church was completely
rebuilt in the 17th century,
partly by Borromini. His bell
tower and dome, best viewed
from the higher ground farther
up Via Capo le Case, are
remarkable for the complex
arrangement of concave and
convex surfaces. The bell
tower is particularly fanciful,
with angel caryatids, flaming
torches resembling ice cream
cones and exaggerated scrolls
like semifolded hearts
supporting a spiky crown.

In 1842, the Virgin Mary
appeared in the church to a
Jewish banker, who promptly
converted to Christianity and
became a missionary. Inside,
the chapel of the Miraculous
Madonna is the first thing
visitors notice. The church is
better known, however, for
the angels that Borromini's
rival, Bernini, carved for the
Ponte Sant'Angelo. Pope
Clement IX declared they
were too lovely to be outside,
so they remained with Bernini's
family until 1729, when they
were moved to the church.

Collegio di Propaganda Fide ❷

Via di Propaganda 1. **Map** 5 A2.
679 69 41. 119. Spagna.
Open to individuals on written request.

BUILT FOR the Jesuits in 1662,
when they were at the
height of their
power, the
Collegio di
Propaganda Fide
(College for the
Propagation of
the Faith) was
Borromini's last
work. The
headquarters
of the Jesuits
had to be a
remarkable
building, but the
extraordinary
facade (now
thickly coated
with grime)
must have
surpassed
even their
expectations.
It is striped with broad
pilasters, between
which the second-
floor windows bend
in, and the central
bay bulges out. A
rigid band divides
the first and second
floors, and the cornice
above the convex central bay
swerves inward. The more
one looks at it, the more
restless it seems. The
architect committed suicide
shortly after completing it.

**Angel by Bernini,
Sant'Andrea delle Fratte**

Entrance to the Jesuit College

Colonna dell'Immacolata ❸

Piazza Mignanelli. **Map** 5 A2.
119. Spagna.

INAUGURATED IN 1857, the
column commemorates
Pope Pius IX's proclamation
of the doctrine of the
Immaculate Conception,
holding that the Virgin Mary
was the only human being
ever to have been born
"without the stain of original
sin." The column itself dates
from ancient Rome. Now
crowned with a statue of the
Virgin Mary, it is one of the
many pagan monuments in
the city to have been
converted to Christian use.

**Portrait of Pope Pius IX
(reigned 1846–78)**

Via Condotti ❹

Map 5 A2. 📟 *81, 90, 90b, 119.*
Ⓜ *Spagna. See Shops and Markets pp322–33.*

Named after the conduits that carried water to the Baths of Agrippa near the Pantheon, Via Condotti is now home to the most traditional of Rome's designer clothes shops. It is also extremely popular for early evening strolls, when elegant perfumed ladies and men in immaculate suits and flowing trench coats mingle with tourists in shorts and sneakers. The most famous shops here are Beltrami (for leather), Ferragamo (for exquisitely crafted and often fantastical shoes), Hermès and Gucci.

Slightly younger designers such as Laura Biagiotti, Gianfranco Ferrè, Gianni Versace and the Fendi sisters have shops on parallel Via Borgognona. Valentino's shops are on Via Maria dei Fiori and Via Bocca di Leone, which cross Via Condotti just below Piazza di Spagna, and Giorgio Armani and Emporio Armani are on nearby Via del Babuino, among the discreet art galleries, exclusive antiques shops and furniture stores.

View along Via Condotti toward the Spanish Steps

Caffè Greco ❺

Via Condotti 86. **Map** 5 A2.
📞 *679 17 00.* 📟 *81, 90, 90b, 119.*
Ⓜ *Spagna.* **Open** *8am–8:45pm Mon–Sat.* **Closed** *Jan 1, two weeks in August, Dec 25.* ♿

This cafe was opened by a Greek (hence *Greco*) in 1760, and throughout the 18th

Caffè Greco, nearly 250 years old

century it was a favorite meeting place for foreign artists. Writers such as Keats, Byron and Goethe and composers Liszt, Wagner and Bizet all breakfasted and drank here. So, too, did Casanova and mad King Ludwig of Bavaria. Today, locals often stand in the crowded foyer to sip espresso; there are also tables in a cozy back room, against walls studded with the portraits of the café's famous customers.

Piazza di Spagna ❻

Map 5 A2. 📟 *119.* Ⓜ *Spagna.*

Shaped like a crooked bow tie and surrounded by tall shuttered houses painted in muted shades of ocher, cream and russet, Piazza di Spagna (Spanish Square) is crowded all day and (in summer) most of the night. The most famous square in Rome, it has long been the haunt of foreign visitors and expatriates.

In the 17th century, Spain's ambassador to the Holy See had his headquarters on the square, and the area around it was deemed to be Spanish territory. Foreigners who unwittingly trespassed were liable to be dragooned into the Spanish army. In the 18th and 19th centuries, Rome was almost as popular with visitors as it is today, and the square stood at the heart of the city's main hotel district. Some travelers came in search of knowledge and artistic inspiration, but most were more interested in gambling, collecting ancient statues to adorn their family homes and conducting love affairs with Italian women.

Not surprisingly, wealthy travelers attracted hordes of beggars, who often produced letters describing their plight, written by scribes who worked in the square.

The Fontana della Barcaccia in the square is the least showy of Rome's Baroque fountains, and it is often completely screened from view by people resting on its rim. It was designed either by the famous Gian Lorenzo Bernini or by his father, Pietro. Because the pressure from the aqueduct that feeds the fountain is extremely low, there are no spectacular cascades or spurts of water. Instead, Bernini constructed a leaking boat – *barcaccia* means "useless old boat" – which lies half-submerged in a shallow pool.

Pope Urban VIII's arms, with the Barberini bees

The bees and suns that decorate the Fontana della Barcaccia are taken from the family coat of arms of Pope Urban VIII Barberini, who commissioned the fountain.

The Fontana della Barcaccia at the foot of the Spanish Steps

Bust of Shelley by Moses Ezekiel

Keats-Shelley Memorial House ❼

Piazza di Spagna 26. **Map** 5 A2.
☎ 678 42 35. 🚌 119. Ⓜ *Spagna.*
Open 9am–1pm & 3–6pm (Oct–
Mar: 2:30–5:30pm) Mon–Fri. **Closed**
public hols. **Adm charge.** 🚫 📷
make reservations in advance. 📷

IN NOVEMBER 1820 the English poet John Keats came to stay with the painter Joseph Severn in a dusty pink house, the Casina Rossa, on the corner of the Spanish Steps. Suffering from consumption, Keats had been sent to Rome by his doctor, in the hope that the mild, dry climate would help the young man's recovery. Depressed because of scathing criticism of his work and tormented by his unrequited love for a young girl named Fanny Brawne, Keats died at 25 the following February.

His death inspired his friend and fellow poet Percy Bysshe Shelley to write the poem "Mourn not for Adonais." In July 1822 Shelley himself was drowned in a boating accident in the Gulf of La Spezia off the coast of Tuscany. Keats, Shelley and Severn are all buried in Rome's Protestant Cemetery (*see p205*).

In 1906 the house was bought by an Anglo-American association and preserved as a memorial and library to honor English Romantic poets. The relics include a lock of Keats's hair, some fragments of Shelley's bones in a tiny urn and a garish Carnival mask picked up by Lord Byron as a souvenir of a trip to Venice. You can visit the room where Keats died, though all the original furniture was burned after his death, on papal orders.

Babington's Tea Rooms ❽

Piazza di Spagna 23. **Map** 5 A2.
☎ 678 60 27. 🚌 119.
Ⓜ *Spagna.* **Open** 9am–11:30pm
Wed–Mon. **Closed** public hols.
♿

THESE AUGUST, old-fashioned tea rooms were opened in 1896 by two Englishwomen, Anna Maria and Isabel Cargill Babington, to serve homesick British tourists scones, jam and pots of Earl Grey tea. The food remains homey – shepherd's pie and chicken supreme for lunch, muffins and cinnamon toast for tea – though these days the menu offers for breakfast pancakes with maple syrup as well as the traditional bacon and eggs.

Providers of English breakfasts to homesick exiles since 1896

Spanish Steps ❾

Scalinata della Trinità dei Monti,
Piazza di Spagna. **Map** 5 A2. 🚌 119.
Ⓜ *Spagna.*

IN THE 17TH century the French owners of Trinità dei Monti decided to link the church with Piazza di Spagna by building a magnificent new flight of steps. They also planned to place an equestrian statue of King Louis XIV at the top. Pope Alexander VII Chigi was not very happy at the

The Spanish Steps in spring with azaleas in full bloom

prospect of erecting a statue of a French monarch in the papal city, and the arguments continued until the 1720s, when an Italian architect, Francesco de Sanctis, produced a design that satisfied both the French and the papacy. The steps, completed in 1726, combine straight sections, curves and terraces to create one of the city's most dramatic and distinctive landmarks.

When the Victorian novelist Charles Dickens visited Rome, he reported that the Spanish Steps were the meeting place for artists' models, who would dress in colorful traditional costumes, hoping to catch the attention of a wealthy artist. The steps are now a popular place to sit, write postcards, take photos, flirt, perform or just watch the passers-by.

Trinità dei Monti ⓾

Piazza della Trinità dei Monti.
Map 5 A2. **☎** 679 41 79. **🚌** 119.
Ⓜ Spagna. **Open** 10am–12:30pm & 4–6pm daily. **✝** **📷**

Trinità dei Monti's bell towers

THE VIEWS of Rome from the platform in front of the facade of Trinità dei Monti, with its twin bell towers, are so beautiful that the church itself is often ignored. It is, however, unusual for Rome, for it was founded by the French in 1495, and although it was later badly damaged, there are still traces of attractive late Gothic latticework in the vaults of the transept. The interconnecting side chapels are decorated with Mannerist paintings, including two fine

works by Daniele da Volterra. A pupil of Michelangelo, Volterra had to paint clothes on the nudes in the *Last Judgment* in the Sistine Chapel, in response to the objections of Pope Pius IV.

Michelangelo's influence is obvious in the muscled bodies shown in the *Deposition* (second chapel on the left). The circles of figures and dancing angels around the Virgin Mary in the *Assumption* (third chapel on the right), have more in common with the graceful style of Raphael.

Villa Medici ⓫

Accademia di Francia a Roma,
Viale della Trinità dei Monti 1.
Map 5 A2. **☎** 676 11. **🚌** 119. **Ⓜ**
Spagna. **Accademia and gardens open** irregularly, so call first.
Exhibitions, concerts.
Adm charge. **📷**

SUPERBLY POSITIONED on the Pincio Hill above Piazza di Spagna, this 16th-century villa has kept the name it assumed when Cardinal Ferdinando de' Medici bought it in 1576. From the terrace visitors can look across the city to Castel Sant'Angelo, from where Queen Christina of Sweden is said to have fired the large cannonball that now sits in the basin of the fountain.

The villa is home to the French Academy,

The 17th-century French painter Nicolas Poussin

which was founded by Louis XIV in 1666 to give select painters the chance to study in Rome. Nicolas Poussin was one of the first advisers to the Academy, Ingres was a director and ex-students include Fragonard and Boucher.

After 1803, when the French Academy moved to the Villa Medici, musicians were also admitted; both Berlioz and Debussy came to Rome as students of the Academy.

All Saints ⓬

Via del Babuino 153B. **Map** 4 F2.
☎ 360 01 881. **🚌** 90, 90b, 119.
Open mornings daily. **Closed** Tue.
✝

IN 1816 THE POPE gave English residents and visitors the right to hold Anglican services in Rome, but it was not until the early 1880s that they acquired a site to build their own church. The architect chosen for the job was G.E. Street, best known in Britain for his Neo-Gothic churches and the London Law Courts. All Saints is also built in Victorian Neo-Gothic, and the interior, though decorated with different-colored Italian marbles, has an unmistakably English air. It even has an organ originally from Huddersfield. Street also designed St-Paul's-within-the-walls in Via Nazionale. Its interior is a jewel of British Pre-Raphaelite art.

19th-century engraving of the inner facade of the Villa Medici

Casa di Goethe ⓭

18–20 Via del Corso. **Map** 4 F1.
🚌 *90, 90b, 119, 926.* **Not open to** *the public.*

THE GERMAN POET, dramatist and novelist Johann Wolfgang von Goethe (1749–1832) lived in this house from 1786 until 1788, working on the journal that eventually formed part of his travel book *The Italian Journey*. He had to contend with Rome's noisy street life, especially during Carnival time, and a number of murders in his area – but Rome for the most part rejuvenated him, and his book went on to become one of the most influential ever to be written about Italy.

Santa Maria dei Miracoli and Santa Maria in Montesanto ⓮

Piazza del Popolo. **Map** 4 F1. 🚌 *90, 90b, 95, 119, 926.* Ⓜ *Flaminio.* **Santa Maria dei Miracoli** ☎ *361 02 50.* **Open** *6am–1pm & 5–7pm Mon–Sat, 8am–1pm & 5–7pm Sun & public hols.* 🚻 📷 ♿ **Santa Maria in Montesanto** ☎ *361 05 94.* **Open** *5–8pm (Nov–Mar: 4–7pm) daily.* **Closed** *Aug.* 🚻 📷

THE TWO CHURCHES at the south end of Piazza del Popolo were designed by the Baroque architect Carlo Rainaldi (1611–91), proof that he could be as ingenious as his more contemporaries, Bernini and Borromini.
To provide a focal point for the piazza, the churches had to look symmetrical, but the site on the

Portrait of Goethe in the Roman countryside by Tischbein (1751–1821)

left was narrower than that on the right. Rainaldi solved the problem by giving Santa Maria dei Miracoli (on the right) a circular dome and Santa Maria in Montesanto an oval one, cleverly squeezing it into the narrower site; however, the sides of the supporting drums facing the piazza are identical.

Pincio Gardens ⓯

Il Pincio. **Map** 4 F1. 🚌 *90, 90b, 95, 119, 926.* Ⓜ *Flaminio.* ♿

THE PINCIO GARDENS lie above Piazza del Popolo, on a hillside that has been so skillfully terraced and richly planted with trees that, from below, the zigzagging road climbing to the gardens is virtually invisible.
There were magnificent gardens on the Pincio Hill in ancient Roman times, but the present gardens were designed in the early 19th century by Giuseppe Valadier (who also re-designed the Piazza del Popolo).

The Pincio Gardens water clock

The broad avenues, lined with umbrella pines, palm trees and evergreen oaks, soon became a fashionable place to stroll, and even this century such diverse characters as Gandhi and Mussolini, Richard Strauss and King Farouk of Egypt patronized the Casina Valadier, an exclusive café and restaurant on the grounds.
From the Pincio's main square, Piazzale Napoleone I, the panoramic views of Rome stretch from the Monte Mario to the Janiculum. For full effect, approach the gardens from the grounds of Villa Borghese *(see pp258–9)* above the Pincio or along Viale della Trinità dei Monti.

The twin churches of Santa Maria di Montesanto (left) and Santa Maria dei Miracoli in a 19th-century view of Piazza del Popolo

The panorama is particularly beautiful at sunset, the traditional time for tourists to take a stroll in the gardens.

One of the most striking features of the park itself is an Egyptian-style obelisk that Emperor Hadrian erected on the tomb of his favorite, the beautiful male slave Antinous. After the slave's premature death (according to some accounts he died saving the emperor's life), Hadrian deified him.

The 19th-century water clock on Via dell'Orologio was designed by a Dominican monk. It was displayed at the Paris Exhibition of 1889.

Traditional Carnival band in Piazza del Popolo

The Casina Valadier restaurant in the Pincio Gardens

Piazza del Popolo ⑯

Map 4 F1. 🚌 90, 90b, 95, 119, 926. Ⓜ Flaminio.

A VAST COBBLED OVAL standing at the apex of the triangle of roads known as the Trident, Piazza del Popolo forms a grand symmetrical antechamber to the heart of Rome. Twin Neoclassical facades stand on either side of the Porta del Popolo; an Egyptian obelisk rises in the center; and the matching domes and porticoes of Santa Maria dei Miracoli and Santa Maria di Montesanto flank the beginning of Via del Corso.

Although it is now one of the most unified squares in Rome, Piazza del Popolo evolved gradually over the centuries. In 1589 the great town-planning pope, Sixtus V, had the obelisk erected in the center by Domenico Fontana.

Over 3,000 years old, the obelisk was originally brought to Rome by Augustus to adorn the Circus Maximus after the conquest of Egypt. Almost a century later Pope Alexander VII commissioned Carlo Rainaldi to build the twin Santa Marias.

In the 19th century the piazza was turned into a grandiose oval by Giuseppe Valadier, the designer of the Pincio Gardens. He also encased Santa Maria del Popolo in a Neoclassical shell to make its south facade fit in better with the overall appearance of the piazza.

In contrast to the piazza's air of ordered rationalism, many of the events staged here were barbaric. In the 18th and 19th centuries, public executions were held in Piazza del Popolo, often as part of the celebration of Carnival. Condemned men were sometimes hammered to death by repeated blows to the temples. The last time a criminal was executed in this way was in 1826, even though the guillotine had by then been adopted as a more scientific means of execution.

The riderless horse races from the piazza down Via del Corso were scarcely more humane: the performance of the runners was enhanced by feeding the horses stimulants, wrapping them in nail-studded ropes and letting off fireworks at their heels.

Santa Maria del Popolo ⑰

See pp138–9.

Porta del Popolo ⑱

Between Piazzale Flaminio and Piazza del Popolo. **Map** 4 F1. 🚌 90, 90b, 95, 119, 926. Ⓜ Flaminio.

T HE VIA FLAMINIA, built in 220 BC to connect Rome with Italy's Adriatic coast, enters the city at Porta del Popolo, a grand 16th-century gate built on the orders of Pope Pius IV Medici. The architect, Nanni di Baccio Bigio, modeled it on a Roman triumphal arch. The outer face has statues of St. Peter and St. Paul on either side of the arch and a huge Medici coat of arms above.

A century later, Pope Alexander VII commissioned Bernini to decorate the inner face to celebrate the arrival in Rome of Queen Christina of Sweden. Lesser visitors were often held up while Customs officers rifled their luggage. The only way to speed things up was with a bribe.

Porta del Popolo's central arch

Santa Maria del Popolo ⑰

ONE OF ROME'S greatest stores of artistic treasures, this early Renaissance church was commissioned by Pope Sixtus IV della Rovere in 1472. Among the artists who worked on the building were Andrea Bregno and Pinturicchio. Later additions were made by Bramante and Bernini. Many illustrious families have chapels here, all decorated with appropriate splendor. The Della Rovere Chapel has delightful Pinturicchio frescoes; the Cerasi Chapel has two Caravaggio masterpieces, the *Conversion of St. Paul* and the *Crucifixion of St. Peter*, but the finest of all is the Chigi Chapel designed by Raphael for his patron, the banker Agostino Chigi. The most striking of the church's many Renaissance tombs are the two by Andrea Sansovino behind the main altar.

★ Chigi Chapel
Raphael designed this chapel, which has an altarpiece by Sebastiano del Piombo. Niches on either side of the altar house sculptures by Bernini and Lorenzetto. Mosaics in the dome show God as creator of the seven heavenly bodies.

Kneeling Skeleton
This floor mosaic of the figure of death was added to the Chigi Chapel in the 17th century.

NERO'S GHOST

Nero lived on in the imagination of the people long after the fall of the Roman Empire. In the Middle Ages, a legend arose that a walnut tree growing here on the spot where his ashes were buried was haunted by the emperor. Ravens roosting in the tree were thought to be demons tormenting him for his hideous crimes. When the first church was built here in 1099 by Pope Paschal II, the tree was cut down, supposedly putting an end to the supernatural events that had terrified local people.

Entrance

Cybo Chapel

STAR FEATURES

★ Chigi Chapel

★ Caravaggio Paintings in Cerasi Chapel

★ Delphic Sibyl

Della Rovere Chapel
Pinturicchio painted the frescoes in the lunettes and the Adoration *above the altar from 1485–9.*

★ **Caravaggio Paintings in Cerasi Chapel**
One of two Caravaggios in the Cerasi Chapel, The Crucifixion of St. Peter uses dramatic fore-shortening to highlight the sheer effort involved in turning the saint's crucifix upside down.

The altarpiece of *The Assumption* is by Annibale Carracci (1540–1609).

Stained Glass
In 1509, French artist Guillaume de Marcillat was invited to provide Rome's first two stained-glass windows.

The Tomb of Ascanio Sforza, who died in 1505, is by Andrea Sansovino.

★ **Delphic Sibyl**
This is one of a series of frescoes by Pinturicchio, some Classical and others biblical, painted from 1508 to 1509 to decorate the apse ceiling.

The altar houses the 13th-century painting known as the *Madonna del Popolo.*

The Tomb of Giovanni della Rovere (1483) is by pupils of Andrea Bregno.

TIMELINE

1213–27 Church enlarged under Gregory IX

Pinturicchio (c 1454–1513)

1485–9 Della Rovere Chapel painted by Pinturicchio

1513–16 Raphael designs and executes Chigi Chapel

1090	1200	1300	1400	1500

1099 Paschal II builds chapel over tombs of the Domitia family (which included Nero) in honor of the Madonna

Pope Paschal II (reigned 1099–1118)

1472–8 Sixtus IV builds church (one of the first Renaissance churches in Rome)

1473 Main altar built

1530–34 Chigi Chapel altarpiece built by Sebastiano del Piombo

Ara Pacis ⑲

Via di Ripetta. **Map** 4 F2.
📞 68 80 68 48. 🚌 81, 90, 90b, 119, 926. **Open** 9am–5pm Tue–Sat, 1am–7pm Sun (last adm: 30 mins before closing).
Adm charge. 📷

Frieze on south wall showing a procession with the family of Augustus

R ECONSTRUCTED at great expense over a period of many years, the Ara Pacis (Altar of Peace) is one of the most significant monuments of ancient Rome. It celebrates the peace created throughout the Mediterranean area by the

Marcus Agrippa *(right)*

Emperor Augustus after victorious campaigns in Gaul and Spain. The monument was commissioned by the Senate in 13 BC and completed four years later. It is a square enclosure on a low platform with the altar in the center. All the surfaces are decorated with magnificent friezes and reliefs carved in Carrara marble. Their high quality indicates that the craftsmen must have been Greek. The reliefs on the north and south walls depict a procession that took place on July 4 in 13 BC; the members

of the emperor's family can be identified, ranked by their position in the succession. Heir apparent at the time was Marcus Agrippa, husband of Augustus's daughter, Julia. All the portraits in the relief are carved with astonishing realism, even the toddler clinging to his mother's skirts.

The tale of the rediscovery of the Ara Pacis dates back to the 16th century, when the first panels were unearthed. One section ended up in Paris, another in Florence. Other finds were made in the late 19th century, when archaeologists finally realized just what they had

discovered. What we see today has all been pieced together since 1938. The reconstruction, in part original, in part facsimile, is enshrined in a large glass hangar, creating a wonderful spectacle when lit up at night.

Livia *(right)*, Augustus's second wife and mother of Tiberius, with an unidentified family member

South wall

East wall

The altar was used once a year for a sacrifice on the anniversary of the monument's inauguration.

West wall

North wall

An acanthus frieze runs around the lower half of the outside wall.

Augustus's young grandson, Lucius

Mausoleum of Augustus ⑳

Piazza Augusto Imperatore. **Map** 4 F2.
🚌 *81, 90, 90b, 119, 926.* **Adm** *by written permission only: apply to Ripartizione X, Piazza Campitelli 7.*
📞 *67 10 20 70.*

NOW JUST a weedy mound, ringed with cypresses and sadly strewn with litter, this was once the most prestigious burial place in Rome. Augustus had the mausoleum built in 28 BC, the year he became sole ruler, as a tomb for himself and his descendants. The circular building was 270 ft (87 m) in diameter with two obelisks (now in Piazza del Quirinale and Piazza dell' Esquilino) at the entrance.

Inside were four concentric passageways (linked by corridors) where the urns containing the ashes of the imperial family were placed. The first to be buried there was Augustus's favorite nephew, Marcellus, who had married Julia, the emperor's daughter. He died in 23 BC, possibly poisoned by Augustus's second wife, Livia, who felt that her son Tiberius would make a more reliable emperor. When Augustus died in AD 14, his ashes were placed in the mausoleum, Tiberius duly became emperor and dynastic poisonings continued to fill the family vault with urns.

This sinister monument was later used as a medieval fortress, a vineyard, a private garden and, even, in the 18th century, as a bullring.

Augustus, the first Roman emperor

Madonna, San Rocco and Sant'Antonio with Victims of the Plague by Il Baciccia (1639–1709)

San Rocco ㉑

Largo San Rocco 1. **Map** 4 F2.
📞 *689 64 16.* 🚌 *81, 90, 90b, 115, 119.* **Open** *7:30–9am & 5– 7:45pm daily.* **Closed** *Aug 17–31.*
✝️ 📷

THIS CHURCH, with a restrained Neoclassical facade by Giuseppe Valadier, the designer of Piazza del Popolo, began life as the chapel of a 16th-century hospital with beds for 50 men – San Rocco was a healer of the plague-stricken. A maternity wing was added for the wives of Tiber bargemen to save them from having to give birth in the insanitary conditions of a boat. The hospital came to be used by unmarried mothers, and one section of the hospital was set aside for women who did not wish to give their names. They were even permitted to wear a veil for the duration of their stay. Unwanted children were sent to an orphanage, and if any mothers or children died they were buried in anonymous graves.

The hospital was abandoned at the turn of the century and demolished in the 1930s during the excavation of the Mausoleum of Augustus. The church has an interesting Baroque altarpiece by Il Baciccia, the artist who decorated the ceiling of the Gesù *(see pp114–15)*.

Santi Ambrogio e Carlo al Corso ㉒

Via del Corso 437. **Map** 4 F2.
📞 *687 83 32.* 🚌 *81, 90, 90b, 119.* **Open** *7:30am–12:30pm & 5–7pm (Oct–Mar: 7:30pm) daily. Ring porter's door to left of church if closed.* 🚻

THIS CHURCH belonged to the Lombard community in Rome and is dedicated to two canonized bishops of Milan, Lombardy's capital. In 1471, Pope Sixtus IV gave the Lombards a church that they dedicated to Sant'Ambrogio, who died in 397. Then in 1610, when Carlo Borromeo was canonized, the church was rebuilt in his honor. Most of the new church was the work of father and son Onorio and Martino Longhi, but the fine dome is by Pietro da Cortona. The altarpiece by Carlo Maratta (1625–1713) is *Gloria dei Santi Ambrogio e Carlo*. An ambulatory leads behind the altar to a chapel housing the heart of San Carlo in a richly decorated reliquary.

Statue of San Carlo by Attilio Selva (1888–1970) behind the apse of Santi Ambrogio e Carlo

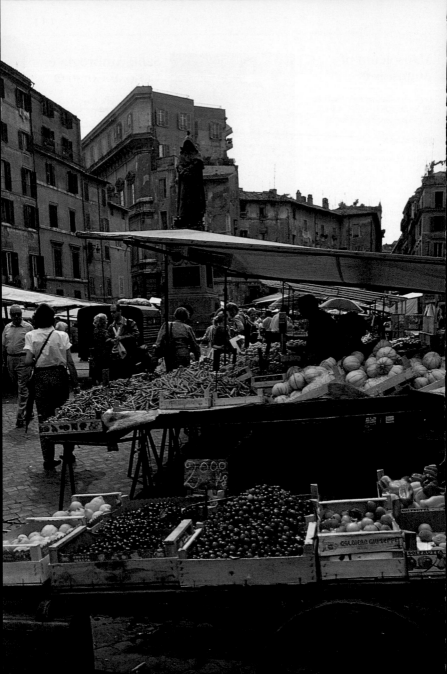

CAMPO DE' FIORI

BETWEEN Corso Vittorio Emanuele II and the Tiber, the city displays many distinct personalities. The open-air market of Campo de' Fiori preserves the lively bohemian atmosphere of the medieval inns that once flourished here, while the area also contains Renaissance palazzi, such as Palazzo Farnese and Palazzo Spada, where powerful Roman families built

18th-century Madonna in Campo de' Fiori

their fortresslike houses near the route of papal processions. Close by, overlooking the picturesque Tiber Island, lies the old Jewish Ghetto, where many traces of daily life from past centuries can still be seen. The Portico of Octavia and the Theater of Marcellus are spectacular examples of the city's many-layered history, built up over the half-ruined remains of ancient Rome.

SIGHTS AT A GLANCE

Churches and Temples
Santissima Trinità dei Pellegrini ❹
Santa Maria dell'Orazione e Morte ❻
San Girolamo della Carità ❽
Sant'Eligio degli Orefici ❾
Santa Maria di Monserrato ❿
San Carlo ai Catinari ⓱
Santa Maria in Campitelli ⓳
San Nicola in Carcere ㉒
San Giovanni dei Fiorentini ㉘

Museums and Galleries
Palazzo Spada ❺

Piccola Farnesina ⓭
Burcardo Theater Museum ⓮

Historic Buildings
Palazzo Pio Righetti ❷
Palazzo del Monte di Pietà ❸
Palazzo Farnese ❼
Palazzo Ricci ⓫
Palazzo della Cancelleria ⓬
Palazzo Cenci ㉕
Casa di Lorenzo Manilio ㉖

Fountains
Fontana delle Tartarughe ⓲

Historic Streets and Piazzas
Campo de' Fiori ❶
Tiber Island ㉓
Ghetto and Synagogue ㉔
Via Giulia ㉗

Ancient Sites
Area Sacra ⓰
Theater of Marcellus ⓴
Portico of Octavia ㉑

Famous Theaters
Teatro Argentina ⓯

GETTING THERE
Most of the streets around Campo de' Fiori are too narrow for buses, but many routes converge on Largo Argentina, a useful starting point for exploring. The 90 and 90b will also take you to Via del Teatro di Marcello. Only three buses, the 46, 62 and 64, go the full length of Corso Vittorio Emanuele II.

SEE ALSO

- ***Street Finder***, maps 4, 8, 11, 12
- ***Where to Stay*** pp294–5
- ***Restaurants*** pp310–11
- ***Via Giulia Walk*** pp276–7

KEY

- Street-by-Street map
- **P** Parking

Fruit stalls beneath the statue of Giordano Bruno in the Campo de' Fiori market

Street by Street: Campo de' Fiori

THIS FASCINATING PART of Renaissance Rome is also an exciting area for shopping and night-life, centered on the market square of Campo de' Fiori. Its stalls supply many nearby restaurants, and young people shop for clothes in Via dei Giubbonari. Popular reasonably priced restaurants and pizzerias keep the area alive late into the night. By day, there are great buildings to admire, though few are open to the public. Two exceptions are the Piccola Farnesina, with its collection of Classical statues, and Palazzo Spada, home to many important paintings.

Sant'Eligio degli Orefici
A small Renaissance church designed by Raphael is concealed behind a later facade 9

Palazzo Ricci
Painted Classical scenes were a favorite form of decoration for the facades of Renaissance houses 11

San Girolamo della Carità
The chief attraction of this church is Borromini's fabulous Spada Chapel 8

Santa Maria di Monserrato
This church, which has strong connections with Spain, houses a Bernini bust of Cardinal Pedro Foix de Montoya 10

Santa Maria dell'Orazione e Morte
A pair of dramatic winged skulls flank the doorway to this church dedicated to the burial of the dead 6

Palazzo Farnese
Michelangelo and other great artists helped to create this monumental Renaissance palazzo 7

KEY

- - - Suggested route

0 meters 75

0 yards 75

Palazzo della Cancelleria
The papal administration ran the affairs of the church from this vast building 12

Piccola Farnesina
This plaque honors Giovanni Barracco. His sculpture collection is housed in the palazzo 13

LOCATOR MAP
See Central Rome Map pp12–13

★ **Campo de' Fiori**
The colorful market makes this one of the city's most entertaining squares 1

Palazzo Pio Righetti
Heraldic eagles stare down from the pediments of the palazzo's windows 2

Palazzo del Monte di Pietà
This was a papal institution where the poor pawned their possessions in order to borrow small sums of money 3

Santissima Trinità dei Pellegrini
The principal role of this church was one of charity, looking after poor pilgrims arriving in Rome 4

★ **Palazzo Spada**
The picture gallery houses a collection started by two wonderfully eccentric 17th-century cardinals 5

STAR SIGHTS

★ Campo de' Fiori

★ Palazzo Spada

Campo de' Fiori ●

Piazza Campo de' Fiori. **Map** 4 E4 & 11 C4. 🚌 46, 62, 64, 70, 81, 87, 90, 90b, 186, 492, 926. See **Markets** p338.

THE CAMPO DE' FIORI (field of Flora), once a meadow, occupies the site of the open space facing the Theater of Pompey. Cardinals and noblemen used to rub shoulders with fishmongers and foreigners in the piazza's market, thus it was one of the liveliest areas of medieval and Renaissance Rome. Today's market retains much of the traditional atmosphere.

In the center of the square is a statue of a hooded figure. This is the philosopher Giordano Bruno, who was burnt at the stake for heresy on this spot in 1600 – a grim reminder of the executions that were held here.

The piazza was surrounded by inns for pilgrims and other travelers. Many of these were once owned by the successful 15th-century courtesan Vannozza Catanei, mistress of Pope Alexander VI Borgia. On the corner between the piazza and Via del Pellegrino is Catanei's shield, which she had decorated with her own coat of arms and those of her husband and her lover, the Borgia pope.

Window pediment with heraldic lion and pine cones, Palazzo Pio Righetti

Palazzo Pio Righetti ●

Piazza del Biscione 89. **Map** 4 E5 & 11 C4. 🚌 46, 62, 64, 70, 81, 87, 90, 186, 492. **Not open** to the public.

THE VAST 17th-century Palazzo Pio Righetti was built over the ruined Theater of Pompey. The windows of the palazzo are decorated with lions and pine cones from the coat of arms of the Pio da Carpi family who lived here.

The curve of the Theater of Pompey, completed in 55 BC, is followed by Via di Grotta Pinta. This was Rome's first permanent theater built of stone and concrete. In places, for example, the basement of the Pancrazio restaurant, you can see early examples of *opus reticulatum* – small square blocks of tufa (porous rock) set diagonally as a facing for a concrete wall.

Palazzo del Monte di Pietà ●

Piazza del Monte di Pietà 33. **Map** 4 E5 & 11 C4. 📞 51 72 66 10. 🚌 44, 56, 60, 65, 75, 170, 710. **Chapel open** 7:40am–6pm Tue–Fri, 7:40am–noon Sat. **Closed** public hols. **Adm** by appt or on request to porter.

THE MONTE, as it is known, is a public institution founded in 1539 by Pope Paul III Farnese as a pawnshop to staunch the usury then rampant in the city. The building still has offices and auction rooms for the sale of unredeemed goods.

The stars with diagonal bands on the huge central plaque decorating the facade are the coat of arms of Pope Clement VIII Aldobrandini,

added when Carlo Maderno enlarged the palace in the 17th century. The clock on the left was added later.

Within, the chapel is a jewel of Baroque architecture, adorned with gilded stucco, marble paneling and reliefs. The decoration makes a perfect setting for the sculptures by Domenico Guidi – a bust of San Carlo Borromeo and a relief of the *Pietà*. There are also splendid reliefs by Giovanni Battista Théudon and Pierre Legros of biblical scenes illustrating the charitable nature of the institution.

Relief by Théudon of *Joseph Lending Grain to the Egyptians* in Palazzo del Monte di Pietà

Santissima Trinità dei Pellegrini ●

Piazza della Trinità dei Pellegrini. **Map** 4 E5 & 11 C5. 📞 686 84 51. 🚌 44, 56, 60, 65, 75, 170, 710 and many other routes. **Closed** for restoration.

THE CHURCH WAS donated in the 16th century to a charitable organization founded by San Filippo Neri to care for the poor and the sick, in particular the many

Market stalls in Campo de' Fiori

Guido Reni's *Holy Trinity*

thousands of paupers who flocked in pilgrimage to Rome during the special holy years known as Jubilees.

The 18th-century façade has niches with statues of the Evangelists by Bernardino Ludovisi. The interior, with Corinthian columns, ends in a horseshoe vault and apse, dominated by Guido Reni's striking altarpiece titled *Holy Trinity* (1625). The frescoes in the lantern are also by Reni.

Other interesting paintings include *St. Gregory the Great Freeing Souls from Purgatory*, by Baldassarre Croce (third chapel to the left); Cavalier d'Arpino's *Virgin and Saints* (second chapel to the left); and a painting by Borgognone (1677) showing the Virgin and recently canonized saints, including San Carlo Borromeo and San Filippo Neri. In the sacristy are depictions of the nobility washing the feet of pilgrims, a custom started by San Filippo.

Fresco in the dome of Santissima Trinità

Palazzo Spada ❺

Piazza Capo di Ferro 13. **Map** 4 E5 & 11 C4. [686 11 58. 44, 46, 62, 64, 65, 70, 87, 90, 492 and many other routes. **Gallery open** 9am–7pm Tue–Sat, 9am–1pm Sun. **Adm charge**. Adm to other rooms by request to Ufficio Personale, Consiglio di Stato [682 71.

THIS MAJESTIC PALAZZO, built around 1540 for Cardinal Capo di Ferro, has an elegant stuccoed courtyard and a façade decorated with reliefs evoking Rome's glorious past.

Cardinal Bernardino Spada, who lived here in the 17th century with his brother, Virginio (also a cardinal), hired Bernini and Borromini to work on the building. The brothers' whimsical delight in false perspectives resulted in a colonnaded gallery by Borromini that appears four times longer than it really is.

The cardinals also amassed a superb private collection of paintings. These are now displayed in the Galleria Spada together with some Classical statues and 18th-century furniture. The wide range of artists represented includes Rubens, Dürer and Guido Reni. Works to look for by lesser artists include *The Visitation* by Andrea del Sarto (1486–1530), *Cain and Abel* by Giovanni Lanfranco (1582–1647) and *The Death of Dido* by Guercino (1591–1666).

Santa Maria dell'Orazione e Morte ❻

Via Giulia. **Map** 4 E5 & 11 B4. 23, 65, 280. **Open** for mass 6pm Sun & public hols.

A PIOUS CONFRATERNITY was formed here in the 16th century to collect the bodies of the unknown dead and give them a Christian burial. The theme of death is stressed in this church, dedicated to St. Mary of Prayer and Death. The doors and windows of Ferdinando Fuga's dramatic Baroque façade are decorated with

winged skulls. Above the central entrance is a *clepsydra* (an ancient hourglass) – symbolic of death.

Offertory box in Santa Maria dell'Orazione e Morte

Palazzo Farnese ❼

Piazza Farnese. **Map** 4 E5 & 11 B4. 46, 62, 64, 70, 71, 87, 90, 492, 926. **Not open** to the public.

AN IMPOSING building that became the prototype for many princely palaces, Palazzo Farnese was originally built for Cardinal Alessandro Farnese, who commissioned the greatest artists of the time to work on its design.

After the cardinal became Pope Paul III in 1534, the building was redesigned by Antonio da Sangallo the Younger. He was assisted in this by Michelangelo, who contributed the great cornice and central window of the main façade, as well as the third level of the courtyard.

Michelangelo had a plan for the Farnese gardens to be connected by a bridge to the Farnese home in Trastevere, Villa Farnesina *(see pp220–21)*. The elegant arch spanning Via Giulia was part of this sadly unrealized scheme. The palazzo was finally completed in 1589, on a less ambitious scale, by Giacomo della Porta. It is now the home of the French embassy.

Majestic façade of Palazzo Farnese

Spada Chapel in San Girolamo

San Girolamo della Carità ⑧

Via di Monserrato 62A. **Map** 4 E5 & 11 B4. 🕿 687 97 86. 🚌 23, 46, 62, 64, 65, 280. **Open** 10am–noon Wed, 10:30–11:30am Sun. 🕇 📷

T HE CHURCH was built on the site of the home of San Filippo Neri, the 16th-century saint from Tuscany. This warm, patient man renewed Rome's spiritual and cultural life with his friendly, open approach to religion. He would have loved the putti shown surrounding his statue in his chapel; they would have reminded him of the Roman urchins he had cared for during his lifetime.

The breathtaking Spada Chapel was designed by Borromini and is unique both

as a work of art and as an illustration of the spirit of the Baroque age. All architectural elements are concealed so that the space of the chapel's interior is defined solely by decorative marblework and statues. Veined jasper and precious multicolored marbles are sculpted to imitate flowery damask and velvet hangings. Even the altar rail is a long swag of jasper drapery held up by a pair of kneeling angels with wooden wings.

Although there are memorials to former members of the Spada family, oddly, there is no indication as to which of the Spadas was responsible for endowing the chapel. It was probably art lover Cardinal Virginio Spada, a follower of San Filippo Neri.

Sant'Eligio degli Orefici ⑨

Via di Sant'Eligio 8A. **Map** 4 D4 & 11 B4. 🕿 686 82 60. 🚌 23, 41, 46, 62, 64, 65, 280. **Open** 10:30am–12:30pm Mon, Tue, Thu & Sat (Fri by request only). When closed inquire at No. 9 Via di Sant'Eligio. **Closed** Aug & Sep. 🕇 📷

T HE NAME of the church records the fact that it was commissioned by a rich corporation of goldsmiths (orefici) in the early 16th century. The original design was by Raphael, who, like his master, Bramante, had acquired a sense of the grandiose from the remains of Roman antiquity. The influence of some of Bramante's works, such as the choir of Santa Maria del Popolo (see p138–9), is evident in the simple way the arches and pilasters define the structure of the walls.

The cupola of Sant' Eligio is attributed to Baldassarre Peruzzi, while the facade was added in the early 17th century by Flaminio Ponzio. Among the various 16th-century painters who decorated the interior was Taddeo Zuccari, who worked on Palazzo Farnese (see p147).

Santa Maria di Monserrato ⑩

Via di Monserrato. **Map** 4 E4 & 11 B3. 🕿 686 58 61. 🚌 23, 41, 46, 62, 64, 65, 280. **Not Open** to the public except by special permission: apply to the rector at the address above. 🕇 📷

An early bust by Bernini of Cardinal Pedro Foix de Montoya

T HE ORIGINS of this, the Spanish national church in Rome, go back to 1506, when a hospice for Spanish pilgrims was begun by a brotherhood of the Virgin of Montserrat in Catalonia. Note Bernini's bust of Pedro Foix de Montoya, the church's benefactor, and Annibale Carracci's painting titled San Diego de Alcalà. There is also a copy of a Sansovino statue of St. James in the third chapel on the left. Some 15th-century tombs by Andrea Bregno and Luigi Capponi are in the courtyard and side chapels.

San Diego by Annibale Carracci

Statue of San Filippo Neri by Pierre Legros

Palazzo Ricci ⓫

Piazza de' Ricci. **Map** 4 D4 & 11 B4.
🚌 23, 46, 62, 64, 65, 280.
Not open to the public.

Part of the frescoed facade of Palazzo Ricci

PALAZZO RICCI was famous for its frescoed facade – now rather faded – originally painted in the 16th century by Polidoro da Caravaggio, a follower of Raphael.

In Renaissance Rome it was common to commission artists to decorate the outsides of their houses with heroes of Classical antiquity. A fresco by a leading artist such as Polidoro, reputedly the inventor of this style of painting, was a conspicuous status symbol. Decorative schemes like this required inventiveness to outshine the other palazzi, a mastery of perspective and, above all, dexterity, since the painting on wet plaster had to be completed before it dried.

Palazzo della Cancelleria ⓬

Piazza della Cancelleria. **Map** 4 E4 & 11 C3. 📞 69 88 48 16. 🚌 44, 46, 62, 64, 70, 81, 87, 90, 90b, 186, 492, 926. **Open** with permit from Vatican only.

THIS PALAZZO, a supreme example of the confident architecture of the Early Renaissance, was begun in 1485. It was financed partly with the gambling winnings of Cardinal Raffaele Riario. Roses, the emblem of the Riario family, adorn the vaults and capitals of the beautiful Doric courtyard. The palazzo's interior was decorated after the Sack of Rome in 1527. Giorgio Vasari boasted that he had completed work on one enormous room in just 100 days; Michelangelo allegedly retorted: "It looks like it." Other Mannerist artists, Perin del Vaga and Francesco Salviati, frescoed the rooms of the cardinal in charge of the Papal Chancellery, the office that gave the palazzo its name when it was installed here by Pope Leo X.

Lily on facade of the Piccola Farnesina

To the right of the main entrance is the unobtrusive church of San Lorenzo in Damaso, founded by Pope Damasus (reigned 366–384). Its surrounding porticoes housed libraries that held the first Papal Archives.

Piccola Farnesina ⓭

Corso Vittorio Emanuele II 166. **Map** 4 E4 & 11 C3. 📞 68 80 68 48. 🚌 46, 62, 64, 70, 81, 87, 90, 90b, 186, 492, 926. **Open** 9am–7pm Tue–Sat, 9am–1pm Sun & public hols. **Adm charge.** 🚫

THIS DELIGHTFUL miniature palazzo acquired its name from the lilies decorating its cornices. These were mistakenly identified as part of the Farnese family crest. In fact, they were part of the coat of arms of a French clergyman, Thomas Leroy, for whom the palazzo was built in 1523.

The entrance is in a new facade, built to overlook Corso Vittorio Emanuele II when the road was constructed at the turn of the century. The original facade to the left of today's entrance is attributed to Antonio da Sangallo the Younger. Note the asymmetrical arrangement of its windows and ledges. The elegant central courtyard also retains its original appearance. The Piccola Farnesina now houses the Museo Barracco, a collection of ancient sculpture assembled during the last century by the

politician Barone Giovanni Barracco. A bust of the baron is in the courtyard. The collection has Assyrian, Egyptian, Greek and Etruscan works as well as Roman ones. Some exhibits are fragmentary, but in this fine Renaissance building they make an attractive display.

Inner courtyard, Piccola Farnesina

Burcardo Theater Museum ⓮

Via del Sudario 44. **Map** 4 F4 & 12 D4. 📞 68 80 67 55. 🚌 44, 46, 56, 60, 62, 64, 70, 81, 90, 90b, 492, 926. **Closed** for restoration until further notice.

THIS LATE 15th-century house belonged to Johannes Burckhardt, chamberlain to Pope Alexander VI Borgia and author of a diary describing Rome under the Borgias. His house now holds Rome's most complete collection of theater literature, with over 30,000 books, plus Chinese puppets and comic masks from the various regions of Italy.

Teatro Argentina ⑮

Via di Torre Argentina. **Map** 4 F4 &
12 D4. [☎] 68 80 46 01. [🚌] 44, 46,
56, 60, 62, 64, 70, 81, 90, 90b, 94,
492, 926. **Plays** performed Oct–Jun.
See **Entertainment** pp346–7.

O NE OF ROME'S most
important theaters was
founded by the powerful
Sforza Cesarini family in 1730,
though the facade dates from
a century later. Many famous
operas were first performed
here. In 1816, for example,
the theater saw the ill-fated
début of Rossini's *Barber of
Seville*, during which the
composer insulted the unap-
preciative audience. Enraged,
the audience pursued him
through the streets of Rome.
Many of Verdi's masterpieces
were first produced here.

Detail of facade, Teatro Argentina

Area Sacra ⑯

Largo di Torre Argentina. **Map** 4 F4 &
12 D4. [🚌] 44, 46, 56, 60, 62, 64, 70,
81, 90, 90b, 94, 492, 926. Apply for
permit to: Ripartizione X (see p367).

T HE REMAINS of four temples
were discovered here
during rebuilding in the 1920s.
Dating from the era of the
Republic, they are among the
oldest to have been found in
Rome. For the purpose of
identification, they are known
as A, B, C and D. The oldest
(temple C) dates back to the
4th century BC. It was placed
on a high platform preceded
by an altar and is typical of
Italic temple plans rather than
the Greek plans. Temple A is
from the 3rd century BC. In
medieval times the small
church of San Nicola was built
over its podium. The remains
of its two apses are still visible.
The column stumps to the
north belonged to a great

***San Carlo at Prayer* by Guido Reni**

portico, known as the
Hecatostylum (portico of 100
columns). In Imperial times
two marble lavatories were
built here – the remains of
one are visible behind temple
A. Behind temples B and C
are remains of a great
platform of tufa blocks. These
have been identified as part
of the Curia of Pompey, a
rectangular building housing a
statue of Pompey, where the
Senate met and where Julius
Caesar was assassinated on
March 15 in 44 BC.

**Area Sacra, with circular ruins of
temple B in the foreground**

San Carlo ai Catinari ⑰

Piazza B Cairoli. **Map** 4 F5 & 12 D4.
[☎] 689 38 74. [🚌] 44, 56, 60, 65, 75,
170, 710, 926. **Open** 7:30am–noon &
4:30–7pm Mon–Sat, 8:30am–12:30pm
& 4:30–7:30pm Sun. [🔲] [📷]

I N 1620 ROME'S Milanese
congregation decided to
honor Cardinal Carlo

Borromeo, with this great
church. It is called "ai
Catinari" because of the
bowlmakers' *(catinari)*
shops in the area. The
solemn travertine facade
was completed in 1638 by
the Roman architect Soria.
The 16th-century basilical
plan is flanked by chapels.
The St. Cecilia chapel was
designed and decorated by
Antonio Gherardi, who
added a family portrait.
The church's paintings and
frescoes by Pietro da Cortona
and Guido Reni are confident,
mature works of the Counter
Reformation, depicting the
life and acts of the recently
canonized San Carlo. On the
sacristy altar is an ornate
crucifix handsomely inlaid
with marble, glass and
mother-of-pearl, by the 16th-
century sculptor Algardi.

Sacristy altar, San Carlo ai Catinari

Fontana delle Tartarughe ⑱

Piazza Mattei. **Map** 4 F5 & 12 D4.
[🚌] 44, 56, 60, 65, 75, 170, 710, 926.

T HE DELIGHTFUL Fontana
delle Tartarughe –
tartarughe are tortoises – was
commissioned by the Mattei
family to decorate "their"
piazza between 1581 and
1588. The design was by
Giacomo della Porta, but the
fountain owes much of its
grace and charm to the four
slender bronze youths, each
resting one foot on the head
of a dolphin, sculpted by
Taddeo Landini. Nearly a
century later an unknown

sculptor was inspired to add the struggling tortoises to complete the composition.

Della Porta's graceful Fontana delle Tartarughe

Santa Maria in Campitelli ⑲

Piazza di Campitelli. **Map** 4 F5 & 12E5. 68 80 39 78. 57, 90, 90b, 92, 94, 95, 716. **Open** 7am–noon & 4–7pm daily.

Cherubs, Santa Maria in Campitelli

IN 17TH-CENTURY ROME the plague could still strike fiercely, and there were no reliable, effective remedies. Many Romans simply prayed for a cure to a sacred medieval icon of the Virgin, the Madonna del Portico. When a particularly lethal outbreak of plague abated in 1656, popular gratitude was so strong that a new church was built to house the icon in appropriate splendor.

The church, designed by Bernini's pupil, Carlo Rainaldi, was completed in 1667. The main elements of the lively Baroque facade are the graceful columns, symbolizing the supporters of the true faith.

Inside the church a fabulous gilded altar tabernacle with spiral columns was designed by Giovanni Antonio de Rossi to contain the image of the Virgin. The side chapels are decorated by some of Rome's finest Baroque painters: Sebastiano Conca, Giovanni Battista Gaulli (known as Il Baciccia) and Luca Giordano.

Theater of Marcellus ⑳

Via del Teatro di Marcello. **Map** 4 A5 & 12 E5. 481 48 00. 57, 90, 90b, 92, 94, 95, 716. **Closed** except for concerts. See **Entertainment** p343.

THE CURVED OUTER WALL of this vast amphitheater has supported generations of Roman buildings. It was built by the Emperor Augustus, who dedicated it to Marcellus, his nephew and son-in-law, who had died at 19 in 23 BC. By the 13th century the theater had been converted into a fortress of the Savelli family. In the 16th century Baldassarre Peruzzi built on the theater's ruins a great palace for the Orsini family, including a garden facing the Tiber. The lower arches were later occupied by humble dwellings and workshops.

Close to the theater stand three beautiful Corinthian columns and a section of frieze. These belonged to the Temple of Apollo, which housed many works of art plundered by the Romans from Greece in the 2nd century BC.

Lavish altar tabernacle in Santa Maria in Campitelli

The Theater of Marcellus by Thomas Hartley Cromek (1809–73)

Portico of Octavia ㉑

Via del Portico d'Ottavia. **Map** 4 F5 & 12 E5. 57, 90, 90b, 92, 94, 95, 716.

BUILT IN HONOR of Augustus's sister, Octavia (the abandoned wife of Mark Antony), this is the only surviving portico of what used to be the monumental piazza of Circus Flaminius.

The rectangular portico enclosed temples dedicated to Jupiter and Juno, decorated with bronze statues. The part we see today is the great central atrium originally covered by marble facings.

In the Middle Ages a great fish market and a church, Sant'Angelo in Pescheria, were built in the ruins of the portico. Because the church was associated with the fishing activities of the nearby riverport, aquatic flora and fauna feature in many of the church's inlays. Links with the Tiber are also seen in the stucco facade on the Fishmonger's Oratory, built in 1689. The church has a fresco of the Madonna and angels painted by the school of Benozzo Gozzoli.

San Nicola in Carcere ㉒

Via del Teatro di Marcello 46. **Map** 5 A5 & 12 E5. 📞 *68 30 71 98.* 🚌 *57, 90, 90b, 92, 94, 95, 716.* **Open** *7:30am–noon & 4–7pm Mon–Sat, 10am–1pm Sun.* **Closed** *Aug–mid-Sep.* 🚶 📷

THE MEDIEVAL CHURCH of San Nicola in Carcere stands on the site of three Roman temples of the Republican era which were converted into a prison in the Middle Ages (*carcere* means "prison"). The temples of Juno, Spes and Janus faced a city gate leading from the Forum Holitorium, the city's vegetable-and-oil market, to the road down to the port on the Tiber. The columns embedded in the walls of the church belonged to two flanking temples whose platforms are now marked by grass lawns.

The church was rebuilt in 1599 and restored in the 19th century, but the bell tower and Roman columns are part of the original design.

Facade and medieval bell tower of San Nicola in Carcere

Tiber Island ㉓

Isola Tiberina. **Map** 8 D1 & 12 D5. 🚌 *15, 23, 97, 774, 780.*

IN ANCIENT TIMES this island, which lay opposite the city's port, had a large structure of white travertine at either end built to resemble the stern and prow of a ship.

Since 293 BC, when a temple was dedicated here to Aesculapius, the god of healing and protector against the plague, the island has been associated with the sick. There is still a hospital here.

Tiber Island, with Ponte Cestio linking it to Trastevere

San Bartolomeo, the church in the island's central piazza, was built on the ruins of the Temple of Aesculapius in the 10th century. Its Romanesque bell tower is a useful landmark, clearly visible from the banks of the Tiber.

From the Ghetto area visitors can reach the island by a footbridge, the Ponte Fabricio. The oldest original bridge over the Tiber still in use, it was built in 62 BC. In medieval times the Pierleoni, and then the Caetani, two powerful families, controlled this strategic point by means of a tower, still in situ. The other bridge to the island, the Ponte Cestio, is inscribed with the names of the Byzantine emperors associated with its restoration in AD 370.

Ghetto and Synagogue ㉔

Synagogue, Lungotevere dei Cenci. **Map** 4 F5 & 12 E5. 📞 *687 50 51.* 🚌 *23, 44, 56, 60, 65, 75, 170, 710, 774.* **Open** *9:30am–1:30pm & 2–5pm (6pm in summer) Mon–Thu, 9:30am–1:30pm (5pm in summer) Fri, 9:30am–12:30pm Sun.* **Closed** *Sat.* 🚫 ♿ 🚶 **Ghetto,** main street is Via del Portico d'Ottavia.

EVEN THOUGH they were first brought to Rome as slaves, Jews were valued for their financial and medical skills during the time of the Roman Empire. In the Middle Ages their relative freedom continued; in fact, the anti-Pope Anacletus came from a converted Jewish family.

Systematic persecution began in the 16th century. From July 25, 1556, all the Jews of Rome were forced to live inside a high-walled enclosure erected on the orders of Pope Paul IV. The ghetto was in a particularly unhealthy part of Rome. Inhabitants were allowed out only during the day. On Sundays they were driven into the church of Sant'Angelo in Pescheria to listen to Christian sermons – a practice abolished only in 1848. Persecution started again under Fascism, when hundreds were sent to German concentration camps.

Today many Jews still live here, and the medieval streets, with shops selling typical Jewish kosher food, retain much of their old character. The imposing synagogue on Lungotevere was built in 1874.

Synagogue overlooking the Tiber

Palazzo Cenci ㉕

Vicolo dei Cenci. **Map** 4 F5 & 12 D5. 🚌 *44, 56, 60, 65, 75, 170, 710.* **Not open** *to the public.*

PALAZZO CENCI belonged to the family of Beatrice Cenci, who was accused, together with her brothers and stepmother, of witchcraft and the murder of her tyrannical father. She was condemned to death and beheaded at Ponte Sant'Angelo in 1599.

Most of the original medieval palazzo has been demolished, and the building visitors see today dates back to the 1570s, even though its forbidding appearance seems medieval.

Heraldic half-moons decorate the main facade on Via del Progresso, while pretty balconies open on the opposite side, where a medieval arch joins the palace to Palazzetto Cenci, designed by Martino Longhi the Elder. Inside is a traditional courtyard with an Ionic-style loggia; many of the rooms retain the original 16th-century decoration that the unfortunate Beatrice would have known as a child.

Balcony of Palazzo Cenci

Casa di Lorenzo Manilio ㉖

Via del Portico d'Ottavia 1D. **Map** 4 F5 & 12 D5. 🚌 *44, 56, 60, 65, 75, 170, 710.* **Not open** to the public.

BEFORE THE RENAISSANCE, most Romans had only vague, confused ideas of their city's glorious past, but after the 15th-century revival of interest in the philosophy and arts of antiquity, some were even encouraged to build houses recalling the splendor of ancient Rome. In 1468 a certain Lorenzo Manilio built a great house for his family, decorating it with an elegant Classical plaque. The Latin inscription dates the building according to the ancient Roman method – 2,221 years

after the foundation of the city – and mentions the owner's name. Original reliefs are embedded in the facades as well as a fragment of an ancient sarcophagus. The Piazza Costaguti facade features windows patriotically inscribed with the legend *Have Roma* (Hail Rome).

Row of Roman busts decorating the Casa di Lorenzo Manilio

Via Giulia ㉗

Map 4 D4 & 11 A3. 🚌 *23, 65, 280.*

THIS PICTURESQUE 16th-century street was built by Bramante for Pope Julius II della Rovere. Lined with aristocratic palazzi dating from the 16th to the 18th centuries, as well as churches and antiques shops, Via Giulia makes a fascinating walk *(see pp276–7).*

Mask fountain in Via Giulia

San Giovanni dei Fiorentini ㉘

Via Acciaioli 2. **Map** 4 D4 & 11 A2. 📞 *68 80 24 01.* 🚌 *23, 46, 62, 64, 65, 280.* **Open** *7–11am & 5–7:30pm (Oct–Mar: 4:30–7pm)* daily. ⛪

THE CHURCH of St. John of the Florentines was built for the large Florentine community living in this area. Pope Leo X wanted it to be an expression of the cultural superiority of Florence over Rome. Started in the early 16th century, the church took over 100 years to build. The principal architect was Antonio da Sangallo the Younger, but many others contributed before Carlo Maderno's elongated cupola was finally completed in 1614. The present facade, recently cleaned and restored, was added in the 18th century.

The church was decorated mainly by Tuscan artists. One interesting exception is the 15th-century statue of San Giovannino by the Sicilian Mino del Reame in a niche above the sacristy. The spectacular high altar houses a marble group by Antonio Raggi, the *Baptism of Christ*. The altar itself is by Borromini, who is buried in the church, along with Carlo Maderno.

This is the only church in Rome where animals are welcomed: the faithful can bring their pets, and an annual Easter lamb-blessing ceremony takes place here.

Antonio Raggi's *Baptism of Christ* in San Giovanni dei Fiorentini

QUIRINAL

1st-century BC stucco in the
Museo Nazionale Romano

ONE OF THE original seven hills of Rome, the Quirinal was a largely residential area in Imperial times. To the east of the hill were the vast Baths of Diocletian, still standing today in front of what is now the main railroad station. Abandoned during the Middle Ages, the district returned to favor in the late 16th century. The prime site was taken by the popes for the Palazzo del Quirinale. Great families such as the Colonna and the Aldobrandini had their palazzi lower down the hill. With the end of papal rule in 1870, the Quirinal became the residence of the kings of Italy, and much of the surrounding area, especially along Via Nazionale, was redeveloped.

SIGHTS AT A GLANCE

Churches
Santi Apostoli ④
San Marcello al Corso ⑥
Santa Maria in Trivio ⑧
Santi Vincenzo e Anastasio ⑩
Sant'Andrea al Quirinale ⑪
San Carlo alle Quattro Fontane ⑫
San Bernardo alle Terme ⑭
Santa Maria degli Angeli ⑰
Santa Maria dei Monti ㉑
Sant'Agata dei Goti ㉒
Santi Domenico e Sisto ㉔

Museums and Galleries
Museo delle Cere ⑤
Accademia Nazionale di San Luca ⑨

Museo Nazionale Romano ⑱
Palazzo delle Esposizioni ⑳

Historic Piazzas
Piazza della Repubblica ⑲

Historic Buildings
Palazzo del Quirinale ②
Palazzo Colonna ③
Baths of Diocletian ⑯

Fountains and Statues
Castor and Pollux ①
Trevi Fountain ⑦
Le Quattro Fontane ⑬
Moses Fountain ⑮

Parks and Gardens
Villa Aldobrandini ㉓

GETTING THERE
The area has Metro stops at Repubblica and Cavour. Useful buses include the 64, 65, 70 and 75 along Via Nazionale and the 71 and 81, which go under the Quirinal through the Traforo Umberto I tunnel. There is no bus to the top of the Quirinal, however. You have to walk up Via XXIV Maggio.

KEY
Street-by-Street map
M Metro station
P Parking

0 meters 300
0 yards 300

SEE ALSO

Fontana delle Naiadi in Piazza della Repubblica

Street by Street: The Quirinal Hill

EVEN THOUGH Palazzo del Quirinale is closed to the public, it is well worth walking up the hill to the palace to see the giant Roman statues of Castor and Pollux in the piazza and enjoy the fine views of the city below. Come down the hill by way of the narrow streets and stairways that lead to one of Rome's unforgettable sights, the Trevi Fountain. Many small churches lie hidden away in the back streets. Toward Piazza Venezia there are grand palazzi, including that of the Colonna, one of Rome's most ancient and powerful families.

Santa Maria in Via is famous for its medieval well and miraculous 13th-century icon of the Madonna.

Santa Maria in Trivio
The attractive facade of this tiny church conceals a rich Baroque interior ⑧

Accademia Nazionale di San Luca
The art academy has works by famous former members, such as Canova and Angelica Kauffmann ⑨

★ Trevi Fountain
Rome's grandest and best-known fountain almost fills the tiny Piazza di Trevi ⑦

Santi Vincenzo e Anastasio
The grand facade of this small Baroque church is on a corner facing the Trevi Fountain ⑩

San Marcello al Corso
This stark Crucifixion by Van Dyck hangs in the sacristy of the church ⑥

Palazzo Odescalchi has a Bernini facade from 1664, with a balustrade and richly decorated cornice. The building faces Santi Apostoli.

Museo delle Cere
The emphasis of this wax museum, opened in 1953, is on horror ⑤

To Piazza Venezia

Palazzo del Quirinale
The old papal palace is now the home of the president of Italy ②

In Piazza del Quirinale, by the president's palace, security is always very strict. Palace guards can often be seen in colorful dress uniform.

Castor and Pollux
The statues are grouped with an obelisk and a fountain ①

Piazza della Pilotta is dominated by the imposing facade of the Gregorian University.

Santi Apostoli
The figures of Christ and the Apostles on the balustrade were added by Carlo Rainaldi in 1681 ④

STAR SIGHT

★ Trevi Fountain

KEY

― ― ― Suggested route

0 meters	75
0 yards	75

Palazzo Colonna
One of the art gallery's finest old masters is Annibale Carracci's The Bean Eater ③

Castor and Pollux ❶

Piazza del Quirinale. **Map** 5 B4.
🚌 *52, 53, 56, 60, 61, 62, 71, 81, 95, 119, 492 and many other routes.*

Quirinal fountain and obelisk with Roman statues of Castor and Pollux

C ASTOR AND POLLUX – the patrons of horsemanship – and their prancing horses stand in splendor in the Piazza del Quirinale. Over 18 ft (5.5 m) high, these statues are huge Roman copies of 5th-century BC Greek originals. They once stood at the entrance to the nearby Baths of Constantine. Pope Sixtus V had them restored and placed here in 1588. Formerly known as the "horse tamers," they gave the square its familiar name of Monte Cavallo (Horse Hill).

The obelisk that stands between them was brought here in 1786 from the Mausoleum of Augustus. In 1818 the composition was completed by the addition of a massive granite basin, once a cattle trough in the Forum.

Palazzo del Quirinale ❷

Piazza del Quirinale. **Map** 5 B3. 🚌 *52, 53, 56, 60, 61, 62, 71, 81, 95, 119, 492 and many other routes.* **Open** *on the 2nd and 4th Sunday of each month.*

B Y THE 1500s, the Vatican had a reputation as an unhealthy location because of the high incidence of malaria, so Pope Gregory XIII chose this superb site on the highest of Rome's seven hills as a summer residence for the popes. Work began in 1574. The Piazza del Quirinale has buildings on three sides, while the fourth is open, giving views of the city to the dome of St. Peter's in the distance.

Many great architects worked on the palace before it assumed its present form in the 1730s. Domenico Fontana designed the main façade; Carlo Maderno, the huge chapel; and Bernini, the narrow wing running the length of Via del Quirinale.

Following the unification of Italy in 1870, it became the official residence of the king; then in 1947 of the president of the republic. For security reasons, the palace and gardens have been closed to the public since 1979.

Canova's monument to Pope Clement XIV in Santi Apostoli, with figures of Humility and Modesty

Palazzo del Quirinale, official residence of the president of Italy

Palazzo Colonna ❸

Via della Pilotta 17. **Map** 5 A4 & 12 F3. 📞 *679 43 62.* 🚌 *57, 64, 65, 70, 75, 81, 170, 492, 710 and many other routes.* **Open** *9am–1pm Sat only (last adm: noon).* **Closed** *Aug.* **Adm charge.** 🚫

P OPE MARTIN V Colonna (reigned 1417–31) began building the palazzo, but most of the structure dates from the 18th century. The art gallery, built by Antonio del Grande between 1654 and 1665, is the only part open to the public. The pictures are numbered but unlabeled, so pick up a guide on the way in. Go up the stairs and through the antechamber leading to a series of three gleaming marble rooms with prominent yellow columns, the Colonna family emblem (*colonna* means "column").

The ceiling frescoes celebrate Marcantonio Colonna's victory over the Turks at the Battle of Lepanto (1571). On the walls are 16th- to 18th-century paintings, including Annibale Carracci's *Bean Eater (see p157)*. The room of landscape paintings, many by Poussin's brother-in-law, Gaspare Dughet, reflects the 18th-century taste of Cardinal Girolamo Colonna. Beyond is a room with a ceiling fresco, the *Apotheosis of Martin V*. The throne room has a chair reserved for visiting popes and a copy of Pisanello's portrait of the portly Martin V.

The gallery also offers a fine view of the private palace garden, site of the ruined Temple of Serapis.

Santi Apostoli ❹

Piazza dei Santi Apostoli. **Map** 5 A4 & 12 F3. 📞 *69 92 19 51.* 🚌 *56, 60, 64, 65, 70, 75, 85, 90, 170, 492 and many other routes.* **Open** *6:30am– noon & 4–7:15pm daily.* ⛪ 📷

T HE ORIGINAL 6th-century church on this site was rebuilt in the 15th century by Popes Martin V Colonna and

Sixtus IV della Rovere, whose oak-tree crest decorates the capitals of the late 15th-century portico. Inside the portico on the left is Canova's 1807 memorial to the engraver Giovanni Volpato. The church itself contains a much larger monument by Canova, his Tomb of Clement XIV (1789).

The Baroque interior by Francesco and Carlo Fontana was completed in 1714. Note the 3D effect of Giovanni Odazzi's painted *Rebel Angels*, who appear to be really falling from the sky. A huge 18th-century altarpiece by Domenico Muratori shows the martyrdom of the Apostles James and Philip, whose tombs are in the crypt.

Museo delle Cere ❺

Piazza dei Santi Apostoli 67.
Map 5 A4 & 12 F3. 679 64 82.
56, 60, 64, 65, 70, 75, 85, 90, 170, 492 and many other routes.
Open 9am–8pm daily. **Adm charge**.

Facade of Rome's wax museum

E XHIBITS in Rome's wax museum include politicians and a re-creation of Mussolini's last cabinet meeting. For the ghoulishly inclined, there is also a vintage electric chair.

San Marcello al Corso ❻

Piazza San Marcello 5. **Map** 5 A4 & 12 F3. 678 08 88. 56, 60, 62, 70, 85, 90, 95, 492. **Open** 7am–noon & 4–7pm Mon–Sat, 8:30am–noon & 4–7pm Sun.

T HIS CHURCH was originally one of the first places of Christian worship in Rome, which were known as *tituli*.

A later Romanesque building burned down in 1519 and was rebuilt by Jacopo Sansovino with a single nave and many richly decorated private chapels on either side.

The third chapel on the right has fine Francesco Salviati frescoes of the Virgin Mary. The decoration of the next chapel was interrupted by the Sack of Rome in 1527. Raphael's follower Perin del Vaga fled, leaving the ceiling frescoes to be completed by Daniele da Volterra and Pellegrino Tibaldi when peace returned to the city.

In the nave stands a splendid Venetian-style double tomb by Sansovino, a memorial to Cardinal Giovanni Michiel (victim of a Borgia poisoning in 1503) and his nephew, Bishop Antonio Orso.

Trevi Fountain ❼

Fontana di Trevi. **Map** 5 A3 & 12 F2.
52, 53, 58, 60, 61, 62, 71, 95, 492 and many other routes.

M OST VISITORS assume that it has always been there, but by the standards of the Eternal City, the Trevi Fountain is a fairly recent creation.

Rome's grandest fountain, the Trevi

Nicola Salvi's theatrical design for Rome's largest and most famous fountain was completed only in 1762. The central figures are Neptune flanked by two Tritons. One struggles to master a very unruly "seahorse," the other leads a far more docile animal. These symbolize the two contrasting moods of the sea.

The site originally marked the terminal of the Aqua Virgo aqueduct built in 19 BC. One of the first-story reliefs shows a young girl (the legendary virgin after whom the aqueduct was named) pointing to the spring from which the water flows.

Chapel in San Marcello al Corso, decorated by Francesco Salviati

Santa Maria in Trivio ⑧

Piazza dei Crociferi 49. **Map** 5 A3 & 12 F2. **[** 678 96 45. **[** 52, 53, 58, 60, 61, 62, 71, 95, 492 and many other routes. **Open** 8:10am–noon, 4–7:30pm daily. **[** **[**

Facade of Santa Maria in Trivio at the turn of the century

IT HAS BEEN SAID that Italian architecture is one of facades, and nowhere is this clearer than in the 1570s facade of Santa Maria in Trivio, delightfully attached to the building behind it. Note the false windows. There is illusion inside, too, particularly in the ceiling frescoes, which show scenes from the New Testament by Antonio Gherardi (1644–1702).

The name of the tiny church probably means "St. Mary-at-the-meeting-of-three-roads." The word *Trivio* has been corrupted to *Trevi*, hence the name of the famous fountain.

Accademia Nazionale di San Luca ⑨

Piazza dell'Accademia di San Luca 77. **Map** 5 A3 & 12 F2. **[** 679 88 50. **[** 52, 53, 56, 58, 60, 61, 62, 71, 81, 95, 119, 492. **Open** 10am–1pm Mon, Wed, Fri and last Sun of month (last adm: 12:15pm). **Closed** Jul, Aug, public hols. **[** **[** see the custodian.

ST. LUKE IS supposed to have been a painter, hence the name of Rome's academy of fine arts. Appropriately, the gallery contains *St. Luke*

Painting a Portrait of the Virgin by Raphael and his followers. The academy's heyday was in the 17th and 18th centuries, when many members made gifts of their work to the collection. Antonio Canova, for example, donated a model for his famous marble group, the *Three Graces*.

Of particular interest are three fascinating self-portraits by women: the 17th-century Italian Lavinia Fontana; the 18th-century Swiss Angelica Kauffmann, whose painting is copied from a portrait of her by Joshua Reynolds; and Elisabeth Vigée-Lebrun, the French painter of the years before the 1789 Revolution.

Santi Vincenzo e Anastasio ⑩

Vicolo dei Modelli 73. **Map** 5 A3 & 12 F2. **[** 678 30 98. **[** 52, 53, 58, 60, 61, 62, 71, 95, 492 and many other routes. **Open** 7am–noon, 3:30–7:30pm daily. **[** **[**

OVERLOOKING the Trevi Fountain is one of the most elaborate Baroque facades in Rome. Its thickets of columns are crowned by

the huge coat of arms of Cardinal Raimondo Mazzarino, who commissioned Martino Longhi the Younger to build the church in 1650. The female bust above the door is of one of the cardinal's famous nieces, either Louis XIV's first love, Maria Mancini (1639–1715), or her younger sister, Ortensia. In the apse, memorial plaques record the popes whose *praecordia* (a part of the heart) are enshrined behind the wall. This gruesome tradition was started at the end of the 16th century by Pope Sixtus V. It continued until Pius X put a stop to it in the early years of this century.

Facade of Santi Vincenzo e Anastasio by Martino Longhi

Self-portrait by Lavinia Fontana in the Accademia Nazionale di San Luca

Interior of Bernini's oval Sant'Andrea al Quirinale

Sant'Andrea al Quirinale ⑪

Via del Quirinale 29. **Map** 5 B3.
474 48 01. 56, 64, 65, 70, 75, 94, 170. **Open** 10am–noon & 4–7pm Wed–Mon (closed in the afternoon in August). **Gratuity** expected by sacristan for showing St. Stanislas's rooms.

KNOWN AS the "Pearl of the Baroque" because of its beautiful roseate marble interior, Sant'Andrea was designed by Bernini and executed by his assistants between 1658 and 1670. It was built for the Jesuits, hence the many IHS emblems (*Iesus Hominum Salvator* – Jesus Savior of Mankind).

The site for the church was wide but shallow, so Bernini pointed the long axis of his oval plan not toward the altar but toward the sides; he then leads the eye around to the altar end. Here he ordered works of art in various media that function not in isolation, but together. The crucified St.

Andrew (Sant' Andrea) of the altarpiece looks up at a stucco version of himself, which in turn is ascending toward the lantern and also the Holy Spirit.

Do not miss the rooms of St. Stanislas Kostka. These quarters of the Jesuit novice, who died in 1568 at 19, reflect not his own spartan taste but the richer style of the 17th-century Jesuits. The Polish saint has been brilliantly immortalized in marble by Pierre Legros (1666–1719).

San Carlo alle Quattro Fontane ⑫

Via del Quirinale 23. **Map** 5 B3.
488 32 61 52, 53, 56, 60, 61, 62, 95, 492. **Open** 9:30am–12:30pm Mon–Sat; 4–6pm Mon–Fri.

IN 1634, the Spanish Trinitarians, an order whose role was to pay the ransom of Christian hostages to the Arabs, commissioned Borromini to design a church and convent at the Quattro Fontane crossroads. The church, so small it would fit inside one of the piers of St. Peter's, is also known as San Carlino.

Although dedicated to Carlo Borromeo, the 16th-century Milanese cardinal canonized in 1620, San Carlo is equally a monument to Borromini. Both the facade and the interior employ bold, fluid curves that give light and life to a cramped site. The oval dome and tiny lantern are particularly ingenious. The undulating lines of the facade are decorated with angels and a statue of San Carlo. Finished in 1667, the facade is one of Borromini's very last works.

There are other delights in the playful inverted shapes in the cloister and the stuccowork in the refectory (now the sacristy), which houses a painting of San Carlo by Orazio Borgianni (1611).

In a small room off the sacristy hangs a portrait of Borromini himself wearing the Trinitarian cross. Borromini committed suicide in 1667, and in the crypt (which may soon be opened to the public) a small curved chapel reserved for him remains empty.

Dome of San Carlo alle Quattro Fontane, lit by concealed windows

Le Quattro Fontane ⑬

Intersection of Via delle Quattro Fontane and Via del Quirinale. **Map** 5 B3. 🚌 *56, 60, 61, 64, 65, 70, 75, 95, 119, 492.* Ⓜ *Barberini.*

Fountain of Strength (or Juno)

T HESE FOUR small fountains are attached to the corners of the buildings at the intersection of two narrow, busy streets. They date from the great redevelopment of Rome during the reign of Sixtus V (1585–90). Each fountain has a statue of a reclining deity. The river god accompanied by the she-wolf is clearly the Tiber; the other male figure may be the Nile or the Aniene. The female figures represent Strength and Fidelity or the goddesses Juno and Diana.

The crossroads is at the highest point of the Quirinal Hill and commands splendid views of three distant landmark obelisks: those placed by Sixtus V in front of Santa Maria Maggiore and Trinità dei Monti and the one that stands in Piazza del Quirinale.

San Bernardo alle Terme ⑭

Via Torino 94. **Map** 5 C3. 🎫 *488 21 22.* 🚌 *60, 61, 62, 65, 492.* Ⓜ *Repubblica.* **Open** *6:30am– 7pm daily.* 🚻 📷 ♿

T HE CHURCH is on the southern side of the piazza of the same name. It was once one of four round

towers that stood at the corners of the ruined Baths of Diocletian (Terme di Diocleziano). Like a smaller-scale Pantheon, the church has a dome with octagonal coffering and a small opening at the top to light the interior. In the great circular wall supporting the dome are eight niches housing huge plaster statues of saints by Camillo Mariani (1567–1611).

It was only in 1598 that Contessa Caterina Nobili Sforza had the idea of transforming this tower into a church. She lies buried beneath one of the fine 18th-century marble altars.

Moses Fountain ⑮

Fontana dell'Acqua Felice, Piazza San Bernardo. **Map** 5 C2. 🚌 *60, 61, 62, 65, 492.* Ⓜ *Repubblica.*

Fontana's Moses Fountain

O FFICIALLY KNOWN as the Fontana dell'Acqua Felice, this fountain owes its popular name to the grotesque

statue of Moses in the central niche. The massive structure with its three elegant arches was designed by Domenico Fontana to mark the terminal of the Acqua Felice aqueduct, so-called because it was one of the many great improvements commissioned by Felice Peretti, Pope Sixtus V. Completed in 1586, it brought clean piped water to this quarter of Rome for the first time.

Pope Sixtus V, the great town planner

The notorious statue of Moses striking water from the rock is larger than life, and the body proportions are wrong. Sculpted by either Prospero Bresciano or Leonardo Sormani, it is a clumsy attempt at re-creating the awesome appearance of Michelangelo's Moses in the church of San Pietro in Vincoli (*see p170*). As soon as it was unveiled to the public, it was said to be frowning at having been created by such an inept sculptor.

The side reliefs also illustrate water stories from the Old Testament: Aaron leading the Israelites to water and Joshua pointing the army toward the Red Sea. The fountain's four lions are copies of Egyptian originals (now in the Vatican Museums), which Sixtus V had put there for public "convenience" and "delight."

Fidelity (or Diana) with her attendant dog, one of the Quattro Fontane

Part of the Museo Nazionale
Romano in the Baths of Diocletian

Baths of Diocletian ⓰

Terme di Diocleziano, Piazza della Repubblica. **Map** 6 D3. 🚌 *57, 65, 75, 170, 492, 910 and many other routes.* Ⓜ *Repubblica, Termini.*

BUILT FROM AD 298 to 306 under the infamous Emperor Diocletian, who was responsible for thousands of Christian deaths, the baths *(see pp22–3)* occupied over 2.5 acres (1 hectare) of ground between the present Piazza dei Cinquecento and Piazza della Repubblica. The baths, the most extensive in Rome, could accommodate up to 3,000 bathers at a time. The best-preserved areas have been adapted to house the church of Santa Maria degli Angeli and the Museo Nazionale Romano.

Santa Maria degli Angeli ⓱

Piazza della Repubblica. **Map** 5 C3. 🕻 *488 08 12.* 🚌 *57, 65, 75, 170, 492, 910 and many other routes.* Ⓜ *Repubblica, Termini.* **Open** *8am–12:30pm & 4–7pm.* 🚻 🅿 ♿ 🔲

INCORPORATED into the ruined Baths of Diocletian by Michelangelo in 1563, this church was so altered in the 18th century by Luigi Vanvitelli it has lost most of its original character. The most striking works of art are the fresco *Martyrdom of St. Sebastian* by Domenichino and the gigantic statue of St. Bruno by Jean-Antoine Houdon. An exhibition in the sacristy gives a detailed account of Michelangelo's original design.

Museo Nazionale Romano ⓲

Viale Enrico de Nicola 79. **Map** 6 D2. 🕻 *48 90 35 07.* 🚌 *57, 65, 75, 170, 492, 910 and many other routes.* Ⓜ *Repubblica, Termini.* **Open** *9am–2pm Tue–Sat, 9am–1pm Sun & public hols (last adm: 30 min before closing).* **Adm charge.** 🅿 ♿

FOUNDED IN 1889, the Museo Nazionale holds most of the antiquities found in Rome since 1870. It has also absorbed pre-existing collections, notably that of the Ludovisi family, to become one of the world's leading museums of Classical art. It occupies the part of the Baths of Diocletian not taken up by the church of Santa Maria degli Angeli, including the former Carthusian monastery, which

Gold coin with head of the
Emperor Diocletian (AD 285–305)

Egyptian relief showing head
crowned with symbolic cobra
in the Museo Nazionale Romano

has a cloister designed by Michelangelo when he was working on Santa Maria.

Unfortunately, the museum is an extreme example of the malaise afflicting many Roman museums. The majority of its rooms, which contain many first-class sarcophagi, mosaics and detached frescoes, are closed to the public. As an end in itself, a visit to the museum therefore gives more frustration than pleasure. However, if visitors have a spare hour while waiting for a train from Termini station, it is worth crossing Piazza dei Cinquecento to see the evocative array of lovely sculptural fragments displayed around the central Renaissance courtyard.

Future plans include a new section of the museum in the former Palazzo Massimo in Piazza dei Cinquecento.

Piazza della Repubblica ⑲

Map 5 C3. 🚍 *4, 16, 36, 38, 60, 61, 62, 65, 75, 192, 492 and many other routes.* Ⓜ *Repubblica.*

Romans often refer to the piazza by its old name, Piazza Esedra, which it was given because it follows the shape of an *exedra* (a semicircular recess) that was part of the Baths of Diocletian. The piazza was part of the redevelopment program undertaken when Rome became capital of a unified Italy. Under its sweeping 19th-century colonnades were once elegant shops, but they have been replaced by banks, travel agencies and cafés.

In the middle of the piazza stands the Fontana delle Naiadi. Mario Rutelli's four naked bronze nymphs caused something of a scandal when they were unveiled in 1901. Each reclines on an aquatic creature symbolizing water in its various forms: a seahorse for the oceans, a water snake for rivers, a swan for lakes and a curious frilled lizard for subterranean streams. The middle figure, added in 1911, is of the sea god Glaucus, who represents man victorious over hostile nature.

Piazza della Repubblica and the Fontana delle Naiadi

Palazzo delle Esposizioni ⑳

Via Nazionale 194 (second entrance in Via Milano). **Map** 5 B4. 🄲 *482 87 60.* 🚍 *56, 64, 65, 70, 75, 94, 170.* **Open** *10am–9pm Wed–Mon (last adm: 8:30pm).* **Closed** *public hols.* **Adm charge.** 🚫 ♿ *Via Milano entrance only.* **Concerts, lectures, films.** *See* **Entertainment** *pp346–7.* 🍴 🖥 📷

Facade of the Palazzo delle Esposizioni

This somewhat grandiose building, with wide steps, Corinthian columns and statues, was designed as an exhibition center by the architect Pio Piacentini and built by the city of Rome in 1882 during the reign of Umberto I. The main entrance looks like a triumphal arch.

The exhibition space has recently been modernized. Exhibitions change every three months, featuring paintings, sculpture, live performances and films. Foreign films are usually shown in the original language. The palazzo also houses the Galleria Comunale d'Arte Moderna, closed to the public since the early 1980s.

Santa Maria dei Monti ㉑

Via Madonna dei Monti 41. **Map** 5 B4. 🄲 *48 55 31.* 🚍 *11, 27, 81.* Ⓜ *Cavour.* **Open** *7am–noon & 5–7:30pm Mon–Sat, 8:30am–1pm Sun, public hols.* ✝ 📷 ♿

Designed by Giacomo della Porta, this church, dating from 1580, has a particularly splendid dome. Over the high altar is a medieval painting of the Madonna, patroness of this quarter of Rome. The altar in the left transept houses the tomb and effigy of the unworldly French saint Benoît-Joseph Labre, who died here in 1783, having spent his life as a solitary pilgrim. While in Rome he slept rough in the ruins of the Colosseum, gave away any charitable gifts he received and came regularly to Santa Maria dei Monti to worship. In his mid-thirties, he collapsed and died outside the church. The foul rags he wore are preserved as relics.

One of the bronze nymphs of the fountain in Piazza della Repubblica

Sant'Agata dei Goti ❷

Via Mazzarino 16 and Via Panisperna.
Map 5 B4. 488 19 94. 57,
64, 65, 70, 81, 170. **Open** 7–9am &
5:30–7pm Mon–Sat, 9:30–10am Sun.

THE GOTHS who gave their
name to this church (*Goti*
are Goths) occupied Rome in
the 6th century AD. They
were Arian heretics who
denied the divinity of Christ.
The church was founded
shortly before the main
Gothic invasions, between
AD 462 and 470, and the
beautiful granite columns date
from this period. The main
altar has a well-preserved
12th-century Cosmatesque
tabernacle, but the most
delightful part of the church
is the charming 18th-century
courtyard built around an
ivy-draped well.

Villa Aldobrandini ❸

Via Panisperna. Entrance to gardens:
Via Mazzarino 1. **Map** 5 B4.
57, 64, 65, 70, 75, 170.
Gardens open dawn–dusk daily.
Villa not open to the public.

BUILT IN the 16th century for
the dukes of Urbino and
acquired for his family by Pope
Clement VIII Aldobrandini
(reigned 1592–1605), the
villa is now government
property and houses an
international law library.

The villa itself, decorated
with the family's six-starred
coat of arms, is closed to the
public, but the gardens and
terraces, hidden behind a
high wall that runs along Via
Nazionale, can be reached
through an iron gate in Via
Mazzarino. Steps lead up past
2nd-century AD ruins into the
recently renovated gardens,
highly recommended as an
oasis of tranquillity in the
center of the city. Gravel
paths lead between formal
lawns and clearly marked
specimen trees, and benches
are provided for the weary.
Since the garden is raised
some 30 ft (10 m) above street
level, the views are excellent.

18th-century courtyard of Sant'Agata dei Goti

Santi Domenico e Sisto ❹

Largo Angelicum 1. **Map** 5 B4.
670 21. 57, 64, 65, 70, 75,
170. **Open** by appt only. **Closed**
Jul–Sep.

Chapel in Santi Domenico e Sisto

THIS CHURCH has a tall,
slender Baroque facade
rising above a steep flight of
steps. This divides into two
curving flights that sweep up
to the terrace in front of the
entrance. The pediment of the
facade is crowned by eight
flaming candlesticks.

The interior has a vaulted
ceiling with a large
fresco, the *Apotheosis of
St. Dominic*, by
Domenico Canuti
(1620–84). The
first chapel on
the right was
decorated by
Bernini, who
may also have
designed the
sculpture of Mary
Magdalene
meeting the
risen Christ in
the Garden of
Gethsemane.   **Facade of Santi**
This fine marble   **Domenico**
group was   **e Sisto**
executed by
Antonio Raggi (1649). Above
the altar is a 15th-century
terra-cotta plaque of the
Madonna and Child. On the
left over a side altar is a large
painting of the Madonna from
the same period, attributed to
Benozzo Gozzoli (1420–97), a
pupil of Fra Angelico.

ESQUILINE

THE ESQUILINE is the largest and highest of Rome's seven hills. In Imperial Rome, the western slopes overlooking the Forum housed the crowded slums of the Suburra. On the eastern side were a few villas belonging to wealthy citizens like Maecenas, patron of the arts and valued adviser to Augustus. The essential character of the place has persisted through two millennia; it is still one of the poorer quarters

Michelangelo's *Rachel* in San Pietro in Vincoli

of the city. The area is now heavily built up, except for a poorly maintained park on the Colle Oppio, a smaller hill to the south of the Esquiline, where you can see the remains of the Baths of Titus, the Baths of Trajan and Nero's Golden House. The area's main interest, however, lies in its churches. Many of these were founded on the sites of private houses where Christians met to worship secretly in the days when their religion was banned.

SIGHTS AT A GLANCE

Churches
San Martino ai Monti **1**
San Pietro in Vincoli **2**
Santa Pudenziana **3**
Santa Maria Maggiore pp172–3 **4**
Santa Prassede **5**
Santa Bibiana **7**

Museums
Museo Nazionale d'Arte Orientale **9**

Historic Piazzas
Piazza Vittorio Emanuele II **8**

Ancient Sites
Auditorium of Maecenas **10**
Nero's Golden House **11**

Arches
Arch of Gallienus **6**

GETTING THERE
This area is close to Termini station and has several other Metro stops: Vittorio Emanuele and Manzoni on line A, Cavour and Colosseo on line B. Bus routes here are a little confusing. Among the most useful are the 93 and 93b from Termini to Santa Maria Maggiore and then along Via Merulana.

SEE ALSO
• *Street Finder*, maps 5, 6
• *Restaurants* pp310–11
• *Mosaics Walk* pp280–81

KEY

⬜	Street-by-Street map
FS	Railway station
M	Metro station
P	Parking

Southern facade of Santa Maria Maggiore by night

Street by Street: The Esquiline Hill

THE SIGHT that draws most people to this unkempt part of Rome is the great basilica of Santa Maria Maggiore. But it is also well worth searching out some of the smaller churches on the Esquiline: Santa Pudenziana and Santa Prassede, with their celebrated mosaics, and San Pietro in Vincoli, home to one of Michelangelo's most famous sculptures. To the south, in the Colle Oppio park, are the scattered remains of the Baths of Trajan.

Santa Pudenziana
The apse of this ancient church has a magnificent 4th-century mosaic of Christ surrounded by the Apostles ❸

Piazza dell'Esquilino
was furnished in 1587 with an obelisk by Pope Sixtus V. This helped to guide pilgrims coming from the north to the important church of Santa Maria Maggiore.

To the Colosseum

PIAZZA DI SAN PIETRO IN VINCOLI

★ **San Pietro in Vincoli**
This church's treasures include Michelangelo's Moses *and the chains that bound St. Peter* ❷

VIA CAVOUR

VIA SFORZA

VIA DEI QUATTRO CANTONI

VIA GIOVANNI LANZA

PIAZZA SAN MARTINO AI M

VIA IN SELCI

VIALE DEL MON

TI Baths of Trajan (A 109) were t first to be built the massive sca later used in the Bat of Diocletian and of Caracall

★ Santa Maria Maggiore
This imposing rear facade was added by Baroque architect Carlo Rainaldi in 1673. Santa Maria's interior is one of the most richly decorated in Rome ❹

LOCATOR MAP
See Central Rome Map pp12–13

The Tomb of Pius V (died 1572) by Domenico Fontana stands in this less well-known Sistine Chapel, under the northeast dome of Santa Maria Maggiore.

Arch of Gallienus
This was built in the 3rd century AD to replace an entrance in the old Servian Wall ❻

To Vittorio Emanuele Metro

★ Santa Prassede
The 9th-century mosaics in the Chapel of San Zeno are among the finest in Rome ❺

The Torre dei Capocci, a restored medieval tower, is one of the area's most distinctive landmarks.

San Martino ai Monti
Its frescoes include 17th-century Roman landscapes and scenes from the life of Elijah by Gaspare Dughet ❶

KEY

— — — Suggested route

| 0 meters | 75 |
| 0 yards | 75 |

STAR SIGHTS

★ Santa Maria Maggiore

★ San Pietro in Vincoli

★ Santa Prassede

San Martino ai Monti ❶

Viale del Monte Oppio 28. **Map** 6 D5.
📞 482 00 93. 🚌 11, 16, 27, 70, 71,
81, 93, 93b, 613. Ⓜ *Cavour, Vittorio
Emanuele.* **Open** 7am–noon & 4:30–
7pm (Oct–Mar: 4:30–6:30pm) daily.
🚹 📷 ♿

**Fresco of old San Giovanni in
Laterano in San Martino ai Monti**

CHRISTIANS have been
worshiping on the site
of this church since the 3rd
century, when they used to
meet in the house of a man
named Equitius. In the 4th
century, after Constantine had
legalized Christianity, Pope
Sylvester I built a church, one
of the very few things he did
during his pontificate. In fact
he was so insignificant that
in the 5th century a more
exciting life was fabricated
for him – which included
tales of him converting
Constantine, curing him of
leprosy and forcing him to
close all pagan temples. Pope
Sylvester's fictional life was
further enhanced in the 8th
century, with the forgery of
a document in which
Constantine offered him
the Imperial crown.

Pope Sylvester's church
was replaced in about
AD 500 by St. Symmachus,
and was rebuilt in the 9th
century and subsequently
transformed completely in
the 1650s. As a result, the
only immediate signs of its
age are the ancient Corinthian
columns dividing the nave
and aisles. The most
interesting features of the
interior are a series of
frescoed landscapes of the
Campagna (the countryside

around Rome) by the 17th-
century French artist Gaspare
Dughet, Poussin's brother-in-
law, in the right aisle. The
frescoes by Filippo Gagliardi,
at either end of the left aisle,
show old St. Peter's and the
interior of San Giovanni in
Laterano before Borromini's
redesign. Though hard to find,
the sacristan can lead visitors
under the church to see the
remains of Equitius's house.

San Pietro in Vincoli ❷

Piazza di San Pietro in Vincoli 4A.
Map 5 C5. 📞 488 28 65. 🚌 11, 27,
81. Ⓜ *Colosseo.* **Open** 7am–12:30pm
& 3:30–7pm (Oct–Mar: 6pm) daily.
🚹 📷 ♿ 👕

ACCORDING TO TRADITION, the
two chains (*vincoli*) used
to shackle St. Peter while he
was being held in the depths

Reliquary with St. Peter's chains

of the Mamertine Prison (*see
p91*) were subsequently taken
to Constantinople. In the 5th
century, Empress Eudoxia
deposited one in a church in
Constantinople and sent the
other to her daughter, Eudoxia,
in Rome. She in turn gave hers
to Pope Leo I, who had this
church built to house it. Some
years later the second chain
was brought to Rome,
where it linked miraculously
with its partner.

The chains are still here,
displayed below the high
altar, but the church is now
best known for Michelangelo's
tomb of Pope Julius II. When
it was commissioned in 1505,
Michelangelo spent eight
months searching for perfect
blocks of marble at Carrara in
Tuscany, but Pope Julius
became more interested in
the building of a new St.
Peter's, and the project
was laid aside. After the
pope's death in 1513,
Michelangelo resumed
work on the tomb but
had finished only the
statues, *Moses* and the
Dying Slaves, when Pope
Paul III persuaded him to
start work on the Sistine
Chapel's *Last Judgment.*
Michelangelo had
planned a vast monument
with over 40 statues, but
the tomb that was built –
mainly by his pupils –
is simply a facade with
six niches for statues. The
Dying Slaves are in Paris
and Florence, but the
tremendous bearded
Moses is here. The horns
on Moses's head should
really be beams of light
– the horns are the result
of the Hebrew original
from the Old Testament
being wrongly translated.

Michelangelo's *Moses* in San Pietro

Apse mosaics in Santa Prassede, showing the saint with St. Paul

Santa Pudenziana ❸

Via Urbana 160. **Map** 5 C4.
📞 481 46 22. 🚌 16, 70, 71, 93, 93b, 613. Ⓜ Cavour.
Open 8am–noon & 3–6pm daily.
✝ 📷

IN THE NORMAL COURSE of events, churches tend to be dedicated to existing saints. In this case, the church, through a linguistic accident, created a brand new saint. In the 1st century AD a Roman senator called Pudens lived on this site and, according to legend, allowed St. Peter to lodge with him. In the 2nd century a bath house was built on this site, and in the 4th century a church was established inside the baths. This was known as the *Ecclesia Pudentiana* (the church of Pudens). In time it was assumed that "Pudentiana" was a woman's name, and a life was created for her – she became the sister of Prassede and was credited with caring for Christian victims of persecution. In 1969 both saints were declared invalid, though both their churches kept their names.

The 19th-century facade of the church retains an 11th-century frieze depicting both Prassede and Pudenziana dressed as crowned Byzantine empresses – the Church's way of asserting that it was as important as the temporal authority of Byzantium.

The apse has a remarkable 4th-century mosaic, clearly influenced by Classical pagan art in its use of subtle colors. The Apostles are represented as Roman senators in togas. Unfortunately, a clumsy attempt at restoration in the 16th century destroyed two of the Apostles and left other figures without their legs.

Santa Maria Maggiore ❹

See pp172–3.

Santa Prassede ❺

Via Santa Prassede 9A. **Map** 6 D4.
📞 488 24 56. 🚌 16, 93, 93b, 613.
Ⓜ Vittorio Emanuele. **Open** 7:30am–noon & 4–6:30pm daily. ✝ 📷 ♿

9th-century mosaics, Santa Prassede

THE CHURCH was founded by Pope Paschal II in the 9th century on the site of a 2nd-century oratory. Artists from Byzantium decorated the church with glittering, jewel-colored mosaics. Those in the apse and choir depict stylized white-robed elders, the haloed elect looking down from the gold-and-blue walls of heaven; spindly-legged lambs; feather-mop palm trees and bright red poppies. In the apse, Santa Prassede and Santa Pudenziana stand on either side of Christ, with the fatherly arms of St. Paul and St. Peter on their shoulders. There are also beautiful mosaics in the Chapel of St. Zeno, built as a mausoleum for Pope Paschal's mother, Theodora.

11th-century frieze and medallions on the facade of Santa Pudenziana

Santa Maria Maggiore ❹

OF ALL THE GREAT Roman basilicas, Santa Maria has the most successful blend of different architectural styles. Its colonnaded triple nave is part of the original 5th-century building. The Cosmatesque marble floor and delightful Romanesque bell tower, with its blue ceramic roundels, are medieval. The Renaissance saw a new coffered ceiling, and the Baroque gave the church twin domes and its imposing front and rear facades. The mosaics are Santa Maria's most famous feature. From the 5th century come the Biblical scenes in the nave and the spectacular mosaics on the triumphal arch. Medieval highlights include a 13th-century enthroned Christ in the loggia.

★ Cappella Paolina
Flaminio Ponzio designed this richly decorated chapel (1611) for Pope Paul V Borghese.

Obelisk in Piazza dell'Esquilino
The Egyptian obelisk was erected by Pope Sixtus V in 1587 as a landmark for pilgrims.

LEGEND OF THE SNOW

In 352, Pope Liberius had a dream in which the Virgin told him to build a church on the spot where he found snow. When it fell on the Esquiline, on the morning of August 5 in the middle of a baking Roman summer, he naturally obeyed. The miracle of the snow is commemorated each year by a service during which thousands of white petals float down from the ceiling of Santa Maria. Originally roses were used, but nowadays the petals are more usually taken from dahlias.

Coffered Ceiling
The gilded ceiling, possibly by Giuliano da Sangallo, was a gift of Alexander VI Borgia at the end of the 15th century. The gold is said to be the first brought from America by Columbus.

TIMELINE

300 AD	600	900	1200	1500	1800

352 Virgin appears to Pope Liberius

432–40 Sixtus III completes church

Pope Gregory VII

1347 Cola di Rienzo crowned Tribune of Rome in Santa Maria

1673 Carlo Rainaldi rebuilds apse

420 Probable founding date

1075 Pope Gregory VII kidnapped by opponents while reading Christmas mass in Santa Maria

Coat of arms of Gregory VII

1288–92 Nicholas IV adds apse and transepts

1743 Ferdinando Fuga adds main facade on orders of Benedict XIV

★ **Coronation of the Virgin Mosaic**
This is the central image of a series of wonderful apse mosaics of the Virgin by Jacopo Torriti (1295).

Baldacchino *(1740s)*
Its columns of red porphyry and bronze were the work of Ferdinando Fuga.

★ **Tomb of Cardinal Rodriguez**
The Gothic tomb (1299) contains magnificent Cosmatesque marblework.

★ **Cappella Sistina**
The chapel was built for Pope Sixtus V (1585–90) by Domenico Fontana and houses the pope's tomb.

Column in Piazza Santa Maria Maggiore
A bronze of the Virgin and Child was added to this ancient marble column in 1615. The column came from the Basilica of Constantine in the Forum.

STAR FEATURES

★ **Cappella Sistina**

★ **Coronation of the Virgin Mosaic**

★ **Cappella Paolina**

★ **Tomb of Cardinal Rodriguez**

Arch erected in memory of Emperor Gallienus

Arch of Gallienus ⓺

Via Carlo Alberto. **Map** 6 D4. 🚍 4, 9, 16, 70, 71. Ⓜ *Vittorio Emanuele.*

Squashed between two buildings just off Via Carlo Alberto is the central arch of an originally three-arched gate erected in memory of Emperor Gallienus, who was assassinated by his Illyrian officers in AD 262. It was built on the site of the old Esquiline Gate in the Servian Wall, parts of which are visible nearby.

Santa Bibiana ⓻

Via Giovanni Giolitti 154.
Map 6 F4. 🄲 446 10 21. 🚍
11, 70, 71. Ⓜ *Vittorio Emanuele.*
Open 7–10am & 4:30–7:30pm daily
(call first). 🛉 📷 ♿

The deceptively simple facade of Santa Bibiana was Bernini's first foray into architecture. It is a clean, economic design with superimposed pilasters and deeply shadowed archways. The church itself was built on the site of the palace belonging to Bibiana's family. This is where the saint was buried after being flogged to death with leaded cords during the brief persecution of the Christians that took place in the reign of Julian the Apostate (361–3). Just inside the church is a small column against which Bibiana is said to have been whipped. Her remains, along with those of her mother, Dafrosa, and her sister, Demetria, who also suffered martyrdom, are preserved in an alabaster urn below the altar. In a niche above the altar stands a statue of Santa Bibiana by Bernini – the first fully clothed figure he ever sculpted. He depicts her standing beside a column, holding the cords with which she was whipped, apparently on the verge of a death swoon.

Early sculpture by Bernini of the martyr Santa Bibiana (1626)

Piazza Vittorio Emanuele II ⓼

Map 6 E5. 🚍 4, 9, 11, 70, 71, 105. 🚊 14, 516, 517. Ⓜ *Vittorio Emanuele. See* **Markets** *p338.*

Piazza vittorio, as it is called for short, is one of the city's main open-air food markets. The arcaded square was built in the urban development undertaken after the unification of Italy in 1870. It was named after Italy's first king, but there is nothing regal about its appearance today. The shabby arcades shelter shops and stalls that sell cheap shoes and clothes.

The equally neglected garden area in the center of— the square contains a number of mysterious ruins – including a large mound; the remains of a Roman fountain from the 3rd century AD; and the Porta Magica, a curious 17th-century doorway inscribed with alchemical signs and formulae.

Museo Nazionale d'Arte Orientale ⓽

Via Merulana 248. **Map** 6 D5.
🄲 487 50 77. 🚍 4, 9, 16, 70, 71,
93, 93b, 613. Ⓜ *Vittorio Emanuele.*
Open 9am–7pm Tue & Thu, 9am–2pm
Wed, Fri & Sat, 9am–1pm Sun.
Adm charge.

The museum occupies part of the late 19th-century Palazzo Brancaccio, which became the home of the Italian Institute of the Middle and Far East in 1957. The collection ranges from prehistoric Iranian ceramics and sculpture from Afghanistan, Nepal, Kashmir and India to 18th-century Tibetan paintings on vellum. From the Far East there are collections of Japanese screen paintings and Chinese jade.

The most unusual exhibits are the finds from the Italian excavation of the ancient civilization of Swat in

4th-century relief from Kashmir

summerhouse – with fountains. Traces of frescoes are on the walls. If visitors look carefully they can make out garden scenes and small figures – including one of a characteristically drunken Dionysus being propped up by a satyr.

Nero's Golden House ⓫

Domus Aurea, Via Labicana 136. **Map** 5 C5. 🏛 699 01 10. 🚌 15, 81, 85, 87, 186. **Closed** for restoration; call the Soprintendenza Archeologica at the above number (8am–1:30pm) to arrange a visit.

Frescoed room in the ruins of Nero's Golden House

AFTER ALLEGEDLY setting fire to Rome in AD 64, Nero decided to build himself an outrageous new palace. It occupied part of the Palatine and most of the Celian and Esquiline hills – an area approximately 25 times the

size of the Colosseum. The vestibule on the Palatine side of the complex contained a colossal gilded statue of Nero. There was an artificial lake, with gardens and woods where imported wild beasts were allowed to roam. According to Suetonius in his life of Nero, the palace walls were adorned with gold and mother-of-pearl, rooms were designed with ceilings that showered guests with flowers or perfumes, the dining hall rotated and the baths were fed with both sulphurous water and seawater.

Tacitus described Nero's debauched garden parties, with banquets served on barges and lakeside brothels serviced by aristocratic women, although, since Nero killed himself in AD 68, he did not have long in his new home.

Nero's successors, anxious to distance themselves from the monster emperor, did their utmost to erase all traces of the palace. Vespasian drained the lake and built the Colosseum (see pp92–5) in its place, Titus and Trajan each erected a complex of baths over the palace, and Hadrian placed the Temple of Venus and Rome (see p87) over the vestibule.

Rooms from one wing of the palace have survived, buried beneath the ruins of the Baths of Trajan on the Oppian Hill. A number of wall paintings can still be seen, but the underground chambers are damp and dangerous. They have been closed to the public since a landslide in 1984.

Nepalese Bodhisattva in the Museo Nazionale d'Arte Orientale

northeast Pakistan. This fascinating culture lasted from the 3rd century BC to about the 10th century AD. Its wonderfully exotic, sensual reliefs show an unusual combination of Hellenistic, Buddhist and Hindu influences.

Auditorium of Maecenas ⓾

Largo Leopardi. **Map** 6 D5. 🚌 4, 9, 16, 70, 71, 81, 93, 93b, 613. Ⓜ Vittorio Emanuele. **Open** 9am–1:30pm Sun. 🚫 ♿

MAECENAS, fop, dandy dresser, gourmet, and patron of the arts, was no mere dilettante; he was also an astute lifelong adviser and colleague of the Emperor Augustus. He was fabulously rich and spent some of his wealth creating a fantastic villa and gardens on the Esquiline Hill, most of which have long disappeared beneath the modern city. The partially reconstructed auditorium, isolated on a traffic island, is the only building that remains.

Inside, a semicircle of tiered seats suggests that it may have been a place for readings and performances. If it was, then Maecenas would have been entertained here by his protégés, the lyric poet Horace and Virgil, author of the Aeneid, reading their latest works. However, water ducts have also been discovered, and it may well have been a nympheum – a kind of

18th-century artist's impression of Nero's Golden House

LATERAN

IN THE MIDDLE AGES, the Lateran Palace was the residence of the popes, and the basilica of San Giovanni beside it rivaled St. Peter's in splendor. After the return of the popes from Avignon at the end of the 14th century, the area declined in importance. Pilgrims still continued to visit San Giovanni and Santa

Cherub from San Giovanni in Laterano

Croce in Gerusalemme, but the area remained sparsely inhabited. Ancient convents slumbered amid gardens and vineyards until Rome became Italy's capital in 1870, and a network of residential streets was laid out to house the influx of newcomers. The main sites of archaeological importance are the Aurelian Wall and the ruins of the Aqueduct of Nero.

SIGHTS AT A GLANCE

Churches
San Giovanni in Laterano pp182–3 ❶
Santa Croce in Gerusalemme ❺
Santi Quattro Coronati ⓫
San Clemente pp186–7 ⓬
Santo Stefano Rotondo ⓭

Shrines
Scala Santa and Sancta Sanctorum ❷

Arches and Gates
Porta Asinaria ❸
Porta Maggiore ❼

Ancient Sites
Amphiteatrum Castrense ❹
Baker's Tomb ❽
Aqueduct of Nero and the Freedmen's Tombs ❾

Museums
Museum of Musical Instruments ❻

Historic Buildings
Villa Wolkonsky ❿

SEE ALSO

GETTING THERE
San Giovanni Metro station on line A is just outside the city wall but handy for many of the sights in the area. The 16, 85, 87, 93 and 93b are among the many buses to Piazza di San Giovanni in Laterano. This can also be reached by the 13 and 30b trams. These are slow, but their routes make them useful for exploring this part of Rome.

KEY

	Street by street map
—	City wall
M	Metro station
P	Parking

0 meters 300
0 yards 300

15th-century apse fresco in Santa Croce in Gerusalemme

Street by Street: Piazza di San Giovanni

Both the basilica of San Giovanni and the Lateran Palace look out over a huge open area, the Piazza di San Giovanni, laid out at the end of the 16th century with an Egyptian obelisk, the oldest in Rome, in the center. Sadly, the traffic streaming in and out of the city through Porta San Giovanni tends to detract from its grandeur. Across the square is the building housing the Scala Santa (the Holy Staircase), one of the most revered relics in Rome and the goal for many pilgrims. The area is also a venue for political rallies, and the feast of St. John on June 23 is celebrated with a fair at which Romans consume vast quantities of snails.

The Chapel of Santa Rufina, originally the portico of the baptistry, has a 5th-century mosaic of spiraling foliage in the apse.

VIA DI SANTO STE...

VIA DELL'AMBA ARADAM

VIA DEI LATERANI

The Cloister of San Giovanni fortunately survived the two fires that destroyed the early basilica. A 13th-century masterpiece of mosaic work, the cloister now houses fragments from the medieval basilica.

Piazza di San Giovanni in Laterano boasts an ancient obelisk and parts of Nero's Aqueduct. This 18th-century painting by Canaletto shows how the piazza once looked.

Star Sight

★ **San Giovanni in Laterano**

Key

— — — Suggested route

0 meters	75
0 yards	75

The Chapel of San Venanzio is decorated with a series of 7th-century mosaics on a gold background. This detail from the apse shows one of the angels beside the central figure of Christ. San Venanzio was an accomplished 6th-century Latin poet.

LOCATOR MAP
See Central Rome Map pp12–13

The Lateran Palace, residence of the popes until 1309, was rebuilt by Domenico Fontana in 1586.

★ **San Giovanni in Laterano**
Borromini's interior dates from the 17th century, but the grand facade by Alessandro Galilei, with its giant statues of Christ and the Apostles, was added in 1735 ❶

Scala Santa
This door at the top of the stair-case leads to the Sancta Sanctorum, the pope's private chapel ❷

The Triclinio Leoniano is a piece of wall and a mosaic from the dining hall of 8th-century Pope Leo III.

Porta Asinaria
This minor gateway, no longer in use, is as old as the Aurelian Wall, dating back to the 3rd century AD ❸

San Giovanni in Laterano ❶

See pp182–3.

Scala Santa and Sancta Sanctorum ❷

Piazza di San Giovanni in Laterano 14. **Map** 9 C1. 70 49 44 89. 4, 15, 16, 81, 85, 87, 186 and many other routes. 13, 30b. San Giovanni. **Open** 6:30–11:50am, 3:30–6:45pm (Oct–Mar 3–6:45pm) daily.

Devout Christians climbing the Scala Santa on their knees

O N THE EAST SIDE of Piazza di San Giovanni in Laterano, a building designed by Domenico Fontana (1589) houses two surviving parts of the old Lateran Palace. One is the pope's private chapel, the Sancta Sanctorum, the other the holy staircase, the Scala Santa. The 28 steps, said to be those that Christ ascended in Pontius Pilate's house during his trial, are supposed to have been brought from Jerusalem by St. Helena, mother of the Emperor Constantine. This belief, however, cannot be traced back any earlier than the 7th century.

The steps were moved to their present site by Pope Sixtus V (reigned 1585–90) when the old Lateran Palace was destroyed. No foot may touch the holy steps, so they are covered by wooden boards. They may be climbed only by the faithful on their knees, a penance that is performed especially on Good Friday. In the vestibule are various 19th-century sculptures, including an *Ecce Homo* by Giosuè Meli (1874).

The Scala Santa and two side stairways lead to the Chapel of St. Lawrence or Sancta Sanctorum (Holy of Holies), built by Pope Nicholas III in 1278. Decorated with fine Cosmatesque marble-work, the chapel contains many important relics, the most precious being an image of Jesus – the *Acheiropoeton,* or "picture painted without hands," said to be the work of St. Luke, assisted by an angel. The image was taken on procession in medieval times to ward off plagues.

Porta Asinaria ❸

Between Piazza di Porta San Giovanni and Piazzale Appio. **Map** 10 D2. 4, 15, 16, 81, 85, 87. 13, 30b. San Giovanni. See **Markets** p339.

T HE PORTA ASINARIA (Gate of the Donkeys) is one of the minor gateways in the Aurelian Wall *(see p196).* Twin circular towers were added and a small enclosure built around the entrance; the remains are still visible today. From outside the walls visitors can see the gate's white travertine facade and two rows of small windows, giving light to two corridors built into the wall above the gateway. In

Porta Asinaria from inside the wall

AD 546 treacherous barbarian soldiers serving in the Roman army opened this gate to the hordes of the Goth Totila, who mercilessly looted the city. In 1084 the Holy Roman Emperor Henry IV entered Rome via Porta Asinaria with the antipope Guibert to oust Pope Gregory VII. The gateway was badly damaged later that year by the pope's rescuer, the Norman Robert Guiscard, who set the whole area around San Giovanni in Laterano on fire.

The area close to the gate, especially in the Via Sannio, is the home of a popular flea-market. During the week, the streets fill with stalls selling cheap clothes, both new and secondhand, shoes and camping equipment; bargains can often be found.

Amphiteatrum Castrense ❹

Between Piazza di Santa Croce in Gerusalemme and Viale Castrense. **Map** 10 E1. 9. 13, 30b. **Not open** to the public.

Columns and bricked-up arches of the Amphiteatrum Castrense

T HIS SMALL 3rd-century amphitheater was used for games and baiting animals. It owes its preservation to the fact that it was incorporated into the Aurelian Wall *(see p196),* which included several existing high buildings in its fortifications. The graceful arches framed by brick semicolumns were blocked up. The amphitheater is best seen from outside the walls, where there is also a very good view of the bell tower of Santa Croce in Gerusalemme.

Discovery and Triumph of the Cross, attributed to Antoniazzo Romano, in Santa Croce in Gerusalemme

Santa Croce in Gerusalemme ❺

Piazza di Santa Croce in Gerusalemme 12. **Map** 10 E1. ☏ *701 47 69.* 🚌 *9.* 🚋 *13, 30b.* **Open** *6am–12:30pm & 3:30–7pm daily.* ✝ 📷 ♿

EMPEROR CONSTANTINE'S mother, St. Helena, founded this church in AD 320 on the grounds of her private palace. Although the church stood at the edge of the city, the relics of the Crucifixion that St. Helena had brought back from Jerusalem made it a center of pilgrimage. Most important were the pieces of Christ's Cross (*croce* means "cross") and part of Pontius Pilate's inscription in Latin, Hebrew and Greek: "Jesus of Nazareth King of the Jews."

In the crypt is a Roman statue of Juno, found at Ostia (*see pp270–71*); it was transformed into a statue of St. Helena by replacing the head and arms and adding a cross. The 15th-century apse fresco shows the medieval legends that arose around the Cross. Helena is shown holding it over a dead youth and restoring him to life. Another episode shows its recovery from the Persians by the Byzantine Emperor Heraclitus after a bloody battle. In the center of the apse is a magnificent tomb by Jacopo Sansovino made for Cardinal Quiñones, Emperor Charles V's confessor (died 1540).

Museum of Musical Instruments ❻

Museo degli Strumenti Musicali, Piazza di Santa Croce in Gerusalemme. **Map** 10 E1. ☏ *701 47 96.* 🚌 *9.* 🚋 *13, 30b.* **Open** *9am–7pm Tue & Thu, 9am–1:30pm Wed, Fri–Sun.* **Closed** *public hols.* **Adm charge.** 📷

ONE OF ROME'S lesser-known museums, this building stands on the site of the Sessorianum, the great Imperial villa belonging to Empress St. Helena, later included in the Aurelian Wall. Opened in 1974, the museum has a collection of over 3,000 instruments from all over the world. It includes instruments typical of the various regions of Italy, and wind, string and percussion instruments of all ages (including Egyptian, Greek and Roman). There are also sections dedicated to church and military music.

The greater part of the collection is composed of Baroque instruments: do not miss the gorgeous Barberini harp, remarkably well preserved, on the first floor in Room 13. There are spinets, harpsichords and clavichords of many different kinds, plus one of the first pianos ever made, dating from 1722.

18th-century statue of St. Helena on the facade of Santa Croce

Art Nouveau entrance to the Museum of Musical Instruments

San Giovanni in Laterano ❶

EARLY IN THE 4th century, the
Laterani family were disgraced
and their land taken by Emperor
Constantine to build Rome's first
Christian basilica. Today's church
retains the original shape but has
been destroyed by fire twice and
rebuilt several times. Borromini
undertook the last major rebuild
of the interior in 1646, and the
main facade is an 18th-century
addition. Before the pope's move
to Avignon in 1309, the adjoining
Lateran Palace was the official papal
residence, and until 1870 all popes were
crowned in the church. The Pope is the
Bishop of Rome, and here in the city's
main cathedral he celebrates Maundy
Thursday mass and attends the
annual blessing of the people.

**Cappella di
San Venanzio**
*This chapel is attached
to the baptistry and is
decorated with 7th-
century mosaics.*

**Entrance
to museum**

Apse

Papal Altar
*Only the Pope
can celebrate mass
at this altar. The
Gothic baldacchino,
decorated with
frescoes, dates from
the 14th century.*

★ Cloisters
*Built by the
Vassalletto family
in about 1220, the
cloisters are remarkable
for their twisted twin columns
and inlaid marble mosaics.*

TIMELINE

AD 313 Constantine gives Laterani site to Pope Melchiades for a church		1144 Church dedicated to San Giovanni in Laterano		1646 Borromini rebuilds interior
314–18 Five-aisled basilical church is built	**896** Church damaged in earthquake	**1309** Papacy moves to Avignon	**1377** Return of popes from Avignon	

AD 300	**800**	**1000**	**1400**	
324 Basilica consecrated by Pope Sylvester I and dedicated to the Redeemer	**904–11** Church rebuilt under Pope Sergius III	**1300** First Holy Year proclaimed	**1360** Church burnt down for second time	**1586** Domenico Fontana builds north facade
		1308 Church destroyed by fire		**1730–40** Alessandro Ga'ilei constructs main facade

★ Baptistry
Though much restored, the domed baptistry dates back to Constantine's time. It assumed its present octagonal shape in AD 432, and the design has served as the model for baptistries throughout the Christian world.

North Facade
This was added by Domenico Fontana in 1586. The Pope gives his blessing from the upper loggia.

Statues of Christ and the Apostles

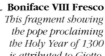

Boniface VIII Fresco
This fragment showing the pope proclaiming the Holy Year of 1300 is attributed to Giotto.

A side door is opened once every 25 years for Holy Year.

Main entrance on east facade

Corsini Chapel
This chapel was built in the 1730s for Pope Clement XII. The altarpiece is a mosaic copy of Guido Reni's painting of Sant'Andrea Corsini.

VISITORS' CHECKLIST

Piazza di San Giovanni in Laterano 4. **Map** 9 C2. ☎ 77 20 79 91. ☒ 4, 15, 16, 85, 87, 93, 93b and other routes to Piazza San Giovanni. Ⓜ San Giovanni. ☒ 13, 30b. **Church and Cloister open** 7am–7pm (Oct–Mar: 6pm Mon–Fri) daily. **Museum open** 9am –1pm & 3–5pm Mon–Fri. **Adm charge** for cloister and museum.
♿ 📷 🚻

STAR FEATURES

★ **Baptistry**

★ **Cloisters**

The original Lateran Palace was almost destroyed by the fire of 1308, which devastated San Giovanni. Pope Sixtus V commissioned Fontana to replace it in 1586.

TRIAL OF A CORPSE

Fear of rival factions led the early popes to extraordinary lengths. An absurd case took place at the Lateran Palace in 897, when Pope Stephen VI tried the corpse of his predecessor, Formosus, for disloyalty to the Church. The corpse was found guilty; its right hand was mutilated, and it was thrown into the Tiber.

Pope Formosus

Porta Maggiore ➐

Piazza di Porta Maggiore. **Map** 6 F5.
🚌 105. 🚋 13, 14, 19, 19b, 516, 517.

ORIGINALLY the two arches of Porta Maggiore were not part of the city wall but part of an aqueduct built for the Emperor Claudius in AD 52. They carried the water of the Aqua Claudia over the Via Labicana and Via Prenestina, two of ancient Rome's main southbound roads. Visitors can still see the original roadway beneath the gate. In the large slabs of basalt – a hard volcanic rock used in all old Roman roads – are the great ruts created by generations of cartwheels. On top of the arches, separate conduits carried the water of two aqueducts, the Aqua Claudia, and its offshoot, the Aqueduct of Nero. They bear inscriptions from the time of the Emperors Vespasian and Titus, who restored them in the years AD 71 and AD 81, respectively. In all, six aqueducts from different water sources entered the city at Porta Maggiore.

The Aqua Claudia was 43 miles (68 km) long, with more than 9 miles (15 km) above ground. Its majestic arches are a strong feature of the Roman countryside, and a brand of mineral water still bears its name. Some arches of the Aqua Claudia were bricked up when it was joined to the 3rd-century Aurelian Wall *(see p196).*

Relief showing breadmaking on the tomb of the baker Eurysaces

Baker's Tomb ➑

Piazzale Labicano. **Map** 6 F5. 🚌 105.
🚋 13, 14, 19, 19b, 516, 517.

IN THE MIDDLE of the tram junction near Porta Maggiore stands the tomb of the rich baker Eurysaces and his wife, Atistia, built in 30 BC. Roman custom forbade burials within city walls, and the roads leading out of cities became lined with tombs and monuments for the middle and upper classes. This tomb is shaped like a baking oven: a low-relief frieze at the top shows Eurysaces presiding over his slaves in the various phases of breadmaking. The inscription proudly asserts his origins and reveals him as a freed slave, probably of Greek origin. Many men like him saved money from their meager slave salaries to earn their freedom and set up businesses, becoming the backbone of Rome's economy.

Relief on the Tomb of the Statilii freedmen

Aqueduct of Nero and the Freedmen's Tombs ➒

Intersection of Via Statilia and Via di Santa Croce in Gerusalemme.
Map 10 D1. 🚌 9, 105. 🚋 13, 14, 19, 19b, 30b. **Apply** for permit: *Ripartizione X, (see p367).*

THE AQUEDUCT was built for Nero in the 1st century AD as an extension of the Aqua Claudia. It was later extended to supply the Imperial residences on the Palatine. Partly incorporated into later buildings, the imposing arches make their way via the Lateran to the Celian Hill. Along the first section of the aqueduct, in Via Statilia, is a small tomb in the shape of a house, dating from the 1st century BC, and bearing the names and likenesses of a small group of freed slaves. Their name, Statilii, indicates that they had been freed by the noble Statilii, the family of Claudius's notorious first wife, Messalina. Servants of families often pooled funds in this way to pay for a dignified burial in a common resting place.

Porta Maggiore, a city gate formed by the arches of an aqueduct

Well-preserved section of Nero's aqueduct near San Giovanni

Villa Wolkonsky ⑩

Via Conte Rosso. **Map** 10 D1.
🚌 *4, 81.* 🚋 *13, 30b.* **Not open** to
the public.

NOW THE RESIDENCE of the
British ambassador, the
villa has a beautiful garden
strewn with Roman remains,
including arches of the Aqua
Claudia and a columbarium,
or collective grave, of the 2nd
century AD. Sadly, garden
parties for British residents
are no longer given here on
the Queen's official birthday.

Santi Quattro Coronati ⑪

Via dei Santi Quattro Coronati 20. **Map**
9 B1. 📞 *70 47 54 27.* 🚌 *15, 81, 85,
87, 118.* 🚋 *13, 30b.* **Open** *9:30am–
noon & 3:30–6pm (Oct–Mar: 9:30am–
noon)* Mon–Sat. 🚻 ◎ ♿

Cloister of Santi Quattro Coronati

THE NAME of this fortified
convent (Four Crowned
Saints) refers to four Christian
soldiers martyred after they
refused to worship a pagan
god. For centuries it was the
bastion of the pope's
residence, the Lateran Palace.
Its high apse still looms over
the houses below, while a
Carolingian tower dominates
the entrance. Erected in the
4th century AD, it was rebuilt
after the invading Normans
set fire to the neighborhood
in 1084. Hidden within is the
garden of the delightful inner
cloister (admission on request),
one of the earliest of its kind,
built around 1220.
    The remains of medieval
frescoes can be seen in the
Chapel of Santa Barbara, but
the convent's main feature is
the Chapel of St. Sylvester –
its remarkable frescoes (1246)
recount the legend of the
conversion to Christianity of

the Emperor Constantine by
Pope Sylvester I (reigned 314–
35), then living as a hermit on
Monte Soratte, north of Rome.
    Stricken by the plague,
Constantine is prescribed a
bath in children's blood, to
the horror of the matrons of
Rome. Unable to bring himself
to obey, Constantine is
visited in a dream by St. Peter
and St. Paul. They advise him
to find Sylvester, who cures
him and baptizes him. The
final scene shows the emperor
kneeling before the pope.
The implied idea of the pope
as heir to the Roman Empire
would affect the whole course
of medieval European history.

San Clemente ⑫

See pp186–7.

Santo Stefano Rotondo ⑬

Via di Santo Stefano 7. **Map** 9 B2.
📞 *70 49 37 17.* 🚌 *15, 118, 673.*
Open *9am–1pm & 3:30–6pm
(summer), 1:50–4:20pm (winter)
Tue–Sat, 3:30–6pm Mon.* 🚫

ONE OF ROME'S earliest
Christian churches, Santo
Stefano Rotondo was built
between 468 and 483. It has an
unusual circular plan with four
chapels in a cruciform. The

**Distinctive circular outline
of Santo Stefano Rotondo**

round inner area was
surrounded by concentric
corridors with 22 Ionic
supporting columns. The high
drum in the center is 72 ft (22
m) high and just as wide. It is
lit by 22 high windows, a few
of them restored or blocked by
restorations carried out under
Pope Nicholas V (reigned
1447–55), who consulted the
Florentine architect Leon
Battista Alberti. The archway in
the center of the church may
have been added during this
period, when the outer
corridor was eliminated.
    In the 16th century the
church walls were frescoed
by Niccolò Pomarancio, with
particularly gruesome
illustrations of the martyrdom
of innumerable saints. Some
of the medieval decor remains
in the chapels: in the first
chapel to the left of the
entrance is a 7th-century
mosaic of Christ with San
Primo and San Feliciano.

Fresco of St. Sylvester and Constantine in Santi Quattro Coronati

San Clemente ⑫

SAN CLEMENTE PROVIDES an opportunity to travel back through three layers of history. At street level, there is a 12th-century church; underneath this lies a 4th-century church; and below that are ancient Roman buildings, including a Temple of Mithras. Mithraism, an all-male fertility cult imported from Persia in the 1st century BC, was a rival to Christianity during the age of Imperial Rome.

The upper levels are dedicated to St. Clement, the fourth pope, who was exiled to the Crimea and martyred by being tied to an anchor and drowned. His life is illustrated in some of the frescoes in the 4th-century church. The site was taken over in the 17th century by Irish Dominicans, who still continue the excavating work begun by Father Mullooly in 1857.

Entrance to the church is through a door in Via di San Giovanni in Laterano.

Paschal Candlestick
This 12th-century spiraling candlestick, striped with glittering mosaic, is a magnificent example of Cosmati work.

18th-Century Facade
Twelfth-century columns were used in the arcade.

★ **Cappella di Santa Caterina**
The restored frescoes by the 15th-century Florentine artist Masolino show scenes from the life of the martyred St. Catherine of Alexandria.

12th-century church

4th-century church

Piscina
This deep pit was discovered in 1967. It could have been used as a font or fountain.

1st- to 3rd-century temple and buildings

TIMELINE

2nd century Site possibly used for secret Christian worship			**1108** New church built over 4th-century church	**1857** Original 4th-century church rediscovered by Father Mullooly	
Late 2nd century Temple of Mithras built	**867** Reputed transfer of remains of San Clemente to Rome				

AD 10	500	1000	1500	1900

90–99 Papacy of St. Clement	**4th century** First church built over courtyard of earlier Roman building		**1667** Church and convent given to Irish Dominicans	
		1084 Church destroyed during Norman invasion led by Robert Guiscard		
AD 64 Nero's fire destroys area			**1861** Church is excavated. Roman ruins discovered	

★ Apse Mosaic
The 12th-century
Triumph of the
Cross *includes
beautifully detailed
animals and
acanthus leaves.*

Schola Cantorum
*The 6th-century
enclosure for the
choir was retained
for the new church,
built in 1108.*

VISITORS' CHECKLIST

Via di San Giovanni in Laterano.
Map 9 B1. 70 45 10 18.
81, 85, 87, 93. Colosseo.
13, 30b. **Open** 9am–12:30pm
& 3:30–6:30pm (Oct–Mar: 6pm)
Mon–Sat, 10am–12:30pm &
3:30–6:30pm Sun. **Adm charge**
to excavations.

**★ Triclinium and
Altar of Mithras**
*The altar, with a
relief of Mithras
slaying the bull,
stands in the
triclinium, a room
used for ritual
banquets.*

**Temple of
Mithras**

**★ 11th-
Century
Frescoes**
*Commissioned by
the de Rapiza family,
one shows the story of a boy
found alive in St. Clement's
tomb beneath the Black Sea.*

Catacomb
*Discovered in
1938 and dating
from the 5th or 6th
century, it contains
16 wall tombs
known as* loculi.

STAR FEATURES

★ Apse Mosaic

**★ Cappella di Santa
Caterina**

**★ 11th-Century
Frescoes**

**★ Triclinium and Altar
of Mithras**

IOVINVSALVMNVS

CARACALLA

THE CELIAN HILL over-looking the Coloss-eum takes its name from Caelius Vibenna, the legendary hero of Rome's struggle with the Tarquins (see pp16–17). In Imperial Rome, this was a fashionable place to live, and some of its van-ished splendor is still appar-ent in the vast ruins of the Baths of Caracalla. Today, thanks to the

Capital from ruins of Baths of Caracalla

Archaeological Zone established at the turn of the century, it is a delight-fully peaceful area, a green wedge stretching from the Aurelian Wall to the heart of the city. Through it runs the cobbled Via di Porta San Sebas-tiano, part of the old Via Appia. It leads to Porta San Sebastiano, one of the best-preserved gates in the ancient city wall.

SIGHTS AT A GLANCE

Churches
Santi Giovanni e Paolo ❶
San Gregorio Magno ❷
Santa Maria in Domnica ❹
San Sisto Vecchio ❻
Santi Nereo e Achilleo ❼
San Cesareo ❽
San Giovanni a Porta Latina ❾
San Giovanni in Oleo ❿
Santa Balbina ⓰

Arches and Gates
Arch of Dolabella ❸
Arch of Drusus ⓭
Porta San Sebastiano and the Aurelian Wall ⓮
Sangallo Bastion ⓯

Historic Buildings
UN Food and Agriculture Organization ⓱
Baths of Caracalla ⓲

Tombs
Columbarium of Pomponius Hylas ⓫
Tomb of the Scipios ⓬

Parks and Gardens
Villa Celimontana ❺

GETTING THERE
Circo Massimo Metro station is handy if you are visiting the churches and parks on the Celian Hill. For the Baths of Caracalla and other sights closer to Porta San Sebastiano, take the 90 or 118 along Viale delle Terme di Caracalla. Other buses, such as the 93, 97 and 613, go to Piazzale Numa Pompilio, a useful central starting point for exploring the area.

SEE ALSO

0 meters   300

0 yards   300

KEY

Street-by-Street map

— City Wall

Ⓜ Metro station

Ⓟ Parking

Mosaic of an athlete from the Baths of Caracalla

Street by Street: The Celian Hill

IN THE COURSE OF A MORNING exploring the green
slopes of the Celian Hill, you will see a fascinating
assortment of archaeological remains and beautiful
churches. A good starting point is the church of San
Gregorio Magno, from where the Clivo di Scauro leads
up to the top of the hill. The steep narrow street passes
the ancient porticoed church of Santi Giovanni e Paolo,
with its beautiful Romanesque bell tower soaring above
the surrounding medieval monastery buildings. Of the
parks on the hill, the best-kept and most peaceful is the
Villa Celimontana, with its formal walks and avenues.
It is a good place for a
picnic, because
few bars or
restaurants
are nearby.

Clivo di Scauro, the
Roman *Clivus Scauri*, leads
up to Santi Giovanni e
Paolo, passing under
the flying buttresses
that support
the church.

VIA DI SAN GREGORIO

CLIVO DI SCAURO

La Vignola is a
delightful Renaissance
pavilion, reconstructed
here in 1911 after it
had been demolished
during the creation of
the Archaeological
Zone around the
Baths of Caracalla.

**To Circo
Massimo
Metro**

**San Gregorio
Magno**
*A monastery and
a chapel were
founded here by
Pope Gregory the
Great at the end of
the 6th century* ❷

★ **Santi Giovanni e Paolo**
*The nave of the church, lit by a blaze
of chandeliers, has been restored
many times and assumed its present
appearance in the 18th century* ❶

★ **Villa Celimontana**
*The delightful 16th-
century villa built for the
Mattei family is now the
center of a public park* ❺

Trams passing over the Celian Hill from the Colosseum rumble up a picturesque narrow track through the Parco del Celio.

LOCATOR MAP
See Central Rome Map pp12–13

Ruins of the Temple of Claudius are visible over a large area of the Celian Hill. These travertine blocks have been incorporated in the base of the bell tower of Santi Giovanni e Paolo.

The gateway of San Tommaso in Formis is decorated with a wonderful 13th-century mosaic showing Christ with two freed slaves, one white, one black.

Arch of Dolabella
Built in the 1st century AD, probably as an entrance to the city, this archway was later incorporated in Nero's aqueduct to the Palatine ❸

STAR SIGHTS

★ **Santi Giovanni e Paolo**

★ **Santa Maria in Domnica**

★ **Villa Celimontana**

★ **Santa Maria in Domnica**
This church is famed for its 9th-century mosaics. These Apostles appear on the triumphal arch above the apse, flanking a medallion containing the figure of Christ ❹

KEY

– – – Suggested route

0 meters 75

0 yards 75

Santi Giovanni e Paolo ❶

Piazza Santi Giovanni e Paolo 13.
Map 9 A1. **[** *700 57 45.* **[** *11, 15, 27, 90, 673.* **[** *13, 30b.*
M *Colosseo or Circo Massimo.*
Open *9–11am & 4–5:30pm daily.*
[ ] [ ] [ ] *church only (not Roman house).*

Santi Giovanni e Paolo is dedicated to two martyred Roman officers whose house stood on this site. Giovanni (John) and Paolo (Paul) had served the first Christian emperor, Constantine. When they were later called to arms by the pagan emperor Julian the Apostate, they refused and were beheaded in their own house in AD 362.

Built toward the end of the 4th century, the church retains many elements of its original structure. The Ionic portico dates from the 12th century, and the apse and bell tower were added by Nicholas Breakspeare, the only English pope, who reigned as Adrian IV (1154–59). The base of the superb 13th-century bell tower was part of the Temple of Claudius that stood on this site. In common with many Romanesque bell towers, it has inlaid marble and ceramic roundels decorating the brickwork.

The interior, remodelled in 1718, has granite piers and columns. A tomb slab in the nave marks the burial place of the martyrs, whose relics are preserved in an urn under the high altar. In a tiny room near the altar, a magnificent 13th-century fresco depicts the figure of Christ flanked by his Apostles (ask the sacristan to unlock the door for you).

Excavations beneath the church have revealed two Roman houses, of the 2nd and 3rd centuries, united and used as a Christian burial place. The two-story construction, with 20 rooms and a labyrinth of corridors, has well-preserved pagan and Christian paintings. The arches to the left of the church were part of a 3rd-century street of shops.

Fresco of Christ and the Apostles in Santi Giovanni e Paolo

San Gregorio Magno ❷

Piazza di San Gregorio. **Map** 8 F2.
[*700 82 27.* **[** *11, 15, 27, 673.*
[*13, 30b.* **M** *Circo Massimo.*
Open *9am–noon & 3:30–6pm daily.*
[ ] [ ]

Facade of San Gregorio Magno

To the English, this is one of the most important churches in Rome, for it was from here that St. Augustine was sent on his mission to convert England to Christianity. The church was founded in AD 575 by San Gregorio Magno (St. Gregory the Great), who turned his family home on this site into a monastery. It was rebuilt in medieval times and restored in 1629–33 by Giovanni Battista Soria. To reach the church you ascend a flight of steps from the street.

The forecourt contains some interesting tombs. To the left is that of Sir Edward Carne, who came to Rome several times between 1529 and 1533 as King Henry VIII's envoy to gain the pope's consent to the annulment of Henry's marriage to Catherine of Aragon.

The interior, remodeled by Francesco Ferrari in the mid-18th century, is typically Baroque, except for the fine mosaic floor and some ancient columns. At the end of the right aisle is the chapel of St. Gregory. Leading off it, another small chapel, believed to have been the saint's own cell, houses his episcopal throne – a Roman chair of sculpted marble. The Salviati Chapel on the left contains a picture of the Virgin said to have spoken to St. Gregory.

Outside, amid the cypresses to the left of the church, stand three small chapels, dedicated to St. Andrew, St. Sylvia (Gregory the Great's mother) and St. Barbara.

Marble throne of Gregory the Great from the 1st century BC

Arch of Dolabella ❸

Via di San Paolo della Croce.
Map 9 A2. 🚌 *15, 673.*

THE ARCH was built in AD 10 by the consuls Cornelius Dolabella and Caius Junius Silanus, possibly on the site of one of the gateways of the old Servian Wall. Made of solid travertine blocks, it was subsequently used to support Nero's extension of the Claudian aqueduct, built to supply the Imperial palace on the Palatine Hill.

The restored Arch of Dolabella

Santa Maria in Domnica ❹

Piazza della Navicella 12. **Map** 9 A2.
📞 *700 15 19.* 🚌 *15, 673.* **Open**
*9am–noon & 3:30–7pm (Oct–Mar:
6pm) daily.* 🔲 ◻ ♿

THE CHURCH overlooks the Piazza della Navicella (little boat), which takes its name from the 16th-century fountain there. It was made

from an ancient stone galley, probably a temple offering made by a Roman traveler on his safe return to the city. The church dates from the 9th century; in the 16th century Pope Leo X added the portico and the coffered ceiling.

In the apse behind the slightly incongruous modern altar is a superb 9th-century mosaic commissioned by Pope Paschal I. Wearing the square halo of the living, the pope appears at the feet of the Virgin and Child. The Virgin, surrounded by a throng of angels, holds a handkerchief in the manner of a fashionable lady at a Byzantine court.

Villa Celimontana ❺

Piazza della Navicella. **Map** 9 A2.
🚌 *15, 81, 85, 87, 90, 673.*
Park open *7am–dusk daily.*

THE DUKES OF MATTEI bought this land in 1553 and transformed the vineyards that covered the hillside into a formal garden. As well as palms and other exotic trees, the garden even has its own Egyptian obelisk. Villa Mattei, built in the 1580s, is now known as Villa Celimontana and houses the Italian Geographical Society.

The Mattei family used to open the park to the public on the day of the Visit of the Seven Churches, an annual event instituted by San Filippo Neri in 1552. Starting from the Chiesa Nuova *(see p124),* Romans went on foot to the city's seven major churches.

When they reached Villa Mattei, they were given a meal of bread, wine, salami, cheese, an egg and two apples. The garden, now owned by the city of Rome, still makes an ideal place for a picnic.

Park of Villa Celimontana

San Sisto Vecchio ❻

Piazzale Numa Pompilio 8. **Map** 9 A3.
📞 *77 20 51 74.* 🚌 *90, 93, 97, 613,
671.* **Open** *9–11am daily.*
Closed *Aug.* 🚫

THIS SMALL CHURCH is of great historical interest, for it was granted to St. Dominic in 1219 by Pope Honorius III. The founder of the Dominican order soon moved his own headquarters to Santa Sabina *(see p204),* San Sisto becoming the first home of the order of Dominican nuns. The best feature of the church itself is the 13th-century bell tower.

Apse mosaic of the Virgin and Child in Santa Maria in Domnica

Santi Nereo e Achilleo ❼

Via di Porta San Sebastiano 4. **Map** 9 A3. 575 79 96. 90, 93, 613, 671. **Open** 10am– noon & 4–6pm Sat–Thu.

AㄷcㄷoRDING to legend, St. Peter, after escaping from prison, was fleeing the city when he lost a bandage from his wounds. The original church was founded here in the 4th century on the spot where the bandage fell, but later it was rededicated to the 1st-century martyrs St.

Detail of mosaic, Santi Nereo e Achilleo

Nereus and St. Achilleus.

Restored at the end of the 16th century, the church has retained many medieval features, including some fine 9th-century mosaics on the triumphal arch. A magnificent pulpit rests on an enormous porphyry pedestal that was found nearby in the Baths of Caracalla. The walls of the side naves are decorated with a series of rather grisly 16th-century frescoes by Niccolò Pomarancio, showing in clinical detail how each of the Apostles was martyred.

Fresco by Niccolò Pomarancio of the *Martyrdom of St. Simon* in Santi Nereo e Achilleo

San Cesareo ❽

Via di Porta San Sebastiano. **Map** 9 A3. 58 23 01 40. **Closed** for restoration.

THIS SPLENDID old church, built over Roman ruins of the 2nd century AD, has been closed since 1988. You can still admire Giacomo della Porta's fine Renaissance facade, but if the workmen will let you in, you can also see Cosmatesque mosaic work and carving to rival that of any church in Rome. The episcopal throne, altar and pulpit are decorated with delightful birds and beasts. The church was restored in the 16th century by Pope Clement VIII, whose coat of arms decorates the ceiling.

San Giovanni a Porta Latina ❾

Via di San Giovanni a Porta Latina. **Map** 9 B3. 70 49 17 77. 4, 90, 118. **Open** 7am–12:15pm & 3–6pm daily. **Donation** expected.

THE CHURCH of "St. John at the Latin Gate" was founded in the 5th century, rebuilt in 720 and restored in 1191. This is one of the most picturesque of the old Roman churches. Classical columns support the medieval portico, and the 12th-century bell tower is superb. A tall cedar tree shades an ancient well standing in the forecourt. The interior has recently been restored, but it preserves the rare simplicity of its early origins, with ancient columns of varying styles lining the aisles. Traces remain of early medieval frescoes. There are 12th-century frescoes showing 46 different scenes from both the Old and New Testaments, which are among the finest of their kind in Rome.

Fresco, San Giovanni a Porta Latina

San Giovanni in Oleo ❿

Via di Porta Latina. **Map** 9 C4. 4, 90. **Closed** for restoration.

Frieze of San Giovanni in Oleo

THE NAME of this charming octagonal Renaissance chapel means "St. John in Oil." The tiny building marks the spot where, according to legend, St. John was boiled in oil – and came out unscathed, or even refreshed. An earlier chapel is said to have existed on the site; the present one was built in the early 16th century. The design has been attributed to Bramante or Antonio da Sangallo the Younger. It was restored by Borromini, who altered the roof, crowning it with a cross supported by a sphere decorated with roses. He also added a terra-cotta frieze of roses and palm leaves. The wall paintings inside the chapel include one of St. John in a cauldron of boiling oil.

Niches for funerary urns in the Columbarium of Pomponius Hylas

Columbarium of Pomponius Hylas ⑪

Via di Porta Latina 10. **Map** 9 B4.
🚌 4, 90. **Open** by appt only: apply to Ripartizione X, Via del Portico d'Ottavia 29 or phone 67 10 20 70.

KNOWN AS a columbarium because it resembles a dovecote (*columba* is the Latin word for dove), this kind of vaulted tomb was normally built by rich Romans to house the cremated remains of their freedmen. Many similar tombs have been uncovered in this part of Rome, which up until the 3rd century AD lay outside the city wall. This one, excavated in 1831, dates from the 1st century AD. An inscription informs us that it is the Tomb of Pomponius Hylas and his wife, Pomponia Vitalinis. Above her name is a "V," which indicates that she was still living when the inscription was made. The tomb was probably a commercial venture. Niches in the interior walls of the columbarium were sold to people who could not afford to build vaults of their own.

Tomb of the Scipios ⑫

Via di Porta San Sebastiano 9.
Map 9 B4. 📞 70 49 00 53. 🚌 4, 90. **Closed** for restoration.

THE SCIPIOS were a family of conquering generals. Southern Italy, Corsica, Algeria, Spain and Asia Minor all fell to their victorious Roman armies. The most famous of all was Publius Cornelius Scipio Africanus, who defeated the great Carthaginian general Hannibal at the Battle of Zama in 202 BC. Scipio Africanus himself was not buried here in the family tomb, but at Liternum near Naples, where he owned a favorite villa. The Tomb of the Scipios was discovered in 1780. It contained various sarcophagi, statues and niches with terra-cotta burial urns. Many of the originals have now been moved to the Vatican Museums, and copies stand in their place.

The earliest sarcophagus was that of Cornelius Scipio Barbatus, consul in 298 BC, for whom the tomb was built. Members of his illustrious family continued to be buried here up to the middle of the 2nd century BC. Excavations in the area have revealed many other archaeological finds: a columbarium similar to that of Pomponius Hylas, a Christian catacomb and a three-story house dating from the 3rd century AD, which was built over the Tomb of the Scipios.

Arch of Drusus ⑬

Via di Porta San Sebastiano.
Map 9 B4.

Arch of Drusus, part of the Aqua Antoniniana aqueduct

ONCE MISTAKENLY identified as a triumphal arch, the Arch of Drusus merely supported the branch aqueduct that supplied the Baths of Caracalla. It was built in the 3rd century AD and so had no connection with Drusus, a stepson of the Emperor Augustus. Monumental in size, it supported the aqueduct across the important main route, Via Appia. The arch still spans right over the old cobbled road, just 160 ft (50 m) short of the well-known gateway Porta San Sebastiano.

Mosaic inscription in the Columbarium of Pomponius Hylas

Fortified gateway of Porta San Sebastiano

Porta San Sebastiano and the Aurelian Wall ⓮

Museo delle Mura, Via di Porta San Sebastiano 18. **Map** 9 B4. ☎ 70 47 52 84. **Open** 9am–7pm Tue–Sat, 9am–1:30pm Sun (last adm: 30 mins before closing). **Closed** public hols. **Adm charge.** ⌀

Most of the Aurelian Wall, begun by the Emperor Aurelian (AD 270–75) and completed by his successor, Probus (AD 276–82), has survived. Aurelian ordered its construction as a defense against marauding Germanic tribes, whose raids were penetrating deeper and deeper into Italy. Some 11 miles (18 km) round, with 18 gates and 381 towers, the wall took in all the seven hills of Rome. It was raised to almost twice its original height by Maxentius (AD 306–12).

Porta San Sebastiano, the gate that leads to the Via Appia Antica *(see p284)* is the largest and best-preserved gateway in the wall. It was rebuilt by the Emperor Honorius in the 5th century AD. Originally the Porta Appia, in Christian times it gradually became known as the Porta San Sebastiano, because the Via Appia led to the Basilica and Catacombs of San Sebastiano, which were popular places of pilgrimage.

It was at this gate that the last triumphal procession to enter the city by the Appian Way was received in state – that of Marcantonio Colonna

after the victory of Lepanto over the Turkish fleet in 1571. Today the gate's towers house a museum containing prints and models illustrating the history of the walls. The views are spectacular, especially out over the unchanging landscape of the Via Appia.

The wall continued to be Rome's main defense until 1870, when it was breached by Italian artillery near Porta Pia, close to today's British Embassy. Many of the gates are still in use, and although the city has spread, most of its noteworthy historical and cultural sights still lie within the walls.

Sangallo Bastion ⓯

Viale di Porta Ardeatina. **Map** 9 A4. ☎ 93, 94, 160, 613, 671. **Closed** for restoration.

Pope Paul III Farnese

Haunted by the memory of the Sack of Rome in 1527 and fearing attack by the Turks, Pope Paul III asked Antonio

da Sangallo the Younger to reinforce the Aurelian Wall. Work on the huge projecting bastion began in 1537. For the moment its massive bulk can be admired only from outside.

Santa Balbina ⓰

Piazza di Santa Balbina 8. **Map** 8 F3. ☎ 578 02 07. ☎ 160. Ⓜ Circo Massimo. **Open** 8am–6pm daily. ⌁

Overlooking the Baths of Caracalla, this isolated church framed by cypresses is dedicated to Santa Balbina, a 2nd-century virgin martyr. Dating back to the 4th century, this is one of the oldest churches in the city. Inside stands the magnificent sculpted and inlaid tomb of Cardinal Stefanus de Surdis, signed by Giovanni di Cosma and dated 1303.

UN Food and Agriculture Organization ⓱

Viale delle Terme di Caracalla. **Map** 8 F2. ☎ 11, 15, 27, 90, 118, 673. ☎ 13, 30b. Ⓜ Circo Massimo. **Closed** to public.

Obelisk of Axum (4th century AD)

The food and Agriculture Organization of the United Nations is based here in a modern building completed in 1951. Before it stands the obelisk of Axum, looted from Ethiopia by Mussolini, who originally commissioned the building to house the Ministry of Italian Africa.

Baths of Caracalla ⑱

Viale delle Terme di Caracalla 52.
Map 9 A3. 575 86 26.
90, 93, 118, 160. **Open** 9am–
dusk Tue–Sat, 9am–1pm Sun, Mon.
Closed public hols. **Adm charge**.
Concerts

COMPLETED by the Emperor Caracalla in AD 217, the baths functioned for about 300 years, until the "plumbing" was destroyed by invading Goths. Over 1,500 bathers at a time could enjoy the facilities. A Roman bath was a long and complicated business, beginning with a sort of Turkish bath, followed by a spell in the *calidarium*, a large, hot room with pools of water to moisten the atmosphere. Then came the lukewarm *tepidarium*, a visit to the large central meeting place, known as the *frigidarium*, and finally a plunge into the *natatio*, an open-air swimming

Fragment of mosaic pavement

pool. For the rich, this was followed by a rubdown with scented woolen cloths. In addition to the baths, there were spaces for exercise, libraries, art galleries and gardens – creating a true leisure center. Most of the rich marble decorations of the baths were removed by the Farnese family in the 16th century to adorn the interior of Palazzo Farnese *(see p147)*.

Part of one of the gymnasia in the Baths of Caracalla

Until recently, open-air operas were staged here – the vocal exertions of the performers are now thought to pose a threat to the structure of this ancient monument.

KEY

☐	Calidarium (very hot)
☐	Tepidarium (lukewarm)
☐	Frigidarium (cold)
☐	Natatio (pool)
☐	Garden

Conference and meeting rooms

Greek and Latin libraries

Water tanks

Stadium

Front entrance

Changing rooms

Gymnasia

Storage room for oils and perfumes

Gymnasium

Conference and meeting room

AVENTINE

THIS IS ONE of the most peaceful areas within the walls of the city. Although it is largely residential, there are some unique historic sights. From the top of the Aventine Hill, crowned by the magnificent basilica of Santa Sabina, there are exceptional views across the river to Trastevere and St. Peter's. At the foot of the hill, ancient Rome is preserved in the two small Temples of the Forum Boarium and the Circus Maximus. The liveliest streets are in Testaccio, with its many stores, restaurants and clubs, while to the south, beside Rome's solitary pyramid, the Protestant Cemetery is a lovely oasis of calm.

Mask fountain in courtyard of Santa Sabina

SIGHTS AT A GLANCE

Churches and Temples
Santa Maria in Cosmedin ❶
San Giorgio in Velabro ❸
San Teodoro ❹
Santa Maria della Consolazione ❺
San Giovanni Decollato ❻
Temples of the Forum Boarium ❽
Santa Sabina ❾
Santi Bonifacio e Alessio ❿
San Saba ⓯

Historic Buildings
Casa dei Crescenzi ❼

Arches
Arch of Janus ❷

Historic Streets and Piazzas
Piazza dei Cavalieri di Malta ⓫

Ancient Sites
Monte Testaccio ⓬
Circus Maximus ⓰

Monuments and Tombs
Protestant Cemetery ⓭
Pyramid of Caius Cestius ⓮

GETTING THERE
The quickest way is by Metro line B to Piramide or Circo Massimo. For a more interesting trip, take a tram – the 13 or 30b. Several buses go down Viale Aventino to Piramide, but the only bus to the top of the Aventine Hill is the 94.

KEY
▢	Street-by-Street map
—	City Wall
M	Metro station
P	Parking

SEE ALSO
- **Street Finder**, maps 7, 8, 12
- **Where to Stay** pp294–5
- **Restaurants** pp310–11

Pines and orange trees on the Aventine Hill with dome of St. Peter's in the distance

Street by Street: Piazza della Bocca della Verità

THE AREA ATTRACTS VISITORS eager to place their hands inside the Bocca della Verità (the Mouth of Truth) in the portico of Santa Maria in Cosmedin. There are many other sights to see in this quiet corner of the city beside the Tiber, which was the site of ancient Rome's first port and its busy cattle market. Substantial Classical remains include two small temples from the Republican age and the Arch of Janus from the later Empire. In the 6th century, the area became home to a Greek community from Byzantium, who founded the churches of San Giorgio in Velabro and Santa Maria in Cosmedin.

Sant'Omobono, a late 16th-century church, now stands in isolation in the middle of an important archaeological site. The remains of sacrificial altars and two temples from the 6th century BC have been discovered.

Casa dei Crescenzi
This 11th-century building used columns and capitals from ancient Roman temples **7**

Ponte Rotto, as this forlorn ruined arch in the Tiber is called, means simply "broken bridge." It was built in the 2nd century BC, and originally named the Pons Aemilius.

★ **Temples of the Forum Boarium**
The tiny round Temple of Hercules and its neighbor, the Temple of Portunus, are the best preserved of Rome's Republican temples **8**

LUNGOTEVERE DEI PIERLEONI

TEVERE

PONTE PALATINO

KEY

- - - Suggested route

0 meters   75
0 yards   75

STAR SIGHTS

★ **Santa Maria in Cosmedin**

★ **Temples of the Forum Boarium**

★ **Santa Maria in Cosmedin**
This medieval church has a mosaic floor and a Gothic altar canopy **1**

Santa Maria della Consolazione
This 16th-century church used to serve a hospital nearby 5

San Teodoro
The 15th-century portal of this ancient round church is decorated with the arms of Pope Nicholas V 4

LOCATOR MAP
See Central Rome Map pp12–13

San Giovanni Decollato
The plain Renaissance facade was completed in about 1504 6

San Giorgio in Velabro
The simple portico of Ionic columns and the Romanesque bell tower date from the 12th century 3

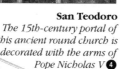

Arch of Janus
This square structure with arches on each side dates from the 4th century AD 2

The Arco degli Argentari, dedicated to the Emperor Septimius Severus in AD 204, is decorated with scenes of religion and war.

The Fontana dei Tritoni by Carlo Bizzaccheri was built here in 1715. The style shows the powerful influence of Bernini.

Bocca della Verità

Santa Maria in Cosmedin **①**

Piazza della Bocca della Verità 18.
Map 8 E1. **(** 678 14 19. **▦** 15, 23, 57, 90, 92, 94, 95, 160, 716. **Open** 9am–1pm & 2:30–6pm daily. (Call first.) ☐ ◎ ⬣ ☐

THIS BEAUTIFUL unadorned church was built in the 6th century on the site of the ancient city's food market. The elegant Romanesque bell tower and portico were added during the 12th century. In the 19th century a Baroque facade was removed and the church restored to its original simplicity. It contains many fine examples of Cosmati work, in particular the mosaic pavement, the raised choir, the bishop's throne and the canopy over the main altar.

Set into the wall of the portico is the Bocca della Verità (Mouth of Truth). This may have been a drain cover dating from before the 4th century BC. Medieval tradition had it that the formidable jaws would snap shut over the hands of those who told lies – a useful trick for testing the faithfulness of spouses.

Arch of Janus **②**

Via del Velabro. **Map** 8 E1. **▦** 15, 57, 90, 92, 95, 160, 716.

PROBABLY DATING from the reign of Constantine, this imposing four-faced marble arch stood at the bustling crossroads on the edge of the Forum Boarium, near the ancient docks. It was an ideal place for merchants and customers to do business in the shade. On the keystones above the four arches are small figures of the goddesses Roma, Juno, Ceres and Minerva. In medieval times the arch used to form the base of a tower fortress. It was restored to its original shape in 1827.

San Giorgio in Velabro **③**

Via del Velabro 19. **Map** 8 E1.
(679 33 35. **▦** 15, 57, 90, 90b, 92, 94, 95, 160, 716, 774, 780.
Closed for restoration.

San Giorgio in Velabro before the 1993 bombing

IN THE HOLLOW of the street named after the Velabrum, the swamp where Romulus and Remus are said to have been found by the she-wolf, is a small church dedicated to St. George, whose bones lie under the altar. The 7th-century basilica has suffered over the centuries from periodic floods, but has been restored to its original appearance, with a double row of assorted granite and marble columns (taken from ancient Roman temples) dividing the triple nave. The austerity of the cool gray interior is relieved by golden frescoes in the apse (attributed to Pietro Cavallini, 1295). The facade and the bell tower date from the 12th century.

Recent testimony to the church's low-lying location is given by the high water-level mark of 1870 in the portico.

San Teodoro **④**

Via di San Teodoro. **Map** 8 E1.
(678 66 24. **▦** 15, 57, 90, 92, 95, 160, 716. **Open** 10:30am–noon Sun.

VISITORS WHO HAPPEN to be in the area on a Sunday morning, will find this round 6th-century church at the foot of the Palatine open for a weekly mass. It is well worth going inside – the 6th-century mosaics in the apse are breathtaking, as is the Florentine cupola (1454). The pretty outer courtyard was designed by Carlo Fontana in 1705.

The church of San Teodoro, one of Rome's hidden treasures

The Arch of Janus, where cattle dealers sheltered from the midday sun

Facade of Santa Maria della Consolazione

Santa Maria della Consolazione ❺

Piazza della Consolazione 84.
Map 5 A5. **📞** 678 46 54. **🚌** 57,
64, 90, 92, 94, 95, 160, 716.
Open 7am–noon daily (afternoons
on request). **Closed** Aug. 🕇 📷
♿

THE CHURCH STANDS near the
foot of the Tarpeian Rock,
which was the site of
numerous public executions.

In 1385, Giordanello degli
Alberini, a condemned
nobleman, paid two gold
florins for an image of the
Virgin Mary to be placed
here, to provide some
consolation to prisoners in
their final moments. From this
came the name of the church
built here in 1470. It was
reconstructed between 1583
and 1606 by Martino Longhi,
who provided the early
Baroque facade.

The church's 11 side chapels
are owned by noble families
and local crafts guild members.
In the presbytery is the famed
image of Mary attributed to
Antoniazzo Romano.

San Giovanni Decollato ❻

Via di San Giovanni Decollato 22.
Map 8 E1. **📞** 699 07 28.
🚌 15, 57, 90, 92, 95, 160, 716.
Closed for restoration.

THE MAIN ALTAR is dominated
by Giorgio Vasari's
Beheading of St. John (1553),
from which the church takes
its name, San Giovanni
Decollato. In
1490, Pope
Innocent VIII
gave this
church site
to a very
specialized
Florentine
fraternal order.
Ghoulishly
attired in black
robes and
hoods, their
task was to
encourage
condemned
prisoners to
repent and to
give them a decent burial
after they had been hanged.
In the cloisters are seven
manholes (one is reserved
for women), which received
the bodies.

The oratory contains a cycle
of frescoes describing the life
of St. John the Baptist, by the
leading Florentine Mannerists
Jacopino del Conte and
Francesco Salviati. In style,
the figures resemble some of
those in the Sistine Chapel.

Casa dei Crescenzi ❼

Via Luigi Petroselli. **Map** 8 E1. **🚌** 15,
23, 57, 90, 92, 94, 95, 160, 716.

STUDDED WITH archaeological
fragments, the house is
what remains of a 12th-century
tower fortress. It was built by
the powerful Crescenzi family
so they could see both the
old docks of Rome (today the
site of the Anagrafe or Public
Records Office) and the
bridge where the family
collected a toll.

Ancient Roman fragments in the Casa dei Crescenzi

Temples of the Forum Boarium ❽

Piazza della Bocca della Verità.
Map 8 E1. **🚌** 15, 23, 57, 90, 92,
94, 95, 160, 716.

Temple of Portunus

THESE MIRACULOUSLY well
preserved Republican
temples, set in a grassy enclave
under the umbrella pines
beside the Tiber, are
particularly appealing by
moonlight. They date from the
2nd century BC and were
saved for posterity when they
were reconsecrated as Christian
churches in the Middle Ages.
They offer rare examples of
combined elements from
Greek and Roman architecture.

The rectangular temple
(formerly known as the Temple
of Fortuna Virilis) was in fact
dedicated to Portunus, the god
of rivers and ports – a
reference to the nearby port of
ancient Rome. Set on a
podium, the temple has four
Ionic travertine columns fluted
at the front and
12 pilasters,
embedded in the
tufa wall of the
cella – the
room that
housed the
image of the
god. Nearby is
the small circular
Temple of
Hercules. It is
often referred to as
the Temple of
Vesta because of
its similarity to the
one in the Forum.

Luminous interior of Santa Sabina

Santa Sabina 9

Piazza Pietro d'Illiria 1. **Map** 8 E2.
 574 35 73. 94. **Open** 9am–
12:45pm & 3:30–6pm daily.

HIGH ON the Aventine stands a perfect early Christian basilica that was founded by Peter of Illyria in AD 422 and restored to its original simplicity early this century. Light filters through high 9th-century windows onto a wide nave framed by white Corinthian columns supporting an arcade with a marble frieze. Over the main door is a 5th-century blue-and-gold mosaic dedicatory inscription; the pulpit, carved choir and bishop's throne are from the 9th century.

The church was given to the Dominicans in the 13th century, and in the nave is the magnificent mosaic tombstone of one of the first leaders of the order, Muñoz de Zamora (died 1300). The side portico has 5th-century paneled doors carved from cypress wood, each bearing scenes from the Bible, including one of the earliest crucifixions in existence.

Santi Bonifacio e Alessio 10

Piazza di Sant'Alessio 23. **Map** 8 D2.
 574 34 46. 94. **Open** 8:30am–noon & 3:30–6:30pm (Oct–Mar: 6pm) daily.

THE CHURCH is dedicated to two early Christian martyrs, whose remains lie under the main altar. Legend has it that Alessio, son of a rich senator living on the site, fled to the East to become a pilgrim and avoid an impending marriage. Returning home after many years, he died as a servant, unrecognized, under the stairs of the family entrance hall, clutching the manuscript of his story for posterity.

The original 5th-century church has undergone substantial changes over the centuries. Noteworthy are the 18th-century facade, with its five arches; the restored Cosmati doorway and pavement; and the magnificent Romanesque five-story bell tower (1217). An 18th-century Baroque chapel by Andrea Bergondi houses part of the famous staircase. Other relics include the well from Alessio's family home and the glowing Byzantine Madonna of the Intercession, brought to Rome from Damascus at the end of the 10th century.

Piazza dei Cavalieri di Malta 11

Map 8 D2. 23, 57, 94, 95, 716.

SURROUNDED BY cypress trees, this ornate walled piazza decorated with obelisks and military trophies was designed by Piranesi in 1765. It is named after the Order of the Knights of Malta (Cavalieri di Malta) whose priory (at No. 3) is famous for the bronze keyhole through which there is a miniature view of St. Peter's, framed by a tree-lined avenue. The priory church, Santa Maria del Priorato, restored and decorated in Neo-classical style by Piranesi in the 18th century, can be visited with permission from the headquarters of the Order. At the southwest corner of the square is the international Benedictine church of Sant'Anselmo, where the strains of Gregorian chants may be heard on Sundays starting at 9:30am.

Doorway of the Priory of the Knights of Malta

Monte Testaccio 12

Via Galvani. **Map** 8 D4. 27, 92.
Closed to public.

FROM ABOUT 140 BC to AD 250, this hill was created by the dumping of millions of *testae* (hence Testaccio) – fragments of the amphorae used to carry goods to the nearby warehouses. The artificial hill is 120 ft (36 m) high, but its full archaeological significance was not realized until the late 18th century.

Facade of Santi Bonifacio e Alessio

Protestant Cemetery ⓑ

Via Caio Cestio 6. **Map** 8 D4.
📞 574 19 00. 🚌 11, 23, 27, 57, 94, 95, 716. 🚊 13, 30b. Ⓜ Piramide.
Open 9am–6pm (Oct–Mar: 5pm)
Tue–Sun (last adm: 30 mins before closing). **Donation** expected. 📷 📱

THE PEACE of this well-tended cemetery beneath the Aurelian Wall is profoundly moving. Non-Catholics, mainly English and German, have been buried here since 1738.

Tombstone of John Keats

In the oldest part are the graves of John Keats (died 1821 – his epitaph reads: "Here lies One Whose Name was writ in Water"), and his friend Joseph Severn (died 1879); not far away are the ashes of Percy Bysshe Shelley (died 1822). Goethe's son, Julius, is also buried here.

Pyramid of Caius Cestius ⓮

Piazzale Ostiense. **Map** 8 E4. 🚌 11, 23, 57, 94, 95. 🚊 13, 30b. Ⓜ Piramide.

Memorial pyramid of Caius Cestius

CAIUS CESTIUS, a wealthy *praetor* (senior Roman magistrate), died in 12 BC. His one claim to fame is his tomb, an imposing pyramid faced in white marble set in the Aurelian Wall near Porta San Paolo. It stands 89 ft (27 m) high and, according to an inscription, took 330 days to build. Unmistakable as a landmark, it must have looked almost as incongruous when it was built as it does today.

Detail of carving on sarcophagus in the portico of San Saba

San Saba ⓯

Via di San Saba. **Map** 8 F3.
📞 574 33 52. 🚌 11, 27, 94, 673. 🚊 13, 30b. **Open** 7am–noon & 4–7pm daily. 📱 📷

TUCKED AWAY in a residential street on the Little Aventine Hill, San Saba began life as an oratory for Palestinian monks fleeing from Arab invasions in the 7th century. The existing church dates from the 10th century and has undergone much restoration. The portico houses a fascinating collection of archaeological remains.

The church has three naves in the Greek style and a short fourth 11th-century nave with vestiges of 13th-century frescoes of the life of St. Nicholas of Bari. Particularly intriguing is a scene of three naked young ladies laying in bed; they are saved from penury by the gift of a bag of gold from St. Nicholas, the future Santa Claus. The beautiful marble inlay in the main door, the floor and the remains of the choir are all 13th-century Cosmati work.

Circus Maximus ⓰

Via del Circo Massimo. **Map** 8 F2.
🚌 11, 15, 27, 90, 94, 118, 673. 🚊 13, 30b. Ⓜ Circo Massimo.

WHAT WAS ONCE ancient Rome's largest stadium is today little more than a long grassy esplanade. Set in the valley between the Palatine and Aventine hills, the Circus Maximus was continually embellished and expanded from the 4th century BC until AD 549, when the last races were held. The grandstands held some 250,000 spectators, cheering wildly at the horse and chariot races, athletic contests and animal fights, and betting furiously throughout.

The Circus had a central dividing barrier *(spina)* with seven large egg-shaped objects on it used for counting the laps of a race. These were joined in 33 BC by seven bronze dolphins that served a similar purpose. In 10 BC, Augustus built the Imperial box under the Palatine and decorated the *spina* with the obelisk that now stands in the center of Piazza del Popolo *(see p137)*. A second obelisk, which was added in the 4th century by Constantius II, is now in Piazza di San Giovanni in Laterano *(see pp178–9)*.

Reconstruction of the Circus Maximus in its heyday

TRASTEVERE

THE PROUD and aggressively independent inhabitants of Trastevere, the area "across the Tiber," consider themselves the most authentic Romans. In this area, one of the most picturesque old quarters of the city, it is still possible to glimpse scenes of everyday life that seem to belong to bygone centuries. There are, however, signs that much of the earthy proletarian character of the place may soon be destroyed by the proliferation of fashionable restau-

Romanesque bell tower

rants, clubs and boutiques. Some of Rome's most fascinating medieval churches lie hidden away in the patchwork of narrow, cobbled backstreets, the only clue to their location being an occasional glimpse of a Romanesque bell tower. Santa Cecilia was built on the site of the martyrdom of the patron saint of music; San Francesco a Ripa commemorates St. Francis of Assisi's visit to Rome; and Santa Maria in Trastevere is the traditional center of the spiritual and social life of the area.

SIGHTS AT A GLANCE

Churches
Santa Maria della Scala ❸
Santa Maria dei
Sette Dolori ❹
Santa Maria in Trastevere
pp212–13 ❻
San Crisogono ❼
Santa Cecilia in Trastevere ❽
San Francesco a Ripa ❾

Museums and Galleries
Sant'Egidio and Museo
del Folklore ❺

Historic Buildings
Casa della Fornarina ❶

Bridges
Ponte Sisto ❷

Parks and Gardens
Villa Sciarra ❿

SEE ALSO

• *Street Finder*, maps 4, 7, 8, 11

• *Where to Stay* pp294–5

• *Restaurants* pp310–11

• *Tiber Walk* pp274–5

KEY

	Street-by-Street map
—	City Wall
P	Parking

GETTING THERE
Nearly all the bus routes that serve this area go along the broad, central Viale di Trastevere. The 75 and 170 are convenient if you are coming from Termini Station or Piazza Venezia. From the Via Veneto area, take the 56 or 60, both of which have their terminus *(capolinea)* in Piazza Sonnino. From the Vatican, it is best to take a 23 or 280 along Lungotevere.

A typical *vicolo* (narrow alleyway) between the densely packed buildings of Trastevere

Street by Street: Trastevere

ALL YEAR ROUND TRASTEVERE is a major attraction both for its restaurants, clubs and movie theaters, and for its picturesque maze of narrow cobbled alleyways. On summer evenings the streets are packed with crowds of pleasure seekers, especially during the noisy local festival, the Festa de Noantri *(see p59).* Everywhere café and restaurant tables spill out over pavements, especially around Piazza di Santa Maria in Trastevere and outside the pizzerias along Viale di Trastevere. There are also kiosks selling slices of watermelon and *grattachecca*, a mixture of syrup and grated ice. It is usually easier to appreciate the antique charm of Trastevere's historic streets in the more tranquil atmosphere of the early morning.

Casa della Fornarina
Raphael's beautiful mistress is said to have lived here. There is now a flourishing restaurant in the back garden ❶

Santa Maria dei Sette Dolori
This church (1643) is a minor work by Borromini ❹

Santa Maria della Scala
The church's unassuming facade conceals a rich Baroque interior ❸

Sant'Egidio and Museo del Folklore
This 17th-century fresco of Sant' Egidio by Pomarancio decorates the left chapel in the church. The convent next door is a museum of Roman life and customs ❺

★ **Santa Maria in Trastevere**
The church is famous for its 12th-century mosaics by Pietro Cavallini. This detail is from a mosaic of the prophet Isaiah to the left of the apse ❻

The fountain of Piazza di Santa Maria in Trastevere by Carlo Fontana (1692) is a popular meeting place. At night it is floodlit, and dozens of young people sit on the steps around its octagonal base.

STAR SIGHT

★ **Santa Maria in Trastevere**

KEY

— — — Suggested route

0 meters   75

0 yards   75

Ponte Sisto
This bridge was built on the orders of Sixtus IV in 1474 to link Trastevere to central Rome ❷

LOCATOR MAP
See Central Rome Map pp12–13

Piazza Belli is named after Giuseppe Gioacchino Belli (1791–1863), who wrote satirical sonnets in Roman dialect rather than academic Italian. At the center of the piazza stands a statue of the poet (1913).

Vicolo del Piede is one of the picturesque narrow streets lined with restaurant tables leading off Piazza di Santa Maria in Trastevere.

The Torre degli Anguillara (13th century) is the only survivor of the many medieval towers that once dominated the Trastevere skyline. The building is home to a society devoted to the study of Dante.

San Crisogono
The Romanesque bell tower dates from the early 12th century. The plain portico is a later addition (1626) but is in keeping with the spirit of this ancient church ❼

Restaurant at the rear of La Fornarina's house

Casa della Fornarina ❶

Via di Santa Dorotea 20. **Map** 4 D5 & 11 B5. 🛈 *581 82 84*. 🚌 *23, 65, 280.* See **Restaurants** *p316.*

NOTHING IS REALLY known about Raphael's model and lover, La Fornarina, yet over the centuries she has acquired a name and even a brief biography. She was called Margherita, her father was a Sienese baker (*La Fornarina* means "the baker's girl") and his shop was here in Trastevere conveniently near Raphael's frescoes in the Villa Farnesina (*see pp220–21*). Behind the house there is now a successful restaurant, Da Romolo.

Margherita's longstanding liaison with Raphael earned her a reputation as a "fallen woman." Worse, Raphael, wishing to be absolved before dying, turned her away from his deathbed. Four months after his death she supposedly took refuge in the convent of Santa Apollonia in Trastevere.

She is generally assumed to have been the model for Raphael's famous portrait of *La Donna Velata* (Woman with a Veil) in the Palazzo Pitti in Florence.

Ponte Sisto ❷

Map 4 E5 & 11 B5. 🚌 *23, 65, 280.*

NAMED AFTER Pope Sixtus IV della Rovere (reigned 1471–84), who commissioned it, this bridge was built by his architect, Baccio Pontelli, to replace an ancient Roman

bridge. Pope Sixtus IV also built the Sistine Chapel (*see pp244–7*) and the Hospital of Santo Spirito (*see p226*), as well as restoring many churches and monuments. His enterprising spirit had to contend with great financial difficulties: his predecessor's collection of precious gems and his own silver plate had to be sold or mortgaged in order to finance his projects.

Pope Sixtus IV probably raised the money he needed to build the bridge by levying a tax on the city's prostitutes. Several popes are known to have used this very unpopular form of taxation.

Pope Sixtus IV

Santa Maria della Scala ❸

Via della Scala. **Map** 4 D5 & 11 B5. 🛈 *58 06 23 30*. 🚌 *23, 65, 280.* **Open** 6:30am–noon & 4–7pm (Oct–Mar: 6:15pm) Mon–Sat, 6:45am–12:15pm Sun and public hols. 🕇

Santa Maria della Scala's altar

THIS CHURCH belongs to a time of great building activity that lasted about 30 years, from the end of the 16th to the early 17th century. Its simple facade contrasts with a rich interior decorated with multicolored marbles and a number of spirited Baroque altars and reliefs.

Santa Maria dei Sette Dolori ❹

Via Garibaldi 27. **Map** 7 B1. 🛈 *589 73 27*. 🚌 *23, 65, 280.* **Closed** to the public.

BORROMINI DESIGNED this church, begun in the early 1640s; and, like many of his projects, it was left incomplete. The rough brick facade and convex and concave surfaces are typical of his work. Rounded corners and the impressive columns accentuate the church's small proportions.

Sant'Egidio and Museo del Folklore ❺

Piazza Sant'Egidio 1. **Map** 7 C1. 🚌 *23, 56, 60, 65, 280.* **Museo del Folklore** 🛈 *581 37 17.* **Open** 9am–6:30pm Tue–Sat, 9am–1:30pm Sun (last adm: 30 mins before closing). **Adm charge. Church open** for services only. 🕇 *8:30pm daily.*

BUILT IN 1630, Sant'Egidio was the church of the adjoining Carmelite convent, one of many founded in the area to shelter the poor and destitute. The convent is now a folklore museum, containing a wealth of material relating to the festivals, pastimes, superstitions and customs of the Romans when they lived under papal rule. There are old paintings and prints of the city and tableaux showing scenes of everyday life in 18th- and 19th-century Rome, including reconstructions of shops and a tavern. The museum also has manuscripts by the much-loved local dialect poets Belli and Trilussa.

Watercolor of public scribe (1880) in the Museo del Folklore

Santa Maria in Trastevere ❻

See pp212–13.

San Crisogono ❼

Piazza Sonnino 44. **Map** 7 C1. 📞 *581 82 25.* 🚌 *56, 60, 75, 170, 710.* **Open** *7–11am & 4–7pm Mon–Sat, 8am–1pm Sun.* **Adm charge** *for excavations.* 🚻 📷 ♿

T HIS CHURCH was built on the site of one of the city's oldest *tituli* (private houses used for Christian worship). An 8th-century church with 11th-century frescoes can still be seen beneath the present church. This dates from the early 12th century, a period of intense building activity in the popular quarters of Rome. San Crisogono was decorated by Pietro Cavallini – the apse mosaic by his school remains.

Most of the columns were taken from previous buildings, including the great porphyry ones of the triumphal arch. The mosaic floor is the result of recycling precious marble from various Roman ruins.

Apse mosaic in San Crisogono

Santa Cecilia in Trastevere ❽

Piazza di Santa Cecilia. **Map** 8 D1. 📞 *589 92 89.* 🚌 *56, 60, 75, 710.* **Open** *10am–noon & 4–6pm daily.* **Adm charge** *for excavations.* **Cavallini fresco** *can be seen 10–11:30am Tue and Thu (donation expected).*

S T. CECILIA, ARISTOCRAT and patron saint of music, was martyred here in AD 230. After an unsuccessful attempt

at scalding her to death, her executioner beheaded her. A church was founded – perhaps in the 4th century – on the site of the saint's house (still to be seen beneath the church, with the remains of a Roman tannery). For a long time her body was missing, but it turned up in the Catacombs of San Callisto *(see p265)*. In the 9th century it was reburied here by Pope Paschal I, who rebuilt the church. A fine apse mosaic survives from this period.

The altar canopy by Arnolfo di Cambio and the fresco of *The Last Judgment* by Pietro Cavallini, reached through the adjoining convent, date from the 13th century, one of the few periods when Rome had a distinctive artistic style of its own. In front of the altar is a statue of St. Cecilia by Stefano Maderno, who used her miraculously preserved remains as a model when she was briefly disinterred in 1599.

San Francesco a Ripa ❾

Piazza San Francesco d'Assisi 88. **Map** 7 C2. 📞 *581 90 20.* 🚌 *44, 75, 170, 710.* **Open** *7–11:30am & 4–7pm daily.* 🚻 📷 ♿

S T. FRANCIS OF ASSISI lived here in a hospice when he visited Rome in 1219, and his stone pillow and crucifix are preserved in his cell. The church was rebuilt by his follower, the nobleman Rodolfo Anguillara, who is portrayed on his tombstone wearing the Franciscan habit.

Entirely rebuilt in the 1680s by Cardinal Pallavicini, the church is rich in sculpture. Particularly flamboyant are the 18th-century Rospigliosi and Pallavicini monuments in the transept chapel. Not to be missed in the Altieri chapel (fourth on the left, along the nave) is Bernini's breathtaking sculpture, *Ecstasy of Beata Ludovica Albertoni.*

Detail of 13th-century fresco by Pietro Cavallini in Santa Cecilia

Villa Sciarra ❿

Via Calandrelli 35. **Map** 7 B2. 🚌 *44, 75, 710.* **Park open** *9am–sunset daily.* **House closed** *for restoration.* ♿

I N ROMAN TIMES the site of this attractive, small public park was a nymph's sanctuary. It is especially picturesque in spring, when its cherry trees and wisterias are in full bloom. The paths through the park are decorated with Romantic follies, fountains and statues, and there are splendid views of the city over the Janiculum bastions.

Bernini's *Ecstasy of Beata Ludovica Albertoni* (1674) in San Francesco a Ripa

Santa Maria in Trastevere ❻

PROBABLY THE FIRST official Christian place of worship to be built in Rome, this basilica became the focus of devotion to the Virgin Mary. According to legend, the church was founded by Pope Callixtus I in the 3rd century, when Christianity was still a minority cult. Today's church is largely a 12th-century building, remarkable for its mosaics, in particular those by Pietro Cavallini. The 22 granite columns in the nave were taken from the ruins of ancient Roman buildings. Despite some 18th-century Baroque additions, Santa Maria has retained its medieval character. This friendly church has strong links with the local community.

Piazza Santa Maria in Trastevere
The piazza in front of the church is the traditional heart of Trastevere. Today it is surrounded by lively bars and restaurants. Carlo Fontana built the octagonal fountain in the late 17th century.

The floor, relaid in the 1870s, is a re-creation of the Cosmatesque mosaic floor of the 13th century.

The bell tower was built in the 12th century. At the top is a small mosaic of the Virgin.

★ Facade Mosaics
The 12th-century mosaic shows Mary feeding the baby Jesus and ten women holding lamps. Eight of the lamps are lit, symbolizing virginity; the veiled women whose lamps have gone out are probably widows.

STAR FEATURES

★ **Cavallini Mosaics**

★ **Facade Mosaics**

MODEST DONORS
Many of Rome's mosaics include a portrait of the pope or cardinal responsible for the building of the church. Often the portrait is dwarfed by the rest of the picture, which glorifies the saint to whom the church is dedicated. On the facade of Santa Maria, two tiny unidentified figures kneel at the Virgin's feet. Were they to stand up, the men would barely reach her knees.

Facade mosaic, detail

The portico was remodeled in 1702 by Carlo Fontana. Statues of four popes decorate the balustrade above.

Front entrance

15th-century wall tabernacle by Mino del Reame

Apse Mosaic
The 12th-century mosaic in the basin of the apse shows the Coronation of the Virgin. She sits on Christ's right hand, surrounded by saints.

VISITORS' CHECKLIST

Piazza Santa Maria in Trastevere.
Map 7 C1. *581 94 43.*
44, 56, 60, 75, 97, 170, 280, 710, 718, 719, 774, 780 to Viale di Trastevere (Piazza Sidney Sonnino); 23, 65 to Lungotevere Raffaello Sanzio. **Open** 7:30am– 1pm & 4–7pm daily. *6pm daily.*

★Cavallini Mosaics
The details in the six mosaics of the Life of the Virgin (1291) display a touching realism.

Madonna della Clemenza
The life-size icon probably dates from the 7th century. A replica is displayed above the altar of the Cappella Altemps.

Tomb of Cardinal Pietro Stefaneschi
The last of his line, Pietro Stefaneschi died in 1417. His tomb is by an otherwise unknown sculptor called Paolo.

TIMELINE

AD 217–22
Church founded by Pope Callixtus I

Pope Innocent II

1291 Pietro Cavallini adds mosaics of scenes from the life of the Virgin for his patron, Bertoldo Stefaneschi

1617 Domenichino designs coffered ceiling with octagonal panel of the Assumption of the Virgin

30 BC	AD 200	1150	1400	1650	1900

38 BC Jet of mineral oil spouts from the ground on this site. Later interpreted as a portent of the coming of Christ

c1138 Pope Innocent II starts rebuilding the church

1580 Martino Longhi the Elder restores church and builds family chapel for Cardinal Marco Sittico Altemps

1702 Pope Clement XI has portico rebuilt

1866–77 Church restored by Virginio Vespignani

JANICULUM

OVERLOOKING THE TIBER
on the Trastevere
side of the river, the
Janiculum Hill has often
played its part in the
defense of the city. The
last occasion was in
1849, when Garibaldi
held off attacking French
troops. The park at the top
of the hill is filled with
monuments to Garibaldi
and his men. A popular
place for walks, the park

**Puppets in the park at the
top of the Janiculum Hill**

provides a welcome escape from the
densely packed streets of Trastevere.

Visitors will often find puppet
shows and other entertainment
and activities for children.
In medieval times, most of
the hill was occupied by
monasteries and con-
vents. Bramante built his
miniature masterpiece, the
Tempietto, in the convent of
San Pietro in Montorio. The
Renaissance also saw the
development of the river-
side area along Via della
Lungara, where the rich
and powerful built large beautiful
houses such as the Villa Farnesina.

SIGHTS AT A GLANCE

Churches and Temples
Sant'Onofrio ❻
San Pietro in Montorio ❼
Tempietto ❽

Museums and Galleries
Palazzo Corsini and Galleria
Nazionale d'Arte Antica ❷

Historic Buildings
Villa Farnesina
pp220–21 ❶

Fountains
Fontana Paola ❾

Monuments
Garibaldi Monument ❺

Arches and Gates
Porta Settimiana ❸

Parks and Gardens
Botanical Gardens ❹

SEE ALSO

GETTING THERE

The Janiculum (Il Gianicolo) is
not the easiest part of Rome to
reach by public transportation.
It can be approached either
from the Vatican area *(see
p223)* or from Trastevere *(see
p207)*. There is only one bus,
the 41, that goes up to the top
of the hill, but the 44, 75 or
710 will take you from Piazza
Venezia to a convenient point
to start your walk. For sights
along Via della Lungara, take
the 23, 65 or 280, which go
along Lungotevere.

KEY

▨ Tour of the Janiculum map

— City Wall

0 meters   300
0 yards   300

The staircase fountain in the Botanical Gardens

A Tour of the Janiculum

THE LONG HIKE to the top of the Janiculum is rewarded by wonderful views over the city. The park's monuments include a lighthouse and statues of Garibaldi and his wife, Anita. There is also a cannon that is fired at noon each day. In Via della Lungara, between the Janiculum and the Tiber, stand Palazzo Corsini, with its national art collection, and the Villa Farnesina, decorated by Raphael for his friend and patron, the fabulously wealthy banker Agostino Chigi.

The Manfredi Lighthouse, built in 1911, was a gift to the city of Rome from Italians in Argentina.

The Monument to Anita Garibaldi by Mario Rutelli was erected in 1932. The great patriot's Brazilian wife lies buried beneath the statue.

Tasso's Oak is a memorial to the poet Torquato Tasso, who liked to sit here in the days before he died in 1595. The tree was struck by lightning in 1843.

The view from Villa Lante, a beautiful Renaissance summer residence, gives a magnificent panorama of the whole city.

Garibaldi Monument
The inscription on the base of the equestrian statue means "Rome or Death" ⑤

ROMA O MORTE

Botanical Gardens
*These were established in
1883 when part of the
grounds of Palazzo
Corsini was given
to the University
of Rome* ❹

★ Palazzo Corsini
*This 15th-century triptych by
Fra Angelico hangs in the
Galleria Nazionale
d'Arte Antica* ❷

LOCATOR MAP
See Central Rome Map pp12–13

★ Villa Farnesina
*The suburban villa of the
banker Agostino Chigi is
celebrated for its frescoes
by Raphael, Baldassarre
Peruzzi and other
Renaissance masters* ❶

Porta Settimiana
*Looking through this
Renaissance gateway from
Via della Lungara, you catch
a glimpse of Trastevere's
warren of narrow streets* ❸

KEY

– – – Suggested route

0 meters   75

0 yards   75

STAR SIGHTS

★ Villa Farnesina

★ Palazzo Corsini and
   Galleria Nazionale
   d'Arte Antica

Villa Farnesina ❶

See pp220–21.

Palazzo Corsini and Galleria Nazionale d'Arte Antica ❷

Via della Lungara 10. **Map** 4 D5 & 11 A5. **☎** 68 80 23 23. **🚌** 23, 41, 65, 280. **Open** 9am–7pm Tue–Fri, 9am–2pm Sat, 9am–1pm Sun & public hols (last adm: 30 mins before closing). **Closed** Jan 1, Aug 15 and Dec 25. **Adm charge.** **Ø** **♿** **📷**

Queen Christina's bedroom in the Palazzo Corsini

THE HISTORY of Palazzo Corsini is intimately entwined with that of Rome. Built for Cardinal Domenico Riario in the late 15th century, it has boasted among its many distinguished guests Bramante, the young Michelangelo, Erasmus and Queen Christina of Sweden, who died here in 1689. The old palazzo was completely rebuilt for Cardinal Neri Corsini by Ferdinando Fuga in 1736. As Via della Lungara is too narrow to allow a good frontal view, Fuga designed the facade so it could be viewed from an angle.

Palazzo Corsini now houses the Galleria Nazionale d'Arte Antica. This outstanding collection includes paintings by Rubens, Van Dyck, Murillo, Caravaggio and Guido Reni, as well as 17th- and 18th-century Italian regional art. The palazzo is also home to the Accademia dei Lincei, a learned society founded in

1603, which once included Galileo among its members.

In 1797 Palazzo Corsini was the backdrop to momentous events: French General Duphot (the fiancé of Napoleon's sister Pauline) was killed here in a skirmish between papal troops and Republicans. The consequent French occupation of the city and the deportation of Pope Pius VI led to the proclamation of a short-lived Roman Republic (1798–9).

Porta Settimiana ❸

Between Via della Scala and Via della Lungara. **Map** 4 D5 & 11 B5. **🚌** 23, 65, 280.

THIS GATE was built in 1498 by Pope Alexander VI Borgia to replace a minor passageway in the Aurelian Wall. The Porta Settimiana marks the start of Via della Lungara, a long straight road built in the early 16th century.

Botanical Gardens ❹

Largo Cristina di Svezia 24, off Via Corsini. **Map** 4 D5. **☎** 686 41 93. **🚌** 23, 65, 280. **Open** 9am–6:30pm (Oct–Mar: 5:30pm) Mon–Sat. **Closed** Sun, public hols.

SEQUOIAS, PALM TREES and splendid collections of orchids and bromeliads are housed in Rome's Botanical Gardens (Orto Botanico). The gardens contain more than 7,000 plant species from all over the world. Indigenous and exotic species are grouped

to illustrate their botanical families and their adaptation to different climates and ecosystems. There are also several interesting examples of such plants as the gingko that have survived virtually unchanged from earlier eras. The gardens were originally part of the Palazzo Corsini but since 1883 have belonged to the University of Rome.

Garibaldi Monument ❺

Piazzale Giuseppe Garibaldi. **Map** 3 C5. **🚌** 41, 44, 75, 710.

Base of the Garibaldi Monument

THIS HUGE equestrian statue is part of a park that commemorates the heroic events witnessed on the Janiculum when the French army attacked the city in 1849. Garibaldi's Republicans fended off the greatly superior French forces for weeks, until the Italians were overwhelmed. Garibaldi and his men escaped. The monument, erected in 1895, was the work of Emilio Gallori. Around the pedestal are four smaller sculptures in bronze showing battle scenes and allegorical figures.

Steps and tiered fountains at the Botanical Gardens

Courtyard of Sant'Onofrio

Sant'Onofrio 6

Piazza di Sant'Onofrio 2. **Map** 3 C4.
(*686 44 98.* **▦** *41.* **Open** *10am–
1.30pm Sun for mass; otherwise adm
by appt only.* **Closed** *Aug, except
saint's feast day on Aug 12.* 📷 ✝
Museum open *by appt only.*

B EATO NICOLA da Forca
Palena, whose tombstone
guards the entrance, founded
this church in 1419 in honor
of the hermit Sant'Onofrio. It
retains the flavor of the 15th
century in the simple shapes
of the portico and the cloister.
In the early 17th century the
portico was decorated with
frescoes by Domenichino.

The monastery next to the
church houses a small museum
dedicated to the 16th-century
poet Torquato Tasso, who
died here in one of the cells.

San Pietro in Montorio 7

Piazza San Pietro in Montorio 2.
Map 7 B1. **(** *581 39 40.* **▦** *41,
44, 75, 710.* **Open** *9am–noon &
4–6:30pm daily. If closed, ring bell at
door to right of church.* 📷 ✝

S AN PIETRO IN MONTORIO – the
church of St. Peter on the
Golden Hill – was founded in
the Middle Ages near the spot
where St. Peter was presumed
to have been crucified. It was
rebuilt by order of Ferdinand
and Isabella of Spain at the
end of the 15th century and
decorated by outstanding
artists of the Renaissance.

The facade is typical of a
time when clean, geometric
shapes derived from Classical
architecture were in vogue.
The single nave ends in a
deep apse that once contained

Raphael's *Transfiguration*,
now in the Vatican. Two wide
chapels, one on either side of
the nave, were decorated by
some of Michelangelo's most
famous pupils. The left chapel
was designed by one of the
few artists Michelangelo
admired, Daniele da Volterra,
who was also responsible for
the altar painting, *Baptism of
Christ*. The chapel on the
right was the work of Giorgio
Vasari, who included a self-
portrait (in black, on the left)
in his biblical altar painting,
Conversion of St. Paul.

The first chapel to the right
of the entrance contains the
powerful *Flagellation*, by
Venetian artist Sebastiano del
Piombo (1518); Michelangelo
is said to have provided the
original drawings. Work by
Bernini and his followers can
be seen in the second chapel
on the left and in the flanking
De Raymondi tombs.

Tempietto 8

Via Garibaldi 33 (in courtyard of San
Pietro in Montorio). **Map** 7 B1.
(*581 39 40.* **▦** *41, 44, 75, 710.*
Open *9am–noon & 4–6:30pm daily.*
See **The History of Rome** *pp30–31.*

I N 1502 BRAMANTE completed
what many consider to be
the first true Renaissance
building in Rome – the
Tempietto. The name means
simply "little temple." Its
circular shape echoes that of
an early Christian
martyrium, a
chapel built on the
site of a saint's
martyrdom. This
was believed to be
the place where St.
Peter was crucified.

Bramante chose
the Doric order for
the 16 columns
surrounding the
domed chapel.
Above the columns
is a Classical frieze
and a delicate
balustrade. Though
the scale of the
Tempietto is tiny,
Bramante's masterly
use of Classical
proportions creates
a satisfyingly

harmonious whole. The
Tempietto illustrates the great
Renaissance dream that Rome
would relive its ancient glory.

Fontana Paola 9

Via Garibaldi. **Map** 7 B1. **▦** *41, 44,
75, 710.*

Fontana Paola, built for Pope Paul V

T HIS MONUMENTAL FOUNTAIN
commemorates the
reopening in 1612 of an
aqueduct originally built by
Emperor Trajan in AD 109.
The aqueduct was renamed
the Acqua Paola after Paul V,
the Borghese pope who
ordered its restoration. When
it was first built, the fountain
had five small basins, but in
1690 Carlo Fontana altered the
design, adding the huge basin
you can see today. Despite
many laws intended to deter
them, generations of Romans
used this convenient pool of
fresh water for bathing and
washing their vegetables.

Bramante's round chapel, the Tempietto

Villa Farnesina **❶**

THE WEALTHY SIENESE BANKER Agostino Chigi, who had established the headquarters of his far-flung financial empire in Rome, commissioned the villa in 1508 from his compatriot Baldassarre Peruzzi. The simple, harmonious design, with a central block and projecting wings, made this one of the earliest true Renaissance villas. The decoration was carried out between 1510 and 1519, and this has recently been restored. Peruzzi frescoed some of the interiors himself. Later, Sebastiano del Piombo, Raphael and his pupils added more elaborate works. The frescoes illustrate Classical myths, and the vault of the main hall, the Sala di Galatea, is adorned with scenes showing the position of the stars at the time of Chigi's birth. Artists, poets, princes, cardinals and the pope himself were entertained here in style by their wealthy host. In 1577 the villa was bought by Cardinal Alessandro Farnese. Since then, it has been known as the Villa Farnesina.

North Facade
The Loggia of Cupid and Psyche looks out on formal gardens that were used for parties and putting on plays.

Entrance

The Wedding of Alexander and Roxanne by Sodoma
Cherubs are shown helping the bride Roxanne prepare for her marriage.

★ Triumph of Galatea by Raphael
The beautiful sea nymph Galatea was one of the 50 daughters of the god Nereus.

The Gabinetto delle Stampe sometimes holds exhibitions of rare prints.

Frescoes in the Room of Galatea
Perseus beheads Medusa in a scene from one of Peruzzi's series of mythological frescoes.

THE ARCHITECT

Baldassarre Peruzzi, painter and architect, arrived in Rome from Siena in 1503, at age 20, becoming Bramante's chief assistant. His architectural designs were typical of Classicism, but his painting owes more to Gothic influences – his figurework is highly stylized. On Raphael's death, he became Head of Works at St. Peter's but was captured in the Sack of Rome *(see p31)*, exiled to Siena until 1535 and died in 1536.

Baldassarre Peruzzi

★ Salone delle Prospettive
Peruzzi's frescoes create the illusion of looking out at views of 16th-century Rome through a marble colonnade.

VISITORS' CHECKLIST

Via della Lungara 230.
Map 4 D5 & 11 A5. 23, 65, 280 to Lungotevere Farnesina.
68 80 17 67. **Open** 9am–1pm Mon–Sat.
Gabinetto delle Stampe *(rare print collection)* 66 98 02 30.
Open 9am–1pm Tue–Sat for occasional exhibitions.

Fresco from the Salone delle Prospettive
This scene shows the Torre delle Milizie (see p90) as it looked in the 1500s.

★ Loggia of Cupid and Psyche
The model for the figure on the left in Raphael's painting of The Three Graces *was Agostino Chigi's mistress, the courtesan Imperia.*

Lunette in the Room of Galatea
Once thought to be by Michelangelo, this giant monochrome head is the work of Peruzzi.

STAR FEATURES

★ **Triumph of Galatea by Raphael**

★ **Loggia of Cupid and Psyche**

★ **Salone delle Prospettive**

VATICAN

A S THE SITE where St. Peter was martyred and buried, the Vatican became the residence of the popes who succeeded him. Decisions reached here have shaped the destiny of Europe, and the great basilica of St. Peter's draws pilgrims from all over the Christian world. The papal palaces beside St. Peter's house the Vatican Museums. With the added attractions of Michelangelo's Sistine Chapel and the Raphael Rooms, their wonderful

Nuns in St. Peter's Square

collections of Classical sculpture make them the finest museums in Rome. The Vatican's position as a state within a state was guaranteed by the Lateran Treaty of 1929, marked by the building of a new road, the Via della Conciliazione. This leads from St. Peter's to Castel Sant' Angelo, a monument to a far grimmer past. Built originally as the Emperor Hadrian's mausoleum, this papal fortress and prison has witnessed many fierce battles for control of the city.

SIGHTS AT A GLANCE

Churches and Temples
St. Peter's pp230–3 ❶
Santo Spirito in Sassia ❹
Santa Maria in Traspontina ❾

Museums and Galleries
Vatican Museums pp234–47 ❷

Historic Buildings
Hospital of Santo Spirito ❺
Palazzo del Commendatore ❻
Palazzo dei Convertendi ❼
Palazzo dei Penitenzieri ❽

Palazzo Torlonia ⓬
Castel Sant'Angelo pp248–9 ⓭
Palazzo di Giustizia ⓮

Gates
Porta Santo Spirito ❸

Historic Streets and Piazzas
The Borgo ❿
Vatican Corridor ⓫

GETTING THERE
The quickest way to reach the area is by Metro line A to Ottaviano. This is especially convenient when visiting the Vatican Museums. The 64 bus runs regularly from Piazza dei Cinquecento in front of Termini Station. Other buses that serve the area include the 23, 81 and 492, which stop in Piazza del Risorgimento. There is a regular shuttle bus between St. Peter's and the Vatican Museums.

| 0 meters | 400 |
| 0 yards | 400 |

KEY
▨ Tour of the Vatican map
— City Wall
Ⓟ Parking

SEE ALSO

Dome of St. Peter's dominating the Vatican skyline

A Tour of the Vatican

THE VATICAN, a center of power for Catholics all over the world and a sovereign state since February 1929, is ruled by the Pope. About 1,000 people live here, staffing the Vatican's facilities. There are shops and a post office; Radio Vatican, broadcasting to the world in over 20 languages; a daily newspaper (*l'Osservatore Romano*), Vatican offices; and a publishing house.

The Madonna of Guadalupe shows the miraculous image of the Madonna that appeared on the cloak of a Mexican Indian in 1531.

Papal heliport

The Grotto of Lourdes is a replica of the grotto in the southwest of France, where in 1858 the Virgin appeared to St. Bernadette.

The Vatican Railway Station, opened in 1930, connects with the line from Rome to Viterbo but is now used only for freight.

Radio Vatican is broadcast from this tower, part of the Leonine Wall built in 847.

The Papal Audience Chamber, by Pier Luigi Nervi, was opened in 1971. It seats up to 12,000.

The information office gives details of tours of the Vatican Gardens.

★ **St. Peter's**
The Chapel of St. Peter is in the grottoes under the basilica. The rich marble decoration was added by Clement VIII at the end of the 16th century ❶

Piazza San Pietro was laid out by Bernini between 1656 and 1667. The narrow space in front of the church opens out into an enormous ellipse flanked by colonnades.

The obelisk was erected here in 1586 with the help of 150 horses and 47 winches.

STAR SIGHTS
★ St. Peter's
★ Vatican Museums

The Eagle Fountain was built to celebrate the arrival of water from the Acqua Paola aqueduct at the Vatican. The eagle is the Borghese crest.

LOCATOR MAP
See Central Rome Map pp12–13

The Casina of Pius IV is a delightful summerhouse in the Vatican Gardens built by Pirro Ligorio in the mid-16th century.

Entrance to Vatican Museums

★**Vatican Museums**
Raphael's Madonna of Foligno *(1513) is just one of the Vatican's many Renaissance masterpieces* ❷

The Galleon Fountain is a perfect scale model of a 17th-century ship in lead, brass and copper. It was made by a Flemish artist for Pope Paul V.

The Cortile della Pigna is mostly the work of Bramante. The niche for the pine cone, once a Roman fountain, was added by Pirro Ligorio in 1562.

KEY

— — — Suggested route

0 meters   75

0 yards   75

To Via della Conciliazione

St. Peter's ❶

See pp230–33.

Vatican Museums ❷

See pp234–47.

Porta Santo Spirito ❸

Via dei Penitenzieri. **Map** 3 C3.
🚌 23, 34, 49, 64, 81, 492.

THIS GATE stands at what was the southern limit of the "Leonine City," the area enclosed within walls by Pope Leo IV as a defense against the Saracens who had sacked Rome in AD 845. The walls measure 2 miles (3 km) in circumference.

Work on the walls started in 846. Pope Leo supervised the huge army of laborers personally, and thanks to his encouragement, the job was completed in four years. He then led a solemn procession to consecrate his massive feat of construction.

Since the time of Pope Leo, the walls have needed much reinforcement and repair. The gateway visible today at Porta Santo Spirito was built by the architect Antonio da Sangallo the Younger in 1543–4. It is framed by two huge bastions that were added in 1564 by

Pope Pius IV Medici. Sadly, Sangallo's design for a monumental entrance to the Vatican was never completed; the principal columns come to an end somewhat abruptly in a modern covering of cement.

Santo Spirito in Sassia ❹

Borgo Santo Spirito 4. **Map** 3 C3.
📞 687 93 10. 🚌 23, 34, 41, 46, 64.
Open *7am–12:30pm & 4–8pm daily.*
🚻 📷 ♿

Nave of Santo Spirito in Sassia

BUILT ON THE SITE of a church erected by King Ine of Wessex, who died in Rome in the 8th century, the church is the work of Antonio da Sangallo the Younger. It was rebuilt (1538–44) after the

Sack of Rome had left it in ruins in 1527. The facade was added under Pope Sixtus V (1585–90). The nave and side chapels are decorated with a series of light, lively frescoes. The pretty bell tower is earlier, dating from the reign of Sixtus IV (1471–84). It was probably the work of the pope's architect Baccio Pontelli, who also built the nearby Hospital of Santo Spirito, and the Ponte Sisto *(see p210)* farther down the River Tiber.

Sixtus V's arms over door of Santo Spirito

Hospital of Santo Spirito ❺

Borgo Santo Spirito 2. **Map** 3 C3.
🚌 23, 34, 41, 46, 64. **Octagonal chapel open** *8:30am–2pm daily.*

THE HOSPITAL is said to have been founded as a result of a nightmare experienced by Pope Innocent III (reigned 1198–1216). In the dream, an angel showed him the bodies of Rome's unwanted babies dredged up from the Tiber in fishing nets. The pope hastened to build a hospice for sick paupers.

In 1475 the hospital was reorganized by Pope Sixtus IV

Fresco of an angel in the octagonal chapel of the Hospital of Santo Spirito

to care for the influx of poor pilgrims expected for the Holy Year. For its day, Sixtus's hospital was a revolutionary building. Cloisters separated the different categories of patient. One is still reserved for orphans and their nurses.

Unwanted infants were passed through a revolving barrel-like contraption known as the *rota*, still visible to the left of the central entrance on Borgo Santo Spirito. This was to guarantee anonymity. Martin Luther, who came here in 1511, was scandalized by the number of abandoned children he saw, believing them to be "the sons of the pope himself."

In the center, under the hospital's conspicuous drum, is an octagonal chapel, where mass was said for patients. This room can be visited; the rest of the building still functions as a hospital.

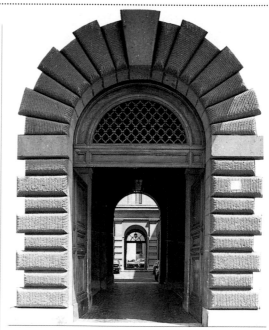

Rusticated doorway of the Palazzo dei Convertendi

The *rota* of Santo Spirito, where mothers left unwanted babies

Palazzo del Commendatore **6**

Borgo Santo Spirito 3. **Map** 3 C3.
🚌 *23, 34, 41, 46, 64.* **Courtyard only open** to the public.

As director of the Hospital of Santo Spirito, the Commendatore not only ran the hospital, he was also responsible for its estates and revenues. This important post was originally given to members of the pope's family.

The palazzo, built next door to the hospital, has a spacious 16th-century frescoed loggia appropriate to the dignity and sobriety of its owners. The frescoes represent the story of the founding of the Hospital of Santo Spirito. To the left of the entrance is the Spezieria, or Pharmacy. This still has the wheel used for grinding the bark of the cinchona tree to produce the drug quinine, first introduced here in 1632 by Jesuits from Peru as a cure for malaria.

Above the courtyard is a splendid clock (1827). The dial is divided into six; it was not until 1846 that the familiar division of the day into two periods of 12 hours was introduced in Rome by Pope Pius IX.

Della Rovere arms

Palazzo dei Convertendi **7**

Via della Conciliazione 43.
Map 3 C3. 🚌 *23, 34, 41, 46, 64.*
Not open to the public.

With the building of Via della Conciliazione in the 1930s, Palazzo dei Convertendi was taken down and later moved to this new site nearby. The house, which is partly attributed to the architect Bramante, is where the artist Raphael died in 1520.

Palazzo dei Penitenzieri **8**

Via della Conciliazione 33. **Map** 3 C3.
📞 *686 54 35.* 🚌 *23, 34, 41, 46, 64.* See **Where to Stay** p295.

The palazzo owes its name to the fact that the place was once home to the confessors (*penitenzieri*) of St. Peter's. Their place has now been taken by tourists, as the building has been converted into the Hotel Columbus.

Originally built by Cardinal Domenico della Rovere in 1480, the palazzo still bears the family's coat of arms, the oak tree (*rovere* means oak), on its graceful courtyard wellhead. On the cardinal's death, the palazzo was acquired by Pope Julius II della Rovere's favorite, Cardinal Francesco Alidosi. Suspected of treason, the cardinal was murdered in 1511 by the pope's nephew, the duke of Urbino, who also took possession of his palazzo. A few of the rooms still contain beautiful frescoes.

View of the Tiber and the Borgo between Castel Sant'Angelo and St. Peter's by Gaspare Vanvitelli (1653–1736)

Santa Maria in Traspontina ❾

Via della Conciliazione 14.
Map 3 C3. 🕿 68 30 00 63.
🚌 23, 34, 41, 46, 64. **Open**
6:30am–noon & 4pm–7:30pm
daily. 🚻 📷 ♿

The facade of the Carmelite church of Santa Maria in Traspontina

THE CHURCH occupies the site of an ancient Roman pyramid, believed in the Middle Ages to have been the Tomb of Romulus. The pyramid was destroyed by Pope Alexander VI Borgia, but representations of it survive on the bronze doors at the entrance to St. Peter's and in a Giotto triptych in the Vatican Pinacoteca *(see p240)*.

The present church was begun in 1566 to replace an earlier one that had been in the line of fire of the cannons defending Castel Sant'Angelo during the Sack of Rome in 1527. The papal artillery officers insisted that the dome of the new church should be as low as possible, so it was built without a supporting drum. The first chapel to the right is dedicated to the gunners' patron saint, Santa Barbara, and is decorated with warlike motifs. In the third chapel on the left are two columns, said to be those to which St. Peter and St. Paul were bound before martyrdom.

The Borgo ❿

Map 3 C3. 🚌 23, 34, 41, 46, 64.

THE WORD BORGO derives from the German *burg*, meaning town. Rome's Borgo is where the first pilgrims to St. Peter's were housed in hostels and hospices, often for quite lengthy periods. The first of these foreign colonies, called "schools," was founded in AD 725 by a Saxon, King Ine of Wessex, who wished to live a life of penance and to be buried near the Tomb of St. Peter. These days hotels and

hostels have made the Borgo a colony of international pilgrims once again. Much of the area's character was destroyed by redevelopment in the 1930s, but it is still enjoyable to explore the old narrow streets on either side of Via della Conciliazione.

Vatican Corridor ⓫

Castel Sant'Angelo to the Vatican.
Map 3 C3. 🚌 23, 34, 41, 46, 64.

Clement VII, who used the Vatican Corridor to evade capture in 1527

LOCALLY KNOWN as the Passetto (small corridor), this long passageway was built into the fortifications during medieval times. Meant to link the Vatican with the fortress of Castel Sant'Angelo, it constituted a fortified escape route that could also be used to control the strategic Borgo area. Arrows and other missiles could be fired from its bastions onto the streets and houses below. The corridor was used in 1494 by Pope Alexander VI Borgia when Rome was invaded by King Charles VIII of France. In 1527 it enabled Pope Clement VII to take refuge in Castel Sant'Angelo as the troops commanded by the Constable of Bourbon began the Sack of Rome.

Palazzo Torlonia ⑫

Via della Conciliazione 30. **Map** 3 C3.
🚌 23, 34, 41, 46, 64. **Not open** to the public.

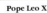
Pope Leo X

THE PALAZZO was built in the late 15th century by the wealthy Cardinal Adriano Castellesi, in a style closely resembling Palazzo della Cancelleria (*see p149*). The cardinal was a much-traveled rogue who collected vast revenues from the bishopric of Bath and Wells, which he was given by his friend King Henry VII of England. In return he gave Henry his palazzo for use as the seat of the English ambassador to the Holy See. Castellesi was finally stripped of his cardinalate by Pope Leo X Medici and disappeared from history.

Since then the palazzo has had many owners and tenants. In the 17th century it was rented for a time by Queen Christina of Sweden. The Torlonia family, who acquired the building in 1820, owed its fortune to the financial genius of shopkeeper-turned-banker Giovanni Torlonia. He lent money to the impoverished Roman nobility and bought up their property during the Napoleonic Wars.

Palazzo Torlonia (1496), unaffected by changes to the surrounding area

Castel Sant'Angelo ⑬

See pp248–9.

Palazzo di Giustizia ⑭

Piazza Cavour. **Map** 4 E3. 🚌 34, 49, 70, 87, 186, 280, 492, 990. **Not open** to the public.

THE MONUMENTAL Palazzo di Giustizia (Palace of Justice) was built between 1889 and 1910 to house the national law courts. Its riverside facade is crowned with a bronze chariot and fronted by giant statues of the great men of Italian law.

The building was supposed to embody the new order replacing the injustices of papal rule, but it has never endeared itself to the Romans. It was soon dubbed the Palazzaccio, roughly the "ugly old palazzo," both for its appearance and for the nature of its business. By the 1970s the building was collapsing under its own weight and may prove impossible to repair.

The ornate travertine facade of the Palazzo di Giustizia

St. Peter's ❶

T HE CENTER of the Roman Catholic faith, St. Peter's draws pilgrims from all over the world. Few are disappointed when they enter the sumptuously decorated basilica beneath Michelangelo's vast dome.

A shrine was erected on the site of St. Peter's tomb in the 2nd century, and the first great basilica, ordered by the Emperor Constantine, was completed around AD 349. By the 15th century it was falling down, so in 1506 Pope Julius II laid the first stone of a new church. It took more than a century to build, and all the great architects of the Roman Renaissance and Baroque had a hand in its design.

★ Dome of St. Peter's
Designed by Michelangelo, though not finished in his lifetime, the spectacular cupola, 435 ft (132.5 m) high, gives unity to the majestic interior of the basilica.

The nave is 690 ft (211.5 m) long.

Papal Altar
The present altar dates from the reign of Clement VIII (1592–1605). The plain slab of marble found in the Forum of Nerva stands under Bernini's baldacchino, over-looking the well of the confessio, the crypt where St. Peter's body is reputedly buried.

Baldacchino
This magnificent canopy of gilded bronze, supported on spiral columns 66 ft (20 m) high, was designed by Bernini in the 17th century.

TIMELINE

AD 60	800	1500	1550	1600
AD 61 Burial of St. Peter		**1506** Julius II lays first stone	**1547** Michelangelo named as chief architect of St. Peter's	**1626** New basilica of St. Peter's consecrated
324 Constantine builds basilica	**1452** Nicholas V plans restoration			**1593** Dome completed
200 Altar built marking grave of St. Peter	**1503** Pope Julius II chooses Bramante as architect for new basilica	**1538** Antonio da Sangallo the Younger made director of works	**1606** Carlo Maderno extends basilica	**1614** Maderno finishes the facade
800 Charlemagne crowned Holy Roman Emperor in St. Peter's		**1514** Raphael director of works	**1564** Death of Michelangelo	

★ View from the Dome
The superb symmetry of Bernini's colonnade can be appreciated from the dome.

VISITORS' CHECKLIST

Piazza San Pietro. **Map** 3 B3.
C 69 88 44 66, 69 88 48 66.
🚌 64 to Piazza San Pietro or 23, 32, 49, 81, 492, 991 to Piazza del Risorgimento. Connecting bus from Vatican Museums.
🚊 19 to Piazza del Risorgimento.
M Ottaviano. **Basilica open** 7am–7pm (Oct–Mar: 6pm).
🕆 📷 🚻 🎞 🚻
Treasury open 9am–6:30pm (Oct–Mar: 5:30pm). **Vatican Grottoes open** 7am–6pm (Oct–Mar: 5pm). **Dome open** 8am–6pm (Oct–Mar: 5pm). **Adm charge** to Treasury and Dome.
Papal audiences: Regular public audiences, usually at 11am on Wed in Papal Audience Chamber, but sometimes in Piazza San Pietro. Tickets (free) from Prefecture of Pontifical Household (north side of piazza). **Open** 9am–1pm Mon–Sat, or write to: Prefettura della Casa Pontificia, 00120 Città del Vaticano. Appearances also at noon on Sundays at the library window to bless the crowd in Piazza San Pietro below.

The two minor cupolas at the corners of the transept are by Vignola.

Pope Urban VIII's Keys
At the base of the columns of the baldacchino, the coat of arms of Pope Urban VIII features the keys to the Kingdom of Heaven.

Facade by Carlo Maderno (1614)

Stairs to the dome

Filarete Door
Finished in 1445, Antonio Averulino's bronze door came from the original basilica.

Entrances

STAR FEATURES

★ Dome of St. Peter's

★ View from the Dome

Piazza San Pietro
On special religious occasions, the Pope appears on a balcony above the square to bless the crowds.

A Guided Tour of St. Peter's

THE BASILICA is 615 ft (187 m) long, and its vast marble-encrusted interior contains 11 chapels and 45 altars in addition to a wealth of precious works of art. Some were salvaged from the original basilica and others commissioned from late Renaissance and Baroque artists, but much of the elaborate decoration is owed to Bernini's work in the mid-17th century. The two side aisles are 250 ft (76 m) long and converge under Michelangelo's enormous dome. The central focus of the building is the Papal Altar beneath Bernini's great baldacchino, filling the space between four massive piers that support the dome. From the basilica you can visit the Grottoes, the Treasury and St. Peter's Sacristy or climb up to the terrace for panoramic views.

⑤ Baldacchino by Bernini
Commissioned by Pope Urban VIII in 1624, the extravagant Baroque canopy dominates the nave and crowns the Papal Altar, at which only the Pope may celebrate mass.

Bernini's Monument to Urban VIII

④ Throne of St. Peter in Glory
In the domed apse, look up to the window above Bernini's Baroque sculpture of 1666. It lights the image of the Holy Spirit, shown as a dove amid clouds, rays of sunlight and flights of angels.

Entrance to Treasury and Sacristy

HISTORICAL PLAN OF THE BASILICA OF ST. PETER'S

St. Peter was buried in AD 64 in a necropolis near his crucifixion site at the Circus of Nero. Constantine built a basilica on the burial site in AD 324. In the 15th century, the old church was found to be unsafe and had to be demolished. It was rebuilt in the 16th and 17th centuries. By 1614, the facade was ready, and in 1626, the new church was consecrated.

Entrance to Necropolis

③ Monument to Pope Alexander VII
Bernini's last work was finished in 1678 and is in an alcove to the left of the transept. The pope sits among the figures of Truth, Justice, Charity and Prudence.

② Monument to Leo XI
On the left beneath the aisle arch is Alessandro Algardi's white marble 1650 monument to Leo XI, whose reign as pope lasted only 27 days.

KEY
- ▢ Circus of Nero
- ▢ Constantinian
- ▢ Renaissance
- ▢ Baroque

KEY
– – – Tour route

⑥ Angelo della Navicella
A fragment of Giotto's beautiful 13th-century mosaic, salvaged from the old basilica, is now in the Grottoes. A later copy of the entire mosaic of Jesus and St. Peter fishing on Lake Tiberias decorates the atrium.

⑦ St. Peter
Until recently this famous 13th-century statue, now attributed to Arnolfo di Cambio, was thought to be a late Roman work. Situated at the end of the nave, it is sculpted in bronze with a delicate filigree halo.

Entrance to Grottoes

The Tabernacle by Bernini is made of gilt bronze in the shape of a temple.

Chapel of St. Sebastian

Stuart Monument by Canova

The Porta Santa (Holy Door) is opened only in Holy Years.

⑧ Pietà
This famous marble sculpture was finished in 1499, when Michelangelo was only 25. It stands in a chapel to one side of the nave, protected by glass since being damaged in 1972.

Filarete Door

Navicella Mosaic

Atrium by Carlo Maderno

① Tomb of Maria Sobieski
The first impressions of the interior of the basilica are of the vast scale and perfect symmetry. Near the entrance is Filippo Barigioni's 18th-century monument to the wife of James Stuart, the Old Pretender.

Vatican Museums ❷

THE BUILDINGS that house one of the world's most important art collections were originally papal palaces built for such Renaissance popes as Sixtus IV, Innocent VIII and Julius II. The long courtyards and galleries, linking Innocent VIII's Belvedere Palace to the other buildings, are by Donato Bramante and were commissioned for Julius II in 1503. Most of the later additions to the buildings were made in the 18th century, when priceless works of art accumulated by earlier popes were first put on display. This complex of museums also houses the Sistine Chapel and the Raphael Rooms, which should not be missed.

★ **Atrium of the Four Gates**
Built by Camporese from 1792 to 1793, this vast domed edifice was the original entrance to the Vatican Museums.

The Belvedere Palace was commissioned in the late 15th century by Pope Innocent VIII.

★ **Cortile della Pigna**
This huge bronze pine cone, part of an ancient Roman fountain, once stood in the courtyard of old St. Peter's. Its niche was designed by Pirro Ligorio.

Cortile della Biblioteca

Cortile del Belvedere

Apartment of Pius V

Sistine Chapel

Borgia Tower

Borgia Apartment

Raphael Loggia

Cortile di San Damaso

STAR FEATURES

★ **Cortile della Pigna**

★ **Atrium of the Four Gates**

★ **Bramante Stairway**

Spiral Ramp
The spectacular stairway up to the museums from the street was designed by Giuseppe Momo in 1932.

Entrance

VISITORS' CHECKLIST

Città del Vaticano. Entrance in Viale Vaticano. **Map** 3 B2. ☎ 69 88 33 33. 🚌 23, 81, 492 to Piazza del Risorgimento or 64 to St. Peter's. Connecting bus between St. Peter's and museums. Ⓜ Ottaviano. 🚊 19 to Piazza del Risorgimento. **Open** 8:45am–1:45pm Mon–Sat and last Sun of month; Apr–Jun: 8:45am–4pm Mon–Fri, 8:45am–1:45pm Sat. **Closed** public & religious hols. Special permit required for Raphael Loggia, Vatican library, Lapidary Gallery and Vatican Archives. **Adm charge**, free last Sun of month. ♿ special routes. 🎧 *Temporary exhibitions, lectures, movies.* 🍴 📷 🛍

Simonetti Stairway
Built in the 1780s with a vaulted ceiling, these stairs were part of the conversion of the Belvedere Palace into the Pio-Clementine Museum.

Cortile Ottagonale
The inner court of the Belvedere Palace was given its octagonal shape in 1773.

★**Bramante Stairway**
Pope Julius II built the spiral staircase within a square tower as an entrance to the palace. The staircase could be ridden up on horseback in case of emergency.

Braccio Nuovo

TIMELINE

1198 Innocent III creates papal palace	**1503** Bramante lays out Belvedere Courtyard **1509** Raphael begins work on Rooms	**1655** Bernini designs Scala Regia	**1756** Foundation of Christian Museum	**1800–23** Chiaramonti Museum founded	**1837** Etruscan Museum founded
1000	**1500**	**1600**	**1700**	**1800**	
1473 Pope Sixtus IV builds Sistine Chapel	**1503–13** Pope Julius II starts Classical sculpture collection	*Bramante (1444–1514)*	**1758** Museum of Pagan Antiquities founded **1776–84** Pius VI enlarges museum	**1822** Braccio Nuovo is opened **1970** Pope Paul VI opens Gregorian Museum of Pagan Antiquities	

Exploring the Vatican Museums

FOUR CENTURIES of papal patronage and connoisseurship have resulted in one of the world's great collections of Classical and Renaissance art. The Vatican houses many of the great archaeological finds of central Italy, including the *Laocoön* group, discovered in 1506 on the Esquiline; the *Apollo del Belvedere*; and the Etruscan bronze known as the *Mars of Todi*. During the Renaissance, parts of the museums were decorated with wonderful frescoes commissioned for the Sistine Chapel, the Raphael Rooms and the Borgia Apartment.

Mars of Todi

Gallery of the Candelabra
Once an open loggia (courtyard gallery), this gallery of Greek and Roman sculpture has a view of the Vatican Gardens.

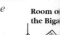
Room of the Biga

Gallery of Tapestries

Etruscan Museum

Siege of Malta
The Gallery of Maps is an important record of 16th-century history and cartography.

Upper floor

Raphael Loggia

Modern Religious Art

Sistine Chapel

Raphael Rooms

Sala dei Misteri
This is one of the rooms of the Borgia Apartment, richly decorated with Pinturicchio frescoes.

GALLERY GUIDE
Visitors have to follow a one-way system. It is best to concentrate on a single collection or to choose one of the suggested itineraries. These are color-coded so that you can follow them throughout the museums. Routes vary in length from 90 minutes to 5 hours. If you are planning a long visit, make sure you allow plenty of time for resting. Conserve your stamina for the Sistine Chapel and the Raphael Rooms; they are 20 to 30 minutes' walk from the entrance, not counting any viewing time along the way.

Gregorian Profane Museum

Pio-Christian Museum

St. Jerome
Leonardo da Vinci's unfinished work, lost but rediscovered in the 19th century, shows the artist's mastery of anatomy.

Entrance

Round Room

Pinacoteca

Pio-Clementine Museum

Room of the Busts
This contains portraits of emperors and other notable Romans.

Greek Cross Room

Stairs up

Egyptian Museum

Stairs down

Braccio Nuovo

Chiaramonti Museum

Vatican Library

Lapidary Gallery

Lower floor

Laocoön
This 1st-century AD marble group depicts the Trojan priest Laocoön and his sons struggling with two snakes.

Room of the Animals
Roman mosaics, like these delightful ducks, decorate the walls and floor of this room of animal sculpture.

Apollo del Belvedere
This Roman copy of a Greek statue of the sun god Apollo perfectly embodies the ideals of Classical beauty.

KEY TO FLOOR PLAN

- Egyptian and Assyrian art
- Greek and Roman art
- Etruscan and Italic art
- Early Christian and medieval art
- 15th- to 19th-century art
- Modern Religious art
- Non-exhibition space
- Temporarily closed

Exploring the Vatican's Collections

THE VATICAN'S GREATEST TREASURES are its Greek and Roman antiquities. These have been on display since the 18th century. The 19th century saw the addition of exciting discoveries from Etruscan tombs and excavations in Egypt. In the Pinacoteca (art gallery) there is a small, choice collection of painting, including works by Raphael, Titian and Leonardo. Works by great painters and sculptors are also displayed throughout the older parts of the museums in the form of sumptuous decorations commissioned by the Renaissance popes.

Colored bas-relief from an Egyptian tomb (c. 2400 BC)

EGYPTIAN AND ASSYRIAN ART

THE EGYPTIAN COLLECTION contains finds from 19th- and 20th-century excavations in Egypt and statues that were brought to Rome in Imperial times. There are also Roman imitations of Egyptian art from Hadrian's Villa (see p269) and from the Campus Martius district of ancient Rome. Egyptian-style statuary from Hadrian's Villa was used to decorate the Greek Cross Room, the entrance to the new wing built in 1780 by Michelangelo Simonetti.

The genuine Egyptian works, exhibited on the lower floor of the Belvedere Palace, include statues, mummies, mummy cases and funerary artifacts. There is also a large collection of documents written on papyrus, the paper the ancient Egyptians made from reeds. Among the main treasures is a colossal granite statue of Queen Tuia, the mother of Rameses II, found on the site of the Horti Sallustiani gardens

(see p251) in 1714. The statue, which dates from the 13th century BC, may have been brought to Rome by the Emperor Caligula (reigned AD 37–41), who had an unhealthy interest in pharaohs and in his own mother, Agrippina.

Also noteworthy are the head of a statue of Mentuhotep IV (21st century BC); the beautiful mummy case of Queen Hetep-heret-es; and the tomb of Iri, the guardian of the Pyramid of Cheops (22nd century BC).

The Assyrian Stairway is decorated with fragments of reliefs from the palaces of the Kings of Nineveh (8th century BC). These depict the military exploits of King Sennacherib and his son, Sargon II, and show scenes from Assyrian and Chaldean mythology.

ETRUSCAN AND OTHER PRE-ROMAN ART

THIS COLLECTION comprises artifacts from pre-Roman civilizations in Etruria and Latium, from Neolithic times to the 1st century BC, when these ancient populations were assimilated into the Roman state. Among the finest objects in the Gregorian Etruscan Museum are those from the Regolini-Galassi tomb, excavated in 1836 at the necropolis of Cerveteri (see p271). The tomb was found intact and yielded numerous everyday household objects, plus a throne, a bed and a funeral cart, all cast in bronze, dating from the 7th century BC. Beautiful black vases, delightful terra-cotta figurines and such bronze statues as the famous *Mars of Todi*, displayed in the Room of the Bronzes, show the Etruscans to have been a highly civilized, sophisticated people.

A number of Greek vases also found in Etruscan tombs are on display in the Vase Collection. The Room of the Italiot Vases contains only vases produced locally in the Greek cities of Southern Italy and in Etruria itself. These date from the 3rd to the 1st century BC.

Etruscan gold clasp (fibula) from the 7th century BC

Head of an athlete in mosaic from the Baths of Caracalla

GREEK AND ROMAN ART

THE GREATER PART of the Vatican Museums is dedicated to Greek and Roman art. Exhibits line connecting corridors and vestibules; walls and floors display fine mosaics; and famous sculptures decorate the main courtyards.

The first serious organization of the collection took place in the reign of Julius II (1503–13) around Bramante's Belvedere Courtyard. The prize pieces form the nucleus of the 18th-century Pio-Clementine Museum. In the pavilions of the Octagonal Courtyard and in the surrounding rooms are sculptures considered among the greatest achievements of Western art. The *Apoxyomenos* (an athlete wiping his body after a race) and the *Apollo del Belvedere* are high-quality Roman copies of Greek originals of about 320 BC. The magnificent *Laocoön*, sculpted by three artists from Rhodes, had long been known to exist from a description by Pliny the Elder. It was rediscovered near the ruins of Nero's Golden House *(see p175)* in 1506. Classical works such as these had a profound influence on Michelangelo and other Renaissance artists.

The much smaller Chiaramonti Museum, named after Pope Pius VII Chiaramonti, was laid out by Canova in the early 19th century. It includes a striking colossal head of the goddess Athene. The Braccio Nuovo, an extension of the Chiaramonti, decorated with Roman floor mosaics, contains a statue of Augustus from the villa of his wife, Livia, at Prima Porta. Its pose is based on the famous *Doryphoros* by the Greek sculptor Polyclitus, a Roman copy of which can be seen on display nearby.

Exhibits in the Vase Rooms range from the Greek geometric style (8th century BC) to black-figure vases from Corinth, such as the famous vase by Exekias, with Achilles and Ajax playing a game similar to checkers (530 BC), and to the later red-figure type, such as the *kylix* (a wide shallow cup) with Oedipus and the Sphinx from the 5th century BC. A stairway links this section to the Gallery of the Candelabra and the Room of the Biga (a two-horse chariot). The horses and harness were added in the 18th century.

The Gregorian Profane Museum, housed in a new wing, charts the evolution of Roman art from dependence upon Greek models to a recognizably Roman style.

The *Doryphoros*, or spear-carrier, a Roman copy in marble of an original Greek bronze

Original Greek works here include large marble fragments from the Parthenon in Athens. There is also a Roman copy of *Athene and Marsyas* by Myron, which was part of the decoration of the Parthenon. Totally Roman in character are two reliefs known as the Rilievi della Cancelleria,

Marble relief of the Emperor Vespasian

because they were discovered beneath the Palazzo della Cancelleria *(see p149)* in the 1930s. They show military parades of the Emperor Vespasian and his son, Domitian. This section also has fine Roman floor mosaics. There are two from the Baths of Caracalla *(see p197)*, depicting athletes and referees. They date from the 3rd century AD. Most striking of all is a mosaic that creates the impression of an unswept floor, covered with debris after a meal. Away from the main Classical collections, in one of the rooms of the Vatican Library, is the *Aldobrandini Wedding*, a beautiful Roman fresco of a bride being prepared for her marriage, dating from the 1st century AD.

Floor mosaic from the Baths of Otricoli in Umbria, in the Round Room

Detail from Giotto's *Stefaneschi Triptych*

EARLY CHRISTIAN AND MEDIEVAL ART

THE MAIN COLLECTION of early Christian antiquities is in the Pio-Christian Museum, founded in the last century by Pope Pius IX and formerly housed in the Lateran Palace. It contains inscriptions and sculpture from catacombs and early Christian basilicas. The sculpture consists chiefly of reliefs decorating sarcophagi, though the most striking work is a free-standing 4th-century statue of the *Good Shepherd*. The sculpture's chief appeal lies in the way it blends biblical episodes with pagan mythology. Christianity adopted Classical images so that its doctrines could be understood in clear visual terms. The idealized pastoral figure of the shepherd, for example, became Christ himself, while bearded philosophers turned into the Apostles. At the same time, Christianity laid claim to be the spiritual and cultural heir of the Roman Empire.

The first two rooms of the Pinacoteca are dedicated to late medieval art, featuring wooden panels tempera-painted that served as altarpieces. The outstanding work is Giotto's altarpiece dating from about 1300, known as the *Stefaneschi Triptych*. It expresses much the same theme as the early Christian works: the continuity between the Classical world of the Roman Empire and the new order of Christian Europe. The crucifixion of St. Peter takes place between two landmarks of ancient Rome, the Pyramid of Caius Cestius *(see p205)*, and the pyramid known in the Middle Ages as the Tomb of Romulus, which stood near the Vatican. The triptych, which decorated the main altar of old St Peter's, includes portraits of Pope St. Celestine V (reigned 1294 – 6), and of the donor, Cardinal Jacopo Stefaneschi, shown offering the triptych to St. Peter.

The Vatican Library has a number of medieval treasures exhibited rather haphazardly in showcases; these include woven and embroidered cloths, reliquaries, enamels and icons. One of the aims of the 18th-century reorganization of the Vatican collections was to glorify Christian works by contrasting them with earlier pagan creations. In the long Lapidary Gallery, over 3,000 stone tablets with Christian and pagan inscriptions are displayed on opposite walls. The world's greatest collection of its kind, it may be visited only with special permission.

15TH- TO 19TH-CENTURY ART

THE RENAISSANCE POPES, many of whom were cultured connoisseurs of the arts, considered it their duty to sponsor the leading painters, sculptors and goldsmiths of

***Pietà* by the Venetian artist Giovanni Bellini (1430 –1516)**

RAPHAEL'S LAST PAINTING

When Raphael died in 1520, the *Transfiguration* was found in his studio, almost complete. The wonderful luminous work was placed at the head of the bier where the great artist's body lay. It depicts the episode in the Gospels in which Christ took three of the Apostles to the top of a mountain, where He appeared to them in divine glory. In the detail shown here, Christ floats above the ground in a halo of ethereal light.

the age. The galleries around the Cortile del Belvedere were all decorated by great artists between the 16th and the 19th century. The Gallery of Tapestries is hung with tapestries woven in Brussels to designs by students of Raphael; the Apartment of Pope Pius V has beautiful 15th-century Flemish tapestries; and the Gallery of Maps is frescoed with 16th-century maps of ancient and contemporary Italy. When you visit the Raphael Rooms *(see pp242–3)*, be sure to also visit the nearby Room of the Chiaroscuri and Pope Nicholas V's tiny private chapel, frescoed by Fra Angelico between 1447 and 1451. Similarly, before reaching the Sistine Chapel *(see pp244–7)*, visit the Borgia Apartment, frescoed in a decorative, flowery style by Pinturicchio and his students in the 1490s. The contrast with Michelangelo's Sistine Chapel ceiling, begun in 1508, could hardly be greater. Another set of fascinating frescoes decorates the Loggia of Raphael, but this requires special permission to visit.

Many important works by Renaissance masters are displayed in the Pinacoteca (art gallery). Highlights among the works by 15th-century painters are a fine *Pietà* by the Venetian Giovanni Bellini and Leonardo da Vinci's unfinished *St. Jerome*. Of the

great 16th-century works, do not miss the fine altarpiece by Titian, the *Crucifixion of St. Peter* by Guido Reni, the *Deposition* by Caravaggio and the *Communion of St. Jerome* by Domenichino. Raphael has a whole room dedicated to his work. It contains the beautiful *Madonna of Foligno* and the *Transfiguration*, as well as eight tapestries made to his designs.

Lunette of the *Adoration of the Magi* by Pinturicchio in the Room of the Liberal Arts in the Borgia Apartment

MODERN RELIGIOUS ART

MODERN ARTISTS exhibited in the Vatican Museums face daunting competition from the great works of the past. Few modern works are displayed conspicuously, the exceptions being Momo's spiral staircase of 1932, which greets visitors as they enter the museums, and Giò Pomodoro's abstract sculpture in the center of the Cortile della Pigna.

In 1973, a contemporary art collection was inaugurated by Pope Paul VI. Housed in the Borgia Apartment, it includes over 800 exhibits by modern artists from all over the world, donated by collectors or the artists themselves. Works in a great variety of media show many contrasting approaches to religious subjects. There are paintings, drawings, engravings and sculptures by 19th- and 20th-century artists, as well as mosaics, stained glass, ceramics and tapestries. Well-known modern painters such as Georges Braque, Paul Klee, Edvard Munch and Graham Sutherland are also represented, and there are drawings by Henry Moore, ceramics by Picasso and stained glass by Fernand Léger. Projects for modern church ornaments include Matisse's decorations for the church of St. Paul de Vence, Luigi Fontana's models for the bronze doors of Milan cathedral and Emilio Greco's panels for the doors of Orvieto cathedral.

***Town with Gothic Cathedral* by Paul Klee (1879–1940)**

Raphael Rooms

POPE JULIUS II'S PRIVATE APARTMENTS were built above those of his hated predecessor, Alexander VI, one of the Borgias, who died in 1503. Julius was impressed with Raphael's work and chose him to redecorate the four rooms *(stanze)*. Raphael and his pupils began the task in 1508, replacing existing works by several better-known artists, including Raphael's own teacher, Perugino. The work took over 16 years, and Raphael himself died before its completion. The frescoes express the religious and philosophical ideals of the Renaissance. They quickly established Raphael's reputation as an artist in Rome, putting him on a par with Michelangelo, then working on the ceiling of the Sistine Chapel.

Detail from *The Expulsion of Heliodorus from the Temple*, showing Pope Julius II watching the scene from his litter

Cortile del Belvedere

KEY TO FLOOR PLAN

① Hall of Constantine

② Room of Heliodorus

③ Room of the Segnatura

④ Room of the Fire in the Borgo

HALL OF CONSTANTINE ①

THE FRESCOES in this room were started in 1517, three years before Raphael's death, but Raphael himself probably had little hand in their execution. As a result, they are not held in the same high regard as those in the other rooms. The work was completed in 1525, during the reign of Pope Clement VII, by Giulio Romano and two other former pupils of Raphael, Giovanni Francesco Penni and Raffaellino del Colle.

The theme of the decoration is the triumph of Christianity over paganism. The four major frescoes show scenes from the life of Constantine and include his *Vision of the Cross* and his victory over his rival Maxentius at *The Battle of the Milvian Bridge*, for which Raphael had provided a preparatory sketch. In both *The Baptism of Constantine* and *The Donation of Constantine*, the figure of Pope Sylvester *(see p170)* was given the features of Clement VII.

ROOM OF HELIODORUS ②

THIS PRIVATE antechamber was decorated by Raphael between 1512 and 1514. The main frescoes show the miraculous protection granted to all the Church's ministers, doctrines and property. The room's name refers to the fresco on the right, *The Expulsion of Heliodorus from the Temple*. This shows a story from Jewish history, in which a thief called Heliodorus is felled

Swiss guards waiting with papal chair in *The Mass at Bolsena*

by a horseman as he tries to make off with the treasure from the Temple of Jerusalem. The scene is witnessed by the pope, borne on a litter by courtiers. The incident is also a thinly veiled reference to Julius II's success in driving foreign armies out of Italy. In *The Meeting of Leo I and Attila*, Raphael pays a similar compliment to the pope's political skill. Pope Leo was originally given the face of Julius II, but after his death, Raphael substituted the features of Julius's successor, Leo X.

The Mass at Bolsena depicts a miracle that occurred in 1263. A priest

***The Battle of the Milvian Bridge*, completed by one of Raphael's assistants**

The Liberation of St. Peter, a three-part composition, shows the saint asleep in his cell in the middle section, led out of prison by an angel on the right, while, on the left, the prison guards cower in terror

master's own plans. The most famous, *The Fire in the Borgo*, was painted from Raphael's designs and reflects his maturity as an artist. It celebrates the miracle that took place in 847, when Pope Leo IV extinguished a fire raging in the Borgo *(see p228)* by making the sign of the cross. The incident is likened to the flight of Aeneas from Troy described by Virgil. The figure of Aeneas appears in the foreground carrying his father on his back. This borrowing of an event from Classical legend shows Raphael's new willingness to experiment. Sadly, his pupils did not always follow his designs faithfully, and this, combined with poor restoration, has spoiled the work.

who doubted that the bread and wine really were the body and blood of Christ suddenly saw the host bleed while he was celebrating mass. Julius II appears in this fresco, accompanied by a colorful group of Swiss guards.

Julius appears again as St. Peter in *The Liberation of St. Peter*. This fresco is remarkable for its dramatic lighting effects, achieved despite the painting's awkward shape and its position above a window.

ROOM OF THE SEGNATURA ③

THE NAME is derived from a special council that met in this room to sign official documents. The frescoes here were completed between 1508 and 1511. The scheme Raphael followed was dictated by Pope Julius II. It reflects the Humanist belief that there could be perfect harmony between Classical culture and Christianity in their mutual search for truth.

The Dispute over the Holy Sacrament, the first fresco completed by Raphael for Pope Julius, represents the triumph of religion and spiritual truth. The consecrated host is shown at the center of the painting. This links the group of learned scholars, who discuss its significance, to the Holy Trinity and the saints floating on clouds up above.

On the opposite wall, *The School of Athens (see p30)* is a bustling scene

centered around the debate on the search for truth between Greek philosophers Plato and Aristotle. It also features portraits of many of Raphael's contemporaries, including Leonardo da Vinci, Bramante and Michelangelo. The other works include a portrait of the bearded Pope Julius II, who in 1511 vowed not to shave until he had rid Italy of all usurpers.

ROOM OF THE *FIRE IN THE BORGO* ④

THIS WAS ORIGINALLY the dining room, but when the decoration was completed under Pope Leo X, it became a music room. All the frescoes exalt the reigning pope by depicting events in the lives of his namesakes, the 9th-century popes Leo III and IV. The main frescoes were finished by two of Raphael's assistants between 1514 and 1517, following their

Detail from *The Fire in the Borgo*, showing Aeneas, the Trojan hero, with his father on his back, fleeing from the fire

The Dispute over the Holy Sacrament, the first fresco completed in the Rooms

Sistine Chapel: The Walls

This is the main chapel in the Vatican Palace, named Cappella Sistina after its founder, Pope Sixtus IV. Its massive walls were frescoed by some of the finest artists of the 15th and 16th centuries, including Michelangelo, Perugino and Botticelli. The 12 paintings on the side walls show parallel episodes from the lives of Moses and of Christ. The decoration of the chapel walls was completed by Michelangelo, who added the great altar wall fresco, *The Last Judgment*.

KEY TO THE FRESCOES: ARTISTS AND SUBJECTS

| 12 | 11 | 10 | 9 | 8 | 7 | | 1 | 2 | 3 | 4 | 5 | 6 |

The Last Judgment

☐ Perugino ☐ Botticelli ☐ Ghirlandaio

☐ Rosselli ☐ Signorelli ☐ Michelangelo

1 Baptism of Christ in the Jordan
2 Temptations of Christ
3 Calling of St Peter and St Andrew
4 Sermon on the Mount
5 Handing over the Keys to St. Peter
6 Last Supper
7 Moses's Journey into Egypt
8 Moses Receiving the Call
9 Crossing of the Red Sea
10 Adoration of the Golden Calf
11 Punishment of the Rebels
12 Last Days of Moses

THE LAST JUDGMENT BY MICHELANGELO

Detail showing figure of Christ

Among Michelangelo's last works in the refurbished Sistine Chapel, *The Last Judgment* was completed in 1541 and is considered the masterpiece of his mature years. Commissioned by Pope Paul III Farnese, the work required the destruction of some earlier frescoes and the removal of two windows above the altar. A new wall was erected which slanted inwards to stop the dust settling on it. Michelangelo worked unassisted on the fresco for seven years.

The painting depicts the souls of the dead rising up to face the wrath of God, a subject rarely used for an altar decoration. It was chosen by the pope as a warning to Catholics to adhere to their faith in the turmoil of the Reformation. In fact the work conveys the artist's own tormented attitude to his faith.

The huge fresco offers none of the soothing certainties of Christian orthodoxy, nor the ordered world view of Classicism. In a dynamic, emotional composition, the figures are caught up in a swirling vortex of motion. The dead are torn from their graves and hauled up to face Christ the Judge, whose athletic, muscular figure is the focus of all the painting's movement.

Christ shows little sympathy for the agitated saints who surround him, clutching the instruments of their martyrdom. Neither is any pity shown toward the damned, hurled downward to the demons in hell. Here Charon, pushing people off his boat into the depths of Hades, and the infernal judge Minos are taken

Looking toward *The Last Judgment*

from Dante's *Inferno*. Minos is given a pair of ass's ears, and is actually a portrait of courtier Biagio da Cesena, who had objected to the nude figures in the fresco. Michelangelo's self-portrait can be spotted on the skin held by the martyr St. Bartholomew. The painting illustrates the artist's belief that suffering is vital in finding faith in God.

St. Bartholomew with his skin, bearing the face of Michelangelo

WALL FRESCOES

Detail from Botticelli's fresco
Temptations of Christ

W HEN THE Sistine Chapel was built, the papacy was a strong political power with vast accumulated wealth. In 1475 Pope Sixtus IV was able to summon some of the greatest painters of his day to decorate the chapel. Among the artists employed were Perugino, who was Raphael's master and is often credited with overseeing the project, Sandro Botticelli, Domenico Ghirlandaio, Cosimo Rosselli and Luca Signorelli. Their work on the chapel's frescoes took from 1481 to 1483.

Although frequently overlooked by visitors who concentrate on Michelangelo's work, the frescoes along the side walls of the chapel include some of the finest works of 15th-century Italian art. The two cycles of frescoes represent scenes from the lives of Moses and Christ. Above them in the spaces between the windows are portraits of the earliest popes, painted by various artists, including Botticelli.

The fresco cycles start at the altar end of the chapel, with the story of Christ on the right-hand wall and that of Moses on the left. Originally there were two paintings, *The Birth of Christ* and *The Finding of Moses*, on the wall behind the altar, but these were both destroyed to make way for Michelangelo's *The Last Judgment*.

The final paintings of the two cycles are also lost. They were on the entrance wall, which collapsed during the 16th century. When the wall was restored, they were replaced with poor substitutes.

As was customary at the time, each fresco contains a series of scenes, linked thematically to the central episode. Hidden meanings and symbols connect each painting with its counterpart on the opposite wall, and there are also many allusions to contemporary events.

The elaborate architectural details in the frescoes include familiar Roman monuments. The Arch of Constantine *(see p91)* provides the backdrop for the *Punishment of the Rebels* by Botticelli, the fifth panel in the cycle of Moses, in which the artist himself appears as the last figure but one on the right. Two similar arches appear in the painting opposite, Perugino's *Handing over the Keys to St. Peter*.

Moses was both spiritual and temporal leader of his people. He called down the wrath of God on those who challenged his decisions, thus

The crowd of onlookers in the *Calling of St. Peter and St. Andrew* by Ghirlandaio

setting a precedent for the power exercised by the pope. In *Handing over the Keys to St. Peter*, Christ confers spiritual

and temporal authority on St. Peter by giving him the keys to the Kingdoms of Heaven and Earth. The golden-domed building in the center of the vast piazza represents both the Temple of Jerusalem and the Church, as founded by Peter, the first pope. The fifth figure on the right is thought to be a self-portrait by Perugino.

Botticelli's *Temptations of Christ* includes a view of the

The central episode in Botticelli's *Punishment of the Rebels*

Hospital of Santo Spirito, rebuilt in 1475 by Sixtus IV *(see p226)*. Here the devil is disguised in the habit of a Franciscan monk. Portraits of both Botticelli and Filippino Lippi are visible in the left hand corner. A portrait of the pope's nephew, Girolamo Riario, appears in the painting of the *Crossing of the Red Sea* by Rosselli, in which the sea is literally red. This painting also commemorates the papal victory at Campomorto in 1482.

Perugino's *Handing over the Keys to St. Peter*

Sistine Chapel: The Ceiling

MICHELANGELO FRESCOED the chapel ceiling for Pope Julius II between 1508 and 1512. Refusing assistance, he worked alone on specially designed scaffolding. The subjects are from the Old Testament – except for the Classical Sibyls, who appear because they were said to have prophesied the birth of Christ. The main picture here shows the ceiling before its recent restoration; the smaller details show the colors revealed after cleaning.

The Creation of Adam
A powerful but tender study of hands shows Adam receiving spiritual grace and intellectual strength from God.

Creation of the Sun and Moon
On the third day, the dynamic figure of God the Creator commands the sun to shed its light on the earth.

KEY

GENESIS 1 God Dividing Light from Darkness; **2** Creation of the Sun and Moon; **3** Separating Waters from Land; **4** Creation of Adam; **5** Creation of Eve; **6** Original Sin; **7** Sacrifice of Noah; **8** The Deluge; **9** Drunkenness of Noah.

ANCESTORS OF CHRIST 26 Solomon with his Mother; **27** Parents of Jesse; **28** Rehoboam with Mother; **29** Asa with Parents; **30** Uzziah with Parents; **31** Hezekiah with Parents; **32** Zerubbabel with Parents; **33** Josiah with Parents.

PROPHETS 14 Jonah; **15** Jeremiah; **18** Daniel; **19** Ezekiel; **22** Isaiah; **23** Joel; **25** Zechariah.

SIBYLS 16 Libyan Sibyl; **17** Persian Sibyl; **20** Cumaean Sibyl; **21** Erythrean Sibyl; **24** Delphic Sibyl.

OLD TESTAMENT SCENES OF SALVATION 10 Punishment of Haman; **11** Moses and the Brazen Serpent; **12** David and Goliath; **13** Judith and Holofernes.

The Creation of Eve
*God has just created Eve
from one of the sleeping
Adam's ribs. The shape of the
tree suggests Christ's Cross.*

Original Sin shows
the tasting of the Tree
of Knowledge and
the expulsion of
Adam and Eve from
the Garden of Eden.

The Ignudi are athletic
male nudes that frame the
main scenes on the ceiling.

The Deluge
concentrates on
the figures of the
people stranded
by the flood.

Delphic Sibyl
*The beautiful prophetess of
the Greek Oracle of Delphi
is portrayed in a moment
of intense inspiration.*

Castel Sant'Angelo ⓭

THE MASSIVE FORTRESS of Castel Sant'Angelo takes its name from the statue of the Archangel Michael on its summit. It began in AD 139 as the Emperor Hadrian's mausoleum. Since then it has had many roles: as part of the Emperor Aurelian's city wall, as a medieval citadel and prison and as the residence of the popes in times of political unrest. From the dank cells in the lower levels to the fine apartments of the Renaissance popes above, a 58-room museum covers all aspects of the castle's history.

Mausoleum of Hadrian
This artist's impression shows the tomb before Aurelian fortified its walls in AD 270 to 275.

Courtyard of Honor
Piles of stone cannonballs decorate the courtyard, once the castle's ammunition store.

The Treasury was probably the original site of Hadrian's burial chamber.

Hall of the Columns

Loggia of Paul III

Hall of the Library

PROTECTING THE POPE

The Vatican Corridor leads from the Vatican Palace to Castel Sant'Angelo. It was built in 1277 to provide an escape route when the pope was in danger. The pentagonal ramparts built around the castle during the 17th century improved its defenses in times of siege.

The Rooms of Clement VIII are inscribed with the family crest of the Aldobrandini pope (1592–1605).

The Hall of Justice is decorated with a fresco of *The Angel of Justice* by Domenico Zaga (1545).

The spiral ramp was the entrance to the mausoleum.

■ Walls and fortifications
☐ Vatican Corridor

★ **View from Terrace**
The castle's terrace, scene of the last act of Puccini's Tosca, *offers splendid views in every direction.*

The Chamber of the Urns housed the ashes of members of Hadrian's family.

STAR FEATURES

★ **Sala Paolina**

★ **View from Terrace**

★ **Staircase of Alexander VI**

VISITORS' CHECKLIST

Lungotevere Castello. **Map** 4 D3 & 11 A1. 687 50 36.
23, 64, 87, 280 to Lungotevere Castello; 34, 49, 70, 81, 186, 926, 990 to Piazza Cavour. Lepanto.
Open 9am–2pm daily (last adm: 1 hr before closing).
Closed public hols.
Adm charge.
10:30am Sun only.
Exhibitions.

Bronze Angel
The gigantic statue of the Archangel Michael is by the 18th-century Flemish sculptor Pieter Verschaffelt.

The Round Hall houses the original model from which Verschaffelt's angel was cast.

★ **Sala Paolina**
The illusionistic frescoes by Perin del Vaga and Pellegrino Tibaldi (1544–7) include one of a courtier entering the room through a painted door.

Hall of Apollo
The room is frescoed with scenes from mythology attributed to the pupils of Perin del Vaga (1548).

Ventilation shaft

★ **Staircase of Alexander VI**
This staircase cuts right through the heart of the building.

Bridge

TIMELINE

AD 100	500	1000	1500	
AD 139 Mausoleum completed by Antoninus Pius	**590** Legendary date of appearance of Archangel Michael above the castle	**1493** Pope Alexander VI restores Vatican Corridor		*Façade of Castel Sant'Angelo*
		1390 Pope Boniface IX remodels the castle		
271 Tomb is incorporated into Aurelian Wall and fortified		**1527** Castle withstands siege during Sack of Rome	**1557** Ramparts built to protect the castle	
AD 130 Hadrian begins family mausoleum	*Cannonballs in the Courtyard of Honor*	**1542–9** Sala Paolina and apartments built for Pope Paul III	**1870** Castle used as barracks and military prison	

VIA VENETO

IN IMPERIAL ROME, this was a suburb where rich families owned luxurious villas and gardens. Ruins from this era can be seen in the excavations in Piazza Sallustio, named after the most extensive gardens in the area, the Horti Sallustiani.

Film director Federico Fellini

After the Sack of Rome in the 5th century, the area reverted to open countryside. Not until the 17th century did it recover its lost splendor, with the building of Palazzo Barberini and the now-vanished Villa Ludovisi.

When Rome became capital of Italy in 1870, the Ludovisi sold their land for development. They kept a plot for a new house, but tax on the profits from the sale was so high that they had to sell that, too. By 1900, Via Veneto had become a street with smart modern hotels and cafés. It featured prominently in Fellini's 1960 film *La Dolce Vita*, a scathing satire on the lives of film stars and the idle rich, but since then it has lost its position as the meeting place of the famous.

SIGHTS AT A GLANCE

Churches and Temples
Santa Maria della Concezione ❸
Santa Susanna ❼
Santa Maria della Vittoria ❽

Historic Buildings
Casino dell'Aurora ❷
Palazzo Barberini ❻

Famous Streets
Via Veneto ❶

Fountains
Fontana delle Api ❹
Fontana del Tritone ❺

SEE ALSO

0 meters   200

0 yards   200

N

GETTING THERE

This is one of the easiest parts of Rome to reach by public transportation. Barberini and Repubblica Metro stations on line A are very handy, and Stazione Termini is only 10 to 15 minutes' walk away. The Via Veneto itself starts at Piazza Barberini, well served by buses from all parts of the city. The 95 goes the whole length of Via Veneto to Porta Pinciana. Other useful routes include the 52, 53, 56, 58 and 60 along Via del Tritone.

KEY

▨	Street-by-Street map
—	City Wall
Ⓜ	Metro station
Ⓟ	Parking

The onset of autumn in Via Veneto

Street by Street: Via Veneto

THE STREETS AROUND VIA VENETO, though within the walls of ancient Rome, contain little dating from before the unification of Italy in 1870. With its hotels, restaurants, bars and travel agencies, the area is the center of 20th-century tourism in the way that Piazza di Spagna was the hub of the tourist trade in the Rome of the 18th-century Grand Tour. However, glimpses of the old city can be seen among the modern streets. These include Santa Maria della Concezione, the church of the Capuchin friars, whose convent once stood in its own gardens. In the 17th century, Palazzo Barberini was built here for the powerful papal family. Bernini's Fontana del Tritone and Fontana delle Api have stood in Piazza Barberini since it was the meeting place of cart tracks entering the city from surrounding vineyards.

Casino dell'Aurora
A pavilion is all that remains of the great Ludovisi estate that once occupied most of this quarter of Rome ❷

Santa Maria della Concezione
This church is best known for the macabre collection of bones in its crypt ❸

Fontana delle Api
Bernini's drinking fountain is decorated with bees, emblem of his Barberini patrons ❹

Fontana del Tritone
Bernini's muscular sea god has been spouting water skyward for 350 years ❺

★ **Palazzo Barberini**
Pietro da Cortona worked on his spectacular ceiling fresco The Triumph of Divine Providence *between 1633 and 1639* ❻

The Porta Pinciana was built in AD 403. Only the central arch of white travertine is original.

Via Veneto
Built during the redevelopment of Rome at the end of the 19th century, this street of smart hotels and spacious pavement cafés enjoyed its heyday during the 1950s and 1960s ❶

Santa Susanna
This church is dedicated to a martyr executed during Diocletian's persecution of Christians in the 3rd century AD ❼

STAR SIGHTS

★ Santa Maria della Vittoria

★ Palazzo Barberini

KEY

– – – Suggested route

0 meters 75

0 yards 75

★ Santa Maria della Vittoria
The highlight of this Baroque church is the Cornaro Chapel, designed to resemble a theater. The center of the stage is occupied by Bernini's thrilling sculpture of the Ecstasy of St. Teresa ❽

Sidewalk café on Via Veneto

Via Veneto ❶

Map 5 B1. 🚌 *52, 53, 56, 58, 58b, 95, 490, 495 and many other routes.* Ⓜ *Barberini.*

VIA VENETO descends in a lazy curve from the Porta Pinciana to Piazza Barberini, lined in its upper reaches with exuberant turn-of-the-century hotels and canopied sidewalk cafés. It was laid out in 1879 over a large estate sold by the Ludovisi family in the great building boom of Rome's first years as capital of Italy. Palazzo Margherita, intended to be the new Ludovisi family palazzo, was completed in 1890. It now houses the American embassy.

In the 1960s this was the most glamorous street in Rome, its cafés patronized by film stars and plagued by the paparazzi. Most of the people drinking in the cafés today are tourists, as film stars now seem to prefer the livelier Bohemian atmosphere of Trastevere.

Palazzo Margherita, the US embassy

Casino dell'Aurora ❷

Via Lombardia 46. **Map** 5 B2. 🄲 *48 39 42.* 🚌 *52, 53, 56, 58.* **Open** *by appt only.*

THE CASINO (a stately country residence) was in a summerhouse on the grounds of the Ludovisi palace. It was built by Cardinal Ludovisi in the 17th century, and frescoed by Guercino. The subject of the ceiling fresco is Aurora, the goddess of dawn. It is a dizzying work creating the impression that the Casino has no roof but lies open to a cloudy sky, across which horses pull Aurora's carriage away from the darkness of night toward the light of day.

Santa Maria della Concezione ❸

Via Veneto 27. **Map** 5 B2. 🄲 *487 11 85.* 🚌 *52, 53, 56, 58, 58b, 490, 495 and many other routes.* Ⓜ *Barberini.* **Open** *7am–noon & 3:45–7:30pm daily.* **Crypt open** *9am–noon & 3–6pm Fri–Wed.* **Donation** *expected.* 🚻 📷

POPE URBAN VIII's brother, Antonio Barberini was a cardinal and a Capuchin friar. In 1626 he founded this plain, unassuming church at what is now the foot of the Via Veneto. When he died, he was buried not in a grand marble sarcophagus like most cardinals, but below a simple flagstone close to the altar, where you can read the bleak epitaph in Latin: "Here lies dust, ashes, nothing."

The grim reality of death is illustrated even more graphically in the crypt beneath the church, where generations of Capuchin friars have decorated the walls of the five vaulted chapels with the bones and skulls of their departed brethren. In all, some 4,000 skeletons were used to create this macabre memento mori. Some of the bones are wired together to form Christian symbols such as crowns of thorns, sacred hearts and crucifixes. There are also a number of complete skeletons, including one of a Barberini princess who died as a child. At the exit, an inscription in Latin reads: "What you are, we used to be. What we are, you will be."

Pope Urban VIII

Fontana delle Api ❹

Piazza Barberini. **Map** 5 B2. 🚌 *52, 53, 56, 58, 58b, 490, 495 and many other routes.* Ⓜ *Barberini.*

THE FOUNTAIN of the bees – *api* are bees, symbol of the Barberini family – is one of Bernini's more modest works. Tucked away in a corner of Piazza Barberini, it is quite easy to miss. Dating from 1644, it pays homage to Pope Urban VIII Barberini, and features rather crablike bees that appear to be sipping the water as it dribbles down into the basin. A Latin inscription informs us that the water is for the use of the public and their animals.

Bernini's Fontana delle Api

Fontana del Tritone ❺

Piazza Barberini. **Map** 5 B3. 🚌 *52, 53, 56, 58, 58b, 490, 495 and many other routes.* Ⓜ *Barberini.*

IN THE CENTER of busy Piazza Barberini is one of Bernini's liveliest fountains, the Triton Fountain. It was created for Pope Urban VIII Barberini in 1642, shortly after the completion of his palace on the ridge above. Acrobatic dolphins stand on their heads, twisting their tails together to support a huge scallop shell on which the sea god Triton kneels, blowing a spindly column of water up into the air through a conch shell. Entwined artistically among the dolphins' tails are the papal tiara, the keys of St. Peter and the Barberini coat of arms.

The Triton and his conch shell in Bernini's Fontana del Tritone

Palazzo Barberini ⑥

Via delle Quattro Fontane 13. **Map** 5 B3. **C** 481 45 91. 🚌 52, 53, 56, 58, 58b, 490, 495 and many other routes. **M** Barberini. **Open** 9am–7pm Tue–Sat, 9am–1pm Sun and public holidays (last adm: 30 mins before closing). **Adm charge**. 📷

WHEN MAFFEI BARBERINI became Pope Urban VIII in 1623, he decided to build a grand palace for his family. The site he chose was then on the fringes of the city, over-looking a ruined temple. The architect, Carlo Maderno, designed it as a typical rural villa, with wings extending into the surrounding gardens. Maderno died in 1629, shortly after the foundations had been laid, and Bernini took over, assisted by Borromini. The peculiar pediments on some of the top-floor windows, and the oval staircase inside, are almost certainly by Borromini.

Of the many sumptuously decorated rooms, the most striking is the Gran Salone, with a dazzling illusionistic ceiling fresco by Pietro da Cortona. The palazzo also houses paintings from the 13th to the 16th centuries, part of the Galleria Nazionale d'Arte Antica, with important works by Filippo Lippi, El Greco and Caravaggio. There is also a Holbein portrait of King Henry VIII of England dressed for his wedding to Anne of Cleves. Of greater local significance are Guido Reni's *Beatrice Cenci*, the young woman executed for planning her father's murder *(see p150)*, and *La Fornarina*, traditionally identified as a portrait of Raphael's mistress, but not painted by him.

Santa Susanna ⑦

Piazza San Bernardo. **Map** 5 C2. **C** 482 75 10. 🚌 16, 36, 37, 60, 61, 62, 910 and many other routes. **M** Repubblica. **Open** 9am–noon & 4pm–7pm Mon–Sat, 10am–noon Sun.

Facade of Santa Susanna

SANTA SUSANNA'S most striking feature is its vigorous Baroque facade by Carlo Maderno, finished in 1603. Christians have worshiped on the site since at least the 4th century. In the nave, there are four huge frescoes by Baldassarre Croce (1558–1628), painted to resemble tapestries. These depict scenes from the life of Susanna, an obscure Roman saint who was martyred here, and the rather better-known life of the Old Testament Susanna, who was spotted bathing in her husband's garden by two lecherous judges.

When it has been restored, Santa Susanna will resume its function as the Catholic church for Americans in Rome.

Santa Maria della Vittoria ⑧

Via XX Settembre 17. **Map** 5 C2. **C** 482 61 90. 🚌 16, 36, 37, 60, 61, 62, 910 and many other routes. **M** Repubblica. **Open** 6:30am–noon & 4:30–7pm daily. 🚻 📷

SANTA MARIA della Vittoria is an intimate Baroque church with a lavishly decorated candlelit interior. It contains one of Bernini's most ambitious sculptural works, the *Ecstasy of St. Teresa* (1646), centerpiece of the Cornaro Chapel, built to resemble a miniature theater. It even has an audience: sculptures of the chapel's benefactor, Cardinal Federico Cornaro, and his ancestors sit in boxes, as if watching and discussing the scene played out in front of them.

Visitors may be shocked or thrilled by the apparently physical nature of St. Teresa's ecstasy. She lies on a cloud, her mouth half-open and her eyelids closed, with rippling drapery covering her body. Looking over her with a smile, which from different angles can appear either tender or cruel, is a curly-haired angel holding an arrow with which he is about to pierce the saint's body for a second time. The marble figures are framed and illuminated by rays of divine light cast out of bronze.

Bernini's astonishing *Ecstasy of St. Teresa*

FARTHER AFIELD

THE MORE INQUISITIVE visitor to Rome might want to try a few excursions to the large parks and some of the more isolated churches on the outskirts of the city. With a day to spare, you can explore the villas of Tivoli and the ruins of the ancient Roman port of Ostia. Traditional haunts of those on

Dish (3rd century BC) in Villa Giulia

the Grand Tour *(see p130)*, such as the catacombs and the ruined aqueducts of Parco Appio Claudio, still offer glimpses of the rapidly vanishing Campagna, the countryside around Rome. More modern sights include the suburb of EUR, built in the Fascist era, and the memorial at the Fosse Ardeatine.

SIGHTS AT A GLANCE

Towns and Areas
EUR ⑭
Tivoli ⑰

Historic Roads
Via Appia Antica ⑦

Churches
Santa Costanza ④
Sant'Agnese fuori le Mura ⑤
San Lorenzo fuori le Mura ⑥
San Paolo fuori le Mura ⑮

Museums and Galleries
Museo Borghese pp260–61 ②
Villa Giulia pp262–3 ③

Parks and Gardens
Villa Borghese ①
Parco Appio Claudio ⑬
Villa Doria Pamphilj ⑯
Villa d'Este ⑱
Villa Gregoriana ⑲

Ancient Sites
Hadrian's Villa ⑳
Ostia Antica ㉑

Tombs and Catacombs
Catacombs of San Callisto ⑧
Catacombs of San Sebastiano ⑨
Catacombs of Domitilla ⑩
Fosse Ardeatine ⑪
Tomb of Cecilia Metella ⑫

KEY

◼ Main sightseeing areas
═══ Motorway

0 kilometers   2
0 miles   1

SIGHTS OUTSIDE ROME

SIGHTS OUTSIDE THE CENTER

Caryatids beside the canal of the Canopus at Hadrian's Villa

Villa Borghese ❶

Map 2 E5. 🚍 *3, 4, 52, 53, 57, 95, 490, 495, 910.* 🚊 *19, 19b, 30b.*
Park open *dawn to sunset.* **Zoo** Viale del Giardino Zoologico. **Map** 2 E4.
📞 *321 65 64.* 🚍 *3, 52, 910.* 🚊 *19, 19b, 30b.* **Open** *8:30am–4:30pm (last adm: 3:30pm) daily.* **Closed** *May 1.*
📷 ♿ 🍴 🏪 🔲

Galleria Nazionale d'Arte Moderna
Viale delle Belle Arti 131. **Map** 2 D4.
📞 *322 41 52.* 🚊 *19, 19b, 30b.*
Open *9am–7pm Tue–Sat, 9am–1pm Sun & public hols.*
🚫 ♿ 📷 🏪 🔲

T HE VILLA and its park were designed in 1605 for Cardinal Scipione Borghese, nephew of Pope Paul V. The park was the first of its kind in Rome. It contained 400 newly planted pine trees; garden sculpture by Bernini's father, Pietro; and dramatic waterworks built by Giovanni Fontana. The layout of the formal gardens was imitated by other prominent Roman families at Villa Ludovisi and Villa Doria Pamphilj, but the cardinal's 18th-century successors preferred a more natural-looking park.

In the early 19th century, Prince Camillo Borghese assembled the family's magnificent art collection in the

British School at Rome, designed by Edwin Lutyens in 1911

Casino Borghese, now the home of the Galleria and Museo Borghese.

In 1902, the park became the property of the Italian state. Within its 4-mile (6-km) circumference, there are now museums and galleries; foreign academies and schools of archaeology; a zoo; a riding school; a grassy amphitheater; an artificial lake; an aviary; and an array of summerhouses, fountains, Neoclassical statuary and exotic follies.

There are several ways into the park, including a monumental entrance on Piazzale Flaminio, built for Prince Camillo Borghese in 1825 by Luigi Canina. Other conveniently sited entrances are at Porta Pinciana at the end of Via Veneto and from the Pincio Gardens *(see p136).* The main attraction of Italian gardens in hot weather is shade, so the long avenues are lined with hedges and trees. Piazza di Siena, a pleasantly grass-covered open amphitheater surrounded by tall umbrella pines, was the inspiration for Ottorino Respighi's famous symphonic poem *The Pines of Rome,* written in 1924. Near Piazza di Siena are the so-called Casina di Raffaello, said to have been owned by Raphael, and the

18th-century Palazzetto dell'Orologio. These were summerhouses from which people enjoyed the beautiful vistas across the park. Many buildings in the park were originally surrounded by formal gardens: the Casino Borghese and the nearby 17th-century Casino della Meridiana and its aviary (the Uccelliera) have both kept their geometrical flower beds. Throughout the park, the intersections of paths and avenues are marked by fountains and statues. West of Piazza di Siena is the Fontana dei Cavalli Marini (the Fountain of the Seahorses), added during the villa's 18th-century remodeling. Walking through the park, you will encounter statues of Byron, Goethe and Victor Hugo, plus a gloomy equestrian King Umberto I.

Statue of the English poet Byron by Thorvaldsen

Dotted about the park are picturesque temples made to look like ruins, including a circular Temple of Diana between Piazza di Siena and Porta Pinciana, and a Temple of Faustina, wife of Emperor Antoninus Pius, on the hill north of Piazza di Siena. The nearby medieval-looking Fortezzuola by Canina contains the works of the sculptor Pietro Canonica, who lived in the building and died there in 1959. In the garden stands Canonica's *Monument to the Alpino and his Mule,* which honors the humblest

Neoclassical Temple of Diana

Ionic temple dedicated to Aesculapius, built on the lake island

protagonists in Italy's alpine battles against Austria in World War I.

In the center of the park is the Giardino del Lago, its main entrance marked by an 18th-century copy of the Arch of Septimius Severus.

The garden has an artificial lake complete with an Ionic Temple to Aesculapius, the god of health, by the 18th-century architect Antonio Asprucci. Rowboats and ducks make the lake a favorite with children; banana trees and bamboo grow around the shore; and the clearings throughout are studded with sculptures.

Surrounded by flower beds south of the lake is the Art Nouveau Fontana dei Fauni, one of the garden's prettiest sculptures. In a clearing close to the entrance on Viale Pietro Canonica are the original Tritons of the Fontana del Moro in Piazza Navona *(see p120)* – they were moved here and for a time replaced by copies in the 19th century.

From the northwest the park is entered by the Viale delle Belle Arti, where the Galleria Nazionale d'Arte Moderna houses an uninspiring collection of 19th- and 20th-century paintings. The Art Nouveau character of the area dates from the International Exhibition held here in 1911, for which pavilions were built by many nations, the most impressive being the British School at Rome, by Edwin Lutyens,

with a facade adapted from the upper west portico of St. Paul's Cathedral in London. Originally a School of Archaeology, the school now offers the chance to study literature, fine arts and history. The statues close by are equally international: they include Simón Bolívar and other liberators of Latin America, as well as the great Persian poet Firdusi.

Beyond the art gallery, in the northeastern corner of the park, lie a somewhat depressing zoo and the Museo Zoologico. A far greater attraction is the pretty 16th-century Villa Giulia, with its world-famous collection of Etruscan and other pre-Roman remains.

GIARDINO ZOOLOGICO

Zoo entrance

Another Renaissance building of importance is the Palazzina of Pius IV, close to the Via Flaminia entrance. It was designed by the architect Vignola in 1552 and then transformed into an elegant apartment for Pius IV's nephew Carlo Borromeo. It is now the home of the Italian Embassy to the Holy See.

Museo Borghese ❷

See pp260–61.

Villa Giulia ❸

See pp262–3.

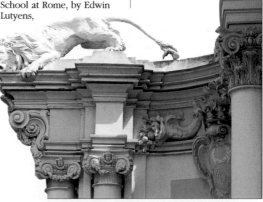

A stone lion guarding the ornate entrance to the Zoo

Museo Borghese ❷

T
HE VILLA AND PARK were laid out by
Cardinal Scipione Borghese, favorite
nephew of Paul V, who had the house
designed for pleasure and entertainment.
The hedonistic cardinal was also an
extravagant patron of the arts, and he
commissioned from the young Bernini
sculptures that now rank among his most
famous works. Scipione also opened his
pleasure park to the public. Today the
villa houses the superb private Borghese
collection of sculpture and paintings in
the Museo and
Galleria Borghese.

Facade of the Villa Borghese
*This painting (1613) by the villa's Flemish
architect Jan van Santen shows the highly
ornate facade of the original design.*

MUSEUM GUIDE

*The museum is
divided into two
sections: the sculpture
collection (Museo
Borghese) occupies
the entire ground
floor and the picture
gallery (Galleria
Borghese) is on the
upper floor. The
Galleria Borghese has
reopened to the public
after extensive
restoration work.*

★ Pluto and Persephone
*One of Bernini's finest works,
this sculpture shows Pluto
carrying off his bride. The
sculptor's astonishing
skill with marble
can be clearly
seen in the
twisting
figures.*

**Sleeping
Hermaphrodite**
*Dated around 150
BC, this is a bronze
Roman copy of the
Greek original by
Polycles. The head and
mattress were added
by Andrea Bergondi
in the 17th century.*

The Egyptian Room
*Frescoes show episodes in
Egyptian history and
Egyptian motifs.*

TIMELINE

1613 15-year-old Bernini sculpts *Aeneas and Anchises*	**Early 1800s** Statues and reliefs are considered too ornate and stripped from the villa's facade	**1809** Much of the collection is sold by Prince Camillo Borghese to France and goes to Louvre	**1902** Villa, grounds and collection bought by the state	
1621–5 Bernini sculpts *Pluto and Persephone*				
1625	**1725**		**1825**	
1622–5 Bernini sculpts *Apollo and Daphne*		**1805** Canova sculpts the semi-nude, reclining Pauline Borghese	**Early 1900s** Balustrade around the forecourt is bought by Lord Astor for the Cliveden estate in England	
1613–15 The Flemish architect Jan van Santen designs and builds Villa Borghese	*Daphne's fingers turning into leaves*			

Rear entrance

★ Apollo and Daphne
Bernini's most famous masterpiece depicts the nymph Daphne fleeing the sun god Apollo at the moment of Daphne's dramatic transformation into a tree.

★ David
Modeling David's face on his own, the 25-year-old Bernini captured the moment before David threw the stone that slew Goliath.

VISITORS' CHECKLIST

Villa Borghese, Piazzale Scipione Borghese 5. **Map** 2 F5. █ *854 85 77.* ▭ *52, 53, 910 to Via Pinciana, 3, 4, 57 to Via Po.* ▭ *19, 30b to Viale delle Belle Arti.* **Open** *9am–7pm Tue–Sat, 9am–1pm Sun (last adm: 30 mins before closing).* **Closed** *public hols.* **Adm charge.** ▣ *no flash. Some of the paintings are on view at the Quaderia della Galleria Borghese al San Michele;* **Map** 8 D2. **Open** *daily.*

★ Pauline Borghese
Napoleon's sister Pauline posed as Venus for the sculptor Canova. Once the statue was completed, Pauline's husband, Camillo Borghese, kept it locked away, even denying Canova access.

Front entrance

Gladiator Mosaic
The floor is decorated with the fragments of a 4th-century AD mosaic from a villa in Torrenova.

KEY TO FLOOR PLAN
☐ Exhibition space
▨ Non-exhibition space

STAR SCULPTURES

★ Pauline Borghese by Canova

★ Apollo and Daphne by Bernini

★ David by Bernini

★ Pluto and Persephone by Bernini

Villa Giulia ③

THIS VILLA was built as a country retreat for Pope Julius III and was designed for entertaining rather than as a permanent home. It once housed an impressive collection of statues – 160 boatloads were sent to the Vatican after the pope died in 1555. The villa, gardens, pavilions and fountains were designed by exceptional architects: Vignola (designer of the Gesù), Vasari and the sculptor Ammannati. Michelangelo also contributed. The villa's main features are its façade, the courtyard and garden, and the *nympheum*. Since 1889, Villa Giulia has housed the Museo Nazionale Etrusco, with its outstanding collection of pre-Roman antiquities from central Italy.

Faliscan Crater of the Dawn
This ornate vase, painted in the free style of the 4th century BC, shows Dawn rising in a chariot.

Chigi Vase
Battle and hunting scenes adorn this Corinthian vase from the 6th century BC.

First floor

★ **Husband and Wife Sarcophagus**
This 6th-century BC masterpiece, from Cerveteri, shows a dead couple at the eternal banquet.

MUSEUM GUIDE
This is the most important Etruscan museum in Italy, housing artifacts from most of the major excavations in Tuscany and Lazio. Rooms **1** *to* **10** *and* **23** *to* **34** *are arranged by site and include Vulci, Todi, Veio and Cerveteri, while private collections are in rooms* **11** *to* **22***.*

Votive Offering
The religious Etruscans made artifacts, such as this model of a boy feeding a bird, in their gods' honor.

TIMELINE

1550 Work begins on Villa Giulia under Pope Julius III	**1655** Queen Christina of Sweden stays in villa as Vatican guest		**1889** Etruscan museum founded	**1919** Castellani private collection donated to museum
		Late 1700s First large-scale studies of Etruscan artefacts		
1550	**1650**	**1750**	**1850**	**1950**
	Late 1500s First, chance finds of Etruscan artefacts raise some scholastic interest		**1908** Barberini private collection bought by the state	**1972** Pesciotti private collection bought by the state
1555 Villa completed	*Corner decoration of bronze chariot used to burn incense*			

Facade

The villa's façade dates from 1552 to 1553. The entrance is designed in the form of a triumphal arch.

VISITORS' CHECKLIST

Piazzale di Villa Giulia 9.
Map 1 C4. 322 65 71.
52, 926 to Viale Bruno
Buozzi, 95, 490, 495 to Viale
Washington. 19, 19b, 30b
to Piazza Thorwaldsen. **Open**
9am–7pm (Oct–Mar: 2pm)
Tue–Sun. **Closed** Jan 1, May 1 &
Dec 25. **Adm charge.**
with seven days' notice.
Concerts: "Notturno Etrusco"
evenings held at the Ninfeo
(Nympheum) on Saturdays
throughout July & August.
Lectures & films.

★ Reconstruction of an Etruscan Temple

Count Adolfo Cozza built the Temple of Alatri here in 1891. He based his design on the accounts of Vitruvius and 19th-century excavations.

Nympheum

Literally, the "area dedicated to the nymphs," this is a sunken courtyard decorated with Classical mosaics, statues and fountains.

STAR EXHIBITS

★ Husband and Wife Sarcophagus

★ Ficoroni Cist

★ Reconstruction of an Etruscan Temple

Main entrance

Ground floor

★ Ficoroni Cist

Engraved and beautifully illustrated, this fine bronze marriage coffer dates from the 4th century BC.

KEY TO FLOORPLAN

☐ Ground floor
☐ First floor
☐ Non-exhibition space

Santa Costanza ❹

Via Nomentana 349. ☎ 861 08 40.
🚌 36, 36b, 37, 60, 136, 137. **Open**
9am–noon Mon–Sat, 4–6pm Tue &
Sat, 4–6pm Sun and public hols.
Adm charge. 📷 ♿ ▣

**Circular interior of 4th-century
church of Santa Costanza**

T HE ROUND CHURCH of Santa
Costanza was originally
built in the early 4th century
as a mausoleum for Emperor
Constantine's daughters,
Constantia and Helena. The
dome and its drum are
supported by a circular arcade
that rests on 12 magnificent
pairs of granite columns. The
ambulatory that runs around
the outside of the central
arcade has a barrel-vaulted
ceiling decorated with
wonderful 4th-century mosaics
of fruit, flowers, animals and
birds and even charming
scenes of a Roman grape
harvest. In a niche on the far
side of the church from the
entrance is a replica of
Constantia's ornately carved
porphyry sarcophagus. The
original was moved to the
Vatican Museums in 1790.

Constantia's sanctity is
somewhat debatable – she
was described by the historian Marcellinus as a Fury
incarnate, constantly goading
her equally unpleasant
husband Hannibalianus to
violence. Her canonization
was probably the result of
some confusion with a saintly
nun of the same name.

Part of the 4th-century mosaic in the ambulatory of Santa Costanza

Sant'Agnese fuori le Mura ❺

Via Nomentana 349. ☎ 861 08 40.
🚌 36, 36b, 37, 60, 136, 137. **Open**
9am–noon Mon–Sat, 4–6pm Tue, Sat,
Sun and public hols. **Adm charge** to
catacombs. 📷 ♿ ▣

T HE CHURCH OF Sant'Agnese
stands among a group of
early Christian buildings that
include the ruins of a covered
cemetery, some extensive
catacombs and the crypt where
the 13-year-old martyr St. Agnes
was buried in AD 304. Agnes
was exposed naked by order of
Emperor Diocletian, furious
that she should have rejected
the advances of a young man
at his court, but her hair
miraculously grew to protect
her modesty. The church is
said to have been built at the
request of the Emperor .
Constantine's daughter
Constantia after she had prayed
at the Tomb of St. Agnes for
delivery from leprosy.

Though much altered over
the centuries, the form and
much of the structure of the
4th-century basilica remain
intact. In the 7th-century apse
mosaic St. Agnes appears as a

bejeweled Byzantine empress
in a stole of gold and a violet
robe. According to tradition,
she appeared like this eight
days after her death holding a
white lamb. Every year on
January 21 two lambs are
blessed on the church altar and
a vestment called the *pallium* is
woven from their wool. Every
newly appointed archbishop is
sent a *pallium* by the Pope.

Steps leading down to Sant'Agnese

San Lorenzo fuori le Mura ❻

Piazzale del Verano 3. ☎ 49 15 11.
🚌 11, 71, 492. 🚋 19, 19b, 30b.
Open 7am–noon & 3:30–6:30pm
daily. 📷 ♿

J UST OUTSIDE the eastern wall
of the city, set off by the
cypresses of the Campo
Verano cemetery, stands the

Apse mosaic in Sant'Agnese, showing the saint flanked by two popes

church of San Lorenzo. Roasted slowly to death in AD 258, San Lorenzo was one of the most revered of Rome's early Christian martyrs. The first basilica erected over his burial place by Constantine was largely rebuilt in 576 by Pope Pelagius II. Close by stood a 5th-century church dedicated to the Virgin Mary. The intriguing bi-level church we see today is the result of these two churches being knocked into one. This process, started in the 8th century, was completed in the 13th century by Pope Honorius III, when the nave, the portico and much of the decoration were added. The remains of San Lorenzo are in the choir of the 6th-century church (beneath the 13th-century high altar).

The church was restored after it was badly damaged by Allied bombers in an air raid during World War II.

Romanesque bell tower of San Lorenzo

Via Appia Antica ❼

📟 *118, 218. See* **Walks** *pp284–5.*

THE FIRST PART of the Via Appia was built in 312 BC by the Censor Appius Claudius Caecus. When it was extended to the ports of Benevento, Taranto and Brindisi in 190 BC, the road became Rome's link with its expanding empire in the East. It was the route taken by the funeral processions of the dictator Sulla (78 BC) and Emperor Augustus (AD 14), and it was along this road that St. Paul was led a prisoner to Rome in AD 56.

Gradually abandoned during the Middle Ages, the road was restored in the mid-16th century by Pope Pius IV. It is lined with ruined family tombs and the collective burial places known as *columbaria*, while beneath the fields on

12th-century cloister of San Lorenzo fuori le Mura

either side lies a vast maze of catacombs. Today the road starts at Porta San Sebastiano *(see p196).* Major Christian sights include the church of Domine Quo Vadis?, built on the spot where St. Peter is said to have met Christ while fleeing from Rome, and the Catacombs of San Callisto and San Sebastiano. Among the tombs lining the road are those of Cecilia Metella *(see p266)* and of Romulus, son of the Emperor Maxentius, who died in AD 309.

Catacombs of San Callisto ❽

Via Appia Antica 110. 📞 *513 67 25.* 📟 *218, 660.* **Open** *8:30am–noon & 2:30–5:30pm (Oct–Mar: 5pm) Thu–Tue.* **Closed** *Feb & public hols.* **Adm charge.** 🚻 🚫 📷 📖 🏛 🅿

IN BURYING their dead in underground cemeteries outside the city walls, the early Christians were simply obeying the laws of the time. They were not forced to use them because of persecution. Because so many saints were buried there, the catacombs later became shrines and places of pilgrimage.

The vast Catacombs of San Callisto are on four different levels and only partly explored. The rooms and connecting passageways are hewn out of volcanic tufa. The dead were

placed in niches, known as *loculi,* which held two or three bodies. The most important rooms were decorated with stucco and frescoes. The area that can be visited includes the Crypt of the Popes, where many of the early popes were buried, and the Crypt of Santa Cecilia, where the saint's body was discovered in 820 before being moved to her church in Trastevere *(see p211).*

Catacombs of San Sebastiano ❾

Via Appia Antica 136. 📞 *788 70 35.* 📟 *218, 660.* **Open** *8:30am–noon & 2.30–5:30pm Fri Wed.* **Closed** *public hols.* **Adm charge.** 🚻 📷 📖 🏛

THE 17TH-CENTURY church of San Sebastiano, above the catacombs, occupies the site of a basilica from the age of Constantine. Preserved at the entrance to the catacombs is the *triclia,* a building that once stood above ground and was used for serving funeral refreshments to parties of mourners. Its walls are covered with graffiti invoking St. Peter and St. Paul, whose remains may have been moved here during one of the periods when the Christians were persecuted by the Roman authorities.

Cypresses lining the Via Appia

Catacombs of Domitilla ⑩

Via delle Sette Chiese 282.
[511 03 42. **]** 94, 218, 613.
Open 8:30am–noon & 2:30–
5:30pm (Oct–Mar: 5pm) Wed–Mon.
Closed Jan. **Adm charge.**

THIS NETWORK of catacombs
is the largest in Rome.
Many of the tombs from the
1st and 2nd centuries AD
have no Christian connection.
In the burial chambers that
can be visited there are
frescoes of both Classical and
Christian scenes, including
one of the earliest depictions
of Christ as the *Good Shepherd*.
Above the catacombs stands
the basilica of Santi Nereo e
Achilleo. After rebuilding and
restoration, little remains of
the original 4th-century church.

Fosse Ardeatine ⑪

Via Ardeatina 174. **[** 513 67 42.
] 218. **Open** 8:30am–5pm daily
(last adm: 30 mins before closing).

ON THE EVENING of March 24,
1944, Nazi forces took 335
prisoners to this abandoned
quarry south of Rome and shot
them point-blank. The execution was in reprisal for a
bomb attack that had killed
32 German soldiers. The
victims included various
political prisoners; 73 Jews;
and 10 other civilians, among
them a priest and a 14-year-
old boy. The Germans blew
up the tunnels where the
massacre had taken place, but
a local peasant had witnessed
the scene and later helped

find the corpses. The site is
now a memorial to the values
of the Resistance against the
Germans, which gave birth to
the modern Italian Republic.
A forbidding bunkerlike
monument houses the rows
of identical tombs containing
the victims. Beside it is a
museum of the Resistance.
Interesting works of modern
sculpture include *The Martyrs*,
by Francesco Coccia, and the
gates shaped like a wall of
thorns by Mirko Basaldella.

**Bronze entrance gates to the Fosse
Ardeatine by Mirko Basaldella**

Tomb of Cecilia Metella ⑫

Via Appia Antica, III Miglio.
[780 24 65. **Open** 9am–1 hr
before sunset (7pm latest)
Tue–Sat, 9am–1pm Mon & Sun.
Closed public hols.

ONE OF THE most famous
landmarks on the Via
Appia Antica is the huge drum-
shaped tomb built for the noble
Cecilia Metella. Her father and
husband were rich patricians
and successful generals of late
Republican Rome, but hardly
anything is known about the

**Fragments of marble relief on the
Tomb of Cecilia Metella**

woman herself. Byron muses
over her unknown destiny in
his poem *Childe Harold*. In
1302, Pope Boniface VIII gave
the tomb to his family, the
Caetani, who incorporated it
in a fortified castle that blocked
the Via Appia, allowing them
to control the traffic on the
road and exact high tolls. The
marble facing of the tomb
was pillaged by Pope Sixtus V
at the end of the 16th century.

Parco Appio Claudio ⑬

Via Lemonia. **]** 557, 558, 650, 663,
664, 765. **Open** 24 hrs daily.

THE PARK covers a large
expanse of land between
the Via Appia Nuova and the
Via Tuscolana. One day it
may become part of one vast
archaeological park stretching
from here to the Colosseum
and the Forum. Its main
features are the remains of
three aqueducts, the Aqua
Marcia dating from 140 BC,
the Aqua Claudia, completed
in AD 52 by the Emperor
Claudius, and the Felice

Ruins of the Aqua Claudia aqueduct (1st century AD) in the Parco Appio Claudio

Aqueduct built by Sixtus V in the 16th century. The arches of Roman aqueducts carried water in separate conduits from two or three different sources *(see pp20–21)*. The area is an excellent place to enjoy uninterrupted views of the Roman Campagna and the Alban hills to the south.

EUR

19th-century mosaic on facade of San Paolo fuori le Mura

93, 97, 197, 293, 493, 765, 771, 791. **M** EUR Fermi, EUR Palasport.
Museo della Civiltà Romana
Piazza G. Agnelli. **[** 592 61 35.
Open 9am–7pm Tue–Sat, 9am–1pm Sun and public hols.
Adm charge.

EUR's Palazzo della Civiltà del Lavoro, the "Square Colosseum"

THE ESPOSIZIONE Universale di Roma (EUR), a suburb to the south of the city, was built originally for an international exhibition, a kind of "Work Olympics," that was planned for 1942 but never took place because of the war. The architecture was intended to glorify Fascism, and to modern eyes the style of the public buildings is very unappealing. The Palazzo della Civiltà del Lavoro (the Palace of the Civilization of Work) is an unmistakable landmark for people arriving from Fiumicino airport.

The scheme was completed in the 1950s. In terms of town planning, EUR has been quite successful. The great marble halls house a number of government offices and museums. The Museo della Civiltà Romana has a vast scale model of Rome at the time of Constantine and casts of the reliefs on the Column of Trajan. To the south of the suburb are a lake and park and the huge domed Palazzo dello Sport built for the 1960 Olympics.

San Paolo fuori le Mura

Via Ostiense 186. **[** 541 03 41.
23, 93b, 170, 223, 673. **M** San Paolo. **Open** 7:30am–6:40pm daily (last adm: 15 mins before closing).

TODAY'S CHURCH IS a faithful if somewhat soulless reconstruction of the great 4th-century basilica destroyed by fire on the night of July 15, 1823. A few fragments of the original church survived. The triumphal arch over the nave is decorated on one side with much-restored 5th-century mosaics. On the other side are mosaics by Pietro Cavallini, originally on the facade. The splendid Venetian apse mosaics (1220) represent the figures of Christ with St. Peter, St. Andrew, St. Paul and St. Luke.

The fine marble canopy over the high altar is signed by the sculptor Arnolfo di Cambio (1285) "together with his partner Pietro," who may have been Pietro Cavallini. Below the altar is the *confessio*, the tomb of St. Paul, whose body was supposed to have been buried here. To the right is an impressive Paschal candlestick by Nicolò di Angelo and Pietro Vassalletto.

The one part of San Paolo spared completely by the fire was the cloister with its pairs of colorful inlaid columns, some octagonal, some spiral, supporting the arcade. Built largely by the Vassalletto family and completed around 1214, it is considered one of the most beautiful in Rome.

Villa Doria Pamphilj

Via di San Pancrazio. 41, 75, 144.
Park open dawn–dusk daily.

ROME'S LARGEST public park, the Villa Doria Pamphilj was laid out in the mid-17th century for Prince Camillo Pamphilj. His uncle, Pope Innocent X, paid for the magnificent summer residence, the Casino del Bel Respiro, and numerous fountains and summerhouses, some of which still survive. Today the park is a popular meeting place for joggers and dog lovers.

Casino del Bel Respiro, Villa Doria Pamphilj

Day Trips around Rome

Tivoli, a favorite place to escape the heat of the Roman summer

Tivoli ⑰

Town is 20 miles (31 km) northeast of Rome. **FS** *from Roma Termini or Tiburtina.* 🚌 *COTRAL from Rebibbia (on Metro line B).*

TIVOLI HAS BEEN a popular summer resort since the days of the Roman Republic. Among the famous men who owned villas here were the poets Catullus and Horace, Caesar's assassins Brutus and Cassius and the Emperors Trajan and Hadrian. Tivoli's main attractions were its clean air and beautiful location on the slopes of the Tiburtini hills, its healthy sulphur springs and the waterfalls of the Aniene – the Emperor Augustus said these had cured him of insomnia. The Romans' luxurious lifestyle was revived in Renaissance times by the owners of the Villa d'Este,

Detail of Fontana dell'Organo at Villa d'Este

the town's most famous sight.

In the Middle Ages, Tivoli suffered frequent invasions since its position made it an ideal base for an advance on Rome. In 1461, Pope Pius II built a fortress here, the Rocca Pia, declaring: "It is easier to regain Rome while possessing Tivoli, than to regain Tivoli while possessing Rome."

After suffering heavy bomb damage in 1944, Tivoli's main buildings and churches were speedily restored. The town's cobbled streets are still lined with medieval houses. The Duomo (cathedral) houses a beautiful 13th-century life-size wooden group representing the *Deposition from the Cross.*

Villa d'Este ⑱

Piazza Trento, Tivoli. 🄲 *0774-31 20 70.* **FS** *Tivoli, then 30 mins walk or local bus (many routes).* **Open** *9am– 1hr before sunset daily.* **Closed** *public hols.* **Adm charge.** 🖵

THE VILLA OCCUPIES the site of an old Benedictine convent. In the 16th century, the estate was developed by Cardinal Ippolito d'Este, son of Lucrezia Borgia. A palace was designed by Pirro Ligorio to make the most of its hilltop situation, but the villa's fame rests more on the terraced gardens and fountains laid out by Ligorio and Giacomo della Porta.

Though the gardens have suffered over the centuries from neglect, the grottoes and fountains still give a vivid impression of the frivolous luxury enjoyed by the princes of the church. From the great loggia of the palace you descend through the shrub-lined paths to the Grotto of Diana and Bernini's Fontana del Bicchierone. Below to the right is the Rometta (little Rome), a model of Tiber Island with allegorical figures and the legendary she-wolf.

The Rometta is at one end of the Viale delle Cento Fontane. Its 100 fountains are in the shape of grotesques, obelisks, ships and the eagles of the d'Este coat of arms, now overgrown with moss. Other fountains have also lost much of their former glory. The Fontana dell'Organo was a water organ, in which the force of the water pumped air through the pipes, but it has long been silent. The garden's lowest level has flower beds, fountains and splendid views out over the plain below.

Terrace of 100 Fountains in the gardens of Villa d'Este

Villa Gregoriana ⑲

Largo Massimo, Tivoli. **FS** *Tivoli, then short walk.* **Open** *Jun–Aug: 10am– 7:30pm; Sep–May: 9:30am–1 hr before sunset daily.* **Adm charge.**

THE MAIN ATTRACTIONS of this steeply sloping wooded park are the waterfalls and grottoes created over the centuries by the River Aniene. The park is named after Pope Gregory XVI, who in the 1830s ordered the building of a tunnel to put an end to the danger of flooding. This created a new waterfall, the Grande Cascata, which plunges 350 ft (108 m) into the valley behind the town.

The Canopus, extensively restored, with replicas of its original caryatids lining the bank of the canal

Hadrian's Villa 20

Villa Adriana, Via Tiburtina. Site is 6 km (4 miles) southwest of Tivoli. **C** *0774-53 02 03.* **FS** *Tivoli, then local bus No. 4.* **COTRAL** *from Rebibbia (on Metro line B).* **Open** *9am–90 mins before sunset daily (last adm: 1 hr before closing).* **Closed** *May 1.* **Adm charge.**

B UILT AS a private summer retreat between AD 118 and 134, Hadrian's Villa was a vast open-air museum of the finest architecture of the Roman world. The grounds of the Imperial palace covered an area of 300 acres (120 hectares) and were filled with full-scale reproductions of the emperor's favorite buildings from Greece and Egypt. Although excavations began here in the 16th century, many of the ruins lying scattered in the surrounding fields have yet to be identified with any certainty. The grounds of the villa make a very picturesque site for a picnic, with scattered fragments of columns lying among olive trees and cypresses.

For an idea of how the whole complex would have looked in its heyday, study the scale model in the building beside the parking area. Important buildings have signs, and several have been partially restored or reconstructed. One of the most impressive is the Maritime Theater. This is a round pool with an island in the middle, surrounded by columns. The island, reached by means of a swing bridge, was probably Hadrian's private studio, where he withdrew from the cares of the Empire to indulge in his favorite pastimes, painting and architecture. There were also theaters; Greek and Latin libraries; two bath houses; extensive housing for guests and the palace staff; and formal gardens with fountains, statues and pools.

Hadrian was a lover of Greek philosophy as well as architecture. One part of the gardens is thought to have been Hadrian's reproduction of the Grove of Academe, where Plato lectured to his students.

Fragment of marble mosaic pavement in the Imperial palace

Hadrian also had a replica of the Stoà Poikile, a beautiful painted colonnade in Athens, from which the Stoic philosophers took their name. Hadrian's Poikile enclosed a piazza with a central pool. The area known as the Hall of the Philosophers near the Poikile was probably a library.

The most ambitious of Hadrian's replicas was the Canopus, a sanctuary of the god Serapis near Alexandria. For this a canal 200 yd (185 m) long was dug and Egyptian statues were imported to decorate the temple and its grounds. This impressive piece of engineering has been restored, and the banks of the canal are lined with caryatids.

Another picturesque spot in the grounds is the Vale of Tempe, the legendary haunt of the goddess Diana, with a stream representing the river Peneios. Below ground, the

Pair of Ionic columns in the vaulted baths of Hadrian's Villa

emperor built a fanciful re-creation of the underworld, Hades, reached through many underground tunnels which linked the various parts of the villa.

Plundered by barbarians who camped here in the 6th and 8th centuries, the villa fell into disrepair. Its marble was burned to make lime for cement, and Renaissance antiquarians contributed further to its destruction. Statues unearthed in the grounds are displayed in museums around Europe. The Vatican's Egyptian Collection *(see p238)* has many fine works that were found here.

Ostia Antica ㉑

Viale dei Romagnoli 717. Site is 16 miles
(25 km) southwest of Rome. **C** *565
00 22 or 565 14 05.* **M** *Magliana on
line B, then train to Ostia Antica.*
Excavations open *winter: 9am–4:30pm
daily; summer: 9am–6pm daily.* **Closed**
May 1. **Museum open** *9am–1pm
daily.* **Closed** *public hols.* **Adm charge**.

Ruins of shops, offices and houses near Ostia's theater

IN REPUBLICAN TIMES Ostia was
Rome's main commercial
port and a military base
defending the coastline and
the mouth of the Tiber. The
port continued to flourish
under the Empire, despite the
development of Portus, a new
port slightly to the northwest,
in the 2nd century AD. Ostia's
decline began in the 4th
century, when a reduction in
trade was followed by the
gradual silting up of the
harbor. Worse was to come
when malaria became endemic
in the area, and the city,
whose population is estimated
to have been nearly 100,000 at
its peak, was as a result
totally abandoned.

Buried for centuries by
sand, the city is remarkably
well preserved. The site is
less spectacular than Pompei
or Herculaneum because
Ostia died a gradual death,
but it gives a more complete
picture of life under the
Roman Empire. People of all
social classes and from all
over the Mediterranean lived
and worked here.

Visitors can understand the
layout of Ostia's streets almost
at a glance. The main road
through the town, the
Decumanus Maximus, would
have been filled with hurrying
slaves and citizens, avoiding
the jostling carriages and
carts, while tradesmen

pursued their business under
the porticoes lining the street.
The floor plans of the public
buildings along the road are
very clear. Many were bath
houses, such as the Baths of
the Cisiarii (carters) and the
grander Baths of Neptune,
named after their fine black-
and-white floor mosaics.
Beside the restored theater,
three large masks, originally
part of the decoration of the
stage, have been mounted
on large blocks of tufa.
Beneath the great brick
arches that supported the
semicircular tiers of seats
were taverns and shops.
Classical plays are put on
here now in the summer.

The Tiber's course has
changed considerably since
Ostia was the port of Rome. It
once flowed past just to the
north of Piazzale delle

**Mask decorating
the theater ·**

Corporazioni, the square
behind the theater. The
corporations were the guilds
of the various trades involved
in fitting out and
supplying ships:
tanners and rope
makers, ship
builders and
timber merchants,
ships' chandlers
and corn weighers.
There were some
60 or 70 offices
around the square.
Mosaics showing
scenes of everyday
life in the port and
the names and
symbols of the
corporations can
still be seen.

There were also offices used
by ship-owners and their
agents from places as far
away as Tunisia and the south
of France, Sardinia and Egypt.
In one office, belonging to a
merchant from the town of
Sabratha in North Africa,
there is a delightful mosaic
of an elephant.

The main cargo coming into
Rome was grain from Africa.
Much of this was distributed
free to prevent social unrest.
Although only men received
this *annona*, or corn ration,
at times over 300,000 were
eligible. In the center of the
square was a temple, probably

Mural from Ostia of merchant ship being loaded with grain

dedicated to Ceres, goddess of the harvest. Among the buildings excavated are many large warehouses in which grain was stored before it was shipped on to Rome.

The Decumanus leads to the Forum and the city's principal temple, erected by Hadrian in the 2nd century AD and dedicated to Jove, Juno and Minerva. In this rather romantic, lonely spot, it is hard to imagine the Forum as a bustling center where justice was dispensed and officials

Floor mosaic of Nereid and sea monster in the House of the Dioscuri

Detail of floor mosaic in the Piazzale delle Corporazioni

met to discuss the city's affairs. In the 18th century it was used as a sheepfold.

Away from the main street are the buildings where Ostia's inhabitants lived. The great majority lived in rented apartments in blocks three or four stories high, known as *insulae*. These varied widely in their comfort and decor. The House of Diana was one of the more elegant ones, with a balcony around the second floor, a private bathhouse and a central courtyard with a cistern where tenants came to get their water. Around the ground floor of the block were shops, taverns and bars selling snacks and drinks. In the bar at the House of Diana you can see the marble counter used by customers buying their sausages and hot wine sweetened with honey.

For the wealthy there were detached houses *(domus)* such as the House of the Dioscuri, which has fine colored mosaics, and the House of Cupid and Psyche, named after a charming statue found there. This is now in the site's small museum, along with other sculptures and reliefs found in Ostia.

Among the houses and shops there are other buildings, including a laundry and the firemen's barracks.

Various religions are practiced in Ostia. There are no fewer than 18 temples dedicated to the Persian god Mithras, as well as a Jewish synagogue dating from the 1st century AD and a Christian basilica. A plaque records the death of St. Augustine's mother in a hotel here in Ostia in AD 387.

ALSO WORTH SEEING

Anagni FS *from Termini (c 50 min).* Picturesque hill town with papal palace and famous Romanesque cathedral.

Bracciano FS *from Termini or Tiburtina (c 90 min).* 🚌 *from Lepanto, on Metro line A (bus c 90 min).* Volcanic lake with villages and wooded hills. Nice for walks or a visit to Orsini Castle. Swimming in summer.

Cerveteri FS *from Termini, Tiburtina or Ostiense to Cerveteri-Ladispoli, then local bus (c 70 min).* 🚌 *from Via Lepanto, on Metro line A (bus c 80 min).* One of the greatest Etruscan cities. Necropolis with complete streets and houses.

Nemi FS *from Anagnina, on Metro line A (bus c 60 min).* Charming village at volcanic lake in the Castelli Romani. Famous for its wine and strawberries.

Palestrina FS *from Rebibbia, on Metro line B (bus c 70 min).* Impressive Roman sanctuary to goddess Fortuna. Museum and the Mosaic of the Nile.

Pompei FS *from Termini. Express train to Pompei (c 160 min) or any train to Naples, then change to local train (c 170 min).* 🚌 *Special bus tours from tourist agents.* Excavations of the wealthy Roman city where the busy daily life was put to an end by the eruption of Vesuvius in AD 79.

Subiaco 🚌 *from Rebibbia, on Metro line B (bus c 120 min).* Birthplace of St. Benedict. Two monasteries to visit.

Tarquinia FS *from Termini or Ostiense (c 180 min).* 🚌 *from Via Lepanto, on Metro line A. Change at Civitavecchia (c 150 min).* Outstanding collection of Etruscan objects and frescoes from Tarquinia's necropolis.

Viterbo FS *from Termini (c 150 min) or COTRAL train from Roma Nord, Piazzale Flaminio, on Metro line A (c 120 min).* 🚌 *from Saxa Rubra reached by the COTRAL train above (bus c 90 min).* Medieval quarter, papal palace and archaeological museum within 13th-century walls.

SIX GUIDED WALKS

ROME IS an excellent city for walking. The distances between major sights in the historic center can easily be covered on foot, and many streets have been pedestrianized. When you get tired, there are plenty of pavement cafés in wonderful settings, such as Piazza Navona and Campo de' Fiori. If you are interested in archaeology, then try a walk across the Forum *(see pp76–87)* and over the Palatine *(see pp96–101) to* take you away from the roaring traffic of modern Rome into a different world of scattered ruins and shady pine trees.

The first of the six suggested walks takes in picturesque quarters on either side of the Tiber, the river that has played such an important part in the city's development. The second

Bernini angel on Ponte Sant'Angelo

walk, along the perfectly straight Via Giulia, gives a vivid impression of the Renaissance city. The next three walks each follow a particular theme. For visitors who wish to savor the glory of ancient Rome, there is a walk taking in the surviving triumphal arches of the emperors. For those who prefer the Middle Ages, there is a tour of early Christian churches with well-preserved mosaics, and for those who enjoy the Roman Baroque, there is a walk concentrating on Bernini's contribution to the city's appearance.

The Romans were famous for their straight roads. The final walk is outside the central sightseeing area, along the best-known Roman road, the Via Appia Antica, parts of which remain after more than 2,000 years of use.

CHOOSING A WALK

Bernini
(pp282–3)

Via Giulia
(pp276–7)

The Six Walks
The routes of the first five walks are marked on the larger map, which also shows the main sightseeing areas of Rome. The smaller inset map shows the location of the Via Appia walk in relation to the central area.

Mosaics
(pp280–81)

Tiber
(pp274–5)

Triumphal Arches
(pp278–9)

KEY

••• Walk routes

— City Wall

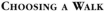

0 kilometers   1

0 miles   0.5

Via Appia Antica
(pp284–5)

Pedestrians strolling across Ponte Sant'Angelo

A Two-Hour Walk by the River Tiber

ROME OWES ITS VERY EXISTENCE to the Tiber; the city grew up around an easy fording point where a marketplace developed. The river could also be a hazard; shallow and torrentlike, it flooded the city every winter up to 1870, when work began on the massive Lungotevere embankments that run along both sides of the river. These provide many fine views from points along their avenues of plane trees. The walk also explores the neighborhoods along the riverside, in particular the Jewish Ghetto and Trastevere, which have preserved much of their character from earlier periods in the colorful history of Rome.

From the old port of Rome to Via dei Funari

Starting from the church of Santa Maria in Cosmedin ① *(see p202)*, cross the piazza to the Temples of the Forum Boarium ② *(see p203)*. This was the cattle market that stood near the city's river port. The river here has preserved two less obvious structures from ancient Rome: the mouth of the Cloaca Maxima ③, the city's great sewer, and one arch of a ruined bridge, known as the Ponte Rotto ④. On Via di Ponte Rotto stands the extraordinary medieval Casa dei Crescenzi ⑤ *(see p203)*, decorated with fragments of Roman temples. Passing the modern Anagrafe (public records office) ⑥, built on the site of the old Roman port, you come to San Nicola in Carcere ⑦ *(see p152)*.

You are now in the Foro Olitorio, Rome's ancient vegetable market. To the east stand the ruins of a Roman portico and the medieval house of the Pierleoni family. Head for the massive Theater

Santa Maria in Cosmedin ①

of Marcellus ⑧ *(see p151)* and look for the three Corinthian columns of the Temple of Apollo beside it. Turn onto Piazza Campitelli and walk up to Santa Maria in Campitelli ⑨ *(see p151)*. The church honors a miraculous image of the Virgin credited with halting the plague in 1656. The 16th-century piazza was the home of Flaminio Ponzio, its architect, who lived at No. 6. Take Via dei Delfini to Piazza Margana, where you can look up at the 14th-century tower of the Margani family ⑩. Retrace your steps, then go up Via dei Funari (Street of the Ropemakers) to the 16th-century facade of Santa Caterina dei Funari ⑪.

The Ghetto

From Piazza Lovatelli, take Via Sant'Angelo in Pescheria, which

leads to the ruined Portico of Octavia ⑫ *(see p151)* in the Jewish Ghetto *(see p152)*. The Roman portico, once Rome's fish market, houses the church of Sant'Angelo in Pescheria. Find the marble plaque on the facade: fish longer than this slab were given to the city's *conservatori* (governors). Turn into the Ghetto: two column stumps belonging to the Portico stand in front of a patched-up doorway made of fragments of Roman sculpture. The cramped buildings and streets around Via del Portico

Main altar of Santa Maria in Campitelli ⑨

Arch of the Ponte Rotto ④

d'Ottavia are typical of old Rome: see the Casa di Lorenzo Manilio ⑬ *(see p153)* and turn down Via delle Cinque Scole, past Palazzo Cenci ⑭ *(see p152)*, toward the river. On Lungotevere, walk past the Synagogue ⑮ *(see p152)* to the small church of San Gregorio ⑯. Here stood the gates of the Ghetto, which were locked at sundown.

Across the river to Trastevere

Crossing to Tiber Island *(see p152)* by Ponte Fabricio, with its two ancient

Classical relief of Medusa above the doorway of Palazzo Cenci ⑭

much of the spirit of old Trastevere. Walk up to the start of Viale di Trastevere at Piazza Belli. After crossing the road, look back

Santa Maria in Trastevere, don't miss the old-fashioned pharmacy at No. 7. The piazza itself, in front of the magnificent church of Santa Maria in Trastevere ㉒ *(see pp212–13)*, has a cheerful atmosphere, and the fountain steps are a favorite meeting place. Go back a little way to Via del Moro. This leads to Piazza Trilussa, dominated by the fountain of the Acqua Paola ㉓, where you emerge out to the bank of the river again. Note the lifelike statue, near the fountain of Roman poet Trilussa, who wrote in the local dialect. From Ponte Sisto ㉔ *(see p210)*, look back to Tiber Island and, beyond it, to the medieval bell tower of Santa Maria in Cosmedin, set against the pine trees on the summit of the Palatine.

The western tip of Tiber Island

0 meters 250
0 yards 250

stone heads on the parapet, you can enjoy a good view of the river in both directions. On the island itself, you should not miss the Pierleoni Tower ⑰ or the church of San Bartolomeo all'Isola ⑱.

Trastevere

As you cross into Trastevere, you can see the medieval house of the powerful Mattei family ⑲, with its fragments of ancient sculpture. Beyond it, Piazza in Piscinula and the surrounding streets retain

KEY

— Walk route

⋇ Good viewing point

at the medieval tower of the Anguillara ⑳ and the statue honoring the poet Gioacchino Belli ㉑ *(see p209)*. As you go down Via della Lungaretta to Piazza

Piazza in Piscinula, old Trastevere

TIPS FOR WALKERS

Starting point: Piazza della Bocca della Verità.
Length: 2 miles (3.5 km).
Getting there: The 15, 23, 57, 90, 90b, 92 and 95 buses all stop near Santa Maria in Cosmedin.
Best time for walk: This walk can be very romantic in the evenings but is enjoyable at any time.
Stopping-off points: Piazza Campitelli and Piazza Margana have typical Roman restaurants, and Via del Portico d'Ottavia features two kosher restaurants and a bakery. Tiber Island has a bar and the famous Sora Lella restaurant (see p314). In Viale Trastevere there are bars and pizzerias of all kinds. Piazza Santa Maria in Trastevere boasts lively bars and restaurants with outdoor tables.

A One-Hour Walk along Via Giulia

L AID OUT BY BRAMANTE for Pope Julius II in the early 16th century, Via Giulia was the first Renaissance street to slice through Rome's jumble of medieval alleys. The original plan included new law courts in a central piazza, but this project was abandoned for lack of cash. The street is now occupied mainly by antiques shops and furniture restorers. On summer evenings, the street is lit with hundreds of oil lamps, and cloisters and courtyards provide romantic settings for a special season of concerts.

Baroque capital on the facade of Sant'Eligio degli Orefici ⑦

From Lungotevere to Largo della Moretta

Starting from Lungotevere dei Tebaldi ① at the eastern end of Via Giulia, you will see ahead of you an archway ② spanning the road. This was the start of Michelangelo's unrealized project linking Palazzo Farnese and its gardens *(see p147)* with the Villa Farnesina *(see pp220–21)* on the other side of the river.

Just before you reach the archway, you will see to your left the curious Fontana del Mascherone ③, in which an ancient grotesque mask and granite basin were combined to create a Baroque fountain.

Beyond the Farnese archway on the left is the lively Baroque facade of the church of Santa Maria dell'Orazione e Morte ④ *(see p147)*. A bit farther along on the same side of the road stands Palazzo Falconieri ⑤, enlarged by Borromini in 1650. Note its two stone falcons glowering at each other across the width of the facade. On the other side of the road, you pass the yellowish facade of Santa Caterina da Siena ⑥, church of the Sienese colony in Rome, which has pretty 18th-century reliefs. The figures of Romulus and Remus symbolize Rome

Relief of Romulus and Remus on Santa Caterina da Siena ⑥

and Siena – there is a legend that the city of Siena was founded by the less fortunate of the twins. After passing the short street that leads down to Sant'Eligio degli Orefici ⑦ *(see p148)* and the facade of Palazzo Ricci ⑧ *(see p149)*, you come to an area of half-demolished buildings around the ruined church of San Filippo Neri ⑨, called Largo della Moretta. If you look to the left down to the river, you can see

Fontana del Mascherone ③

Ponte Mazzini and the huge prison of Regina Coeli on the other side of the Tiber. At this point you may like to make a small detour to the right to the beginning of Via del Pellegrino, where there is an inscription ⑩ defining the *pomerium*, or boundary, of the city in the time of the Emperor Claudius.

From Largo della Moretta to the Sofas of Via Giulia

Farther on, facing the narrow Vicolo del Malpasso, are the imposing prisons, the Carceri

Nuove ⑪, built by Pope Innocent X Pamphilj in 1655. When first opened, they were a model of humane treatment of prisoners, but they were replaced by the Regina Coeli prison across the river at the end of the 19th century. The buildings now house offices of the Ministry of Justice and a small Museum of Crime.

At the corner of Via del Gonfalone, a small side street running down to the river,

KEY

—   Walk route

⁂   Good viewing point

0 meters		250
0 yards		250

[Map showing Via Giulia walk route with numbered points ⑫ through ⑳, labeled streets including Ponte Vittorio Emanuele II, Ponte Pr. Amedeo, Via della Lungara, Lungotevere dei Tebaldi, Lungotevere Gianicolense, Via di San Francesco di Sales, Ponte Mazzini, and the Tevere river]

Farnese archway across Via Giulia, built to a design by Michelangelo ②

you can see part of the foundations of Julius II's planned law courts. Just down the street stands the small Oratorio di Santa Lucia del Gonfalone ⑫, which is often used for concerts.

The next interesting facade is Carlo Rainaldi's 17th-century Santa Maria del Suffragio ⑬ on the left. On the same side is San Biagio degli Armeni ⑭, the Armenian church in Rome. It is often referred to by local people as San Biagio della Pagnotta (of the loaf of bread). The nickname originates from

the traditional distribution of bread to the poor that took place on the saint's feast day.

On the corner there are more travertine blocks belonging to the foundations of Julius II's projected law courts, known because of their curious shape as the "Sofas of Via Giulia."

The Florentine Quarter

Your next stop should be the imposing Palazzo Sacchetti at No. 66 ⑮. Originally this was the house of Antonio da Sangallo the Younger, the architect of Palazzo Farnese, but it was greatly enlarged by later owners. The porticoed courtyard houses a 15th-century Madonna and a striking Roman relief of the 3rd century AD. Just opposite Palazzo Sacchetti is the beautiful late Renaissance portal of Palazzo Donarelli ⑯. The 16th-century house at No. 93 is richly decorated with stuccoes and coats of arms ⑰. No. 85 is another typical Renaissance palazzo with a heavily rusticated ground floor ⑱. There is a tradition

Detail on the side of the door of Santa Maria del Suffragio ⑬

Plaque honoring Antonio da Sangallo on Palazzo Sacchetti ⑮

that, like many houses of the period, it once belonged to Raphael. Palazzo Clarelli ⑲ was built by Antonio da Sangallo the Younger as his own house. The inscription above the doorway bears the name of Duke Cosimo II de' Medici, whose family later bought the palazzo.

This whole area used to be inhabited by a flourishing Florentine colony, which had its own water mills built on pontoons along the Tiber. Their national church is San Giovanni dei Fiorentini ⑳ (see p153), the final great landmark at the end of Via Giulia. Many Florentine artists and architects had a hand in its design, including Sangallo and Jacopo Sansovino.

Coat of arms of Pope Paul III Farnese on the facade of Via Giulia No. 93 ⑰

TIPS FOR WALKERS

Starting point: Lungotevere dei Tebaldi, by Ponte Sisto.
Length: 1,100 yds (1 km).
Getting there: Take either a 46, 62 or 64 to Corso Vittorio Emanuele II, then walk down Via dei Pettinari or a 23, 65 or 280 along Lungotevere.
Best time for walk: On summer evenings, the street is lit by oil lamps. At Christmas, crèches are on display in shop windows.
Stopping-off points: There are bars in Via Giulia, at Nos. 21 and 84. Campo de' Fiori has better bars, with outdoor tables, and a wide choice of places to eat. These include a Chinese restaurant in Via dei Giubbonari and a fried fish restaurant in Piazza Santa Barbara dei Librai (closed Sun).

A 90-Minute Tour of Rome's Triumphal Arches

ROME'S GREATEST GIFT to architecture was the arch, and the Roman people's highest tribute to its victorious generals was the triumphal arch. In Imperial times, arches were erected to honor an emperor's campaign victories almost as a matter of course, promoting his personal cult and ensuring his subsequent deification. Spectacular processions passed through these arches. Conquering generals, cheered by rapturous crowds, rode in their chariots to the Capitol, accompanied by their legions bearing spoils from their campaigns.

Part of the Via Sacra, once spanned by the Arch of Augustus ③

Arches of the Forum

This walk through the Forum and around the base of the Palatine takes in Rome's three great surviving triumphal arches and two arches of more

Relief of barbarian captives on the Arch of Septimius Severus ①

humble design that were used simply as places of business. It starts from the Arch of

Emperor Septimius Severus ① and his sons, Geta and Caracalla *(see p83)*, in the Forum. Erected in AD 203, it celebrates a successful campaign in the Middle East. Eight years later when Caracalla had his brother killed, all mention of Geta was removed from the inscription.

Look up at the reliefs showing phases of the campaigns. Set in tiers, they are probably the sculptural counterparts of the paintings illustrating the general's feats that were borne aloft in the triumphal procession. On the right, the inhabitants of a fortified city surrender to the Romans' siege machines. Below are smaller friezes showing the triumphal procession itself.

Heading east, make your way through the Forum to the ruins of the Temple of Julius Caesar ②. The temple was built by Augustus in 42 BC, on the site where Caesar's body was cremated after Mark Antony's famous funerary oration. A nearby sign marks the ruins of the Arch of Augustus ③, spanning the Via Sacra between the Temple of Castor and Pollux ④ *(see p84)* and the Temple of Caesar. This arch, erected after Augustus had defeated Mark Antony and Cleopatra, was demolished in 1545, and its materials were used in the

Capital from Temple of Castor and Pollux ④

new St. Peter's. From here, proceed uphill toward the elegant Arch of Titus ⑤ *(see p87)*. Compared with Septimius Severus's arch, it shows an earlier, simpler style. Look up at the beautiful lettering of the inscription before you examine the inner bas-reliefs. These show

KEY

—	Walk route
✳	Good viewing point
Ⓜ	Metro station

0 meters	250
0 yards	250

Arch of Titus in a 19th-century watercolor by the English artist Thomas Hartley Cromek ⑤

Arches of Domitian's extension to the Claudian Aqueduct ⑨

Four-sided Arch of Janus ⑬

through the arch would have been carrying building materials quarried from the Forum's various ruins.

Arch of Constantine

Leave the Forum by heading down the hill toward the Colosseum ⑥ *(see pp92–5)* and the nearby Arch of Constantine ⑦ *(see p91)*. This arch, hastily built to commemorate the emperor's victory over his rival Maxentius in AD 312, is a patchwork of reliefs from different periods. Stand on the Via di San Gregorio side and compare the earlier panels at the top (AD 180–193) with the hectic battle scenes just above the smaller arches, sculpted in AD 315. In the curious dwarf-like soldiers, you can see the transition from Classicism to a cruder medieval style of sculpture.

Now take Via di San Gregorio, which runs along the valley between the Palatine and Celian hills. This was the ancient route taken by most triumphal processions. Passing the entrance to the Palatine ⑧ and the well-preserved arches of the Claudian Aqueduct ⑨ on the right, you come to Piazza di Porta Capena ⑩, named after the gate that stood here to mark the beginning of the Via Appia *(see p284)*. After rounding the back of the Palatine, follow Via dei Cerchi, which runs alongside the grassy area that preserves the oval outline of the Circus Maximus ⑪ *(see p205)*.

Arches of the Forum Boarium

When you reach the church of Sant'Anastasia ⑫, turn right up Via di San Teodoro, then take the first left down Via del Velabro. Straddling the street is the four-sided Arch of Janus ⑬ *(see p202)*, erected in the 3rd century AD: not a triumphal arch but a covered area where merchants could take shelter from the sun or rain when discussing business. Like the Arch of Titus, it became part of a fortress built by the Frangipane family during the Middle Ages.

Tucked away beside the nearby church of San Giorgio in Velabro ⑭ *(see p202)* is what looks like a large rectangular doorway. This is the Arco degli Argentari, or Moneychangers' Arch ⑮. Look up at the inscription, which notes that it was erected by local silversmiths in honor of Septimius Severus and his family in AD 204. As in the emperor's triumphal arch, the name of Geta has been obliterated by his brother and murderer, Caracalla. Geta's figure has also been removed from among the portraits on the panels inside the arch. Triumph in Imperial Rome could be very short-lived.

Roman legionaries carrying the spoils looted from the conquest of Jerusalem; heralds holding plaques with the names of vanquished peoples and cities; and Titus riding in triumph in his chariot.

The medieval Frangipane family turned the Colosseum into a vast impregnable stronghold and incorporated the Arch of Titus into their fortifications. Notice the wheelmarks scratched on the inside walls of the arch by generations of carts; they indicate the steady rise in the level of the Forum before it was eventually excavated in the 18th and 19th centuries. Many of the carts that passed

A Three-Hour Tour of Rome's Best Mosaics

IN IMITATION of the audience chambers of Imperial palaces, Rome's early Christian churches were decorated with brilliant mosaics. These were pieced together from cubes of marble, colored stone and fragments of glass. To create a golden background, gold leaf was placed between pieces of glass. These were then heated so that they fused. The glorious colors and subjects portrayed gave the faithful a glimpse of the heavenly court of the King of Kings. This walk concentrates on a few of the churches decorated in this wonderful medium.

Apse mosaic in the Chapel of Santa Rufina ③

San Giovanni

Start from Piazza di Porta San Giovanni, where you can visit the heavily restored mosaic that was originally in the banqueting hall of Pope Leo III (reigned 795–816) ①, showing Christ among the Apostles. On the left are Pope Sylvester and the Emperor Constantine, on the right, Pope Leo and Charlemagne, just before he was crowned

Obelisk and side facade of San Giovanni in Laterano ②

Holy Roman Emperor in AD 800. Inside the church of San Giovanni in Laterano ② *(see pp182–3)*, the 13th-century apse mosaic shows Christ as he appeared miraculously during the consecration of the church. In the panels by the windows, look for the small figures of two Franciscan friars; these are the artists Jacopo Torriti *(left)* and Jacopo de Camerino *(right)*. Leave by

the exit on the right near the splendid 16th-century organ and head for the octagonal Baptistry of San Giovanni ③, where the Chapel of Santa Rufina has a beautiful apse mosaic in green, azure and gold, dating from the 5th century. In the neighboring Chapel of San Venanzio there are golden 7th-century mosaics, showing the strong influence of the Eastern Church at this time.

Santo Stefano Rotondo to San Clemente

Leave the piazza by the narrow road that leads to the round church of Santo Stefano Rotondo ④ *(see p185)*. One of its chapels contains a 7th-century Byzantine mosaic honoring two martyrs buried here. Farther on, in Piazza della Navicella, is the church of Santa Maria in Domnica ⑤ *(see p193)*. It houses the superb mosaics commissioned by Pope Paschal I, who gave new impetus to Rome's mosaic production in the 9th century. He is represented kneeling beside the Virgin. On leaving the church, notice the facade of San Tommaso in Formis ⑥, which has a charming mosaic of Christ flanked by two freed slaves, one black and one white, dating from the 13th

Ceiling mosaic, Baptistry of San Giovanni ③

acanthus leaves. San Clemente also has a fine 12th-century Cosmatesque mosaic floor.

The Colle Oppio
Passing the old entrance to the church, cross Via Labicana and walk up the hill to the small Colle Oppio park ⑨. This has fine views of the Colosseum and contains the ruins of Nero's Golden House ⑩ *(see p175)* and the Baths of

Interior of Baptistry of San Giovanni ③

century. From here, head up the steep hill, past the forbidding apse of Santi Quattro Coronati ⑦ *(see p185)*, to the fascinating church of San Clemente ⑧ *(see pp186–7)*. Its 12th-century apse mosaic shows the cross set in a swirling pattern of

Trajan ⑪. Across the park lie San Martino ai Monti ⑫ *(see p170)*, which has a 6th-century mosaic portrait of Pope St. Sylvester in the crypt, and Santa Prassede ⑬ *(see p171)*. Here the Chapel of St. Zeno contains the most important Byzantine mosaics in Rome, reminiscent of the fabulous mosaics of Ravenna. Pope Paschal I erected the chapel as a mausoleum for his

14th-century facade mosaics by Filippo Rusuti. Inside, the 5th-century mosaics in the nave depict Old Testament stories, while the triumphal arch has scenes relating to the birth of Christ, including one of the Magi wearing striped stockings. In the apse is a Coronation of the Virgin by Jacopo Torriti (1295).

On leaving Santa Maria, pass the obelisk ⑮ in the piazza behind the church and go downhill to Via Urbana and Santa Pudenziana ⑯ *(see p171)*. The figures in the apse mosaic, one of the oldest in Rome (AD 390), are remarkable for their naturalism. The two women with crowns are traditionally identified as Santa Prassede and Santa Pudenziana.

Mosaic saint in Santa Prassede ⑬

When you leave the church, you can either retrace your steps to Santa Maria Maggiore or walk down Via Urbana to Via Cavour Metro station.

11th-century frieze above the doorway of Santa Pudenziana ⑯

mother, Theodora. The apse and triumphal arch of the church itself also have fine mosaics. When you move on to Santa Maria Maggiore ⑭ *(see pp172–3)*, go to the column in the center of the piazza in front of the church to see the beautiful

KEY
— Walk route
— City Wall
☼ Good viewing point
Ⓜ Metro station

0 meters 250
0 yards 250

TIPS FOR WALKERS

Starting point: Piazza di Porta San Giovanni.
Length: 2 miles (3.5 km).
Getting there: The nearest Metro station is San Giovanni, on line A, in Piazzale Appio, just outside Porta San Giovanni. The 81, 85 and 87 buses and the 13 and 30b trams stop in front of San Giovanni in Laterano.
Best time for walk: It is advisable to go in the morning, in order to to appreciate the mosaics in the best possible light.
Stopping-off points: The bars and restaurants in Piazza del Colosseo are popular with artists, who like to draw the Colosseum on the paper tablecloths. In the Parco del Colle Oppio is a small café kiosk with tables. There are several bars around Santa Maria Maggiore, some of which have outdoor tables.

A Two-Hour Walk around Bernini's Rome

GIAN LORENZO BERNINI (1598–1680) is the artist who probably left the strongest personal mark on the appearance of the city of Rome. Favorite architect, sculptor and town planner to three successive popes, he turned Rome into a uniquely Baroque city. This walk traces his enormous influence on the development and appearance of the center of Rome. It starts from the busy Largo di Santa Susanna just north of Termini Station, at the church of Santa Maria della Vittoria.

Facade of Santa Maria in Via ⑬

Bernini's Fontana del Tritone ②

Quirinale. The long wing of the Palazzo del Quirinale ⑦ *(see p158)*, nicknamed the Manica Lunga (long sleeve), is by Bernini. On the other side of the road is the facade of Sant'Andrea al Quirinale ⑧ *(see p161)*, one of Bernini's greatest churches. When you reach the Piazza del Quirinale ⑨, note the doorway of the palazzo, attributed to Bernini. From the piazza, go up the

composer Donizetti lived at No. 77 and turn into Via Santa Maria in Via, where the church ⑬ has a fine Baroque

Through Piazza Barberini

Santa Maria della Vittoria ① *(see p255)* houses the Cornaro Chapel, the setting for one of Bernini's most revolutionary and controversial sculptures, the *Ecstasy of St. Teresa* (1646). From here take Via Barberini to Piazza Barberini. In its center is Bernini's dramatic Fontana del Tritone ② *(see p254)*, and at one side stands the more modest Fontana delle Api ③ *(see p254)*. As you go up Via delle Quattro Fontane, you catch a glimpse of Palazzo Barberini ④ *(see p255)* built by Bernini and several other artists for Pope Urban VIII. The gateway and cornices are decorated with the bees that made up part of the Barberini family crest. Next make your way to the crossroads, decorated by Le Quattro Fontane ⑤ *(see p162)*, to enjoy the splendid views in all four directions.

Passing the diminutive San Carlo alle Quattro Fontane ⑥ *(see p161)*, built by Bernini's rival Borromini, take Via del

stairs to Via della Dataria and into Vicolo Scanderbeg, which leads to a small piazza with the same name ⑩. Scanderbeg was the nickname of the Albanian prince Giorgio Castriota (1403–68), the "Terror of the Turks." His portrait is preserved on the house where he lived.

The Trevi Fountain

Go along the narrow Vicolo dei Modelli ⑪, where male models waited to be chosen by artists, then turn toward the Trevi Fountain ⑫ *(see p159)*. Its energy is clearly inspired by Bernini's work, a tribute to his lasting influence on Roman taste. Leave the piazza along Via delle Muratte, where the

Neptune Fountain at the north end of Piazza Navona ⑱

facade by Bernini's follower Carlo Rainaldi. At the top of this street, turn left down to Via del Corso. On the other side of the road, you will see the towering Column of Marcus Aurelius ⑭ *(see p113)* in Piazza Colonna. Beyond this is Palazzo Montecitorio ⑮, begun in 1650 by Bernini and now the home of the Italian parliament *(see p112).*

Pantheon to Piazza Navona
Via in Aquiro leads you to the Pantheon ⑯ *(see pp110–11).* Refusing Pope Urban VIII's request for him to redecorate

Collegio Innocenziano by Bernini's rival Borromini in Piazza Navona ⑱

Angel on Ponte Sant'Angelo

the dome, Bernini said that although St. Peter's had a hundred defects, the Pantheon did not have any. From the Pantheon, make a small detour to Piazza della Minerva, where you can see the bizarre Bernini obelisk, supported by a small elephant, by the church of Santa Maria sopra Minerva ⑰ *(see p108).* Then retrace your steps and take Salita dei Crescenzi to

reach the fabulous Piazza Navona ⑱ *(see p120),* which was remodeled by Bernini for Pope Innocent X Pamphilj. The design for the central fountain, the Fontana dei

Fiumi *(see p120),* was by Bernini, though the figures symbolic of the four rivers were sculpted by other artists. The central figure in the Fontana del Moro, however, is by Bernini himself. Bernini's contemporaries were fascinated by the innovative use of shells, rocks and other natural forms in his fountains, and his expert handling of water to create constant movement.

An extended walk
More energetic walkers may want to head toward the river to see the Ponte Sant'Angelo and its Bernini angels, and then go on to St. Peter's *(see pp230–33),* where they can admire Bernini's great colonnaded piazza in front of the church, the papal tombs, his altar decorations and the bronze baldacchino.

TIPS FOR WALKERS

Starting point: Largo di Santa Susanna.
Length: 2 miles (3.5 km).
Getting there: Take Metro line A to Repubblica or any bus to Termini, then walk. Buses 60, 61, 62 and 137 stop in Via Barberini.
Best time for walk: Go either between 9am and noon for good lighting conditions in the churches or between 4 and 7pm.
Stopping-off points: The Piazza Barberini and Fontana di Trevi areas have lots of bars and pizzerias for tourists. The many elegant cafés en route include the famous Caffè Giolitti (see p109), and there is a vast choice of outdoor cafés and restaurants around Piazza della Rotonda and Piazza Navona.

KEY

— Walk route

⚶ Good viewing point

Ⓜ Metro station

| 0 meters | 250 |
| 0 yards | 250 |

A 90-Minute Walk along the Via Appia Antica

LINED WITH CYPRESSES AND PINES as it was when the ancient Romans came here by torchlight to bury their dead, the Via Appia is wonderfully atmospheric. The fields are strewn with ruined tombs set against the picturesque background of the Alban hills to the south. Although the marble or travertine stone facings of most tombs have been plundered, a few statues and reliefs survive or have been replaced by copies.

Capo di Bove

Start from the Tomb of Cecilia Metella ① *(see p266)*. In the Middle Ages, this area acquired the name Capo di Bove (ox head) from the frieze of festoons and ox heads still visible on the tomb. On

Gothic windows in the church of San Nicola ②

Tomb of Sixtus Pompeus the Righteous ⑨

the other side of the road, you can see the ruined Gothic church of San Nicola ②, which, like the Tomb of Cecilia Metella, was part of the medieval fortress of the Caetani family.

Proceed to the crossroads ③, where many original Roman paving slabs, huge blocks of extremely durable volcanic basalt, are still in place. Just

on both sides of the Appia, are other tombs, some still capped with the remains of the medieval towers that were built over them. On the right, after passing some private villas, you come to a military zone around the Forte Appio ⑤, one of a series of forts built around the city in the 19th century. On the left, a little farther on, stand the ruins of the Tomb of Marcus Servilius ⑥, showing fragments of reliefs excavated in 1808 by the Neoclassical sculptor Antonio Canova. He was one of the first to work on the principle that excavated tombs and their inscriptions and reliefs should be allowed to remain in situ. On the other side of the road stands a tomb with a relief of a man, naked except for a short cape, known as the

"Heroic Relief" ⑦. On the left of the road are the ruins known as the Tomb of Seneca ⑧. The great moralist Seneca owned a villa near here, where he committed suicide in AD 65 on the orders of Nero. The next major tomb is that of the family of Sixtus Pompeus the Righteous, a freed slave of the 1st century AD ⑨. The verse inscription records the father's sadness at having to bury his own children, who died young.

The ruined church of San Nicola ②

past the next turn (Via Capo di Bove), you will see on your left the nucleus of a great mausoleum overgrown with ivy, known as the Torre di Capo di Bove ④. Beyond it,

Artist's impression of how the mausoleums and tombs lining the Via Appia looked in the 2nd century AD

Section of the Via Appia Antica, showing original Roman paving

From Via dei Lugari to Via di Tor Carbone

Just past Via dei Lugari on the right, screened by trees, is the Tomb of Pope St. Urban (reigned 222–30) ⑩. Set back from the road on the left stands a large ruined podium, probably part of a Temple of Jupiter ⑪. The next stretch was excavated by the architect Luigi Canina early in the 19th century. On the right is the Tomb of Caius Licinius ⑫, followed by a smaller Doric tomb ⑬ and the imposing Tomb of Hilarius

Fuscus ⑭, with five portrait busts in relief of members of his family. Next comes the Tomb of Tiberius Claudius Secondinus ⑮, where a group of freedmen of the Imperial household were buried in the 2nd century AD.

Passing a large ruined columbarium, you reach the Tomb of Quintus Apuleius ⑯ and the reconstructed Tomb of the Rabirii freed slaves (1st century BC) ⑰. This has a frieze of three half-length figures above an inscription.

The figure on the right is a priestess of Isis. Behind her you can see the outline of a *sistrum*, the metal rattle used at ceremonies of the cult.

The majority of the tombs are little more than shapeless stacks of eroded brickwork. Two exceptions in the last stretch of this walk are the Tomb of the Festoons ⑱, with its reconstructed frieze of festive putti, and the Tomb of the Frontispiece ⑲, which has a copy of a relief with four portraits. The two central figures are holding hands.

When you reach Via di Tor Carbone, the Via Appia still stretches out ahead of you in a straight line; if you wish to extend your walk, there are many more tombs and ruined villas to visit along the way.

KEY

— Walk route

❊ Good viewing point

| 0 meters | 250 |
| 0 yards | 250 |

Figure on the Tomb of the Heroic Relief ⑦

TIPS FOR WALKERS

Starting point: Tomb of Cecilia Metella.

Length: 2 miles (3 km).

Getting there: Take the 118 bus from San Giovanni in Laterano or the Colosseum. On the way back, the 118 goes along the Via Appia Pignatelli. Allow plenty of time for waiting for the bus.

Best time for walk: Go fairly early, before it gets too hot.

Stopping-off points: There is a bar near the church of Domine Quo Vadis?, before the start of the walk, but it is best to bring your own refreshment. There are also several well-established restaurants on the first stretch of the Appia, including the Cecilia Metella, Via Appia Antica 125/127 (phone: 513 67 43; closed Mon).

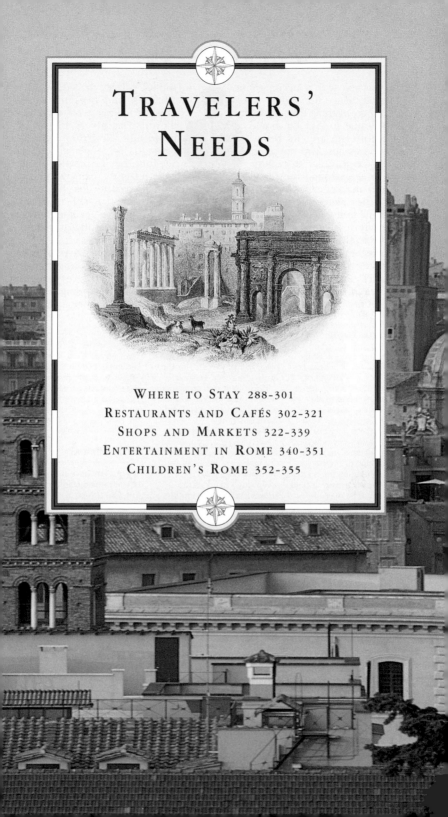

TRAVELERS'
NEEDS

WHERE TO STAY

ROME HAS BEEN a major tourist center since the Middle Ages, when pilgrims from all over Europe came to visit the home of Catholicism and its relic-packed churches. The nostalgic can still sleep in a 15th-century hotel or stay around the Campo de' Fiori market, where visiting ecclesiastics were entertained by courtesans in the Renaissance era. Those who prefer their history a little less raffish can stay in an ex-monastery, convent or a still-functioning religious house. Romantics can sleep in the house once occupied by Keats, while the celebrity-conscious can stay

Porter at the Majestic Hotel

in former palaces graced by VIPs of the past and present. Rome offers the full range of accommodations, mainly in historical buildings. *Pensione* (guesthouse) is no longer an official category, but in practice many places retain the name and more personal character that has made them so popular with travelers. Other possibilities include hostels, residential hotels and accommodations with kitchens.

The 72 hotels we have selected are listed in the *Choosing a Hotel* chart *(pp294–5)*, organized *(pp296–301)* according to their price category and area.

WHERE TO LOOK

AROUND the Spanish Steps and Piazza di Spagna lies the traditional heartland of foreign visitors, with some of the most exclusive smaller hotels. Similar places can be found all over the center, to the west of Via del Corso.

While moderately priced accommodations are rare in central Rome, the advantages of staying right on the doorstep of the city's many ancient sights cannot be overestimated; you can walk to the major areas of interest and easily return at midday for a shower, meal and siesta.

If the less expensive hotels we have recommended in the center are full, try the Borgo – close to the Vatican – or the lively quarter of Trastevere.

Those in search of glamour should head for Via Veneto, which has many grand and luxurious hotels.

If you're looking for a peaceful retreat, try the area around the Aventine or one of the high-class hotels next to the Villa Borghese park.

Although many of the streets immediately around Termini Station are somewhat seedy, the area is nonetheless a convenient stopover for travelers. There's also a

concentration of cheap hotels, with some decent (if basic) ones among them. The hotels recommended lie in a fairly safe area on the east side of the station. The approach to the center from Termini has a number of good hotels that are particularly suitable for the business traveler.

HOTEL PRICES

ROME MAY have cheaper accommodations than London or New York, but rates for comparable establishments have caught up. Prices are set by the state, and hotels must display the official rate on the door of each room. VAT is usually included and has been taken into account in the price categories on page 291.

It is rare, but not unheard of, for Roman hotels to have low- and high-season rates, so it can be worth bargaining since you will inevitably be quoted the official rate – even in the winter months before and after Christmas, when competition is less strong. Discounts for long-term visitors and groups are often negotiable.

Rooms without a bathroom can cost about 30% less. Single travelers will find few bargains: though it is possible to find a single room for 60% of the price of a double, on the average you'll pay 70%,

The Verdi Room in Via Veneto's Majestic Hotel *(see p301)*

The Plaza Minerva *(see p296)*

and occasionally up to 90%. Where breakfast is included in the quoted price, you can ask for the relevant amount to be deducted from your bill if you don't want the meal.

HIDDEN EXTRAS

EVEN IF the room price includes service, you are still expected to tip at least L1,000 for room service and around L2,000 for bellboys.

Hotels will often add hefty surcharges to international phone calls and may charge extra for parking and air conditioning. The cost of drinks in minibars can be high – you can buy a cheaper supply from local shops.

FACILITIES

HOTEL STANDARDS have improved of late – you can expect air-conditioning and some bathrooms with hair dryers in middle-range establishments and direct-dial phones in middle-to-lower price rooms, although budget travelers staying in cheaper hotels shouldn't expect much more than a clean room.

Because most hotels occupy historic buildings, room sizes can vary dramatically even within the same establishment (and this is often reflected in the

pricing), so don't be afraid to ask to see your room before you check in. For the same reason, swimming pools are few and far between, but roof terraces or gardens are common across the range.

First-class hotels will usually have some degree of soundproofing; otherwise, noise levels can be dreadful, in which case ask for a room facing away from the road. The chart on pages 294 to 295 indicates which hotels have a quiet location – this covers both peaceful neighborhoods and certain quiet streets in busy areas.

Parking in central Rome is a problem, though a few hotels have a limited number of parking spaces of their own.

Business visitors to the capital are well provided for, with hotel facilities ranging from fax machines to meeting and conference rooms *(see pp294–5)*.

MAKING RESERVATIONS

THE ITALIAN postal service tends to be unreliable, so it is safer to reserve by phone or fax. You should do this at least two months in advance if you want a particular hotel in May, June, September or October; Easter and Christmas are also busy.

If a deposit is required, you can pay by credit card or international money order. Under Italian law a reservation is valid as soon as the deposit is paid, so you're likely to lose money if you cancel. If you arrive by train, people may approach you at the station with offers of accommodations.

The Portoghesi Hotel *(see p296)*

They can be of some use if you are looking for a budget hotel, but you should exercise the usual caution. A better bet if you haven't reserved a room anywhere in advance is to head for one of the tourist board offices. Here, staff will reserve you a room within your price range.

Villa San Pio garden *(see p299)*

CHECKING IN AND OUT

ITALIAN HOTELIERS are legally obliged to register you with the police, which is the reason they always ask for your passport. They usually hold on to it for a few hours, but you will need it if you're going to change money. Everyone in Italy is supposed to carry with them some sort of identification.

In some of Rome's cheaper *pensioni,* don't be surprised if you are asked to pay in advance. To speed up the checking-out process, mention in advance if you intend to pay by credit card.

The Locarno *(see p297)*

TOURIST BOARDS

THE PROVINCIAL and state tourist boards can provide advice on accommodations and reserve rooms.

Rome Provincial Tourist Board (EPT)
Via Parigi 5, 00185.
[48 89 92 55.

EPT Leonardo da Vinci Airport, Fiumicino, 00054.
[65 95 44 71.

EPT Termini Station,
Piazza dei Cinquecento, 00185.
[482 30 78 or 487 12 70.

Italian State Tourist Board (ENIT)
Via Marghera 2, 00185.
[497 11.

The reception area of the Regina Hotel Baglioni *(see p301)*

DISABLED TRAVELERS

Provision for the disabled is very poor. Small hotels that occupy parts of buildings sometimes offer only rooms that must be reached via several flights of stairs, while certain establishments can accommodate disabled guests only on the ground floor or have only one or two rooms that are appropriate. Ramps, wide doorways and bathroom handrails are rare.

Our entries for wheelchair access in the listings below rely on the establishments' own assessments; any specific requirements should be checked before reserving.

There is a private organization, Associazione Nazionale dei Andicappati at via Tommaso Fortifiocca 100, which gives advice to disabled travelers. They can be contacted on 781 07 72.

TRAVELING WITH CHILDREN

Italians love children, and they are usually welcome across the range of hotels. Facilities, however, tend to be unimpressive. Most hotels can provide cribs or small beds, but highchairs, children's meals and babysitting services are rare. However, many establishments – especially smaller, family-run ones – go out of their way to be helpful.

Many hotels do not have any special rates for children, especially in high season, and charge a standard rate if you require an extra bed in a room, whether it's for a baby

or an adult; this can add anything from a few thousand lire to 40% on to the price of a double room. For a family with older children, two-room suites are sometimes to be found. For hotels providing children's facilities, see Choosing a Hotel *(pp294–5)*.

APARTMENTS

Anyone staying for more than one or two weeks should consider renting an apartment, which can be arranged through an agency. **International Services** has a list of studios and apartments; the **Landmark Trust** rents an apartment (reserved three years in advance) in the house where Keats died, near the Spanish Steps.

RESERVING APARTMENTS

International Services
Via del Babuino 79, 00187.
[36 00 00 18. FAX 36 00 00 37.

Landmark Trust
Shottesbrooke, Maidenhead SL6 3SW, Great Britain.
[01628-82 59 25. FAX 01628-82 54 17 (UK phone number).

RESIDENTIAL HOTELS

If you want the comfort and privacy of your own apartment coupled with the services of a hotel, you could opt to stay in a *residenza*. Prices range from around L500,000 to over L3 million for a week in a two-bedded room, though some *residenze* are available only for two-week or monthly lets. A full

list is available from tourist board offices *(see p289)*; the following are some of the most central:

Residence Babuino
Via del Babuino 172, 00187.
[361 16 63.

Di Ripetta
Via di Ripetta 231, 00186.
[323 11 44. FAX 320 39 59.

In Trastevere
Vicolo Moroni 35, 00153.
[581 27 68.

Ripa
Via Orti di Trastevere 1, 00153.
[586 11.

Vittoria
Via Vittoria 60, 00187.
[679 75 33.

RELIGIOUS INSTITUTIONS

If you don't mind an early curfew when the rest of Rome is still swinging, quite a few religious institutions take in paying guests. You do not have to be a practicing Catholic to stay in one of these, but be sure to reserve well in advance since all of the following places cater to groups of students and pilgrims. **Domus Mariae** and **Istituto Madri Pie** are near the Vatican; **Congregazione Suore dello Spirito Santo** is farther out of town, 4 miles (6 km) west of the center. Prices are near those of the cheapest hotels.

Domus Mariae
Via Aurelia 481, 00165.
[663 88 23.

The Gregoriana *(see p297)*

Istituto Madri Pie

Via A. de Gasperi 4, 00165.
C 63 19 67.

Congregazione Suore dello Spirito Santo

Via della Pineta Sacchetti 227, 00168.
C 305 31 01.

Facade of the Excelsior *(see p301)*

BUDGET ACCOMMODATIONS

EVEN IF YOU'RE TRAVELING on a shoestring, it's possible to find a clean, decent room in Rome. Dormitory accommodations can be found at rock-bottom prices in simple establishments, such as the **Ottaviano.** Youth hostels are a good option – and not just for the young. The **Ostello del Foro Italico** provides bed, breakfast and shower at a very reasonable price.

Women can get single, double or triple rooms at the **Young Women's Christian Association** (YWCA). Its location near Termini Station is convenient but somewhat unsafe, so take care if arriving at night. The **Protezione della Giovane** organization has an information office for

women under 25; they will try to find you somewhere safe and cheap to stay.

HOSTEL AND DORMITORY ADDRESSES

Ottaviano

Via Ottaviano 6, 00192.
C 39 73 72 53, or 39 73 81 38.

Associazione Italiana Alberghi per la Gioventù

(Youth Hostel Association)
Via Cavour 44, 00184.
C 487 11 52.

Ostello del Foro Italico

Viale delle Olimpiadi 61, 00194.
C 323 62 79.

Residenza Universitaria de Lollis

Via Cesare de Lollis 20, 00185.
Rooms in August only. Details from Youth Hostel Association, above.

YWCA

Via C. Balbo 4, 00184.
C 488 39 17.

Protezione della Giovane

Via Urbana 158.
C 488 14 89.

CAMPING

MOST CAMPSITES are well out of town – suitable for an occasional excursion into Rome – with the exception of **Flaminio**, which is near the Olympic Village, 4 miles (6 km) north of the center.

Flaminio

Via Flaminia Nuova 821, 00191.
C 333 26 04.

USING THE LISTINGS

The hotels on pages 296 to 301 are organized according to area and price. The symbols after the hotel's address show the facilities it offers.

꤭ rooms with bath and/or shower available
1 single-rate rooms available
↟↟ rooms for more than two people available, or an extra bed can be put in a double room
24 24-hour room service available
TV television in all rooms
Y minibar in all rooms
✈ nonsmoking rooms available
✿ rooms with good view
▤ air-conditioning in all rooms
≈ swimming pool in hotel
✿ business facilities: message-taking service, fax machine for guests, desk and telephone in each room and a meeting room within the hotel
✿ child cribs and baby-sitting service
✿ wheelchair access (phone for details)
✿ elevator
✿ pets allowed in bedrooms (confirm that you are bringing a pet). The majority of hotels accept guide dogs.
P hotel parking available
◐ garden/terrace open to guests
Y bar
¶¶ restaurant
ℹ tourist information
✆ credit cards accepted
AE American Express
DC Diners Club
MC MasterCard/Access
V VISA
JCB Japanese Credit Bureau

Price categories for a double room with bath or shower, including breakfast, tax and service:
L under L100,000
LL L100,000–L199,000
LLL L200,000–L299,000
LLLL L300,000–L400,000
LLLLL over L400,000

The pool in the Aldrovandi Palace garden *(see p301)*

Rome's Best: Hotels

Rᴏᴍᴀɴ ʜᴏᴛᴇʟs ʀᴀɴɢᴇ from frescoed palaces and fin-de-siècle bastions of faded glamour to family-run guesthouses. Most are within easy reach of restaurants, shops and transportation. Whatever the price level, all the hotels shown on this map have something special to offer, whether it's a chic location or a roof terrace with soaring views of the city. The only drawback is that these places and the others listed on pages 294 to 301 are exceptions to the many less outstanding hotels, so you should reserve well in advance. The hotels shown here are the best in their particular style or price range.

Hotel Raphaël

Sole al Pantheon
The writers Jean Paul Sartre and Simone de Beauvoir stayed in this superbly located – and recently refurbished – 15th-century palazzo. (See p296.)

N

0 meters 500
0 yards 500

Raphael
Full of antiques and art, the Raphael offers a central location. (See p297.)

Piaz Spa

Pia de Roto

Vatican

Piazza Navona

Campo de' Fiori

Janiculum

Campo de' Fiori
Central Rome's best bargain offers small well-furnished rooms and terrific views from the sixth-floor roof terrace. (See p298.)

Trastevere

Teatro di Pompeo
This guesthouse-style hotel was built on the ruins of an ancient theater. (See p299.)

Sant'Anselmo
To be sure of getting a room, reserve well in advance at this peacefully located Roman villa. An added bonus is the lovely secluded garden. (See p299.)

Villa Borghese
Delightful public rooms and a cool, shaded courtyard with a leafy canopy above, create an unpretentious and relaxed atmosphere in this pleasantly informal hotel.
(See p301.)

Hassler
Luxurious suites and an air of faded grandeur remind visitors of the Hassler's heyday. The rooftop restaurant is Rome's most famous.
(See p298.)

Carriage
The serene atmosphere makes this city-center hotel a special haven.
(See p297.)

Via Veneto

Quirinal

Esquiline

Grand
Good service and extensive facilities are the main features of this old-fashioned luxury hotel.
(See p299.)

Forum

Palatine

Caracalla

Lateran

Scalinata di Spagna
The prized location at the top of the Spanish Steps and a large private terrace make this hotel a popular choice with visitors.
(See p298.)

Inghilterra
Sip a cocktail in the Inghilterra's clublike bar, once frequented by Ernest Hemingway. (See p298.)

Choosing a Hotel

THE 71 HOTELS listed in the following pages have all been inspected and assessed. This selection chart includes some of the features that may affect your hotel choice. The hotels are listed alphabetically within their price category. For more detailed information, see pages 296 to 301.

Hotel	Price	Number of Rooms	Large Rooms	Business Facilities	Hotel Parking	Recommended Restaurant	Close to Shops and Restaurants	Quiet Location	24-Hour Room Service
FORUM (see p296)									
Forum	ⓁⓁⓁⓁ	76		■					●
PIAZZA DELLA ROTONDA (see p296)									
Abruzzi	Ⓛ	25					●		
Mimosa	Ⓛ	11					●	■	
Santa Chiara	ⓁⓁⓁ	97					●		
Sole al Pantheon	ⓁⓁⓁⓁ	30					●		●
Colonna Palace	ⓁⓁⓁⓁⓁ	110	●				●		
Holiday Inn Crowne Plaza Minerva	ⓁⓁⓁⓁⓁ	134	●	■			●	■	●
Nazionale	ⓁⓁⓁⓁ	87	●	■			●		●
PIAZZA NAVONA (see p296)									
Navona	Ⓛ	26					●	■	
Due Torri	ⓁⓁⓁ	26					●	■	
Genio	ⓁⓁⓁ	60					●		
Portoghesi	ⓁⓁⓁ	27				●	●	■	
Raphael	ⓁⓁⓁⓁ	63					●	■	
PIAZZA DI SPAGNA (see p297)									
Jonella	Ⓛ	9					●		
Firenze	ⓁⓁ	25	●				●		●
Lydia	ⓁⓁ	17					●		
Margutta	ⓁⓁ	21					●	■	
Suisse	ⓁⓁ	13	●				●	■	
Carriage	ⓁⓁⓁ	27	●				●		
Condotti	ⓁⓁⓁ	17	●				●		●
Gregoriana	ⓁⓁⓁ	19				●	●	■	●
Homs	ⓁⓁⓁ	50				●	●	■	
Locarno	ⓁⓁⓁ	38		■		●	●		
Mozart	ⓁⓁⓁ	31					●	■	
Piazza di Spagna	ⓁⓁⓁ	16					●		
Scalinata di Spagna	ⓁⓁⓁ	15				●	●		●
Manfredi	ⓁⓁⓁⓁ	15		■			●	■	●
Borgognoni	ⓁⓁⓁⓁⓁ	50		■	●		●	■	
Hassler	ⓁⓁⓁⓁⓁ	100	●	■	●	■	●	■	
Inghilterra	ⓁⓁⓁⓁⓁ	105		■			●	■	●
Valadier	ⓁⓁⓁⓁⓁ	38		■			●	■	
CAMPO DE' FIORI (see p298)									
Campo de' Fiori	ⓁⓁ	27					●	■	
Piccolo	ⓁⓁ	15					●		
Pomezia	ⓁⓁ	22					●		
Rinascimento	ⓁⓁ	19					●	■	
Smeraldo	ⓁⓁ	35					●		
Sole	ⓁⓁ	58		■	●		●	■	
Della Lunetta	ⓁⓁⓁ	36					●	■	
Teatro di Pompeo	ⓁⓁⓁⓁ	12		■	●		●	■	

Price categories for a double room per night, including breakfast, tax and service:
Ⓛ under L100,000
ⓁⓁ L100,000–L199,000
ⓁⓁⓁ L200,000–L299,000
ⓁⓁⓁⓁ L300,000–L400,000
ⓁⓁⓁⓁⓁ over L400,000.

HOTEL PARKING
Car parking facilities attached to the hotel or in the hotel complex.

CLOSE TO SHOPS AND RESTAURANTS
Within a 5-minute walk of a good area for shops, bars, cafés and restaurants.

BUSINESS FACILITIES
Message-taking service, fax machine for guest use, desk and telephone in each room and a meeting room that is available within the hotel.

	Price	NUMBER OF ROOMS	LARGE ROOMS	BUSINESS FACILITIES	HOTEL PARKING	RECOMMENDED RESTAURANT	CLOSE TO SHOPS AND RESTAURANTS	QUIET LOCATION	24-HOUR ROOM SERVICE
QUIRINAL *(see p299)*									
Grand	ⓁⓁⓁⓁⓁ	171	●	■		■			●
TERMINI *(see p299)*									
Cervia	Ⓛ	26							
Gexim	Ⓛ	9						■	
Katty	Ⓛ	11							
Mari	Ⓛ	13	●						
Restivo	Ⓛ	6							
Canada	ⓁⓁⓁ	70	●	■	●				
AVENTINE *(see p299)*									
Aventino	ⓁⓁ	23	●	■				■	●
Sant'Anselmo	ⓁⓁ	46		■				■	●
Villa San Pio	ⓁⓁ	59	●	■	●			■	●
Domus Aventina	ⓁⓁⓁ	26	●	■	●			■	●
TRASTEVERE *(see p300)*									
Carmel	Ⓛ	10							
Manara	Ⓛ	7					●		
VATICAN *(see p300)*									
Alimandi	ⓁⓁ	30						■	
Amalia	ⓁⓁ	30					●		
Columbus	ⓁⓁⓁ	92		●	●				●
Atlante Star	ⓁⓁⓁⓁ	70	●	■	●		●		●
VIA VENETO *(see p300)*									
Merano	ⓁⓁ	32					●		
Oxford	ⓁⓁⓁ	58		■	●		●		
Alexandra	ⓁⓁⓁⓁ	45			●		●		
Imperiale	ⓁⓁⓁⓁ	95			●		●		●
Pullman Boston	ⓁⓁⓁⓁ	124	●	■			●	■	
Residenza	ⓁⓁⓁⓁ	29	●				●		
Romantik Barocco	ⓁⓁⓁⓁ	28		■			●		
Victoria	ⓁⓁⓁⓁ	120		■			●	■	●
Bernini Bristol	ⓁⓁⓁⓁⓁ	126	●	■			●		●
Excelsior	ⓁⓁⓁⓁⓁ	327	●	■	●		●		●
Majestic	ⓁⓁⓁⓁⓁ	96			●		●		
Regina Hotel Baglioni	ⓁⓁⓁⓁⓁ	130	●	■	●		●		
VILLA BORGHESE *(see p301)*									
Villa Borghese	ⓁⓁⓁ	31			●				●
Aldrovandi Palace	ⓁⓁⓁⓁⓁ	140		■	●				
Lord Byron	ⓁⓁⓁⓁⓁ	37		■		■		■	●

FORUM

Forum

Via Tor de' Conti 25, 00184. **Map** 5 B5.
📞 679 24 46. **FAX** 678 64 79.
TX 62 25 49. **Rooms:** 76. 🛏 1
♨ 24 TV 🍷 ☂ 🍽 🔒 📶 👤
🍴 ☰ AE, DC, MC, V.
Ⓛ Ⓛ Ⓛ Ⓛ

Occupying a palace built out of
materials from the ruins of the
nearby Imperial Fora, the Forum
is an old-fashioned hotel. It features
mellow wood-paneled public
rooms, and a sunny roof terrace
restaurant giving wonderful views
over the archaeological center.

PIAZZA DELLA ROTONDA

Abruzzi

Piazza della Rotonda 69, 00186.
Map 4 F4 & 12 D3. 📞 679 20 21.
Rooms: 25. 1 ♨ Ⓛ

The Abruzzi provides clean, basic
rooms with terra-cotta-tiled floors
in an ochre-colored palazzo overlooking the Pantheon. The rooms
at the back, while not the best, are
quiet. No breakfast is served.

Mimosa

Via di Santa Chiara 61, 00186. **Map**
4 F4 & 12 D3. 📞 68 80 17 53. **Rooms:**
11. 🛏 1. 1 ♨ Ⓛ

The Mimosa is a clean, if slightly
scruffy, family-run hotel close to
the Pantheon. Rooms are cool, and
the five communal bathrooms and
showers are immaculate. The hotel
is popular with visiting student
groups, so reserve well ahead.

Santa Chiara

Via di Santa Chiara 21, 00186.
Map 4 F4 & 12 D3. 📞 687 29 79.
FAX 687 31 44. **Rooms:** 97. 🛏 1 ♨
TV 🍷 ☰ 📶 ☰ AE, DC, MC, V,
JCB. Ⓛ Ⓛ Ⓛ

Conveniently located in the historic
center, the Santa Chiara occupies
an apricot-washed palazzo. Public
rooms are cool, particularly the
marble reception area and the
lounge. Bedrooms are carpeted
and have good-quality furnishings
and marble bathrooms. Street-
facing rooms can be noisy.

Sole al Pantheon

Piazza della Rotonda 63, 00186.
Map 4 F4 & 12 D3. 📞 678 04 41.
FAX 69 94 06 89. **Rooms:** 30. 🛏 1
♨ 24 TV 🍷 ☰ 📶
☰ AE, DC, MC, V. Ⓛ Ⓛ Ⓛ Ⓛ

A hotel since 1467, the Sole boasts
an illustrious list of former
guests – from Renaissance writer
Ariosto to Jean-Paul Sartre and
Simone de Beauvoir. Its location
opposite the Pantheon is
unbeatable, and though it has
been modernized (60% of the
rooms now have Jacuzzis), there
are still bedrooms with painted,
paneled ceilings.

Colonna Palace

Piazza di Montecitorio 12, 00186.
Map 4 F3 & 12 E2. 📞 678 13 41.
FAX 679 44 96. **TX** 62 14 67 CIFCOL.
Rooms: 110. 🛏 1 ♨ TV 🍷 ☂
☰ 📶 🍷 👤 ☰ AE, DC, MC, V.
Ⓛ Ⓛ Ⓛ Ⓛ

The Colonna Palace stands on the
same piazza as Italy's Chamber of
Deputies, and so the area attracts
politicians as well as tourists.
Bedrooms are spacious, though
the bathrooms are small. Breakfast
is served in a basement room
livened up by frescoes. There are
lovely views from the impressive
roof garden, where a Jacuzzi has
recently been installed.

Holiday Inn Crowne Plaza Minerva

Piazza della Minerva 69, 00186.
Map 4 F4 & 12 D3. 📞 69 94 18 88.
FAX 679 41 65. **TX** 62 00 91 HINMIN.
Rooms: 134. 🛏 1 ♨ 24 TV 🍷
☂ 🔒 ☰ 📶 👤 🍷 🍴
👤 ☰ AE, DC, MC, V, JCB.
Ⓛ Ⓛ Ⓛ Ⓛ

Occupying Palazzo Fonseca
behind the Pantheon, this is
Rome's newest luxury hotel. The
interior was designed by Post-
Modern architect Portoghesi, and
its centerpiece is the lounge,
canopied in semi-translucent
Venetian glass and presided over
by a statue of Minerva. The large
bedrooms are decorated in shades
of beige and coral. Views from the
roof terrace are magnificent,
stretching over the Pantheon,
St. Peter's and the Janiculum Hill.

Nazionale

Piazza di Montecitorio 131, 00186.
Map 4 F3 & 12 E2. 📞 678 92 51.
FAX 678 66 77. **TX** 62 14 27. **Rooms:**
87. 🛏 1 ♨ TV 🍷 ☂ ☰ 🔒
🍷 👤 ☰ AE, DC, MC, V, JCB.
Ⓛ Ⓛ Ⓛ Ⓛ

Home to Robert de Niro while he
was making *Godfather II*, the
Nazionale is usually frequented
by visiting tourists, businesspeople
and politicians – it stands right
on the corner of the Chamber
of Deputies. Public rooms are
comfortable, particularly the
lounge, with its brocade sofas and
flower arrangements. Some of the

rooms are huge, and most are
partially furnished with British and
Italian antiques.

PIAZZA NAVONA

Navona

Via dei Sediari 8, 00186. **Map** 4 F4 &
12 D3. 📞 686 42 03. **Rooms:** 21.
🛏 18. 1 ♨ ☂ 🍷 🍴 Ⓛ

This hotel's superb location –
across from Piazza Navona and
five minutes' stroll from the
Pantheon – means that it's hard to
find a room here unless you
reserve well in advance. The hotel
is run largely by the owners'
Australian son-in-law, who is
extremely helpful. Bedrooms are
basic, and some have bathrooms.
The restaurant opens for groups
of 15 or more.

Due Torri

Vicolo del Leonetto 23–25, 00186.
Map 4 E3 & 11 C1. 📞 687 69 83.
FAX 686 54 42. **Rooms:** 26. 🛏 1
♨ TV 🍷 ☰ 📶 👤 🍴 ☰ AE,
DC, MC, V. Ⓛ Ⓛ Ⓛ

This amiable hotel is a short walk
from both Piazza Navona and the
Spanish Steps, tucked into an
alleyway in the artisans' district
of the old town. Bedrooms vary:
some are stylish, others plain and
rather small. The lounge is both
elegant and homey, with looped-
back drapes, statuettes, an
immense gilt-framed mirror and
pink velvet sofas.

Genio

Via Zanardelli 28, 00186. **Map** 4 E3 &
11 C2. 📞 683 37 81. **FAX** 68 30 72 46.
Rooms: 64. 🛏 1 ♨ TV 🍷 ☰
📶 👤 ☰ AE, DC, MC, V, JCB.
Ⓛ Ⓛ Ⓛ

On a fairly busy road just behind
Piazza Navona, the Genio's
bedrooms are ordinary, though
comfortable. The location,
however, and a roof terrace where
you can picnic with your own
food, make it worth considering.

Portoghesi

Via dei Portoghesi 1, 00186.
Map 4 E3 & 11 C2. 📞 686 42 31.
FAX 687 69 76. **Rooms:** 27. 🛏 1
♨ TV ☰ 📶 👤 ☰ MC, V.
Ⓛ Ⓛ Ⓛ

Ideally located on a cobbled street
a brief walk from Piazza Navona,
the Portoghesi is a simple hotel,
with slightly dated bedrooms. The
public rooms, however, are
elegant, and there's a roof terrace
looking out to the dome of the
Portuguese community's church
next door.

Raphael

Largo Febo 2, 00186. **Map** 4 E3 & 11 C2. 68 28 31. FAX 687 89 93. TX 62 23 96 RHOTEL. **Rooms**: 63. [symbols] AE, DC, MC, V. ⓁⓁⓁⓁⓁ

The Raphael is curtained with ivy and situated on a cobbled street just off Piazza Navona. The big reception lounge has the air of an exhibition hall, being full of antique statues, modern sculpture and even a painted sled. There is a restaurant in the basement whose outstanding feature is an ornate wine cabinet. Bedrooms are decorated with parquet floors, marbled walls and 18th-century-style furniture as well as paisley curtains. The rooms on the top floor offer terrific views.

PIAZZA DI SPAGNA

Jonella

Via della Croce 41, 00187. **Map** 4 F2. 679 79 66. **Rooms**: 5. 1 Ⓛ

The Jonella occupies an orange-colored palazzo on one of the most attractive shopping streets in the Piazza di Spagna area. The decor is somewhat ordinary, but the location and low prices make this place worth considering. The owner occasionally pops out to shop, so if you arrive when no-one's there, be patient and wait for someone to return.

Firenze

Via Due Macelli 106, 00187. **Map** 5 A2 & 12 F1. 679 72 40. FAX 678 56 36. **Rooms**: 25. [symbols] AE, MC, V. ⓁⓁ

The Firenze lies a short distance from Piazza di Spagna on a busy main road. The owner has set her elegant stamp on the hotel: Chinese urns and gilt-framed mirrors greet you in the entrance hall, and the bedrooms are large and beautifully decorated. There is also a leafy terrace where you can take breakfast.

Lydia

Via Sistina 42, 00187. **Map** 5 B2. 679 38 15. FAX 679 72 63. TX 62 33 13. **Rooms**: 28. 6. [symbols] AE, DC, MC, V. ⓁⓁ

The Lydia is a pleasant hotel, popular with students, on a busy road a few minutes' walk from the Spanish Steps. Rooms have pale-blue walls and pastel bedcovers, and two retain their old ceiling frescoes. If you're not fortunate enough to get one of these, content yourself with breakfasting

in the chandelier-lit dining room, which is also decorated with beautiful frescoes. Some of the street-facing rooms can be noisy.

Margutta

Via Laurina 34, 00187. **Map** 4 F1. 679 84 40, 322 36 74. **Rooms**: 21. [symbols] AE, DC, MC, V. ⓁⓁ

The Margutta sits on a quiet cobbled street just below the Piazza del Popolo. You'll be able to forget the worn facade and slightly grubby seats in the lobby as soon as you get to your room, which will have white walls and green wrought-iron bedsteads and candleholders. If you want to stay in one of the three attic rooms that share a pretty roof terrace, be sure to book well in advance.

Suisse

Via Gregoriana 54–56, 00187. **Map** 5 A2 & 12 F1. 678 36 49. FAX 678 12 58. **Rooms**: 13. 8. [symbols] ⓁⓁ

Occupying the third floor of a dusty palazzo (the entrance is at No. 54), the Suisse is a pleasant small hotel with friendly staff. Chinese prints hang along the corridors and in the rooms. The rooms also have polished floors, molded ceilings and marble-topped dressers and tables. Breakfast is served in the bedrooms.

Carriage

Via delle Carrozze 36, 00187. **Map** 5 A2. 699 01 24. FAX 678 82 79. TX 62 62 46. **Rooms**: 27. [symbols] AE, DC, MC, V, JCB. ⓁⓁⓁ

Situated on a street where the nobility used to park their carriages, this hotel's elegance is immediately evident in the reception area, with its paneling, candelabra and gilt-framed mirrors. The rooms are just as impressive, decorated in a serene shade of blue, with some antique furniture. Two rooms open on to the leafy terra-cotta-tiled public terrace; two have their own private terraces.

Condotti

Via Mario de' Fiori 37, 00187. **Map** 5 A2 & 12 F1. 679 47 69. FAX 679 04 57. **Rooms**: 17. 1 [symbols] AE, DC, MC, V, JCB. ⓁⓁⓁ

Close to Piazza di Spagna and in the heart of the designer shopping district, the Condotti is a comfortable, inviting hotel. Rooms are medium to large and well decorated. One room has its own small terrace, and three others share one.

Gregoriana

Via Gregoriana 18, 00187. **Map** 5 A2 & 12 F1. 679 42 69. FAX 678 42 58. **Rooms**: 19. 1 24 [symbols] ⓁⓁⓁ

The Gregoriana is a stylishly congenial hotel, situated close to the Spanish Steps on a tree-lined, quiet street of elegant palazzi. The first- and third-floor corridors are papered with a leopard-spotted print, while that of the second floor is in the style of William Morris. The rooms are all the same: black lacquer doors, terra-cotta-colored carpets, flowery wallpaper and 1920s drawings on the walls. There are no public rooms, so breakfast and drinks are served in the bedrooms.

Homs

Via della Vite 71–72, 00187. **Map** 5 A3 & 12 F1. 679 29 76. FAX 678 04 82. **Rooms**: 50. 1 [symbols] AE, DC, MC, V. ⓁⓁⓁ

On one of the quieter, less pretentious shopping streets in the Piazza di Spagna area, the Homs has clean, pleasant rooms with dark-green carpets, white walls and white bathrooms. The breakfast room opens out on to a pleasant terrace.

Locarno

Via della Penna 22, 00186. **Map** 4 F1. 361 08 41, 361 08 42, 361 08 43. FAX 321 52 49. **Rooms**: 38. [symbols] AE, DC, MC, V, JCB. ⓁⓁⓁ

Situated on a small, busy side-street near the Tiber, a brief walk from Piazza del Popolo, the Locarno is an attractive 1920s hotel with an Art Nouveau door and swags of lilac growing across its facade. Old-fashioned touches remain, with a grandfather clock and Tiffany lamp in the reception area, and a marble-topped bar of polished wood. Outside, there's a patio packed with greenery and kept cool by a tiny fountain.

Mozart

Via dei Greci 23, 00187. **Map** 4 F2. 36 00 19 15. FAX 678 42 71. **Rooms**: 31. 1 [symbols] AE, DC, MC, V, JCB. ⓁⓁⓁ

Located on a cobbled street between Piazza del Popolo and Piazza di Spagna, the Mozart is immediately appealing. The attractively worn decor includes a Venetian mirror. There's a small breakfast room, as well as a bar/café, which opens off the reception area. Rooms have ceramic-tiled or parquet floors, and bathrooms tend to be small, most having only a shower.

Piazza di Spagna

Via Mario de' Fiori 61, 00187. **Map** 5 A2 & 12 F1. 679 30 61, 679 64 12. **FAX** 679 06 54. **Rooms**: 16.

AE, MC, V.

Close to the designer boutiques of Via Condotti, this attractive, small hotel has simple but good-sized rooms with tiled floors. A couple of bathrooms offer Jacuzzis. The breakfast room and bar are tiny, so most residents decide to take breakfast in their own rooms.

Scalinata di Spagna

Piazza Trinità dei Monti 17, 00187. **Map** 5 A2. 679 30 06. **FAX** 69 94 05 06. **Rooms**: 15.

AE, MC, V.

This hotel occupies a small 18th-century villa at the top of the Spanish Steps. Breakfast is served at a communal table under the gaze of a parrot. Some of the rooms retain their old paneled ceilings. Reserve far in advance if you want to stay in one of the rooms that open out on to the large terrace.

Manfredi

Via Margutta 61, 00187. **Map** 5 A2. 320 76 76, 320 76 95. **FAX** 320 77 36. **Rooms**: 16.

AE, MC, V, JCB.

This pretty family run hotel is excellently located, just off Piazza di Spagna, on a peaceful cobbled street of art galleries and antiques shops. The reception area and bar/breakfast room are paved with marble and decorated in soft pastels. Bedrooms are all soundproofed with pale fabric wallcoverings and coordinated furnishings.

Borgognoni

Via del Bufalo 126, 00187. **Map** 5 A3 & 12 F1. 69 94 15 05. **FAX** 69 94 15 01. **TX** 62 30 74 BUFALO. **Rooms**: 50.

AE, DC, MC, V, JCB.

This elegant hotel is just off Piazza San Silvestro, five minutes from the Spanish Steps. In the public rooms, a modern style is coupled with traditional oil paintings. The bedrooms – some with terraces – are beautifully understated.

Hassler

Piazza Trinità dei Monti 6, 00187. **Map** 5 A2. 678 26 51. **FAX** 678 99 91. **TX** 61 02 08. **Rooms**: 100.

AE, MC, V, JCB.

Standing at the top of the Spanish Steps, with magnificent views of Rome from its roof terrace, restaurant *(see p313)* and suites, the Hassler was once host to royalty and the glitterati of Europe and America. Its *dolce vita* days are over, but the lounges and bedrooms lit by Venetian glass chandeliers, the wood-paneled bar and the marble bathrooms retain the air of a more extravagant era.

Inghilterra

Via Bocca di Leone 14, 00187. **Map** 5 A2. 69 9 81. **FAX** 69 92 22 43. **TX** 61 45 52. **Rooms**: 105.

AE, DC, MC, V.

Liszt and Hemingway are among the writers, artists and musicians who have stayed here. In the heart of Rome's designer shopping area and close to the Spanish Steps, it's still a desirable place to stay. The bedrooms are individually decorated and furnished. The bar could have been lifted straight from a London gentlemen's club, and the restaurant's walls, painted with garden views and sky-frescoed ceiling, create the illusion of dining in the open.

Valadier

Via della Fontanella 15, 00187. **Map** 4 F1. 361 19 98. **FAX** 320 15 58. **TX** 62 08 73. **Rooms**: 38.

AE, DC, MC, V, JCB.

Slickly decorated with shiny wood and marble, the Valadier styles itself as an intimate hideaway for those on a romantic visit to Rome. Public rooms are tailor-made for seduction, with low sofas, marble floors and Oriental rugs. If you believe the hotel's publicity, the bizarre art selection is there to provide shy Casanovas with conversation openers.

CAMPO DE' FIORI

Campo de' Fiori

Via del Biscione 6, 00186. **Map** 4 E4 & 11 C4. 687 48 86. **FAX** 687 60 03. **Rooms**: 27.

MC, V.

This very reasonable mid-range hotel occupies a well-kept house,

just off the Campo de' Fiori market square. You enter the tiny reception area along a passageway in which mirrors intriguingly repeat a series of columns into an illusory optical suggestion of infinity. The small bedrooms have beams and paisley furnishings or sky-painted ceilings, lacy walls and frilly bedcovers. On the sixth floor, a split-level roof garden gives vertiginous but aesthetically rewarding views over the Pantheon, the Victor Emmanuel monument and St. Peter's.

Piccolo

Via dei Chiavari 32, 00186. **Map** 4 E4 & 11 C4. 68 80 25 60. **Rooms**: 15.

AE, MC, V.

Close to Piazza Campo de' Fiori, the Piccolo is a family-run hotel at the lowest end of the price range. There is, however, nothing cheap about the atmosphere. Cool and serene, featuring clean, simple rooms of various sizes, the Piccolo also has a separate, bar/breakfast room with a television.

Pomezia

Via dei Chiavari 12, 00186. **Map** 4 E4 & 12 D4. 686 13 71. **Rooms**: 22.

AE, DC, MC, V.

In the heart of the lively Campo de' Fiori district, the Pomezia was renovated and now has spotless, simply decorated rooms and a bar in the reception area to welcome weary arrivals.

Rinascimento

Via del Pellegrino 122, 00186. **Map** 4 E4 & 11 B3. 687 48 13. **FAX** 683 35 18. **TX** 62 02 07 HTLRIN. **Rooms**: 19.

AE, MC, V.

With an appealing location in the Campo de' Fiori district, close to artisans' workshops and a variety of trattorias, the Rinascimento is housed in an old palazzo with stone arched windows. The bedrooms, however, tend to be slightly worn and have rather cramped bathrooms.

Smeraldo

Vicolo dei Chiodaroli 9, 00186. **Map** 4 F5 & 12 D4. 687 59 29. **FAX** 68 80 54 95. **Rooms**: 35.

AE, MC, V.

Situated in the heart of the bustling Campo de' Fiori quarter, the Smeraldo offers an oasis of serenity, with clean, simple rooms in an ocher-washed building with shutters over the windows.

Sole

Via del Biscione 76, 00186. **Map** 4 E4 & 11 C4. **[** 68 80 68 73, 68 80 52 58. FAX 689 37 87. **Rooms:** 58. 🛏 31. 🔟
🎃 📺 🔧 🐕 🔌 P 🅿️ ① ① Ⓛ

Possibly the oldest hotel in Rome, this appealing establishment occupies a palazzo just off the central market square of Campo de' Fiori. Rooms are furnished in a slightly haphazard way, but with some character. There are small sitting areas and a leafy, sunny terrace with a drink-and-snack machine. No breakfast is served.

Della Lunetta

Piazza del Paradiso 68, 00186. **Map** 4 E4 & 11 C4. **[** 686 10 80, 686 36 87. FAX 689 20 28. **Rooms:** 36. 🛏 13. 🔟 🎃 🅿️ ① Ⓛ ①

On a tiny crumbling piazza, midway between Corso Vittorio Emanuele and Piazza Campo de' Fiori, the Lunetta is a popular well-maintained little hotel with neat, clean rooms and a courtyard. More bathrooms are gradually being installed, and a rooftop garden is being renovated. No breakfast is served.

Teatro di Pompeo

Largo del Pallaro 8, 00186. **Map** 4 E4 & 11 C4. **[** 68 30 01 70, 687 25 66. FAX 689 55 31. **Rooms:** 12. 🛏 🔟 🎃 📺 🔧 🌡 ☎ 🔧 🐕 🔌 P 🅿️ ① ⏁ 🌐 AE, DC, MC, V. Ⓛ Ⓛ Ⓛ Ⓛ

This courteously run small hotel sits over the ruins of the first permanent theater in the city, which was completed in 55 BC by Pompey the Great. You can eat breakfast among the original theater arches, and the bar has a terra-cotta floor and marble tables.

Grand

Via V. E. Orlando 3, 00185. **Map** 5 C2. **[** 47 09. FAX 474 73 07. TX 61 02 10. **Rooms:** 170. 🛏 🔟 🎃 🎃 📺 🔧 ☰ 🔧 🐕 🗣 🌡 ① ① 🌐 AE, DC, MC, V, JCB. Ⓛ Ⓛ Ⓛ Ⓛ Ⓛ

To step into the Grand is to enter another world. Cherubs cavort over the reception area; flowers and fruit are carved on the walls of the lounge, and rich pastel rugs lie on the parquet floor. Facilities include a sauna, a beauty salon, a hairdresser, and a restaurant renowned as one of the most beautiful in the country. The standard of bedrooms varies, but you might find yourself in an antique bed reading by the light of a genuine Venetian lamp.

Cervia

Via Palestro 55, 00185. **Map** 6 E2. **[** 49 10 57. FAX 49 10 56. **Rooms:** 27. 🛏 7. 🔟 🎃 🌐 MC, V. Ⓛ

The Cervia is a 20-room hotel housed in the same palazzo as the Mari and the Restivo. Some of the rooms have been refurbished with sponge-painted walls and private bathrooms, and these are a very good value. The rest, however, tend to be a bit more basic. The public areas are immaculate, and there is also a pleasant modern bar/breakfast room.

Gexim

Via Palestro 34, 00185. **Map** 6 E2. **[** 446 02 11, 444 13 11. FAX 444 13 11. **Closed** last 2 wks in Aug. **Rooms:** 9. 🛏 5. 🔟 🎃 🐕 Ⓛ

Don't be put off by the shabby exterior of the palazzo – the Gexim, which occupies part of the third floor, is a cut above most cheap hotels. Pastel-painted walls are hung with prints of Impressionist paintings, and all the bedrooms, bathrooms and public rooms are spotless. The hotel has recently been renovated.

Katty

Via Palestro 35, 00185. **Map** 6 E2. **[** 444 12 16. **Rooms:** 11. 🛏 2. 🔟 🎃 Ⓛ

The Katty has clean, basic rooms, some of which have an occasional piece of antique furniture. It's extremely popular with British and American students, so either reserve in advance or turn up early, ideally between 8 and 9am. No breakfast is served.

Mari

Via Palestro 55, 00185. **Map** 6 E2. **[** 446 21 37. FAX 482 83 13. **Rooms:** 21. 🛏 10. 🔟 🎃 🌐 MC, V. Ⓛ

This friendly hotel run by three women has clean, pleasant rooms with no frills. If it's full, Mari 2 nearby at Via Calatafimi 38 (phone: 474 03 71) has more rooms (half with bathrooms) and is also a good deal. There is a 5% surcharge for paying with credit cards.

Restivo

Via Palestro 55, 00185. **Map** 6 E2. **[** 446 21 72. **Rooms:** 6. 🔟 🎃 Ⓛ

In the same building as the Mari, the Restivo has six immaculately maintained bedrooms. The elderly owner has a hall full of gifts and postcards from grateful guests who often return again and again.

Canada

Via Vicenza 58, 00185. **Map** 6 E2. **[** 445 77 70. FAX 445 07 49. TX 61 30 37 CANADA. **Rooms:** 70. 🛏 🔟 🎃 📺 🔧 🐕 🗣 ① 🌡 🌐 AE, DC, MC, V, JCB. Ⓛ Ⓛ Ⓛ

Outside the center, behind Termini Station, the Canada is an above-average mid-range hotel. Rooms are very comfortable, and there's a pleasant lounge with attractive cane seats and comfortable sofas. The service is courteous.

Aventino

Via San Domenico 10, 00153. **Map** 8 D2. **[** 574 51 74, 578 32 14. FAX 578 36 04. **Rooms:** 23. 🛏 🔟 🎃 🔧 🐕 🌡 🌐 AE, DC, MC, V. Ⓛ Ⓛ

Run by the owners of Villa San Pio and Sant'Anselmo, the Aventino is more modest, with large but fairly simple rooms. However, its lush garden location is gorgeous, and the breakfast room, with a magnificent armoire and stained glass, is a reminder of headier days.

Sant'Anselmo

Piazza di Sant'Anselmo 2, 00153. **Map** 8 D2. **[** 574 51 74. FAX 578 36 04. **Rooms:** 46. 🛏 🔟 🎃 🔧 🐕 🌡 ① 🌐 AE, DC, MC, V. Ⓛ Ⓛ

This pretty villa, among the gardens of the peaceful Aventine, is within walking distance of the Colosseum. The entrance hall's ceiling is stenciled with flowers; there are chandeliers and corridors with floors of inlaid marble. The lounge looks out on to the hotel's secluded garden. Some rooms have hand-painted antique furniture. Reserve well in advance.

Villa San Pio

Via Sant'Anselmo 19, 00153. **Map** 8 E3. **[** 578 32 14, 574 35 47. FAX 578 36 04. **Rooms:** 59. 🛏 🔟 🎃 🔧 🐕 🗣 🔌 P 🅿️ ① 🌡 🌐 AE, DC, MC, V. Ⓛ Ⓛ

The Villa San Pio occupies a yellow-and-ocher villa set in a garden graced with statues. The elegant entrance hall is furnished with velvet and brocade chairs, a painted grandfather clock and an 18th-century Venetian tapestry. While some of the rooms are simple, others have embroidered bedspreads and flower-stenciled furniture; still others open on to the garden. There are two bars. Breakfast or drinks can be taken in the bedrooms or garden.

For key to symbols *see p291.*

Domus Aventina

Via di Santa Prisca 11B, 00153. **Map** 8 E2. **(** 574 61 35. **FAX** 57 30 00 44. **Rooms**: 26. 🛏 1 🎱 24 TV 📺 ☷ 🍽 🛎 P 🅿 🍸 🍴 🗘 *AE, DC, MC, V, JCB.* Ⓛ Ⓛ Ⓛ

This immaculate hotel occupies a 14th-century convent situated at the foot of the Aventine Hill. Rooms are large and simply decorated in pastel tones, and there are wonderful views of the Celian Hill from many of the balconies – 18 rooms have them – and from the huge terrace.

TRASTEVERE

Carmel

Via Mameli 11, 00153. **Map** 7 C2. **(** 580 99 21. **Rooms**: 10. 🛏 9. 1 🎱 Ⓛ

The Carmel is a few notches up from the Manara, the only other Trastevere area hotel. The most appealing feature is a terrace with a leafy canopy, potted plants and garden furniture. A few of the rooms open off the terrace. All ten rooms are spotless, and most have bathrooms. The owner is not eager to have children stay, and you have to reserve in advance since she closes the hotel when she thinks trade will be slack.

Manara

Via Manara 25, 00153. **Map** 7 C1. **(** 581 47 13. **Rooms**: 7. 🛏 1. 🎱 Ⓛ

The Manara lies just off the main market square of Trastevere. For those planning to spend most of their nights in the local trattorias, bars and clubs, it's a good budget choice. All the rooms are simple and extremely clean, but only one has an en suite bathroom.

VATICAN

Alimandi

Via Tunisi 8, 00192. **Map** 3 B2. **(** 39 72 39 48. **FAX** 39 72 39 43. **Rooms**: 32. 🛏 26. 1 🎱 TV 📺 🍽 P 🅿 🍸 🗘 *AE, MC, V.* Ⓛ Ⓛ

On a quietish street just below the entrance to the Vatican Museums, the Alimandi is a simple *pensione* at the cheap end of its price range – hence its popularity with young travelers. Rooms are clean and adequate. The outstanding feature of this guesthouse is a lovely, large roof terrace, where you can sit and have a barbecue, if you arrange in advance.

Amalia

Via Germanico 66, 00192. **Map** 3 C2. **(** 39 72 33 54, 39 72 33 56. **FAX** 39 72 33 65. **Rooms**: 30. 🛏 20. 1 TV 📺 🍽 🍸 🗘 *AE, MC, V.* Ⓛ Ⓛ

Situated between the Ottaviano Metro station and the Vatican, the Amalia attracts mainly Italian visitors. It has spotless rooms arranged on three floors, a lounge with a bar and a coffee machine off the reception area.

Columbus

Via della Conciliazione 33, 00193. **Map** 3 C3. **(** 686 54 35. **FAX** 686 48 74. **TX** 62 00 96. **Rooms**: 92. 🛏 1 🎱 TV 🍸 ☷ 🍽 🛎 🍴 🗘 🍽 P 🅿 🍴 🗘 *AE, DC, MC, V.* Ⓛ Ⓛ Ⓛ

Perfect for anyone wishing to stay near the Vatican, the Columbus occupies an austere former monastery. Heavy wrought-iron light fixtures hang from the vaults in the reception hall; the magnificent upper lounge has a beamed ceiling and terra-cotta floor; the function room – housed in the old refectory – has kept its frescoes; and there is a walled terrace garden. The bedrooms are well-equipped, though the beds are narrow.

Atlante Star

Via Vitelleschi 34, 00193. **Map** 3 C2. **(** 687 32 33. **FAX** 687 23 00. **TX** 62 23 55. **Rooms**: 70. 🛏 1 🎱 24 TV 📺 ☷ 🍽 🛎 🍴 🗘 P 🅿 🍸 🍴 🗘 *AE, DC, MC, V, JCB.* Ⓛ Ⓛ Ⓛ Ⓛ

This hotel is a good option if you're in Rome on business and need on-site office facilities. The rooftop restaurant has panoramic views of St. Peter's, but both service and atmosphere leave much to be desired. Double rooms are modest in size, and singles can be cramped, some of them with only a shower. Avoid street-facing rooms since they can be noisy.

VIA VENETO

Merano

Via Veneto 155, 00187. **Map** 5 B2. **(** 482 17 96. **FAX** 482 18 10. **Rooms**: 30. 🛏 1 🎱 📺 🍴 🍴 🗘 *AE, DC, MC, V.* Ⓛ Ⓛ

The Merano is a friendly small *pensione* in a 19th-century palazzo that also houses a piano bar and hairdresser. The decor is a little dated, and relatively high prices, for what is essentially a guesthouse, reflect the upscale location. The hotel's best feature is its sunny parquet-floored breakfast room.

Oxford

Via Boncompagni 89, 00187. **Map** 5 C1. **(** 48 82 89 52. **FAX** 42 81 53 49. **TX** 63 03 92. **Rooms**: 58. 🛏 1 TV 📺 🍽 🛎 🍴 🗘 🍴 🗘 🍴 🍴 🗘 *AE, DC, MC, V, JCB.* Ⓛ Ⓛ Ⓛ

On a quiet road off Piazza dei Fiumi, about ten minutes' walk from Via Veneto, the Oxford has stylish public rooms: comfortable sofas of shocking pink and modern pictures in the reception area; striped sofas and abstract art in the bar. The bedrooms are more dated, with hessian-covered walls and candlewick bedspreads.

Alexandra

Via Veneto 18, 00187. **Map** 5 B2. **(** 488 19 43, 488 19 44. **FAX** 487 18 04. **TX** 62 26 55. **Rooms**: 45. 🛏 1 🎱 TV 📺 🍽 🛎 🍴 P 🅿 🍴 🍴 🗘 *AE, DC, MC, V, JCB.* Ⓛ Ⓛ Ⓛ Ⓛ

One of the less expensive hotels on the upscale Via Veneto, the Alexandra has a pleasant conservatory-style breakfast room and a lounge decorated with chintz and brocade. All the bedrooms are unique, and you may just as easily end up in a room furnished with antiques as one with splash-painted walls. If you are a light sleeper, ask for an internal room, since the windows do not block out all the traffic noise.

Imperiale

Via Veneto 24, 00187. **Map** 5 B2. **(** 482 63 51. **FAX** 482 63 51. **TX** 62 10 71. **Rooms**: 95. 🛏 1 🎱 24 TV 📺 🍽 🛎 🍴 🗘 🍴 🗘 *AE, DC, MC, V.* Ⓛ Ⓛ Ⓛ Ⓛ

One of the more reasonably priced Via Veneto hotels, the Imperiale lacks the panache of its more glamorous neighbors, but the friendly staff make for a good relaxed atmosphere. The lounge is more of a place to wait than to spend an evening; however, the bar is quite pleasant, and the bedrooms are well decorated, with pretty coordinating furnishings and small marble bathrooms.

Pullman Boston

Via Lombardia 47, 00187. **Map** 5 B2. **(** 47 80 21. **FAX** 482 10 19. **TX** 62 22 47. **Rooms**: 124. 🛏 1 🎱 TV 📺 🍽 🛎 🍴 🗘 🍴 🍴 🗘 *AE, DC, MC, V, JCB.* Ⓛ Ⓛ Ⓛ Ⓛ

Overlooking the beautifully kept grounds of the Villas Medici and Ludovisi, the Boston is a quiet old-fashioned hotel, convenient for both the Via Veneto and the Spanish Steps. The rooms are decorated in pastel shades, and some are very large. Views from the roof terrace stretch from the Villa Borghese right up to St. Peter's and the Vatican City.

Residenza

Via Emilia 22–24, 00187. **Map** 5 B2.
【 488 07 89. **FAX** 48 57 21.
Rooms: 29. 🛏 📶 🎴 TV Y 🏢
P Y 🍴 ⚙ MC, V.
ⓁⓁⓁ

The Residenza is an elegant hotel that occupies a villa on a quiet road off the Via Veneto. Kilim rugs decorate the lounges. There is a canopied terrace with pine furniture, plus a terra-cotta-tiled roof garden, edged with potted plants. The bedrooms are less stylish than the public rooms, but are comfortable, large and well-equipped.

Romantik Barocco Hotel

Piazza Barberini 9 (entrance on Via della Purificazione 4), 00187.
Map 5 B3. 【 487 20 01. **FAX** 48 59 94. **Rooms:** 28. 🛏 📶 🎴 TV Y 🏢 🛗 🍴 ⚙ AE, DC, MC, V, JCB. ⓁⓁⓁⓁ

Occupying a restored palazzo at the bottom of Via Veneto, the Barocco is ideal for anyone who prefers a small hotel. Bedrooms are pleasant with unobtrusive décor, and some have working areas. There are two small lounges (one with a bar) and a restaurant.

Victoria

Via Campania 41, 00187. **Map** 5 B1.
【 47 39 31. **FAX** 487 18 90.
TX 61 02 12. **Rooms:** 120. 🛏 📶
🎴 24 TV Y 🏢 🏊 🏢 🛗
🍴 ⚙ 🎴 🍴 🛗 ⚙ AE, DC, MC, V. ⓁⓁⓁⓁ

Situated on a quiet road at the top of Via Veneto and overlooking the walls abutting the Porta Pinciana, the Victoria prides itself on being a "hotel for individuals," keeping its personal touch by refusing large group reservations. It is renowned for good service. There are stylish public rooms and an attractive roof terrace, but the bedrooms are rather small and uninspired.

Bernini Bristol

Piazza Barberini 23, 00187. **Map** 5 B3.
【 488 30 51. **FAX** 482 42 66.
TX 61 05 54. **Rooms:** 126. 🛏 📶
🎴 24 TV Y 🏢 🏊 🏢 🛗
🍴 🛗 Y 🍴 ⚙ AE, DC, MC, V, JCB.
ⓁⓁⓁⓁ

This unprepossessing brick building overlooks a busy piazza that has Bernini's Triton fountain as its centerpiece. The marble-laden hotel is comfortable, with a roof garden, but the decor is

uninspiring and the atmosphere more conducive to work than pleasure. The central location and facilities ensure a steady stream of business visitors.

Excelsior

Via Veneto 125, 00187. **Map** 5 B1.
【 474 58 20. **FAX** 482 62 05. **TX** 61 02 32. **Rooms:** 327. 🛏 📶 🎴 24 TV Y 🏢 🏊 🏢 🛗 🍴 P Y 🍴 🛗 ⚙ AE, DC, MC, V, JCB. ⓁⓁⓁⓁ

Exotically sculpted balconies supported by statues set the tone for this extravagant hotel, which houses boutiques, saunas, a restaurant and a famous piano bar. Public rooms are sumptuous, with marble walls and floors, rich carpets and brocade furnishings – and the corridors are paneled with silk or imitation marble. The bedrooms are spacious, with chandeliers, gilded wooden paneling and ornate bathrooms.

Majestic

Via Veneto 50, 00187. **Map** 5 B2.
【 48 68 41, 482 80 14. **FAX** 488 09 84, 488 56 57. **TX** 62 22 62. **Rooms:** 96.
🛏 📶 🎴 TV Y 🏢 🏊 P 🛗
Y 🍴 🛗 ⚙ AE, DC, MC, V, JCB.
ⓁⓁⓁⓁ

Founded in 1889, the Majestic is the oldest of Via Veneto's hotels. Since its five-year refurbishment, it has played host to such international stars as Madonna, Pavarotti, and Stallone. Most of the furniture and much of the décor in the public rooms are original, down to the startling gilded lime-green lounge. Bedrooms and corridors are decorated in a bold, bright style, particularly on the fifth floor, where carpets with a zig-zag pattern provide the background to chintz and brocade.

Regina Hotel Baglioni

Via Veneto 72, 00187. **Map** 5 B2.
【 47 68 51. **FAX** 48 54 83. **TX** 62 08 63.
Rooms: 130. 🛏 📶 🎴 TV Y 🏢
🏊 🏢 🛗 🍴 P Y 🍴 🛗
⚙ AE, DC, MC, V. ⓁⓁⓁⓁ

The exuberance of the Baglioni's exterior – it is painted vanilla and strawberry pink and decorated with grimacing masks – continues in the reception area, where a wrought-iron staircase is guarded by the statue of a sea god. The bedrooms are painted in vivid shades of coral, aqua and blue, and many are very spacious. Double glazing in the rooms overlooking Via Veneto cuts down on some of the noise, but light sleepers might still prefer to ask for a room at the back of the hotel when reserving.

VILLA BORGHESE

Villa Borghese

Via Pinciana.31, 00198. **Map** 2 F5.
【 841 41 00. **FAX** 844 26 36.
Rooms: 31. 🛏 📶 📶 🎴 24 TV Y 🏢 P 🛗 Y 🍴 🛗 ⚙ AE, DC, MC, V, JCB. ⓁⓁⓁ

This immediately likable hotel occupies a villa close to Villa Borghese. Although the hotel is on a rather busy main road, the atmosphere is pleasant: more that of a private home than a hotel. Public rooms include an intimate old-fashioned bar, a lounge with comfortable sofas and floral soft furnishings, and there is a courtyard sheltered by a pretty ivy-covered pergola. The rooms are on the small side but they are tastefully decorated.

Aldrovandi Palace

Via Aldrovandi 15, 00197. **Map** 2 E4.
【 322 39 93. **FAX** 322 14 35.
TX 61 61 41 ALDROV. **Rooms:** 140.
🛏 📶 📶 TV Y 🏢 🏊 🏢 🛗
P 🛗 Y 🍴 🛗 ⚙ AE, DC, MC, V, JCB. ⓁⓁⓁⓁⓁ

Among the most restful luxury hotels in the city, the Aldrovandi is just outside the center of Rome on a fairly busy road overlooking Villa Borghese. The reception lounge is elegant, decorated with rich soft furnishings, carpets, chandeliers and lots of vases of fresh flowers. The real highlight of the hotel, however, is the sunny garden with its attractive swimming pool, which is overlooked by an airy restaurant.

Lord Byron

Via de Notaris 5, 00197. **Map** 2 D4.
【 361 30 41. **FAX** 322 04 05.
TX 61 12 17 HBYRON. **Closed** Sun & last 2 wks in Aug. **Rooms:** 37. 🛏 📶 🎴 24 TV Y 🏢 🏊 🏢 🛗 🛗 Y 🛗 🍴 ⚙ AE, DC, MC, V. ⓁⓁⓁⓁ

This refined small hotel is housed in a dazzling white building in the residential district of Parioli, but there is nothing ascetic about its rooms today. The lounge is lavishly furnished with antiques and tapestry-seated chairs, and the tiny sitting room has large sofas and old-fashioned portraits. The restaurant is decorated with plenty of chintz and fresh flowers and serves some of the best food in Rome. All the bedrooms have tapestry and floral soft furnishings with marble coffee tables and are provided with a full decanter of port, which comes with the compliments of the management.

RESTAURANTS AND CAFES

I N ROME, eating out can be both a joy and an entertainment. On warm summer evenings tables flow out onto every conceivable open space, and diners dedicate long hours to the popular social activity of people watching (and of being noticed and admired themselves) in a confusion of passers-by, street performers, rose sellers and traffic. Although Romans have always loved to linger at the table, the lavish feasts of ancient Rome have been scaled down and today's cooking is based on simplicity, freshness and good quality local raw ingredients in

Waiter at Alberto Ciarla
(see p316)

what is essentially a seasonal cuisine. Fast food is gradually arriving, but it is fundamentally alien to the Roman temperament and way of life.

The 66 restaurants reviewed in this chapter have been selected from the best that Rome can offer across all price ranges. The chart on pages 310 and 311 will help narrow down your selection, and the map on page 308 shows the highlights of the list. The section *Light Meals and Snacks*, featured on pages 318 to 321, has details of recommended cafés, pizzerias, wine bars and other places for more casual eating.

WHERE TO FIND GOOD RESTAURANTS

E VERY AREA of the city has its own culinary delights. True Roman cooking can be found in the old slaughter-house area of Testaccio and in the Jewish quarter (the Ghetto) near Campo de' Fiori. Around the university, in San Lorenzo, northeast of the city center, you will find lots of cheap pizzerias and *trattorias*.

Near Termini station there's a good selection of African – particularly Ethiopian and Eritrean – restaurants. For dining outdoors, which often means in beautifully secluded piazzas or in impressively ancient parts of the city, try the restaurants in the narrow streets of Trastevere (the old

artists' quarter); around Campo de' Fiori, or along the old Via Appia Antica.

TYPES OF RESTAURANTS

I N GENERAL, a *trattoria* is an unassuming family-run establishment with good home cooking, while a *ristorante* is more elegant and thus more expensive.

Many eating places – where paper tablecloths give a clue to low prices – simply have no name. They offer an open doorway and, more often than not, excellent basic home cooking. Some of them offer a great deal more, and your chances of finding authentic Roman cooking are higher in the best of these establishments than in more expensive restaurants.

There will probably be times when you don't want a full restaurant meal, and Rome offers a huge variety of places for more casual eating *(see pp318–21)*. One type of place offering snacks or more substantial dishes is the *enoteca*, which

Fresh artichokes, a Roman specialty

doubles as a well-stocked wine shop for browsers and connoisseurs.

The sign *Vino e Cucina* (wine and food), sadly fast disappearing, holds the same promise. Other places for a sit-down, informal lunch or dinner are *birrerie*, which are not only for beer drinkers but also offer pizzas or even four-course meals.

There's plenty of interesting take-out food sold throughout the day – *pizza al taglio* (pizza by the slice) is available all over the city. For full-size pizzas, choose places with wood stoves *(forno a legna)* for better results than from electric ovens. Other take-out foods such as whole roast chickens, potatoes or *supplì* (fried rice croquettes) can be had from *rosticcerie*. A self-service *tavola calda* will serve an impressive array of hot food and is ideal for lunch.

VEGETARIAN FOOD

P URELY VEGETARIAN restaurants are largely unknown in Rome, but everywhere you'll find pasta or rice dishes (*risotto*) using interesting combinations of vegetables, salads, artichokes cooked in different ways or vegetables stuffed and then baked in the oven. Most menus are very adaptable.

The interior of Relais le Jardin *(see p317)*

The Price of a Meal

WHAT YOU PAY will clearly depend on your choice of establishment. In a *tavola calda*, or Roman pizzeria, for example, you can often eat for as little as L15,000 a head. A local *trattoria* costs perhaps L25,000, whereas in a restaurant expect to pay around L50,000 and up. Bottled wine, as opposed to a jug or carafe of house wine *(vino della casa)*, commands higher prices but should offer a more interesting range of tastes *(see p306)*. House wine is usually acceptable, though.

Reading the Menu

NOT EVERY restaurant automatically provides a menu – the waiter will often tell you the day's specialities *(piatti del giorno)*, usually not mentioned on the standard menu but almost always worth ordering. If you are not sure about these, you can always ask for *la lista* (the menu) and then allow yourself to be guided.

A meal could begin with *antipasti* (appetizers) or *primi piatti* – the latter consisting of *pasta asciutta* (pasta with some kind of sauce), *pasta in brodo* (clear broth with pasta in it), *pasta al forno* (baked pasta), risotto or a substantial soup. You then move on to the *secondi*, the main meat or fish course, for which you'll need to order vegetables *(contorni)* separately if you would like them. Afterward you have a choice of *formaggi* (cheeses), *frutta* (fruit) or *dolci* (desserts). Romans don't usually eat

One of many Trastevere cafés

Outdoor café life in the piazza outside Santa Maria in Trastevere

cheese as well as a sweet dish, but cheese often comes with such fruit as pears, figs and melon. Strong espresso coffee and perhaps a liqueur *(amaro* or *digestivo)* rounds off the meal *(see p306)*. You may want to skip the first course, or you may prefer to choose a salad or vegetable dish. Pasta alone tends not to be seen as a full meal.

Opening Times

RESTAURANTS are generally open from about noon to 3pm and from 8 to 11pm or much later. The busiest times tend to be 9 to 9:30pm for dinner and 1 to 1:30pm for lunch. Dinner is generally the preferred time for more relaxed eating, particularly in summer, when it begins and ends late as the heat of the day subsides. Bars are open all day, often from the early hours, serving all kinds of drinks (alcohol can be sold at any time of day) and snacks. The quietest month is August, when many restaurant owners take their annual vacation (shown by *Chiuso per Ferie* signs).

Reserving a Table

MAKING A RESERVATION *(prenotazione)* is generally advisable, especially for Sunday lunch and often for Saturday evening. Also, check the weekly closing day: many places are closed on Monday, and Sunday evening can also be difficult for reservations.

In summer try to reserve a shady table outside, since air-conditioning is not universal, and indoors the atmosphere may be stuffy.

Wheelchair Access

ROME is slowly adapting to the needs of those in wheelchairs, but a call to the restaurant in advance will help secure the right table.

Taking Children Along

CHILDREN are very welcome, particularly in family-run places. You can usually order half-portions (but expect to pay more than half), or just ask for an extra plate. Highchairs *(seggioline)* may also be available in some establishments.

Using the Listings

Key to symbols in the listings on pp312 to 317.

🍴 fixed-price menus
🚭 nonsmoking area
Ⓥ vegetarian dishes
🧒 child portions and sometimes highchairs
♿ wheelchair access
👔 jacket and tie required
🎵 live music
🪑 tables outside
🍷 exceptional wine list
★ highly recommended
💳 credit cards accepted
AE American Express
DC Diners Club
MC MasterCard/Access
V VISA
JCB Japanese Credit Bureau

Price categories for a three-course meal for one, including a half bottle of house wine, cover charge, tax and service:
Ⓛ up to L35,000
ⓁⓁ L35,000–L55,000
ⓁⓁⓁ L55,000–L75,000
ⓁⓁⓁⓁ L75,000–L100,000
ⓁⓁⓁⓁⓁ over L100,000

What to Eat in Rome

Bulb of fresh garlic

THE TRADITIONAL *cucina romanesca* has always relied on local markets full of fresh seasonal vegetables, fruit, cheese and meat from the nearby countryside, plus seafood from the Mediterranean. As in the rest of Italy, pasta is an important part of the menu; one popular dish is the famous *spaghetti alla carbonara*, which was devised in Rome. Many genuinely Roman meat dishes are based on the so-called *quinto quarto* (fifth quarter) – head, innards, tail, pig's feet and so on. Highly flavored with olive oil, herbs, lard, bacon *(pancetta)* or pig's cheek *(guanciale)*, they become a culinary delight. Fish from the Mediterranean is excellent. In season, mushrooms and artichokes may be served in dozens of different ways. *Misticanza* is also good in season: it's a fresh mix of salad leaves, including the peppery *rughetta* (arugula) and *puntarelle* (curly endive shoots, often served with anchovy dressing). For dessert, be sure to try Italian ice cream or puddings such as the classic *tiramisù*.

Maritozzi alla Panna
These soft buns with raisins and candied peel are filled with whipped cream.

Bruschetta
Toasted bread is rubbed with garlic and olive oil; tomatoes can be added.

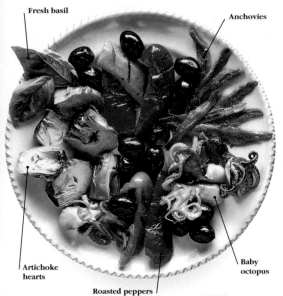

Fresh basil

Anchovies

Artichoke hearts

Baby octopus

Roasted peppers

Supplì
Fried rice croquettes stuffed with mozzarella make a tasty snack.

Antipasti
Italian appetizers may include olives, cured meats, seafood and grilled or preserved vegetables.

Olive Oil and Vinegar
Always on the table, these are for dressing salads and flavoring antipasti.

Filetti di Baccalà
A Jewish specialty, deep-fried cod filets are a typical Roman snack or first course.

Risotto alla Romana
Liver, sweetbreads, Marsala and Romano cheese are used to make this risotto.

TYPICAL ITALIAN PASTA

Penne rigate (quills)

Farfalle (butterflies)

Fusilli (spirals)

Conchigliette (shells)

Cappelletti (small hats)

Bucatini all'Amatriciana
Pasta tubes are served with bacon, tomatoes and onion, with grated Romano on top.

Spaghetti alla Carbonara
Chopped bacon, eggs and cheese are used to prepare this famous local dish.

Gnocchi alla Romana
Small potato or semolina dumplings are served with tomatoes or with butter.

Fiori di Zucca e Carciofi Fritti
Squash blossoms in batter and whole artichokes deep-fried are popular antipasti.

Coda alla Vaccinara
A traditional Roman dish, this is made from braised oxtail with tomatoes.

Saltimbocca alla Romana
Veal with Parma ham and sage, this tasty dish is also served rolled and skewered.

Fave al Guanciale
Fresh springtime broad beans are simmered with bacon and onion.

Parmesan

Italian Cheeses
Parmesan is the best-known Italian cheese, but Rome's classic is pecorino Romano, made from ewe's milk. The mature, hard version is often used grated, but fresh Romano can be eaten as a dessert cheese. Mild buffalo-milk mozzarella is the classic one for pizza.

Mozzarella

Crostata di Ricotta
This Roman cheesecake is filled with ricotta, Marsala and lemon.

Tiramisù
Mascarpone cheese, coffee and chocolate are combined for this wonderful dessert.

What to Drink in Rome

ITALY IS ONE OF Europe's most significant wine-producing countries, keeping up a tradition started in the hills around Rome over 2,000 years ago. Today, wine **Roman mosaic** is usually drunk with meals as a **showing bird** matter of course, and knowing the **and vines** difference between *rosso* (red) and *bianco* (white) may be all the vocabulary you need to get by. Beer is widely available too, as well as good selections of apéritifs and digestifs. Rome's drinking water, another debt to the ancient Romans, is particularly good, fresh and sweet, and in abundant supply.

The vineyards of Frascati, southeast of Rome

WHITE WINE

Orvieto   **Frascati**

VINES THRIVE in the warm climate of Lazio, the region around Rome, producing abundant supplies of inexpensive dry white wine for the city's cafés and restaurants. It is usually sold by the carafe. Of local bottled wines, Frascati is the best known, but Castelli Romani, Marino, Colli Albani and Velletri are very similar in style. All are made from one grape variety, the Trebbiano, though better quality versions contain a dash of Malvasia for perfume and flavor. Other central Italian whites worth trying are Orvieto and Verdicchio. Quality white wines from all over Italy, including fine whites from Friuli in the northeast, are widely available in Rome.

Calcaia comes from Barberani, a reliable producer of Orvieto.

Bigi produces good quality Orvieto, especially the single-vineyard Torricella.

Casal Pilozzo is an easy-drinking white wine from Frascati producers, Colli di Catone. Choose the youngest vintage.

Colle Gaio, with its rich, fruity flavor, stands out among the dry white Frascatis.

WINE TYPE	GOOD VINTAGES	GOOD PRODUCERS
WHITE WINE		
Friuli (Pinot Bianco, Chardonnay, Pinot Grigio, Sauvignon)	The most recent	Gravner, Jermann, Puiatti, Schiopetto, Volpe Pasini
Orvieto/ Orvieto Classico	The most recent	Antinori, Barberani, Bigi, Il Palazzone
RED WINE		
Chianti/ Chianti Classico/ Chianti Rufina	90, 88, 85	Antinori, Castello di Ama, Castello di Cacchiano, Castello di Volpaia, Felsina Berardenga, Fontodi, Frescobaldi, Isole e Olena, Il Palazzino, Riecine, Rocca delle Macie, Ruffino, Vecchie Terre di Montefili, Villa Cafaggio
Brunello di Montalcino/ Vino Nobile di Montepulciano	90, 88, 85	Altesino, Avignonesi, Biondi Santi, Caparzo, Case Basse, Lisini, Il Poggione, Poliziano, Villa Banfi
Barolo/ Barbaresco	90, 89, 88, 85, 82, 78	Aldo Conterno, Altare, Ceretto, Clerico, Gaja, Giacomo Conterno, Giacosa, Mascarello, Ratti, Voerzio

RED WINE

Tuscan table wine   Barolo

THOUGH SOME local red wine is made, most of the bottled red wine in Rome comes from other parts of Italy. Tuscany and Piedmont produce very good everyday drinking wines as well as top-grade ones like Barolo. Price should reflect quality – try Dolcetto, Rosso di Montalcino or Montepulciano, all affordable reds.

Montepulciano d'Abruzzo, a rich and juicy red wine, is always a good choice. It is produced in the Abruzzi region.

Chianti Classico Riserva is older and stronger than a normal Chianti Classico.

Torre Ercolana is produced in small quantities and is generally regarded as one of Lazio's best red wines. It is made from Cesanese and Cabernet grapes and requires at least five years' aging.

READING THE LABEL

Chianti Classico

ITALY has a two-tier system for labeling quality wine. DOC *(denominazione di origine controllata)* means you can be sure the wine is from the region declared on the label and is made from designated grape varieties. A higher classification – DOCG *(denominazione di origine controllata e garantita)* – is given to top wines such as the reds Barolo, Barbaresco, Chianti Classico and Brunello di Montalcino.

APÉRITIFS AND OTHER DRINKS

BITTER, herb-flavored drinks like Martini, Campari or Aperol are the most popular apéritifs. (Ask for an *analcolico* if you prefer a non-alcoholic one.) Italians drink their apéritifs neat or with ice and soda. Strong, herby after-dinner drinks, known as *digestivi* or *amari*, are worth trying if you need to settle your stomach. Italian brandy and grappa can be very fiery. Italian beer, popular with pizza, is made in

Campari lager style.

SOFT DRINKS

ITALIAN FRUIT juices are good and most bars squeeze fresh orange juice *(spremuta)* on the spot. Iced tea and coffee are refreshing in summer, and fruit-flavored tea, such as peach, is very popular.

Refrigerated storage for wine and beer

DRINKING WATER

Unlike many Mediterranean cities, Rome benefits from a constant supply of fresh drinking water, piped down from the hills through a system of pipes and aqueducts that has changed little from ancient Roman times. Only if there is a sign saying *acqua non potabile* is the water not safe to drink.

One of Rome's many fresh water drinking fountains

Coffee is almost more important to Roman life than wine. For strong black coffee, have expresso at any time of day. Try milky cappuccino for breakfast or mid-afternoon or, for extra milk, caffè latte.

Espresso

Cappuccino

Caffè latte

Rome's Best: Restaurants and Cafés

ROME IS KNOWN less for luxury restaurants than for atmospheric places where the focus is on the social side of dining and on regional cooking. An amazing variety can be found. Many places specialize, often priding themselves on being the best of their kind – whether they offer superb espresso or traditional foods such as deep-fried salted cod *(baccalà)*. Other restaurants can offer especially beautiful settings or are known as the best places to be seen. The selection here shows some of the many highlights of a city where eating is taken very seriously indeed.

Caffè Giolitti
This historic ice cream shop serves a variety of flavors, to eat in or take out. (See p320.)

Romolo nel Giardino della Fornarina
For romantic Roman eating, Romolo is best in the summer, with its walled garden, candlelit tables and guitar music.
(See p316.)

Il Delfino
This snack bar at Largo Argentina sells everything from whole chickens on the spit to salads, sandwiches and supplì *(rice croquettes): a feast for the eye.*
(See p320.)

Vatican

Piazza Navona

Campo de' Fiori

Janiculum

Trastevere

Filetti di Baccalà
This small, crowded place serves tasty fried fillets of cod – one of Rome's most traditional dishes – and offers a truly Roman experience. (See p320.)

Piperno
For over a century, traditional Roman/Jewish cooking has been the specialty of Piperno, in the heart of the Jewish Ghetto. (See p314.)

Babington's Tea Rooms
This old-fashioned genteel establishment at the foot of the Spanish Steps serves English tea and cakes. (See p320.)

Caffè Greco
Famous as the haunt of writers, artists and intellectuals in the 19th century, this café still retains the faded grandeur shown in this painting. (See p320.)

Piazza di Spagna

Via Veneto

zza della otonda

Quirinal

Tazza d'Oro
This figure graces the wall on the outside of Tazza d'Oro, where you will find some of the best coffee in Rome – the espresso is rated highly by connoisseurs. (See p320.)

Capitol

Esquiline

Forum

Palatine

Lateran

Aventine

Caracalla

| 0 meters | 500 |
| 0 yards | 500 |

Sora Lella
This Roman trattoria *is famous for its setting on the Isola Tiberina and for the fashionable crowd that it attracts.* (See p314.)

Vecchia Roma
Summer is the best time to eat here and make the most of the quiet and lovely Baroque piazza. (See p314.)

Choosing a Restaurant

THE RESTAURANTS in this guide have been selected for their good value or exceptional food. This chart highlights some of the factors that may influence your choice. Entries are alphabetical within price category. For more details on the restaurants, see pages 312 to 317. Information on cafés and wine bars is on pages 318 to 321.

	Price	Fixed Price Menu	Vegetarian Dishes	Tables Outside	Seafood Specialties	Late Opening	Air-Conditioning	Attractive Setting
PIAZZA DELLA ROTONDA (see p312)								
Da Gino	Ⓛ							
Il Buco	ⓁⓁ	●		●			■	
Vecchia Locanda	ⓁⓁⓁ		■	●	■	●	■	●
Sangallo	ⓁⓁⓁⓁ	●				●	■	
La Rosetta ★	ⓁⓁⓁⓁⓁ				■			
El Toulà	ⓁⓁⓁⓁ	●	■				■	
PIAZZA NAVONA (see p312)								
La Taverna	ⓁⓁ	●		●			■	●
Nel Regno del Re Ferdinando	ⓁⓁⓁ		■		■	●	■	
Osteria dell'Antiquario	ⓁⓁⓁ	●		●			■	●
Il Convivio ★	ⓁⓁⓁⓁ	●			■			
Papà Giovanni	ⓁⓁⓁⓁ		■				■	
PIAZZA DI SPAGNA (see p313)								
Al 34	ⓁⓁ		■	●			■	
Birreria Viennese	ⓁⓁ	●				●	■	
Fiaschetteria Beltramme	ⓁⓁ				■			
Mario alle Vite	ⓁⓁ			●			■	
Porto di Ripetta	ⓁⓁⓁ	●			■		■	
Sogo-Asahi	ⓁⓁⓁⓁ	●			■			
Hassler Roof Restaurant	ⓁⓁⓁⓁⓁ						■	●
CAMPO DE' FIORI (see p313)								
Bella Shanghai	Ⓛ	●	■				■	
Al Pompiere	ⓁⓁ							
Le Maschere	ⓁⓁⓁ		■	●		●	■	
Il Cardinale	ⓁⓁⓁ		■		■			
Il Drappo	ⓁⓁⓁ	●		●		●	■	
Piperno	ⓁⓁⓁ			●	■			
Sora Lella	ⓁⓁⓁ						■	
Taverna Giulia	ⓁⓁⓁ			●		●	■	
Vecchia Roma	ⓁⓁⓁ		■	●			■	●
Camponeschi	ⓁⓁⓁⓁⓁ			●	■	●		●
QUIRINAL (see p314)								
Colline Emiliane	ⓁⓁ						■	
Al Moro	ⓁⓁⓁ				■		■	
Il Posto Accanto	ⓁⓁⓁ		■		■			
Quadrifoglio	ⓁⓁⓁ					●	■	
TERMINI (see p314)								
Gemma alla Lupa	Ⓛ	●	■	●			■	
Coriolano	ⓁⓁⓁⓁⓁ		■		■		■	

Price categories for a three-course meal for one, half a bottle of house wine and all unavoidable extra charges such as cover, service and tax:
Ⓛ up to L35,000
ⓁⓁ L35–55,000
ⓁⓁⓁ L55–75,000
ⓁⓁⓁⓁ L75–100,000
ⓁⓁⓁⓁⓁ over L100,000.

★ Means highly recommended.

FIXED PRICE MENU
Restaurant offering *menu turistico* (tourist menu): usually three or four courses without wine or coffee, for a set price.

VEGETARIAN DISHES
Restaurant specializing in seafood or fish or serving good seafood selection.

LATE OPENING
Last orders on or after 11:30pm.

ATTRACTIVE SETTING
Restaurant set in a pretty piazza or having a garden terrace or a lovely view.

Restaurant	Price	Fixed Price Menu	Vegetarian Dishes	Tables Outside	Seafood Specialties	Late Opening	Air-Conditioning	Attractive Setting
ESQUILINE (see p315)								
La Tana del Grillo	ⓁⓁ							
Trattoria Monti	ⓁⓁ	●	■					
Cicilardone	ⓁⓁⓁ							
Agata e Romeo	ⓁⓁⓁⓁ	●				●	■	
LATERAN (see p315)								
Alfredo a Via Gabi	ⓁⓁ						■	
Cannavota	ⓁⓁⓁ	●			■		■	
Charly's Saucière	ⓁⓁⓁ				■	●	■	
AVENTINE (see p315)								
Perilli a Testaccio	ⓁⓁ						■	
Checchino dal 1887 ★	ⓁⓁⓁⓁ				●			
TRASTEVERE (see p316)								
Da Lucia	Ⓛ			●				
Romolo nel Giardino della Fornarina	ⓁⓁ			●		●	■	●
La Taverna di Bambù	ⓁⓁ		■			●	■	
La Cornucopia	ⓁⓁⓁ	●		●	■	●	■	●
Da Paris	ⓁⓁⓁ			●	■		■	●
Peccati di Gola	ⓁⓁⓁ			●	■			
Tentativo ★	ⓁⓁⓁ	●				●	■	
Cul De Sac 2 ★	ⓁⓁⓁⓁ						■	
Alberto Ciarla ★	ⓁⓁⓁⓁⓁ	●		●	■	●	■	
JANICULUM (see p316)								
Al Tocco	ⓁⓁⓁ		■		■	●	■	
VATICAN (see p316)								
Macondo	Ⓛ		■	●	■			
San Luigi	ⓁⓁⓁ		■				■	
VIA VENETO (see p317)								
Cantina Cantarini	Ⓛ			●	■	●		
Tullio	ⓁⓁⓁ		■		■			
Andrea	ⓁⓁⓁⓁ		■		■			
Giovanni	ⓁⓁⓁⓁ	●			■			
San Benedetto	ⓁⓁⓁⓁ	●			■			
George's ★	ⓁⓁⓁⓁ		■	●		●	■	●
Le Sans Souci ★	ⓁⓁⓁⓁⓁ		■		■	●	■	
VILLA BORGHESE (see p317)								
Al Ceppo	ⓁⓁⓁ		■	●	■		■	
Relais la Piscine ★	ⓁⓁⓁⓁⓁ	●		●	■		■	●
Relais le Jardin ★	ⓁⓁⓁⓁ				■		■	

PIAZZA DELLA ROTONDA

Da Gino

Vicolo Rosini 4 (Piazza del Parlamento). **Map** 4 F3 & 12 D1. 687 34 34. **Open** 12:45–3pm & 8–10:30pm Mon–Sat. **Closed** Aug.

Journalists, politicians and the initiated scramble for a seat under the kitschy frescoed pergola of this ancient, ultra-Roman *trattoria* to feast on traditional daily dishes: *gnocchi* and *osso buco* (Thursdays), *baccalà* (Fridays), tripe (Saturdays), plus classic sturdy soups, dutifully executed Roman standards and delectable homemade *tiramisù*.

Il Buco

Via di Sant'Ignazio 8. **Map** 4 F4 & 12 E3. 678 32 98 & 678 44 67. **Open** 12:30–4pm & 7pm–midnight Tue–Sun. **Closed** Aug 10–Sep 1. AE, DC, MC, V.

Much has happened since the tiny *buco* (hole) opened in 1891 – the small *osteria* has become a large restaurant, yet the calm atmosphere, unfailing courtesy and formidable Tuscan menu remain. From the traditional *crostini* (liver pâté canapés), robust *ribollita* (thick vegetable soup) and huge Florentine steaks, to the final *tozzetti* (almond biscuits) with *vin santo* (dessert wine), this is a truly Tuscan experience.

Vecchia Locanda

Vicolo Sinibaldi 2. **Map** 4 F4 & 12 D3. 68 80 28 31. **Open** 12:30–3pm & 7pm–midnight Mon–Sat. AE.

Visit this small family-run Ligurian restaurant in summer, when tables line the secluded arched street. Meals are prepared with great care, and the service is impeccable. The menu features imaginative combinations of herbs and vegetables: *risotto* with zucchini blossoms, *porcini* crêpes, stuffed truffled rabbit and lots of fresh fish. There's a good selection of French and regional wines.

Sangallo

Vicolo della Vaccarella 11. **Map** 4 F3 & 12 D2. 686 55 49. **Open** 7pm–1am Mon–Sat. **Closed** Aug. AE, DC, MC, V.

In this small, intimate and elegant bistro, Albert and his family conjure up dishes from their native Provence and other regions (*bouillabaisse, cassoulet, coq au vin*), together with equally delicious classic Mediterranean standards (*couscous, paella*). Try the light, fragrant desserts and excellent French and Italian wines.

La Rosetta

Via della Rosetta 9. **Map** 4 F4 & 12 D2. 68 30 88 41. **Open** 1–3pm & 7:30–11:30pm Mon–Sat. **Closed** 3 wks Aug & Christmas. ★ AE, DC, MC, V.

Despite the exorbitant prices, people flock nightly (having reserved in advance) for a seat in the tightly packed elegant rooms. Fresh fish and seafood arrive daily from Sicily and, cooked in the simplest ways, achieve culinary perfection. Enthusiastic waiters and quality French and Italian wines, particularly the Sicilian whites, complement the cuisine.

El Toulà

Via della Lupa 29B. **Map** 4 F3 & 12 D1. 687 34 98. **Open** 1–3pm & 8–11pm Tue–Fri, 8–11pm Mon & Sat. **Closed** Aug & Christmas. V AE, DC, MC, V.

El Toulà is justly renowned as one of the most exclusive, traditional and luxurious restaurants in Rome. The Venetian-inspired cooking is exactingly prepared to the highest standards, with forays into the best classic international cuisine. In its dignified, formal surroundings, the service is also exemplary.

PIAZZA NAVONA

La Taverna

Via del Banco di Santo Spirito 58. **Map** 4 D3 & 11 A2. 686 41 16. **Open** noon–3pm & 7–11pm Tue–Sun. AE, DC, MC, V, JCB.

Tourists and local residents mingle in Giovanni's crowded Roman *trattoria* to enjoy the family atmosphere and traditional regional cooking. Particularly appreciated are the *rigatoni all'amatriciana*; *coda alla vaccinara*, and, on Thursday, Friday and Saturday, respectively, *gnocchi, baccalà* and tripe.

Nel Regno del Re Ferdinando

Via dei Banchi Nuovi 8. **Map** 4 D4 & 11 B2. 68 80 11 67. **Open** 8pm–1am Mon–Sat. **Closed** Aug. V AE, MC, V.

Reminiscent of a classic 19th-century *taverna*, Re Ferdinando is a rare representative in Rome of the southern Campania region. Delights include some colorful vegetable and fish antipasti, and *maccheroni*. Another specialty is *sartù di riso* (a savory rice mold covered in tomato sauce, cheese and breadcrumbs and baked in the oven). The Neapolitan desserts are delicious. There is a separate nonsmoking room. Good regional wines include many from Ischia.

Osteria dell'Antiquario

Piazzetta San Simeone 27. **Map** 4 E3 & 11 B2. 687 96 94. **Open** 8–11:30pm Mon–Sat. **Closed** Aug 15 & Dec 20–Jan 7. AE DC, MC, V, JCB.

In the comfort of the elegantly restructured rooms of an old antiques shop, Giorgio Nisti offers an unusual menu dictated by the whims of the chef and the daily market, with traditional dishes creatively adapted to contemporary health-conscious tastes. There is an impressive choice of regional, French and California wines.

Il Convivio

Via dell'Orso 44. **Map** 4 E3 & 11 C2. 686 94 32. **Open** 1–2:30pm & 8–10:30pm Mon–Fri, 8–10:30pm Sun. **Closed** 2 weeks Aug–Sep. ★ AE, DC, MC, V.

An air of sophisticated tranquillity pervades this intimate restaurant, one of the very best specializing in modern creative cookery. Its young chef, one of the three brother/owners from the Marches, creates both subtle and unusual combinations of flavors. The highly personalized menu evolves with the seasons, and the staff is highly attentive. The wine list is extensive.

Papà Giovanni

Via dei Sediari 4. **Map** 4 F4 & 12 D3. 686 53 08. **Open** 1–3pm, 8–11:30pm Mon–Sat. **Closed** Aug & public hols. V MC, V.

Nearly 60 years have passed since Papà Giovanni first sold his country wines in Rome; the bottles lining the walls are testimony to the past and to the superb cellar of Giovanni's son, Renato Sentuti. Here diners sample the best of the lighter Roman cuisine. Offered are such classics as *cacio e pepe*, salt cod and tripe, as well as exotic salads and truffled dishes. Desserts include ricotta soufflé with strawberry sauce, hot chocolate profiteroles and exquisite sorbets.

PIAZZA DI SPAGNA

Al 34

Via Mario de' Fiori 34. **Map** 5 A2.
679 50 91. **Open** noon–3pm &
7:30–11pm Tue–Sun. **Closed** Aug.
AE, DC, MC, V, JCB.

For a comfortable chat or a
romantic tête-à-tête, Al 34 provides
the perfect setting. Predominantly
featuring southern Italian cooking,
the extensive menu offers an
esoteric selection, particularly
where vegetables and herbs are
served with pasta, meat and fish.
Given the atmosphere and
location, the prices are reasonable.

Birreria Viennese

Via della Croce 21. **Map** 5 A2.
679 55 69. **Open** 11:30am–
midnight Thu–Tue. **Closed** Jul 15–
Aug 15. AE, DC, MC, V,
JCB.

The stained-glass entrance leads to
a long crowded room where
traditional beers and Austrian
specialties have been sampled for
more than 60 years. Try sausages,
goulash, *Wienerschnitzel*,
sauerkraut or the massive *piatto di
legno della Transilvania* (a
wooden platter heaped with
delights, for two). Wine is also
available. The staff is extremely
helpful and courteous.

Fiaschetteria Beltramme

Via della Croce 39. **Map** 4 F2. **Open**
12:10–3pm & 7:45–10:30pm Mon–
Sat. **Closed** Dec 23–Jan 7.

This small Roman *trattoria* proudly
displays its glorious past; signed
photos and paintings line the long
walls, and the crowded tables
make sharing – and new
friendships – inevitable. The family
atmosphere is enhanced by
traditional basic fare – *pasta e ceci*,
minestra di fagioli, fresh fish and
typical meat dishes. Efficient,
speedy service means this is not a
place for lingering over dinner.

Mario alla Vite

Via della Vite 55. **Map** 5 A3 & 12 E1.
678 38 18. **Open** 12:30–3pm &
7:30–11pm Mon–Sat. **Closed** Aug.
AE, DC, MC, V, JCB.

Despite an exclusive address,
Mario has kept prices reasonable,
and his food is still simple, honest
Tuscan fare. Elbow-to-elbow
dining, haphazard service and
noisy confusion seem inevitable.
Nevertheless, the food is worth it –
traditional *fagioli al fiasco*
(cannellini beans in oil), *ribollita*
(thick vegetable soup), Florentine

steaks and delicious pastries are
the attractions, along with a wide
selection of wines.

Porto di Ripetta

Via di Ripetta 250. **Map** 4 F2.
361 23 76. **Open** 1–3pm &
8pm–midnight Mon–Sat. **Closed**
Aug. AE, DC, MC,
V.

The fame of this restaurant
depends largely on the genius of
chef Maria Romani. With the fish
that arrives daily from her native
Marches, she creates inspired
combinations such as soup with
fish and broad beans or giant
prawns with artichokes. The food
is expensive but worth it; the
business lunch is much cheaper.
There's a selection of excellent
wines to choose from.

Sogo-Asahi

Via di Propaganda 22. **Map** 5 A2.
678 60 93. **Open** noon–2:30pm
& 7:30–10.30pm Mon–Sat.
AE, DC, MC, V, JCB.

This appealing luxury restaurant
is a find for lovers of Japanese
cooking. Traditional specialties
are elegantly served by helpful
and knowledgeable waiters:
sashimi (raw fish) and melt-in-the-
mouth tempura are accompanied
by saké, Japanese beer or a good
Italian wine. The special menus
are particularly inexpensive at
lunch. Sogo-Asahi opens in
August, when most of Rome's
restaurants are closed.

Hassler Roof Restaurant

Piazza Trinità dei Monti 6. **Map** 5 A2.
678 26 51. **Open** 7:30–11:30am,
noon–2:30pm & 7:30–10pm
Mon–Sat, 7:30–11:30am,
12:30–3pm & 7:30–10pm Sun.
AE, DC, MC, V, JCB.

Perched on the sixth floor of the
Hotel Hassler, overlooking the
Spanish Steps, this roof restaurant
commands a breathtaking view of
Rome. Come for the gargantuan
but pricey Sunday brunch. The
wine list is excellent, the hovering
waiter attentive but discreet. In the
evening, when prices are higher,
there's piano music.

CAMPO DE' FIORI

Bella Shanghai

Corso Vittorio Emanuele II 333.
Map 4 E4 & 11 C3. 686 16 84.
Open 11am–3pm & 6pm–midnight
daily. AE, MC, V.

This cheerful Vietnamese
restaurant offers a respectable
alternative to Italian food. Eat by
candlelight in a relaxed atmosphere and try the wide selection of
relatively inexpensive dishes. A
waiter patiently explains the menu
for first-timers; recommended are
the fried ravioli starters, chicken in
foil *(pollo d'argento)* and the *tre
delizie* (three delights – beef,
chicken and prawns in a special
sauce). There are also affordable
Italian wines, tea, ginseng liqueur
and a selection of grappas.

Al Pompiere

Via S. M. dei Calderari 38. **Map** 4 F5
& 12 D5. 686 83 77. **Open** noon–
3pm & 7:30–11pm Mon–Sat.
Closed last week Jul & all Aug.
V.

In the heart of the Jewish Ghetto,
Al Pompiere occupies the first
floor of the 16th-century Palazzo
Cenci-Bolognetti. Under its
frescoed open-beamed ceilings, in
a homey atmosphere, all the
classic dishes of the substantial
Roman cuisine are expertly served:
among them fried zucchini flowers
with anchovies, *rigatoni con la
pajata* and baby lamb.

Le Maschere

Via Monte della Farina 29.
Map 4 F5 & 12 D4. 687 94 44.
Open 7pm–midnight Tue–Sun
(May–Oct: noon–3pm also). **Closed**
Nov. AE, DC, MC, V,
JCB.

You'll feel an agreeable sensation
of being in the country as you
cross the spacious tiled hall and
descend to the rustic indoor
terrace with its high reed-lined
ceiling, a roofed grill and eerily lit
wall masks. Candles on the tables
and the subdued conversational
hum lull you in preparation for the
fiery Calabrian food to come.
Charming service and good
Calabrian house wine (plus a short
list) ensure an enjoyable evening.

Il Cardinale

Via delle Carceri 6. **Map** 4 D4 & 11 B3.
686 93 36. **Open** 7:30–11:30pm
Mon–Sat. **Closed** Aug.
AE, DC, MC, V.

For genuine regional cooking
using the best ingredients from the
Castelli Romani, this small, elegant
yet comfortable restaurant near
Via Giulia is highly recommended.
Dishes range from tasty robust
soups to such specialties as
zucchine alla velletrana (baked
squash) and *crema al cocco*
(coconut *crème brûlée*). There are
particularly good wines also
from Lazio.

For key to symbols *see p303.*

Il Drappo

Vicolo del Malpasso 9. **Map** 4 D4 & 11 B3. 687 73 65. **Open** 8pm–midnight Mon–Sat. **Closed** Jan 1, Easter, Aug 1–15, Dec 25. AE.

A small, intimate restaurant with ceiling drapes (hence the name), plants and candlelight, Il Drappo provides an authentic taste of Sardinia – traditional dishes imbued with flashes of culinary creativity. Everything is evocative of the island, including the wines. Try the *seada* (sweet cheese-filled ravioli) for dessert followed by the *mirto* liqueur at the end.

Piperno

Via Monte de' Cenci. **Map** 4 F5 & 12 D5. 68 80 66 29. **Open** 12:30–3pm & 8–11pm Tue–Sat, 12:30–3pm Sun. **Closed** Easter, Aug & Christmas. AE, DC, MC, V.

Piperno, in the heart of the old Jewish Ghetto, has been famed for over a century for its traditional Jewish/Roman dishes. Despite the competition, the restaurant is still unbeaten for lightly fried zucchini flowers, vegetable *fritto misto*, *carciofi alla giudia*, tripe and superb fish, served in plain surroundings. Service is familiarly attentive and timely. The house wine is excellent Frascati. Reserve well in advance.

Sora Lella

Via Ponte Quattro Capi 16, Isola Tiberina. **Map** 8 D1. 686 16 01. **Open** 1–2:30pm & 8–10:40pm Mon–Sat. **Closed** 30 days over Aug and Sep. AE, MC, V.

Founded by the exuberant Roman actress Sora Lella, this small, bright *trattoria* is a well-known place to people watch. Sora Lella is now run by Lella's son, Aldo. Dishes are based on traditional Roman cuisine, but prices are very high for an essentially simple style of cooking. Go instead for the beautiful location on the Isola Tiberina, the often glamorous clientele and the good service.

Taverna Giulia

Vicolo dell'Oro 23. **Map** 4 D4 & 11 A2. 686 97 68 & 689 37 20. **Open** 12:30–3:30pm & 7:30pm–midnight Mon–Sat. **Closed** Aug. AE, DC, MC, V.

Taverna Giulia's customers respect the quiet comfort of its ancient dining rooms and discreet service as well as the superb Genoese and Ligurian food. Salmon and mozzarella canapés, *pansoti* (ravioli) in nut sauce, stockfish *alla genovese* and perfect *crème brûlée* are complemented by Ligurian wines and *Sciacchetrà* (dessert wine) served with almond biscuits.

Vecchia Roma

Piazza Campitelli 18. **Map** 4 F5 & 12 E5. 686 46 04. **Open** 1–4pm & 8–11:30pm Thu–Tue. **Closed** 2 weeks Aug. AE, DC, MC.

Set in a quiet, atmospheric piazza, this is one of the best places to go on a summer evening. Reliable Roman cooking is offered, with tempting antipasti, simply cooked fish and grilled meats, plus a connoisseur's wine list. Specialties are summer salads and, in winter, numerous variations of polenta. Added pleasures are the 18th-century interior and the excellent service.

Camponeschi

Piazza Farnese 50. **Map** 4 E5 & 11 C4. 687 49 27. **Open** 8pm–1am Mon–Sat. **Closed** 10 days Aug. AE, DC, MC, V.

Camponeschi is set in one of the most attractive piazzas in Rome, especially beautiful in summer. The extensive menu includes modern and regional Italian cooking, creative Mediterranean fish and meat dishes, soufflés and refined French specialties. There's a varied regional, French and Californian wine list.

Colline Emiliane

Via degli Avignonesi 22. **Map** 5 B3. 481 75 38. **Open** 12:45–2:45pm & 7:45–10:45pm Sat–Thu. **Closed** Aug.

Regional dishes are the hallmark of this small family *trattoria*: one unpretentious room presenting a welcome haven from the nearby Via del Tritone. Enjoy food typical of the northern province of Emilia Romagna – salamis and cold meats, homemade pastas (tagliatelle, tortellini), boiled meats with *salsa verde* (spinach, onion and anchovy sauce) and strictly Emilian wines.

Al Moro

Vicolo delle Bollette 13. **Map** 5 A3 & 12 F2. 678 34 95. **Open** 1–3:30pm & 8–11:30pm Mon–Sat. **Closed** Aug.

Franco Romagnoli's *trattoria* is a reliable choice for traditional Roman cooking that uses fresh local ingredients. Noisy and crowded, it has closely packed tables that do not encourage intimate dining. Classic dishes are served: *bucatini all'amatriciana*, *spaghetti alla Moro* (special carbonara), fried vegetables, excellent *baccalà alla Moro* (salt cod), tripe and *abbacchio*. The wine list is vast.

Il Posto Accanto

Via del Boschetto 36A. **Map** 5 B4. 474 30 02. **Open** 12:30–3pm Mon–Fri, 7:45–10pm Mon–Sat. **Closed** 2 weeks Aug. AE, DC, MC, V.

Tiny, intimate and elegant, this family-run restaurant owes its success to a carefully chosen short menu revolving around homemade pasta (excellent *tagliolini con asparagi* and *ravioli con zenzero* – ginger), simply prepared fish and meat, top-quality vegetables and familiar desserts *(tiramisù)*, often prepared within sight of the lucky diners. There is a range of wines, as well as good grappas.

Quadrifoglio

Via del Boschetto 19. **Map** 5 B4. 482 60 96. **Open** 8pm–midnight Mon–Sat. **Closed** Aug. AE, DC, MC, V.

Chef Pino Forlenza has researched diligently to reproduce authentic dishes from Naples, Campania and the tip of Africa. They are tailored to modern tastes with carefully selected raw ingredients and delivered with southern hospitality and courteous service. Most of the wines are from Campania.

Gemma alla Lupa

Via Marghera 39. **Map** 6 E3. 49 12 30. **Open** noon–3:30pm, 7–11pm Mon–Sat. **Closed** 2 weeks Aug.

Gemma's is a modest, family-run, typically Roman *trattoria* serving substantial portions of orthodox Roman cooking. The main features are its bustling atmosphere and speedy service. However, it is a good choice where you eat well, despite the low prices.

Coriolano

Via Ancona 14. **Map** 6 D1. 44 24 98 63. **Open** noon–3pm & 7:30–11pm Mon–Sat. **Closed** Aug. AE, DC, MC, V.

This small restaurant aims at perfection with its lacy tablecloths and crystal glasses. The Italian menu selections change with the seasons and use only fresh raw ingredients, including fish. Specialties include homemade *ravioli di ricotta e spinaci*, *capretto* (kid) and chocolate *zuppa del contadino*.

ESQUILINE

La Tana del Grillo

Via Alfieri 4. **Map** 6 E5.
【 70 45 35 17. **Open** 12:30–2:30pm & 7:30–11pm Tue–Sat, 7:30–11pm Mon. **Closed** Aug.
🎴 ⛄ 🈺 *AE, DC, MC, V.*
Ⓛ Ⓛ

Marisa Balboni runs an elegant and characteristically hospitable Emilian restaurant. Clients are pampered, from the cushioned chairs, restful prints and attractive tableware to the wholesome food served with courtesy and care. Particularly recommended are the *polpettone all'emiliana* (meat loaf), *salame al sugo ferrarese* (Ferrarese salami) and *cappellacci con la zucca* (pumpkin-stuffed pasta).

Trattoria Monti

Via di San Vito 13A. **Map** 6 D4.
【 446 65 73. **Open** 12:30–3pm & 7:30–11pm Wed–Mon. **Closed** Aug 18–Sep 12, Dec 24–Jan 3.
Ⓥ ⛄
🄴 *DC, MC, V.* Ⓛ Ⓛ

This unpretentious local *trattoria* serves delicate, creative regional dishes from the Marches region. Franca Camerucci cooks, while her husband, Mario, is an attentive waiter and expert sommelier. Specialties include fried stuffed olives, artichokes and *ciauscolo* (salami); *tortello al rosso d'uova* (fresh pasta stuffed with ricotta, spinach and tomato); and *tacchino all'aceto balsamico* (lightly vinegared turkey slices). There is a good Verdicchio house wine and a commendable wine list.

Cicilardone

Via Farini 12. **Map** 6 D4.
【 48 35 49. **Open** noon–3pm Tue–Sat & 7.30pm–midnight Mon–Sat. **Closed** mid 2 wks Aug.
🄴 *AE, DC, MC, V, JCB.*
Ⓛ Ⓛ Ⓛ

Ring at Cicilardone's door and your host – Domenico Lucia – will greet you like an old friend and converse about the gastronomic delights from the region of Basilicata. Try the *menu di assaggini* – a number of dishes to give you an idea of the regional taste, including traditional pastas and hot chocolate profiteroles. There are some unusual southern wines.

Agata e Romeo

Via Carlo Alberto 45. **Map** 6 D4.
【 446 61 15. **Open** 1–2:30pm & 8–11:30pm Mon–Sat. **Closed** 2 wks Aug.
🎴 Ⓥ ⛄ 🈺 🍷
🄴 *AE, DC, MC, V.* Ⓛ Ⓛ Ⓛ Ⓛ

One of the newer *trattoria*-turned-restaurants, its increasing prices sadly reflect recent popular acclaim. Nevertheless, Agata's skill in producing a changing menu of predominantly Roman and southern Italian dishes, and Romeo's impeccable service and range of carefully chosen wines, are hard to beat. Well-spaced, elegantly set tables are ideal for tranquil eating.

LATERAN

Alfredo a Via Gabi

Via Gabi 36. **Map** 10 D3.
【 77 20 67 92. **Open** noon–3pm & 7:30–11pm Wed–Mon. **Closed** Aug. Ⓛ Ⓛ

This is a spacious local *trattoria* with a pavement pergola for outdoor eating. Specialties from Rome and the Marches – served in ample portions – include *tonnarelli ai sapori di bosco* (pasta with mushrooms), excellent *porcini* (in season), *straccetti all'ortica* (meat in nettle sauce), and *panna cotta* (rich *crème caramel*) with fruit or chocolate. Service is cheerful and friendly.

Cannavota

Piazza San Giovanni in Laterano 20.
Map 9 C1. **【** 77 20 50 07. **Open** 12:30–4pm & 7:45–11pm Thu–Tue. **Closed** Aug 1–20. 🎴
🄴 *AE, DC, MC, V.* Ⓛ Ⓛ Ⓛ

Join the enthusiastic regulars who crowd this friendly restaurant if you are feeling especially hungry. Portions are generous, the cooking is traditional Italian and the service is swift. Seafood – prawns, in particular – is excellent, but meat is also featured on the menu.

Charly's Saucière

Via San Giovanni in Laterano 270.
Map 9 B1. **【** 70 49 47 00. **Open** 12:45–2:30pm & 8pm–midnight Tue–Fri, 8pm–midnight Mon & Sat. **Closed** 2 wks Aug. ⛄ 🄴 *AE, MC, V.*
Ⓛ Ⓛ Ⓛ

An old-style, unsurprising and well-established French restaurant, this has scarcely altered over the years and is especially warm and intimate on a winter evening. Diners choose from French and Swiss fare: pâtés, onion soup, cheese soufflé, fondues, *rösti*,

steaks in a variety of sauces, and crêpes, accompanied by a small but careful selection of wines. The service is always highly professional and attentive.

AVENTINE

Perilli a Testaccio

Via Marmorata 39. **Map** 8 D3.
【 574 24 15. **Open** 12:30–3pm, 7:30–11pm Thu–Tue.
Closed Aug. ⛄ Ⓛ Ⓛ

In the heart of Testaccio, this archetypal Roman *trattoria* is always packed with hungry regulars (and the occasional famous face). Offered are giant-size quantities of robust traditional fare – *rigatoni alla pajata*, *spaghetti alla carbonara* (served in king-size bowls), *coda alla vaccinara*, *carciofi alla romana*. Everything is efficiently served. Ignore the noise and awful murals and enjoy yourself.

Checchino dal 1887

Via di Monte Testaccio 30. **Map** 8 D4.
【 574 38 16. **Open** Oct–May: 12.30–3pm & 8–11pm Tue–Sat, 12.30–3pm Sun; Jun, Jul & Sep: 12.30–3pm & 8–11pm Tue–Sat.
Closed Aug, 1 wk at Christmas. ⛄
🈺 🍷 ★ 🄴 *AE, DC, MC, V.*
Ⓛ Ⓛ Ⓛ Ⓛ

Historic home of Roman cuisine for over 100 years, Checchino specializes in authentic dishes using the *quinto quarto* (offal, tripe, intestines and tail), originally discarded by the old slaughterhouse opposite. At the old convent tables under vaulted ceilings, with an open fire in winter, Ninetta Mariani and her two sommelier sons offer traditional *rigatoni alla pajata*, *coda alla vaccinara*, *crostata di ricotta*, a superb cheese tray and an extraordinary wine selection. Carved into the artificial Monte de' Cocci (made from broken amphoras), its cool, natural wine cellar deserves a special visit.

TRASTEVERE

Da Lucia

Vicolo del Mattonato 2. **Map** 7 B1.
【 580 36 01. **Open** 1–4pm & 8pm–midnight Tue–Sun. **Closed** 2 weeks Aug, 1 wk Christmas. ⛄ 🈺 Ⓛ

Head for this well-worn popular *trattoria* off Via Garibaldi if you like genuine Roman cooking. You won't be disappointed by the *pasta e ceci*, *baccalà*, *pollo con i peperoni* (chicken with peppers), boiled meats and, incongruously, Milanese risotto. The service is unreliable, the wine basic. Outdoor tables make a more attractive dining area in summer.

Romolo nel Giardino della Fornarina

Via Porta Settimiana 8. **Map** 4 D5 & 11 B5. 581 82 84. **Open** noon–3pm & 7:30pm–midnight Tue–Sun. **Closed** Aug 3–26. AE, DC, MC, V. See p210.

A Roman institution, this was said to have been the home of La Fornarina, Raphael's celebrated mistress and model. Its atmosphere is best enjoyed on a summer evening. Eat out by candlelight in the walled courtyard, to the accompaniment of a melancholy guitar. The food is Roman, including fried *mozzarella alla Fornarina* and *cervella e carciofi* (brains and artichokes).

La Taverna di Bambù

Via Santa Dorotea 2 (Piazza Trilussa). **Map** 4 E5. 580 60 65. **Open** 7pm–midnight daily. **Closed** Aug. MC, V.

An intimate Chinese restaurant, this is well known for its freshly prepared dishes served in abundant portions. A few Italianate specialties, such as pizza with onions, are offered as a concession to the host city, but the authentic Cantonese dishes – such as crispy beef and spare ribs in orange sauce – are excellent and well complemented by a selective, extensive list of Italian wines.

La Cornucopia

Piazza in Piscinula 18. **Map** 8 D1. 580 03 80. **Open** 8–11pm Mon–Sat. AE, MC, V.

One of the better, more expensive fish restaurants in Trastevere, it is particularly recommended for its candlelight, elegant settings and, in summer, comfortable tables outside in the piazza. Dishes are mostly Mediterranean, with excellent antipasti, unusual pasta, such simply cooked fish as *spigola al vapore* (steamed sea bass) and selected meats. The Castelli house white is recommended.

Da Paris

Piazza San Calisto 7A. **Map** 7 C1. 581 53 78. **Open** 12:30–3pm & 8–11pm Tue–Sun, 12:30–3pm Sun. **Closed** Aug. AE, DC, MC, V.

This classic Roman/Jewish restaurant is a firm favorite with choosy diners in Trastevere. Jole Cappellanti's homemade pasta and traditional dishes are a must and include *minestra di arzilla* (skate) and *trippa* (tripe) *alla romana*. The *fritto misto vegetale* is extraordinary, the fish fresh. There are good desserts and the owner's personal choice of wines.

Peccati di Gola

Piazza dei Ponziani 7A. **Map** 8 D1. 581 45 29. **Open** 12.30–3pm, 8–11:30pm Tue–Sun. **Closed** 10 days Jan, 10–15 days Sep. AE, DC, MC, V, JCB.

Situated in a quiet, ivy-clad piazza, Peccati di Gola (literally, "gluttony") is renowned for its Calabrian and Mediterranean fish cuisine successfully interpreted for modern tastes. There is delicious antipasto and a tantalizing choice of fresh seafood, risotti and fish.

Tentativo

Via della Luce 5. **Map** 8 D1. 589 52 34. **Open** 12:30–2:30pm & 8:30–11:30pm Mon–Sat. **Closed** Aug 15–Sep 1. ★ AE, MC, V.

Its full intriguing and ambitious name, *Tentativo di Descrizione di un Banchetto a Roma* ("an attempt to describe a Roman banquet") suggests the nature of this refined and intimate restaurant with its exclusive ultramodern decor. The creative nouvelle cuisine offers an adventurous but delicious variety of tastes. Service is discreet, genteel and attentive.

Cul de Sac 2

Vicolo dell'Atleta 21. **Map** 8 D1. 581 33 24. **Open** 8–11pm Tue–Fri, 8–11:30pm Sat, 12:30–2:30pm Sun. **Closed** Aug. ★ AE, DC, MC, V.

Cul de Sac 2 has emerged as both a wine lover's mecca (with over 650 labels to choose from) and the most innovative and stylish restaurant in the capital. Guy, the chef, creates French-inspired recipes for pasta, fish, meat, extraordinary game and desserts. Trastevere's magical setting, the elegant white rooms with their antiques and the obliging service complete the exceptional appeal.

Alberto Ciarla

Piazza San Cosimato 40. **Map** 7 C1. 581 86 68. **Open** 8pm–midnight Mon–Sat. **Closed** 15 days Aug, 15 days Jan. ★ AE, DC, MC, V, JCB.

This is the quintessential restaurant for fish lovers – at least, those who are prepared to splurge. The elegant, dark decor is dramatically lit by candlelight. Perfectly executed dishes range from the simple to the elaborately creative and include traditional and contemporary fare plus a few unusual meat dishes. Ciarla, who is president of the Italian sommeliers, provides an exceptional wine list, including many fine French and Californian wines.

JANICULUM

Al Tocco

Via San Pancrazio 1, Piazzale Aurelio 7. **Map** 7 A1. 581 52 74. **Open** noon–3pm & 8pm–midnight Tue–Sun. **Closed** Aug 18–30. V AE, DC, MC, V.

In this attractive, ivy-clad 15th-century restaurant, Danilo Albanesi has succeeded in creating the hospitable atmosphere of a tasteful private home, complete with faded photographs, old lace and heavily laden sideboards. He brings alive ancient culinary traditions of the Tuscan Maremma: rustic soups, fish, grilled foods and simple yet mouth-watering desserts. Try the choice, mainly Tuscan, wines.

VATICAN

Macondo

Via Marianna Dionigi 37. **Map** 4 E2. 321 26 01. **Open** 1–3pm & 7:30–11pm Mon–Sat. **Closed** mid-Aug–mid-Sep. V

This brightly decorated, friendly little Caribbean restaurant is just the place to visit if you fancy a change from Italian cuisine. The food is fresh, light, and plentiful and is always beautifully presented. The star dish is *pabellon criollo* (strips of beef, black beans, rice and fried plantain). Try such starters as *patacones y guacamole* (plantains and avocado dip), remembering to leave room for desserts such as the banana cake soaked in banana liquor. There is a good selection of wines at various prices as well as cocktails and Venezuelan rums.

San Luigi

Via Mocenigo 10. **Map** 3 B2. 39 72 07 04. **Open** 11:30am–3pm & 6–11pm Mon–Sat. **Closed** Aug. V AE, MC, V.

If you have just spent hours in the Vatican Museums, the pleasure of a relaxing restaurant with 19th-century decor and soft music will soothe your aching limbs. A fixed menu is offered at lunch and a choice of traditional Neapolitan and creative dishes in the evening. Pastas and desserts are particularly successful. There's a choice of good French and Italian wines.

VIA VENETO

Cantina Cantarini

Piazza Sallustio 12. **Map** 5 C2.
€ 48 55 28. **Open** noon–3pm & 7pm–midnight Mon–Sat. **Closed** Aug, Dec 25–Jan 6. 🔲 🗐 AE, DC, MC, V, JCB. Ⓛ

Hidden away on a small square, this popular local *trattoria* is remarkable for its good natured waiters. Meat is on the menu from Monday to Wednesday, and fish the rest of the week. Typical dishes are *alla marchigiana* (from the Marches) and an amazingly light and delicious vegetable-and-veal *fritto misto*.

Tullio

Via San Nicola da Tolentino 26.
Map 5 B2. **€** 474 55 60. **Open** 12:30–3:30pm & 7:30–11pm Mon–Sat. **Closed** Aug. 🔳 🗐 AE, DC, MC, V, JCB. ⓁⓁⓁ

This genuine Tuscan restaurant is frequented by an enthusiastic clientele for its generous helpings and fair prices. Typical dishes include *porcini* in every possible form, *pasta e fagioli*, grilled meat and fish and Florentine steaks – served in agreeable surroundings by courteous, speedy waiters.

Andrea

Via Sardegna 26. **Map** 5 C1.
€ 482 18 91, 474 05 57. **Open** 12:30–3pm & 7:45–11pm Mon–Fri, 7:45–11pm Sat. **Closed** Aug. 🔳 🗐 AE, DC, MC, V, JCB. ⓁⓁⓁ

This congenial, refined restaurant offers a superb array of antipasti, ranging from humble *supplì* (rice croquettes) to regal lobster (try it in *insalata catalana*). Leave room for the impressive seasonal first and second courses and for desserts. There is an extensive choice of French and Italian wines.

Giovanni

Via Marche 64. **Map** 5 B1.
€ 482 18 34. **Open** 12:30–3pm & 7:30–11pm Sun–Thu, 12:30–3pm Fri. **Closed** Aug. 🍴 🗐 MC, DC, AE, V. ⓁⓁⓁ

A throng of satisfied regulars crowd this classic, well-established restaurant near Via Veneto. The efficient, reliable service is hard to beat. The place is run on traditional lines by the Sbrega family, with a strong regional influence from Lazio and the Marches. They serve such fresh pasta dishes as *tagliolini all'amatriciana*, vegetable soups, boned chicken with rice, unbeatable roast lamb, *osso buco*, fresh fish and *millefeuilles*. The house wines are good.

San Benedetto

Via Romagna 20–22. **Map** 5 C1.
€ 474 39 81, 488 28 20.
Open Oct–Mar: 12:30–4pm & 7:30–10:30pm Tue–Sat; Apr–Sep: 12:30–4pm & 7:30–10:30pm Mon–Fri. **Closed** Aug 10 –22, Christmas–New Year. 🍴 🗐 🗐 AE, DC, MC, V. ⓁⓁⓁ

San Benedetto del Tronto in the Marches is the inspiration behind Pier Luigi Camiscioni's restaurant. Local fish is expertly cooked *alla marchigiana*. In addition, there are delicious antipasti (mussels, fresh sardines), soups and simple fried and grilled fish. Follow these with fruity desserts and excellent cheese and dessert wine from the Marches.

George's

Via Marche 7. **Map** 5 B2.
€ 42 08 45 75. **Open** 12:30– 3pm & 7:30pm–2am Mon–Sat. **Closed** Aug. 🔳 🍴 🎵 🔲 ★ 🗐 AE, DC, MC, V, JCB. ⓁⓁⓁⓁ

Visit this slightly tarnished survivor from the *dolce vita* era for its nostalgic air of luxurious elegance, softly illuminated rooms, garden terrace, tinkling piano music and impeccable service. George's offers tempting and expertly prepared international dishes and a good selection of French and Italian wines.

Le Sans Souci

Via Sicilia 20. **Map** 5 C1.
€ 482 18 14. **Open** 8pm–2am Tue–Sun. **Closed** Aug. 🔳 🍴 🎵 🔲 ★ 🗐 AE, DC, MC, V, JCB. ⓁⓁⓁⓁ

This restaurant has overcome a glitzy fame to emerge as a sound exponent of elaborate French and Italian cuisine. The decor is black and gold throughout, with 17th-century gilt mirrors and chandeliers. In the sophisticated anteroom you can drink an apéritif at your leisure and consult the menu and magnificent wine list. As you might expect, the service is eagerly efficient.

VILLA BORGHESE

Al Ceppo

Via Panama 2. **Map** 2 F3.
€ 841 96 96. **Open** 12:30–3pm & 8–11pm Tue –Sun. **Closed** 3 wks Aug. 🔳 🍴 🔲 🗐 🔲 🗐 AE, DC, MC, V, JCB. ⓁⓁⓁ

In 20 years, two sisters from the Marches, Cristina and Marisella Milozzi, have won an affectionate following of regulars in this exclusive, notoriously diffident area of Rome. Patrons are attracted by the consistently reliable food and the hospitable yet refined family atmosphere. The strictly seasonal menu concentrates on traditional dishes with a touch of invention, as well as excellent grilled meats, home-made desserts and Italian wines.

Relais la Piscine dell'Aldrovandi Palace Hotel

Via G Mangili 6. **Map** 2 D4.
€ 321 61 26. **Open** 12:30–3pm & 7:30–11pm daily. 🍴 🔲 🔲 🔲 ★ 🗐 AE, DC, MC, V. ⓁⓁⓁⓁ

The autonomous restaurant of the Aldrovandi Palace Hotel is especially beautiful in summer, when tables are set on the terrace by the pool. Jean Luc Frenat, the young Breton chef, produces an excellent, typically Mediterranean nouvelle cuisine, using prime meat and fish, vegetables and herbs. This is accompanied by meticulous service, wonderful desserts and a fully comprehensive wine list. Business lunches are a specialty.

Relais le Jardin dell'Hotel Lord Byron

Via Giuseppe de Notaris 5.
Map 2 D4. **€** 322 45 41. **Open** 12:30–2:30pm & 8–11pm Mon–Sat. **Closed** Aug. 🍴 🔲 🔲 🎵 🔲 ★ 🗐 AE, DC, MC, V, JCB. ⓁⓁⓁⓁ

For many, this is Rome's greatest restaurant, located in the quiet, exclusive and green area of Parioli. Diners here are undaunted by absolutely top prices, high-class, impeccably correct service, and haute cuisine at its finest. The inspired chef draws predominantly on traditional Italian regional cooking, with exceptionally creative combinations of fruit, herbs and vegetables served with top-quality meats and fish. To finish, there are homemade desserts and pastries; the list of French, Italian and Californian wines offers many outstanding choices.

For key to symbols *see p303*.

Light Meals and Snacks

WHERE SHOULD YOU GO for a casual bite to eat? Rome has the ability to satisfy the all-important stomach at most hours of the day and night. A network of *gelaterie, pasticcerie,* pizzerias, wine bars, *rosticcerie* and *tavole calde* mean that many varieties of good food and drink are always just around the corner.

Start with a classic breakfast at your local stand-up bar: cappuccino and a hot *cornetto* (similar to a croissant). A heavy morning's sightseeing may leave you ready for an apéritif in one of Rome's elegant 19th-century bars, followed by lunch at a wine bar or Roman-style fast-food place. In the afternoon, there are plenty of opportunities for coffee and cakes at a *pasticceria,* while the late-night bars, especially those with tables outside, are a source of entertainment. Here you can sip a drink or linger over the final ice cream of the day.

PIZZERIAS

ROMAN PIZZERIAS are the natural choice for informal eating: they are noisy, convivial and fun. Most open only at night, when the wood ovens are lit and the embers glow reassuringly up until last orders. Look for the *Forno a Legna* (wood-burning oven) sign – electric ovens simply don't produce the same results. In the best pizzerias you sit in view of the vast marble slabs where the *pizzaioli* flatten the dough and whip the pizzas in and out of the oven on long-handled peels. Turnover is quick, so you may not be encouraged to linger.

To start you might try a *bruschetta* (toasted tomato or garlic bread), some *supplì* (fried rice balls), fried zucchini flowers or *filetti di baccalà* (battered cod filets), or a plate of cannellini beans in oil. Follow this with a *calzone* (folded-over pizza) or the classic Roman pizza – round, thin and crunchy – with various toppings: *napoletana* (tomatoes, anchovies, mozzarella), *margherita* (without anchovies), *capricciosa* (ham, artichokes, eggs, olives) and anything else the *pizzaiolo* fancies. Draft beer is the classic thing to drink, but wine is always available. You should expect to pay around L15,000 a head for a meal. The most representative Roman pizzerias, from all

points of view, are **Da Baffetto** (look for the line outside) and its offspring, **La Montecarlo**; also try **Remo** in Testaccio and **Ivo** in Trastevere, where tables line the road in summer. **Osteria Picchioni** and restaurant-cum-pizzeria **Manuia** prepare delicious, elaborate gourmet combinations. Another popular place not to be missed is **Panattoni**, where a huge variety of customers patiently line up for a sidewalk seat on Viale Trastevere in summer or clamor for one of the marble-topped tables (hence the restaurant's nickname "the mortuary") inside.

ENOTECHE (WINE BARS)

ENOTECHE offer a fine selection of wines from Italy and around the world. They are usually run by experts, eager to share their knowledge about the best combinations of wine and food. Some *enoteche* are simply shops for browsing. Others, like **Achilli al Parlamento** and **Bevitoria Navona**, offer the traditional *mescita* – wine and champagne tasting by the glass, accompanied by snacks and canapés. Their prices are reasonable: about L1,500 for a glass on tap, L3,000 upward for a quality wine, to about L8,000 for champagne. **Vineria Reggio** in Campo de' Fiori is a typical spot for

mescita, especially at night. Here professionals, residents and tourists alike meet for an apéritif or gather round a table to share a bottle.

For more substantial food for as little as L20,000 to L25,000 a head, try the bistro- or restaurant-style *enoteche,* open from lunch until late. Particularly recommended are the innovative **Cul de Sac 1**, **Trimani Wine Bar**, the tiny **Il Tajut** serving specialties from Friuli and **Cavour 313**.

BIRRERIE (BEER HOUSES)

ROMAN *BIRRERIE* had their heyday in the early years of this century. The few that have survived the competition from subsequent pizzerias and *enoteche* are some of the best: German-style beer houses where you can still enjoy beer and substantial snacks in traditional wood-paneled rooms. The quiet **Premiata Fabbrica Birra Peroni**, serving classic beer-drinkers' fare, is worth a visit for its authentic turn-of-the-century air of decadence, as is the permanently crowded **Fratelli Tempera**. Another place that attracts Italians and foreigners alike is the **Birreria Viennese/Wiener Bierhaus**, with its excellent Transylvanian specialties, which come heaped generously on wooden plates. If you eat here or in the **Birreria Bavarese**, you'll spend around L30,000 to L50,000. Elsewhere will be cheaper if you want to concentrate more on drinking.

FAST FOOD

ROME HAS PLENTY OF homespun fast-food options for when you need something quick and inexpensive to eat. Slices of freshly baked pizza are available for one or two thousand lire from *pizza al taglio* shops. Many of these places also sell spit-roasted chickens, *supplì* and other traditional pizzeria fare. *Rosticcerie* offer deliciously tasty roast chicken and potatoes, as well as ready-made pasta dishes, cooked vegetables, salads and desserts – useful for picnics or for making a complete take-out meal. For a similarly speedy but sit-down snack, bars with a *tavola calda* (hot table) have the same kind of selection, especially at lunch; one of the largest and most popular is **Il Delfino** at Largo Argentina. Vegetarians should seek out the **Centro Macrobiotico** near Piazza di Spagna. The **McDonald's** hamburger outlet in Piazza di Spagna also offers a good range of fresh mixed salads.

Most *alimentari* (grocery shops) will make you up a *panino* (filled roll). Especially delicious are **Paladini's** hot plain pizza pockets stuffed with choices from the shop's counters; here you can also have a glass of wine. Try one of the region's specialties if you see the sign *Porchetta*: whole aromatic roast pig with crackling, sliced into *rosette* (rolls) or thick country-bread sandwiches – there is a good stall selling these at the tram stop in Viale Carlo Felice opposite San Giovanni in Laterano. At the hole-in-the-wall **Er Buchetto** you can even sit down in relative comfort with a glass of wine. For a really typical Roman snack, make a late-afternoon detour to **Filetti di Baccalà**, which serves, as the name suggests, fried cod fillets.

BARS, CAFÉS AND TEA ROOMS

ROMAN BARS are the city's lifeline: they are places to meet, eat, drink, buy supplies of milk and coffee, make phone calls or use the bathroom. Some of them are small, stand-up, basic one-counter bars for grabbing a quick *cornetto* and cappuccino; others are quite luxurious grandiose affairs doubling as cake shops, ice cream parlors, tea rooms or *tavola calda*, or all of these in one. Most open early at around 7:30am, and close late, particularly on weekends, well past midnight or 2am. In summer, tables cover the available

outdoor space, and the fight for a place in the shade begins. Traditionally elegant – and pricey – bars for people-watching are the conveniently located **Rosati** and **Doney**, as well as **Caffè Greco**, the 19th-century haunt of artists, writers and composers *(see p133)*, and the carefully restored **La Caffettiera** at the Pantheon. Another popular and well-established bar is the **Antico Caffè della Pace**. **Minim's de Paris**, **Caffè Flores** (with piano music) and **Selarum** in Trastevere are recommended for late-night drinks, as is **Zodiaco** on Monte Mario for its panoramic views.

Earlier in the day, Rome's favored meeting places are its tea rooms. **Babington's** *(see p134)* is the place to go for an expensive cup of tea and cakes in genteel surroundings; **Dolci e Doni** is more relaxed. Try a *gran caffè speciale* at the counters of **Sant'Eustachio** or one of Rome's best espressos at **Tazza d'Oro**. **Ciampini al Café du Jardin**, with its garden setting and rooftop views, is unbeatable in summer, particularly at the apéritif hour, as is the **Bar Parnaso** in Parioli.

Museum cafés are seldom open, or worth visiting. A welcome exception, however, is the café of the **Palazzo delle Esposizioni**, open throughout the day *(see p164)*. If you're stuck for choice, try one of the grander, larger bars such as **Alemagna** – where you can stand, sit, eat and drink at any time of the day, well into the night.

PASTICCERIE (PASTRY SHOPS)

ON SUNDAY mornings you'll often see Romans emerging from the local *pasticceria* with a beautifully wrapped package. This can contain dainty individual pastries, whole cakes or tarts, traditional Easter *colombe* (doves) or Christmas *panettoni* (huge cakes with raisins and candied peel) all for consumption by large gatherings of friends, relatives

or family after lunch. The window displays of Rome's cake shops are often fantastic. These, and the aroma of brewing coffee, might tempt you in for a hot *cornetto* or a brioche in the early morning, a midday *pizzetta* or savory tart, or a choux pastry or fruit tart later in the afternoon.

GELATERIE (ICE CREAM PARLORS)

ICE CREAM *(gelato)* is one of summer's particular delights, and nowhere more so than in Rome. Every well-equipped bar has its tubs of homemade ice cream, and in the *gelaterie* the choice is endless – water ices made with a phenomenal variety of fruit; lemon and coffee *granite* (crushed ice); as well as more exotic ice cream specialties such as rice, *zuppa inglese* (English trifle), *zabaglione, tiramisù* and After Eight.

Choose as many varieties as the size of your cone or cup will hold, topped with cream *(panna)*, and then go for a stroll or take a break and enjoy an ornate creation with all the trimmings served to you at a table. *Gelaterie* are open all day until late at night, when they become evening entertainment.

Tre Scalini in Piazza Navona is a famous spot for enjoying the expensive yet so heavenly chocolate *tartufo*, while a summer evening in EUR, especially with children, nearly always ends in a trip to **Giolitti**, known historically for ice cream; try also the strategically placed, crowded original parlor near the Pantheon *(see p109)*, also serving coffee and pastries. In the same area is the popular **Gelateria della Palma**.

Adults may prefer to pick their nighttime treat at **Chalet del Lago**, again in EUR, while sitting beside the lake. If you happen across a small kiosk bearing the sign *Grattachecche* (most likely in Trastevere and Testaccio), try one of Rome's oldest traditions – ice grated on the spot and enlivened with a variety of classic flavorings.

DIRECTORY

FORUM

Pizzeria
Alle Carrete
Via della Madonna dei
Monti. **Map** 5 B5.

PIAZZA DELLA ROTONDA

Pizzerias
Barroccio
Via dei Pastini 13.
Map 4 F4 & 12 D2.

Er Faciolaro
Via dei Pastini 123.
Map 4 F4 & 12 D2.

Wine Bars
Achilli al Parlamento
Via dei Prefetti 15.
Map 4 F3 & 12 D1.

Corsi
Via del Gesù 88.
Map 4 F4 & 12 E3.

Spiriti
Via di Sant'Eustachio 5.
Map 4 F4 & 12 D3.

Fast Food
Fiocco di Neve
Via del Pantheon 51.
Map 4 F4 & 12 D2.

Bars, Cafés and Tea Rooms
La Caffettiera
Piazza di Pietra 65.
Map 4 F3 & 12 E2.

Camilloni
Piazza Sant'Eustachio 54.
Map 4 F4 & 12 D3.

Ciampini
Piazza S. Lorenzo in Lucina
29. **Map** 4 F3 & 12 D1.

Sant'Eustachio
Piazza Sant'Eustachio 82.
Map 4 F4 & 12 D3.

Tazza d'Oro
Via degli Orfani 82/84.
Map 4 F4 & 12 D2.

Teichner
Piazza S. Lorenzo in Lucina
17. **Map** 4 F3 & 12 E1.

Ice Cream Parlors
Gelateria della Palma
Via della Maddalena 20.
Map 4 F3 & 12 D2.

Giolitti
Via Uffici del Vicario 40.
Map 4 F3 & 12 D2.

PIAZZA NAVONA

Pizzerias
Da Baffetto (Volpetti)
Via del Governo Vecchio
114. **Map** 4 E4 & 11 B3.

Corallo
Via del Corallo 10.
Map 4 E4 & 11 B3.

La Montecarlo
Vicolo Savelli 12/13.
Map 4 E4 & 11 C3.

Wine Bars
Bevitoria Navona
Piazza Navona 72.
Map 4 E4 & 11 C2.

Cul de Sac 1
Piazza Pasquino 73.
Map 4 E4 & 11 C3.

Fast Food
Paladini
Via del Governo Vecchio
28/29. **Map** 4 E4 & 11 B3.

Bars, Cafés and Tea Rooms
Antico Caffè della Pace
Via della Pace 5.
Map 4 E4 & 11 C3.

Pastry Shops
A Bella Napoli
Corso Vittorio Emanuele II
246. **Map** 4 E4 & 11 B3.

Ice Cream Parlors
Tre Scalini
Piazza Navona 28.
Map 4 E4 & 11 C3.

PIAZZA DI SPAGNA

Pizzerias
La Capricciosa
Largo dei Lombardi 8.
Map 4 F2.

Il Leoncino
Via del Leoncino 28.
Map 4 F2.

Wine Bars
Buccone
Via di Ripetta 19.
Map 4 F1.

Roffi Isabelli
Via della Croce 76 A.
Map 5 A2.

Beer Houses
Birreria Bavarese
Via Vittoria 47. **Map** 5 A2.

Birreria Viennese/
Wiener Bierhaus
Via della Croce 21.
Map 5 A2.

Fast Food
Centro Macrobiotico
Via della Vite 14.
Map 5 A3.

Fior Fiore
Via della Croce 17–18.
Map 5 A2.

McDonald's
Piazza di Spagna 46.
Map 5 A2.

Bars, Cafés and Tea Rooms
Alemagna
Via del Corso 181.
Map 5 A3.

Babington's Tea Rooms
Piazza di Spagna 23.
Map 5 A2.

Caffè Greco
Via Condotti 86.
Map 5 A2.

Ciampini al Café
du Jardin
Piazza Trinità dei Monti.
Map 5 A2.

Dolci e Doni
Via delle Carrozze 85 B.
Map 4 F2.

Rosati
Piazza del Popolo 5.
Map 4 F1.

Pastry Shops
Krechel
Via Frattina 134.
Map 5 A2.

CAMPO DE' FIORI

Wine Bars
Bottega del Vino
da Beve
Via Santa Maria del Pianto
9A/11.
Map 4 F5 & 12 D5.

Il Goccetto
Via dei Banchi Vecchi 14.
Map 4 D4 & 11 B3.

Vineria Reggio
Piazza Campo de' Fiori 15.
Map 4 E4 & 11 C4.

Fast Food
Il Delfino
Corso Vittorio Emanuele II
67. **Map** 4 F4 & 12 D4.

Filetti di Baccalà
Largo dei Librari 88.
Map 4 E5 & 11 C4.

Da Giovanni
Piazza Campo de' Fiori 39.
Map 4 E4 & 11 C4.

Bars, Cafés and Tea Rooms
Alberto Pica
Via della Seggiola 12.
Map 4 F5 & 12 D5.

Caffè Flores
Lungotevere dei Vallati
25/27. **Map** 4 E5 & 11 C5.

Pastry Shops
Bernasconi
Largo di Torre Argentina 1.
Map 4 F4 & 12 D4.

La Dolceroma
Via del Portico d'Ottavia
20B. **Map** 4 F5 & 12 E5.

Il Forno del Ghetto
Via del Portico d'Ottavia 2.
Map 4 F5 & 12 E5.

QUIRINAL

Pizzerias
Est! Est! Est!
Via Principe Amedeo 4A.
Map 6 D3.

I Rioni
Via dei SS. Quattro
Coronati 24. **Map** 9 B1.

Wine Bars
Cavour 313
Via Cavour 313.
Map 5 B5.

Beer Houses
Albrecht
Via Rasella 52. **Map** 5 B3.

Fratelli Tempera
Via San Marcello 19.
Map 5 A4 & 12 F3.

Fast Food
Bar del Palazzo del
Yogobar
Via Mazzarino 8–10.
Map 5 B4.

Er Buchetto
Via del Viminale 2.
Map 5 C3.

McDonald's
Piazza della Repubblica
40. **Map** 5 C3.

Nadia e Davide
Via Milano 33.
Map 5 B4.

**Bars, Cafés and
Tea Rooms**
**Palazzo delle
Esposizioni**
Via Milano 9.
Map 5 B4.

TERMINI

Pizzerias
La Bruschetta
Via Ancona 35.
Map 6 D1.

Formula 1
Via degli Equi 13.
Map 6 F4.

Le Maschere
Via degli Umbri 8–14.
Map 6 F4.

Wine Bar
Trimani Wine Bar
Via Cernaia 37B.
Map 6 D2.

Beer House
**Premiata Fabbrica
Birra Peroni**
Via Brescia 24–32.
Map 6 D1.

Pastry Shop
La Partenopea
Via Appia Nuova 198.
Map 10 E3.

ESQUILINE

Pizzeria
Osteria Picchioni
Via del Boschetto 16.
Map 5 B4.

Beer House
Marconi
Via di Santa Prassede 9C.
Map 6 D4.

Fast Food
Cottini
Via Merulana 286.
Map 6 D4.

**Palazzo del Freddo di
Giovanni Fassi**
Via Principe Eugenio
65–67. **Map** 6 E5.

**Bars, Cafés and
Tea Rooms**
Ristoro della Salute
Piazza del Colosseo 2.
Map 9 A1.

LATERAN

Fast Food
**Viale Carlo Felice
Porchetta Stall**
Viale Carlo Felice.
Map 10 D1.

Ice Cream Parlors
**Premiate Gelaterie
Fantasia**
Via La Spezia 100–102.
Map 10 E1.

AVENTINE

Pizzerias
Remo
Piazza Santa Maria
Liberatrice 44. **Map** 8 D3.

Taverna Cestia
Via della Piramide Cestia
67. **Map** 8 E3

Wine Bar
Palombi
Piazza Testaccio 38–41.
Map 8 D3.

TRASTEVERE

Pizzerias
Almacrì
Via F. Benaglia 3.
Map 7 B4.

Da Gildo
Via della Scala 31A.
Map 4 D5 & 11 B5.

Ivo
Via di San Francesco a
Ripa 158. **Map** 7 C1.

Panattoni
Viale Trastevere 53.
Map 7 C1.

Ar Popi Popi
Via delle Fratte di
Trastevere 45. **Map** 7 C1.

Da Vittorio
Via di San Cosimato 14A.
Map 7 C1.

Wine Bars
**Il Cantiniere di Santa
Dorotea**
Via di S. Dorotea 9.
Map 4 D5 & 11 B5.

Ferrara
Via dell'Arco di San
Calisto 36. **Map** 7 C1.

Fast Food
McDonald's
Piazza Sonnino 39–40.
Map 8 D1.

**Bars, Cafés and
Tea Rooms**
Selarum
Via dei Fienaroli 12.
Map 7 C1.

Pastry Shop
Valzani
Via del Moro 37B.
Map 7 C1.

Ice Cream Parlors
La Fonte della Salute
Via Cardinale Marmaggi
2/4/6. **Map** 7 C1.

Sacchetti
Piazza San Cosimato 62.
Map 7 C1.

VATICAN

Pizzerias
Pizzeria San Marco
Via Tacito 29.
Map 4 D2.

Il Tempio della Pizza
Viale Giulio Cesare 91.
Map 3 C1.

Wine Bar
**Il Simposio di Piero
Costantini**
Piazza Cavour 16.
Map 4 E2.

Beer House
Tiroler Keller
Via G. Vitelleschi 23.
Map 3 C2.

VIA VENETO

Wine Bar
Marchetti
Via Sicilia 144.
Map 5 C1.

**Bars, Cafés and
Tea Rooms**
Doney
Via Veneto 145.
Map 5 B2.

EUR

Fast Food
McDonald's
Piazzale Don Luigi Sturzo
21–22.

**Bars, Cafés and
Tea Rooms**
Chalet del Lago
Lake, EUR.

Ice Cream Parlors
Giolitti
Casina dei Tre Laghi, Viale
Oceania 90.

FARTHER AFIELD

Wine Bars
Guerrini
Viale Regina Margherita
205–207.

Semidivino
Via Alessandria 230.

Il Tajut
Via Albenga 44.
Map 10 E3.

Fast Food
Svizzera Siciliana
Piazza Pio XI 10–11.

**Bars, Cafés and
Tea Rooms**
Bar Parnaso
Piazza delle Muse 22.
Map 2 E2.

Il Cigno
Viale Parioli 16.
Map 2 E3.

Duse
Via Eleonora Duse 1E.
Map 2 F2.

Pannocchi
Via Bergamo 56.
Map 6 D1.

San Filippo
Via di Villa San Filippo
8/10. **Map** 2 F2.

Zodiaco
Viale Parco Mellini 90.

Pastry Shops
Euclide
Via F. Civinini 119.
Map 2 D3.

SHOPS AND MARKETS

ROME HAS BEEN a thriving center for design and cosmopolitan shopping since ancient times. In the heyday of the empire, the finest craftspeople were drawn to Rome, and artifacts and produce of all kinds, including gold, furs, wine and slaves, were imported from far-flung corners of the empire to service the needs of the wealthy Roman population.

Shopping in Rome today in many ways reflects this diverse tradition. Italian designers have

Window shopping in Rome, an absorbing pastime

an international reputation for their luxuriously chic style in fashion, knitwear and leather goods (especially shoes and handbags), as well as in interior design, fabrics, ceramics and glass. The artisan tradition of fine workmanship is strong, and the love of design is apparent in the smallest items. Rome is not a city for bargains (though it often offers better value than Florence or Milan), but even window shopping is a memorable event.

BEST BUYS

LEATHER GOODS of all kinds, including shoes and bags, are a good buy here. Ready-to-wear Italian designer clothes are not cheap, but they are certainly less expensive than designer fashion in other countries. Armani jeans are a good example *(see p327)*. You are also likely to find designer lighting fixtures at lower prices here. Both modern and traditional Italian ceramics and handicrafts can be very beautifully made, and, if you have time to wander around the back streets, unusual unique gifts can often be found.

SALES

SALE TIME *(saldi)* is from mid-July to mid-September and the period from just before Christmas to the first week in March. Top designers

(see p326) slash prices by half, but their clothes are still very expensive even then. Good bargains can be found in the young designer shops *(see p327)*, and good-quality large shoe sizes are sold very cheaply (most Italians have small feet). Both of the Cesari shops *(see pp 328 and 333)* are well known for their sales. In general, though, sales in Rome do not offer huge discounts.

Both the original and the sale price should be quoted on each reduced item. *Liquidazioni* (closing-down sales) are usually genuine and can sometimes be worth investigating. However, other signs in shop windows, such as *Vendite Promozionali* (special introductory prices) and *Sconti* (discounts) are often only lures to get you into the shop. The sign on the door saying *Entrata Libera* means "Browsers Welcome."

Antiques at Acanto *(see p336)*

WHEN TO SHOP

SHOPS ARE GENERALLY open from 9am to 1pm and from 3:30 to 7:30pm (4 to 8pm in the summer months). Some of the shops in the center stay open all day from 10:30am to 7:30pm. Most shops are closed on Sunday (except immediately before Christmas). Shops are also closed on Monday morning, apart from food and technical supply stores, which close on Thursday afternoons in winter and Saturday afternoons in summer.

August brings the city to a virtual standstill as Roman families escape the heat and go to the sea or the mountains. Signs saying *Chiuso per Ferie* (Closed for Vacation) appear everywhere in the shops. Most shops close for at least two weeks around August 15, the national holiday.

Flower stalls in Piazza Campo de' Fiori *(see p338)*

SHOPPING ETIQUETTE

APART FROM a few department stores, most Roman shops are small, specializing in just one field. Browsing at leisure may at first seem daunting if you are used to large shopping centers. Customers will almost always receive better attention if they dress smartly – the emphasis on *fare la bella figura* (making a good impression) is taken seriously.

Sizes are not always uniform, so it's wise to try clothes on if possible before buying, since refunds and exchanges are not usually given.

Stylish leather gloves on display

HOW TO PAY

MOST SHOPS now accept all the major credit cards, whose signs are displayed on the shop window. Some will also accept foreign currency, though the exchange rate may not be good. When you make a purchase, you are bound by Italian law to leave the shop with a *ricevuta fiscale* (receipt). You can try asking for a discount if paying cash, and you may be lucky, though many shops have a *prezzi fissi* (fixed prices) sign.

VAT EXEMPTION

VALUE-ADDED TAX – VAT (IVA in Italy) – ranges from 12% on clothing to 35% on luxury items such as jewelry and furs. Marked or advertised prices normally include the IVA. It is possible for non–European Community citizens to obtain an IVA refund for individual purchases that exceed L650,000, but be prepared for a long and bureaucratic process. The simplest method is to shop at a place displaying the "Euro Free Tax" sign.

Present your passport when you make your purchase and fill in a form from the shop; the shop then deducts the IVA, gives you a copy of the form, and sends their copy to the Euro Free Tax Organization in Milan, which will then deal with the paperwork.

If you wish to buy something from a shop that is not part of the "Euro Free Tax" scheme, you must get the Italian Customs to stamp the vendor's receipt at your departure, showing them the purchased article, and then mail the stamped receipt back to the shop, which should then send you a refund.

Mercato delle Stampe *(see p338)*

DEPARTMENT STORES AND SHOPPING CENTERS

DEPARTMENT STORES, known as *grandi magazzini*, are few and far between in Rome. **La Rinascente** and **Coin** are good for ready-to-wear clothes, household linens and haberdashery and have well-stocked perfume counters. La Rinascente gives 10% discount to tourists on perfumes and cosmetics if you show your passport. The **Standa** and **Upim** chain stores offer moderately priced medium-quality clothes and household goods.

Another alternative for the zealous shopper is to head for one of Rome's two shopping centers. **Cinecittà Due Centro Commerciale**, built in 1988, offers around 100 shops plus bars, banks,

Bargains in Via Sannio *(see p339)*

and restaurants within easy reach of the center by Metro (line A to Cinecittà). An even bigger center, called **I Granai**, has now opened in Via Laurentina, reachable by Metro (line B to Laurentina).

Cinecittà Due Centro Commerciale
Via Tuscolana. **Map** 10 E2.
📞 722 09 10.

Coin
Piazzale Appio 7. **Map** 10 D2.
📞 708 00 20.

I Granai
Via del Tintoretto.
📞 51 95 57 77.

La Rinascente
Via del Corso 189. **Map** 5 A3 & 12 E2.
📞 679 76 91.

Piazza Fiume. **Map** 6 D1.
📞 884 12 31.

Standa
Via Cola di Rienzo 173. **Map** 4 D2.
📞 324 32 83.

Viale Trastevere 60. **Map** 7 C2.
📞 589 53 42.

Via Appia Nuova 181. **Map** 10 D2.
📞 702 48 96.

Upim
Via del Tritone 172. **Map** 5 A3.
📞 678 33 36.

Via Nazionale 211. **Map** 5 C3.
📞 48 45 02.

Piazza S. Maria Maggiore. **Map** 6 D4.
📞 446 55 79.

Craftsmen near Piazza Navona

Rome's Best: Shopping Streets and Markets

THE MOST INTERESTING shops in Rome are in the old center, so shopping is easy to combine with sightseeing. The shops are often housed in medieval or Renaissance buildings, and their window displays can be exquisite. Just like shopkeepers in the past, today's traders tend to specialize in one type of merchandise. Street names often refer to the old tradesmen: locksmiths in Via dei Chiavari, leather jerkin makers in Via dei Giubbonari and chair makers in Via dei Sediari. Today, antiques merchants have taken over from the rosary sellers on Via dei Coronari. The top names in fashion and modern design dominate the Via Condotti area, and the artisan-craftsperson tradition is still strong around Campo de' Fiori and Piazza Navona.

Via dei Coronari

Art Nouveau and antiques enthusiasts will love browsing in the shops that line this charming street just northwest of Piazza Navona. But be prepared for high prices as most of the items are imported.

Via Cola di Rienzo

Situated close to the Vatican Museums, this long wide street has the finest food shops and is also good for clothes, books and gifts.

Vatican

Piazza Navona

Janiculum

Via del Pellegrino

Bookstores and art shops abound here next to working artisans in the historic center. Don't miss the mirror-lined alley near Campo de' Fiori.

Camp de' Fio

Trasteve

Via dei Cappellari

This narrow medieval street is a great place for watching furniture restorers and other artisans plying their crafts in the open air.

Porta Portese

You can buy anything from antiques to a tin whistle at Trastevere's Sunday-morning flea market. (See p339.)

Via Margutta
Upscale antiques shops mix with genteel restaurants on this peaceful cobbled street.

Via del Babuino
This street is renowned for designer furniture, lighting and glass, as well as interesting antiques and fashion shops.

DESIGNER SHOPPING

All the well-known stars of the Italian fashion scene, plus exclusive jewelers, gift shops, shoe designers and tailors, are concentrated in this cluster of chic and stylish shopping streets by the Spanish Steps *(see pp326–31)*. Romans love to stroll here in the early evening.

Via Borgognona
Crowds flock here to buy, or just gaze at, high-fashion clothes, shoes, leather bags and other accessories.

0 meters	500
0 yards	500

Testaccio Market
A visual feast of fruit and vegetables greets the eye in this lively market. (See p338.)

Men's and Women's Fashion

ITALY IS ONE of the leading lights in high-class fashion, or *alta moda*. Many of the most famous designers are based in Milan, but Rome is home to a cluster of sophisticated and internationally distinguished fashion houses. There is also a wonderful selection of *alta moda* shops. Boutiques displaying an eclectic mix of designer goods are next door to prestigious showrooms devoted to single collections. But even those unable to splurge on genuine designer wear will delight in a stroll down the exclusive streets that radiate out from the Piazza di Spagna, where the window displays are not merely creative but truly spectacular.

Custom-made fashions are beyond most budgets, but designers also offer ready-to-wear alternatives in their boutiques. While not cheap, these provide style at a price far less than that of a tailor-made garment.

WOMEN'S HIGH FASHION

ROME'S MOST famous designer internationally is probably **Valentino**. However, one of the first houses to make a name for Roman fashion was **Sorelle Fontana**. This was *the* salon to be dressed by during the 1950s heyday of Rome's *dolce vita*. Sorelle Fontana has been dressing high society since the 1930s and stocks a wide selection of ready-to-wear clothes and accessories.

Fendi occupies a large tract of the fashion street Via Borgognona. Fendi made its name with high-fashion furs, then branched out into leather goods, accessories and ready-to-wear, collaborating with Karl Lagerfeld, who designed the coveted double-F logo that emblazons its very collectible products. Third-generation family members design the younger, less expensive Fendissime line.

For well over a decade, **Laura Biagiotti** has reigned as Rome's queen of discreet, conservative couture. From her headquarters in a castle just outside Rome, she designs a range of timelessly elegant knitwear and silk separates for women who don't want to sacrifice style for comfort. She is famous for her use of cashmere and white as well as her creative use of fabrics and quality of finish. Her flagship showroom in Via Borgognona stocks her complete collection, which now includes hosiery,

perfumes, swimwear and leather goods. Her scarves make wonderful presents and are often reduced in price during sales; other items from previous collections are available in the shop all year round at very good discounts.

Other internationally known Rome-based designers include **Renato Balestra** for tailored suits and glamorous evening-wear and **Roberto Capucci**, who uses wonderful textures and fabrics in classy suits. **Raniero Gattinoni** produces elegant suits and blouses for both his custom-made and off-the-rack showrooms. **Mila Schön**'s specialty is dramatic eveningwear.

Other luminaries of Italian fashion with shops in Rome include **Giorgio Armani**, **Gianfranco Ferrè, Gianni Versace** and **Trussardi**. A rising star in ready-to-wear is **Genny**. Based in Ancona, the Genny design team produces classic, elegant and always stylish collections.

If you're looking for clothes from unconventional designers, **Gente** is the place to go – its Roman showrooms have exclusive rights to the couture collections of avant-garde stylists such as Dolce & Gabbana and Moschino, plus Europeans such as Jean Paul Gaultier. **Max & Co** also has a number of branches here. Chic suits and separates are the mainstays of this popular label. The quality of fabric and finish is superb, and, with suits available for around L1,000,000, its prices are much lower than those of other *alta moda* designers' ready-to-wear lines.

MEN'S TAILORS AND DESIGNER WEAR

ITALIAN MEN are every bit as fashion conscious as the women, and there is no shortage of choice in Rome for the well-dressed man. Suits generally begin at around L1,000,000, jackets at L750,000 and trousers at L250,000.

Most of the "star" designers of women's *alta moda* have a shop for men, like **Valentino Uomo** and **Versus by Versace**. The designs are less dramatic than the women's, with the accent on understated sophistication and casual sportiness. Valentino's distinctive monogrammed accessories are relatively affordable.

Battistoni is probably the most prestigious designer concentrating on menswear. Giorgio Battistoni and family's fine custom-made shirts and suits have been in demand with film stars and high society

VALENTINO

One of the high priests of Italian fashion, **Valentino Garavani** opened the doors of his Roman atelier in 1959 to a distinguished clientele that included Sophia Loren, Audrey Hepburn and Jackie Kennedy, and has never looked back. He has created some of the most dramatic and flattering evening dresses of the last

three decades. In the 1970s, he began designing ready-to-wear lines for both men and women alongside his *alta moda* collections, and you can now find his very distinctive "V" logo on a wide range of accessories. Valentino's salon is in a huge palazzo in Piazza Mignanelli, and he also has a separate ready-to-wear boutique nearby (see p330).

for 50 years. **Etro** sells classically cut clothes and accessories for men and women in exotic Italian-designed printed fabrics.

Carlo Palazzi's Baroque palazzo setting offers elegant ready-to-wear, and the master tailor Peppino Scarapazzi will also make to measure. **Davide Cenci** has been a mecca since 1926 for those in search of the English country gentleman look. **Brioni** offers traditional tailor-made and their own ready-to-wear men's clothing. **Trussardi** sells beautifully tailored classics, and **Polidori Uomo** offers classics custom-made or ready-to-wear, from its own gorgeous tweeds and wools. **Testa** has impeccably tailored suits that appeal to the younger set, and **Enzo Ceci** is popular for ready-to-wear *alta moda* designs. **Degli Effetti** stocks more avant-garde designers, such as Romeo Gigli and Jean Paul Gaultier.

YOUNG DESIGNER WEAR

T HERE IS A HUGE choice for the young. Top designers Valentino and Armani offer their leading fashions translated into more affordable lines at **Oliver** and **Emporio Armani** (Armani jeans are a very good buy at about L100,000). Fendi has its Fendissime line, and MaxMara's Penny Black label can be found in its **Max & Co** branches. Targeted at the younger set, these are good places to pick up stylish, sporty numbers. **Henry Cottons** is another very collectible designer label. Average prices are L100,000 for a shirt, L400,000 for raincoats, L800,000 for suits.

Energie is a big hit and has two shops with some of the best window displays in Rome. Teenagers flock here for jeans and T-shirts. **Aria**, **Babilonia** and **Box 233** are also very popular these days.

Bacillario, **Cantiere del Nord** and **Eventi** represent the more avant-garde styles – *dark*, as they call it here – fusing Gothic, New Age and punk influences, with outrageous window creations. **Luna e**

L'altra offers trendy unconventional designer clothes in a pleasant, friendly atmosphere.

HIGH STREET FASHION

R OME IS NOT a good place to look for everyday wear, since there is a distinct lack of mid-price shops bridging the huge gap between the dazzlingly priced *alta moda* designer exclusives and the ultracheap goods sold in markets *(see pp338–9)*. Lower-budget shops do exist, but quality is often poor. If you have the stamina, you may find a bargain along Via del Corso, Via del Tritone, Via Nazionale, Via Cavour, Via Cola di Rienzo, Via Ottaviano or Via dei Giubbonari.

The most convenient places to shop are department stores such as La Rinascente, Standa and Upim *(see p323)*. They may not sound exciting, but you can browse at leisure and find nice things. It's also worth trying shops mentioned under "Young Designer Wear" – particularly the *alta moda* designers' cheaper lines, such as **Emporio Armani** and **Max & Co**. At **Discount dell'Alta Moda** and **Discount System** you can find end-of-season designer labels at 50% less than the boutique prices. **Scala Quattordici** is a good place to buy simple linen dresses made by the owner. And while you don't need to come to Rome to shop at **Benetton**, there are many shops here which sell the authentic garments in their universal colors.

KNITWEAR

K NITWEAR is a particular strength in Italian design, and in Rome there are plenty of specialist shops. **Laura Biagiotti** is celebrated for her luxurious cashmere separates, and **Missoni** for spectacular kaleidoscopic patterns and colors. Krizia no longer has a shop in Rome but its sophisticated knitware is available from **Liz**.

Choses de Cachemire has cashmere cardigans, pullovers and knitted suits. **Miranda** offers beautiful handmade

items, from wool scarves for less than L100,000 to coats for around L500,000. Other shops, such as the **Luisa Spagnoli** outlets, offer a wider selection, including lower-priced items.

LINGERIE

T HIS IS ANOTHER Italian specialty excelling in both style and quality, with lines such as La Perla exported worldwide. Lingerie is traditionally sold in leading household linen shops *(see p333)* – **Cesari**, for example, is La Perla's main outlet in Rome. There are also boutiques specializing in lingerie and swimwear.

Liberti has a range of swimwear that's ideal for Italian beaches, as well as lingerie and women's night attire. **Brighenti** is said to be where film stars go for their lingerie. **Tomassini** has original designs by Luisa Romagnoli. **Schostal** has more traditional underwear, with a very good men's section.

SECONDHAND CLOTHES

T HOSE WHO are willing to browse will find a wide variety of secondhand clothes, whether inspired by a collector's interest in vintage clothes or a low budget. Apart from Via Sannio and Porta Portese markets *(see p339)*, which have many secondhand clothes stalls, the mecca is Via del Governo Vecchio. Among the best shops in this ancient street off Campo de' Fiori are **Mai Visto**, with a range of leather jackets in every color, as well as clothes from the 1970s onwards, and **Moon**, which has mostly 1920s dresses and some hats and jewelry.

Le Gallinelle offers a marvelous selection of period hats and sells both secondhand and vintage clothes. At **Via dei Chiavari 40** you can find smart clothes from the 1920s onward, and owner Solange also does some dressmaking on the spot and sells at reasonable prices. **Maga Morgana** will make reproductions of period dresses and costumes to order. Via del Pellegrino is also a good street for second-hand clothes.

Shoes and Accessories

ITALY'S LEATHER INDUSTRY is renowned all over the world, and shoes, bags and belts are a good buy in Rome. Accessories in general are not just an afterthought but an integral part of an outfit for the well-dressed Roman. The choice of stylish jewelry, scarves, ties and other accessories is excellent.

SHOES

ROME IS FULL of shoe stores, ranging from high-quality stores in the Via Condotti area (where prices tend to start at L250,000) to the more economical shops around the Trevi fountain, and every big market has its bargain shoe stalls on its fringes.

Probably the best-known shop is **Ferragamo** – one of the world's top shoe stores. It stocks classic yet fashion-conscious shoes, as well as women's clothing and leather goods – the silk signature scarves are quite a feature.

Fratelli Rossetti is a close contender for the number one position. Founded by brothers Renzo and Renato over 30 years ago, this company produces classic men's shoes and beautiful, dressy low-heeled shoes for women that reflect the most up-to-the-minute trends. Along with **Campanile** in Via Condotti it represents the epitome of elegance. Its prices, of course, are sky-high but why not buy something small, and at least you'll have the bag! **Bruno Magli**, Bologna's well-known star, has dressy patent-leather pumps and other classic styles.

Beltrami is an amazing store boasting a spacious storefront. It sells bags as well as men's and women's shoes in classic and innovative styles. **De Bach** has colorful styles for women.

Rome's own **Raphael Salato** has three extremely elegant, high-priced shops: his shoes are genuine masterpieces of craftsmanship, and many are made of intricately embroidered leather. Neapolitan **Mario Valentino** is another Rome-based designer, with an impressive flagship shop on Via Frattina. He designs leather clothing, bags and accessories as well as

shoes – all beautifully tailored and expensive.

Via Frattina also has other, more moderately-priced shoe stores such as **Pollini** and **Ramirez**. Pollini makes boots and bags for men and women in trendy and imaginative styles. **Fausto Santini** stocks original, colorful designs for the younger set at more reasonable prices.

The same goes for **I Cervone**, which specializes in highly colorful women's shoes. **Borino** stocks simple and elegant, low-heeled designs. The **Mr Boots** shops stock a wide range of trendy boots and casual shoes for men and women, while **Dominici** sells witty, smart and affordable footware for women.

Guido Pasquali is a younger designer whose work combines an exciting freshness with a regard for the timeless dictates of good taste; his boots in particular are worth looking out for.

LEATHER BAGS AND ACCESSORIES

THE MOST FAMOUS of Rome's leather shops is trendy to-the-nth **Gucci**, a dandy's paradise selling shoes, suitcases, handbags, wallets, belts and other accessories. It has a fashion boutique for men and women and is well known for its silk ties and scarves. **Fendi** also has exquisite leather goods as well as some lower-priced lines in synthetic materials and a range of gift items. Although their famous "stripe" line leather-finished synthetic handbags cost as much as L250,000 (and their all-leather ones start at L300,000), at least they are cheaper to buy here than abroad. **Valextra** has high-quality, fairly traditional briefcases, handbags, wallets and purses from Milan. **Skin**,

Ginocchi and the more economical suede and leather factory **Pappagallo** are all in the Via Sistina area.

Mandarina Duck's brightly colored fabric bags and line of luggage are very much in fashion and make an attractive (and vegetarian) alternative to the more traditional leather styles.

There are also some great places to buy artisan leatherwork. **Sirni** is at the top end of the scale with elegant bags and briefcases made in a workshop at the back. **Anna Maria Pirozzi** makes everything – from belts to handbags – herself, and has a tiny workshop in Via Panisperna. Prices are very reasonable and she will even make special items to order. **Marco Marinucci** also has a workshop, where bags, belts, wallets and shoes are made.

CLASSIC JEWELRY

WHAT CARTIER is to Paris, Tiffany & Co. is to New York and Asprey's is to London, **Bulgari** is to Rome. This internationally revered jeweler's has passers-by glued to the windows gazing at its large fat gemstones. These "windows" are rather curious small boxes inserted into a wall with one or two pieces of jewelry in each of them, which adds to the feeling of looking at precious items in a case at a museum. Bulgari's watches, especially the men's, are popular and very elegant, as are the famous mesh necklaces. It specializes in large, colorful stones in High Renaissance-style settings but also produces contemporary designs. This was one of Andy Warhol's favorite shops, and it is the most palatial shop on Via Condotti. Inside, the shop's atmosphere is one of almost religious awe and contemplation.

Buccellati is an offshoot of the famous Florentine dynasty, which was begun by Mario Buccellati in the 1920s and patronized by the poet Gabriele D'Annunzio. Its delicately engraved designs are inspired by the Italian Renaissance, and are real classics displaying superb craftsmanship.

Ansuini designs are fashionable yet classic, with strong, imaginative themes being introduced for each new collection. **Massoni**, founded in 1790, is one of Rome's oldest jewelry houses. Its refined one-of-a-kind pieces and brooches are quite outstanding. At **Moroni Gioielli** you will also find imaginative, unique pieces of the highest-quality workmanship. **Petocchi**, which was jeweler to the former Italian monarchy (1861–1946), the House of Savoy, has both traditional and contemporary styles on display.

Peroso is an old-fashioned store that has been going since 1891 and specializes in antique jewelry and silverware. **Boncompagni Sturni** sells traditional designs with the emphasis on quality and craftsmanship. You have to ring the bell to be admitted to both of these stores, and they are extremely expensive.

Ouroboros is known for less expensive handmade gold and silver items. Traditional jewelry can be bought more cheaply in the Via dei Pettinari and Piazza del Monte di Pietà.

COSTUME JEWELRY

For less conventional tastes, there are several shops selling innovative, avant-garde pieces, often using semiprecious metals and stones. **Via dei Coronari 193** is worth trying. **Via dei Pettinari 80** has an exciting mixture of Art Nouveau items and many other types of contemporary designs.

Delettré produces bold, unique designs influenced by Art Deco styles. You are as likely to find rock crystal here as diamonds. Their logo of a crescent moon and five stars was specially designed by Karl Lagerfeld.

Tempi Moderni has an interesting collection of Art Deco and Liberty period jewelry. You can also find some nice pieces from the 1920s and 1930s in Cose Così (*see p336*). **Bozart** is the place for trendy, flashy costume jewelry. **Siragusa** puts beautiful 3rd- and 4th-century BC beads and coins into handmade gold chains, in a museum-like shop just off the Piazza di Spagna.

TRADITIONAL GOLDSMITHS AND SILVERSMITHS

The mainstay of Rome's jewelry industry is still the traditional artisan goldsmith and silversmith, working to order in tiny studio workshops. These are concentrated in the old Jewish Ghetto area, Campo de' Fiori, Ponte Sisto near Via Giulia, and Montepietà (where the pawnbrokers live). Artisan jewelry can also be found in Via dei Coronari, Via dell'Orso, Via del Pellegrino. The jewelers create individual pieces to their own designs and have often learned their profession from their parents and grandparents. They also do repair work, or take old gold jewelry, melt it down and make it into something to suit you. **Oddi e Seghetti** produces some traditional artisan jewelry and always works to customers' commissions.

GLOVES, HATS AND HOSIERY

If you're looking for top quality, you will find an expensive line of gloves and scarves at **Merola**. **Di Cori** and **Sermoneta** stock every imaginable kind of glove. **Catello d'Auria** specializes in gloves and hosiery. The **Anticoli** gloves factory is one of the oldest in Rome and has a large selection at reasonable prices. It also sells belts, scarves, ties and handbags. **Borsalino** is the place for hats. **Calza e Calze** has the best range of hosiery in Rome – the friendly staff will serve you with almost any color or pattern of tights and stockings that you could wish for.

SIZE CHART

For Australian sizes follow British and American convention.

Children's clothing

Italian	2-3	4-5	6-7	8-9	10-11	12	14	14+ (years)
British	2-3	4-5	6-7	8-9	10-11	12	14	14+ (years)
American	2-3	4-5	6-6x	7-8	10	12	14	16 (size)

Children's shoes

Italian	24	25½	27	28	29	30	32	33	34
British	7	8	9	10	11	12	13	1	2
American	7½	8½	9½	10½	11½	12½	13½	1½	2½

Women's dresses, coats and skirts

Italian	38	40	42	44	46	48	50
British	8	10	12	14	16	18	20
American	6	8	10	12	14	16	18

Women's blouses and sweaters

Italian	81	84	87	90	93	96	99 (cms)
British	31	32	34	36	38	40	42 (inches)
American	6	8	10	12	14	16	18 (size)

Women's shoes

Italian	36	37	38	39	40	41
British	3	4	5	6	7	8
American	5	6	7	8	9	10

Men's suits

Italian	44	46	48	50	52	54	56	58 (size)
British	34	36	38	40	42	44	46	48 (inches)
American	34	36	38	40	42	44	46	48 (inches)

Men's shirts (collar size)

Italian	36	38	39	41	42	43	44	45 (cms)
British	14	15	15½	16	16½	17	17½	18 (inches)
American	14	15	15½	16	16½	17	17½	18 (inches)

Men's shoes

Italian	39	40	41	42	43	44	45	46
British	6	7	7½	8	9	10	11	12
American	7	7½	8	8½	9½	10½	11	11½

DIRECTORY

WOMEN'S HIGH FASHION

Fendi
Via Borgognona 36A/39.
Map 5 A2. 679 76 41.

Genny
Piazza di Spagna 27.
Map 5 A2. 679 60 74.

Gente
Via del Babuino 82.
Map 4 F1. 320 76 71.
Also: Via Frattina 69.
Map 5 A2. 678 91 32.
Also: Via dei Due Macelli 62. **Map** 5 A3 & 12 F1.
679 27 27.

Gianfranco Ferrè
Via Borgognona 42C.
Map 5 A2. 679 00 50.

Gianni Versace
Via Bocca di Leone 26.
Map 5 A2.

Giorgio Armani
Via Condotti 77.
Map 5 A2. 699 14 61.
Also: Via del Babuino 140.
Map 4 F1. 679 68 98.

Laura Biagiotti
Via Borgognona 43–44.
Map 5 A2. 679 12 05.

MaxMara
Via Condotti 46.
Map 5 A2. 678 79 46.
Also: Via Frattina 28.
Map 5 A2. 679 36 38.

Mila Schön
Via Condotti 64.
Map 5 A2. 678 48 05.

Raniero Gattinoni
Piazza di Spagna 91.
Map 5 A2. 679 53 61.

Renato Balestra
Via Sistina 67. **Map** 5 A2.
679 55 37.

Roberto Capucci
Via Gregoriana 56.
Map 5 A2. 679 51 80.

Sorelle Fontana
Salita S. Sebastianello 6.
Map 5 A2. 679 86 52.

Trussardi
Via Condotti 49.
Map 5 A2. 679 21 51.

Valentino
Piazza Mignanelli 22.
Map 5 A2. 673 91.

Also: Via Bocca di Leone 15.
Map 5 A2. 679 58 62.
Also: Via Gregoriana 24.
Map 5 A2. 673 91.

MEN'S TAILORS AND DESIGNER WEAR

Battistoni
Via Condotti 57 & 61A.
Map 5 A2. 678 62 41.

Brioni
Via Barberini 79.
Map 5 C2. 488 47 65.

Carlo Palazzi
Via Borgognona 7E.
Map 5 A2. 678 91 43.

Davide Cenci
Via Campo Marzio 1–7.
Map 4 F3 & 12 D2.
699 06 81.

Degli Effetti
Piazza Capranica 75–79.
Map 4 F3 & 12 D2.
679 02 02.

Enzo Ceci
Via della Vite 52.
Map 5 A3 & 12 E1.
679 88 82.

Etro
Via del Babuino 102.
Map 5 A2. 678 82 57.

Polidori Uomo
Via Borgognona 4A.
Map 5 A2. 678 48 42.

Testa
Via Borgognona 13.
Map 5 A2. 679 61 74.
Also: Via Frattina 104.
Map 5 A2. 679 06 60.

Trussardi
See Women's High Fashion.

Valentino Uomo
Via Condotti 12.
Map 5 A2. 678 36 56.

Versace Uomo
Via Borgognona 29.
Map 5 A2. 679 52 92.

YOUNG DESIGNER WEAR

Aria
Via Nazionale 239.
Map 5 C3. 48 44 21.

Babilonia
Via del Corso 185.
Map 4 F3 & 12 E1.
678 66 41.

Bacillario
Via Laurina 43. **Map** 4 F1.

Box 233
Via Nazionale 233.
Map 5 C3. 481 45 18.

Cantiere del Nord
Via del Corso 187.
Map 5 A3 & 12 E2.
678 66 41.

Emporio Armani
Via del Babuino 140.
Map 4 F1. 678 84 54.

Energie
Via del Corso 408–409.
Map 4 F2.
687 12 58, 687 10 04.
Also: Via del Corso
486–487. **Map** 4 F2.
322 70 46.

Eventi
Via dei Serpenti 134.
Map 5 B4. 48 49 60.

Henry Cottons
Via del Babuino 75.
Map 4 F1. 679 08 36.
Also: Via Appia Nuova 51.
Map 10 D2. 700 89 87.

Luna e L'Altra
Via del Governo
Vecchio 105.
Map 4 E4 & 11 B3.
68 80 49 95.

Max & Co
Via Nazionale 56.
Map 5 C3.
48 90 31 10.
Also: Via Appia Nuova
201–203. **Map** 10 D2.
701 44 13.
Also: Via Salaria 59–61.
Map 6 D1. 854 67 15.

Oliver
Via del Babuino 61.
Map 4 F1. 360 01 90.

HIGH STREET FASHION

Benetton
Via Condotti 59.
Map 5 A2. 679 79 82.

Discount dell'Alta Moda
Via di Gesù e Maria 16A.
Map 4 F2. 361 37 96.

Discount System
Via del Viminale 35.
Map 5 C3. 474 65 45.

Emporio Armani
See Young Designer Wear.

Max & Co
See Young Designer Wear.

Scala Quattordici
Via della Scala 14.
Map 4 D5 & 11 B5.

KNITWEAR

Choses de Cachemire
Via del Babuino 105.
Map 4 F1. 679 84 88.

Laura Biagiotti
See Women's High Fashion.

Liz
Via Appici Nuovo 90.
Map 10 D2. 700 36 09.

Luisa Spagnoli
Via del Corso 385.
Map 5 A4 & 12 F3.
679 39 83.
Also: Via Vittorio
Veneto 130. **Map** 5 B1.
488 58 81.
Also: Via Frattina 116.
Map 5 A2.
679 55 17.
Also: Via Barberini 84.
Map 5 C2.
488 07 57.

Miranda
Via Francesco Crispi 44.
Map 5 B2.

Missoni Sport
Via del Babuino 96A–97.
Map 4 F1.
679 79 71.

Missoni Uomo
Piazza di Spagna 78.
Map 5 A2.
679 25 55.

LINGERIE

Brighenti
Via Frattina 7–8.
Map 5 A2.
679 14 84.

Cesari
Via del Babuiro 195.
Map 5 B3.
361 34 51.

Liberti
Via del Tritone 101.
Map 12 F1.
488 22 46.

Schostal
Via del Corso 158.
Map 4 F3 & 12 E1.
679 12 40.

Tomassini
Via Sistina 119. **Map** 5 A2.
[488 19 09.

SECONDHAND CLOTHES

Le Gallinelle
Via del Boschetto 76.
Map 5 B4. [488 10 17.

Maga Morgana
Via del Governo Vecchio
27. **Map** 4 E4 & 11 C3.
[687 99 95.

Mai Visto
Via del Governo Vecchio
85. **Map** 11 C3.
[687 20 26.

Moon
Via del Governo Vecchio
89A. **Map** 4 E4 & 11 B3.

Via dei Chiavari 40
Via dei Chiavari 40.
Map 4 E4 & 11 C4.

SHOES

Beltrami
Via Condotti 84.
Map 5 A2. [679 13 30.

Borino
Via dei Pettinari 86.
Map 4 E5 & 11 C5.
[687 56 70.

Bruno Magli
Via Vittorio Veneto 70A.
Map 5 B2. [488 43 55.

Campanile
Via Condotti 58.
Map 5 A2. [678 30 41.

De Bach
Via del Babuino 123.
Map 4 F1.

Dominici
Via del Corso 14.
Map 12 E1. [361 05 91.

Fausto Santini
Via Frattina 122.
Map 5 A2. [678 41 14.

Ferragamo
Via Condotti 73–74.
Map 5 A2. [679 15 65.
Also: Via Condotti 66.
Map 5 A2. [678 11 30.

Fratelli Rossetti
Via Borgognona 5A.
Map 5 A2. [678 26 76.

Guido Pasquali
Via Bocca di Leone 5.
Map 5 A2.
[679 50 23.

I Cervone
Via del Corso 99.
Map 4 F2.
[678 35 22.

Mario Valentino
Via Frattina 84.
Map 5 A2 & 12 E1.
[679 12 46.

Mr Boots
Piazza Trilussa 33.
Map 4 E5.
[580 38 20.
Also: Piazza Redi Roma 10.
Map 10 D3.
[77 20 86 72.
Also: Via A Brunetti 2.
Map 4 F1.
[321 57 33.

Pollini
Via Frattina 22–24.
Map 5 A2 & 12 E1.
[678 90 28.

Ramirez
Via del Corso 73.
Map 4 F3 & 12 E1.

Raphael Salato
Via Veneto 149.
Map 5 B1.
[482 18 16.

LEATHER GOODS

Anna Maria Pirozzi
Via Panisperna 65.
Map 5 B4.

Fendi
See Women's High Fashion.

Ginocchi
Via Sistina 35. **Map** 5 B2
[488 39 25.

Gucci
Via Condotti 8. **Map** 5 A2.
[678 93 40.

Mandarina Duck
Via di Propaganda 1.
Map 5 A2.
[69 94 03 20.

Marco Marinucci
Via del Lungaretta 65A.
Map 7 C1.

Pappagallo
Via Francesco Crispi 115.
Map 5 B2.
[678 30 11.

Sirni
Via della Stelletta 33.
Map 4 F3 & 12 D2.
[68 80 52 46.

Skin
Via dei Due Macelli 59.
Map 5 A3 & 12 F1.
[679 58 56.

Valextra
Via del Babuino 94.
Map 4 F1.
[679 23 23.

CLASSIC JEWELRY

Ansuini
Via del Babuino 150D.
Map 4 F1.
[36 00 21 99.

Boncompagni Sturni
Via del Babuino 115.
Map 4 F1. [678 38 47.

Buccellati
Via Condotti 31.
Map 5 A2. [679 03 29.

Bulgari
Via Condotti 10.
Map 5 A2. [679 38 76.

Massoni
Largo Carlo Goldoni 48.
Map 4 F2 & 12 E1.
[678 26 79.

Moroni Gioielli
Via Belsiana 32 A.
Map 4 F2. [678 04 66.

Ouroboros
Via di Sant'Eustachio 14.
Map 4 F4 & 12 D3.

Peroso
Via Sistina 29.
Map 5 B3. [474 79 52.

Petocchi
Piazza di Spagna 23.
Map 5 A2. [679 39 47.

COSTUME JEWELRY

Bozart
Via Bocca di Leone 4.
Map 5 A2.
[678 10 26.

Delettré
Via Fontanella Borghese.
Map 4 F2.
[678 19 12.

Siragusa
Via delle Carrozze 64.
Map 5 A2.
[679 70 85.

Tempi Moderni
Via del Governo Vecchio
108. **Map** 4 E4 & 11 B3.
[687 70 07.

Via dei Coronari 193
Via dei Coronari 193.
Map 4 E3 & 11 B2.
[68 80 15 03.

Via dei Pettinari 80
Via dei Pettinari 80.
Map 4 E5 & 11 C5.

TRADITIONAL GOLDSMITHS AND SILVERSMITHS

Oddi e Seghetti
Via del Cancello 18.
Map 4 E3 & 11 C2.
[68 80 26 43.

GLOVES, HATS AND HOSIERY

Anticoli
Via Lombardia 4.
Map 5 B2. [488 44 82.

Borsalino
Via IV Novembre 157B.
Map 5 A4 & 12 F3.
[679 41 92.

Calza e Calze
Via della Croce 78.
Map 4 F2.

Catello d'Auria
Via dei Due Macelli 55.
Map 5 A2 & 12 F1.
[679 33 64.

Di Cori
Piazza di Spagna 53.
Map 5 A2. [678 44 39.

Merola
Via del Corso 143.
Map 4 F3 & 12 E1.
[679 19 61.

Sermoneta
Piazza di Spagna 61.
Map 5 A2.
[679 19 60.

Interior Design

ITALIAN DESIGN belongs to a long-established tradition based on the skills of the master craftsperson, and some firms have a history going back hundreds of years. Rome's stylish interior design shops are worth seeking out, even if it's only to look around and enjoy the ambience. You might well pick up some design ideas for your home, as well as find some interesting or unusual things to buy.

FURNITURE

A WORLD-FAMOUS name in furniture design is **Cassina**: here its expensive hi-tech designs can be bought for far less than they would be abroad. Its style features stark, clean-lined tables, armchairs and sofas in glass, tubular steel and leather in the tradition of architect-designed furniture by Le Corbusier, Eileen Gray, and Vico Magistretti. Merchandise can be shipped abroad.

Stildomus, farther down the street, has a long, narrow showroom displaying very fine modern wood furniture. **Fontana Arte** sells highly original furniture and lamps made almost entirely of glass.

Take a look at the nearby **Studio Punto Tre** if you want something different: it's packed with strangely painted chests of drawers, Egyptian-style artifacts and small bits and pieces that would make good presents. **Alivar**, near the Capitol, sells impeccable reproductions of the "classics" of modern furniture, such as Aalto, Le Corbusier and Mackintosh, at reasonable prices.

Spazio Sette, near Largo Argentina, has a spectacular showroom on three levels in the Palazzo Lazzaroni, a former cardinal's palace. It is one of Rome's premier home furnishing stores, and, apart from furniture, it stocks items that would make interesting gifts. The furniture – modern, laminated, stack-up chairs and so forth, plus vases, glass, bowls, and kitchen equipment – is jumbled together in a fascinating display.

Magazzini Forma & Memoria is in a cleverly converted old printing works on the edge of the Tiber, not far from St. Peter's. It has four levels of display space for the latest in furniture and design items from Italy and else-where. In the basement are a reading area, a health-food bar and an exhibition space. All this plus panoramic views at the top make it a fascinating place to visit.

LIGHTING FIXTURES

L IGHTING FIXTURES are one of the most popular and more easily transportable items, and there are a number of superb showrooms to visit. **Flos Arteluce** is a merger of two design houses whose Roman showroom displays its lights as if they were museum exhibits. The design style is minimalist – plenty of black and white, chrome and steel.

Nearby **Artemide** is, like Flos Arteluce, a design house in its own right and is similarly well-known abroad. Its Rome showroom is elegant, with expensive high-tech lighting design similar to that of Flos Arteluce. **Borghini** sells less famous names, and so is more economical.

Italian lighting and other electrical equipment are designed for 220–240 volts. If you are going to use an item in countries with lower voltages, always ask the shop whether the product needs a transformer, because this can depend on the model. Lighting fixtures generally take screw bulbs, although bayonet bulbs of some designer models may also be ordered.

KITCHENS AND BATHROOMS

A LTHOUGH YOU won't be able to take one home with you, you may enjoy looking at a few of the ultramodern high-tech kitchens sold in Rome. For an overview of the latest designs, visit **La Residenza**, which stocks a selection of over a dozen kitchen sets from about 9 or more Italian manufacturers. **Coas Tradizione Casa** in Piazza Cardelli has some interesting combinations in a centrally located showroom.

Italian bathroom shops concentrate almost entirely on modern design. **Odorisio** is the equivalent of La Residenza for bathrooms, and has some luxurious examples. **Ravasini**, nearby, sells very decorative floral fixtures with matching accessories. **Andreucci** also has a bathroom shop stocking all the latest styles.

TILES

T HE ITALIAN ceramic tile tradition is an ancient one. A great variety of tiles is displayed in kitchen and bath-room showrooms, but there are also specialty shops. The most beautiful and the most expensive is **Farnese**, looking ancient Roman in style with its mosaic tables. Di Donato uses old-fashioned methods to design and produce the tiles – hence the cost. He is influenced by Roman and Pompeiian art but also produces modern one-of-a-kind designs.

Ceramiche Musa specializes in modern tiles with decorative floral and ancient Roman motifs popular with visitors. **Via Giulia** sells period tiles, in limited editions. You can become owner of an Art Nouveau tile for around L30,000 to L60,000, but older or rarer examples can cost more.

GLASS

D ECORATIVE GLASS objects are popular to buy in Rome. **Navona Venetian Glass,** just behind Piazza Navona, sells Murano and other glass items at reasonable prices. This shop is open on Sundays – which can be useful for vistors on short trips to Rome. **Archimede Seguso** also specializes in Murano glass but includes smaller pieces and gift-sized items.

Tupini, the Roman equivalent of the Harrods china department, has quality glass, china and silverware. **Arteque** is a very beautiful shop, with a more traditional flavor. For less expensive gifts, try **Stilvetro**. It is the ideal place for pasta bowls, glass, and ceramics.

Shipment home can usually be arranged at any of these glass establishments so you may make your purchase without worrying about transporting it home.

FABRICS

SUMPTUOUS furnishing fabrics are what **Cesari** in Via del Babuino is renowned for. It also has a linen and lingerie shop *(see p327)*. **Il Sigillo**

offers fabrics and wallpapers made to order from a rich assortment of samples. At **Galtrucco** you can choose material for a suit which they will make to measure so that your individual taste can be combined with their professional expertise.

Bises has two shops in Via del Gesù, No. 91 for silks and fashion fabrics and No. 63 that specialises in furnishing materials.

If you are looking for worthwhile bargains, take a wander around the old Jewish quarter that runs from Largo Argentina down to the Tiber; it is full of cheaper fabric shops, such as **Paganini**. At sale time, remnants *(scampoli)* can be really good value, and you could just the right fabric at just the right price.

HOUSEHOLD LINENS AND KITCHENWARE

A SELECTION of lovely sheets can be found at **Frette**.

If you enjoy designer kitchenware, don't miss **C.u.c.i.n.a.** in the cellars of No. 118 Via del Babuino. It stocks kitchen utensils from all over the world, as well as pots and pans in both rustic and high-tech styles and countless space-saving accessories. **Single** specializes in stainless steel designs such as Alessi and sells wooden breadboards and assorted containers.

For the budget conscious, there is also **Salvoni**, whose basement is well stocked with cut-price gift ideas. You'll find an arrary of household and kitchenware, including silver, china and crystal items.

Books and Gifts

ROME OFFERS A HUGE SELECTION for gift buying. There are products from all over Italy as well as locally produced artisanwares. Seeking out the smaller shops can be an adventure in itself, as many are in attractive parts of the city that you might not otherwise visit.

Some of the artisan ceramics are very unusual; there are also beautiful books on Italian art and architecture, plus wonderful paper products. Food gifts and drinks are always welcome – especially if they are something really special, such as 20-year-old balsamic vinegar. In addition to the usual souvenirs, there is an abundance of religious artifacts – for obvious reasons – and Michelangelo masterpieces are the most popular icons for T-shirts, statuettes and postcards.

BOOKSHOPS

ROME IS RICH in bookshops, from the encyclopedic to the very specialized. Italian books, both hardcover and softcover, are generally very attractive but also tend to be quite expensive.

Rizzoli, Rome's largest bookshop, has a wide selection on art and cookery, among other subjects, and many books in English and other foreign languages. **Feltrinelli** has three shops in the capital. The most important is situated in Via del Babuino and offers a wide selection of contemporary literature. Milanese **Franco Maria Ricci** offers very beautiful art books, as well as its own glossy magazine, *FMR*. **Libreria Godel** is also good for browsing – it carries books on Rome, great postcards, art calendars and secondhand art books.

Remainder has half-price bargains and sells games for children, too. There are many discount bargains as well as secondhand book stalls in Via delle Terme di Diocleziano and in Largo della Fontanella di Borghese.

MULTIMEDIA AND MUSIC

ROME'S BIGGEST music store is **Ricordi**. In addition to records, cassettes and CDs, it sells musical instruments and musical scores in its four central outlets. By contrast, **Discoteca Frattina** is quite a small, handy music shop that also sells videocassettes. The multimedia shop **Mondadori** sells greeting cards, posters and videos and has good map and music departments as well as books.

STATIONERY AND PAPERCRAFT

THE DELIGHTFUL **Papirus** sells papercraft, boxes, obelisks, picture frames and other desk items. **Laboratorio Scatole** offers pretty marbled notebooks, writing paper, files and boxes in various sizes.

Pineider, stationery suppliers to the Roman gentry, will print exquisite visiting cards for you. They also sell handsome leather-bound desk diaries. Just as classy, though less traditional, **Vertecchi** is filled with original paper gifts: boxes of every size and shape, paper tablecloths and napkins, wrapping paper and dazzling Christmas decorations.

ARTISAN HANDICRAFTS

SPACIOUS and artistically rustic, **La Galleria** is filled with authentic artisanwares, including handwoven textiles and beautiful ceramics that owner Clotilde Sambuco chooses from all parts of Italy. Domenico and Lavinia Sarti's **Bottega Artigiana** nearby is a small shop with ceramics made by the couple in their Anzio studio. You can buy vases and urns in unglazed terra-cotta and attractive terra-cotta light fixtures. **Arti e Mestieri** is the workshop of a friendly mother and daughter who make original articles in wood and terra-cotta. For a really original gift, go to **Opificio Romano**, a workshop that reproduces ancient Roman and Pompeian mosaics, where they will re-create any design you choose to order.

SOUVENIRS AND RELIGIOUS ARTIFACTS

MOST OF the tobacco shops in central Rome sell postcards, stamps and a variety of souvenirs, and many cheap and sometimes appealingly kitsch souvenirs are sold by the mobile stalls around the major tourist attractions.

Bookshops near the main basilicas, such as **Libreria Belardetti**, sell souvenirs and religious mementos. Other shops specialize in religious articles for both the clergy and the layperson. Facing the Vatican gates in Via di Porta Angelica are several shops, such as **Al Pellegrino Cattolico**, selling mementos to visitors and tourists.

FOOD

ONE OF THE unusual things about shopping in Rome is the absence of large-scale supermarkets in the center. It has been local government policy to keep them out in order to protect the little *alimentari*, or delicatessens. There are hundreds of these, not on the main shopping streets, but in small side streets running off them or in the "village" districts, such as Monti, Trastevere, the Ghetto, Borgo and Campo de' Fiori. They are often crammed from floor to ceiling with all the irresistible delicacies that are typical of Italy.

Here you can buy, the day before your departure, your supply of parmesan and pecorino Romano cheese *(see p305)*, Parma ham or prosciutto di montagna, attractive bottles of dark-green extra-virgin unfiltered olive oil, dried porcini mushrooms and sun-dried tomatoes to take home (but check Customs restrictions first). Food is by no means cheap, and most of the above are considered luxury items.

Pietro Franchi is without doubt the most exclusive delicatessen in the city, and its windows are a visual feast of seafood platters, pâtés, cheeses and cold meats. Next door is the famous coffee shop **Castroni**, which has Rome's largest selection of imported products from all over the world. It also stocks Italian olive oils, balsamic vinegars, honeys and preserves and of course coffee.

Via della Croce deserves a special mention for its good selection of well-stocked *alimentari* like **Fratelli Fabbi**. Specialty food shops like **Fior Fiore** sell exquisite little cakes of almond and orange peel; ricotta cheese; and piles of artichoke-, spinach- and tomato-flavored pasta; plus thin, crispy pizza straight from the oven.

Azienda Agricola is a tiny shop selling specialty food products. Enjoy the display of beautifully packaged bottles of olive oil flavored with garlic or herbs, pâtés made of black or green olives, plus jars of truffles, asparagus and artichokes and their own preserves. They all make ideal and much-appreciated gifts.

Cheese lovers can usually find lots of Italian varieties in any of the small *alimentari* in the city, but it's also worth trying the local cow, sheep and buffalo milk cheeses that are sold at the **Cisternino Cooperativa fra Produttori di Latte di Lazio** near Piazza Campo de' Fiori.

Boxes of chocolates and traditional confectionery and cakes such as *torrone* and *panettone* can be bought from good-quality bars. **L'Albero del Pane** sells wonderful wholemeal and rye flour breads and other health foods.

WINE

WINE IS GENERALLY sold in *alimentari* and also in supermarkets. There are, however, many specialty shops (look for the sign *Enoteca)* with a huge stock of wines and spirits. They invariably have a little bar where they serve wine and light snacks or canapés. Here you can find Italian wines, and usually local wines, mostly white, from the nearby Frascati, Colli Albani and Marino vineyards, on tap. One of the most select is **Enoteca Buccone**, which is housed in an old coach-house. Another well-known one is **Antica Enoteca**, which has an old-world feeling to it. The **Enoteca del Corso** is more modern, with a good selection of Italian grappa and jars of marinated fruits. **Enoteca Corsi** in Via del Gesù is also worth a visit.

DIRECTORY

BOOKSHOPS

Feltrinelli
Via del Babuino 39–41.
Map 5 A2.
☎ 36 00 18 42.

Franco Maria Ricci
Via Borgognona 4D.
Map 5 A2. ☎ 679 34 66.

Libreria Godel
Via Poli 45. **Map** 5 A3 &
12 F2. ☎ 679 87 16.

Remainder
Piazza San Silvestro 28.
Map 5 A3 & 12 E1.
☎ 679 28 24.

Rizzoli
Largo Chigi 15. **Map** 5 A3
& 12 E2. ☎ 679 66 41.

MULTIMEDIA AND MUSIC

Discoteca Frattina
Via Frattina 50–51.
Map 5 A2. ☎ 679 14 93.

Mondadori
Piazza Cola di Rienzo 81–83.
Map 4 D2. ☎ 321 03 23.

Ricordi
Via Battisti 120 C. **Map** 5
A4 & 12 F3. ☎ 679 80 22.

STATIONERY AND PAPERCRAFT

Laboratorio Scatole
Via della Stelletta 27.
Map 4 F3 & 12 D2.
☎ 68 80 20 53.

Papirus
Via Capo Le Case 55A.
Map 5 A3 & 12 F1.

Pineider
Via dei Due Macelli 68.
Map 5 A2 & 12 F1.
☎ 679 58 84;
Also: Via della Fontanella
Borghese 22. **Map** 4 F3 &
11 D1. ☎ 68 30 80 14.

Vertecchi
Via della Croce 70.
Map 4 F2. ☎ 678 31 10.

ARTISAN HANDICRAFTS

Bottega Artigiana
Via Santa Dorotea 21.
Map 4 D5 & 11 B5.
☎ 588 20 79.

La Galleria
Via della Pelliccia 29A–30.
Map 7 C1. ☎ 581 66 14.

Arti e Mestieri
Via dei Cappellari 57.
Map 4 E4 & 11 C4.
☎ 683 25 21.

Opificio Romano
Via dei Gigli d'Oro 9–10.
Map 4 E3 & 11 C2.
☎ 68 80 27 62.

SOUVENIRS AND RELIGIOUS ARTIFACTS

Al Pellegrino Cattolico
Via di Porta Angelica 83.
Map 3 C2. ☎ 68 80 23 51.

Libreria Belardetti
Via della Conciliazione 4.
Map 3 C3. ☎ 686 55 02.

FOOD

L'Albero del Pane
Via Santa Maria del Pianto
19–20. **Map** 4 F5 & 12 D5.
☎ 686 50 16.

Azienda Agricola
Vicolo della Torretta 3.
Map 4 F3 & 12 D1.
☎ 687 58 08.

Castroni
Via Cola di Rienzo 196.
Map 4 D2. ☎ 687 43 83.

Cisternino Cooperativa fra Produttori di Latte di Lazio
Vicolo del Gallo 20.
Map 4 E5 & 11 C4.
☎ 687 28 75.

Fior Fiore
Via della Croce 17–18.
Map 5 A2. ☎ 679 13 86.

Fratelli Fabbi
Via della Croce 27.
Map 5 A2. ☎ 679 06 12.

Pietro Franchi
Via Cola di Rienzo 204.
Map 4 D2. ☎ 683 26 69.

WINE

Antica Enoteca
Via della Croce 76B.
Map 5 A2. ☎ 679 08 96.

Enoteca Buccone
Via di Ripetta 19. **Map**
4 F1. ☎ 361 21 54.

Enoteca Corsi
Via del Gesù 88. **Map** 4 F4
& 12 E3. ☎ 679 08 21.

Enoteca del Corso
Corso Vittorio
Emanuele II 293–5.
Map 4 D4 & 11 A3.
☎ 68 80 15 94.

Art and Antiques

Rome's art and antiques shops range from exclusive establishments to contemporary art galleries. In response to a fashion for collecting early 20th-century artifacts, new dealers and galleries are springing up throughout Rome – Venini's Murano glass is popular, as are lighting and furniture. Many more sell general bric-a-brac and jewelry. Copies of antique prints can be picked up for a fraction of the originals' price. Rome is not good for bargain antiques, but it's worth looking in shops along Via dei Cappellari and Via del Pellegrino or going to the Porta Portese Sunday market *(see p339)*.

ANTIQUES AND OLD MASTER PAINTINGS

There are antiques shops dotted all over the center of Rome, though the cream tend to be concentrated in distinct areas. Discreet haggling in the shops is accepted practice, but even if you get a reduction in price, make sure the dealer provides the relevant export documents.

The famous Via del Babuino and to a lesser extent Via Margutta, which is more famous for its art galleries, are home to around 30 of Rome's grandest showrooms for antique furniture, Old Master paintings and objets d'art.

W Apolloni is one of the city's most respected and prestigious shops, attracting museums and professional collectors, along with the interested browser, with fine 17th-century paintings, furniture and rare silver.

Cesare Lampronti, aided and complemented by his partner, Carlo Peruzzi, is a top dealer in 16th- to 18th-century European paintings, with an emphasis on Roman and Italian works.

Amedeo di Castro, apparently no relation to the other four di Castros on this street, is a fourth-generation dealer in bas-relief sculptures and exquisite pieces from the 18th and early 19th centuries.

Via Giulia *(see p153)* has over 20 high-quality antiques shops to choose from. Definitely worth a visit is **La Chimera**, a temple to owner Paola Cipriani's love of simply elegant Neoclassical furniture and paintings. She also sells the occasional modern piece. Another shop not to miss on Via Giulia is **Antiquariato Valligiano**. It's the only place in Rome where you can find 19th-century Italian country furniture – a rustic antidote for those overpowered by the grandiose Baroque.

Via Monserrato, running parallel, is worth scouring for slightly lower quality pieces at more attainable prices.

Via dei Coronari is almost exclusively devoted to antiques, with over 40 shops lining both sides of this picturesque street. Quality is very high – as are the prices. It is a good place for Baroque and Empire elaborately inlaid vases, secretaries and consoles.

L'Art Nouveau specializes in high-quality Art Nouveau (usually called *Liberty* here). The **Art Deco Gallery** sells furniture and sculpture from that period.

Piero Taloni has a superb collection of lighting fixtures from the Baroque through to Art Deco periods.

Slightly farther away lies Via della Stelletta, which is home to a handful of unusual and fascinating shops.

Acanto is an inexpensively priced Aladdin's cave with an eclectic mix of objets d'art. It is the perfect place to search for religious memorabilia, Italian curiosities and prints.

Bilenchi is yet another specialist, but in exquisite, turn-of-the-century lamps. Another relatively undiscovered area is Via del Boschetto and Via Panisperna. Shops here tend to specialize in early 20th-century artifacts, with some English Victorian pieces thrown in.

Retrospettiva is strong on top designers and craftspeople selling furniture, Murano glass and Faenza pottery from 1900 to 1950. **Passato Prossimo** has some curious bygones, including a collection of Bakelite and plastic jewelry of the 1940s and 1950s. And **Antichità di Antonella e Maria Teresa** offers a dazzling collection of Art Deco and Liberty lamps.

Of course there are many perennial favorites apart from these streets. The best way to discover them is through word of mouth or just by chance as you stroll along. **Cose Così** is a charming little shop full of small decorative pieces from 1800 to 1940 (watches, silver, glass, frames, vases and jewelry). **Manasse** is the best place to head for if you're after antique jewelry, icons and Fabergé eggs.

Anticaja e Petrella has an eccentric collection of used junk and printed ephemera stored under Sant'Andrea della Valle *(see p123)*.

MODERN ART

Rome is rich in avant-garde galleries exhibiting paintings by recognized modern masters through to the up-and-coming generation of young, mainly Italian, artists.

Rome's art galleries are usually open 10am to 1pm and 5 to 8pm Tuesday to Saturday. Some open only in the afternoon; others also stay open on Monday afternoon. The best times to visit are in the afternoons and early evenings.

As with Rome's antiques shops, the art galleries tend to be concentrated in a couple of distinct areas. The largest of these covers the triangle area between Via del Babuino and Via di Ripetta and adjoining streets, known locally as the Trident.

The pioneering **Agenzia d'Arte Moderna**, founded in 1913, promoted Futurism from the start and other modern art movements as well. There are works by Burri and Kounellis always on display.

Sperone, under the owner-directorship of Gian Enzo Sperone, shows works by American artists like Ray Smith, Julio Galan and Jonathan Lasker. Also included are Italian artists like Gallo, Bianchi, Dessi, Paladino and Merzi.

Apollodoro, which sells interesting design artifacts, has an entrance modeled on Borromini's illusionistic per-spective in the garden gallery of Palazzo Spada *(see p147)*.

One of this area's highlights is the Via Margutta art fair *(see p339)*, which usually takes place around Christmas and in springtime.

Via Giulia and its surround-ings is the next area to investigate: **Galleria Giulia** is a gallery-cum-bookshop with work by artists such as Argeles, Boille, Cano, Cascella, Echaurren, Erba and Lionni, as well as by Bauhaus artists and German Expressionists.

Fabio Sargentini at **L'Attico** follows the latest trends in Italian art from Del Giudice to Corsini and Fabiani.

Trastevere is possibly better for more innovative ventures: The **Galleria Bondho** (previously Alessandra Bonomo) spotlights young Italian and foreign painters, such as Schifano, Boetti, Twombly, Nunzio, Tremlett, LeWitt, Dokoupil. **De' Florio Arte** works with established and emerging contemporary artists from Italy and abroad in a gallery which has retained a real sense of history. In a stupendous villa a few miles outside Rome, **Mauro Vigneti** specializes in both Italian and international artists working in Rome.

ANTIQUE PRINTS AND PHOTOGRAPHS

THE JUSTIFIABLY celebrated **Nardecchia**, named after its cultivated owner, Plinio, is the cream of Rome's print dealers. Look for originals by the 18th-century engraver

Piranesi and views of the city and ancient Roman life.

Another Roman institution, **Casali**, has been trading for over 100 years. The family now runs two shops specializing in 16th- to 19th-century drawings and engravings of Roman scenes ranging from museum-standard Piranesi down to relatively inexpensive and delightfully decorative floral scenes by unknowns.

The Florence-based **Alinari** family is renowned for its sepia photographs of Italy from 1890 onward, including shots of Rome at the turn of the century. At its Roman outlet, prices of photographs from the original plates start at around L30,000 and mounted prints at L500,000. Larger sizes can be mounted on wood or board.

Another place definitely worth heading for in search of that perfect print of old Rome and some enjoyable, relaxing, and maybe persuasive, browsing is the **Mercato delle Stampe** *(see p338)*.

Outdoor Markets

R OME'S OUTDOOR MARKETS are essential to visit if you're interested in experiencing the exuberance and vitality for which Romans are renowned. The markets are wonderfully vivid visually too, as Italian stallholders and vendors have raised the display of even the humblest vegetable to an art form.

The city is dotted with popular, small outdoor food markets, and there are several fascinating well-established ones near the center, along with the most famous flea market over in Trastevere.

It is important to keep your wits about you in all these markets, because pickpockets work with lightning speed in the bustling crowds. However, Roman markets provide such a vibrant source of entertainment, it would be a shame to let such caveats deter you from joining in the fun.

The street fairs that take place throughout the year offer various pleaures and also normally sell a good variety of local produce, handicrafts and clothes. Seasonal fairs also occur, especially around Christmas, when you can stock up on Italian specialties and gifts.

Campo de' Fiori

Piazza Campo de' Fiori. **Map** 4 E4 & 11 C4. ▥ *44, 46, 62, 64, 70, 81, 90, 90b, 492.* **Open** *7am–1:30pm Mon–Sat. See p146.*

Right in the heart of the old city, Rome's most picturesque market is also its most historical. Its name, Campo de' Fiori, which translates as "field of flowers," sometimes misleads people into expecting a flower market. In fact, the name is said to derive from Campus Florae (Flora's square) – Flora being the lover of the great Roman general Pompey. A market has actually been held for many centuries in this now somewhat shabby, but still beautiful, piazza.

Every morning except Sunday, the piazza is transformed by an array of stalls selling colorful fruit and vegetables, meat, poultry and fish. One or two stalls specialize in legumes, rice, dried fruit and nuts, and there are also flower stalls situated near the fountain. But the huge open baskets of ready-stripped broccoli and spinach, various chopped vegetables for minestrone and freshly prepared green salad mixes are the main attraction for visitors. They provide a real visual display as well as an edible feast.

The excellent delicatessen shops on the square and bread shops nearby complement the market. They make it a great place to stock up for an impromptu picnic if the weather turns out fine and you're tempted to do some *al fresco* dining in one of Rome's many attractive parks.

Mercato delle Stampe

Largo della Fontanella di Borghese. **Map** 4 F3 & 12 D1. ▥ *119, also routes to Via Tomacelli.* **Open** *7am– 1pm Mon–Sat.*

This market is a veritable haven for lovers of old prints, books (both genuine antiquarian and less costly secondhand), magazines and other printed ephemera. The quality varies, but it is a good deal more specialized than the *banche*, or stalls, near Termini station which are a more obvious tourist trap. Italian-speaking collectors can enjoy a field day leafing through back issues of specialty magazines. Other visitors might prefer the wonderful selection of illustrated art books and old prints of Rome. It is a good place to pick up that Piranesi print of your favorite Roman vista, ruin or church – but be prepared to bargain hard.

Mercato dei Fiori

Via Trionfale. **Map** 3 B1. ▥ *Ottaviano.* ▥ *23, 70.* **Open** *10:30am–1pm Tue.*

Essentially a trade market, the Flower Market, just north of Via Andrea Doria, is open to the public only on Tuesdays. Housed in a covered hall, it has two floors brimming over with cut flowers upstairs and all kinds of potted plants on the lower floor. Anyone who has an interest in flowers will enjoy this wonderful array of Mediterranean blooms, which are for sale at giveaway prices.

Mercato Andrea Doria

Via Andrea Doria. **Map** 3 B1. ▥ *Ottaviano.* ▥ *23, 70.* **Open** *7am–1pm Mon–Sat.*

The market used to stretch the whole length of this wide avenue. It has now been reorganized onto a huge square of open ground between Via Santamaura and Via Tunisi. Apart from the magnificent displays of fruit and vegetables, it has numerous stalls selling meat, poultry, fish and groceries, as well as an interesting clothes and shoe section. Situated northwest of the Vatican Museums, it is a little off the normal beaten track and has remained very much a Roman market that caters to the needs of the large local population.

Mercato di Piazza Vittorio

Piazza Vittorio Emanuele II. **Map** 6 E5. ▥ *Vittorio Emanuele.* ▥ *4, 9.* **Open** *7am–2pm Mon–Sat. See p174.*

Bustling Piazza Vittorio was, until recently, perhaps the most Roman of the city's larger markets.

Organized as a cramped corridor of stalls around a central garden, it is the place where bargain-hunting *popolari*, Rome's bustling shoppers, buy their food. Stallholders offer cheap prices if you buy by the kilo, but watch out for bad fruit.

Lately it has become more international and now features African and Asian food stalls.

Sadly, the market's days are numbered: the city council says that it defaces the 19th-century square. Some stalls have moved to the new site in Via Giolitti; others won't go. The battle is on, but make a visit before a splash of Roman color is lost forever.

Mercato di Testaccio

Piazza Testaccio. **Map** 8 D3. ▥ *Piramide.* ▥ *11, 27.* **Open** *7:30am–1:30pm Mon–Sat.*

The covered market at Testaccio occupies the central area of the Testaccio piazza. The few cheap clothing and shoe stalls skirting the outside are unremarkable, but the inside is well worth a visit. Lined with butchers, grocers and fishsellers, the whole central area is given over to fruit and vegetables – a theater-set array of seductive colors and textures. Very popular with local residents, it offers super-fresh, high-quality produce and reasonable prices. Much of this market's charm for visitors lies in its compact size and relaxed, friendly atmosphere.

Porta Portese

Via Portuense & Via Ippolito Nievo.
Map 7 C3. 🚌 *170, 280, 718, 719.*
Open 6:30am–2pm Sun.

The *mercato delle pulci*, or flea market, is relatively new in Roman terms. Established shortly after the end of World War II, it is said to have grown out of the thriving black market that operated at Tor di Nona opposite Castel Sant' Angelo during those lean years. Stall holders from as far away as Naples start setting up shop in the early hours of the morning – if you happen to be strolling in that direction after a late night on the town in Trastevere, it's well worth pausing just to watch.

Anything and everything seems to be for sale, piled high on stalls in carefully arranged disorder – clothes, shoes, bags, luggage, camping equipment, linen, towels, pots, pans, kitchen utensils, plants, pets, spare parts, cassettes and CDs, old LPs and 78s.

Furniture stalls tend to be concentrated around Piazza Ippolito Nievo along with what they call "antiques," though you may have to sort through an awful lot of junk before finding a real one. And then you will have to bargain for it. The technique is to offer them half the asked price and then walk away. Many go just to haggle but usually end up buying something anyway.

There are also secondhand clothes – leather or sheepskin coats and jackets go for L10,000 – with many of the Via Sannio stall holders relocating here for the Sunday trade. The stretch along Via Ippolito Nievo is monopolized by "*i Russi di Porta Portese,*" immigrant Russian stallholders selling caviar, icons (authenticity uncertain), lace, other ethnic handicrafts, old cameras and binoculars. A must if you have a Sunday morning to spare.

Mercato di Via Sannio

Via Sannio. **Map** 9 C2. Ⓜ *San Giovanni.* 🚌 *16, 81, 87.* **Open** 8am–1pm Mon–Fri & 8am–6pm Sat.

In the 1960s and 1970s this used to be Italy's answer to Carnaby Street or Soho. Today, at first glance, it doesn't seem to have anything very special to offer. Random stalls sell inexpensive casual clothes, shoes, bags, belts, jewelry, toys, kitchen utensils and music cassettes. However, toward the end of the street is a large covered section that extends back to the Aurelian Wall *(see p196)*. Here visitors will find many stalls piled high with secondhand clothes at very low prices for those who like to

rummage for bargains. There is also a section that sells military-style goods plus camping and fishing equipment.

Some of these stalls move their wares to Porta Portese on Sunday morning.

Local Markets

Generally open 7am–1pm Mon–Sat.

Piazza delle Coppelle (**map** 4 F3 & 12 D2), near the Pantheon, is probably the most picturesque of all the outdoor food markets around the city. A tiny market devoted to food and fruit and

flowers, it offers a charming splash of color in the heart of the city.

Piazza San Cosimato (**map** 7 C1) in Trastevere hosts another lively local market selling tempting cheeses and salami.

There is a fairly big market on **Via Alessandria** (**map** 6 D1) in Nomentana, and other smaller ones in **Via della Pace** (**map** 4 E4 & 11 C3) near Piazza Navona, and in **Via Balbo** (**map** 5 C4) and **Via Milazzo** (**map** 6 E3) near Termini Station. You can also visit the trade market, the **Mercato Generale** (**map** 8 D5), in Via Ostiense, which is open to the public after 10am.

STREET FAIRS

A special and interesting feature of shopping in Rome is the street fair.

The **Expo Tevere** exhibition starts each year between mid-June and mid-July on both sides of the river bank between the Sant'Angelo and Cavour bridges. Its stalls display Italian regional arts and crafts and also sell pasta, jam, olive oil, wines and liqueurs. Most items are cheaper than in the shops. The exhibition opens in the evening (6pm–1am). The entrance fee is minimal and also includes a ferry trip across the Tiber.

There are two antiques fairs, both known as the **Fiera dell'Antiquariato**, that take place in Via dei Coronari. The first starts in the second half of May, 10am to 1pm and 4pm to 11pm daily. It makes a memorable scene at night, when lighted torches line the carpeted street. The second goes along Via dell'Orso as well and normally occurs in mid-October (or late September), Monday to Thursday from 3 to 11pm and Friday and Saturday from 10am to 11pm. Stalls sell leatherwork, jewelry and gifts.

The **Via Margutta Art Fair** usually takes place around Christmas and in springtime. Set in one of the most charming and exclusive streets of the city, it's an event not to be missed - although it's more

for browsing because prices are very high. The utterly glamorous **Spanish Steps Alta Moda Fashion Show** is a fairly new event and doesn't have a set date. The seating space is filled by invitation only. However, the public can squeeze in the back to enjoy this display of Italian designer fashion. So far it has been held mid- to late July.

Befana, the traditional Epiphany fair in Piazza Navona (mid-December until January 6) is now rather low-key but still fascinating for those who have never seen it. Stalls selling clay statues for nativities and sweets that look like pieces of coal are the main attraction.

Natale Oggi is a well-established event taking place near Christmas in the Fiera di Roma at EUR, and it is worth visiting to have a look at the special Italian Christmas treats.

Via Giulia hosts art fairs now and then, plus open evenings when the antiques and art galleries stay open late offering food and wine to all visitors.

Every year Trastevere hosts its very own carnival, known as the **Noantri** festival, around late July, when Viale Trastevere becomes overrun with the typical *porchetta* stalls *(see p341)*, party lights, gift stalls and people.

The details given here may change, so check the local listings or at the tourist office *(see p359)*.

ENTERTAINMENT IN ROME

THERE'S A PARTICULAR excitement attached to Roman entertainment. Football and opera, for example, are both worth experiencing for sheer atmosphere alone, whether or not you are a fan. The jazz scene is especially good, with international stars appearing alongside local talent. And concerts and films take on an added dimension when performances take place beneath the stars in the many open-air arenas spread

Gregory Peck and Audrey Hepburn in *Roman Holiday*

across the city. Unexpectedly, given the general shutdown among shops, restaurants and museums, the summer remains Rome's liveliest time for live music and other cultural events. Rome's many graceful Renaissance squares, vast parks, villa gardens, Classical ruins and other open spaces host various major arts festivals. If you prefer sports, or want to try out some Roman nightclubs, there's plenty to choose from.

WHAT'S HAPPENING

THE HANDIEST source of information about what's happening is *Trovaroma,* the weekly Thursday supplement to *La Repubblica* newspaper. It has a day-by-day rundown of what's on and where, and covers music, exhibitions,

Lester Bowie at Alpheus *(see p344)*

theater, movies, guided tours, restaurants and children's entertainment. There is also a monthly listings publication, *Info Rome,* which is written in English and Italian. Daily newspapers like *Il Messaggero, Il Manifesto, Paese Sera* and *La Repubblica* usually give the evening's entertainment listings.

Two biweekly magazines, *Wanted in Rome* and *Metropolitan,* provide less detailed listings in English. They can be found in Via Veneto newsstands or at English bookshops. Also worth getting hold of is *Carnet di Roma,* available at the beginning of each month from the EPT *(see p359);* it gives details in English of

classical music, festivals, theater and exhibitions in the city and surroundings.

Punctuality is not what Italians are renowned for, so don't be surprised if some events start slightly later than advertised in listings.

RESERVING TICKETS

RESERVING in advance is not part of Italian lifestyle. Two ticket agencies that will reserve theater tickets for you (for a small fee) are **Gesman** and **Box Office**. As a rule, theaters themselves do not accept telephone reservations – you have to visit the box office in person. They will charge you a *prevendita* supplement (about 10% of the normal price) for any tickets sold in advance. The price of a theater ticket can be anywhere between L10,000 and L70,000.

Tickets for classical concerts are usually sold on the spot, and are sometimes for that night only, an arrangement that favors the last-minute

decision to go. Opera is the exception. Tickets are sold months in advance, with just a few held back until two days before the performance.

One of the many stages at Alpheus

It is usually easier (and also cheaper) to get tickets for the Caracalla Festival, which takes place in the summer.

The **Teatro dell'Opera** box office *(see p343)* handles sales for both summer and winter seasons, and they have a high-tech reservation system, with a computer that color-codes unsold seats.

Tickets for most big rock and jazz events can be bought at **Orbis**; **Prontospettacolo**; and larger record shops, such as **Rinascita**.

Remember that if you're trying to get hold of a ticket for a particular performance that has already sold out, you're extremely unlikely to be able to obtain one from

Member of contemporary dance group Momix *(see p343)*

unofficial sources – there are few ticket scalpers in Rome, except at major football matches, such as important finals.

DISCOUNT TICKETS

THEATERS and concert venues tend not to offer discounts on tickets since performances are so often oversubscribed. Movie theaters, however, offer people over 60 and disabled people a 30% reduction on weekdays. In recent years the Comune di Roma has sponsored reduced-price movie tickets on one day a week (usually Wednesday), but this may be discontinued. Some clubs at the beach resorts, such as Fregene, offer reductions: watch for *due per uno* coupons in local bars; they allow two people entrance for the price of one.

FACILITIES FOR THE DISABLED

FEW ROMAN venues provide easy access for people with restricted mobility, and any disabled visitors and their companions are likely to find the lack of provision for them very frustrating.

The situation does improve a little in summer, however, when a great many performances in the city are held in the open air. The Baths of Caracalla have wheelchair access, as do the classical concerts held in the beautiful gardens of Villa Giulia *(see pp262–3)*. For more general information on provisions for the disabled, see page 359.

The Teatro dell'Opera *(see p342)*

Performance in the Classical setting of the Baths of Caracalla *(see p342)*

OPEN-AIR ENTERTAINMENT

OPEN-AIR OPERA, movies, classical music and jazz concerts fill the calendar from late June until the end of September. These performances outdoors can be wonderful, with spectacular settings and enthusiastic audiences. Some of them are grand affairs, but small events may be just as evocative – a guitar recital in the cloisters of Santa Maria della Pace *(see p342)*, for example, or jazz in the beautiful gardens of Villa Doria Pamphilj *(see p344)*.

Singers performing the *Barber of Seville*

Many movie theaters roll back their ceilings in summer for open-air screenings or else move to outdoor arenas, and there are also annual open-air movie festivals. The Cineporto along the Tiber and the Festival di Massenzio offer films, food and small exhibitions in July and August. Theater, too, moves outside in summer. Greek and Roman plays are staged at Ostia Antica *(see p270)*, and other shows take place at the Anfiteatro del Tasso *(see p347)*.

Rome's most important summer festival is monthlong RomaEuropa, with main performances in the grounds of the Villa Medici. There are other, smaller festivals, too, but times and venues change from year to year, so it's best to watch for posters around the city for the most up-to-date information. More traditional is Trastevere's community festival, Festa de Noantri *(see p59)*, with music, fireworks and processions. This religious festival is on the Saturday after July 16, but celebrations continue well into August, so pace yourself for a long party! The Festa dell'Unità, run by the PDS (the former Communist Party), but not limited to politics, is generally held in September. The celebration includes games, stalls, food and drink.

Finally, if you like your entertainment less structured, and somewhat more leisurely, you can always do as the Romans do and take part in the *passeggiata* (early-evening stroll) – the city's favorite spots are Piazza Navona *(see p120)* and along Via del Corso.

TICKET AGENCIES

Gesman
Via Angelo Emo 65.
Map 3 A2. (39 74 07 89.

Box Office
Viale Giulio Cesare 88. **Map** 3 C1.
Box office tickets for classical music, rock, pop and jazz concerts and some sporting events.
(372 02 16.

Orbis
Piazza dell'Esquilino 37.
Map 6 D4. (47 44 776.

Prontospettacolo
Telephone bookings only.
(39 38 72 97.

Classical Music and Dance

CLASSICAL CONCERTS take place in a surprising number of venues: tickets for opera premieres may be hard to get, but those for soloists, groups or orchestras playing in gardens, churches, villas or ancient ruins are more available. World-renowned soloists and orchestras make appearances throughout the year; past visitors have included Luciano Pavarotti and Placido Domingo, Catherine Malfitano and prima ballerina Sylvie Guillem.

Programs are generally international in scope, but some festivals are dedicated to one of Italy's very own, such as Palestrina, the great 16th-century master of polyphonic church music, or Arcangelo Corelli, inventor of the Baroque *concerto grosso*.

MUSIC IN CHURCHES

ONE OF ROME'S main attractions for classical music lovers is the rich repertoire that can be heard in the city's churches. Always sacred in theme (by decree of Pope John Paul II), music is mainly performed as concerts rather than during services.

Programs are posted around the city and outside the churches. You will often find very good musicians playing in the main churches, while the smaller, out-of-the-way churches frequently play host to young musicians and to amateur choirs as well.

St. Peter's (see p230) hosts one major RAI (national broadcasting company) concert on December 5 attended by the pope and free for the general public. It has two established choirs. The Coro della Cappella Giulia sing at the 10:30am mass and 5pm vespers on Sunday. The Coro della Cappella Sistina sing whenever the pope celebrates mass here, as on June 29 (St. Peter's and St. Paul's day).

Important choral masses also take place on January 25 in **San Paolo fuori le Mura** (see p267), when the Pope attends; on June 24 in **San Giovanni in Laterano** (p182); and on December 31 at the **Gesù** (pp114–5), where the *Te Deum* is sung. The church of **Sant'Ignazio di Loyola** (p106) is another favorite venue for choral concerts.

Gregorian chant can be heard in **Sant'Apollinare** (p127) at 11am on Sundays and during religious festivals.

Easter and Christmas are great times for affordable but chilly concerts: there is usually neither an entrance fee nor heating!

ORCHESTRAL, CHAMBER AND CHORAL MUSIC

THE **Auditorium di Santa Cecilia**, the national broadcasting company's **Foro Italico** and **Teatro dell' Opera** are Rome's three main auditoriums, with their own resident orchestras and choirs. The Orchestra e Coro dell' Accademia di Santa Cecilia is the top orchestra, but the Orchestra e Coro di Roma della RAI is also good. All three offer interestingly varied seasons that include visiting groups and soloists from all over the world.

The season at the **Teatro Olimpico** usually offers very good chamber music, some orchestral concerts and ballet, with at least one concert a week. They are advertised on large yellow posters with red borders, easily identifiable in the streets and a hallmark for high-level performances.

The Concerti del Tempietto concert series Festival Musicale delle Nazioni concentrates on the composers of a different country each month on Saturdays (9pm) and Sundays (5:45pm) between November and June at the **Sala Baldini**.

Ticket prices for classical concerts vary depending on performers and venue. The **Auditorium del Foro Italico** sells tickets for most concerts for under L20,000; a ticket for the **Teatro Olimpico** costs

between L25,000 and L40,000, but seats for an important concert at **Teatro dell'Opera** may cost as much as L150,000.

The Associazione Musicale Romana sponsors three annual festivals in the **Palazzo della Cancelleria** (see p149): the Festival Internazionale di Cembalo (harpsichord festival) in March; Musica al Palazzo in May; and the Festival Internazionale di Organo in September.

It's always worth checking which musicians are playing at the **Teatro Ghione**, the **Oratorio del Gonfalone**, the **Aula La Sapienza**, or the **Sala Accademica di Via dei Greci**.

OPEN-AIR SUMMER CONCERTS

IN THE SUMMER, music lovers can enjoy concerts in cloisters, palazzo courtyards and ancient ruins. Concerts can be one-time events or part of a festival, regular fixtures or impromptu. Do as the Romans do: don't plan until the last moment and keep an eye on the posters and listings pages (see p340) for the latest details.

Open-air opera and dance once had their home in the majestic Baths of Caracalla, but this venue is no longer used. Classical concerts are often part of festivals like RomaEuropa (see p341), but there are also a number of open-air festivals and concert series dedicated specifically to classical music. Among the more interesting of these is the Stagione Estiva dell'Orchestra dell'Accademia di Santa Cecilia held at the Ninfeo (nympheum) on the grounds of **Villa Giulia** (see p263). Also listed as the Concerti a Villa Giulia, the concerts begin in July, with tickets under L20,000.

The Associazione Musicale Romana organizes Serenate in Chiostro – a lively and varied program of concerts held during July in the cloisters of **Santa Maria della Pace** (see p121), with tickets on sale for under L20,000.

Estate al Tempietto (listed also as Concerti del Tempietto) is the Tempietto orchestra's summer treat, with concerts every evening from July to September in the **Area Archeologica del Teatro di Marcello** *(see p151)*. They're held in the adjacent basilica of San Nicola in Carcere if it rains.

Festival Villa Pamphilj in Musica, in July, is a series of concerts in the gardens of **Villa Doria Pamphilj** *(see p267)*. Programs range from comic opera to jazz and 20th-century classical music.

Brass bands can be heard in the **Pincio Gardens** *(see p136)* on Sunday mornings from the end of April until mid-July – they usually strike up at around 10:30am.

CONTEMPORARY MUSIC

THE **Auditorium del Foro Italico**, the **Auditorium di Santa Cecilia** and the Accademia Filarmonica Romana (usually at the **Teatro Olimpico**) sometimes include modern pieces in their programs but these are generally less popular than the classics; there is no set venue with a regular contemporary program.

International names appear on festival programs and at special concerts. The most interesting festivals are Nuovi

Spazi Musicali (now part of RomaEuropa) in the summer, with free concerts transmitted on Italian radio, and the Festival Nuova Consonanza in autumn. Works of modern Italian composers are performed in the Rassegna Nuova Musica Italiana concert series two or three times a year. Also well worth attending are performances by scholars of the French Academy at **Villa Medici** *(see p135)*.

OPERA

ITALY AND OPERA are to many people synonymous. Critics will tell you (justifiably) that Rome's opera is nowhere near the standard of that at Milan's La Scala, or Naples's San Carlo. But that doesn't mean it's not worth visiting – world-class singers do appear here *(see p38)*, mainly in premieres or solo recitals. However you judge the quality of the performances, the surroundings in which they take place are often incomparable. In summer, the visual spectacle of *Aïda*, performed in the open air, is simply magnificent.

The season starts late at **Teatro dell'Opera**, between November and January. In recent years, programs have concentrated on the great popular operas rather than on staging experimental

productions or historical adaptations. Tickets range from L25,000 to L250,000. Until recently the Teatro dell'Opera would move outdoors in July and August, to stage opera and ballet in the ancient baths of Caracalla. This celebrated tradition has now stopped as vibrations caused by the basso profundos and by the nimble corps de ballet were deemed to pose a threat to the Baths' structure.

BALLET AND DANCE

OPPORTUNITIES to watch ballet or contemporary dance are fairly limited in Rome. The opera house's resident company, Corpo di Ballo del Teatro dell'Opera di Roma, performs the great classics as well as Roland Petit–style modern choreographies. Performances are staged at **Teatro dell'Opera**.

Contemporary dance is most likely found during the summer festivals, but foreign companies often perform at **Teatro Olimpico** as well. American modern dance groups of the Moses Pendleton school – Pilobolus, Momix, ISO and Daniel Ezralow – are popular visitors. Traditional folk dancers and acrobats from China and companies such as the Moscow Circus and Moisseiev Dance Company usually perform at the **Teatro Tenda a Strisce**.

Rock, Jazz, Folk and World Music

ROME'S NON-CLASSICAL MUSIC SCENE is unpredictable, but if you have the patience, you'll come across a huge variety of music at the many clubs, as well as open-air events with such foreign stars as Madonna, Michael Jackson and Dire Straits. Publicity is often disorganized, but the "Music Box" section of *Trovaroma (see p340)* gives an idea of what you can choose from.

It's not possible to reserve tickets in advance at the smaller venues – just turn up with everyone else. You will need to buy a *tessera* (membership card) though, costing anything from L1,000 to L20,000. Well-known musicians may mean a further entrance fee, but local groups are generally included in the membership.

ROCK MUSIC

BIG ROCK CONCERTS are held at EUR in the **Palazzo dello Sport**, or in a stadium: the **Stadio Flaminio**, the **Stadio Olimpico**, or out-of-the-way **Ippodromo Capannelle**. Get there at least an hour before the gates open for a good seat. Testaccio's **Villaggio Globale Il Mattatoio** (a converted abattoir) is a large-scale stand-up venue for concerts and other events. The facilities are basic, and again, the large crowds mean you should turn up early.

Rome also has several lively clubs and discos which play rock music. Loyal devotees head for the good clubs in large numbers. Some are unpretentious and friendly and some, which are rather sumptuous and stylish, are frequented by the rich and famous. Entrance for the top spots can cost up to L40,000. A venue to be aware of is **Osiris**, near Campo de' Fiori, which puts on rock, mainstream pop and world music. Check what's on, too, at the **Antica Carboneria**; at **Black Out**, with concerts held on Thursdays; at the **Piper '90**; and, in the Vatican area, at **Il Castello**, a converted movie theater with rock and jazz festivals and a club.

Forte Prenestino is an interesting place – a former prison, it was taken over by squatters a few years ago and turned into a social center housing rock concerts, debates and art exhibitions. Nearer the center are more traditional establishments. **Big Mama**, the trendy **Palladium** and **Caffè Caruso** are well-known, popular venues for a great variety of live bands.

JAZZ

ROME'S TASTE for jazz has developed over the years as a result of visits from American and other foreign musicians. Miles Davis played one of his last concerts at the Roma Jazz Festival, for instance, and guitarist Pat Metheny, Sonny Rollins, Gil Evans' Band, the Lounge Lizards, Spyrogyra, and Joe Zawinul's Syndicate are frequent visitors. Roma Jazz takes place every year, generally in July, with performances at the **Foro Italico** *(see p351)*, sometimes listed as the Stadio del Tennis in *Trovaroma*. Tickets, which cost around L35,000 to 40,000, are obtainable from Orbis *(see p341)* and other agents.

Outside festival times, the best jazz musicians play at **Palladium**, near San Paolo fuori le Mura, or at **Airport Café** and **Alpheus**. **Alpheus** is unique in offering separate concert halls and interesting festivals featuring high-quality jazz ensembles every night. Other, smaller venues, some of which encourage budding talent, include **Vicolo 49** where you are welcome to join in. Some of Rome's music schools also double as showcases for new performers – these include **Mississippi Blues**, **Saint Louis Music City**, **Ciac Musica** and **Alexanderplatz**.

In summer, many of the music festivals take place outdoors at night. Jazz has featured in the Festival Villa Pamphilj in Musica in recent years, held every July and organized by I Concerti nel Parco. Tickets, costing around L15,000, are available from the Villa Pamphilj itself.

In winter, try two pub-style spots open until late: **La Finestra sul Cortile** and **Stardust** – the latter offers jazz on Tuesdays and a pianist on other nights. Or try what's offered at **Caffè Latino**, **Caffè Caruso**, **Fonclea**, **Melvyn's** and **Antica Carboneria**.

There's a wide range of artists to watch for. Pianist Antonello Salis plays a mix of jazz and Caribbean rhythms. Crystal White and the Super-naturals are a resident Roman jazz-funk formation. Guitar lovers may enjoy Eddie Palermo's fusion, and the major names to be aware of in jazz groups are Roberto Gatto, Maurizio Gianmarco, Massimo Moriconi and Massimo Urbani. Rome's other well-known bands include Orizzonte degli Eventi (fusion), Sestetto Swing di Roma (swing) and Area 2 (not strictly Roman), who play jazz rock.

FOLK MUSIC

AT THE FOREFRONT of folk music in Rome for 30 years, **Folkstudio** in Trastevere is well worth a visit. Founded back in the 1960s, its cramped rooms have an informal, friendly, participatory atmosphere that welcomed up-and-coming stars such as Bob Dylan – a fact that is fondly remembered here. Irish folk music and American country and western are much in demand, as well as the regional strains of Italian folk music. No drinks are sold, so bring your own. You'll need to buy a membership card to enter, costing around L10,000.

A recent arrival on Rome's folk music scene is the **Shamrock** in the Colosseum area, offering country and bluegrass music. If you want to eat, too, head for **Fonclea** near St. Peter's, but check out *Trovaroma* to see who's playing – country music is played only on some nights.

In some of Rome's Irish pubs, you may be lucky and find some spontaneous music-making going on. Places to try are the **Fiddler's Elbow** and **Druid's Den**, both in the Santa Maria Maggiore area. Also find out where the Kay McCarthy Ensemble or Square Dance is performing.

WORLD MUSIC

A STRONG Latin American colony has made its home in Rome since the 1970s. Latin American music is no passing fad here; Romans dance the night away together with the many Brazilian, Argentinian and Peruvian residents and merengue, salsa and soca are all very popular. For the last few years, an open-air summer Caribe festival has taken place in Villa Borghese with live music and other attractions. It's by no means a certain annual event, but its worth keeping an eye out for.

Many venues offer similar opportunities to enjoy Latin American music throughout the year: **El Charango** has South American food as well as music and a small dance area. At **Yes Brazil** the owner and beautiful long-legged waitresses sway with the clientele to the bossa nova, offering a double delight of music and movement. Various musicians alternate way into the night: try to see the guitarist Giovanna Marinuzzi, who plays lively Brazilian music, and be sure to reserve front tables ahead of time. Also watch for resident Brazilian musicians Brenazil, Carlos de Lima and Alvinho, and local salsa band Xenaya, or check what's on at the **Caffè Latino** and **La Cabaña** in the Ghetto, at **Caffè Caruso** in Testaccio and the **Bossa Nova** or **Melvyn's** in Trastevere.

Other regional musical styles have less of a presence, but are nevertheless available for the aficionado. Lovers of African music should seek out performances by Sanganà or Akwaba. African and Italian musicians play together with Pietro dall'Oglio's group at various places in the city.

Movies and Theater

MOVIEGOING IS A POPULAR pastime in Rome, with around 40 films playing on an average weekday; theater-goers, however, have far less choice.

The great majority of Roman movie theaters are *prima visione* (first run) and show the latest international films in dubbed versions. The smaller art theaters are more likely to show subtitled versions of foreign films.

Theater productions are performed in Italian whether the plays are national classics or by foreign playwrights. The main theaters offer a selection by great Italian playwrights. There are also performances of traditional cabaret, avant-garde theater and dance theater. Theater tickets cost between L10,000 and L70,000 and can generally be bought in advance only by visiting the theater box office in person, or through agencies such as **Gesman** and **Box Office** *(see p341)*.

MOVIES (*PRIMA VISIONE*)

THERE ARE OVER 80 *prima visione* movie theaters in the city. The best in Rome in terms of both decor and comfort are the **Fiamma** (two screens), **Barberini** (three screens) and **Rivoli**.

As a rule, foreign films are dubbed into Italian rather than subtitled (Italian dubbers are considered among the best in the world), but the **Alcazar** has showings in the original language – mainly English – on Mondays.

Tickets for new films generally cost around L10,000, but a few theaters listed as *prima visione* charge less, namely **Capranichetta**, **Diamante** and **Cinema Roma**. Senior citizens and disabled people are normally entitled to a 30% reduction on weekdays. The Comune di Roma sponsors a reduced-ticket day (normally it's Wednesday). Check the newspaper or *Trovaroma* for accurate details *(see p340)*.

ART MOVIE THEATERS

THERE ARE TWO main types of art movie theaters in Rome: the *cine-clubs* and the *cinema d'essai*. Both are good if you're interested in catching older classics and new foreign films as well as films by some of the contemporary Italian directors. The *d'essai* theaters now and then show films in the original language (indicated by *v.o.* for *versione originale* in the listings). Try the **Azzurro Scipioni** (one of the few to remain open throughout summer) or the **Nuovo Sacher**. Some of the smaller theaters like the **Labirinto**, are called *cine-clubs* and require membership.

The multimedia arts center **Palazzo delle Esposizioni** usually shows interesting series of international films in the Sala Rossellini (prior reservations are advised).

Cartoons and children's favorites are shown at **Dei Piccoli**. The evening showings for adults, often in the original language, are listed as Dei Piccoli Sera.

The **Tibur**, a small theater with a varied program, is one of the few places where students get a reduction.

ENGLISH-LANGUAGE FILMS

IN ADDITION TO occasional undubbed showings of British, American and Australasian films in art theaters and the **Alcazar**, Rome has its own English-language movie theater, the **Pasquino**, in Trastevere. Titles change every few days (tickets cost around L7,000).

SUMMER MOVIES

MANY ROMAN movie theaters have retractable ceilings used in summer, while other theaters close for the summer. The **Nuovo Sacher** has an outdoor arena that is used for summer screenings.

Rome also has two summer movie festivals: Cineporto and Massenzio. These show several films each night from 9pm until the small hours, with food and drinks on sale and often live music during the intervals. Cineporto (every night, July–September) has a fixed venue in the Parco della Farnesina, but Massenzio moves around (see listings).

It's also worth checking the listings pages *(see p340)* for retrospectives or avant-garde film programs at the **Azzurro Scipioni** and the open-air arts festivals, like Roma-Europa *(see p341)* and Festa dell'Unità *(see p341)*. Sci-fi enthusiasts will surely enjoy the Fantafestival (early June), a science-fiction, fantasy and horror film festival.

MAINSTREAM THEATER

THE BACKBONE of Rome's theatrical repertoire is Luigi Pirandello's dramas and comedies by 18th-century Venetian Carlo Goldoni and 20th-century Neapolitan Eduardo de Filippo. Major foreign playwrights are also performed from time to time.

The best classic productions are staged at the **Teatro Argentina**, **Teatro Quirino**, **Teatro Valle**, **Teatro Eliseo** and **Teatro Piccolo Eliseo**. **Teatro Argentina**, originally an opera house, is state-owned and home of Rome's permanent theater company. The **Quirino** and **Valle** host productions from other Italian cities. The **Valle** alternates between productions of great Italian classics by famous companies and lesser-known modernist works. Plays at the **Quirino** often feature famous Italian actors. The **Eliseo** and **Piccolo Eliseo** are among the best of the private theaters. Agatha Christie and Alfred Hitchcock are often on at the **Teatro Stabile del Giallo**, which runs crime and detective thrillers, while **Teatro Vittoria** goes in for Noël Coward or Raymond Queneau. The program at

Teatro Sistina usually includes musicals by visiting foreign companies and shows by popular Italian actors.

CONTEMPORARY THEATER

THE HOMES OF contemporary theater are the **Tordinona**, **Politecnico**, **Ateneo** (inside the university), plus a host of small theaters, ingeniously rigged up in cellars, garages, small apartments or tents. The **Colosseo** and **La Scaletta** host some alternative fringe-type productions (known here as *teatro off*), while the **Tordinona**, the **Politecnico** and the **Ateneo** tend to stage works by contemporary authors and occasional avant-garde productions. Some, like the **Teatro dei Cocci**, put on drama school productions.

FOLK, CABARET AND PUPPET THEATER

ROMAN AND Neapolitan folk songs and cabaret can be enjoyed in one of Trastevere's traditional lively cabaret restaurants like **Ciceruacchio**, **Fantasie di Trastevere**, or **Meo Patacca**.

Puppet theater is another tradition. Shows generally take place early in the evening on weekends and sometimes during the week at **Teatro Verde**; **Teatro Villa Lazzaroni**; **Teatro Mongiovino**; and the **English Puppet Theater**, where puppeteers will recite in English if there is enough demand. In the summer, traveling Neapolitan and Sicilian marionette companies give special performances.

OPEN-AIR THEATER

THE OPEN-AIR summer theater season usually features Greek and Roman plays at **Ostia Antica** *(see pp270–71)*.

The **Anfiteatro Quercia del Tasso** in the Janiculum park takes its name from the oak tree under which 16th century poet Tasso used to sit. The theater has no fixed genre (both Plato and Noël Coward were offered recently, for instance), and tickets cost around L20,000.

Nearby is a permanent Neapolitan street puppet theater booth featuring *Pulcinella* (the Italian original of Punch). Shows are usually in the afternoons, with morning shows on Sundays; children love them.

Nightclubs

THE CENTER OF ROMAN NIGHTLIFE used to be the Via Veneto area so effectively portrayed by Fellini in his film *La Dolce Vita*. The place still offers plenty of action, but new, less formal and more affordable clubs have emerged, with a more vibrant atmosphere and appealing to a younger and more diverse crowd.

With the new clubs come new areas. The picturesque narrow streets in Trastevere, the Piazza Navona and the Pantheon areas are becoming more popular. Testaccio, too, has become a new mecca for Roman clubbers.

WHAT'S OFFERED

AS IN ANY OTHER major city, Rome's nightlife is constantly changing. Roman club-goers are an extremely varied group, and most clubs arrange different nights to appeal to different tastes – so it's essential to keep up-to-date on what's happening by checking in a magazine like *Trovaroma (see p340)*.

For a more direct source of information, head for the bars around the Piazza Navona and Campo de' Fiori areas. At about 10:30pm the narrow streets and piazzas swarm with people, and any interesting event will soon become common knowledge. *Buoni* (free or reduced-price tickets) may be handed out.

ADMISSION

PREFERRED CLUBBING nights for Romans are Thursday, Friday and, of course, Saturday, when you should expect to pay around L35,000 for entrance. Lines for the most popular places can be long, but provided you arrive before midnight you'll avoid the crush.

Some clubs require a *tessera* (membership card) that you can buy on the spot and that usually replaces the entrance fee. Your ticket, or *tessera*, usually includes a free first drink; your second could well be expensive – as much as L20,000 in some of the plusher clubs.

In these smarter places, how you look is all-important: a jacket and tie are a must, and usually you need an invitation or a personal introduction to get in. It should not be difficult to gain entrance to the traditional discos as long as you dress in designer casual wear, but watch out! A black T-shirt could make you too *alternativo*. All-male groups are never welcome, and in more exclusive clubs neither are unaccompanied men.

CLUBS AND BARS

AN ELEGANT NIGHT out could start in one of the refined piano bars, such as the **Blue Bar**; the **Little Bar** frequented by the English-speaking community; or the intimate **Tartarughino**, popular with politicians and financiers. Livelier places are the American-style bars, such as **Hemingway**. If you prefer the arts world, head for **Zelig**, **Bar della Pace**, **Le Cornacchie**, and **La Vetrina**.

To continue, head for **Gilda**, a favorite with the Roman jet set, featuring two elegant restaurants, a large glitzy dance floor and many VIPs. The famous nightclub of the 1960s, **Jackie O**, has been revamped in lavish style, with a lush interior and an expensive restaurant. In a similar vein and not to be missed are **Open Gate**, **Gossip Café**, and **Notorious**.

The hottest club among the younger and trendier is **Alien**. This club offers house, techno and hip-hop, along with stages, wild lighting effects and "happenings." A smaller dance floor offers a more mellow music selection. Equally funky is the relatively new **Tatum**, which also offers soul and dance music.

An unforgettable place for dancing in a blitzkrieg of beat is **Radio Londra**, designed to look like a World War II bunker, where hard dance music and free entrance attract huge crowds of jive bombers. On **Argonauta**, a moored paddle steamer on the Tiber, you can dance, strut or grove to anything from techno to reggae on Fridays and Saturdays.

The more traditional disco is at its best at **Piper '90**, the oldest and biggest Roman disco, which totally revamps its interior every season. It's especially popular with the younger crowd, as is **Veleno. New York, New York** offers music from the 1940s and 1950s on some nights, jazz funk on others. There are some disco bars worth noting, too, like **Drunken Ship** and **Fandango**.

To find out about events in the more unusual Roman clubs, start the evening at the **Vineria**. The old abattoir *(il Mattatoio)* at Testaccio is the setting for **Villaggio Globale**, a social center hosting concerts, shows, discos and parties. **Circolo degli Artisti** is another social center with a large dance floor, bar, theater and video room, situated in the old milk center. Two converted movie theaters, **Castello** in the Vatican area and **Palladium** in the southern suburbs, provide many concerts and events.

GAY AND LESBIAN

THE GAY AND LESBIAN SCENE is quite active. Many clubs have fixed gay nights as well as special events, especially during the Maratona Gay Festival in May. The most famous gay club is **Alibi**, where music is a mixture of underground and 1970s hits. **Angelo Azzurro** offers hi-energy and house in Post-Modern surroundings. Watch for events organized by **Circolo Mario Mieli di Cultura Omosessuale** or go to bars such as **Hangar** to find out what's on. For lesbians there is less choice; try **Panico** on a Sunday evening. Women- only nights take place at **Galaxia** on Friday and Sunday.

JAZZ, SALSA AND AFRICAN

THERE ARE many jazz clubs *(see p344)*. The following mix live music with dancing and drinking. **Caffè Latino** (membership club) is best at the weekend. For South American music, try **Yes Brazil** and **Drink Music**, with live bands and lots of people, or **Caffè Caruso** (membership club) for salsa. **Alpheus** is a four-roomed venue where different kinds of music events take place simultaneously.

African clubs like **Fantasy** (free on Fridays) are lively, friendly and cheap.

CLUBBING IN SUMMER

IN SUMMER, when everything closes down in the city, head for the Roman seaside resorts. At Fregene, for instance, there are 13 clubs; all pretty much the same, where the dress is designer-label casuals. Take along your swimsuit since much of the fun takes place in and around the pools. Names include **Gilda on the Beach**, **Tattou** and **Miraggio** – the latter two popular with a younger crowd. **Sogno del Mare** features live concerts by well-known bands, a swimming pool and a spacious, pleasant environment. Most of these seaside clubs have restaurants attached to them as well.

LATE CLUBS

MOST ROMAN clubs stay open until 3 or 4am, but the informal and lively **Blue Zone** (a club that, unlike most, is opcn on Mondays) and the smarter **Decó** both stay open until dawn.

Before heading off to bed, join other diehard clubbers at any of the city's 24-hour bars for a final drink and head for one of the early-morning bakers to buy sweet *cornetti* hot from the oven.

DIRECTORY

Alibi
Via di Monte Testaccio 44.
Map 8 D4. 574 34 48.

Alien
Via Velletri 13. **Map** 6 D1.
841 22 12.

Alpheus
Via del Commercio 36/8.
Map 8 D5. 574 98 26.

Angelo Azzurro
Via Card. Merry del Val 13.
Map 7 C1. 580 04 72.

Antico Caffè della Pace
Via della Pace 2/5.
Map 4 E4 & 11 C2.
686 12 16.

Argonauta
Lungotevere degli Artigiani.
Map 7 C4. 556 54 40.

Blue Bar
Via dei Soldati 25.
Map 4 E3 & 11 C2.

Blue Zone
Via Campania 37 A.
Map 5 B1. 482 18 90.

Caffè Caruso
Via di Monte Testaccio 36.
Map 8 D4. 574 50 19.

Caffè Latino
Via di Monte Testaccio 96.
Map 8 D4. 574 40 20.

Il Castello
Via di Porta Castello 44.
Map 4 D3. 686 83 28.

Circolo degli Artisti
Via Lamarmora 28.
Map 6 E5. 446 49 68.

Le Cornacchie
Piazza Rondanini 53.
Map 4 F4 & 12 D2.

Decó
Via C. Beccaria 22.
Map 4 E1. 361 12 40.

Drink Music
Via Natale del Grande 4.
Map 7 C1. 580 02 86.

Drunken Ship
Campo de' Fiori 20/21.
68 30 05 35.

Fandango
Corso Vittorio Emanuele
286. **Map** 4 D3 & 11 B3.

Fantasy
Via Alba 42. **Map** 10 F3.
701 67 41.

Galaxia
Piazza Bulgarelli 41.
881 10 43.

Gilda
Via Mario de' Fiori 97.
Map 5 A2 & 12 F1.
678 48 38.

Gossip Café
Via Romagnosi 11 A.
Map 4 E1. 361 13 48.

Hangar
Via in Selci 69. **Map** 5 C5.

Hemingway
Piazza delle Coppelle 10.
Map 4 F3 & 12 D2.
686 44 90.

Jackie O
Via Boncompagni 11.
Map 5 B2. 488 54 57.

Little Bar
Via Gregoriana 54 A.
Map 5 A2.

Circolo Mario Mieli di Cultura Omosessuale
Via Ostiense 202.
541 39 85.

New York, New York
Via Ostia 29. **Map** 3 B1.
372 40 61.

Notorious
Via San Nicola da
Tolentino 22. **Map** 5 B2.
474 68 88.

Open Gate
Via San Nicola da
Tolentino 4. **Map** 5 C2.
482 44 64.

Palladium
Piazza B. Romano 8.
511 02 03.

Panico
Via di Panico 13. **Map** 4 D3
& 11 B2. 68 30 07 49.

Piper '90
Via Tagliamento 9.
855 53 98.

Radio Londra
Via Monte Testaccio 67.
Map 8 D4.

Tartarughino
Via della Scrofa 1.
Map 4 F3 & 12 D2.

Tatum
Via Luciani 52. **Map** 2 D3.
322 12 51.

Veleno
Via Sardegna 27.
Map 5 B1. 482 18 38.

La Vetrina
Via della Vetrina 20.
Map 4 E3 & 11 B2.

Villaggio Globale
Lungotevere Testaccio. **Map** 8 D4. 57 30 03 29.

Vineria
Campo de' Fiori 5.
Map 4 E4 & 11 C4.

Yes Brazil
Via S. Francesco a Ripa 103.
Map 7 C2. 581 62 67.

Zelig
Via Monterone 74.
Map 4 F4 & 12 D3.
687 92 09.

SUMMER CLUBS

Gilda on the Beach
Lungomare di Ponente 11.
665 06 49.

Miraggio
Lungomare di Ponente 95.
646 39 50.

Sogno del Mare
Lungomare di Ponente 25.
66 56 05 40.

Tattou
Via Francavilla a Mare.
646 38 38.

Sports

DON'T BE SURPRISED if the peace of a Sunday afternoon in Rome is interrupted by people shouting and honking car horns. It simply means that one of the home soccer teams has won at the stadium, and the whole town will vibrate with the excitement.

Soccer is the national sport (some would say obsession), but other sports also manage to attract a large following. Roman sports fans are never at a loss for varied and well-organized events and activities.

Times and venues for most spectator sports are listed in *Trovaroma (see p340)*, as well as the local sections of *La Gazzetta dello Sport* or *Corriere dello Sport*.

SOCCER

AN ITALIAN SOCCER MATCH is an experience not to miss for the quality of the play, the excitable crowds and the fun atmosphere. Soccer fan troublemakers are rare.

Rome has two teams, Roma and Lazio, and they take turns playing at the **Stadio Olimpico** on Sunday afternoons at 3pm, in the Campionato Italiano (Italian championship league). Seats can be scarce, so get tickets in advance from the stadium (L15,000 to L150,000). The cheapest tickets are in the La Tribuna stand; middle-range and most expensive, are in Le Catinate and Le Curve, respectively.

On Wednesday evenings, there are international competitions – the Coppa delle Coppe (European Cup Winners Cup), the UEFA cup and the Coppa dei Campioni (European Championship Cup). In between these, teams battle it out for the national Coppa Italia.

TENNIS

A MAJOR EVENT, the International Championships go on at **Foro Italico** for two weeks in May. The world's top tennis stars thrash it out on clay courts at 1 and 8:30pm from Tuesday to Friday, and at 1pm only on weekends. Buy tickets in advance either directly from the Foro Italico or from a ticket agency.

If you wish to play yourself, there are now over 350 tennis clubs in Rome. It is often essential to reserve at least a week in advance, and there's usually a moderate court fee.

Clubs where membership is not required are the **Centro Sportivo Italiano** and the **Circolo Stampa** in northern Rome and the **Oasis di Pace**, just off the Via Appia Antica. The big hotels offer tennis for a reasonable price. **St. Peter's Holiday Inn** requires a small annual membership fee on top of the court price, which includes the gym and the pool (in the summer).

HORSE RACING, TROTTING, AND LEISURE RIDING

IMPORTANT RACES include the Derby in June and the Premio Roma in November. There are trotting races at the **Ippodromo di Tor di Valle** and flat races and steeple chases at **Ippodromo delle Capannelle**.

The International Horse Show is held at the end of April and the beginning of May in Piazza di Siena, Villa Borghese *(see p258)*. It is one of the most important social and sporting events in the calendar, and the setting makes it a great attraction.

For a ride in the countryside around Rome, try the **Centro Ippico Fiano Romano**. Most riding clubs in the city do not accept short-term members.

GOLF

EVEN THE MOST ELITE golf clubs will accept a touring golfer with a home membership and handicap. Most clubs are closed on Mondays and on weekends, when they host competitions, and guests cannot play. Prices range from L50,000 to L80,000.

The **Olgiata Golf Club** is open to everybody from Tuesday to Thursday and to guests accompanied by a member on Friday to Sunday. **Country Club Castel Gandolfo** is the newest club, and **Circolo Golf Roma** the oldest and most prestigious. Within the city ring road is the course at the **Sheraton Hotel** (closed Tuesday).

Two of the many important competitions taking place on the various golf courses in and around Rome are the National Championships in October and the Rome Masters in April.

CAR AND MOTORCYCLE RACING

FORMULA 1 and Formula 3 races take place on Sundays at **Valle Lunga**; be prepared for some relatively expensive entrance fees. Frequently on Saturdays official trials are open to spectators, and on some nonracing Sundays Italy's car designers show new models.

GREYHOUND RACING

THE **Cinodromo** track has shed its sleazy image, and the entrance fee and bets are inexpensive. There is usually a lively, animated crowd of all ages in attendance. Races are run every Wednesday and Thursday at 6:30pm and on Sundays at 10:15am.

ROWING

IN MID-JUNE, a British Oxbridge crew challenges the historic Aniene crew to a race taking place alternately on the Thames and the Tiber. The best place to view this from is between the Margherita and the Sant' Angelo bridges. The race usually starts at around 6pm. Another event is the battle between the Roma and Lazio crews, from Ponte Milvio to Ponte Flaminio, on the same variable date as the Roma-Lazio soccer Derby.

SWIMMING

SWIMMING POOLS are few and definitely not geared to the short-term visitor. You often have to pay an expensive membership and on top of that a monthly fee. It's also essential, in most pools, to produce a medical certificate assuring your good health.

The state-owned pools can be slightly cheaper, but you still have to pay an initial membership fee.

It's better to try the outdoor pools, often part of the big hotels. The **Shangri-La Hotel** opens its pool to non-residents from July to September. For a higher entrance fee, swim at the **Hilton**, which also opens its pool in summer. The best deal is on Sunday when the sports club and swimming pool **La Margherita** opens to non-members from 10am to 1pm for a reasonable charge. **Piscina delle Rose** in EUR is an Olympic-sized pool (often deserted in the morning) open from June to September 9am to 5:30pm during the week, 9am to 7pm at weekends.

HEALTH CLUBS

JUST AS THE swimming pools, Roman health clubs usually require both a membership and monthly payments. For just a short stay in Rome, try the hotel facilities, or, if you are willing to pay, head for one of the private clubs. Use of club facilities may be negotiable – you could be lucky and find that you are waved through for the price of a guest pass.

The **Roman Sports Center** welcomes day members for a reasonable price, and you can use the swimming pools, gym and sauna. The facilities are open from 9am to 10pm. Wear Lycra since normal shorts are not allowed. The **Centro Internazionale di Danza** (Sep–Jul) offers cheap aerobic and dance classes for non-members on Mondays, Wednesdays and Fridays at 6:30pm; you don't need to reserve.

JOGGING AND CYCLING

ROME'S PERFECT climate and stunning scenery attract thousands of well-dressed joggers and cyclists into the city's many parks. Early in the morning or on a Sunday, you'll find the more popular locations looking more like a high-speed fashion show than a track to work up a sweat.

At **Villa Doria Pamphilj** *(see p267)*, is an extensive park situated above the Janiculum, where you can choose among three tracks, plenty of open spaces and a network of paths. **Villa Borghese** *(see p258)* is another vast popular place with a running track.

Alternatively, jog under the acacia trees and palms at Villa Torlonia; on the spotlit track at Villa Glori; or combine sport with culture by running the **Via Appia Antica** *(see p265)* branching off into Parco Caffarella. Other favorites are Viale delle Terme di Caracalla, Circo Massimo, Parco degli Aquedotti and Parco di Colle Oppio.

All of the above are also ideal for cyclists, and you can rent bikes from many places, including **Collalti**, **Via del Corso** and **I Bike Roma**.

Organized bike trips are advertised in *Trovaroma*.

DIRECTORY

FOOTBALL

Stadio Olimpico
Viale dei Gladiatori.
[323 24 52.

TENNIS

Circolo Stampa
Piazza Mancini 19.
Map 1 A2.
[323 24 52.

Centro Sportivo Italiano
Lungotevere Flaminio 55.
Map 1 A3. **[** 361 00 36.

Foro Italico
Viale dei Gladiatori 31.
[321 90 64.

Oasis di Pace
Via degli Eugenii 2.
[718 45 50.

St. Peter's Holiday Inn
Via Aurelia Antica 415.
[66 42.

HORSE RACING AND RIDING

Centro Ippico Fiano Romano
Between Via Tiberina and Capena.
[0765 45 50 19.

Ippodromo delle Capannelle
Via Appia Nuova 1255.
[718 31 43, 34 56.

Ippodromo di Tor di Valle
Via del Mare km.9.
[592 02 69.

GOLF

Circolo Golf Roma
Via Acqua Santa 3.
[780 34 07.

Country Club Castel Gandolfo
Via di Santo Spirito 13.
[931 23 01, 30 84.

Olgiata Golf Club
Largo dell'Olgiata 15.
[30 88 91 41.

Sheraton Golf Hotel
Viale Parco dei Medici 22.
[655 34 77.

CAR RACING

Valle Lunga
Autodromo di Roma,
Via Cassia km.32.
[904 10 27.

GREYHOUND RACING

Cinodromo
Via della Vasca Navale 6.
[556 62 58.

SWIMMING

Hilton Hotel
Via Cadlolo 101.
[350 91.

La Margherita
Via Monti Tiburtini 511.
[451 05 52.

Piscina delle Rose
Viale America 20.
[592 67 17.

Shangri-La Hotel
Viale Algeria 141.
[591 64 41.

HEALTH CLUBS

Centro Internazionale di Danza
Via San Francesco di Sales 14. **Map** 4 D5 & 11 A4.
[588 55 28.

Roman Sports Center
Viale del Galoppatoio 33.
Map 5 A1. **[** 320 16 67.

BICYCLING

I Bike Roma
Villa Borghese car park.
Map 5 A1. **[** 322 52 40.

Collalti
Via del Pellegrino 82.
Map 4 E4 & 11 B3.
[68 80 10 84.

Via del Corso
Piazza S. Lorenzo in Lucina. **Map** 4 F3 & 12 E1.
[68 75 14.

CHILDREN'S ROME

ITALIANS LOVE HAVING children around, and you can be sure yours will be made welcome wherever they go. But there are few special facilities for children, and the heat, crowds and lack of clean public bathrooms mean that Rome is not an ideal city for a vacation with those under seven. It does, however, have plenty to offer slightly older children, especially those who may have an inter-

Renaissance cherub from the Villa Farnesina

est in history or art. The temptation may be to wear yourself and your children out by packing too many sights into one day. Plan in advance and leave plenty of time to wander around the city, looking at the unusual fountains and monuments, watching knife grinders at work in the markets and spending hours agonizing over the choice of ice cream flavors and special pizza toppings.

PRACTICAL ADVICE

IF YOU ARE bringing your children to Rome, try to come in early spring or late autumn, when the weather is good, but not too hot. Easter is best avoided, since the city is more crowded than usual, and you're constantly jostled on packed buses and streets. Where you stay is crucial. A hotel near the Villa Borghese park will give your children plenty of chance to relax and let off steam, though you may end up spending a lot of time and money to get to and from the town center. A hotel in the old center is ideal, so you can easily go back during the day for a rest and a clean bathroom. Since hygienic toilets and changing facilities are rare within the city, it is really not advisable to bring a baby to Rome unless you are visiting friends or family. As with many historic cities, Rome may not instantly appeal to all children, but there is plenty to inspire their imaginations. Use this book to make the buildings and history come alive. Children might also enjoy learning a few Italian words and phrases so they can order food and buy things by themselves.

Jogging in Villa Borghese

If lingering over drinks on the café terraces is what you enjoy best, bring your off-spring something to keep them busy once they have finished with their treat: crayons and paper, a computer game or a Walk-man. Alternatively, most other adults are very tolerant of children running around and making a noise while they relax and, if yours are reasonably outgoing, they could join in with the local children playing ball games in early evenings on piazzas like Campo de' Fiori.

If you feel the need for a total break, most hotels will be able to provide a baby-sitter or help you to contact a qualified baby-sitting agency.

In the event of sickness or an accident, see pages 360–61 for information and a list of emergency numbers.

Fairground in the Villa Borghese park

GETTING AROUND

BUMPY COBBLES, narrow streets without sidewalks and overcrowded buses make pushing strollers around tiring work. You will, however, inevitably find some people willing to help you haul a carriage up steps in a Metro station or onto a bus. Mothers with young children are usually allowed ahead in lines and may be offered seats on buses. The Metro is often less crowded. Kids under 3 ft 3 in (1 m) tall travel free on public transportation.

Although the city is not good for cyclists, families with older children could rent bikes to ride along the Via Appia Antica or to take on a regional train into the country. The bike rental hut in the Pincio gardens has free baby seats.

Anyone over the age of 14 can ride a scooter under 50 cc, although Rome is not the best place for novices (*see p378*).

A rental bike with free baby seat

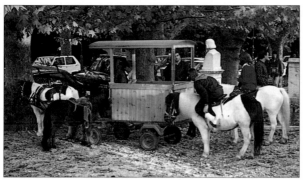
Pony-pulled trains in the Villa Borghese park

EATING OUT

CHILDREN ARE normally warmly welcomed in neighborhood pizzerias and trattorias, and highchairs are often available for toddlers and babies. If there's no highchair, you can expect the waiters to improvise for you with armloads of cushions or telephone directories. Most places are perfectly happy to serve half portions or to let children share meals.

In trattorias it can sometimes be difficult to be exactly sure what a certain dish contains (especially when there is no menu, and the dishes of the day are reeled off, usually at top speed, by the waiter), so picky eaters are likely to be happier in pizzerias *(see pp318–21)*. Here they can choose their own topping (remember

that *prosciutto,* which is usually translated in menus as ham, is cured). The most entertaining pizzerias for kids are the old-fashioned ones where they can watch the chefs pound, stretch and flip the pizza dough. The best places get busy from around 7:30pm, so it is wise to go early to avoid having to get in line. If all else fails, there are three branches of McDonald's.

PICNICS

PICNICS IN THE parks are ideal, and shopping for the food is often half the fun. There's no problem finding small cartons of fruit juice and branded canned drinks, but except in supermarkets (the branch of Standa on Viale Trastevere is the most convenient) they are

extremely expensive. The water from drinking fountains is safe, so it's worth carrying plastic cups around.

In addition to picnic food from bakeries and markets, there are lots of scrumptious takeout foods. Many of them are appealing but messy, so it's wise to bring paper napkins. Try deep-fried fruit and vegetables from Cose Fritte on Via di Ripetta and *supplì al telefono,* rice croquettes with a gooey string of mozzarella inside, from *pizza al taglio* outlets. A *tramezzino* comes quite close to an American sandwich, but if your kids are miserable without peanut butter, you can find it (and other foreign foods) at Ruggieri on Campo de' Fiori.

Feeding pigeons on Piazza Navona

ICE CREAM

ROME, OF COURSE, is famous for ice cream; you and your children are likely to be tempted at every turn. Real ice cream fans may even want to plan their day's sightseeing around one of the best *gelaterie (see pp319–21).* It's far cheaper to buy either a cone or tub of ice cream to eat in the street, but in some of the more traditional places it's worth paying to sit down. At Fassi, they have an old-fashioned ice cream-making machine on display, and at Giolitti, you can enjoy gargantuan sundaes in the elegant parlor *(see p109).*

Investigating some of the hundreds of Italian ice cream flavors

Sightseeing with Children

Entrance to the Villa Borghese Zoo

GENERAL TIPS

ROME DOES NOT have many museums with the sort of hands-on exhibits and activities that many other cities provide for children. Instead, it has other things to entertain visitors. Bernini's marble elephant *(see p108)* and the fat *facchino*, or porter, *(p107)* delight most children. The Capuchin cemetery at Santa Maria della Concezione *(p254)*, the catacombs *(pp264–7)* and the Mamertine Prison *(p91)* are for the young with more ghoulish imaginations.

Look for details like the dirty toenails on figures in Caravaggio's paintings; the Etruscan votives, which were offered to the gods, at the Villa Giulia *(pp262–3)*; and the illusory collapsing ceiling in the Chiesa Nuova, as well as the fake dome of Sant' Ignazio di Loyola *(see p106)*.

Museums your children will enjoy include the Museo delle Arti e Tradizioni Popolari at EUR, with its antique toys and nativity scene *(p267)*, and the Museo delle Mura, which explores the length of the Aurelian Wall *(p196)*.

Among the churches, St. Peter's, where they can climb to the top of the dome *(see p230)*, and San Clemente, where they can descend to the underground mithreum *(see pp186–7)*, are most fun.

At the Vatican children will like the statues and mosaics in the Animal Gallery and the Sistine Ceiling *(p246)*, especially when they find out that Michelangelo had to paint it hunched up on a scaffolding platform.

ANCIENT RUINS

THE ANCIENT RUINS best appreciated by children are the Colosseum *(see pp92–5)*, and Trajan's Markets *(see pp 88–9)*. You can still make out what both these buildings looked like from their remains. The scant ruins of the Forum and Palatine, on the other hand, may not appeal so strongly. Ostia Antica, where the remains include a theater, shop and 20-seater public toilet, is much more likely to interest them *(see pp270–71)*.

Mosaic from the Vatican

MOSAICS

THERE ARE SCORES of vivid, sometimes quirky, mosaics in buildings all over Rome. Many of these are particularly appealing to children. Details in the mosaics range from brilliantly colored flowers, leaves, animals and buildings (in the churches of San Clemente, Santa Prassede and Santa Maria in Trastevere, *see p186, p171 and pp212–13*) to the debris of a banquet (in the Vatican's Museo Gregorio Profano, *see pp234–5*).

Model trains in Villa Borghese

ENTERTAINMENT

ROME'S CULTURAL offerings for children are a bit sparse. To find out what's on, check the movie pages of the newspapers and the listings in *Trovaroma (see p340)*. Most theaters and cinemas have reduced entrance tickets for children, although these are only useful if your children are able to speak Italian.

Language is not a barrier in cartoons and puppet shows. There are cartoons at Villa Borghese's Cinema dei Piccoli and traditional puppet shows every afternoon except Wednesday up on the Janiculum hill. If your hotel has a TV, you'll find plenty of cartoons there to keep your kids entertained.

Stall at the Befana Christmas toy fair on Piazza Navona

Resting on the curb side

One of the most appealing times for children to be in Rome is over Christmas, when Piazza Navona hosts the Befana toy fair, where stalls sell toys and sweets.

PARKS

VILLA BORGHESE *(see p258)* has rowboats to rent and ducks to feed; pony and pony-cart rides; bikes to rent; a mini-cinema; a small fun fair; and a zoo. Villa Celimontana *(see p193)* has bike trails, and open-air theater performances in the summer. The amusement park LUNEUR at EUR *(see p267)* is old-fashioned but can be fun. The Bomarzo Monster Park, 60 miles (95 km) north of Rome, was built in the 16th century for a mad duke. Children can clamber over its giant stone monsters.

TOYS

A VISIT TO a Roman toyshop is a treat. **Menasci** sells wooden toys, **Città del Sole** has delightful educational toys and games, and **Al Sogno** is a wonderland of stuffed animals.

Città del Sole
Via della Scrofa 65. **Map** 4 F3 & 12 D2.
687 54 04.

Menasci
Via Napoleone III 72. **Map** 5 A3 & 12 F2. 678 19 81.

Al Sogno
Piazza Navona 53. **Map** 4 E4 & 11 C3.
686 41 98.

CHILDREN'S CLOTHES

Italians adore dressing their children up, and on Sunday afternoons in particular, you are likely to encounter young children dressed as if they had walked straight out of a costume drama: girls in frills and flounces and boys in velvet breeches or knee-length shorts.

Many shops sell beautifully handcrafted children's shoes and clothes – the downside is that they can often be expensive and impractical: dry-clean-only clothes are common, and shoes are not made for mud.

Lavori Artigianili Femminili sells handmade silk and wool clothes for children up to eight. **Succo d'Arancio** sells smart casuals and **Children's Club** offers Italian styles made from classic Liberty fabrics.

Lavori Artigianili Femminili
Via Capo le Case 6. **Map** 5 A3 & 12 F1.
679 29 92.

Succo d'Arancio
Via dell'Arancio 36. **Map** 4 F2 & 12 D1.
687 62 52.

Children's Club
Via della Frezza 61–2. **Map** 4 F2.
322 18 98.

SURVIVAL
GUIDE

PRACTICAL INFORMATION

R OMANS OFTEN SEEM unconcerned by the priceless art treasures and ancient ruins that lie so casually among the buildings and workings of their hectic 20th-century city. Visitors nearly always find these wonders very exciting, but it's not always easy to actually see them. Relaxed local attitudes make for hundreds of variations on opening hours. Most places close for several hours over lunch and reopen in the late afternoon; some

museums are open in the mornings only. Bank and shop hours can be just as difficult to pin down. On a more positive note, many of the main sights are within easy walking distance of one another. Start your day early and wear comfortable shoes for the Roman cobblestones. Rome can be a delight-fully informal city to visit, but remember to observe dress rules to cover up in churches, as this is one area where the Italians are very strict.

MUSEUMS AND MONUMENTS

M ANY MUSEUMS open only in the mornings and close all day on Mondays. If you are particularly eager to see a specific monument or museum, make sure it's open before you set out. There is usually an admission charge for museums and monuments, though some are free on Sundays. All churches are free, and many contain works of art that are worthy of the world's greatest museums. Some of Rome's sights are accessible only on personal application or by written appointment. Examples include Nero's Aqueduct or the gardens at the Vatican. The *Area by Area* section of this guide gives opening times for each sight and tells you whether there is an admission charge. The **EPT** publishes a useful leaflet called *Musei e Monumenti di Roma*, which gives details of current exhibitions at Rome's main museums and galleries.

EPT's guide to current exhibitions

Museum entry cards are available from museums and tourist offices or by writing in advance to **L'Associazione Nazionale Museidon**. The cards admit you without extra charge to most museums, galleries and exhibition centers in the city. They are valid for two, four or seven consecutive days and cost from around L15,000 to L50,000.

Typical traffic congestion in Via delle Quattro Fontane

TOURIST INFORMATION

T HE SERVICE at the main provincial tourist office (**EPT**) is better than at the crowded station. You should be able to pick up details of special tours here. EPT also helps with accommodation *(see p289)*. Besides the official tourist offices, good travel agents such as **CIT**, **Wagons Lits** or the **American Express** office can also be helpful to visitors. For information on Italian cities and areas outside Rome,

ITALIA ®

ENTE NAZIONALE ITALIANO PER IL TURISMO

ENIT logo

contact **ENIT** (the National Tourist Board), who have offices in all the main cities.

A word of warning: any information you obtain in Italy should be regarded as only approximate; prices and opening times change often, without warning. Even sights that are normally open for regular hours can be closed for what seem to be unbelievably long periods of restoration *(chiuso per restauro)* or because of a sudden strike *(sciopero)*.

The 119 electric minibus: useful for the historic center

ENTERTAINMENT INFORMATION

THE WEEKLY *Trovaroma*, in *La Repubblica*, is the main guide to what's on. The bilingual fortnightly *Un Ospite a Roma* (A Guest in Rome) also has entertainment listings and is available free from newsagents. Listings in English are also

Trovaroma in *Metropolitan* and *Wanted in Rome*. Full entertainment information is on page 340.

GUIDED TOURS

SEVERAL COMPANIES offer tours of Rome with English-speaking guides; these include **CIT**, **American Express**, **Green Line Tours** and **Carrani Tours**. Full-day city tours including lunch cost around L95,000–110,000; half-day tours around L40,000–50,000. Alternatively, the 110 ATAC bus passes many of the main sights in Rome on a three-hour circuit. The total journey will cost you around L6,000. Tour guides can be hired at many of the major sights, such as the Roman Forum (*see pp78–87*). Employ only the official guides and make sure you establish the fee in advance; on average they charge around L100,000 for a half-day's tour.

ATAC, the Rome bus company

VISITING CHURCHES

MANY OF ITALY's churches are very dark, but they usually have light meters to illuminate chapels and works of art. The meters are coin-operated (L100, L200 or L500 coins accepted). Recorded information in several languages is often available at coin-operated machines. Dress codes are firmly upheld in Roman churches; St. Peter's (*see pp230–33*) is especially strict.

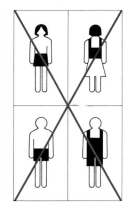

Unacceptable dress in church: both sexes should cover torsos and upper arms.

ETIQUETTE

PEOPLE IN ROME are generally courteous and friendly to foreign visitors. Remember to show consideration for local residents and workers.

Italians are delighted at any effort to speak their language, so it's worth learning a few phrases (*see p431*). Italians tend to drink only with meals and are unlikely to be seen drunk – drunkenness is frowned upon. Smoking is common in bars and restaurants but banned on public transportation.

Roman style

TIPPING

FOREIGNERS ARE expected to tip, although Italians themselves don't often do so. Leave a few coins in bars or cafés; in restaurants where service is not included, leave around 10%. Keep L1,000 or L2,000 notes and coins handy for taxi drivers, sacristans, chambermaids, doormen, porters and usherettes.

ROME FOR THE DISABLED

ROME IS not particularly well organized to cater for the disabled. Its uneven cobbles and crowded pavements aren't suitable for those in wheelchairs, and even the most agile must be alert when crossing busy roads. Look before crossing at traffic lights and pedestrian crossings – not all vehicles stop when you expect. The seriously disabled will need to arrange help. Ramps, elevators and modified toilets exist in a few places, including Termini station and the Colosseum.

If you have no escort, consider a specially-designed package tour, or contact an organization for disabled travelers before you arrive.

The Vatican Museums, Sistine Chapel and St. Peter's are all accessible by wheel-chair. The Vatican Museums (*see pp234–237*) are very accommodating and will offer staff help if needed.

PUBLIC TOILETS

PUBLIC TOILETS are few and far between. There are clean ones by the Colosseum (with facilities for the disabled), at St. Peter's and in the Rinascente store (*see p323*). Most cafés let you use theirs if you ask. Take your own paper.

USEFUL ADDRESSES

American Express
Piazza di Spagna 38. **Map** 5 A2.
[676 41.

Associazione Nazionale Museidon
Via A. Silvani 23, 00139 Rome.

Carrani Tours
Via V. E. Orlando 95. **Map** 5 C3.
[488 05 10.

CIT
Piazza della Repubblica 65.
Map 5 C3. [474 65 55.

ENIT
Via Marghera 2. **Map** 6 E3.
[497 11.

EPT
Via Parigi 5. **Map** 5 C2.
[48 89 92 53. **Open** 9am–1:30pm, 2–7pm Mon–Sat.

Green Line Tours
Via Farini 5A. **Map** 6 D4.
[474 48 57.

Personal Security and Health

ON THE WHOLE, Rome is a safe, unthreatening place for visitors, but petty street crime is a problem. Don't carry more money than you'll need for the day and leave other valuables or documents in a hotel safe. Cameras are less likely to be snatched if they're in a carrier bag rather than an obvious case. Take particular care in crowded places, such as stations, or on full buses, and steer clear of bands of innocent-looking children – they may be skillful professional pickpockets.

Pharmacy sign

ADVICE FOR VISITORS

TAKE OUT ADEQUATE property insurance before you travel (it is difficult to arrange once you are in Italy), and guard your belongings all the time once you're in Rome. Some hotels have personal safes in the bedrooms. You can program these with your own number. (Don't use your date of birth; it's on your passport and registration slip.) To be prepared for all eventualities, keep a separate photocopy of all your vital documents, such as your passport, to minimize the problem of replacing them, and take a spare photograph or two. Traveler's checks are the safest way to carry large amounts of cash. Keep the receipts separate from the checks for a refund in case you lose them.

Be wary of bag-snatchers on mopeds who operate on quiet streets. You might want to wear a discreet money belt or a securely fastened, long-strapped shoulder bag, while

Mounted police

equipment like video cameras should be disguised. Pickpockets (sometimes children) adopt highly sophisticated distraction techniques with cards or newspapers while they deftly separate you from your possessions in seconds. Be especially cautious in market places or on public transportation. Bus route No. 64, which runs between Termini station and the Vatican, is notorious for pickpockets. Thefts from cars are

also common. Nothing portable like a jacket or bag should be left visible inside a car on Rome's streets, and don't carry luggage on a roof rack. The streets to the east and south of Termini station and around the Colosseum are well known for prostitution and drug-peddling and unsavory at night.

Women traveling alone (or even in small groups) may need to take extra care. Italian society is male-dominated, and women who are out without male escorts attract more attention than they do in much of the rest of Europe and North America.

Beware of unauthorized minicab drivers, who are probably not insured and frequently overcharge. They operate in particular near the airport, waiting to profit from

Distinctive *carabinieri* motorcycle

***Carabiniere* – a member of the military police**

***Carabiniere* in traffic police uniform**

Municipal policeman directing traffic

new arrivals. Avoid unofficial vendors and tour guides; instead stick to the official tourist agencies *(see p289 and pp358–9)*.

Police car

POLICE

THE VIGILI URBANI, or municipal police, wear blue uniforms in winter and white in summer and can most often be seen regulating traffic. The *carabinieri* are the military police, in red striped trousers. They deal with everything from fine art thefts to speeding offenses. *La polizia* (the state police) wear blue uniforms with white belts and berets, and they specialize in serious crime. Any of these should be able to help you.

Green cross ambulance

Italian fire engine

MEDICAL MATTERS

NO INOCULATIONS are required for Rome, but take mosquito repellent and sun screen in the summer. The Tiber is polluted, but the water from the taps and from many street fountains is piped straight from the hills, and is fresh and palatable.

Non-EU visitors should take out insurance to cover everything, including emergencies. For insurance claims, make sure you keep all receipts for medical treatment and any medicines prescribed.

If you need urgent medical attention, contact the First Aid

Carabinieri in dress uniform

(Pronto Soccorso) department of a main hospital such as **Policlinico Umberto I**, or check the Yellow Pages *(Pagine Gialle)* for a doctor *(medico)* or dentist *(dentista)*. Pharmacists post late-opening hours on their doors (several stay open all night), and can usually supply the local equivalent of foreign medicines. They are well-trained to deal with minor ailments and can prescribe a variety of drugs without a doctor's prescription.

Farmacia Internazionale Capranica and **Farmacia Internazionale Barberini** stock American and British pharmaceutical products.

Many of the words for minor complaints and remedies are similiar in Italian, for example *lassativo* (laxative), *aspirina* (aspirin), and *tranquillante* (tranquilizer).

Farmacia Internazionale Barberini
Piazza Barberini 49. **Map** 5 B3.
📞 482 54 56.

Farmacia Internazionale Capranica
Piazza Capranica 96. **Map** 4 F3 & 12 D2. 📞 679 46 80.

Policlinico Umberto I
Viale del Policlinico 155. **Map** 6 F2.
📞 499 71.

LOST PROPERTY

IF YOU WANT to make an insurance claim, report your loss to any police station, and get a signed form. For lost passports, go to your embassy or consulate; for lost traveler's checks, go to the issuing company's office *(see p362)*.

Termini station has a police office on platform 1. Or, contact the **Ufficio Stranieri**.

Lost Property on Buses
📞 581 60 40. **Open** *Tue–Thu.*

Lost Property on the Metro
📞 57 53 36 80.

Ufficio Stranieri
Via Genova 2. **Map** 5 B3.
📞 46 86 29 87 *(24 hrs), English spoken.*

Commissariato di Polizia – a police station

EMERGENCY TELEPHONE NUMBERS

Ambulance
📞 55 10.

Automobile Club d'Italia
Car accidents and breakdowns.
📞 116.

Fire
📞 115.

First Aid
📞 482 67 41.

General SOS
📞 113.
Free from any telephone.

Police
📞 112 (Carabinieri) *or* 46 86 (La Polizia).

Samaritans
📞 70 45 44 44.
Line open *1pm–10pm daily.*

Traffic Police
📞 676 91.

Banking and Local Currency

MONEY SERVICES are not always fast in Rome. Transactions can involve considerable paperwork and a lot of waiting around. On the whole, bank exchange rates are more favorable than those in travel agents and hotels – the deal just takes longer to complete. Small change is indispensable – especially the L100, L200 or L500 coins needed for telephones, tips and illuminating works of art and chapels in churches *(see p359)*.

Eagle sculpture on the Ministry of Finance

CHANGING MONEY

IT'S BEST to have at least some local currency when you arrive, so you won't have to change money immediately. However, there are increasing numbers of convenient electronic exchange machines at arrival points. There are now several throughout the city, too. Multilingual instructions are available. You simply feed in up to 14 bills of the same foreign currency, and should get some lire back. Exchange rates vary from place to place. The Banco di Santo Spirito office at Fiumicino Airport offers reasonable rates.

For the best rates, change money at a bank (look for the sign *Cambio*). Hotels tend to give poor rates, even if they charge modest commissions. At the Vatican Museums *(see p235)*, you aren't charged any commission. The American Express office *(see p359)* offers good rates and is open on Saturday mornings. Cardholders may withdraw up to $1,000 (or 500 pounds sterling) a week from the cash machine, but you pay a fee for this service and need a PIN (personal identification number) to use your card.

Automatic exchange machine

CREDIT CARDS

CREDIT CARDS, which used to be regarded with great suspicion in Italy, are now much more widely accepted in larger hotels, shops and restaurants in Rome. Some places, however, prefer Eurocheques, which can be cleared faster. All major credit and charge cards (American Express, Access/MasterCard, VISA, Diners Card) are well known. Banks and cash dispensers are more likely to accept VISA cards for cash advances, but Access (MasterCard) is accepted by more retail outlets in Italy. Take both if you have them. Paying for anything in foreign currency will almost always be expensive.

TRAVELER'S CHECKS

IF YOU OPT for traveler's checks, choose a well-known name, such as Thomas Cook or American Express, or take those issued through a major bank. Most issuers charge a 1% commission on traveler's checks. Get some small denominations, so you won't be left with huge amounts of Italian currency at the end of your trip. But don't forget that the minimum commission charged for each transaction (and the amount of time involved) may make changing small amounts of money uneconomical. Always record the traveler's check numbers and refund addresses separately from the checks themselves in case they are stolen. Some places will charge you for each check.

Check the exchange rates before you travel and decide whether lire, dollar or sterling checks are more appropriate. Lire cheques are issued only by Italian banks and may be more difficult to cash in Italy than dollar or sterling ones.

OPENING HOURS

BANKS ARE USUALLY open from 8:30am–1:20pm on Monday to Friday. Some larger branches also open from about 3 to 4:30pm, but opening times vary, and banks are closed for public holidays and on weekends. Bureaux de Change have hours similar to shops. The exchange office at Termini Station *(see p372)* is open on Sunday mornings.

USING BANKS

QUEUES IN BANKS can be long, and the forms involved in changing money can take up a lot of time. You usually have to line up first at the *cambio*, then at the *cassa* to obtain your cash. Take some form of identity with you, such as a passport. Metal objects may set off emergency detectors as you enter.

Exchange office at one of the Italian national banks

One of the major Italian banks

The Bank of Rome, which has branches in other Italian cities

CURRENCY

ITALY'S CURRENCY unit is the *lira* (plural *lire*) and is usually abbreviated L or £. It became the national currency during the unification process in the mid-19th century.

Lira means pound, and the English pound is referred to as *lira sterlina* to distinguish it.

Telephone tokens *(gettoni)* are worth L200, and you may get some *gettoni* in your change instead of coins.

Shops and bars will not always change large notes, so it is wise to ask for smaller denominations of bank notes when you change money. Coins are often in short supply.

The prospect of carrying around millions of units of currency may at first seem alarming. Plans to alter the basic unit have still not been realized, but you'll find in practice that the last three zeros are often ignored in spoken Italian: *sessanta* will usually mean L60,000 and not, as one may think, L60.

Bank Notes

Italian bank notes come in denominations of L100,000, L50,000, L10,000, L5,000, L2,000 and L1,000, which are easily identifiable by their colors and the historic people portrayed. Notes increase in size progressively according to their value. The lira is never divided into smaller units.

1,000 lire

2,000 lire

5,000 lire

10,000 lire

50,000 lire

100,000 lire

Coins

Coins, shown here at actual size, are in denominations of L500, L200, L100 and L50. Old L100 and L50 coins are still in use, and there are L10 and L20 coins of minute value. Telephone gettoni *are worth L200.*

50 lire (new)

100 lire (new)

500 lire

50 lire (old)

100 lire (old)

200 lire

Gettone (200 lire)

Using Rome's Telephones

THE ROME TELEPHONE SYSTEM has recently undergone a major upheaval. Many numbers have been changed, and new equipment has been installed alongside older machinery. Until the overhaul is complete, you may need a degree of patience when using the phone. At present, telephone numbers can have any number of digits from four to about nine.

Telephone company logo

TELEPHONE OFFICES

TELEPHONE OFFICES (*Telefoni*) are run by Telecom Italia (previously called SIP) and offer a convenient way of making long-distance or private calls. At the *Telefono* there will be several metered telephones, each in its own soundproofed booth. An assistant will assign you a booth and meter your call once you have been connected to the number you want. You pay on your way out. No premium is charged on this service, but *Telefoni* opening hours rarely

Telephone sign

coincide with Italy's cheapest-rate calling times. The one at the **Palazzo delle Poste** on Piazza San Silvestro is an exception – it stays open 24 hours a day. There are other *Telefoni* throughout Rome, including ones at Fiumicino Airport, Termini Railway Station, other major post offices and the underground car park at Villa Borghese. To send international telegrams, go to a post office and dial 186 or call **Telecom**.
Useful information Telecom
[573 41; Palazzo delle Poste, Via Calabria 46. **Map** 5 A3 & 12 E1.

TELEPHONE RATES

THE CHEAPEST times to phone within Italy are 10pm to 8am from Monday to Saturday and all day Sunday. If this is inconvenient, it is also relatively inexpensive to call during weekday evenings between 6:30pm and 10pm; or after 1pm on Saturday. But check what time is best if you are making international calls: time variations throughout the world make a difference in cheap rates. Telephoning from hotel rooms is expensive and is sometimes marked up by several hundred percent. In general, telephone calls cost more from Italy than they do from North America.

USING A SIP COIN AND CARD TELEPHONE

1 Lift the receiver and wait for the dial tone.

2 If you use coins or *gettoni*, insert them in the slot at the top. The slot for telephone cards is lower down.

3 The display shows how much credit is left.

4 Dial the number and wait to be connected.

5 If you still have credit and want to make a second call, press the "follow-on call" button.

6 If your telephone card is about to expire, place a new one in the telephone card slot. When the old card expires, it will feed through automatically.

7 After your call is finished, unused coins or *gettoni* are returned from the left-hand slot. Cards are returned from the slot on the right.

Telephone cards have values of L5,000 or L10,000.

To use a card, break off the marked corner and insert, arrow first.

L500

Gettone

L200

L100

USING PUBLIC TELEPHONES

Newer SIP PAYPHONES, or *interurbani*, are orange; from these you can dial both long distance and some international calls directly. Pay phones take L100, L200 and L500 coins. For long-distance direct-dial calls, have at least L2,000 of change ready. If you don't put enough coins in to start with, the telephone simply retains your money and disconnects you. After a successful call, however, any unused coins are usually returned.

New sign

Old sign for telephone

The most up-to-date pay phones (pictured opposite) take SIP telephone cards (ask for a *scheda* or *carta telefonica*) costing L5,000 or L10,000, as well as coins. Some payphones will now only accept cards. Cards are

REACHING THE RIGHT NUMBER

Gettoni and stamps are available here

- The telephone code for Rome is 06.
- General information on calls within Europe is on 176. Reverse charge and credit card calls are also accepted.
  - European operator assistance is on 15.
  - Intercontinental operator assistance is on 170.
  - General telephone information is on 180.
  - You can dial direct to the operator in Australia, Canada and the US through the Countrydirect service. Dial 172 followed by: 1061 for Australia; 1001 for Canada; 1011 for AT&T, US; 1022 for MCI, US; and 1877 for US Sprint.
  - *See also* Emergency Numbers *p361*.

available from shops, bars and tobacconists displaying the black-and-white T sign. Break off the marked corner and insert the card arrow first; the value of the unexpired units will show on a display window. After your call, the card can be retrieved and reused until its value expires.

Older-style phones tend to be found in bars and cafés. These phones will accept only tokens *(gettoni)*, costing L200, which can be

purchased at shops, bars, newsstands, post offices or special vending machines. To use these phones insert the *gettone*, dial, wait for an answer and then push the knob to make the token drop; this connects you.

For long-distance calls on older telephones, seek out a *telefono a scatti,* or metered phone. Ask the bar owner if you can phone, and the call will be metered. You pay him or her when finished.

Sending Letters

The ITALIAN postal service is not especially efficient, and it is said that letters traveled faster in the days of the old Roman Empire than they do today, in spite of modern technology. For leisurely postcards, the service is usually fine, but expect anything sent abroad to take its

Rome letters   Other destinations

Italian state post box

Post Office sign

time; the Italian postal service is particularly slow in August, when it can take up to a month for a postcard to reach the US. For anything urgent or important, it's better to use the more expensive express system, which knocks a day or two off the delivery time, or registered post. Otherwise, you can buy ordinary stamps *(francobolli)* at tobacconists with the black-and-white T sign as well as in post offices. Branch post office hours are generally from around 8:30am

until 2pm (8:30am to noon on Saturdays and the last day of the month), but main offices stay open 24 hours a day or well into the evening for some services (such as registered post). Among the 24-hour ones are Piazza San Silvestro, at Termini and at the airport. Italian mail boxes are red.

HELD MAIL

Letters and parcels that are to be picked up at the post office are sent care of *(c/o)* Palazzo delle Poste, Roma, *Fermo Posta.* Print the surname clearly in block capitals and underline it to make sure the letters are filed correctly. To collect your mail, you have to show your passport and pay a small charge. American Express mail holding is free to clients.

VATICAN MAIL
The Vatican postal service costs the same as the state mail, but is faster. Buy cards and stamps at the post office near the Vatican Museums entrance, or in Piazza San Pietro. Letters bearing Vatican stamps can only be posted in blue Vatican post boxes.

Vatican post office sign

Vatican postage stamps

Postage stamps

Airmail sticker

Additional Information

Fiumicino airport, point of arrival for most visitors to Rome

CUSTOMS AND IMMIGRATION

Citizens of the United States, Canada, Australia, New Zealand or the UK do not need visas for stays of up to three months, but all non-European Community (non-EC) residents require full passports. British citizens may use a Visitor's Card. For longer stays, a visa should be obtained from your nearest Italian embassy or consulate before you travel. You won't usually need any vaccination certificates, but you should check if you have stopped over in tropical or Middle Eastern zones. Duty-free allowances are as follows:

Non-European Community residents are allowed to bring in 400 cigarettes, 100 cigars, 200 cigarillos or 500 grams of tobacco; 1 liter of spirits or 2 liters of wine; 50 grams of perfume. Goods such as watches and cameras may be imported freely for personal or professional use. EC residents no longer have to "declare" goods, but random checks are made to guard against the likes of drug traffickers.

The refund system for Value Added Tax (IVA in Italy) for non-EC residents is very complex (see p323), and it is only worth reclaiming if you have spent a lot of money in a single outlet.

Strictly speaking, all visitors to Italy have to register with the police, presenting a passport within three days of their arrival. In practice, the vast majority of visitors have this procedure taken care of for them by their hotels, when they first register. If you are

staying elsewhere, contact a local police department for advice, or telephone the **Questura** (police station).

Questura
📞 46 86.

CATHOLIC SERVICES

For many catholics, a visit to Rome means an audience with the pope. General audiences are usually held every Wednesday at 11am (10am in hot weather) in St. Peter's square, the Audiences room, or at the summer residence at Castel Gandolfo. To attend an audience, apply to the **Prefettura della Casa Pontificia** before your visit. (Rome travel agencies may be able to arrange an audience as part of a coach tour during your stay.) There is no charge. Mass is held daily in the main churches of Rome (High Mass is on Sunday.) Churches where confession is heard include St. Peter's (see pp230–33), San Giovanni in Laterano (pp182–3), San Paolo fuori le Mura (p264), Santa Maria Maggiore (pp172–3), the Gesù (pp114–15), Santa Sabina (p204) and Sant'Ignazio (p106). English-speaking Catholic churches include San Silvestro (Piazza San Silvestro) and San Tommaso di Canterbury (Via di Monserrato 45).

Confession box, Gesù

Prefettura della Casa Pontificia
Città del Vaticano, 00120. **Map** 3 B3.
📞 69 82.

An international Student Identity Card (ISIC) or a Youth International Educational Exchange Card (YIEE) are worth having for reductions on museum and other charges.

Students on the steps of Santa Maria Maggiore

Contact the **Centro Turistico Studentesco** for information. The **Associazione Italiana Alberghi per la Gioventù** (the Italian YHA) has four hostels in the city. **Casa dello Studente** lists student hostels. **Transalpino** is for rail discounts.

ISIC card

Associazione Italiana Alberghi per la Gioventù
Via Cavour 44, 00184. **Map** 3 D3.
📞 487 11 52.

Casa dello Studente
Viale Ministero degli Affari Esteri 6.

Centro Turistico Studentesco
Via Genova 16. **Map** 5 C3. 📞 467 92 71. (Branches at Via Appia Nuova 434 and Corso Vittorio Emanuele 297.)

Transalpino
Piazza Esquilino 8A. **Map** 6 D4.
📞 487 08 70. (Branch at Stazione Termini, in main gallery).

The pope on his balcony at St. Peter's

Newspapers available in Rome

NEWSPAPERS, TV, RADIO

ROME'S MAIN newspapers are *La Repubblica* and *Il Messaggero*. British and American newspapers are readily available, and the *International Herald Tribune* is sold on the day of issue. The state TV channels are RAI Uno, Due and Tre; all of them are politically aligned. The advent of satellite and cable TV means there are European channels in many languages, plus sport and CNN news in English. The BBC World Service is broadcast on radio on 15.070MHz (short wave) in the mornings and 648KHz (medium wave) at night. Vatican Radio on 93.3MHz and 105MHz (FM) broadcasts news in English.

EMBASSIES AND CONSULATES

IF YOU LOSE your passport or need other help, contact your national embassy or consulate as listed below.

Australia
Via Alessandria 215. **Map** 6 E1.
(854 27 21

Canada
Via G.B. De Rossi 27.
(44 59 81.

New Zealand
Via Zara 28.
(440 29 28.

United Kingdom
Via XX Settembre 80A. **Map** 6 D2.
(482 55 51.

United States
Via Veneto 119A/121. **Map** 5 B2.
(467 41.

ELECTRICAL ADAPTERS

ELECTRIC CURRENT in Italy is 220V AC, with two-pin round-pronged plugs. Adapters can be purchased in most countries. In most hotels of three or more stars, there are hair dryers and shaving outlets in all the bedrooms.

Shaving outlet in hotel bedroom for 110V or 220V

Standard Italian plug

ROME TIME

ROME IS ONE HOUR ahead of Greenwich Mean Time (GMT). Examples of the time difference with Rome for other major cities are as follows: London: -1 hour; New York: -6 hours; Dallas: -7 hours; Los Angeles: -9 hours; Perth: +7 hours; Sydney: +9 hours; Auckland: +11 hours; Tokyo: +8 hours. These figures can vary slightly for brief periods with local changes in summer. For all official purposes, the Italians use the 24-hour clock.

CONVERSION TABLE

Imperial to Metric
1 inch   = 2.54 centimeters
1 foot   = 30 centimeters
1 mile   = 1.6 kilometers
1 ounce   = 28 grams
1 pound   = 454 grams
1 US pint = 0.5 liters
1 US gallon = 3.8 liters

Metric to Imperial
1 centimeter = 0.4 inches
1 meter   = 3 feet 3 inches
1 kilometer = 0.6 miles
1 gram   = 0.04 ounces
1 kilogram   = 2.2 pounds
1 liter   = 2 US pints

SIGHTSEEING PERMITS

TO VISIT certain sights in Rome, you need to obtain a written permit and book the time of your visit in advance. This applies particularly to archaeological sites, which may sometimes be closed during excavations. Write to:

Comune di Roma Ripartizione X
Piazza Campitelli 7. **Map** 4 F5 & 12 E5.
(67 10 20 70. **FAX** 67 10 31 18.

To speed things up, deliver your application in person to the *protocollo* on the third floor. Once your application has been received, set a time for your visit by calling Signor Natale of the:

Ufficio Monumenti Antichi e Scavi, Via del Portico d'Ottavia 29. **Map** 4 F5 & 12 E5. **Map** 4 F5 & 12 E5.
(67 10 38 19, 67 10 20 71 or 67 10 24 75. **FAX** 67 10 31 18.

OTHER RELIGIOUS SERVICES

Anglican
All Saints, Via del Babuino 153.
Map 4 F2. **(** 36 00 18 81.

American Episcopal
St. Paul's, Via Napoli 58. **Map** 5 C3.
(488 33 39.

Jewish
Sinagoga, Lungotevere Cenci.
Map 4 F5 & 12 D5. **(** 687 50 51.

Methodist
Via Firenze 38. **Map** 5 C3.
(481 48 11.

Mosque
Viale della Moschea (Parioli district).
Map 2 F1. **(** 808 21 67.

Presbyterian
St. Andrew's, Via XX Settembre 7.
Map 5 C3. **(** 482 76 27.

The Mosque in Parioli

GETTING TO ROME

MANY NATIONAL AIRLINES, including Italy's Alitalia, fly directly to Rome from most European cities and several in North America and Australia. There are no direct flights from New Zealand, but passengers can catch connections from either Frankfurt or London.

Alitalia aircraft

Rome also has train and coach links with the rest of Europe. These take a lot longer than flights (about 24 hours from London, compared with about three), but tend to cost about the same, so are worthwhile only if you want to travel overland. The trains are often crowded in summer.

Part of the new extension to Fiumicino Airport

BY AIR

IF YOU'RE FLYING from the United States, **TWA**, Delta and United Airlines operate regular direct scheduled flights to Rome, with services from about half a dozen cities (including New York, Boston, Washington, Los Angeles and Chicago). Flying time from New York is about 8 ½ hours and it's about 13 hours from Los Angeles. **Canadian Airlines** flies from Montreal and Toronto, **Qantas** from Melbourne and

Alitalia flight tickets

Sydney. The Italian state airline, **Alitalia**, also flies between Rome and New York, San Francisco, Philadelphia, Boston, Chicago, Detroit, Washington, Montreal, Toronto and Sydney. It may, however, be considerably cheaper for intercontinental travelers to take a budget flight to London, Paris, Frankfurt or Amsterdam and continue the journey to Rome from there. **British Airways** and Alitalia operate direct scheduled flights from London Heathrow to Rome, and you can fly from Manchester. Among the airlines using Rome as an intercontinental transit point are **Philippine Airlines**, Sudan Airways and Ethiopian Airlines: fares are cheaper, but flights are often less frequent and sometimes subject to long delays.

APEX (advanced purchase excursion), PEX, or SuperPEX fares generally offer the best value in scheduled flights, but must be purchased in advance (for example, 7 or 14 days ahead in the UK; 21 days in the US). They are subject to penalty clauses if you cancel, so take out insurance as soon as you buy your ticket.

The new ticket hall at Ostiense

If you're based in the UK, it's worth checking in the small ads of newspapers for discount charters (though even in low season these are becoming increasingly rare). Regular charters run all year round. Most leave from Gatwick and Luton, but there are one or two flights a week from Manchester, and it's usually possible to fly from Glasgow and Birmingham. Fares vary greatly, peaking in summer and in Holy Week for the Pope's Easter blessing.

If you want to reserve flights during your stay in Rome, travel agents, such as the **American Express** office, should be able to help.

Easy-to-follow signs at Ostiense

AIRLINE NUMBERS

Alitalia
📞 656 21 or 656 43.

American Express
📞 676 41.

British Airways
📞 47 48 05 01 or 65 01 15 13.

Canadian Airlines
📞 655 71 17 or 652 90 47.

Qantas
📞 48 65 58 or 65 01 01 46.

TWA
📞 1-800-892-4141.

PACKAGE VACATIONS

Package vacations to Rome can be much cheaper than booking transportation and accommodation separately. For European visitors, there are weekend packages and two- or three-place deals; Rome is frequently packaged with Florence and Venice. The city can also be part of a Europe-wide tour. Most package companies provide free transportation from the airport to your hotel. The more expensive ones may include a tour guide.

AIRPORTS

Rome has two international airports. Leonardo da Vinci – commonly known as Fiumicino – handles most

Ciampino, a more basic airport used by most charter flights

scheduled flights and is about 18 miles (30 km) southwest of the city. The other airport is Ciampino, about 9 miles (15 km) southeast and used by the majority of charter flights. Major car rental firms have rental offices at both airports, though you may find it less harrowing to get into the city center on public transportation or by taxi.

Shuttle bus to car-rental lots at Fiumicino

From Fiumicino there's a train to Tiburtina Station (6:15am–midnight; 25 min journey). If you're lucky, the ticket office (which also sells Metro tickets) will be open; if not, you'll have to tackle the automatic ticket machine *(see p373)*. A faster – and more expensive – train leaves Fiumicino each hour, bound for Termini (7:50am–10:05pm, return trains departing hourly 7am–9:15pm). Ostiense is linked with Piramide Metro by a series of escalators, travelators and overpasses. At Piramide Metro you can catch a subway train to the city center. This Metro line stops at 9pm on weekdays and at 11:30pm on Saturdays and Sundays, though. Taxis can be difficult to find at Ostiense after 9pm, but there's a bus (the No. 95) to Piazza Venezia.

The swiftest way to get to the center from Ciampino is by bus to Anagnina Metro station, then by a subway train to Termini. Taxis from both airports are expensive; use only official cabs, and, make sure that the fare meter is switched on and showing only the minimum charge before you leave.

One of the overhead walkways linking the air terminal at Ostiense station with Piramide Metro station

KEY

🚌 Bus to Termini
Ⓕ Railway to Ostiense
Ⓟ Multistory garage
– – – Future extension
——— New ring road

Taxi stand

The International Terminal will have better facilities for passengers.

The Domestic Terminal has a restaurant, shops, and three bars.

Domestic pier

Overhead walkways

From Rome

To Rome

THE FUTURE FIUMICINO
Fiumicino airport is currently being extended. The plans include a new international terminal, and improved road access.

Arriving in Rome

THIS MAP shows the main bus, rail and Metro links used by travelers arriving in Rome. The connections between Rome's two airports and the city center are shown, as well as links between Rome and the rest of Italy and the international rail routes from neighboring European countries. Travel information, including details of journey times and service frequency, is listed separately in each box.

FS *National connections*
*Links to Flaminio from **Viterbo** (2 hrs), **Bracciano** (90 mins).*

Flaminio

FS *Coastal route from Northern Italy*
*Links with Termini station. **Marseille** (11 hrs), **Nice** (9 hrs), **Turin** (7 hrs 30 mins), **Genova** (6 hrs), **Pisa** (3 hrs 30 mins).*

Lepanto

Ottaviano

Piazza di Spagna

Spagna

Barberini

Vatican

Piazza Navona

Piazza della Rotonda

KEY

- ✈ Airport *see pp368–9*
- **FS** Railway *see pp368–9*
- 🚌 Coach & Bus Link *see pp374–7*
- **M** Metro *see pp376–7*
- ▬ Airport Link *see pp368–9*
- ▬ State Rail Link *see pp374–5*
- ▬ Metro Line A *see pp376–7*
- ▬ Metro Line B *see pp376–7*
- ▪▪ Walkway *see pp372–3*

San Pietro

Janiculum

Campo de' Fiori

Capitol

Forum

Palatin

Trastevere

Ostiense station, linked to Piramide Metro

Circo Massimo

Aventine

Piramide

✈ **LEONARDO DA VINCI (FIUMICINO)**
Direct train links to Ostiense, Tiburtina and Termini. Linked with Piramide Metro station.
FS *Fiumicino–Tiburtina every 20 mins. Fiumicino–Termini every 60 mins.*
🚌 *Fiumicino–Lepanto (via Fregene) every 30 mins.*
🚌 *Fiumicino–Ostiense (via Fiumicino village) every 45 mins.*

Trastevere

Ostiense

M *Line B, southbound*
Stops after Piramide are: Garbatella, San Paolo Basilica, Marconi, Magliana, EUR Palasport, EUR Fermi and Laurentina (end station).

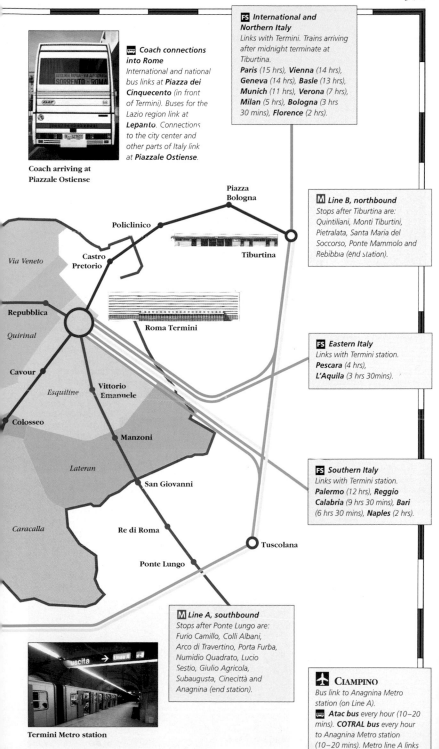

🚌 **Coach connections into Rome**
*International and national bus links at **Piazza dei Cinquecento** (in front of Termini). Buses for the Lazio region link at **Lepanto**. Connections to the city center and other parts of Italy link at **Piazzale Ostiense**.*

Coach arriving at Piazzale Ostiense

🚆 **International and Northern Italy**
Links with Termini. Trains arriving after midnight terminate at Tiburtina.
Paris *(15 hrs),* **Vienna** *(14 hrs),* **Geneva** *(14 hrs),* **Basle** *(13 hrs),* **Munich** *(11 hrs),* **Verona** *(7 hrs),* **Milan** *(5 hrs),* **Bologna** *(3 hrs 30 mins),* **Florence** *(2 hrs).*

Ⓜ Line B, northbound
Stops after Tiburtina are: Quintiliani, Monti Tiburtini, Pietralata, Santa Maria del Soccorso, Ponte Mammolo and Rebibbia (end station).

Piazza Bologna

Policlinico

Via Veneto

Castro Pretorio

Tiburtina

Repubblica

Quirinal

Roma Termini

🚆 **Eastern Italy**
Links with Termini station.
Pescara *(4 hrs),* **L'Aquila** *(3 hrs 30mins).*

Cavour

Vittorio Emanuele

Esquiline

Colosseo

Manzoni

Lateran

San Giovanni

🚆 **Southern Italy**
Links with Termini station.
Palermo *(12 hrs),* **Reggio Calabria** *(9 hrs 30 mins),* **Bari** *(6 hrs 30 mins),* **Naples** *(2 hrs).*

Caracalla

Re di Roma

Tuscolana

Ponte Lungo

Ⓜ Line A, southbound
Stops after Ponte Lungo are: Furio Camillo, Colli Albani, Arco di Travertino, Porta Furba, Numidio Quadrato, Lucio Sestio, Giulio Agricola, Subaugusta, Cinecittà and Anagnina (end station).

Termini Metro station

✈ **CIAMPINO**
Bus link to Anagnina Metro station (on Line A).
🚌 *Atac bus every hour (10–20 mins).* **COTRAL bus** *every hour to Anagnina Metro station (10–20 mins). Metro line A links with Termini station.*

Reaching Rome by Train, Coach or Car

ANY OVERLAND journey to Rome is fastest by train, though there are coach connections to most major European cities. Within Italy, journeys between large cities are usually also best done by train, but when traveling from towns that are not on the main Intercity railroad routes, coaches can be quicker. For drivers, the Italian Automobile Club *(see p361)* provides free assistance and excellent maps to members of affiliated automobile clubs from all over the world.

A Pendolino – Italy's fastest train

The foyer of Stazione Termini

STAZIONE TERMINI

STAZIONE TERMINI, Rome's main train station, is also the hub of the urban transportation system. Beneath it is the only interchange between the city's two Metro lines, and directly outside, on Piazza dei Cinquecento, is the central bus terminal. Though it is one of Rome's most stunning 20th-century buildings, it also has many unsavory aspects, so it is unwise to linger longer than necessary.

FS logo

If you arrive late, aim to leave the neighborhood as swiftly as you can. There are usually taxis (go to the official stand), even in the small hours, and most of the city's night buses start at Termini.

In summer, the station gets very crowded, and you can expect long lines at ticket booths, bureaux de change and both the transportation and tourist information offices. There is a left luggage office; a police station where you should report anything lost or stolen on a train or in the station; and a small Citalia office where you can exchange money as well as get travel information. In the foyer, you will find an international telephone office *(see p364)*, a bookshop, a post office and a tobacconist (where you can stock up on bus and Metro tickets). Other facilities at the station include a burger bar; a café; a ticket office for Transalpino; and, downstairs in the gloomy Metro subway, a hairdresser and an *albergo diurno* (day hotel), where, for a price, you can freshen up with a bath or shower.

Of Rome's other stations, four are most likely to be of interest to tourists. They are

BINARIO 17

Platform sign

← **uscita**

Exit sign

Ostiense and Trastevere, for trains to Fiumicino Airport and Viterbo *(see p271)*; Tiburtina, for some of the trains on the north-south line through Italy; and Roma Nord for trains to Prima Porta.

TRAVELING BY TRAIN

ITALIAN STATE RAILWAYS (Ferrovie dello Stato, or FS) have several levels of service, from Locale trains that stop at every station, to the Pendolino, a super-fast and luxurious train, which offers first- and second-class service: The Pendolino runs between Rome and Milan, Turin, Genoa, Bari, Naples and Venice. You have to reserve, and you're charged hefty supplements for the privileges of speed, hostess service and free newspapers. You also pay a supplement on Intercity trains. These trains are for fast long-distance journeys and have both first- and second-class carriages. They run from Rome to Venice, Milan, Florence and Naples. You should reserve in high season and on weekends. Reservations are required on some services

Termini, the heart of Italy's rail network and Rome's transportation system

An international Eurocity train

which are marked in the timetable by a black R on a white background. Some staff at the **Reservation Office** speak English, but it may be easier to go in person to the station, or to a travel agent displaying the FS symbol.

From Rome, you can also take international or Eurocity (EC) trains to destinations all over Europe. It's worth reserving a seat, especially during the summer when trains become crowded.

Stazione Termini Booking Office
Via Giolitti 22. **C** 47 75.

MACHINES FOR FS RAIL TICKETS

These self-service machines are easy to use, and most have instructions in four languages on a printed panel.

1 Select your destination.

3 Take your ticket and change.

2 The price is shown on the display. Insert coins, notes, or an American Express or Diners Club card.

Date **Length of journey** **Price of ticket**

Destination **Class** **Number of adults and children traveling**

COACH TRAVEL

Most regional and long-distance coaches are blue

LONG-DISTANCE coaches terminate at Tiburtina, which is the city's main coach station. Information and tickets for Euroline coaches to European cities are available from **Lazzi Express**. The **Appian Line** offers regular services within Italy. Its itineraries include Florence, Naples, Capri, Sorrento, Pompeii, Venice and Assisi. Local buses, serving villages and towns within the Lazio region, are run by **COTRAL**. All bus stations used by COTRAL are linked

to Metro stations. Tickets for COTRAL services are bought on the spot and cannot be reserved in advance. Some day trips from Rome by bus are described on pages 268 to 271.

Appian Line
Piazza dell'Esquilino 6–7. **C** 488 41 51.

COTRAL
C 591 55 51.

Lazzi Express
Via Tagliamento 27. **C** 884 08 40.

TRAVELING BY CAR

TO DRIVE YOUR own car in Italy, you need an international Green Card (for insurance purposes) and the vehicle registration document. A translation of your driving license, available at Italian tourist offices abroad, is also useful. Wearing seat belts is

Blue signs showing A roads and green signs showing motorways

compulsory in Italy. You must also carry a warning triangle in case of breakdown. Main routes to Rome connect with the Grande Raccordo Anulare (GRA), Rome's ringroad.

Tolls are charged on all Italian motorways. You can buy gas coupons and magnetic motorway toll cards from automobile organizations before entering Italy.

Euroline coach running between Rome and the rest of Europe

GETTING AROUND ROME

ROME'S CENTER is compact, and, although walking absolutely everywhere would be far too overly ambitious, it is a city in which you can spend much of your time on foot. Since the main streets in the center are usually clogged with traffic, driving and cycling are not recommended, but courageous motorcycle or scooter riders can have great fun buzzing around on a rented Vespa. Traveling by bus and tram can be very slow, so use overland public transportation only when you have a long way to go. The Metro, designed to connect the suburbs with the center, has no stops in the historic city center near the Pantheon or Piazza Navona, though it is the swiftest way of crossing the city.

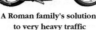

A Roman family's solution to very heavy traffic

WALKING

WANDERING through Rome's old center is one of the most enjoyable aspects of being in the city. You can take in the architectural details while absorbing the streetlife and stopping as you want at will, or peek into any church, shop or bar that catches your eye. You can easily see several of the main tourist sights in a few hours. The Colosseum, for example, is only about 1.5 miles (2.5 km) from the Spanish Steps. Your route could pass by the Forum, Piazza Venezia and several churches; other sights, such as the Trevi Fountain, the Galleria Doria Pamphilj and the Pantheon, are just a short detour away.

Explore the city area by area, using public transportation when distances are too far.

Only very small patches of central Rome have sidewalks, and a street that is closed to cars will still be used by cyclists and scooter riders. There have been many plans to create more traffic-free zones, and even to ban anything on wheels from some parts of the city – but imposing such measures on a population as insubordinate as Rome's is not easily done.

If you find the summer heat hard to bear, remember that the narrow cobbled streets get little sunlight and remain relatively cool, while walking into an open piazza can be like stepping into a furnace.

During the height of summer, you'll have a more enjoyable time if you follow the example of the Italians. Walk slowly on the shady side of the street; have a long lunch followed by a siesta in the hottest part of the day. You can continue exploring in the late afternoon, when churches and shops reopen and the streets are at their liveliest. Wandering at night is worthwhile, for the streets are cool and many facades floodlit.

Directions for walkers

Pedestrian crossing: only slightly safer than the open road

CROSSING ROADS

FIRST IMPRESSIONS suggest there can be only two sorts of pedestrian in Rome: the quick and the dead. Even if you cross roads by sets of traffic lights and pedestrian crossings strictly in your favor, there is sure to be some van or Vespa hurtling toward you with apparently homicidal intent. Fortunately, Roman drivers have quick reactions. The pious would attribute this to the protection of Santa Francesca Romana *(see p87)*, cynics to the fact that, according to Italian insurance law, drivers are responsible for any road accident. Whatever the inspiration, accidents are quite rare. The best tactic is to be as alert and confident

Avanti: Go! Pedestrians have right of way

Alt: Stop! Traffic has right of way

Pedestrian crossing   **Watch out for children**

as Romans. The roads are very busy. When crossing try to leave as large a gap as possible between yourself and oncoming traffic. Step purposefully into the road, facing approaching motorists with a determined glare. The trick now is to keep going steadily: don't hesitate or change your course and don't run. As long as a driver can see you, he or she should stop or at least swerve, albeit at the last moment.

Pedestrians and drivers must both take particular care at night, when the traffic lights are switched to a constantly flashing amber, turning the crossings into free-for-alls.

STREET SIGNS

THEORETICALLY, although it may not always seem to be the case, pedestrians have right of way at crossings when the green *avanti* sign is lit up. The red sign *alt* means you must wait. Underground crossings are indicated by a sign reading *sottopassaggio*.

It is easy to get lost in the maze of streets and piazzas that comprise the historic center. Until you know your way around, you can follow the yellow signs marking routes between the sights and piazzas of particular interest to tourists. Routes leading to general landmarks are indicated by signs on a silver-gray background.

No stopping

No parking

One-way street

No through road

DRIVING

DRIVING IN CENTRAL Rome can be an extremely intimidating experience for visitors. The flamboyant aggression of Italian drivers is notorious; pedestrians step out into the roads without warning; and the one-way system operating in much of the center makes retaining a sense of direction impossible. You'll also find motorists passing on the

wrong side, while scooters and Vespas zoom among the lanes of traffic and go the wrong way down one-way streets. A rule to remember is to give way to the right. Unless you are accustomed to driving in Italian cities, leave your car at home – or failing that, in a guarded parking area.

Car thefts are rife in Rome, so never leave anything of value in your car, even out of sight: areas such as Campo de' Fiori are patrolled by gangs watching for anyone leaving cameras, fur coats and other costly items in their trunks. You should also remove your car radio – you won't be the only person carrying one into a bar, restaurant or disco.

Take extra care driving at night. Not only do traffic lights switch to flashing amber, but many Italians are astonishingly cavalier about driving under the influence of alcohol or drugs.

PARKING

THE MOST convenient parking area is below the Villa Borghese. Much of the city center is reserved for residents with permits, and there are thousands of drivers with fake permits, which exacerbates the problem. If you do find a legal place to park, you may return and find you've been hemmed in by double-parked cars. Locations of some of the most useful parking areas are on page 379.

Directions to parking areas

GASOLINE

GAS IS VERY expensive. It can be bought from roadside pumps throughout the city, as well as from regular garages, though the former don't always sell lead-free gas (*senza piombo*). In the afternoon and at night, many pumps are self-service, operated by banknotes or credit cards. Late-night gas stations are listed on page 379.

The state gas company logo

ILLEGAL PARKING

Rome's traffic police are vigilant. If you've parked illegally, your car may be clamped or (if it's causing an obstruction) towed away, so phone 676 91 to check before reporting it stolen. No-parking zones should be clearly marked, but look carefully, in case the sign is hidden by a tree.

Signpost for a tow-away area (*zona rimozione*)

A tow truck at work

Traveling by Bus, Tram and Metro

R OME'S PUBLIC TRANSPORTATION system is comparatively cheap and comprehensive, and it is just as efficient as the busy streets allow. Priests, nuns, tourists, pilgrims, professionals and pickpockets all pile aboard, transforming the buses and trams into mobile saunas during the summer. Short distances are better covered on foot, because heavy traffic often blocks the roads. Getting off at the right stop can be difficult, but other passengers will usually help if you ask for directions. Always keep a tight hold on your valuables.

BUSES AND TRAMS

R OME'S PUBLIC bus and tram company is called **ATAC** (Azienda Tramvie e Autobus del Comune di Roma). Scores of its orange buses and a handful of rattling trams cover most parts of the city. They run from early morning until about midnight. There are also a few night buses.

Apart from one electric minibus (No. 119), no buses can run through the narrow streets of the historic center. But there are plenty of bus routes to take you within a short walk of the main sights *(see map inside back cover)*.

Rome's new yellow bus stops comprehensively list the details of routes taken by all the buses using that stop. There are, however, still a number of old-style bus stops left. These list only a few of

ATAC bus No. 64

Rome-Gubbio bus

the streets and piazzas that the buses pass and are mystifying until you know Rome well.

USING BUSES AND TRAMS

T HE MAIN TERMINUS is on Piazza dei Cinquecento outside Termini Station, but there are other major route hubs throughout the city, most usefully those at Largo Argentina, Piazza Venezia and Piazza del Risorgimento. Information on using the transportation system can be obtained from ATAC kiosks. Tickets can be bought from automatic machines found at main bus stops and also at Metro and train stations.

Most day buses have only a driver; night buses usually also have a conductor who issues tickets. (You can't buy tickets on day buses.)

During the day, if you have a normal ticket, you should board the bus at the back. There will be an orange machine there to time-stamp your ticket. Timed tickets, *biglietto integrale a tempo* (BIT), are valid for 75 minutes or until the end of the journey, if you board before the end of the 75 minutes. BIT tickets can be used for travel on all buses and trams and for one-way journeys on the Metro or train.

INFORMATION

ATAC
Piazza dei Cinquecento.
Map 6 D3.
[46 95 44 44;
46 95 22 00.
Open 7:30am–7pm daily.

BIG ticket for one day's unlimited travel

75-minute BIT tickets

Monthly passes

TICKETS

T ICKETS FOR CITY buses, trams and Metros have to be bought before you travel. You can buy them at bars, newsstands and tobacconists, as well as at Metro stations and bus termini. Watch for places displaying ATAC (bus and tram), COTRAL (Metro) and FS (train) stickers. Most of the outlets selling tickets close by mid-evening but there are automatic ticket machines, at main bus stops and train and Metro stations, which take both coins and notes and usually distribute change.

BIT tickets are valid for 75 minutes, during which time you can hop on and off as many buses, trams and Metros as you like. If you are going to make four or more journeys in one day, it's worth buying a *biglietto integrato giornaliero*

FERMATA

New-style bus stop listing details of routes served

A Roman tram in the orange livery of ATAC

(BIG) ticket. These give you a day's travel on the buses, trams and the Metros and one-way on urban train lines, except for Fiumicino airport. There are also available weekly tickets and monthly (calendar month) passes which are valid on all transportation, with special discounts for students and people over 65. Fare dodging is common but incurs a hefty on-the-spot fine.

METROPOLITANA

Rome's subway system, the Metropolitana, has two lines (A and B) that cross the city in a rough X shape, converging at Termini Station *(see inside back cover and pp370-71).* Line A (red) leads from Ottaviano near the Vatican to Anagnina in the southeast of the city,

Metro logo

where buses go to Ciampino airport. Line B (blue) runs from Rebibbia in the northeast, where you can catch a bus to Tivoli, down to EUR in the southwest, where buses leave for the coast. Stations are clearly marked by the Metro logo, a large white M on a red background.

The system was designed to ferry commuters in from the suburbs, so is not very useful within the center, but the Metro is a relatively speedy way of crossing the city. Useful stations are Colosseo, Spagna, San Giovanni, Ottaviano and Piramide (for trains to Fiumicino). Metro Line C is due to be completed by 2000, linking St Peter's to the Colosseum. Line A runs from 5:30am–11:30pm and Line B 5:30am–10:30pm.

USEFUL BUS AND TRAM ROUTES

This map shows a selection of buses that go through interesting parts of the city with good views of major sights. The 64 is always full of tourists, since it is the one route from Termini to St. Peter's. The other routes are likely to be less crowded. The 30b tram follows a leisurely route around the southeast of the city, while the 23 goes along the Tiber.

KEY

FS Railway station

M Metro station

━━ Bus route 23

━━ Tram route 30b

━━ Bus route 56

━━ Bus route 64

━━ Bus route 119

BIKE AND MOPED RENTAL

Rome's NARROW streets and heavy traffic, combined with the seven steep hills on which it was built, make it a challenging place for even the most serious of cyclists. However, there are a few areas, such as the Villa Borghese, the banks of the Tiber and some pockets in the historic center (around the Pantheon and Piazza Navona), where cycling can be a relaxing way to see the city. Make sure that you have a loud bell though – places that are good for cyclists tend to be popular with walkers and strollers too.

Mopeds *(motorini)* and scooters, called Vespas or

Horse-drawn carriages outside the Pantheon

A Vespa scooter and helmet

wasps in Italy because of the buzzing noise they make, are an efficient way of getting through the traffic. You may want to stick to quiet streets to begin with, though.

Although motorcyclists have to wear helmets by law, moped riders over 18 don't. However, you can rent helmets from most rental shops in Rome.

Bikes and mopeds can be rented from **Collalti**, **Roma Rent**, **Scoot-a-Long**, **St. Peter Moto** and **Scooters for Rent**. **Biciroma** rents from several spots in the old center and a **telephone hire service** operates in the summer and autumn.

You may have to leave a credit card as deposit when you pick up the bike.

HORSE-DRAWN CARRIAGES

These ARE NOT as popular in Rome as in Florence, but you can hire horse-drawn caleches *(carrozzelle)* for a gentle tour of the historic center. Carriages carry up to five people and can be hired from many points: Piazza di Spagna, the Colosseum, Trevi Fountain, St. Peter's, Via Veneto, Villa Borghese, Piazza Venezia and Piazza Navona. Trips last half an hour, an hour, half a day or a day. They tend to be expensive, but prices for longer rides are negotiable; establish the price before you leave and make sure you understand whether the rate is per person or for the whole carriage.

TAXIS

OFFICIAL TAXIS in Rome are yellow and must bear the "taxi" sign on the roof. Use only these taxis, not those offered by hawkers at stations and tourist spots; official taxi drivers do not look for customers.

Taxi stand signpost Yellow taxis can be hailed either at specially marked stands or on the street (drivers are not supposed to stop in the street but many do). You can nearly always find them at the main tourist sights, at airports and

Official yellow taxi

stations (including Termini and Ostiense). Roman taxi drivers are not renowned for their friendliness and may even refuse to take you too far from the lucrative city center.

Taxis aren't a cheap way of getting about, so unless you have heavy luggage or screaming toddlers, public transportation is usually a better option.

Taxi drivers always charge supplements for baggage, late-night trips (10pm–7am) and trips on Sundays or public holidays. As with taxis elsewhere, the fare meter continues running while you're at a standstill, so traffic jams can

Taxis lining up at Fiumicino

become expensive. Drivers may also take suspiciously circuitous routes to your destination. Taxi drivers in Rome expect tips from visitors. Native Romans generally give small amounts or nothing at all, but you'll be expected to give at least 10% of the fare.

You can book in advance from **Cosmos Radio Taxi**, **Società Cooperativa Autoradiotaxi Roma** or **Società la Capitale Radio Taxi**. There is a surcharge for taxis booked in advance.

CAR RENTAL

IN ITALY car rental is usually expensive, while gas prices are among the highest-priced in Europe. Major international companies (**Avis, Europcar, Hertz** and **Eurodollar**) have rental offices at airports and within the city center. However, you may get a better deal by booking a car ahead through a travel agent or tour operator before you leave. Local firms (such as **Maggiore**) are generally a lot cheaper, but check that breakdown service and collision damage waiver are included in the rental price.

Prospective renters should be aged 21 or over and have held a driving license for at least one year. Theoretically, you should also hold an international license

Roman car number plate

(available from your national automobile association), but most car rental firms do not usually insist on this.

Accident rates on Italian roads are very high, so insure yourself to the hilt. It's also a good idea to join an internationally affiliated automobile association (such as the AA in Britain or the AAA in the US). If you break down in Italy, phone for **ACI** (Italian Automobile Club) assistance. They will tow anyone without charge, but only members of affiliated associations get free repairs. There is also a Roman automobile club (**AC Roma**) with its own assistance center.

Details of current road and traffic conditions (in Italian) are available from a special **Road Conditions** number. You'll find more information on driving and parking in Rome on page 375.

Car rental offices at Fiumicino airport

STREET FINDER

MAP REFERENCES given with sights, restaurants, hotels, shops and entertainment venues refer to the maps in this section (*see* How the Map References Work *opposite*). A complete index of the street names and places of interest marked on the maps follows on pages 382–91. The key map below shows the area of Rome covered by the *Street Finder*. This includes the sightseeing areas (which are color-coded) as well as the whole of central Rome with all the districts important for restaurants, hotels and entertainment venues. Because the historic center is so packed with sights, there is a large-scale map of this area on pages 11 and 12.

0 kilometers　　2

0 miles　　　　1

How the Map References Work

The first figure tells you which Street Finder map to turn to.

Trevi Fountain ⑦

Fontana di Trevi. **Map 5 A3** & **12 F2**. 🚌 52, 53, 58, 60, 61, 62, 71, 95, 492 and many other routes.

The letter and number are a grid reference. You will find the letters at the top and bottom of the map and the numbers at the sides.

The second reference refers to the large-scale maps of central Rome (11 & 12). It is read in exactly the same way as the first.

The map continues on map 8 of the Street Finder.

The key to the abbreviations used in the Street Finder is on page 382.

KEY TO STREET FINDER

▢	Major sight
▢	Places of interest
▢	Railway station
Ⓜ	Metro station
🚌	Bus terminus
🚋	Tram terminus
🅿	Main car parks
🛈	Tourist information office
✚	Hospital with emergency unit
🚓	Police station
✝	Church
✡	Synagogue
⊠	Post office
=	Railway line
—	One-way street
⋮	Steps
▬	City wall

SCALE OF MAPS 1–10

0 meters	250	
		1:13,000
0 yards	250	

SCALE OF MAPS 11 & 12

0 meters	150	
		1:8,000
0 yards	150	

Street Finder Index

KEY TO ABBREVIATIONS USED IN THE STREET FINDER

B.go	Borgo	**M.te**	Monte	**Reg.**	Regina
d.	di, del, dell',	**P.**	Piazza	**S.**	San, Sant', Santa
	dello, della, dei,	**P.etta**	Piazzetta	**S. M.**	Santa Maria
	delle, degli	**P.le**	Piazzale	**SS.**	Santi, Santissima
Gall.	Galleria	**Princ.**	Principe	**V.**	Via
L.go	Largo	**P.ta**	Porta	**Vic.**	Vicolo
Lungot.	Lungotevere	**P.te**	Ponte	**V.le**	Viale

General Index

Acknowledgments

DORLING KINDERSLEY would like to thank the following people whose contributions and assistance have made the preparation of this book possible.

MAIN CONTRIBUTORS

Olivia Ercoli is an art historian and tour guide who has lived all her life in Rome. Bilingual in English and Italian, she lectures on art history and writes on a range of subjects for English and Italian publications.

Travel writer Ros Belford conceived the idea of the Virago Woman's Guides, of which she is now series editor, and wrote the *Virago Woman's Guide to Rome*. She has traveled widely in Europe and as well as writing guide books contributes to a variety of publications, including *The Guardian*.

Roberta Mitchell heads the editorial section of the UN's Publishing Division in Rome, where she has lived for many years. An experienced writer and editor with extensive knowledge of the city, she has contributed to a number of guides to Rome, including the *American Express Guide to Rome*.

CONTRIBUTORS

Sam Cole, Mary Jane Cryan Pancani, Daphne Wilson Ercoli, Laura Ercoli, Lindsay Hunt, Adrian James, Christopher McDowall, Davina Palmer, Rodney Palmer, Debra Shipley.

DORLING KINDERSLEY wishes to thank the following editors and researchers at Websters International Publishers: Sandy Carr, Matthew Barrell, Siobhan Bremner, Serena Cross, Valeria Fabbri, Annie Galpin, Gemma Hancock, Celia Woolfrey.

ADDITIONAL PHOTOGRAPHY

Andy Crawford, Philip Enticknap, Steve Gorton, Neil Mersh, Poppy, David Sutherland.

ADDITIONAL ILLUSTRATIONS

Anne Bowes, Robin Carter, Gillie Newman, Chris D. Orr.

ADDITIONAL PICTURE RESEARCH

Sharon Buckley.

CARTOGRAPHY

Advanced Illustration (Cheshire), Contour Publishing (Derby), Euromap Limited (Berkshire). Street Finder maps: ERA Maptec Ltd. (Dublin) adapted with permission from original survey and mapping from Shobunsha (Japan).

CARTOGRAPHIC RESEARCH

James Anderson, Donna Rispoli, Joan Russell.

RESEARCH ASSISTANCE

Janet Abbott, Flaminia Allvin, Licia Bronzin, Lupus Sabene.

DESIGN AND EDITORIAL ASSISTANCE

Hilary Bird, Vanessa Courtier, Claire Edwards, Simon Farbrother, Vanessa Hamilton, Marcus Hardy, Sasha Heseltine, Sally Ann Hibbard, Stephanie Jackson, Steve Knowlden, Mary Lambert, Janette Leung, Jane Middleton, Fiona Morgan, Helen Partington, Naomi Peck, Carolyn Pyrah, Salim Qurashi, Jane Shaw, Clare Sullivan, Andrew Szudek, Daphne Trotter, Diana Vowles.

SPECIAL ASSISTANCE

Dottore Riccardo Baldini, Signor Mario di Bartolomeo of the Soprintendenza dei Beni Artistici e Storici di Roma, Belloni, Dorling Kindersley picture department, David Gleave MW, Debbie Harris, Emma Hutton and Cooling Brown Partnership, Dottoressa Todaro and Signora Camimiti at the Ministero dell'Interno, Trestini.

PHOTOGRAPHY PERMISSIONS

DORLING KINDERSLEY would like to thank the following for their kind permission to photograph at their establishments: Bathsheba Abse at the Keats-Shelley Memorial House, Accademia dei Lincei, Accanto, Aeroporti di Roma, Aldrovandi Palace, Alpheus, Banco di Santo Spirito at Palazzo del Monte di Pietà, Rory Bruck at Babington's, Caffè Giolitti, Caffè Latino, Comune di Roma (Ripartizione X), Comunità Ebraica di Roma, Guido Cornini at Monumenti Musei e Gallerie Ponteficie, Direzione Sanitaria Ospedale di Santo Spirito, Dottoressa Laura Falsini at the

Soprintendenza Archeologica di Etruria Meridionale, Hotel Gregoriana, Hotel Majestic, Hotel Regina Baglioni, Marco Marchetti at Ente EUR, Dottoressa Mercalli at the Museo Nazionale di Castel Sant'Angelo, Ministero dell'Interno, Plaza Minerva, Ristorante Alberto Ciarla, Ristorante Filetti di Baccalà, Ristorante Romolo, Signor Rulli and Signor Angeli at the Soprintendenza Archeologica di Roma, Soprintendenza Archeologica per il Lazio, Soprintendenza per i Beni Ambientali e Architettonici, Soprintendenza per i Beni Artistici e Storici di Roma, Daniela Tabo at the Musei Capitolini, Villa d'Este, Villa San Pio, Mrs. Marjorie Weeke at St. Peter's

PICTURE CREDITS

t = top; tl = top left; tc = top center; tr = top right; cla = center left above; ca = center above; cra = center right above; cl = center left; c = center; cr = center right; clb = center left below; cb = center below; crb = center right below; bl = bottom left; b = bottom; bc = bottom center; br = bottom right.

Every effort has been made to trace the copyright holders and we apologize in advance for any unintentional omissions. We would be pleased to insert the appropriate acknowledgments in any subsequent edition of this publication.

Works of art have been reproduced with the permission of the following copyright holders: © DACS: Città con Cattedrale Gotica, 1925 by Paul Klee 241b.

The publishers are grateful to the following individuals, companies and picture libraries for permission to reproduce their photographs:

ACCADEMIA NAZIONALE DI SAN LUCA, Rome: 160b; AFE: 57b, 61cr; Sandro Battaglia 59c, 61clb, 61br, 324br; Louise Goldman 157t; G. La Malfa 251t; AGENZIA SINTESI: Fabio Fiorani 360br, 361t, 361b; Antonella di Girolamo 361c; Marco Marcotulli 360bc; R. Venturi 360bl; ALITALIA: 368t, 369cl; ALLSPORT: David Cannon 39br; ANCIENT ART AND ARCHITECTURE: 16bl, 20tl, 21tl, 25bc, 34crb, 35tc, 44cl; ARTOTHEK, Stadelsches Kunstinstitut Frankfurt, Goethe in the Roman Campagna by J.H.W. Tischbein 136t.

BIBLIOTECA REALE, Torino: 28–29c; BRIDGEMAN ART LIBRARY: 18br, 37tr; Agnew & Sons, London 51tr; Antikenmuseum Staatliches Museum, Berlin 19bl; Biblioteca Publica Episcopal, Barcelona/Index 114bl; Bibliothèque da la Sorbonne 28c, British Museum, London 27ctr; Chateau de Versailles, France/Giraudon 33tr, 54cl; Christie's, London 40, 55tr, 68b, 95t; The Fine Art Society, London 151tr, 279tl; Galleria degli Uffizi, Florence 31bl; Greek Museum, University of Newcastle-upon-Tyne 16br; King Street Galleries, London 33br; Louvre, Paris/Lauros-Giraudon 56br; Louvre, Paris/Giraudon 26br; Roy Miles Gallery, 29 Bruton St, London 228t; Musée des Beaux-Arts, Nantes 53t; Museo e Gallerie Nazionali di Capodimonte, Naples, Detail from the predella of San Ludovico by Simone Martini 26tr; Musée Condé, Chantilly f.71v Très Riches Heures, 26tc; Museum of Fine Arts, Budapest 110bl; Museo Archeologico di Villa Giulia 48cl; Museo Poldi Pezzoli, Milan 54tr; Palazzo Doria Pamphilj, Rome 107b; Piacenza Town Hall, Italy/Index 27br; Private Collection 19br, 22bl, 24br, 27tr, 178b; Pushkin Museum, Moscow 111t; Sotheby's, London 18bl; Spink & Son Ltd., London 163b; Vatican Museums & Galleries 41ca, 237tr.

CEPHAS PICTURE LIBRARY: Mick Rock 306tr; VANESSA COURTIER: 355t.

CM DIXON: 17bl, 24c, 268b, 269t, 269b.

ECOLE NATIONALE SUPERIEURE DES BEAUX-ARTS: 21cr, 22–23, 248t, 284–285b; ENTE NAZIONALE ITALIANO PER IL TURISMO: 358cl, cr; ET ARCHIVE: 14, 17tr, 17clb, 18tr, 19tc, 23t, 27cl, 28tl, 31br, 32br, 37br, 48tl, 306tl; MARY EVANS PICTURE LIBRARY: 9, 18cl, 23cl, 24cl, 29br, 30cb, 30b, 31t, 34tl, 34cr, 34bl, 54tl, 56tl, 67bl, 74t, 81b, 91t, 92b, 94bl, 127c, 135t, 135b, 213b.

CORALDO FALSINI: 38–39c, 340b, 341t, 341c; WERNER FORMAN ARCHIVE: 17cr, 20bl, 22tl, 23cr, 23bl, 23br, 47tr, 155t, 163tr, 175c; FOLKLORE MUSEUM, Rome: 210br.

GARDEN PICTURE LIBRARY: Bob Challinor 172cb; GIRAUDON: 15b, 28br, 36br, 55tl; RONALD GRANT: 52br, 340t.

SONIA HALLIDAY: 19c, 22br, 25cl; Laura Lushington 24bl; ROBERT HARDING PICTURE LIBRARY: 23cra, 32bl, 79cr, 177t, 268c, 353c; Mario Carrieri 35tr; Caffè Greco, Rome by

Ludwig Passini 309tr; John G. Ross 38tl, 59cl, 341b; Sheila Terry 39cl; G. White 59br; MICHAEL HOLFORD: 70b; HULTON DEUTSCH: 36tl, 38bc, 57cr, 63, 175b, 287c, 357c.

MAGNUM: Erich Lessing 15t, 17tl, 89br; MANSELL COLLECTION: 19tr, 25bl, 26bc, 31cl, 54bc, 55tc, 56cl, 57cl, 75cl, 75cr, 78tc, 93b, 112c, 122t, 125tr, 126tl, 132br, 133cr, 136bl, 139bl, 139br, 162tr, 172bl, 172 br, 183br, 192bl, 196bl, 210c, 220bl, 227cr, 229cr; Alinari 80br, 141bl, 160tl, 174t, 254b; Anderson 78cr, 138bl, 163tl, 228b; MORO ROMA: 36cl, 37cl, 38br, 39tr, 39bl.

NATIONAL PORTRAIT GALLERY, London: 55cr, 55b, 56tr, 57tr; © NIPPON TELEVISION NETWORK CORPORATION, Tokyo 1992: 244t, 245t, 245bl, 245br.

LA REPUBBLICA TROVAROMA: 359tl; REX FEATURES: Sipa 366br; Today 39cr.

SCALA: 94t, 278cl, Casa di Augusto 97t, Chiesa del Gesù 115t, Galleria Borghese 32cla, 260tr, Galleria Colonna 157b, Galleria Doria Pamphilj 46br, 105cr, Galleria Spada 46cl, Galleria degli Uffizi 16–17, 27bl, Museo d'Arte Orientale 174t, 174br, Musei Capitolini 47bl, Museo della Civiltà Romana 48tr, 48b, Museo delle Terme 21tr, Museo Napoleonico 49cr, Museo Nazionale, Napoli 21cl, Museo Nazionale, Ravenna 22cl, Museo del Risorgimento, Milano 36clb, 36–37c, Museo del Risorgimento, Roma 37tl, Museo di San Marco 54bl, Palazzo Barberini 253bl, Palazzo Ducale 8, 19tr, Palazzo della Farnesina 220ct, Palazzo Madama 20cl, Palazzo Venezia 47cr, 66bl, San Carlo alle Quattro Fontane 33cl, 33cr, Santa Cecilia in Trastevere 32tl, San Clemente 35bl, Santa Costanza 24–25c, Santa Maria Antiqua 24tl, Santa Maria dell'Anima 121t, Santa Maria Maggiore 43tr, Santa Maria del Popolo 139tr, 139c, Santa Prassede 26bl, 28bl, Santa Sabina 25tc, 29cl, Vatican Museums 19bc, 25t, 25cr, 25cra, 27cr, 29tl, 29cr, 30tl, 30ct, 31cr, 31bc, 32cr, 32clb, 41tr, 46tl, 48cr, 49bl, 224bl, 225cr, 235t, 238tl, 238br, 240t, 240b, 241t, 241c, 241b, 242tl, 242c, 242b, 243t, 243c, 243b, 244–245c, 246cl, 246cr, 246b, 247tl, 247c, 247cr, 247b; TONY STONE: Richard Passmore 1c.

TOPHAM PICTURE SOURCE: 38cl.

ZEFA: 2, 39tl, 230cl, 231br, 356–7, 358t, 372t; Eric Carle 58t; Kohlhas 231t.

Thanks also to Dottoressa Giulia De Marchi of L'ACCADEMIA NAZIONALE DI SAN LUCA, Rome for 160b, Rettore Padre Libianchi of LA CHIESA DI SANT'IGNAZIO DI LOYOLA for 106t, ENTE NAZIONALE PER IL TURISMO, HASSLER HOTEL, Rome for 293tl, GRAND HOTEL, Rome for 293crb and to LA REPUBBLICA TROVAROMA.

Phrase Book

IN EMERGENCY

Help!	Aiuto!	*eye-yoo-toh*
Stop!	Fermate!	*fair-mah-teh*
Call a doctor	Chiama un medico	*kee-ah-mah oon meh-dee-koh*
Call an ambulance	Chiama un' ambulanza	*kee-ah-mah oon am-boo-lan-tsa*
Call the police	Chiama la polizia	*kee-ah-mah lah pol-ee-tsee-ah*
Call the fire department	Chiama i pompieri	*kee-ah-mah ee pom-pee-air-ee*
Where is the telephone?	Dov'è il telefono?	*dov-eh eel teh-leh-foh-noh?*
The nearest hospital?	L'ospedale più vicino?	*loss-peh-dah-leh pee-oo vee-chee-noh?*

COMMUNICATION ESSENTIALS

Yes/No	Sì/No	*see/noh*
Please	Per favore	*pair fah-vor-eh*
Thank you	Grazie	*grah-tsee-eh*
Excuse me	Mi scusi	*mee skoo-zee*
Hello	Buon giorno	*bwon jor-noh*
Good bye	Arrivederci	*ah-ree-veh-dair-chee*
Good evening	Buona sera	*bwon-ah sair-ah*
morning	la mattina	*lah mah-tee-nah*
afternoon	il pomeriggio	*eel poh-meh-ree-joh*
evening	la sera	*lah sair-ah*
yesterday	ieri	*ee-air-ee*
today	oggi	*oh-jee*
tomorrow	domani	*doh-mah-nee*
here	qui	*kwee*
there	la	*lah*
What?	Quale?	*kwah-leh?*
When?	Quando?	*kwan-doh?*
Why?	Perchè?	*pair-keh?*
Where?	Dove?	*doh-veh*

USEFUL PHRASES

How are you?	Come sta?	*koh-meh stah?*
Very well, thank you.	Molto bene, grazie.	*moll-toh beh-neh grah-tsee-eh*
Pleased to meet you.	Piacere di conoscerla.	*pee-ah-chair-eh dee coh-noh-shair-lah*
See you soon.	A più tardi.	*ah pee-oo tar-dee*
That's fine.	Va bene.	*va beh-neh*
Where is/are ...?	Dov'è/Dove sono ...?	*dov-eh/doveh soh-noh?*
How long does it take to get to ...?	Quanto tempo ci vuole per andare a ...?	*kwan-toh tem-poh chee voo-oh-leh pair an-dar-eh ah...?*
How do I get to ...?	Come faccio per arrivare a ...?	*koh-meh fah-choh pair arri-var-eh ah..?*
Do you speak English?	Parla inglese?	*par-lah een-gleh-zeh?*
I don't understand.	Non capisco.	*non ka-pee-skoh*
Could you speak more slowly, please?	Può parlare più lentamente, per favore?	*pwoh par-lah-reh pee-oo len-ta-men-teh pair fah-vor-eh*
I'm sorry.	Mi dispiace.	*mee dee-spee-ah-cheh*

USEFUL WORDS

big	grande	*gran-deh*
small	piccolo	*pee-koh-loh*
hot	caldo	*kal-doh*
cold	freddo	*fred-doh*
good	buono	*bwoh-noh*
bad	cattivo	*kat-tee-voh*
enough	basta	*bas-tah*
well	bene	*beh-neh*
open	aperto	*ah-pair-toh*
closed	chiuso	*kee-oo-zoh*
left	a sinistra	*ah see-nee-strah*
right	a destra	*ah dess-trah*
straight ahead	sempre dritto	*sem-preh dree-toh*
near	vicino	*vee-chee-noh*
far	lontano	*lon-tah-noh*
up	su	*soo*
down	giù	*joo*
early	presto	*press-toh*
late	tardi	*tar-dee*
entrance	entrata	*en-trah-tah*
exit	uscita	*oo-shee-ta*
toilet	il gabinetto	*eel gab-bee-net-toh*
free, unoccupied	libero	*lee-bair-oh*
free, no charge	gratuito	*grah-too-ee-toh*

MAKING A TELEPHONE CALL

I'd like to place a long-distance call.	Vorrei fare una interurbana.	*vor-ray far-eh oona in-tair-oor-bah-nah*
I'd like to make a collect call.	Vorrei fare una telefonata a carico del destinatario.	*vor-ray far-eh oona teb-leb-fon-ah-tab ab kar-ee-koh dell dess-tee-nah-tar-ree-oh*
I'll try again later.	Ritelefono più tardi.	*ree-teh-leh-foh-noh pee-oo tar-dee*
Can I leave a message?	Posso lasciare un messaggio?	*poss-oh lash-ah-reh oon mess-sah-joh?*
Hold on	Un attimo, per favore	*oon ah-tee-moh, pair fah-vor-eh*
Could you speak up a little please?	Può parlare più forte, per favore?	*pwoh par-lah-reh pee-oo for-teh, pair fah-vor-eh?*
local call	la telefonata locale	*lah teh-leh-fon-ah-ta loh-kah-leh*

SHOPPING

How much does this cost?	Quant'è, per favore?	*kwan-teh pair fah-vor-eh?*
I would like ...	Vorrei ...	*vor-ray*
Do you have ...?	Avete ...?	*ah-veh-teh.. ?*
I'm just looking.	Sto soltanto guardando.	*stoh sol-tan-toh gwar-dan-doh*
Do you take credit cards?	Accettate carte di credito?	*ah-chet-tah-teh kar-teh dee creh-dee-toh?*
What time do you open/close?	A che ora apre/ chiude?	*ah keh or-ah ah-preh/kee-oo-deh?*
this one	questo	*kweh-stoh*
that one	quello	*kwell-oh*
expensive	caro	*kar-oh*
cheap	a buon prezzo	*ah bwon pret-soh*
size, clothes	la taglia	*lah tah-lee-ah*
size, shoes	il numero	*eel noo-mair-oh*
white	bianco	*bee-ang-koh*
black	nero	*neh-roh*
red	rosso	*ross-oh*
yellow	giallo	*jal-loh*
green	verde	*vair-deh*
blue	blu	*bloo*
brown	marrone	*mar-roh-neh*

TYPES OF SHOP

antiques dealer	l'antiquario	*lan-tee-kwah-ree-oh*
bakery	la panetteria	*lah pah-net-tair-ree-ah*
bank	la banca	*lah bang-kah*
bookshop	la libreria	*lah lee-breh-ree-ah*
butcher's	la macelleria	*lah mah-chell-eh-ree-ah*
cake shop	la pasticceria	*lah pas-tee-chair-ee-ah*
department store	il grande magazzino	*eel gran-deh mag-gad-zee-noh*
delicatessen	la salumeria	*lah sah-loo-meh-ree-ah*
drugstore	la farmacia	*lah far-mah-chee-ah*
fish seller	la pescheria	*lah pess-keh-ree-ah*
florist	il fioraio	*eel fee-or-eye-oh*
greengrocer	il fruttivendolo	*eel froo-tee-ven-doh-loh*
grocery	alimentari	*ah-lee-men-tah-ree*
hairdresser	il parrucchiere	*eel par-oo-kee-air-eh*
ice cream parlor	la gelateria	*lah jel-lah-tair-ree-ah*
market	il mercato	*eel mair-kah-toh*
newsstand	l'edicola	*leh-dee-koh-lah*
post office	l'ufficio postale	*loo-fee-choh pos-tah-leh*
shoe store	il negozio di scarpe	*eel neh-goh-tsioh dee skar-peh*
supermarket	il supermercato	*su-pair-mair-kah-toh*
tobacconist	il tabaccaio	*eel tah-bak-eye-oh*
travel agency	l'agenzia di viaggi	*lah-jen-tsee-ah deh vee-ad-jee*

SIGHTSEEING

art gallery	la pinacoteca	*lah peena-koh-teh-kah*
bus stop	la fermata dell'autobus	*lah fair-mah-tah dell ow-toh-booss*
church	la chiesa	*lah kee-eh-zah*
	la basilica	*lah bah-seel-i-kah*
garden	il giardino	*eel jar-dee-no*
library	la biblioteca	*lah beeb-lee-oh-teh-kah*
museum	il museo	*eel moo-zeh-oh*
railway station	la stazione	*lah stah-tsee-oh-neh*
tourist information	l'ufficio turistico	*loo-fee-choh too-ree-stee-koh*
closed for the public holiday	chiuso per la festa	*kee-oo-zoh pair lah fess-tah*

STAYING IN A HOTEL

Do you have any vacant rooms?	Avete camere libere?	ah-veh-teh kah-mair-eh lee-bair-eh?
double room	una camera doppia	oona kah-mair-ah dob-pee-ah
with double bed	con letto matrimoniale	kon let-toh mah-tree-moh-nee-ah-leh
twin room	una camera con due letti	oona kah-mair-ah kon doo-eh let-tee
single room	una camera singola	oona kah-mair-ah sing-goh-lah
room with a bath, shower	una camera con bagno, con doccia	oona kah-mair-ah kon ban-yoh, kon dot-chah
porter	il facchino	eel fah-kee-noh
key	la chiave	lah kee-ah-veh
I have a reservation.	Ho fatto una prenotazione.	oh fat-toh oona preh-noh-tah-tsee-oh-neh

EATING OUT

Have you got a table for ...?	Avete una tavola per ...?	ah-veh-teh oona tah-voh-lah pair ...?
I'd like to reserve a table.	Vorrei riservare una tavola.	vor-ray ree-sair-vah-reh oona tah-voh-lah
breakfast	colazione	koh-lah-tsee-oh-neh
lunch	pranzo	pran-tsoh
dinner	cena	cheh-nah
The bill, please.	Il conto, per favore.	eel kon-toh pair fah-vor-eh
I am a vegetarian.	Sono vegetariano/a.	soh-noh veh-jeh-tar ee-ah-noh/nah
waitress	cameriera	kah-mair-ee-air-ah
waiter	cameriere	kah-mair-ee-air-eh
fixed price	il menù a prezzo fisso	eel meh-noo ah pret-soh fee-soh
menu		
dish of the day	piatto del giorno	pee-ah-toh dell jor-no
starter	antipasto	an-tee-pass-toh
first course	il primo	eel pree-moh
main course	il secondo	eel seh-kon-doh
vegetables	il contorno	eel kon-tor-noh
dessert	il dolce	eel doll-cheh
cover charge	il coperto	eel koh-pair-toh
wine list	la lista dei vini	lah ee-stah day vee-nee
rare	al sangue	al sang-gweh
medium	al puntino	al poon-tee-noh
well done	ben cotto	ben kot-toh
glass	il bicchiere	eel bee-kee-air-eh
bottle	la bottiglia	lah bot-teel-yah
knife	il coltello	eel kol-tell-oh
fork	la forchetta	lah for-ket-tah
spoon	il cucchiaio	eel koo-kee-eye-oh

MENU DECODER

apple	la mela	lah meh-lah
artichoke	il carciofo	eel kar-choff-oh
baked	al forno	al for-noh
beans	i fagioli	ee fah-job-lee
beef	il manzo	eel man-tsoh
beer	la birra	lah beer-rah
boiled	lesso	less-oh
bread	il pane	eel pah-neh
broth	il brodo	eel brob-doh
butter	il burro	eel boor-oh
cake	la torta	lah tor-tah
cheese	il formaggio	eel for-mad-job
chicken	il pollo	eel poll-oh
baby clams	le vongole	leh von-gob-leh
coffee	il caffè	eel kah-feh
dry	secco	sek-koh
duck	l'anatra	lah-nah-trah
egg	l'uovo	loo-oh-voh
eggplant	la melanzana	lah meh-lan-tsah-nah
fish	il pesce	eel pesh-eh
french fries	patatine fritte	pah-tah-teen-eh free-teh
fresh fruit	frutta fresca	froo-tah fress-kah
garlic	l'aglio	labl-yoh
grapes	l'uva	loo-vah
grilled	alla griglia	ah-lah greel-yah
ham	il prosciutto	eel pro-shoo-toh
cooked/cured	cotto/crudo	kot-toh/kroo-doh
ice cream	il gelato	eel jel-lah-toh
lamb	l'abbacchio	lah-back-kee-oh
lobster	l'aragosta	lah-rah-goss-tah
meat	la carne	la kar-neh
milk	il latte	eel labt-teh

mineral water fizzy/still	l'acqua minerale gasata/naturale	lah-kwah mee-nair-ah-leh gab-zah-tah/nah-too-rah-leh
mushrooms	i funghi	ee foon-gee
oil	l'olio	loll-yoh
olive	l'oliva	lob-lee-vah
onion	la cipolla	lah chee-poll-ah
orange	l'arancia	lah-ran-chah
orange/lemon juice	succo d'arancia/ di limone	soo-koh dah-ran-chah/ dee lee-mob-neh
peach	la pesca	lah pess-kah
pepper	il pepe	eel peh-peh
pork	carne di maiale	kar-neh dee mah-yah-leh
potatoes	le patate	leh pah-tah-teh
prawns	i gamberi	ee gam-bair-ee
rice	il riso	eel ree-zoh
roast	arrosto	ar-ross-toh
roll	il panino	eel pah-nee-noh
salad	l'insalata	leen-sah-lah-tah
salt	il sale	eel sah-leh
sausage	la salsiccia	lah sal-see-chah
seafood	frutti di mare	froo-tee dee mab-reh
soup	la zuppa, la minestra	lah tsoo-pah, lah mee-ness-trah
steak	la bistecca	lah bee-stek-kah
strawberries	le fragole	leh frah-gob-leh
sugar	lo zucchero	lob zoo-kair-oh
tea	il tè	eel teh
herb tea	la tisana	lah tee-zah-nah
tomato	il pomodoro	eel pob-mob-dor-oh
tuna	il tonno	ton-noh
veal	il vitello	vee-tell-oh
vegetables	i legumi	ee leb-goo-mee
vinegar	l'aceto	lah-cheh-toh
water	l'acqua	lah-kwah
red wine	vino rosso	vee-noh ross-oh
white wine	vino bianco	vee-noh bee-ang-koh
zucchini	gli zucchini	lyee dzoo-kee-nee

NUMBERS

1	uno	oo-noh
2	due	doo-eh
3	tre	treh
4	quattro	kwat-roh
5	cinque	ching-kweh
6	sei	say-ee
7	sette	set-teh
8	otto	ot-toh
9	nove	nob-veh
10	dieci	dee-eh-chee
11	undici	oon-dee-chee
12	dodici	dob-dee-chee
13	tredici	tray-dee-chee
14	quattordici	kwat-tor-dee-chee
15	quindici	kwin-dee-chee
16	sedici	say-dee-chee
17	diciassette	dee-chah-set-teh
18	diciotto	dee-chot-toh
19	diciannove	dee-chah-nob-veh
20	venti	ven-tee
30	trenta	tren-tah
40	quaranta	kwah-ran-tah
50	cinquanta	ching-kwan-tah
60	sessanta	sess-an-tah
70	settanta	set-tan-tah
80	ottanta	ot-tan-tah
90	novanta	nob-van-tah
100	cento	chen-toh
1,000	mille	mee-leh
2,000	duemila	doo-eh mee-lah
5,000	cinquemila	ching-kweh mee-lah
1,000,000	un milione	oon meel-yob-neh

TIME

one minute	un minuto	oon mee-noo-toh
one hour	un'ora	oon or-ah
half an hour	mezz'ora	medz-or-ah
a day	un giorno	oon jor-noh
a week	una settimana	oona set-tee-mah-nah
Monday	lunedì	loo-neh-dee
Tuesday	martedì	mar-teh-dee
Wednesday	mercoledì	mair-koh-leh-dee
Thursday	giovedì	job-veh-dee
Friday	venerdì	ven-air-dee
Saturday	sabato	sab-bah-toh
Sunday	domenica	dob-meh-nee-kah